First published 2001 by

Philip's, a division of
Octopus Publishing Group Ltd
2–4 Heron Quays
London E14 4JP

Second edition 2003
Third impression 2005

ISBN-10 0-540-08466-2 (spiral-bound)
ISBN-10 0-540-08467-0 (perfect-bound)

ISBN-13 978-0-540-08466-1 (spiral-bound)
ISBN-13 978-0-540-08467-8 (perfect-bound)

© Philip's 2004

Printed and bound in Spain
by Cayfosa-Quebecor.

London

Contents

II	**Key to map pages**
IV	Administrative and Postcode boundaries
VI	**Key to map symbols**
1	**Street maps**
77	**Keys to enlarged map pages and symbols**
78	**Enlarged street maps**
174	**Index**
267	**List of numbered locations**
280	London Underground
282	Central London theatres and cinemas

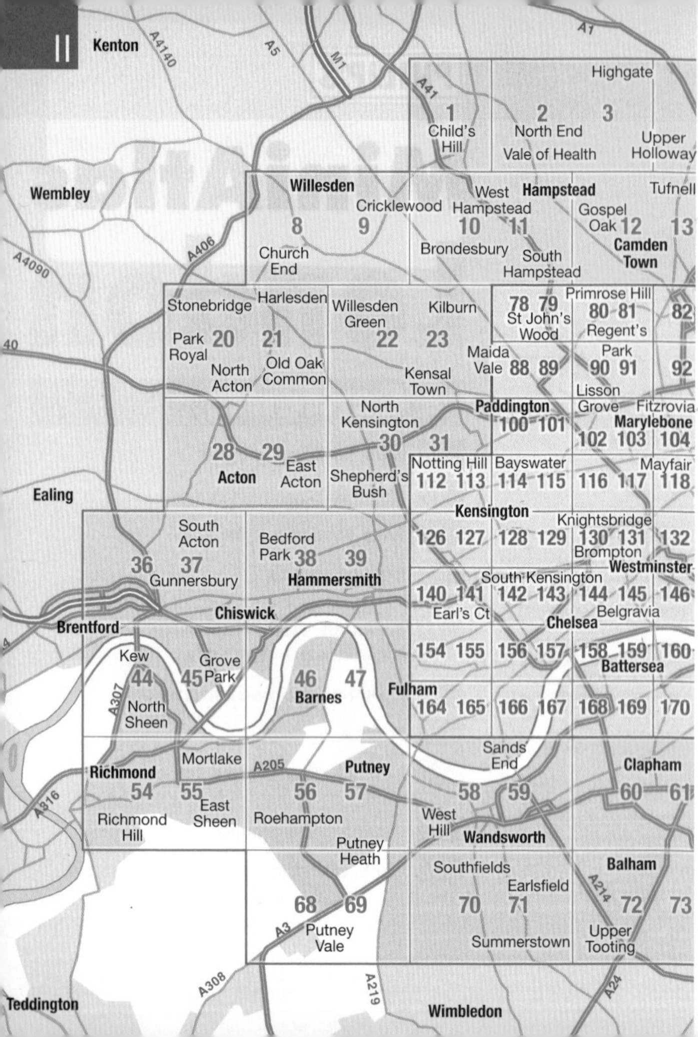

Kenton

Highgate

1 Child's Hill

2 North End Vale of Health

3

Upper Holloway

Wembley

Willesden

West Hampstead

Tufnell

Cricklewood

Hampstead

8

9

10 Brondesbury

11

Gospel Oak 12

13

Church End

South Hampstead

Camden Town

Stonebridge

Harlesden

Willesden Green

Kilburn

78 79 St John's Wood

Primrose Hill 80 81

82

Park Royal 20

21

22

23

Regent's Park

North Acton

Old Oak Common

Kensal Town

Maida Vale

88 89

90 91

92

Lisson Grove

Fitzrovia

North Kensington 30

Paddington 100 101

Marylebone

28 29

31

102 103 104

Acton

East Acton

Shepherd's Bush

Notting Hill 112 113

Bayswater 114 115

116 117 118

Mayfair

Ealing

Kensington

Knightsbridge

South Acton

Bedford Park 38

36 37

39

126 127 128 129

130 131 132

Brompton

Gunnersbury

Hammersmith

140 141 Earl's Ct

South Kensington 142 143

Westminster

144 145 146

Belgravia

Chiswick

Chelsea

Brentford

154 155

156 157

158 159 160

Battersea

Kew 44

Grove 45 Park

46 47

Fulham

North Sheen

Barnes

164 165

166 167

168 169 170

Richmond

Mortlake

Putney

Sands End

Clapham

54 55

56 57

58 59

60 61

Richmond Hill

East Sheen

Roehampton

West Hill

Wandsworth

Putney Heath

Southfields

Balham

Earlsfield

68 69

70 71

72 73

Putney Vale

Summerstown

Upper Tooting

Teddington

Wimbledon

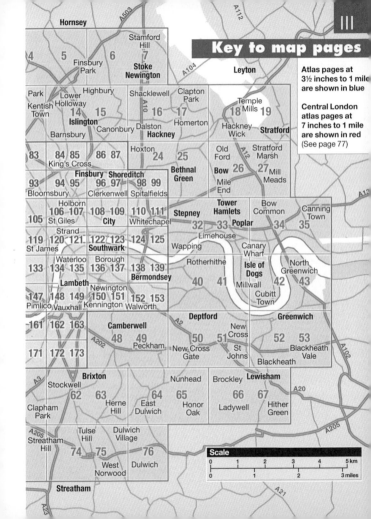

Hornsey

A503

A112

Stamford Hill

Key to map pages

4 5 Finsbury Park 6 7 **Stoke Newington**

A104

Leyton

Atlas pages at 3½ inches to 1 mile are shown in blue

Central London atlas pages at 7 inches to 1 mile are shown in red (See page 77)

Park Kentish Town | Lower Holloway | Highbury | Shacklewell | Clapton Park | Temple Mills 18 19

14 15 **Islington** 16 17 Homerton | Hackney Wick | **Stratford**

Barnsbury | Canonbury Dalston **Hackney**

A10

83 84 85 86 87 King's Cross | Hoxton 24 25 | Old Ford | Stratford Marsh

A12

93 94 95 **Finsbury Shoreditch** 96 97 98 99 | Bethnal Green | **Bow** 26 27 Mill Meads

Bloomsbury | Clerkenwell Spitalfields | Mile End

105 106 107 108 109 110 111 Holborn St Giles | **Stepney** | Tower Hamlets 32 33 **Poplar** | Bow Common | Canning Town

119 120 121 122 123 124 125 Strand St James | Waterloo | **Southwark** Whitechapel | Limehouse | 34 35

133 134 135 136 137 138 139 | Wapping | Canary Wharf | North Greenwich

147 148 149 150 151 152 153 Pimlico Vauxhall | Waterloo | Borough **Bermondsey** | Rotherhithe | **Isle of Dogs** 40 41 Millwall 42 43

-161 162 163 | Lambeth | Newington Kennington Walworth | Cubitt Town

171 172 173 | **Camberwell** 48 49 Peckham | **Deptford** 50 51 | New Cross | 52 53 **Greenwich**

A202 | New Cross Gate | St Johns | Blackheath Vale

A2 | Blackheath

A102

Brixton

Stockwell 62 63 Herne Hill | 64 East Dulwich | **Nunhead** 65 Honor Oak | **Brockley** 66 Ladywell | **Lewisham** 67 Hither Green

A3 | Clapham Park | A20

A205

A202

Tulse Hill | Dulwich Village

A205 Streatham Hill 74 75 76 | Dulwich

West Norwood

Streatham

A23

A21

Scale					
0	1	2	3	4	5 km
0		1		2	3 miles

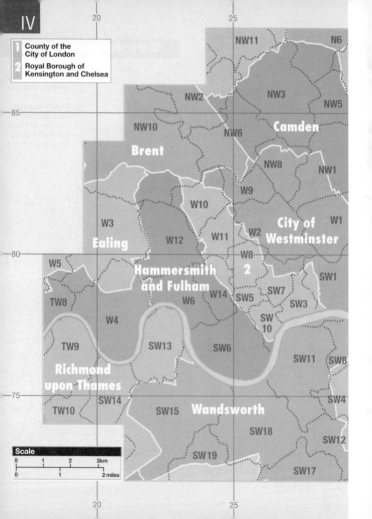

IV

Scale
0   1   2   3km
0   1   2 miles

1 County of the
City of London
2 Royal Borough of
Kensington and Chelsea

NW11
N6
NW2
NW3
NW5
85
NW10
Camden
NW6
Brent
NW8
NW1
W9
W10
W1
W3
W11
W2
City of
Westminster
Ealing
W12
W8
80
W5
2
Hammersmith
and Fulham
SW1
TW8
W6
W14
SW5
SW7
SW3
W4
SW10
TW9
SW13
SW6
SW11
SW8
Richmond
upon Thames
75
SW14
SW4
TW10
SW15
Wandsworth
SW18
SW12
SW19
SW17

20
25

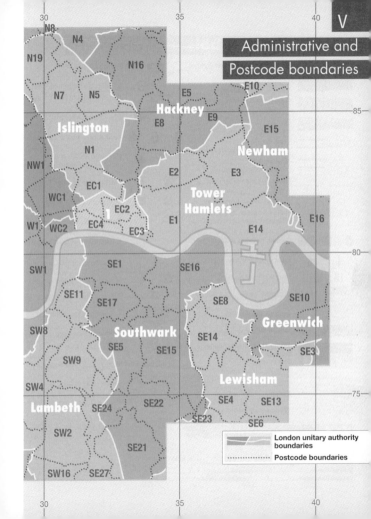

Administrative and
Postcode boundaries

London unitary authority boundaries

Postcode boundaries

Key to map symbols

(22a)	**Motorway** with junction number
	Primary route – single, dual carriageway
	A road – single, dual carriageway
	B road – single, dual carriageway
	Through-route – single, dual carriageway
	Minor road – single, dual carriageway
	Road under construction
	Rural track, private road or narrow road in urban area
	Path, bridleway, byway open to all traffic, road used as public path
	Tunnel, covered road
	Gate or barrier, car pound
P P&R	Parking, park and ride
Three Legged Cross	Junction name
	Pedestrianised area
	Restricted access area
	Congestion Charge Zone boundary Roads within the zone are outlined in red
	Houses, important buildings
	Woods, parkland/common

	Railway with station
	London Underground station
	Docklands Light Railway station
	Bus or coach station
♦ ♦ ♦	Ambulance, police, fire station
H ✚	Hospital, accident and emergency entrance
	Market, public amenity site
i PO	Information centre, post office
VILLA House	Roman, non-Roman antiquity
100 ·304	House number, spot height – in metres
✝	Christian place of worship
☾ ✡	Mosque, synagogue
▣	Other place of worship
65	Adjoining page number
NW6	Postcode boundary
City of Westminster	Unitary authority boundary
	Water, tidal water
	River or canal – minor, major Stream

Scale

3½ inches to 1 mile   1:18103

0	220yds	440yds	660yds	½ mile

0	250m	500m	750m	1km

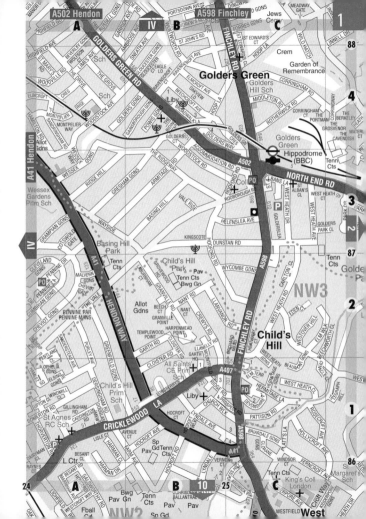

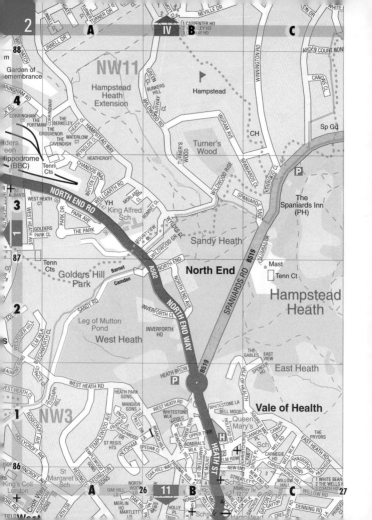

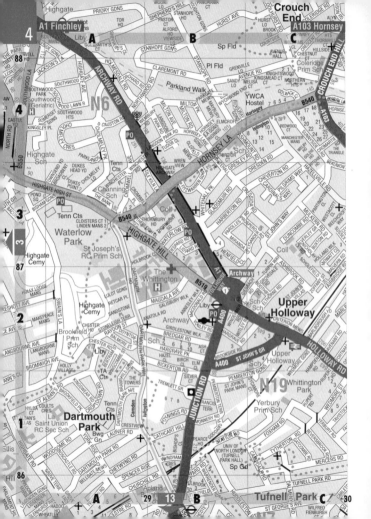

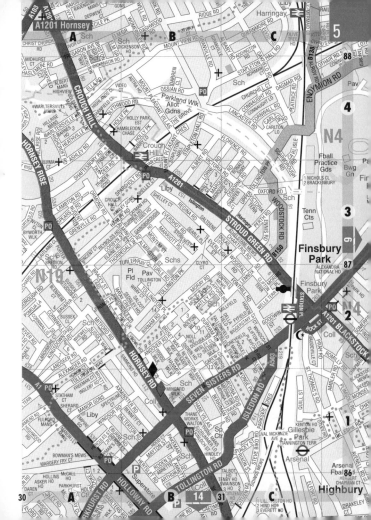

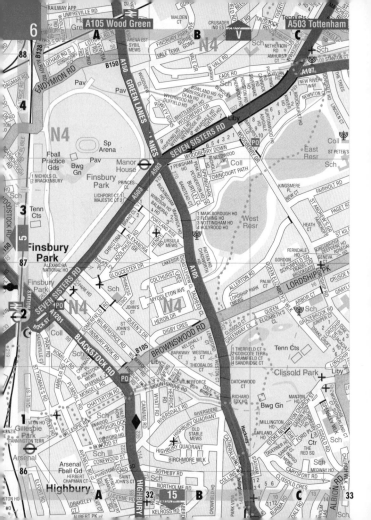

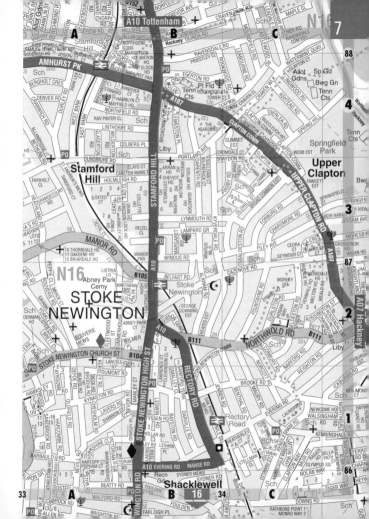

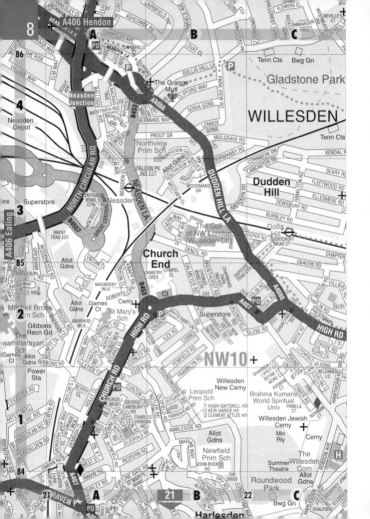

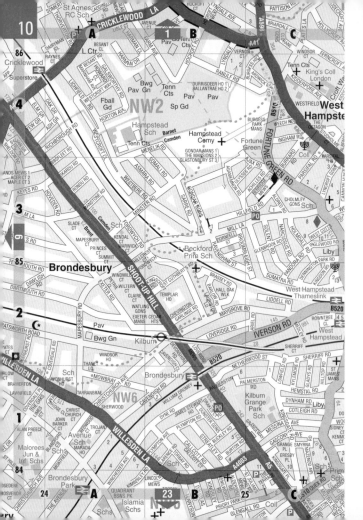

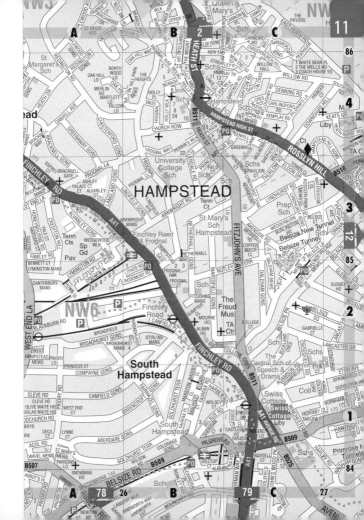

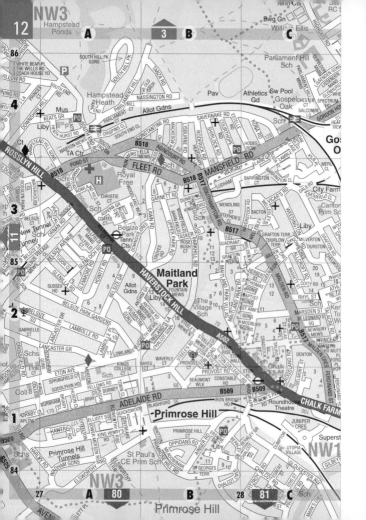

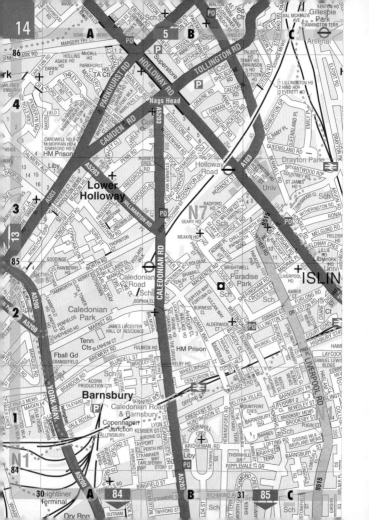

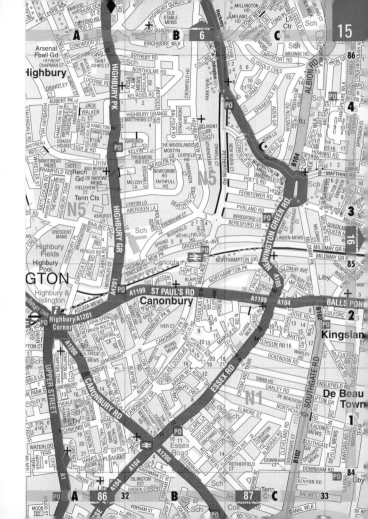

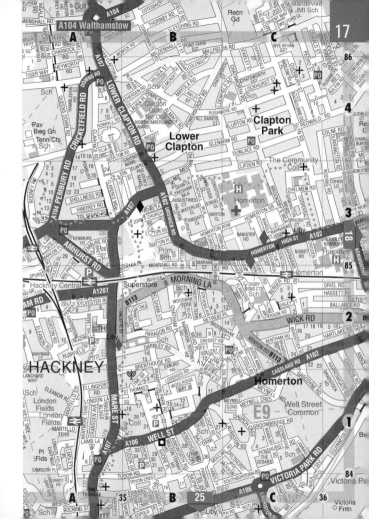

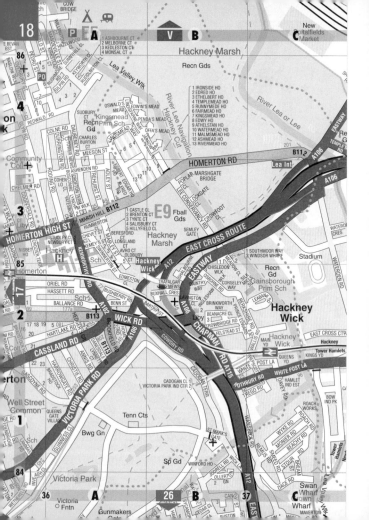

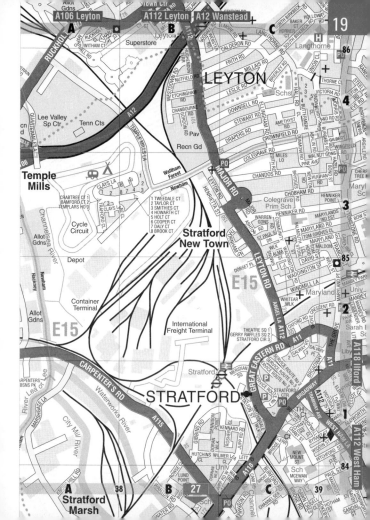

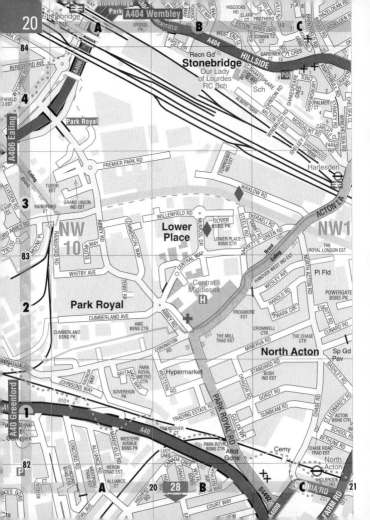

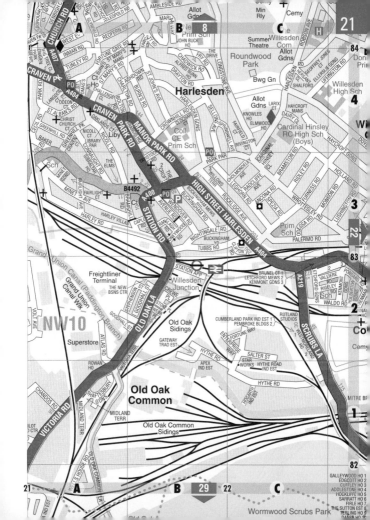

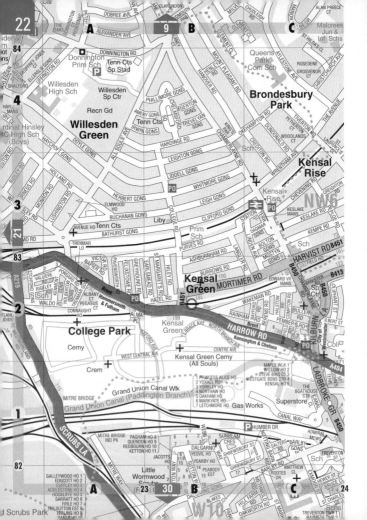

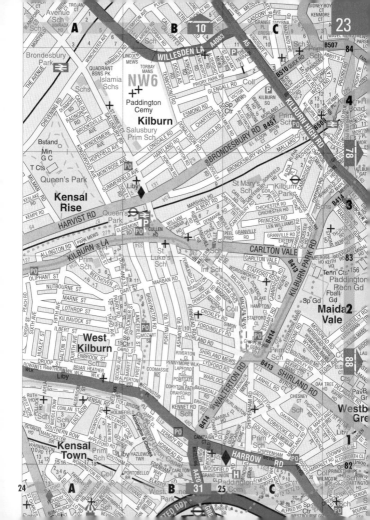

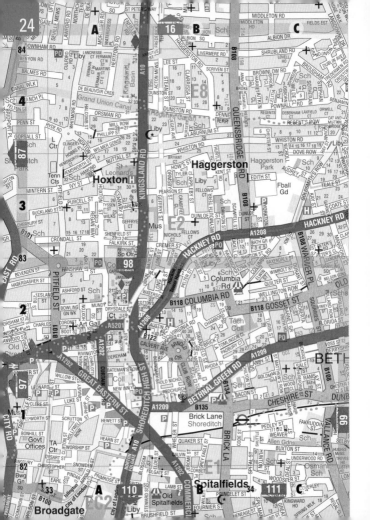

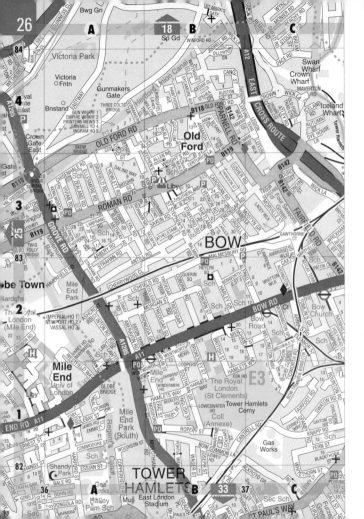

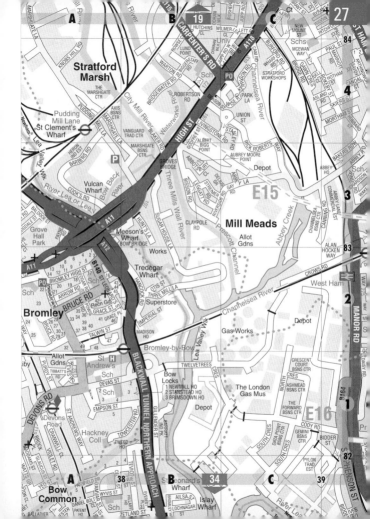

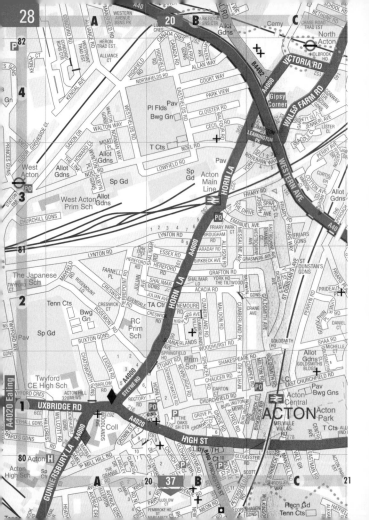

A40
WESTERN
AVENUE BSNS PK
SCHOOL RD
BETHUNE RD
A
20
B
C
CHASE ROAD
TRAD EST

CONCORD RD
WESTPOINT TRAD EST
CRES
CANADA CRES
PARK ROYAL
BSNS CTS
Allot
Gdns
North
Acton
Cemy
HOLBROOK HO

P 82
KENDAL CT
ALLIANCE RD
HERON
TRAD EST
ALLIANCE
CT
CANADA RD
WILFRID
CANADA RD
ALLAN WAY
VICTORIA RD
B4002

S GDNS
Gn
4
HIGHFIELD
RD
NORTHFIELDS AVE
COURT WAY
PARK VIEW
Gipsy
Corner
WALES FARM RD
DENWAY
A4000

GROVESIDE CL
GROVE DR
WALTON
GDNS
WESTFIELDS RD
NORMAN WAY
SAXON DR
MOAT
CT
Pl Flds
Pav
Bwg Gn
CLOISTER RD
CECIL RD
BALFOUR RD
LEAMINGTON
ROSEBANK WAY
GARRETT CL
LISTER CT
JENNER AVE
PERRY AVE

PRINCES GDNS
West
Acton
3
HOWARD CT
THE LINK
NOEL RD
ALWYN AVE
T Cts
NOEL RD
LOWFIELD RD
Sp
Gd
Pav
Acton
Main
Line
FRIARY RD
THE DRIVE
SPA RD
ST JOSEPH'S AVE
WESTERN AVE
CURTIS
DR
Allot
Gdns
A40

STATION RD
West Acton
Prim Sch
Allot
Gdns
Allot
Gdns
HORN LA
PO
EMANUEL AVE
FRIARY PARK
BROUGHAM
TESSAL NE AVE
GRASMERE AVE
EASTBOURNE
WESTBOURNE
FRIARS WAY
ST DUNSTAN'S
GDNS
FRIARS PL LA
FRIARS RD

CHURCHILL GDNS
81
LYNTON RD
1 2 3 4 5
LYNTON RD
FARADAY RD
ALLISON RD
BIRKBECK RD
YORK HO
ACACIA RD
The Japanese
Sch
MATFIELD
ROSEMOUNT
LO
OAK
TREE
SHALIMAR
ESSEX RD
HEREFORD
PL
HEREFORD
SHALIMAR
The Tiltwood
GDNS
ST DUNSTAN'S RD
PRIDEAU

2
Tenn Cts
Bwg
Gn
Sp Gd
Pav
FARNELL
RD
CRESWICK RD
ROSEMOUNT
RD
CRESWICK RD
BUXTON GDNS
PERREPOINT RD
JULIAN AVE
EDENDALE
NEMOURE
CRESWICK
HORN LA
TA Ctr
RC
Prim
Sch
HIGH
CUMBERLAND RD
MALDON RD
CUMBERLAND
PK
CRANE
AVE
CUMBERLAND AVE
GOLDSMITH AVE
GOLDSMITH
(HO)
Allot
Gdns
MICHELLE
CT
DANIEL
CT
SHAA RD
VYNER RD

A4020 Ealing
1
UXBRIDGE RD
Twyford
CE High Sch
TWYFORD CRES
WHITEHALL GDNS
HILLCREST
CHATSWORTH GDNS
BARLOW
LECKER RD
STEYNE RD
1 2
HORN LA
RECTORY
A4020
KING
SUMMERLANDS
SPRINGFIELD
RD
STUART RD
NEWBURGH RD
WOODHURST RD
SHAKESPEARE RD
Prim
Sch
CHAUCER RD
DARTON
CHURCHFIELD RD
MILTON RD
NAPIER RD
LC
East Churchfield RD
GOLDSMITH'S
BLDGS
CENTRAL AVE
P
BURLINGTON
Pav
Bwg Gns
T Cts
ACTON
Acton
Central
Acton
Park
MELVILLE
VILLAS
RD

80
Acton
Coll
A4020
Acton
High Sch
GUNNERSBURY LA
A4000
WOODLANDS
AVE
WILCOTT RD
MILL HILL RD
CROWN ST
HIGH ST
THE
OAKS
SCH CTR
P
CROMES
P
GROVE PL
P
P
FRED RD
P
SCOTT
P
GLOUCESTER
THE GRANGE
WINCHESTER RD
BIRKBECK RD
VALE RD
EASTMAN RD
CROSS LEY
WAY

H
A
20
37
B
C
21
Acton
High Sch
WOODLANDS AVE
AVENUE RD N
MEON RD
PEMBROKE HO
COPENHAGEN
GDNS
WILKINSON
Recn Gd
Tenn Cts
HATFIEL

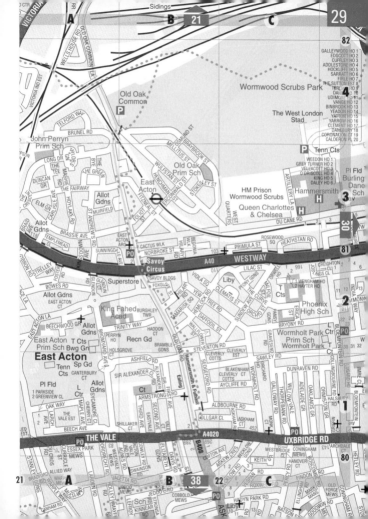

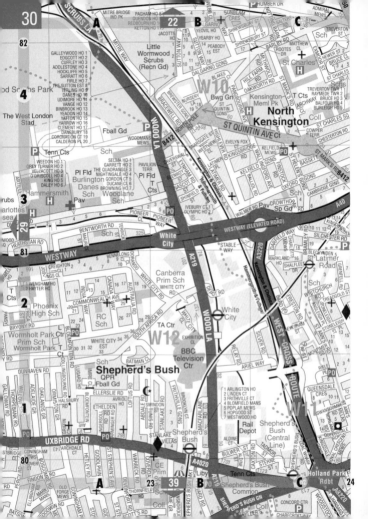

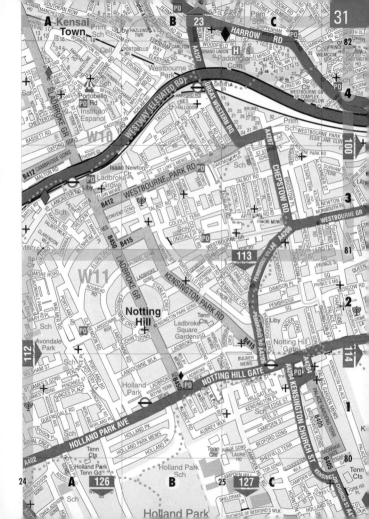

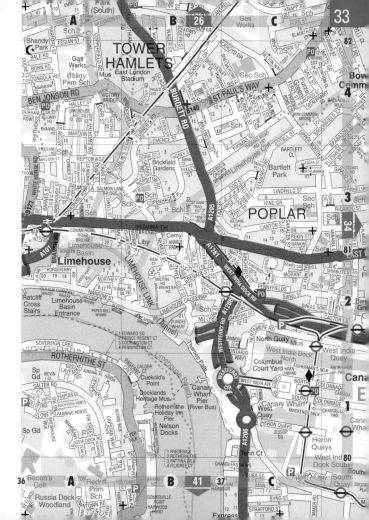

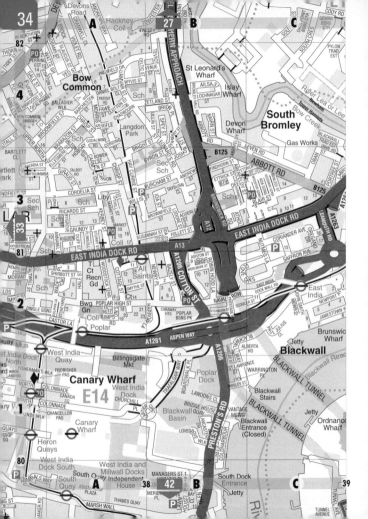

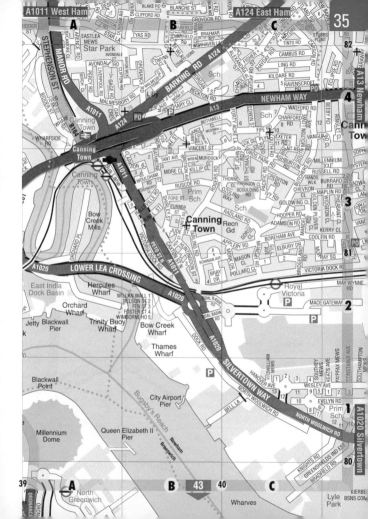

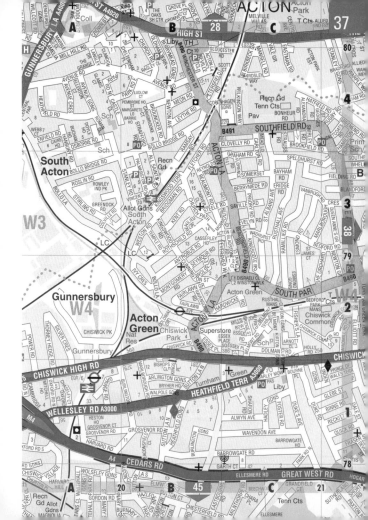

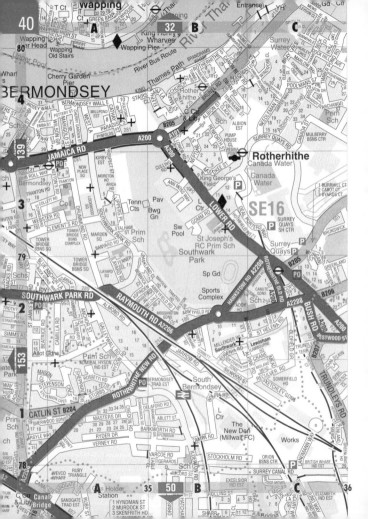

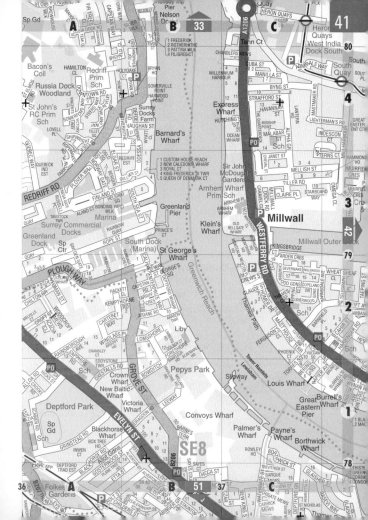

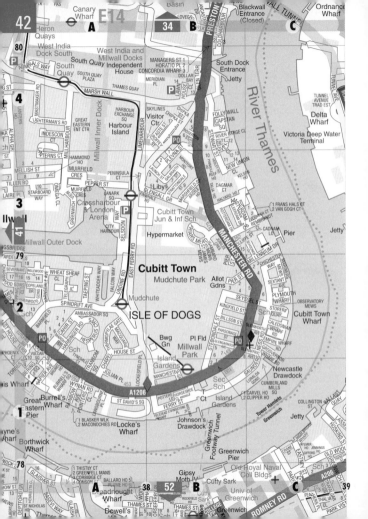

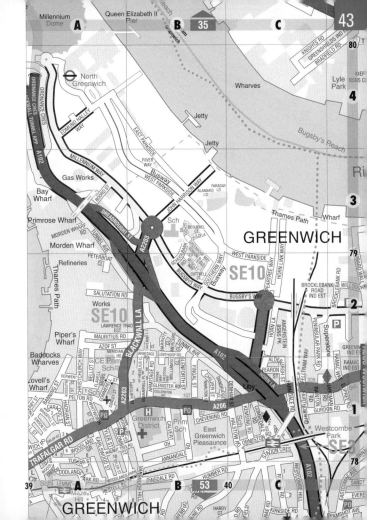

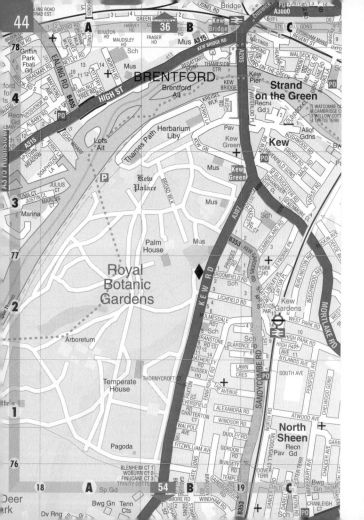

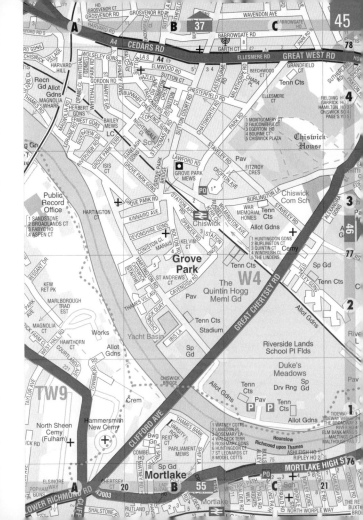

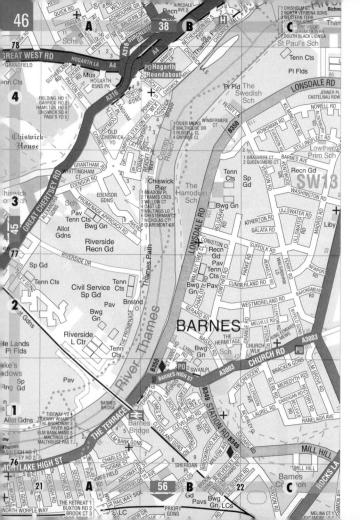

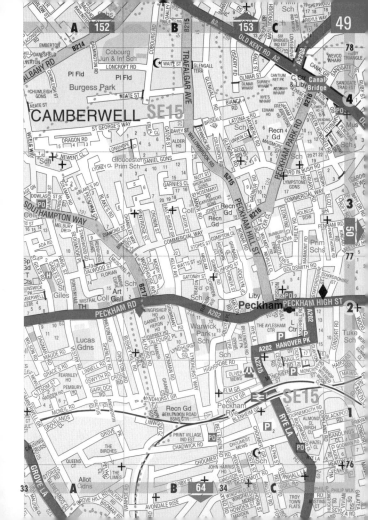

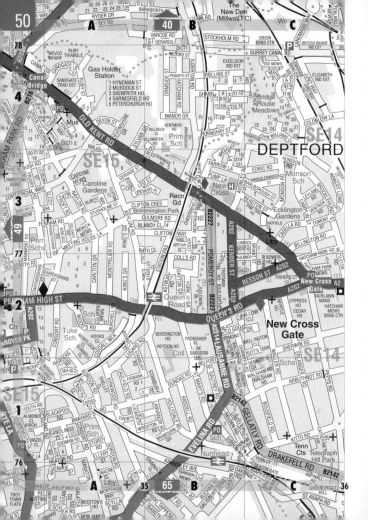

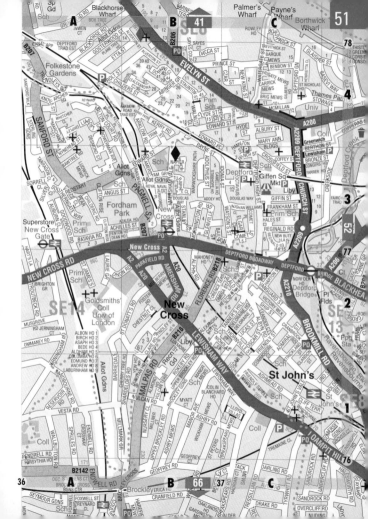

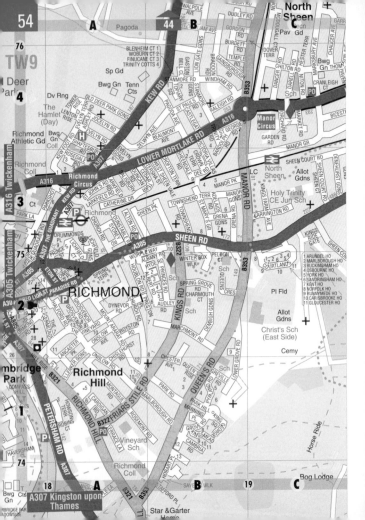

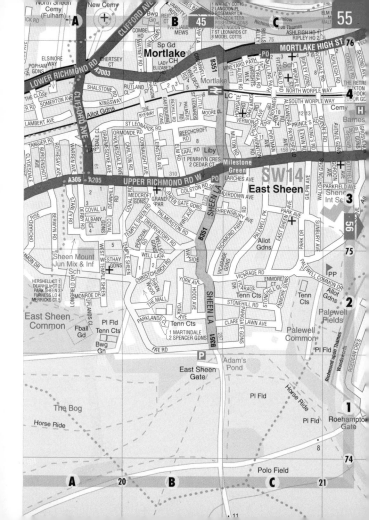

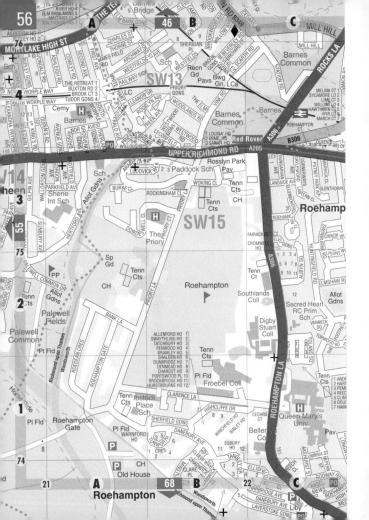

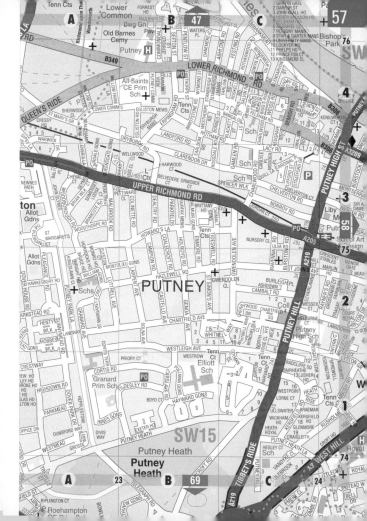

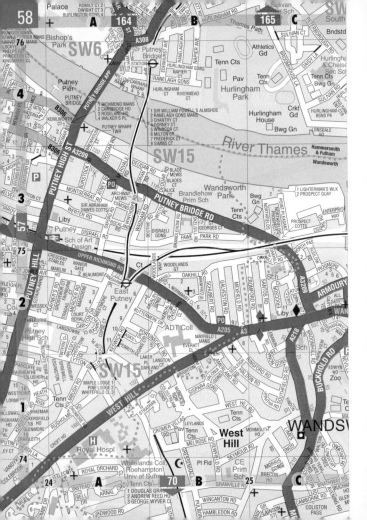

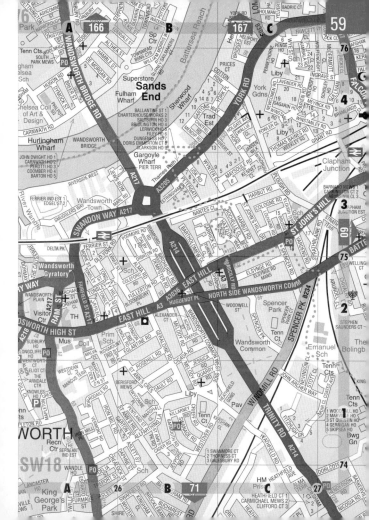

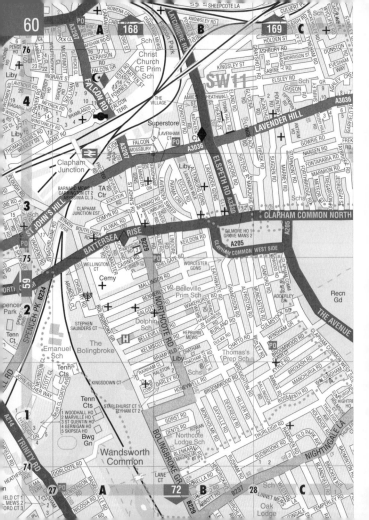

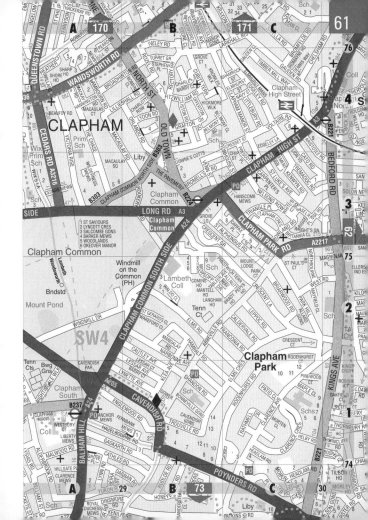

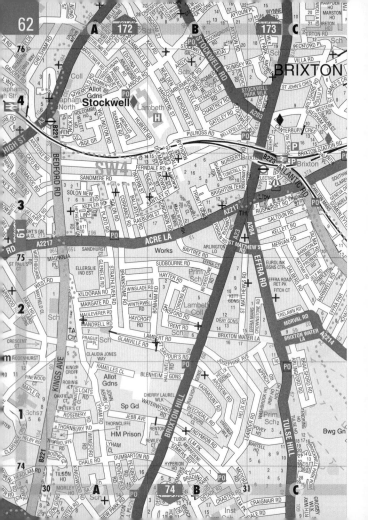

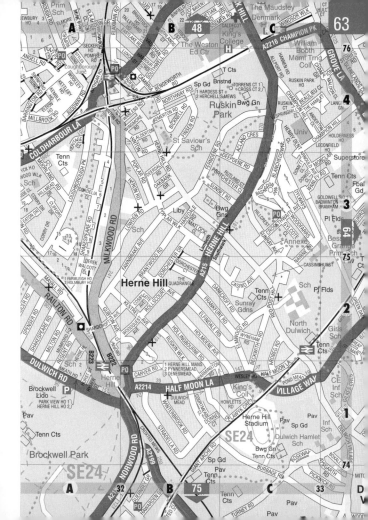

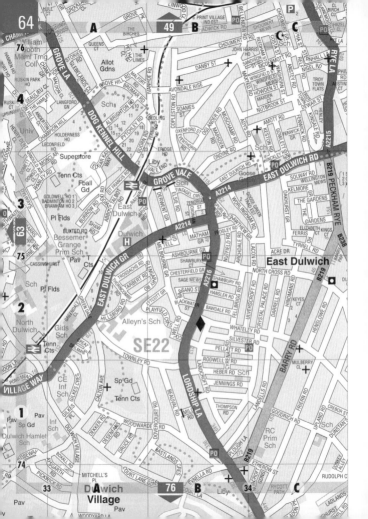

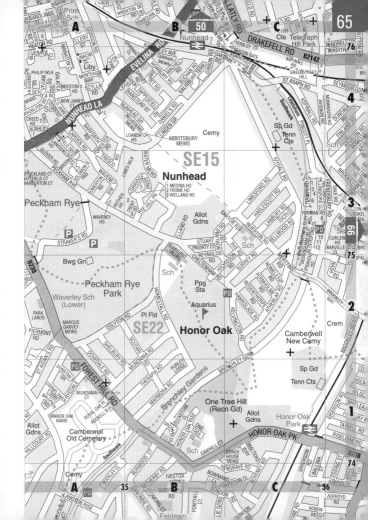

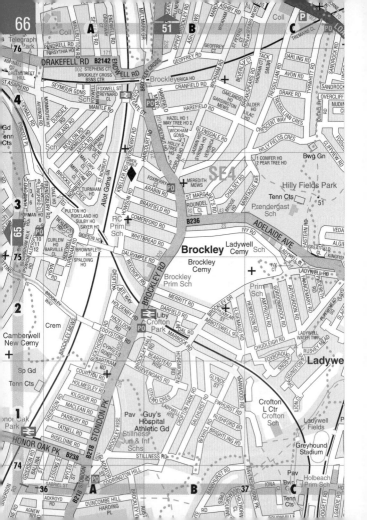

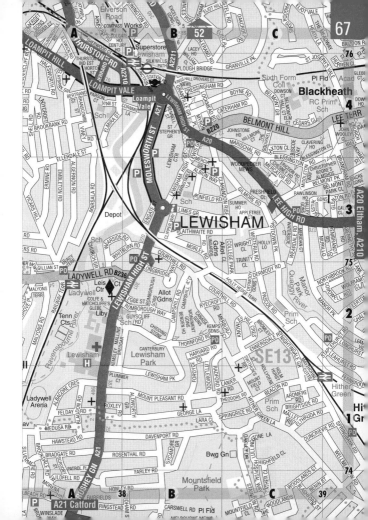

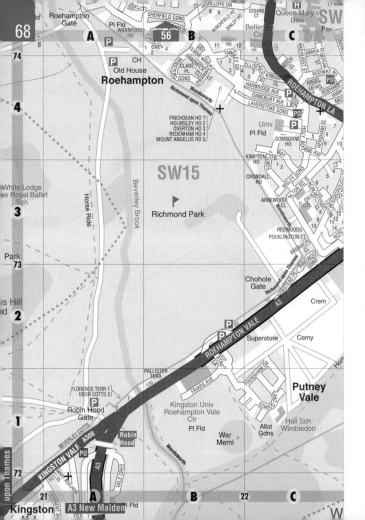

74

4

3

Park
73

s Hill
d

2

1

72

21

Roehampton Gate

A P

PI Fld
WARNFORD
HO

SHERFIELD GDNS

56

B

CEDARS
CT

Queen Mary's
Univ

Belleve
Co

SW

C Pav

8

2 CRES 4

CH
P
Old House

Roehampton

KINGS
CLARE
PL

CHADWICK
GDNS

WINCHFIELD HO
BINLEY HO

EGBURY
HO

11 12

TANGLEY GR

UMBRIA ST

ARCHWOOD ST

RODWAY RD

ANGEL WK

ROEHAMPTON LA

HIGH

PO

Wandsworth
Richmond upon Thames

+

ELLISFIELD DR

HARBRIDGE AVE
DANEBURY AVE Liby

LAVERSTOKE GDNS

5

P

P

+

SW15

FINCHDEAN HO 1
HOLMSLEY HO 2
OVERTON HO 3
REDENHAM HO 4
MOUNT ANGELUS RD 5

Univ
PI Fld

P

SOMBORNE
HO

FONTLEY WAY

PINE AVE

White Lodge
e Royal Ballet
Sch

3

Horse Ride

Beverley Brook

▶

Richmond Park

KIMPTON
HO

CRONDALL
HO

IBSLEY GDNS

ARNEWOOD
CL

Wandsworth

Sch

REDWOODS
POCKLINGTON CT

Chohole
Gate

Richmond upon Thames

BREAMORE
CL

LONGWOOD
GDNS

Crem

Crem

Cemy

A3

P
P

ROEHAMPTON VALE

Superstore

Cemy

Putney
Vale

Hors

PALLISTER
TERR

196

FRIARS AVE

FRENSHAM DR

STROUD CRES

Kingston Univ
Roehampton Vale
Ctr
PI Fld

Allot
Gdns

Hall Sch
Wimbledon

FLORENCE TERR 1
EBOR COTTS 2

P
Robin Hood
Gate

BEVERLEY COTTS

KINGSTON VALE A308

Robin
Hood

PO

A3

VALE CRES

Wandsworth

War
Meml

+

A A3 New Malden

22

upon Thames

Kingston

PI Fld

B

C

W

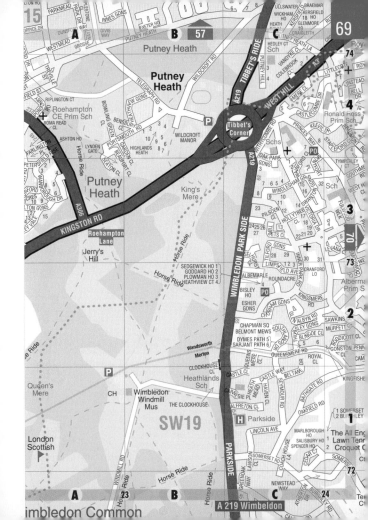

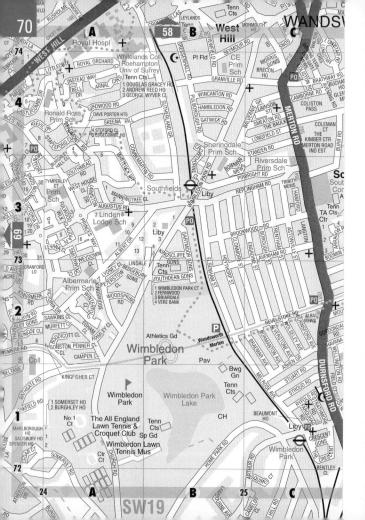

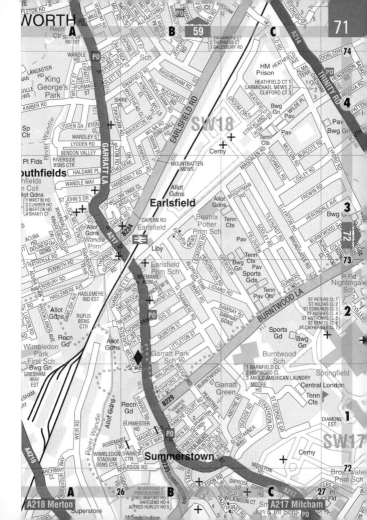

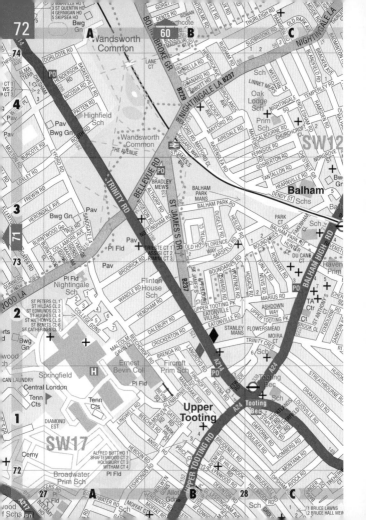

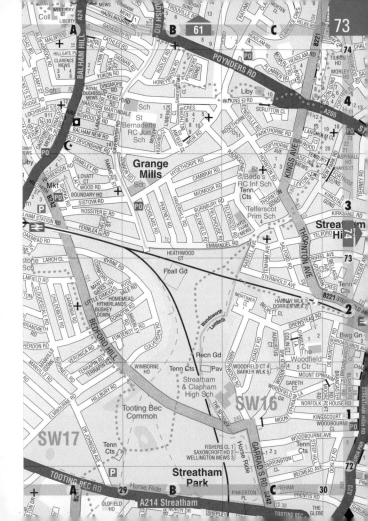

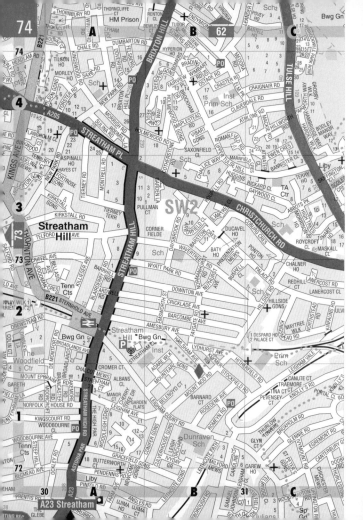

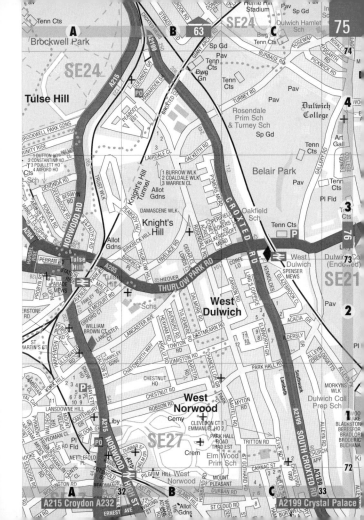

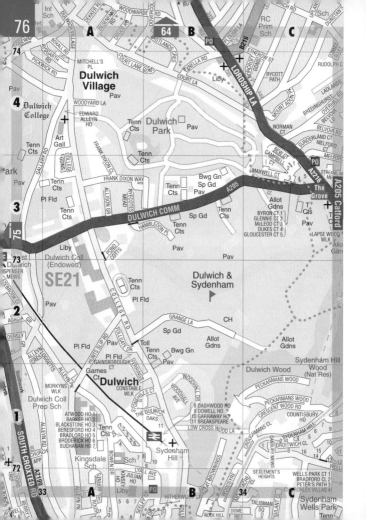

Key to enlarged map pages

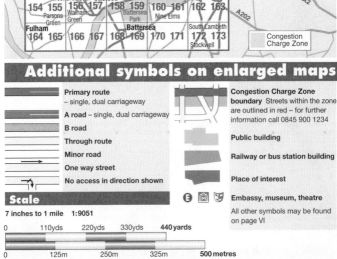

78 79 St John's Wood	Primrose Hill 80 81 Regent's	82 83 Somers Town	Islington 84 85 King's Cross	86 87		A10
Maida Vale 88 89 Westbourne Green	Park 90 91 Lisson Grove	92 93	St Pancras Finsbury 94 95 Bloomsbury	Shoreditch 96 97	Bethnal 98 99 Green	
Paddington 100 101	Marylebone 102 103	Fitzrovia 104 105	Holborn 106 107 St Giles Strand	108 109 City	Spitalfields 110 111 Whitechapel	A11 A13
Notting Hill 112 113	Bayswater 114 115 Kensington	116 117 Hyde Park	Mayfair 118 119 St James	120 121 South Bank	Southwark 122 123	124 125 St George in the East
Kensington Holland Pk 126 127 West Kensington	Gardens 128 129 South Kensington	Knightsbridge 130 131 Brompton	Green Park 132 133 Westminster	Waterloo 134 135 The Borough	136 137	138 139 Bermondsey
140 141 Earl's Ct	142 143	Belgravia 144 145	Pimlico 146 147	Lambeth 148 149 Vauxhall Kennington	Newington 150 151 Walworth	152 153
West Brompton Chelsea 154 155 Parsons Green	Walham 156 157 Green	158 159 Battersea Park	160 161 Nine Elms	162 163	A202	A2
Fulham 164 165	Battersea 166 167	168 169	170 171	South Lambeth 172 173 Stockwell		

Congestion Charge Zone

Additional symbols on enlarged maps

Primary route
– single, dual carriageway

A road – single, dual carriageway

B road

Through route

Minor road

One way street

No access in direction shown

**Congestion Charge Zone
boundary** Streets within the zone
are outlined in red – for further
information call 0845 900 1234

Public building

Railway or bus station building

Place of interest

E 🏛 🛡 **Embassy, museum, theatre**

All other symbols may be found
on page VI

Scale

7 inches to 1 mile   1:9051

0	110yds	220yds	330yds	**440 yards**

0	125m	250m	325m	**500 metres**

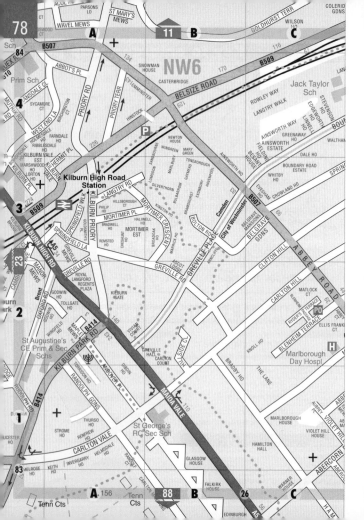

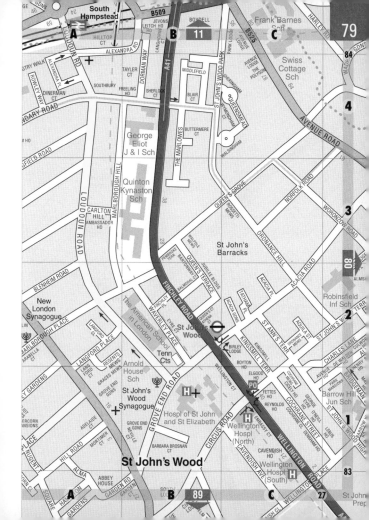

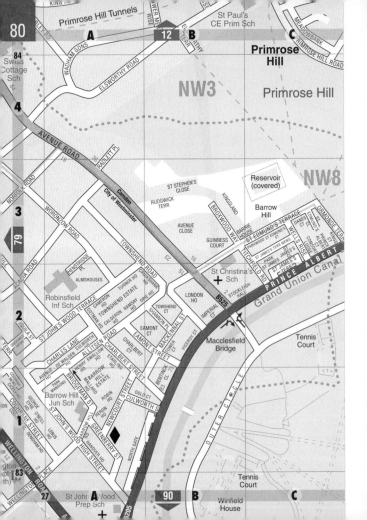

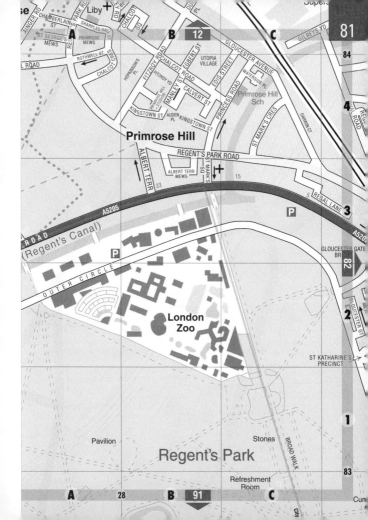

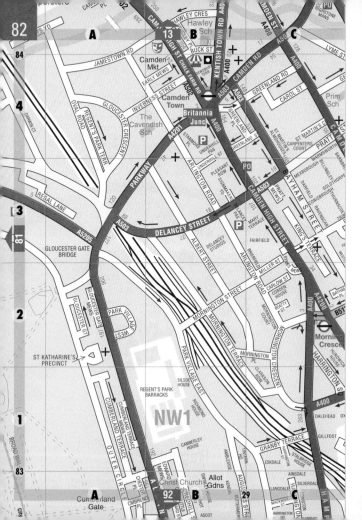

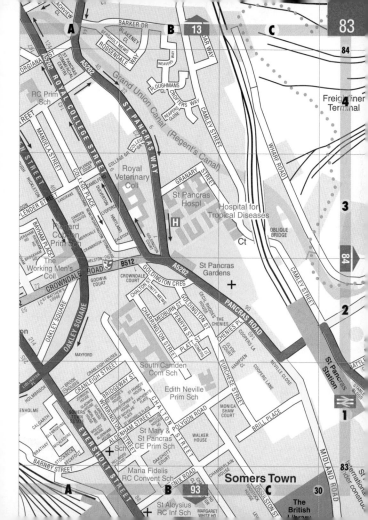

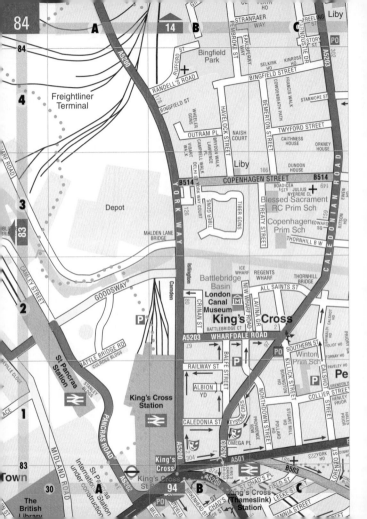

SHOREDITCH

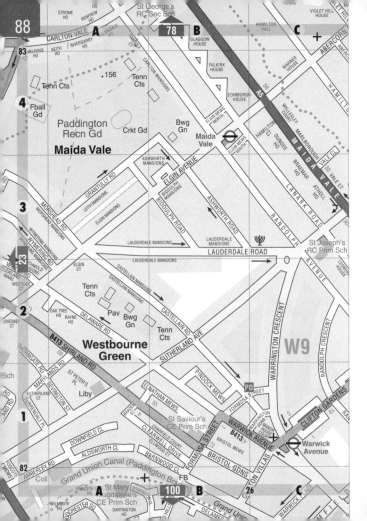

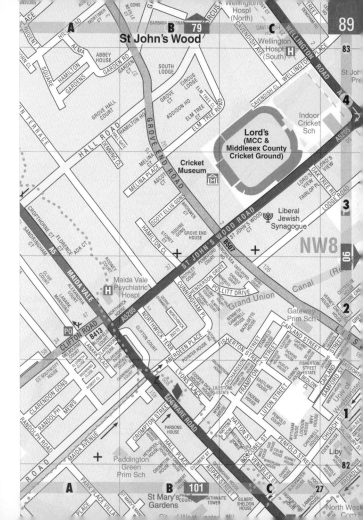

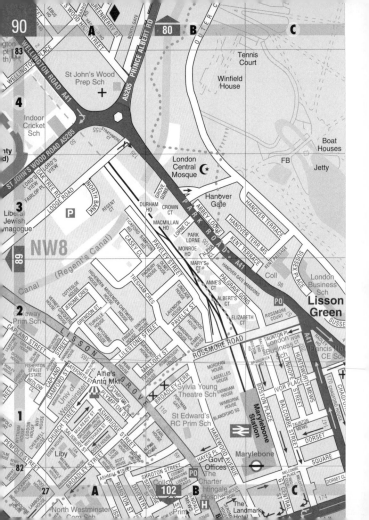

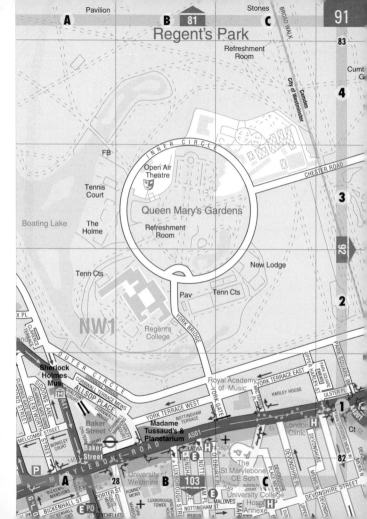

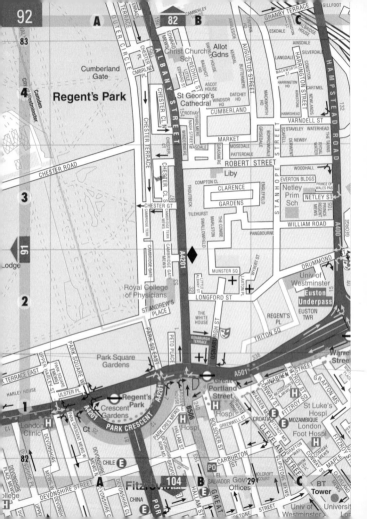

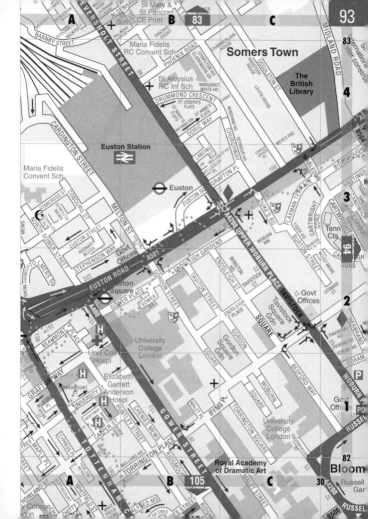

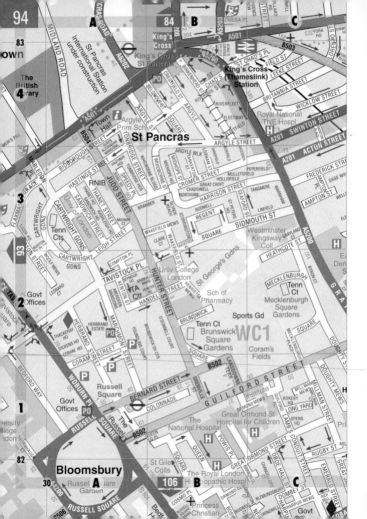

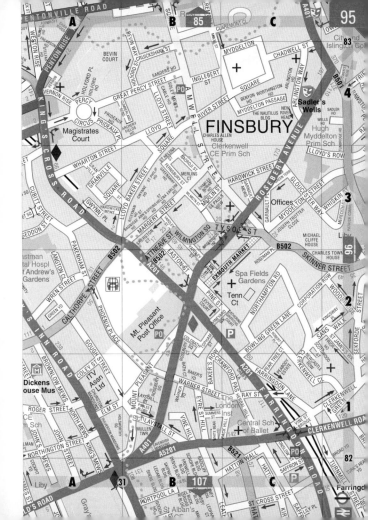

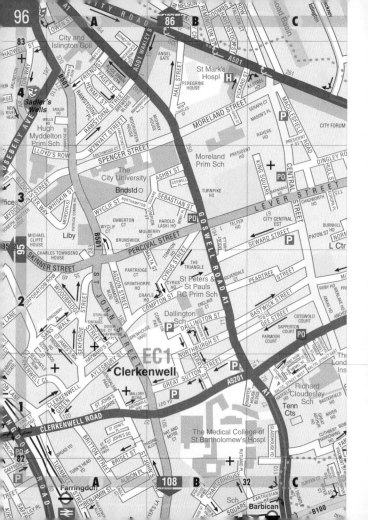

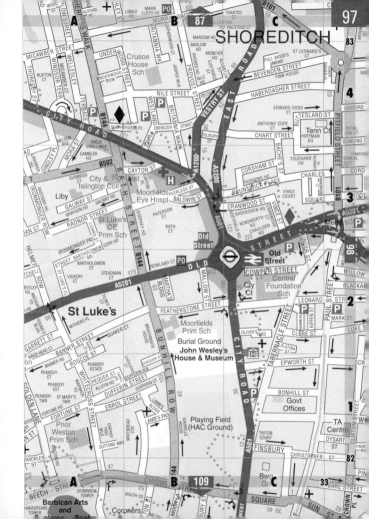

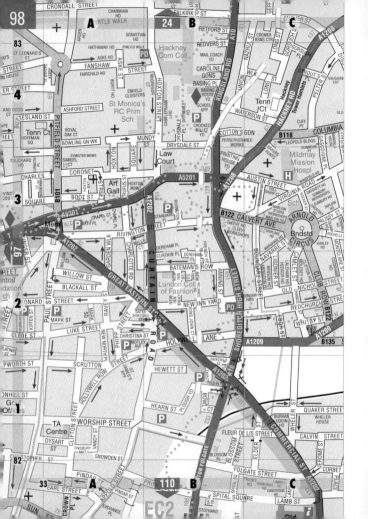

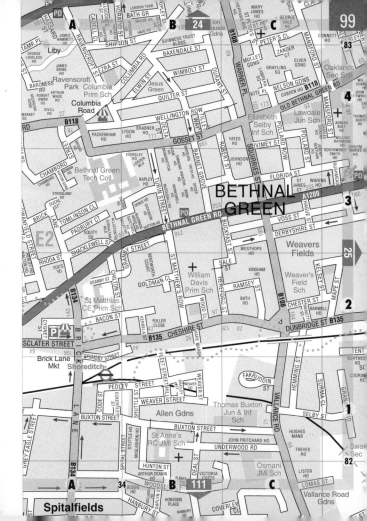

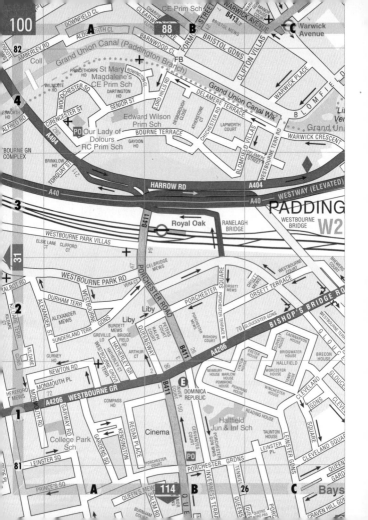

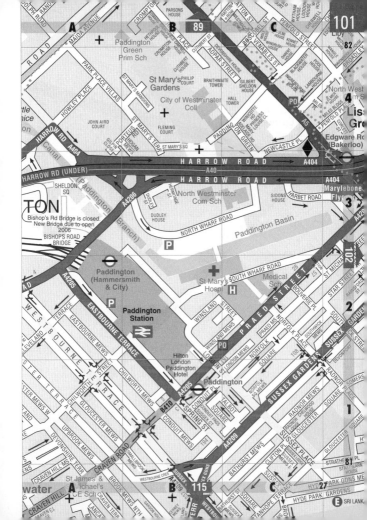

A   MAIDA AVENUE
B   89
C   82

Paddington
Green
Prim Sch

PARSONS
HOUSE

PENFOLD STREET

St Mary's
Gardens

PHILIP
COURT

City of Westminster
Coll

Braithwaite
Tower

Gilbert
Sheldon House

North West
m S

4

Lis
Gre

HALL
TOWER

Edgware Rd
(Bakerloo)

JOHN AIRD
COURT

FLEMING
COURT

PADDINGTON GREEN

A5

NEWCASTLE PL

HARROW ROAD   A404

HARROW ROAD (UNDER)   A40

HARROW ROAD   A404

Marylebone
Flyo

SHELDON
SQ

TON
Bishop's Rd Bridge is closed.
New Bridge due to open
2006
BISHOPS ROAD
BRIDGE

North Westminster
Com Sch

SIDONS
HOUSE

TARBET ROAD

3

A42

HEAD AGE

DUDLEY
HOUSE

NORTH WHARF ROAD

Paddington Basin

102

P

Paddington
(Hammersmith
& City)

SOUTH WHARF ROAD

St Mary's
Hosp

H

Medical
Sch

STAR STREET

2

P

Paddington
Station

PRAED STREET

EASTBOURNE TERRACE

WINSLAND STREET

Hilton
London
Paddington
Hotel

PO

NORFOLK PLACE

SUSSEX GARDE

SUSSEX

CHILWORTH MEWS

Paddington

B410

CONDUIT STREET

TALBOT
SQUARE

NORFOLK
SQUARE

SUSSEX GARDENS

RADNOR MEWS

1

GLOUCESTER MEWS

SPRING STREET

CONDUIT MEWS

SUSSEX PLACE

RADNOR
SQUARE

UPBROOK MEWS

BATHURST MEWS

CLIFTON

81

DEVONSHIRE MEWS

GLOUCESTER
SQUARE

STRATHE
PL

A   CRAVEN HILL
water

St James &
Michael's
CE Sch

B   115

WESTBOURNE CRES

C   27

HYDE PARK GARDENS

E   SRI LANK

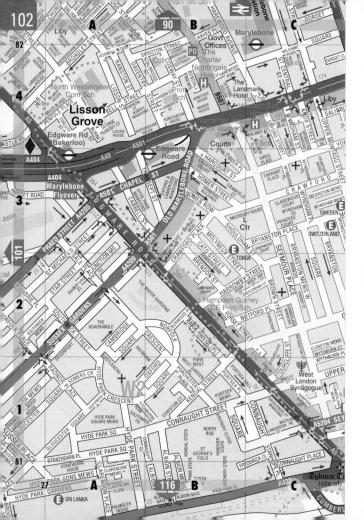

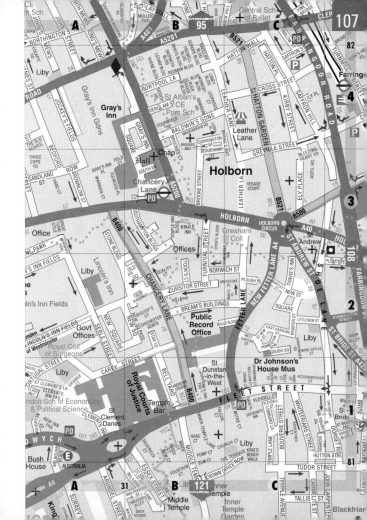

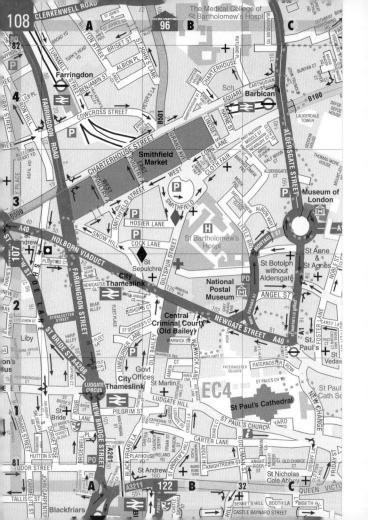

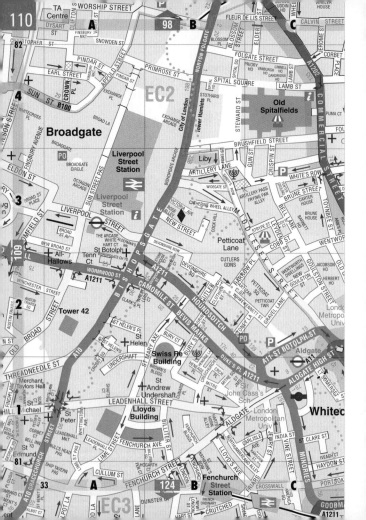

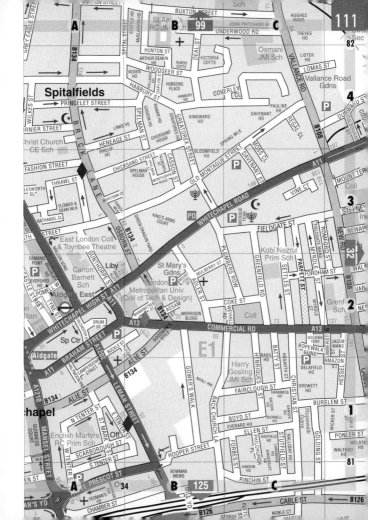

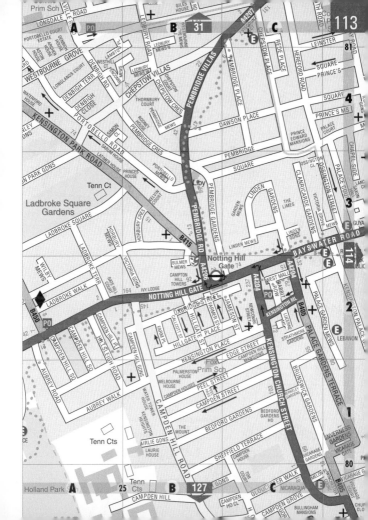

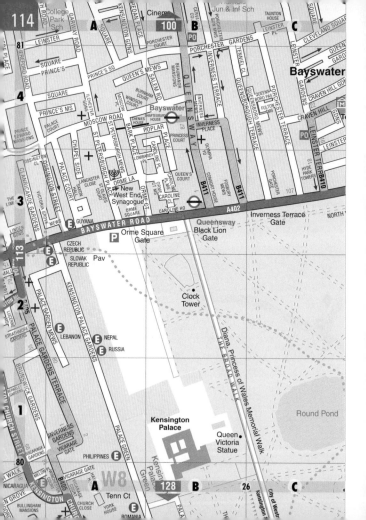

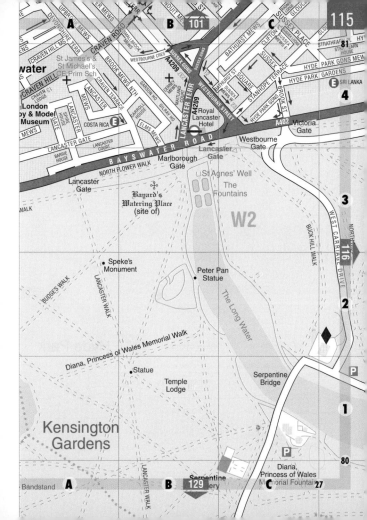

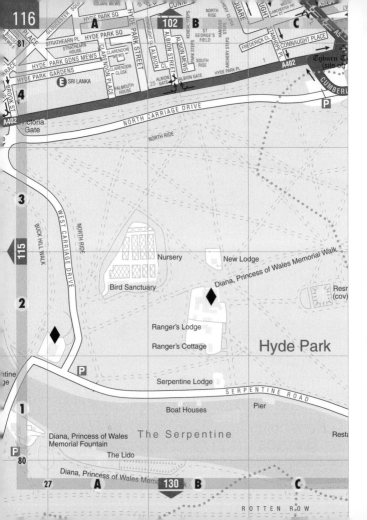

A

81

GLOUCESTER SQ

SQUARE MEWS

HYDE PARK SQ

STRATHEARN PL   HYDE PARK SQ

STRATHEARN
HOUSE

HYDE PARK GDNS MEWS

HYDE PARK GARDENS

CLARENDON
MEWS

CLARENDON
CLOSE

FALMOUTH
HOUSE

B

NORTH
RISE

ST
GEORGE'S
FIELD

SOUTH
RISE

ALBION
MEWS

25 ALBION
GATE

ALBION GATE

HYDE PARK PL

C

NORTH
LANCHESTER CT
WEST

FREDERICK CL   CONNAUGHT PLACE

CONNAUGHT PLACE

A402

Tyburn T
(site of

4

E Sri Lanka

A402

Victoria
Gate

NORTH CARRIAGE DRIVE

NORTH RIDE

P

CUMBERL

3

WEST CARRIAGE DRIVE

NORTH RIDE

BUCK HILL WALK

◀ **115**

Nursery

New Lodge

Diana, Princess of Wales Memorial Walk

Bird Sanctuary

Resr
(cov)

2

◆

◆

Ranger's Lodge

Ranger's Cottage

Hyde Park

P

Serpentine Lodge

SERPENTINE ROAD

1

ntine
ge

Boat Houses

Pier

Resta

P

80

Diana, Princess of Wales
Memorial Fountain

The Serpentine

The Lido

Diana, Princess of Wales Memor

27

A

▼ **130**

B

C

ROTTEN ROW

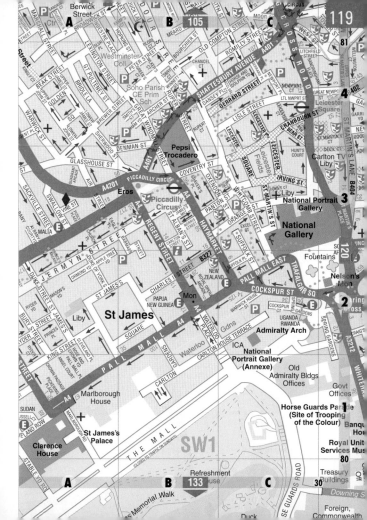

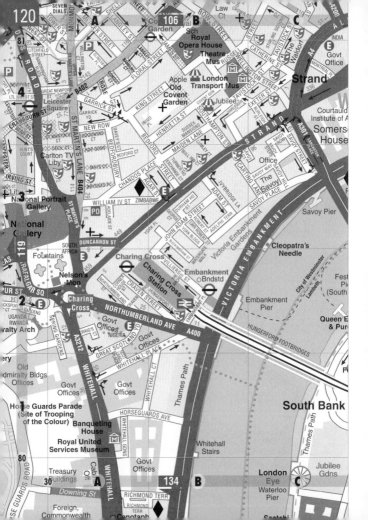

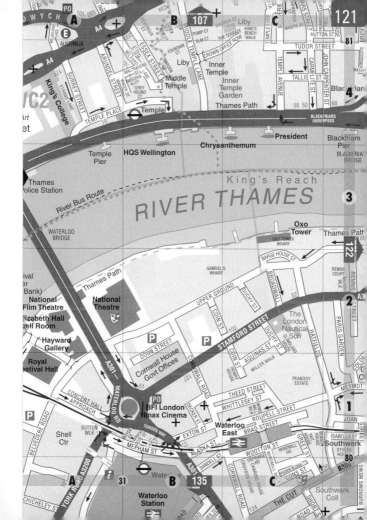

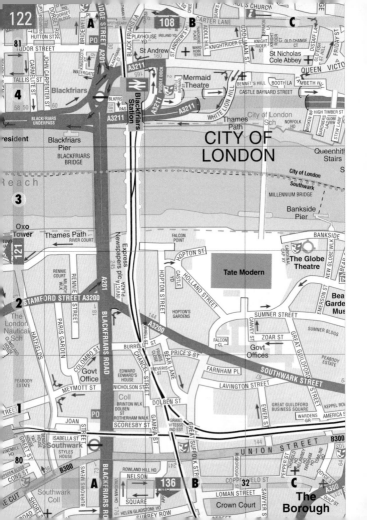

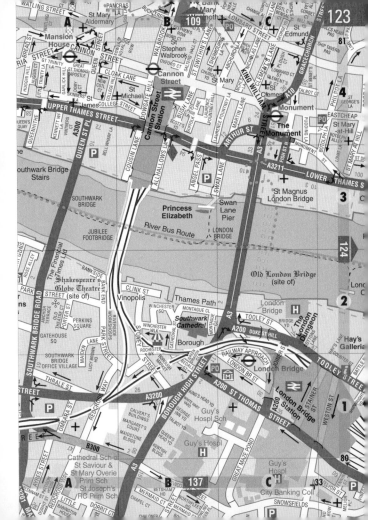

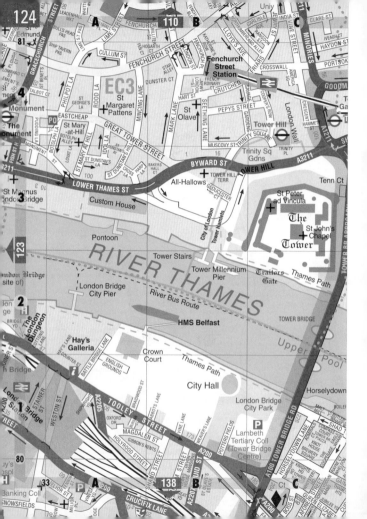

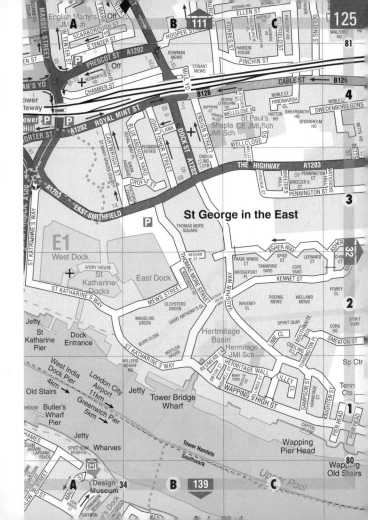

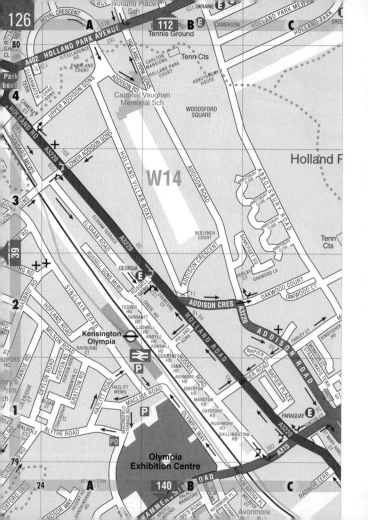

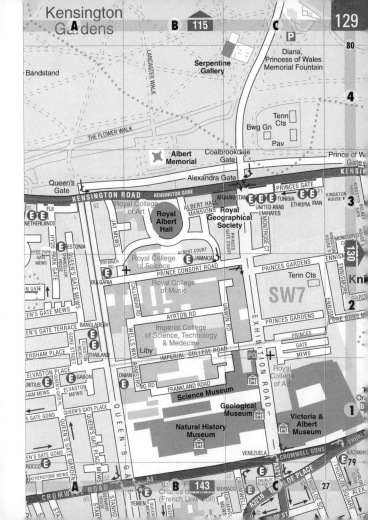

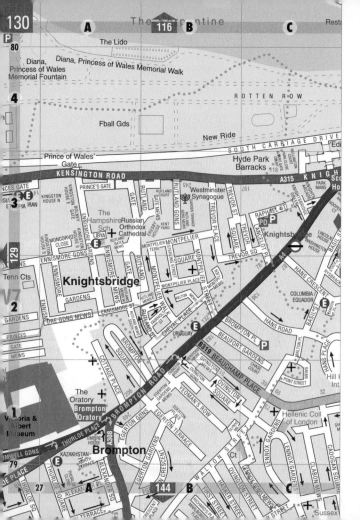

A **116** B C Resta

P
80
The Lido

Diana, Diana, Princess of Wales Memorial Walk
Princess of Wales
Memorial Fountain

4
ROTTEN ROW

Fball Gds

New Ride

SOUTH CARRIAGE DRIVE Edi

Prince of Wales'
Gate
Hyde Park
Barracks

KENSINGTON ROAD A315 KNIGH

NCES GATE Westminster PRINCE'S GATE Synagogue
3 E Kingston RUTLAND Park
SIA House N GATE RAPHAEL ST Mans
ROMA IRAN PO Ho
Kingston GATE Russian P
House S Gate Orthodox Cathedral Knightsbridge LINCOLN
The Hampshire HOUSE
LIBYA E Sch E Knightsbridge WASHINGTON
MONCORVO Kingston Gardens Montpelier HOUSE BASIL
CLOSE Terr HANS CRESCENT
129 ENNISMORE GDNS Montpelier RYBRACKS
Tenn Cts ENNISMORE Square COLUMBIA
Knightsbridge EQUADOR E
ENNISMORE GARDENS Montpelier Place BASIL ST
V7 GARDENS ENNISMORE ST HANS ROAD HANS PLACE
2 Rutland CHEVAL PLACE Hill H
GARDENS ORE GDNS MEWS Mews E Int
PRINCES URUGUAY BEAUFORT GARDENS
GATE COTTAGE PLACE B319 BEAUCHAMP PLACE P CHASE
MEWS SQUARE BROMPTON ROAD Court PONT STREET
EGERTON GDNS YEOMAN'S ROW
The EGERTON GARDENS MEWS Hellenic Coll
Oratory OVINGTON SQUARE of London
Brompton THURLOE EGERTON GDNS EGERTON TERRACE WALTON STR
Oratory PLACE A308 Ct LENNOX GARDENS
Victoria & EMPIRE Brompton OVINGTON SQUARE MEWS CADOGAN
Albert HOUSE LENNOX GARDENS
Museum 79 KAZAKHSTAN E CRESCENT
OMWELL GDNS THURLOE PL LENNOX CLABON
GE PLACE EGERTON GARDENS OVINGTON STREET
THURLOE SQUARE
27 A 144 B HASKER STREET C
ALEXAN EG FIRST STREET Sussex

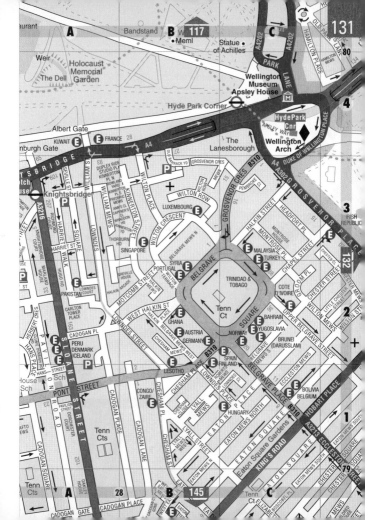

A   Bandstand   **B** W 117   **C** A4202

Restaurant

• Meml

Statue
of Achilles

80

Weir

Holocaust
Memorial
Garden

The Dell

Wellington
Museum
Apsley House

4

Albert Gate

Hyde Park Corner

Hyde Park
Cnr

KUWAIT E FRANCE 28

Edinburgh Gate

The
Lanesborough

Wellington
Arch

APSLEY WAY

DUKE OF WELLINGTON PLACE

3

IRISH
REPUBLIC

Knightsbridge

BRIDGE

A3216

SEVILLE ST

WILLIAM S

DUPLEX RIDE
STUDIO PL
KINNERTON
PL N
KINNERTON
YARD

FREDERIC
MEWS

ANN'S CL

CAPENER'S
CL

WILTON ROW

P

GROSVENOR CRES

B310

GROSVENOR CRES

A302 GROSVENOR PLACE

132

Hatch
House

HARRIET WALK

HUGO RD

WILLIAM MEWS

KINNERTON STREET

WILTON PLACE

LUXEMBOURG E

WILTON CRESCENT

PEMBROKE

HALKIN STREET

HEADFORT PL

MONTROSE
PL

MONTROSE
CT

CHAPEL STREET

MALAYSIA E
E TURKEY

2

WILTON MEWS

LITTLE CHESTER MEWS

CHESTER STREET

HARRIET STREET

SQUARE

LOWNDES

THORBURN
HO

SINGAPORE E

BELGRAVE MEWS W

SYRIA E

PORTUGAL E

WILTON
TERRACE

BELGRAVE

TRINIDAD &
TOBAGO

CHESTER STREET

COTE
D'IVOIRE E

UPPER BELGRAVE STREET

WILTON MEWS

PAKISTAN E

CARLTON
TOWER
PLACE

GREVILLE
HOUSE

HALKIN ARCADE

MOTCOMBE STREET

HALKIN ST

HALKIN
PLACE

WEST HALKIN ST

GHANA E

SQUARE

Tenn
Ct

BAHRAIN E

NORWAY E

E YUGOSLAVIA

BRUNEI
(DARUSSLAM)

1

CADOGAN PL

HERBERT CRES

PAVILION

SLOANE

LOWNDES STREET

BELGRAVE MEWS S

E AUSTRIA

CHESHAM
PLACE

GERMANY E

BELGRAVE
MEWS E

SPAIN
E FINLAND

BELGRAVE PLACE

B310

ECCLESTON MEWS

E BOLIVIA
BELGIUM

HOBART PLACE

79

HANS
PLACE

PERU E
DENMARK
ICELAND

P

LESOTHO E

CHESHAM MEWS

P319

CHESHAM STREET

ECCLESTON STREET

PONT STREET

SLOANE

PAVILION RD

DORCHESTER
COURT

AFTO
MEWS

House
Sch

Sch

CONGO/
ZAIRE E

CHESHAM PL

LYALL
MEWS

CHESHAM PL

LYALL
MEWS W

LYALL ST

E HUNGARY

EATON
PLACE

A3216 ECCLESTON STREET

CHESTER

CADOGAN PLACE

CADOGAN PLACE

CADOGAN LANE

CHESHAM PLACE

EATON MEWS N

EATON MEWS W

EATON SQUARE

EATON SQUARE

Eaton Square Gardens

KING'S ROAD

EATON MEWS NORTH

EATON MEWS SOUTH

ECCLESTON STREET SOUTH

MEWS

Tenn
Cts

DAKLEY HOUSE

28

EATON

WEST EATON

145

Tenn
Ct

ELIZABETH

BOSCOBEL PL

MEWS

CADOGAN GATE

CADOGAN PLACE

A   **B**   **C**

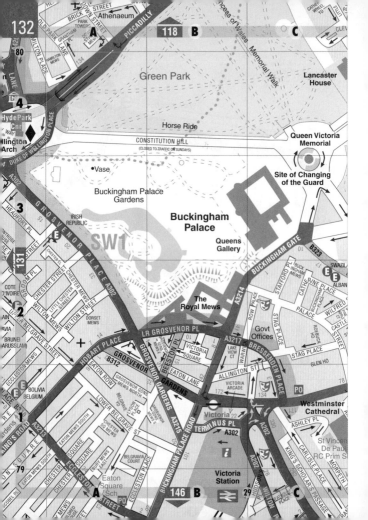

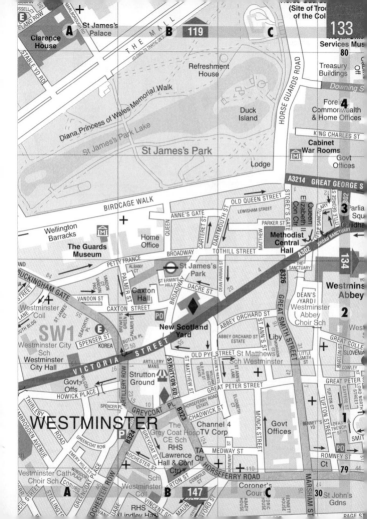

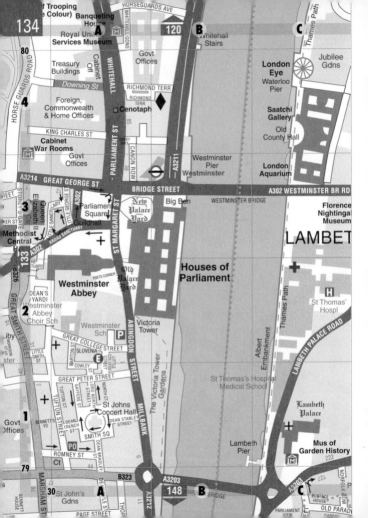

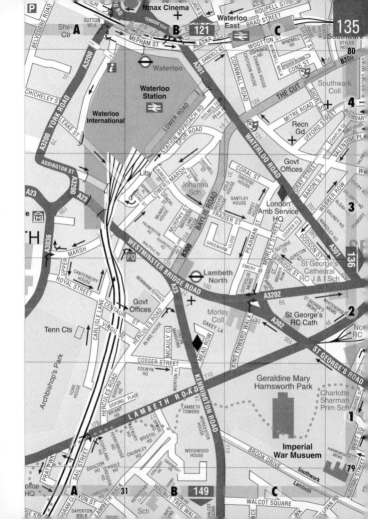

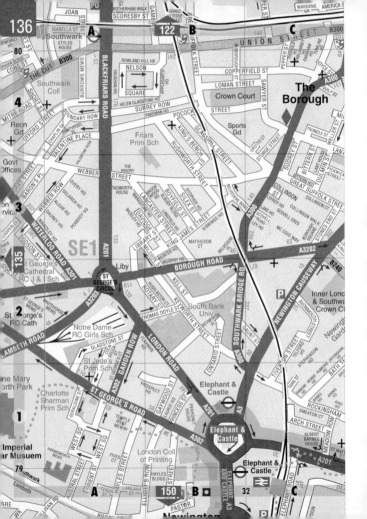

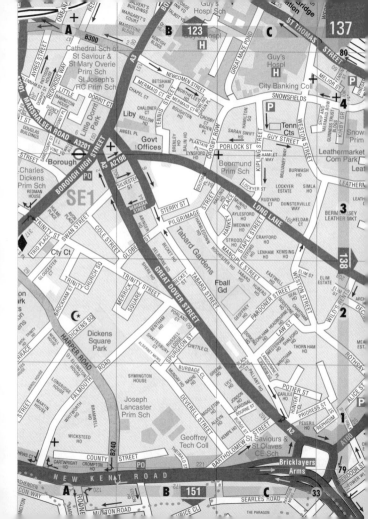

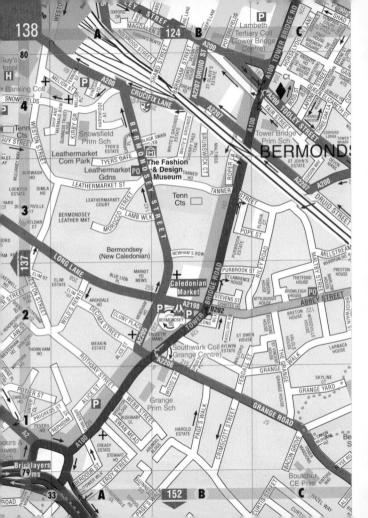

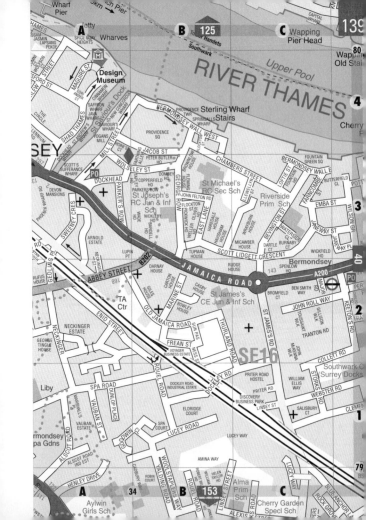

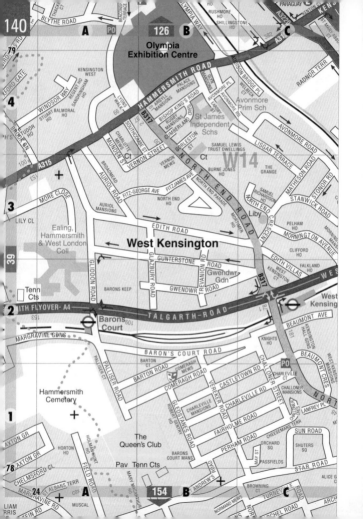

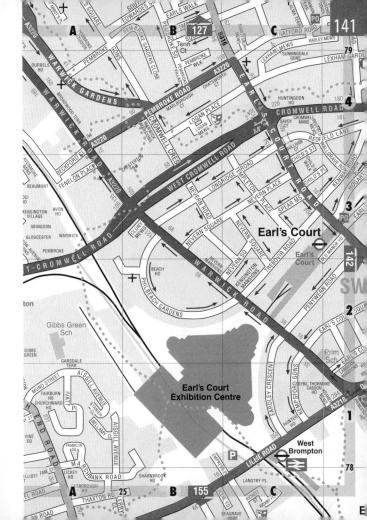

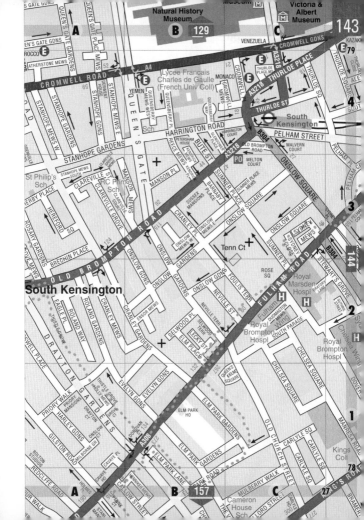

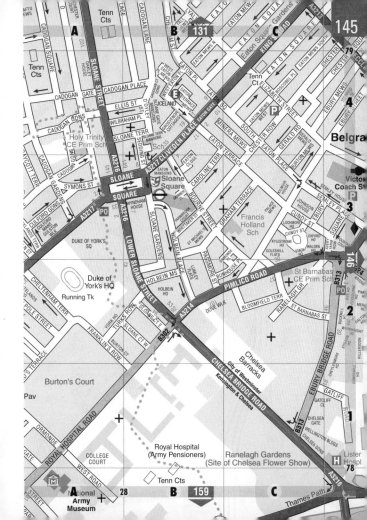

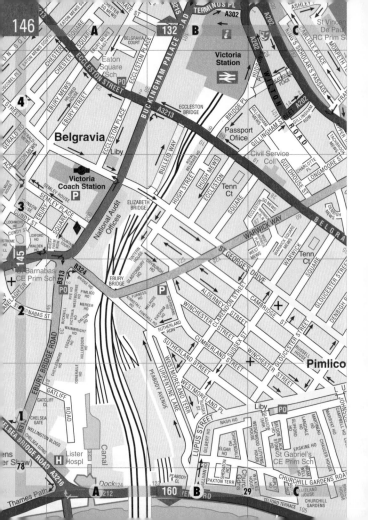

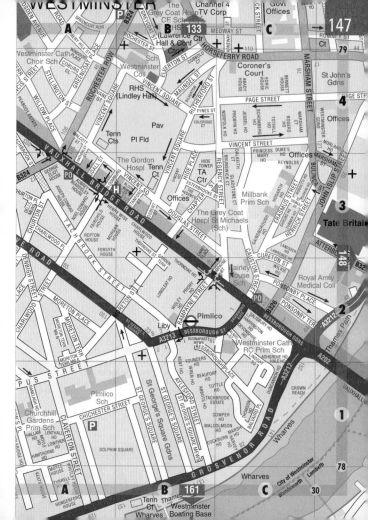

A   134   B   C

Lambeth
Pier

Mus of
Garden History

SMITH SQ

PO

ROMNEY ST

Ct

79

St John's
Gdns

PAGE STREET

B323

A3203

A3212

LAMBETH BRIDGE

A3203

NORFOLK ROW

EUSTACE
HOUSE

OLD PARADE

GABRIEL
HOUSE

222

121

PARLIAMENT
VIEW
APARTMENTS

4

Offices

Offices

REYNOLDS
HO

DUKE'S
HO

Millbank
Tower

Tate Britain

147

3

ATTERBURY ST   B326

Royal Army
Medical Coll

PONSONBY PLACE

2

PONSONBY TER

1

Wharves

78

30   A

MARSHAM STREET

THORNEY STREET

DEAN RYLE ST

MARSHAM ST

MORLAND
HO

JOHN ISLIP STREET

MILLBANK

ISLIP STREET

HERRICK STREET

BULINCA ST

HOGARTH
HO

ERASMUS ST

ROGERS
HO

A3212

Thames Path

VAUXHALL BRIDGE

BRIDGEFOOT

CROWN
REACH

City of Westminster
Wandsworth   Lambeth

ST GEORGE
WHARF

RIVER THAMES

Fire Brigade
Pier

Fire Brigade
HQ

Thames Path

ALBERT EMBANKMENT

Gunhouse
Stairs
(site of)

LAMBETH HIGH STREET

Recn
Gd

WHITGIFT
HO

WHITGIFT ST

A3036

SALAMANCA STREET

SALAMANCA PL

RANDALL ROAD

RANDALL ROW

LINWORTH ST

GLASSHOUSE WALK

LAUD ST

VAUXHALL WALK

Vauxhall

New Spring
Gdns Wk

VAUXHALL
WALK

Spring
Gardens

GODING STREET

DARLEY
HOUSE

LEOPOLD
WALK

Vauxhall
Cross

Vauxhall

Vauxhall

A3204

A202

AUCKLAND ST

P

ARDEN HO

COVERLEY
PL

LILAC
PL

PEDLERS
Park

HAYMANS
POINT

JONATHAN STREET

WORGAN STREET

ANNE HOUSE

HONEY
HOUSE

JAMESON
HOUSE

TYERS STREET

ARROWSMITH HO

WICKHAM STREET

Va
Pr

Vauxhall
City Farm

OSWALD'S PLACE

TYER

SIMPSON
ST

St Anne's
RC Prim
Sch

PIPPIN
CT

A3203

DURHAM STREET

CARLEYFORD RD

A3204

A30

162   B   SLAMBETH P   C

Thames Path

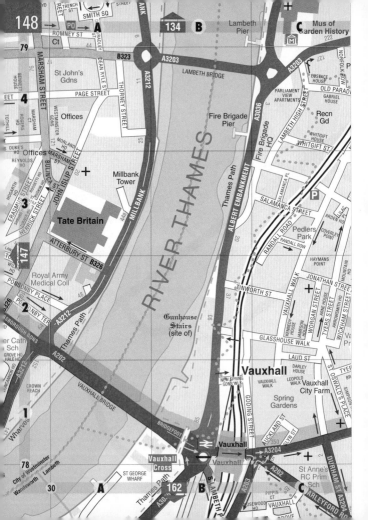

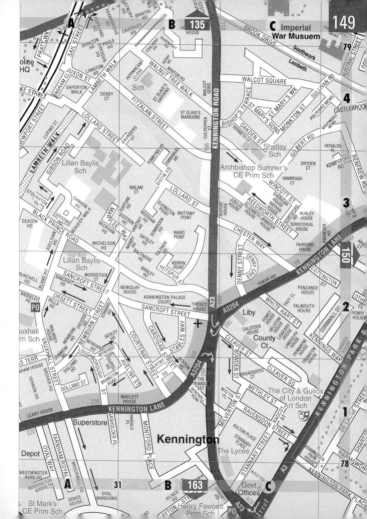

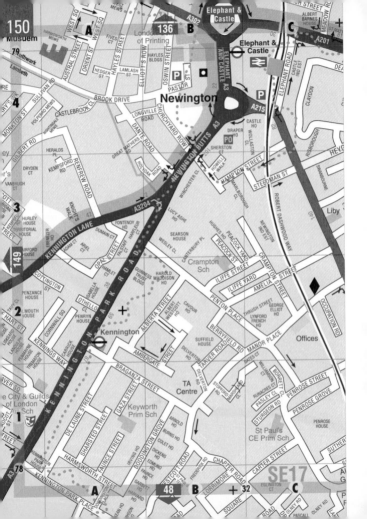

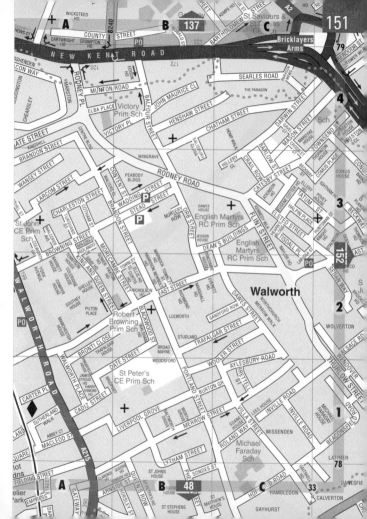

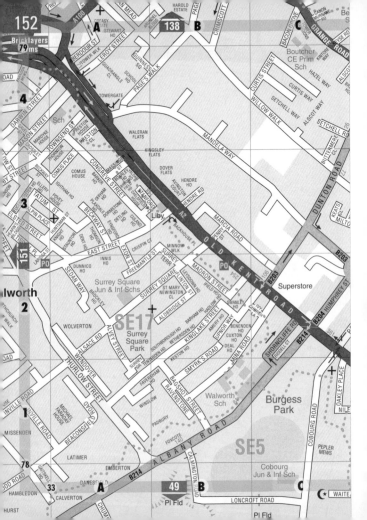

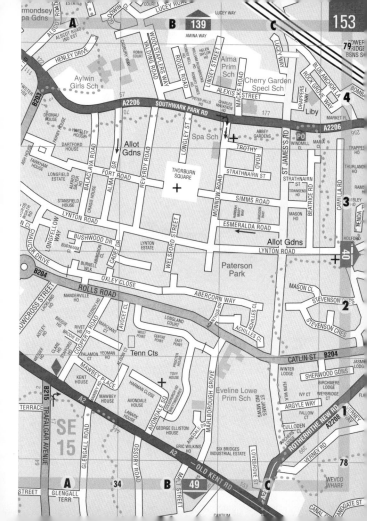

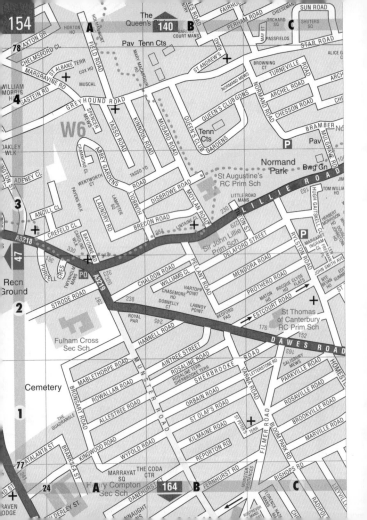

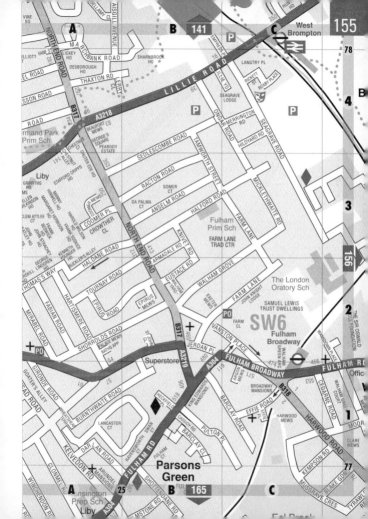

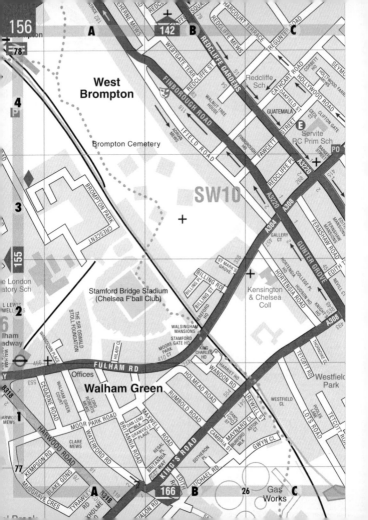

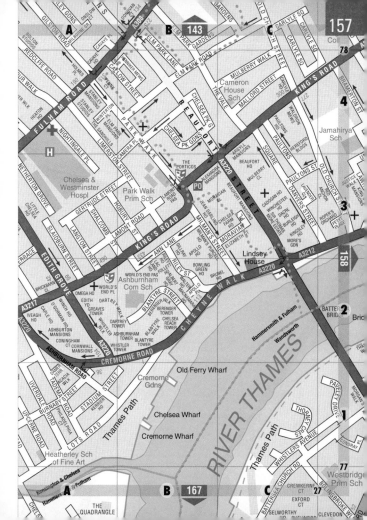

A   B   143   C

78

GILSTON ROAD

FULHAM ROAD

CAREY

ELM PARK GARDENS

ELM PARK ROAD

ELM PARK LANE

CALLOW STREET

KING'S ROAD

CARLYLE SQ

CARLYLE SQ

OLD CHURCH STREET

MULBERRY WALK

4

BRAMERTON ST

OLD CHURCH STREET

Cameron House Sch

MALLORD STREET

THE VALE

Jamahirya Sch

NIGHTINGALE PL

H

Chelsea & Westminster Hospl

NETHERTON GROVE

GERTRUDE STREET

SHALCOMB

LANGTON STREET

LAMONT ROAD

Park Walk Prim Sch

BEAUFORT STREET

PARK WALK

CAMERA PL

LIMERSTON STREET

HOBURY

CHELSEA PK GDNS

THE PORTICOS

ALEXANDRA MANSIONS

CHELSEA PK GDNS

BEAUFORT STREET

PAULTONS SQUARE

PAULTONS ST

HEREFORD BLDGS

Beaufort HO

ARGYLL MANSIONS

PO

MORAVIAN CL

JEAN DARLING CT

Chelsea Farm HO

BEAUFORT MANSIONS

CADOGAN HO

WINCHESTER HO

DACRE HO

KINGSLEY HO

MORE'S GDN

ROPER'S ORCHARD

PETYT PLACE

DANVERS STREET

OLD CHURCH STREET

MOLESWORTH

BURLEIGH HO

3

KING'S ROAD

MORAVIAN

ANN LANE

GILBEY

RILEY ST

APOLLO PL

Elizabeth

A3212

A3220

Lindsey House

A3212

158

77

MITMAN STREET

TADEMA'S WHARF

BLANTYRE STREET

World's End Pas

Ashburnham Com Sch

World's End Pl

EDITH YD

OMEGA HO

WINCH HO

O'GORMAN HO

GREAVES TOWER

DARTREY WALK

BLANTYRE STREET

BERENGER TOWER

BLANTYRE TOWER

CHELSEA REACH TOWER

WHISTLER TOWER

DARTREY TOWER

ASHBURNHAM TOWER

BLANTYRE TOWER

FOLLETT ST

BRUNEL HO

BOWLING GREEN HO

CHEYNE WALK

BATTERSEA BRIDGE

2

Bric

EDITH GROVE

A3217

IVEAGH HO

CAPLE HO

ASHBURTON MANSIONS

CONINGHAM

CORNWALL MANSIONS

A3220

ASHBURNHAM ROAD

CREMORNE ROAD

Hammersmith & Fulham

Wandsworth

ACACIA WALK

BURNABY STREET

UVERDALE ROAD

TETCOTT ROAD

PHILADELPHIA CT

KENYON HO

LOTS ROAD

STADIUM STREET

Cremorne Gdns

Old Ferry Wharf

Thames Path

Chelsea Wharf

Cremorne Wharf

RIVER THAMES

PAVELEY DRIVE

THORNEY

WHISTLERS AVENUE

MORGAN'S WALK

SUNDRAY

1

Thames Path

Heatherley Sch of Fine Art

UPCERNE ROAD

Kensington & Chelsea

Hammersmith & Fulham

A   B   167   C

Westbridge Prim Sch

77

CREWKERNE CT

BATTERSEA CHURCH RD

EXFORD CT

SELWORTHY

CLEVEDON

27

BOLLINGBROKE WK

THE QUADRANGLE

Kings Coll

Offices

A

B

C

KING'S COURT N
KING'S COURT S

CHELSEA MANOR ST

Chelsea TOWERS

FLOOD ST

CHELSEA MANOR ST

REDESDALE ST

REDBURN STREET

CHRISTCHURCH STREET
CHRISTCHURCH ST

CAVERSHAM ST

Christchurch
CE Prim Sch

KING'S ROAD A3217   A3204

BRAMERTON ST

GLEBE PLACE

OAKLEY STREET

MARGARETTA TERR

MANOR STREET ESTATE

GROVE HO

ALPHA PL

FLOOD STREET

OAKLEY GARDENS

PHENE ST

CHEYNE ROW

ST LOO AVE

ST LUKE

OAKLEY ST

ROBINSON ST

DILKE ST

CHEYNE GDNS

ROSSETTI GDNS MANSIONS

CHEYNE ST

B302

The
English
Gardening Sch

4

78

Jamahirya
Sch

UPPER CHEYNE ROW

Carlyle's
House

JUSTICE WALK
LAWRENCE STREET

CHELSEA EMBAN

Chelsea
Physic Garden

Thames Path

CHEYNE WALK

CHELSEA EMBAN

ADAIR HO

PIER HO

B304

CHEYNE MEWS

PAULTONS SQ

HEREFORD BLDGS

PAULTONS ST

OLD CHURCH STREET

DANVERS STREET

CHELSEA SQ

JUSTICE WALK
LORDSHIP PLACE
CARLYLE MANS

ROPER'S ORCHARD
PETYT PLACE

CHEYNE WALK

A3031

Cadogan Pier

3

MORE'S

157 A3212

RIVER T

Chel

ALBERT BRIDGE
(SUSPENSION)

Terrace Wa

Thames Path

2

uth & F

Wandsworth

BATTERSEA
BRIDGE

BridgeWharf

THAMES WALK

ALBION WHARF

RIVERSIDE

WATERSIDE POINT

GREAT EASTERN WHARF

GRANDMORE CT

ANHALT ROAD

CARRIAGE DRIVE NORTH

Pav

Festival P
Gard

HESTER ROAD

ELCHO STREET

Ransome's
Dock

RASTOCK ST

HOWIE ST

PARKGATE ROAD

ST MARY LE-PARK CT

ALBANY MANSIONS

ALBERT BRIDGE ROAD

P

P

1

THORNE CL

PAVELEY DRIVE

ROBINSON WALK

KINGSMILL

Bsns Ctr

Royal Coll of Art
Sculpture Sch

Govt
Offices

JUER STREET

SEARLES CL

WORFIELD ST

WORFIELD ST

CARRIAGE DRIVE WEST

SW

WHISTLERS AVENUE

CONDRAY PL

PO

B306

BATTERSEA BRIDGE ROAD

Westbridge
Prim Sch

MUSGRAVE CT

HYDE LA

HENRY CL

ETHELBURGA ST

HERON HO

MASSEY NE

JAGGER HO

ALBERT ST

BA

77

CREWKERNE CT

EXFORD CT

27

BRYNMAER RD
BOLINGBROKE WI

CLEVEDON CT

RANDALL CL

168

VILL

A

B

C

ath

ELWORTHY CL CHELWOOD

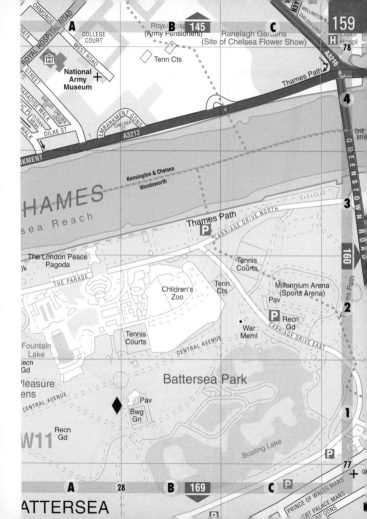

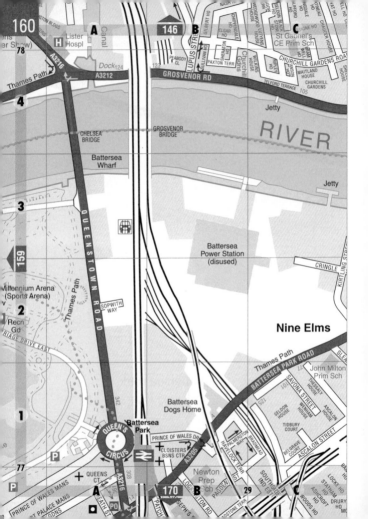

160

H Lister Hospl

78

A3216

Canal

A 146

B

GILBERT HO

NASH HO

ELGAR HO

LUPUS STR

C St Gabriel's CE Prim Sch

CHURCHILL GARDENS ROAD

PEABODY CL

PAXTON TERR

123

124

Dock

A3212

GROSVENOR RD

TELFORD TERRACE

CHURCHILL GARDENS

105

4

Thames Path

CHELSEA BRIDGE

GROSVENOR BRIDGE

Battersea Wharf

RIVER

Jetty

Jetty

3

QUEENSTOWN ROAD

Battersea Power Station (disused)

CRINGLE

KIRTLING STREET

159

Millennium Arena (Sports Arena)

2

Recn Gd

RIAGE DRIVE EAST

Thames Path

SOPWITH WAY

Nine Elms

Thames Path

BATTERSEA PARK ROAD

SLEA

John Milton Prim Sch

SAVONA STREET

THESSALY

SELDON HOUSE

WYNDHAM HOUSE

ASCALON HOUSE

TIDBURY COURT

1

342

Battersea Dogs Home

QUEEN'S CIRCUS

Battersea Park

HARTINGTON

WARE

PALMERSTON WAY

BROADMED

BELGRAVE COURT

ASCALON STREET

308

PRINCE OF WALES DR

CLOISTERS BSNS CTR

HAVELOCK TERR

SOUTHSIDE IND EST

77

P

QUEENS CT

A3216

Newton Prep Sch

PADDEN

29

C

STATHAM

LOCKE HO

ASHCROFT HO

DRURY HO

A 170 B

TON RD

SETH'S

MISTONE TERR

WOODS HO

P

PRINCE OF WALES MANS

PO

PATCH

ST PALACE MANS

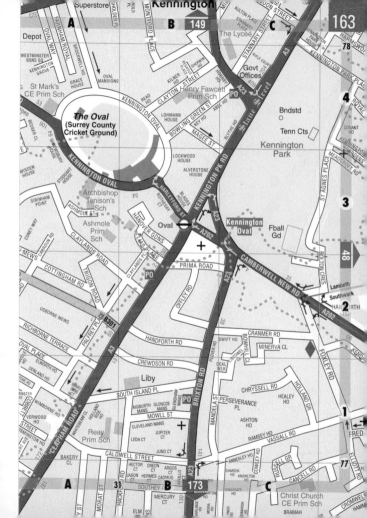

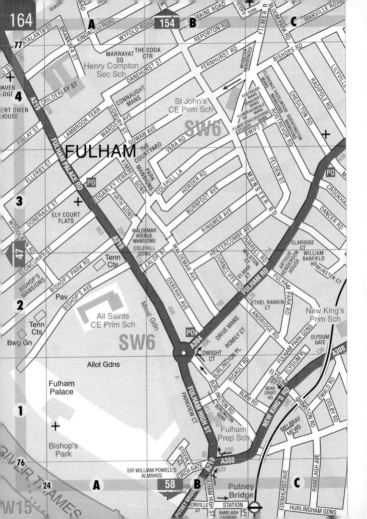

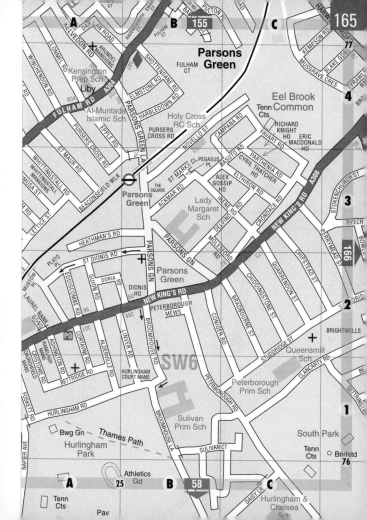

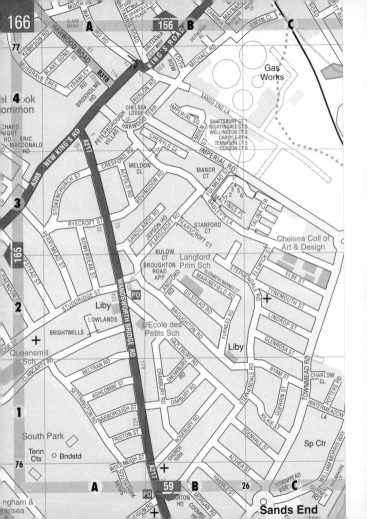

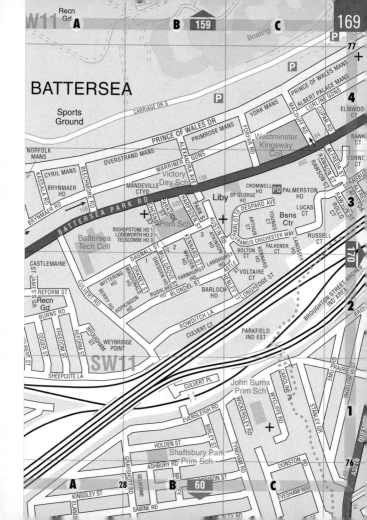

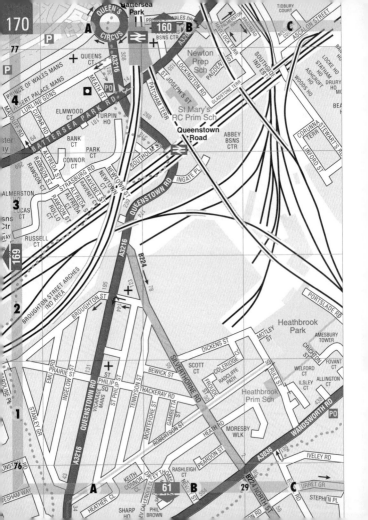

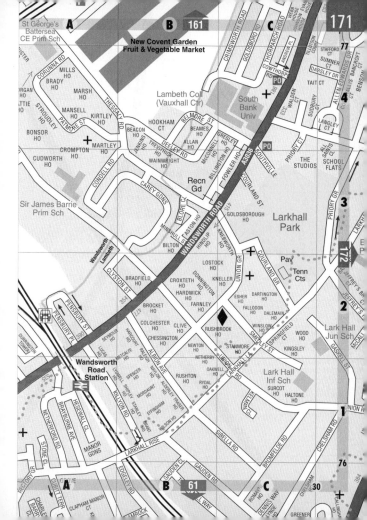

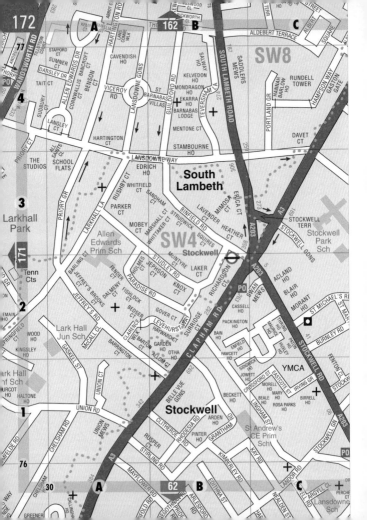

Index

Church Rd **6** Beckenham BR2..........**53** C6 **228** C6

Place name	Location number	Locality, town or village	Postcode district	Standard scale reference	Enlarged scale reference
May be abbreviated on the map	Present when a number indicates the place's position in a crowded area of mapping	Shown when more than one place (outside London postal districts) has the same name	District for the indexed place	Page number and grid reference for the standard mapping	Page number and grid reference for the central London enlarged mapping, underlined in red

Public and commercial buildings are highlighted in magenta
Places of interest are highlighted in blue with a star ★

Index of localities, towns and villages

A
Acton 28 C1
Acton Green 37 B2

B
Balham 72 C3
Barbican 109 A3
Barnes 14 A1
Barnsbury 14 A1
Battersea 169 A4
Bayswater 114 C4
Bedford Park 38 A3
Belgravia 146 A4
Belsize Park 12 A3
Bermondsey 40 A4
Bethnal Green 25 A2
Blackheath
  Vale 53 B1
Blackwall 34 C2
Bloomsbury 106 A4
Borough The 136 C4
Bow 26 B3
Bow Common 34 A4
Brixton 62 C4
Broadgate 110 A4
Brockley 66 B3
Bromley
  (Tower Hamlets) ... 27 A4
Brompton 130 A1
Brondesbury 10 A2
Brondesbury
  Park 22 C4
Brook Green 39 C2

C
Camberwell 48 B2
Camden Town 13 A1
Canary Wharf 34 A1
Canning Town 35 B3
Canonbury 15 B2
Chelsea 144 B1
Child's Hill 1 C6
Chiswick 38 B1
Church End
  (Brent) 8 B2
City of London 122 B4
Clapham 61 A4
Clapham
  Common 61 A3
Clapham Junction 60 A3
Clapton Park 17 C4
Clerkenwell 96 A1
College Park 22 A2
Covent Garden 120 B4
Cricklewood 9 B4
Cubitt Town 42 B2

D
Dalston 16 C2
Dartmouth Park 4 A1
De Beauvoir Town 16 A1
Deptford 50 C3
Dollis Hill 9 A4
Dudden Hill 8 C3
Dulwich 76 A2
Dulwich Village 76 A4

E
Earl's Court 141 C1
Earlsfield 71 B3
East Acton 29 A1
East Dulwich 64 C2
East Sheen 55 C3
Euston 93 A3

F
Finsbury 95 C4
Finsbury Park 5 C3
Fitzrovia 104 A4
Fulham 47 C1

G
Globe Town 25 C2
Gospel Oak 12 B2
Greenwich 53 A4
Grove Park
  (Hounslow) 45 B2
Gunnersbury 37 A2

H
Hackney 17 A2
Hackney Wick 18 C2
Haggerston 24 B3
Hammersmith 39 B2
Hampstead 11 B3
Harlesden 21 B4
Herne Hill 63 B2
Highbury 15 A4
Highgate 3 C4
Holborn 107 C3

Homerton
Homerton 17 C1
Honor Oak 65 B2
Hoxton 24 A3
Hyde Park 116 C2

I
Isle of Dogs 42 B2
Islington 14 C2

K
Kennington 149 B1
Kensal Green 22 B2
Kensal Rise 22 C3
Kensal Town 23 A1
Kensington 127 C3
Kentish Town 13 B2
Kew 44 C4
Kilburn 23 B4
King's Cross 84 C2
Kingsland 16 A2
Knightsbridge 130 A1

L
Ladywell 66 C2
Lambeth 134 C3
Lewisham 67 B3
Leyton 19 C4
Limehouse 33 A2
Lisson Green 90 B2
Lisson Grove 102 A4
Lower Clapton 17 B4
Lower Holloway 14 A3
Lower Place 20 B3

M
Maida Vale 88 A4
Maitland Park 12 C2
Marylebone 104 B2
Mayfair 118 A3
Mile End 26 A1
Mill Meads 27 C3
Millwall 41 C3
Mortlake 55 B4

N
New Cross 51 B2
New Cross Gate 50 C2
Newington 150 B4
Nine Elms 160 C2
North Acton 20 C2
North End 2 B2
North Kensington 30 C4
North Sheen 44 C1
Notting Hill 112 C3
Nunhead 65 B3

O
Old Ford 26 B4
Old Oak Common 21 B1

P
Paddington 100 C3
Park Royal 20 A2
Parsons Green 165 B4
Peckham 49 A2
Pentonville 85 A1
Pimlico 146 C1
Poplar 33 C2

Primrose Hill 12 B1
Putney 57 B2
Putney Heath 57 B1
Putney Vale 68 C1

R
Ratcliff 32 C2
Regent's Park 92 A4
Richmond 54 A2
Richmond Hill 54 A1
Roehampton 68 A4
Rotherhithe 40 C3

S
Sands End 59 B4
Shacklewell 16 B4
Shadwell 32 B2
Shepherd's Bush . . . 30 A1

Shoreditch 87 C1
Soho 105 B1
Somers Town 93 C4
South Acton 37 A3
South Bank 120 C1
South Bromley 34 C4
South Hackney 25 B4
South Hampstead . . . 11 B1
South
  Kensington 143 A3
South Lambeth 172 B3
Southfields 71 A3
Southwark 40 B2
Spitalfields 110 A4
St George in
  the East 32 A2
St Giles 106 A2
St James 119 B2

St John's 51 C1
St John's Wood 79 B1
St Luke's 97 A2
St Pancras 94 B4
Stamford Hill 7 A3
Stepney 32 C4
Stockwell 62 A4
Stoke Newington . . . 7 A2
Stonebridge 20 B4
Strand 120 C4
Strand on
  the Green 44 C4
Stratford 19 B1
Stratford Marsh 27 A4
Stratford New Town . 19 B3
Streatham Hill 74 A3
Summerstown 71 B1

T
Temple Mills 19 A3
Tower Hamlets 33 B4
Tufnell Park 13 C4
Tulse Hill 75 A4

U
Upper Holloway 4 C2
Upper Tooting 72 B1

V
Vale of Health 2 C1
Vauxhall 148 B1

W
Walham Green 156 A1
Walworth 151 C2
Wandsworth 58 C1

Wapping 32 A1
Waterloo 135 B4
West Brompton 156 A4
West Dulwich 75 A2
West Hampstead . . . 10 C4
West Hill 58 B1
West Kensington . . . 140 B3
West Kilburn 23 A2
West Norwood 75 B1
Westbourne Green . . 88 A2
Westminster 133 A1
Whitechapel 110 C1
Willesden 8 C4
Willesden Green . . . 22 A4
Wimbledon Park . . . 70 B2

Abbreviations used in the index

Acad	Academy	Ent Ctr	Enterprise Centre	Mus	Museum
App	Approach	Ent Pk	Enterprise Park	Obsy	Observatory
Arc	Arcade	Est	Estate	Orch	Orchard
Art Gall	Art Gallery	Ex Ctr	Exhibition Centre	Par	Parade
Ave	Avenue	Ex Hall	Exhibition Hall	Pas	Passage
Bglws	Bungalows	Fst	First	Pav	Pavilion
Bldgs	Buildings	Gdn	Garden	Pk	Park
Bsns Ctr	Business Centre	Gdns	Gardens	Pl	Place
Bsns Pk	Business Park	Gn	Green	Prec	Precinct
Bvd	Boulevard	Gr	Grove	Prep	Preparatory
Cath	Cathedral, Catholic	Gram	Grammar	Prim	Primary
CE	Church of England	Her Ctr	Heritage Centre	Prom	Promenade
Cemy	Cemetery	Ho	House	RC	Roman Catholic
Cir	Circus	Hospl	Hospital	Rd	Road
Circ	Circle	Hts	Heights	Rdbt	Roundabout
Cl	Close	Ind Est	Industrial Estate	Ret Pk	Retail Park
Cnr	Corner	Inf	Infant	Sch	School
Coll	College	Inst	Institute	Sec	Secondary
Com	Community	Int	International	Sh Ctr	Shopping Centre
Comm	Common	Intc	Interchange	Sp	Sports
Comp	Comprehensive	Jun	Junior	Specl	Special
Con Ctr	Conference Centre	Junc	Junction	Sports Ctr	Sports Centre
Cotts	Cottages	La	Lane	Sq	Square
Cres	Crescent	L Ctr	Leisure Centre	St	Street, Saint
Cswy	Causeway	Liby	Library	Sta	Station
Ct	Court	Mans	Mansions	Stad	Stadium
Ctr	Centre	Mdw/s	Meadow/s	Tech	Technical/Technology
Crkt	Cricket	Meml	Memorial	Terr	Terrace
Ctry Pk	Country Park	Mid	Middle	Trad Est	Trading Estate
Cty	County	Mix	Mixed	Twr/s	Tower/s
Ctyd	Courtyard	Mkt	Market	Univ	University
Dr	Drive	Mon	Monument	Wlk	Walk

A

Abady Ho SW1 . . . . **147** C4
Abberley Mews **9**
  SW8 . . . . .61 C4
Abbess Cl SW7 . . . . . . .75 A3
Abbeville Mews **3**
  SW4 . . . . .61 C3
Abbeville Rd SW4 . . . .61 C3
Abbey Bsns Ctr
  SW8 . . . . .170 B4
Abbey Ct NW8 . . . . . . .78 C2
SE17 . . . . .151 A1
3 London W12 . . . . . .38 A3
Abbeyfield Rd SE16 . .40 B2
Abbey Gdns NW8 . . . . .79 A1
  W6 . . . . .154 A3
Abbey Ho NW8 . . . . . . .89 A4
Abbey La E15 . . . . .27 C3
Abbey Lo NW8 . . . . . . .90 B3
Abbey Orchard St
  SW1 . . . . .133 C2
Abbey Orchard Street
  Est SW1 . . . . .133 C2
Abbey Rd NW8 . . . . . . .78 C2
Wembley NW10 . . . . . .20 A3
Abbey St SE1 . . . . .138 C2
Abbey Tutorial Coll
  W2 . . . . .31 C3 113 A4
Abbot Cl SW8 . . . . . . .162 A1
Abbot Ct SW8 . . . . . . .162 A1
Abbotsbury Cl E15 . . .27 B3
  W14 . . . . .126 C3
Abbotsbury Ho
  W14 . . . . .126 B4
Abbotsbury Mews
  SE15 . . . . .65 B4
Abbotsbury Rd
  W14 . . . . .126 C3
Abbotshade Rd **3**
  SE16 . . . . .32 C1
Abbots Ho SW1 . . . . . .147 B1
  W14 . . . . .126 C1
Abbots La SE1 . . . . . . .124 B1
Abbots Pk SW2 . . . . . .74 C3
Abbot's Pl NW6 . . . . . .78 A4
Abbot St E8 . . . . .16 B2
Abbotstone Ho **4** E5 . .7 C2
Abbotstone Rd
  SW15 . . . . .57 B4
Abbotswell Rd SE4 . . .66 B2
Abbotswood Rd
London SE22 . . . . .64 A3
Streatham SW16 . . . . . .73 C1
Abbott Ho SW12 . . . . .72 B4
Abbott Rd E14 . . . . . . .34 C3
Abbotts Cl N1 . . . . .15 B2
Abchurch La EC2,
  EC4 . . . . .123 C4
Abchurch Yd EC4 . . . .123 B4
Abdale Rd W12 . . . . . . .30 A1
Abel Ho SE11 . . . . .163 B4
Aberavon Rd E3 . . . . . .26 A2
Abercorn Cl NW8 . . . . .88 C4
Abercorn Ho SE10 . . . .52 A3
Abercorn Mans
  NW8 . . . . .79 A1
Abercorn Mews **1**
  TW10 . . . . .54 B3
Abercorn Pl NW8 . . . . .78 C1
Abercorn Way SE1 . . .153 B2
Abercrombie Ho **1**
  W12 . . . . .30 A2

Abercrombie St
  SW11 . . . . .168 B2
Aberdale Ct **22**
  SE16 . . . . .40 C4
Aberdare Gdns
  NW6 . . . . .11 A1
Aberdeen Ct W2 . . . . . .89 B1
London N5 . . . . .15 B3
Aberdeen La N5 . . . . . .15 B3
Aberdeen Mans
  WC1 . . . . .94 A2
Aberdeen Pk N5 . . . . . .15 B3
Aberdeen Pl NW8 . . . . .89 B2
Aberdeen Rd
London N5 . . . . .15 B4
London NW10 . . . . .8 B3
Aberdeen Terr SE3 . . .52 C1
Aberdour St SE1 . . . . .152 A4
Aberfeldy Ho SE5 . . . .48 A3
Aberfeldy St E14 . . . . .34 B3
Abersham Rd E8 . . . . .16 B3
Abingdon W14 . . . . . . .141 A3
Abingdon Cl SE1 . . . . .153 A2
London NW1 . . . . .13 C2
Abingdon Ct W8 . . . . .127 C1
Abingdon Gdns
  W8 . . . . .127 C1
Abingdon Ho E2 . . . . .98 C2
Abingdon Mans
  W8 . . . . .127 C1
Abingdon Rd W8 . . . . .127 C1
Abingdon St SW1 . . . .134 A2
Abingdon Villas
  W8 . . . . .127 C1
Abinger Gr SE8 . . . . . . .51 B4
Abinger Ho SE1 . . . . . .137 B3
Abinger Mews W9 . . . .23 C1
Abinger Rd W4 . . . . . . .38 A3
Ablett St SE16 . . . . .40 B1
Abney Gdns **5** N16 . . .7 B2
Abney Park Cemetery★
  N16 . . . . .7 A2
Abney Park Ct N16 . . . .7 B2
Aborfield **3** NW5 . . .13 B3
Aboyne Rd SW17 . . . . .71 C1
Abyssinia Cl SW11 . . .60 A3
Abyssinia Rd SW11 . . .60 A3
Acacia Cl SE8 . . . . .41 A2
Acacia Gdns NW8 . . . .79 C2
Acacia Gr SE21 . . . . . . .75 C2
Acacia Ho N16 . . . . .6 C2
Acacia Pl NW8 . . . . . . .79 C2
Acacia Rd
London NW8 . . . . .79 C2
Acacia Wlk SW10 . . . .157 A1
Academy **1** E2 . . . . . .25 B3
Academy The **3** N19 . .4 B3
Acanthus Dr SE1 . . . . .153 B2
Acanthus Rd SW11 . . .60 C4
Accommodation Rd
  NW11 . . . . .1 B3
Acer Ct **3** NW2 . . . . . .1 A1
Acfold Rd SW6 . . . . . .166 A3
Achilles Cl SE1 . . . . . .153 C2
Achilles Ho **16** E2 . . .25 A3
Achilles Rd NW6 . . . . .10 C3
Achilles St SE14 . . . . . .51 A3
Achilles Way W1 . . . . .117 C1
Acklam Rd W10 . . . . . .31 B4
Ackmar Rd SW6 . . . . .165 B3
Ackroyd Dr E3 . . . . .33 C4
Acland Burghley Sch
  NW5 . . . . .13 A4
Acland Cres SE5 . . . . . .63 C4
Acland Ho SW9 . . . . . .172 C2
Acol Ct **3** NW6 . . . . . .10 C1
Acol Rd NW6 . . . . .11 A1

Acorn Gdns W3 . . . . . .28 C4
Acorn Par **7** SE15 . . .50 A3
Acorn Production Ctr
  N7 . . . . .14 A1
Acorns The **3**
  SW19 . . . . .69 C3
Acorn Wharf SE15 . . . .49 C4
Acorn Wlk SE16 . . . . . .33 A1
Acre Dr SE22 . . . . .64 C3
Acre La SW2 . . . . .62 B3
Acris St SW18 . . . . .59 B2
Acton Bsns Ctr
  NW10 . . . . .20 C1
Acton Central Ind Est **8**
  W3 . . . . .28 C1
Acton Central Sta
  W3 . . . . .28 B1
Acton High Sch W3 . . .36 C4
Acton Hill Mews
  W3 . . . . .28 A1
Acton Ho **6** E8 . . . . . .24 B4
  5 London W3 . . . . . .28 B3
Acton Hospl W3 . . . . . .36 C4
Acton La
Acton NW10 . . . . .20 C4
London W3 . . . . .37 B4
Acton W3 . . . . .37 B2
Acton Main Line Sta
  W3 . . . . .28 B3
Acton Mews E8 . . . . . . .24 B4
Acton Park Est W3 . . . .37 C4
Acton St WC1 . . . . .94 C3
Acton Town Sta W3 . . .36 C4
Acton Vale Ind Pk
  W3 . . . . .29 B1
Acuba Ho SW18 . . . . . .71 A3
Acuba Rd SW18 . . . . . .71 A2
Ada Ct N1 . . . . .86 C3
  W9 . . . . .89 A3
Ada Gdns E14 . . . . .34 C3
  E15 . . . . .27 C4
Adair Ho SW3 . . . . . . .158 B4
Adair Rd W10 . . . . .23 A1
Adair Twr **7** W10 . . . .23 A1
Ada Kennedy Ct **6**
  SE10 . . . . .52 B3
Adam Ct SE11 . . . . . . .150 A3
Adam & Eve Ct
  W1 . . . . .105 A2
Adam & Eve Mews
  W8 . . . . .127 C2
Adamfields NW3 . . . . .11 C1
Adams Gardens Est **5**
  SE16 . . . . .40 B4
Adams Ho **8** E14 . . . . .34 C3
Adamson Rd E16 . . . . .35 C3
London NW3 . . . . .11 C2
Adams Pl N7 . . . . .14 B3
Adam's Row W1 . . . . .117 C3
Adam St WC2 . . . . .120 B3
Adam Wlk SW6 . . . . . .47 B3
Ada Pl E2 . . . . .24 C4
Ada Rd SE5 . . . . .49 A3
Adare Wlk SW16,
  SW2 . . . . .74 B2
Ada St E8 . . . . .25 A4
Adderley St SW11 . . . .60 C2
Adderley St E14 . . . . . .34 B3
Addey Ho SE8 . . . . .51 B3
Addey & Stanhope Sch
  SE14 . . . . .51 C2
Addington Ct **7**
  SW14 . . . . .55 C4
Addington Ho
  SW9 . . . . .173 A1
Addington Rd E3 . . . . .26 C2
Addington Sq SE5 . . . .48 C3

Addington St SE1 . . . .135 A3
Addison Ave
  W11 . . . . .31 A1 112 A1
Addison Bridge Pl
  W14 . . . . .140 C4
Addison Cres W14 . . . .39 C3
Addison Gdns W14 . . .39 C3
Addison Gr W4 . . . . . . .38 A3
Addison Ho NW8 . . . . .89 B4
Addison Park Mans **1**
  W14 . . . . .39 C4
Addison Pl
  W11 . . . . .31 A1 112 A1
Addison Prim Sch
  W14 . . . . .39 C3
Addison Rd W14 . . . . .126 C2
Addle Hill EC4 . . . . . . .108 B1
Addle St EC2 . . . . .109 A3
Addlestone Ho W10 . . .30 B4
Addy Ho SE16 . . . . .40 B2
Adela Ho **9** W6 . . . . . . .39 B1
Adelaide Ave SE4 . . . .66 C3
Adelaide Cl SW9 . . . . .62 C3
Adelaide Ct NW8 . . . . .79 A1
Adelaide Gr W12 . . . . .29 C1
Adelaide Rd
London NW3 . . . . .12 A1
  2 London SW18 . . .58 C2
Richmond TW9 . . . . . . .54 B3
Adelaide St WC2 . . . . .120 A3
Adela St W10 . . . . .23 A1
Adelina Gr E1 . . . . .32 B4
Adelina Mews
  SW12 . . . . .73 C3
Adeline Pl WC1 . . . . . .105 C3
Adelphi Ct **20** SE16 . . .40 C4
Adelphi Terr WC2 . . . .120 B3
Adeney Cl W6 . . . . .47 C4
Aden Gr N16 . . . . .15 C4
Aden Ho **12** E1 . . . . . . .32 C4
Aden Lo N16 . . . . .15 C4
Adeyfield Ho EC1 . . . . .97 C3
Adie Rd W6 . . . . .39 B3
Adisham Ho **4** E5 . . . .17 A3
Adler St E1 . . . . .111 B2
Adley St E5 . . . . .18 A3
Admiral Ct W1 . . . . . . .103 B3
London SW1 . . . . .167 A4
Admiral Hyson Ind Est
  SE16 . . . . .40 A1
Admiral Mews W10 . . .22 C1
Admiral Pl SE16 . . . . . .33 A1
Admirals Ct SE1 . . . . .124 C1
  57 Putney SW19 . . . .69 C3
Admirals Gate SE10 . .52 A2
Admiral Sq SW10 . . . .167 A4
Admiral St SE8 . . . . . . .51 C2
Admirals Way E14 . . . .41 C4
Admiral's Wlk NW3 . . .2 B1
Admiralty Arch★
  SW1 . . . . .119 C2
Admiralty Cl **3** SE8 . .51 C2
Admiral Wlk W9 . . . . . .31 C4
Adolphus Rd N4 . . . . . . .6 A3
Adolphus St SE8 . . . . . .51 B3
Adpar St W2 . . . . .101 B4
Adrian Bolt Ho **2**
  E2 . . . . .25 A2
Adrian Ho N1 . . . . .85 A3
  SW8 . . . . .162 A2
Adrian Mews
  SW10 . . . . .156 B4
Adriatic Ho **18** E1 . . . .25 C1
Adron Ho **5** SE16 . . . .40 B2
Adstock Ho **5** N1 . . . .15 A1
ADT Coll SW15 . . . . . . .58 B2

Adventurers Ct **4**
  E14 . . . . .34 C2
Adys Lawn NW2 . . . . . . .9 A2
Adys Rd SE15 . . . . .64 B4
Affleck St N1 . . . . .85 A1
Afghan Rd SW11 . . . . .168 A1
Agamemnon Rd
  NW6 . . . . .10 B3
Agar Gr NW1 . . . . .13 C1
Agar Pl NW1 . . . . .13 B1
Agar St WC2 . . . . .120 B3
Agate Rd W6 . . . . .39 B3
Agatha Cl E1 . . . . .32 B1
Agave Rd NW2 . . . . .9 B4
Agdon St EC1 . . . . .96 A2
Agincourt Rd NW3 . . .12 B4
Agnes Ct **13** SW18 . . .59 C3
Agnes Ho **13** W11 . . . .30 C2
Agnes Rd W3 . . . . .38 B4
Agnes St E14 . . . . .33 B3
Aigburth Mans
  SW9 . . . . .163 B1
Ailsa St E14 . . . . .34 B4
Ainger Rd NW3 . . . . . . .12 B1
Ainsdale NW1 . . . . .92 C4
Ainsdale Dr SE1 . . . . .153 B1
Ainsley St E2 . . . . .25 A2
Ainsty St **14** SE16 . . .40 B4
Ainsworth Est NW8 . . .78 C4
Ainsworth Ho NW8 . . .78 B3
Ainsworth Rd E9 . . . . .17 B1
Ainsworth Way
  NW8 . . . . .78 C4
Aintree St SW6 . . . . . .154 B2
Aird Ho SE1 . . . . .136 C1
Airdrie Cl N1 . . . . .14 B1
Airedale Ave W4 . . . . .38 B1
Airedale Ave S W4 . . .38 B1
Airedale Rd SW12 . . . .72 B4
Airlie Gdns
  W8 . . . . .31 C1 113 B1
Air St W1 . . . . .119 A3
Aisgill Ave SW5 . . . . . .141 A1
Aiten Pl W6 . . . . .38 C2
Aithan Ho **8** E14 . . . .33 B3
Aitken Cl E8 . . . . .24 C4
Ajax Ho **18** E2 . . . . . . .25 A3
Ajax Rd NW6 . . . . .10 C3
Akbar Ho **7** E14 . . . . .42 A2
Akehurst St SW15 . . . .68 C4
Akenside **3**
  NW3 . . . . .11 C3
Akenside Rd NW3 . . . .11 C3
Akerman Rd SW9 . . . .48 A2
Akintaro Ho **7** SE8 . .51 B4
Alamaro Lo SE10 . . . . .43 B3
Aland Ct SE16 . . . . .41 A3
Alan Preece Ct NW6 . .9 C1
Alaska St SE1 . . . . .121 B1
Albacore Cres SE13 . .67 A1
Alba Mews SW18,
  SW19 . . . . .70 C2
Alban Ho NW3 . . . . . . .11 C3
Albans Cl SW16 . . . . . .74 A1
Albany W1 . . . . .118 C3
Albany Cl SW14 . . . . . .55 A3
Albany Ct NW1 . . . . . . .133 B2
London NW10 . . . . .22 A3
Albany Ctyd W1 . . . . .119 A3
Albany Ho **2** TW8 . . .44 A4
Albany Mans SW11 . . .158 B1
Albany Mews SE5 . . . .48 B4
London N1 . . . . .14 C1
Albany Par **4** TW8 . .44 A4
Albany Pas **7** TW10 . .54 A2
Albany Pl N7 . . . . .14 C4

Albany Rd SE5 ... 49 A4
Richmond TW10 ... 54 A2
Albany St NW1 ... 92 B4
Albany Terr 6 TW10 ... 54 B2
Alba Pl W11 ... 31 B3
Albemarle SW19 ... 69 C2
Albemarle Ho SE8 ... 41 B2
Albemarle Mans NW3 ... 11 A4
Albemarle Prim Sch SW19 ... 70 A2
Albemarle St W1 ... 118 C3
Albemarle Way EC1 ... 96 A1
Albermarle Ho 3 SW9 ... 62 C4
Alberta Ct 1 TW10 ... 54 B2
Alberta Ho E14 ... 34 B1
Alberta St SE17 ... 150 B2
Albert Ave SW8 ... 162 C1
Albert Barnes Ho SE1 ... 136 C1
Albert Bigg Point E15 ... 27 B4
Albert Bridge Rd SW11 ... 158 C1
Albert Cl 11 E9 ... 25 A4
Albert Cotts E1 ... 111 B4
Albert Ct SW7 ... 129 B3
9 Putney SW19 ... 70 A3
Albert Dr SW19 ... 70 A3
Albert Emb SE1 ... 148 B3
Albert Gate Ct SW1 ... 130 C3
Albert Gdns E1 ... 32 C3
Albert Gray Ho SW10 ... 157 B2
Albert Hall Mans SW7 ... 129 B3
Albert Mans SW11 ... 168 C4
London N8 ... 5 A4
Albert Memorial* SW7 ... 129 B3
Albert Mews W8 ... 128 C2
Albert Palace Mans SW11 ... 169 C4
Albert Pl W8 ... 128 B3
Albert Rd NW6 ... 23 B3
London N4 ... 5 B4
Richmond TW10 ... 54 B2
Albert's Ct NW1 ... 90 B1
Albert Sq SW8 ... 162 C1
Albert St NW1 ... 82 B3
Albert Starr Ho 7 SE8 ... 40 C2
Albert Studios SW11 ... 168 C4
Albert Terr NW1 ... 81 B3
London NW10 ... 20 B4
Albert Terr Mews NW1 ... 81 B3
Albert Way SE15 ... 50 A3
Albert Westcott Ho SE17 ... 150 B2
Albion Ave SW8 ... 171 B1
Albion Cl W2 ... 116 B4
Albion Ct 7 W6 ... 39 A2
Albion Dr E8 ... 16 C1
Albion Est SE16 ... 40 B4
Albion Gate W2 ... 116 B4
Albion Gdns 1 W6 ... 39 A2
Albion Gr N16 ... 16 A4
Albion Mews N1 ... 85 B4
W2 ... 116 B4
6 London W6 ... 39 A2
Albion Pl EC1 ... 108 A4
EC2 ... 109 C3
Albion Pl *continued*
London W6 ... 39 A2
Albion Prim Sch SE16 ... 40 B4
Albion Rd N16 ... 15 C4
Albion Sq E8 ... 16 B1
Albion St SE16 ... 40 B4
W2 ... 116 B4
Albion Terr E8 ... 16 B1
Albion Way EC1 ... 108 C3
London SE13 ... 67 B3
Albion Wharf SW11 ... 158 A2
Albion Yd N1 ... 84 B1
Albon Ho
London SE14 ... 51 B2
Wandsworth SW18 ... 59 A1
Albrighton Rd SE5, SE22 ... 64 A4
Albury Bldgs SE1 ... 136 B3
Albury Lo 7 SW2 ... 74 B4
Albury St SE8 ... 51 C4
Albyn Rd SE8 ... 51 C2
Alconbury Rd E5 ... 7 C2
Aldbourne Rd W12 ... 29 C1
Aldbridge St SE17 ... 152 B2
Aldburgh Mews W1 ... 103 C2
Aldbury Ho SW3 ... 144 A3
Aldebert Terr SW8 ... 162 C1
Aldeburgh St SE10 ... 43 C1
Aldenham Ho NW1 ... 83 A1
Aldenham St NW1 ... 83 B1
Alden Ho E8 ... 25 A4
Aldensley Rd W6 ... 39 A3
Alderbrook Prim Sch SW12 ... 73 A4
Alderbrook Rd SW12 ... 61 A1
Alderbury Rd SW13 ... 46 C4
Aldergrove Ho 3 E5 ... 7 C2
Alder Ho SE15 ... 49 B4
1 London NW3 ... 12 B2
London SE4 ... 66 C4
Alderley Ho SW8 ... 171 B1
Alder Lo SW6 ... 47 C2
Aldermanbury EC2 ... 109 A2
Aldermanbury Sq EC2 ... 109 A3
Alderman's Wlk EC2 ... 110 A3
Alder Mews 9 N19 ... 4 B2
Alderney Ho 16 N1 ... 15 B2
Alderney Mews SE1 ... 137 B1
Alderney Rd E1 ... 25 C1
Alderney St SW1 ... 146 B2
Alder Rd SW14 ... 55 C4
Aldersford Cl SE4 ... 65 C3
Aldersgate Ct EC1 ... 108 C3
Aldersgate St EC1 ... 108 C3
Aldershot Rd NW6 ... 23 B4
Alderson St W10 ... 23 A1
Alderton Rd SE24 ... 63 B4
Alderville Rd SW6 ... 165 A1
Alderwick Ct N7 ... 14 B2
Aldford St W1 ... 117 C2
Aldgate EC3 ... 110 B1
Aldgate East Sta E1 ... 111 A2
Aldgate High St EC3 ... 110 C1
Aldgate Sta EC3 ... 110 C1
Aldham Ho SE4 ... 51 B2
Aldine Ct W12 ... 30 B1
Aldine St W12 ... 39 B4
Aldington Ct 1 E8 ... 16 C1
Aldred Rd NW6 ... 10 C3
Aldren Rd SW17 ... 71 B1
Aldrich Terr SW18 ... 71 B2
Aldrick Ho N1 ... 85 A2
Aldridge Ct W11 ... 31 B4
Aldridge Rd Villas W11 ... 31 B4
Aldsworth Cl W9 ... 88 A1
Aldworth Gr SE13 ... 67 B1
Aldwych WC2 ... 107 A1
Aldwych Bldgs WC2 ... 106 B2
Aldwyn Ho SW8 ... 162 A1
Alexander Ave NW10 ... 9 A1
Alexander Ct SW18 ... 59 B2
Alexander Ho 9 E14 ... 41 C3
Alexander Mews W2 ... 100 A2
Alexander Pl SW7 ... 144 A4
Alexander Rd N19 ... 5 A2
Alexander Sq SW3 ... 144 A4
Alexander St W2 ... 31 C3
Alexandra Ave SW11 ... 169 B3
Alexandra Cl SE8 ... 51 B4
Alexandra Cotts SE14 ... 51 B2
Alexandra Ct W9 ... 89 A2
4 London N16 ... 16 B4
5 London W12 ... 38 C4
Alexandra Gdns W4 ... 46 A3
Alexandra Gr N4 ... 6 A3
Alexandra Ho 13 W6 ... 39 B1
Alexandra Mans SW3 ... 157 B3
6 London NW6 ... 10 C3
Alexandra National Ho N4 ... 6 A2
Alexandra Pl NW8 ... 79 A4
Alexandra Rd
London NW8 ... 11 C1
London W4 ... 37 C4
Mortlake SW14 ... 55 C4
Richmond TW9 ... 44 B3
Alexandra St E16 ... 35 C4
5 SE14 ... 51 A3
Alex Gossip Ho SW6 ... 165 B3
Alexis St SE16 ... 153 C4
Alfearn Rd E5 ... 17 B4
Alford Ct N1 ... 87 A1
Alford Pl N1 ... 87 A1
Alfreda Ct SW11 ... 170 A3
Alfreda St SW11 ... 170 A3
Alfred Butt Ho SW17 ... 72 B1
Alfred Cl W4 ... 37 C2
Alfred Ho E9 ... 18 A3
Alfred Mews W1, WC1 ... 105 B4
Alfred Nunn Ho NW10 ... 21 B4
Alfred Pl WC1 ... 105 B4
Alfred Rd W2 ... 31 C4
London W3 ... 28 B1
Alfred Salter Ho SE1 ... 153 A3
Alfred Salter Prim Sch SE16 ... 40 C4
Alfred St E3 ... 26 B2
Alfriston Cl SW19 ... 69 C1
Alfriston Rd SW11 ... 60 B2
Algar Ho SE1 ... 136 A3
Algarve Rd SW18 ... 71 A3
Algernon Rd NW6 ... 23 C4
Algernon Rd *continued*
London SE13 ... 67 A3
Algiers Rd SE13 ... 66 C3
Alice Ct SW15 ... 58 B3
Alice Gilliott Ct W14 ... 155 A4
Alice La E3 ... 26 B4
Alice Owen Tech Ctr EC1 ... 96 A4
Alice Shepherd Ho 7 E14 ... 42 B4
Alice St SE1 ... 138 A1
Alice Walker Cl 8 SE24 ... 63 A3
Alie St E1 ... 111 A1
Alison Ct SE1 ... 153 B1
Aliwal Rd SW11 ... 60 A3
Alkerden Rd W4 ... 38 A1
Alkham Rd N16 ... 7 B2
Allam Ho W11 ... 112 A4
Allanbridge N16 ... 7 A4
Allan Ho SW8 ... 171 B4
Allan Way W3 ... 28 B4
Allard Gdns SW4 ... 61 C2
Allardyce St SW4, SW9 ... 62 B3
Allbrook Ho 4 SW15 ... 68 C4
Allcroft Rd NW5 ... 12 C2
Allendale Cl SE5 ... 48 C2
Allendale Sch W8 ... 127 C2
Allen Edwards Dr SW8 ... 172 A4
Allen Edwards Prim Sch SW4 ... 172 A3
Allenford Ho 1 SW15 ... 56 B1
All England Lawn Tennis & Croquet Club The SW19 ... 70 A1
Allen Ho W8 ... 127 C2
Allen Mans W8 ... 127 C2
Allen Rd E3 ... 26 B3
London N16 ... 16 A4
Allensbury Pl
London NW1 ... 14 A1
7 London NW1 ... 13 C1
Allen St W8 ... 127 C1
Allenswood 12 SW19 ... 70 A3
Allerdale Ho 7 N4 ... 6 C4
Allerton Ho N1 ... 87 C1
Allerton Rd N16 ... 6 B2
Allerton St N1 ... 97 C4
Allerton Wlk 11 N7 ... 5 B2
Allestree Rd SW6 ... 154 A1
Alleyn Cres SE21 ... 75 C2
Alleyn Ho EC1 ... 97 A1
SE1 ... 137 B1
Alleyn Pk SE21 ... 76 A1
Alleyn Rd SE21 ... 76 A1
Alleyn's Sch SE22 ... 64 A2
Allfarthing La SW18 ... 59 B1
Allfarthing Prim Sch SW18 ... 59 B1
Allgood St 10 E2 ... 24 B3
Allhallows La EC4 ... 123 B3
Alliance Ct W3 ... 28 A4
Alliance Rd W3 ... 20 A1
Allied Ind Est W3 ... 29 A1
Allied Way W3 ... 38 A4
Allingham Ct NW3 ... 12 A3
Allingham St N1 ... 86 C2
Allington Ct SW8 ... 170 C1
Allington Rd W10 ... 23 A3
Allington St SW1 ... 132 B1
Allison Cl SE10 ... 52 B2
Allison Gr SE21 ... 76 A3
Allison Rd W3 ... 28 B2
Alliston Ho E2 ... 99 A3
Allitsen Rd NW8 ... 80 A2
Allnutt Way SW4 ... 61 C2
Alloa Rd SE8 ... 41 A1
Allom Ct SW4 ... 172 B1
Allonby Ho E14 ... 33 A4
Alloway Rd E3 ... 26 A2
Allport Ho SE5 ... 63 C4
Allport Mews 33 E1 ... 25 B1
All Saints CE Prim Sch SW15 ... 57 B4
All Saints' CE Prim Sch
London NW2 ... 1 B1
London SE3 ... 53 A1
All Saints Ct 9 E1 ... 32 B2
London E5 ... 17 B4
All Saints Dr SE3 ... 53 B1
All Saints Pas SW18 ... 58 C2
All Saints Rd W11 ... 31 B3
All Saints' Rd W3 ... 37 B3
All Saints St N1 ... 84 C2
All Saints Sta E14 ... 34 A2
Allsop Pl NW1 ... 91 A1
All Souls' Ave NW10 ... 22 A4
All Souls CE Prim Sch W1 ... 104 C4
All Souls Pl W1 ... 104 B3
Alma Birk Ho 1 NW6 ... 10 B1
Almack Rd E5 ... 17 B4
Alma Gr SE1 ... 153 A3
Alma Ho 7 TW8 ... 44 A4
Alma Pl NW10 ... 22 A4
Alma Prim Sch SE16 ... 153 C4
Alma Rd SW18 ... 59 B2
Alma Sq NW8 ... 89 A4
Alma St London E15 ... 19 C2
London NW5 ... 13 A2
Alma Terr W8 ... 127 C1
Wandsworth SW18 ... 71 C4
Almeida St 10 N1 ... 15 A1
Almeric Rd SW11 ... 60 B3
Almington St N4 ... 5 B3
Almond Ave W5 ... 36 A3
Almond Cl SE15 ... 49 C1
Almond Ho SE4 ... 51 B1
Almond Rd SE16 ... 40 A2
Almorah Rd N1 ... 15 C1
Al-Muntada Islamic Sch SW6 ... 164 C2
Alperton St W10 ... 23 B1
Alphabet Sq E3 ... 33 C4
Alpha Cl NW8 ... 90 B3
Alpha Ct 6 NW5 ... 13 A2
Alpha Gr E14 ... 41 C4
Alpha Ho NW6 ... 23 C3
NW8 ... 90 B1
19 London SW4 ... 62 B3
Alpha Pl NW6 ... 23 C3
SW3 ... 158 B4
Alpha Rd SE14 ... 51 B2
Alpha St SE15 ... 49 C1
Alpine Gr 36 E9 ... 17 B1
Alpine Rd SE16 ... 40 C1
Alroy Rd N4 ... 5 C4
Alsace Rd SE17 ... 152 A2
Al Sadiq & Al Zahra Schs NW6 ... 23 A4
Alscot Rd SE1 ... 139 A1
Alscot Road Ind Est SE1 ... 139 A1
Alscot Way SE1 ... 152 C4

Altenburg Gdns
SW11 . . . . .60 B3
Althea St SW6 . . . . . .59 A4
Althope Mews
SW11 . . . . .167 C3
Althorp Rd SW17 . .72 B3
Alton Ho 3 E3 . . . . . .27 A2
Alton Rd
Richmond TW10,TW9 .54 A3
Roehampton SW15 . . .68 C3
Alton St E14 . . . . .34 A4
Alumni Ct SE1 . . . . .139 A4
Alvanley Ct NW3 . . . .11 A3
Alvanley Gdns NW6 .11 A3
Alvanley Ho W4 . . .173 B4
Alverstone Ave
SW18,SW19 . . . . .70 C2
Alverstone Ho
SE11 . . . . .163 B3
Alverstone Rd NW2 .9 B1
Alverton St SE8 . . . .51 B4
Alvey St SE17 . . . . . .152 A2
Alvington Cres E8 . .16 B3
Alwyn Ave W4 . . . . . .37 C1
Alwyne La N1 . . . . . . .15 A1
Alwyne Pl N1 . . . . . . .15 B1
Alwyne Rd N1 . . . . . .15 A1
Alwyne Sq N1 . . . . . .15 B2
Alwyne Villas N1 . . .15 A1
Alwyn Gdns W3 . . . .28 A3
Alzette Ho 11 E2 . . . .25 C3
Amazon St E1 . . . . . .32 A3
Ambassador Ct 9
NW6 . . . . .10 C3
Ambassador Ho
NW8 . . . . .79 A3
Ambassador Sq E14 .42 A2
Amber Ct N7 . . . . . . .14 C2
Ambergate St
SE17 . . . . .150 B2
Amberley Ct 2
SW9 . . . . .63 A4
Amberley Rd W9 . . .31 C4
Ambler Prim Sch N4 .6 A2
Ambler Rd N4 . . . . . .6 A1
Ambleside N1 . . . . .82 B1
13 Putney SW19 . . .70 A3
Ambleside Ct E9 . . .17 B3
Ambleside Point 11
SE15 . . . . .50 B3
Ambleside Rd NW10 .8 B1
Ambrosden Ave
SW1 . . . . .133 A1
Ambrose Ho 9 E14 .33 C4
Ambrose Mews
SW11 . . . . .168 C3
Ambrose St SE16 . . .40 A2
Ambrose Wlk E3 . . .26 C3
AMC Bsns Ctr NW10 .20 A2
Amelia Cl W3 . . . . . .37 A4
Amelia Ho 5 W6 . . .39 B1
Amelia St SE17 . . . .150 C2
Amen Cnr EC4 . . . . .108 B1
Amen Ct EC4 . . . . . .108 B1
American Coll The
W1 . . . . .103 C2
American Sch in London
The NW8 . . . . .79 B2
America Sq EC3 . . . .124 C4
America St SE1 . . . .122 C1
Amerland Rd SW18 .58 B1
Amersham Gr SE14 .51 B3
Amersham Rd SE14 .51 B2

Amersham Vale
SE14,SE8 . . . . .51 B3
Amery Gdns NW10 .22 A4
Amery Ho SE17 . . . .152 B2
Amesbury Ave SW2 .74 B2
Amesbury Twr
SW8 . . . . .170 C2
Ames Cotts 3 E3 . . .33 A4
Ames Ho 10 E2 . . . . .25 C3
Amethyst Rd E15 . . .19 C4
Amhurst Ct N4 . . . . . .6 C4
Amhurst Par N16 . . . .7 B4
Amhurst Pk N4,N16 . .7 A4
Amhurst Rd E8,N16 .16 C4
Amhurst Terr E8 . . . .16 C4
Amias Ho EC1 . . . . . .96 C2
Amiel St 31 E1 . . . . .25 B1
Amies St SW11 . . . . .60 B4
Amigo Ho SE1 . . . . .135 C2
Amina Way SE16 . . .139 B1
Amner Rd SW11 . . . .60 C1
Amor Rd W6 . . . . . . .39 B3
Amory Ho N1 . . . . . . .85 A2
Amott Rd SE15 . . . . .64 C4
Amoy Pl E14 . . . . .33 C2
Ampton Pl WC1 . . . .94 C3
Ampton St WC1 . . . .94 C3
Amstel Ct 11 SE15 . .49 B3
Amsterdam Rd E14 .42 B3
Amwell St EC1 . . . . . .95 B4
Amyruth Rd SE4 . . . .66 C2
Anatola Rd N19 . . . . .4 B2
Anchorage Point
E14 . . . . .41 C4
Anchor Ho EC1 . . . . .96 C2
Anchor Mews SW12 .61 A1
Anchor Ret Pk E1 . . .25 B1
Anchor Ter SE1 . . . .123 A2
Anchor Yd EC1 . . . . .97 A2
Ancill Cl W6 . . . . . . .154 A3
Ancona Rd NW10 . . .21 C3
Andalus Rd SW9 . . .62 A4
Andaman Ho 3 E1 . .33 A4
Anderson Cl W3 . . . .28 C3
Anderson Ho 10 E14 34 B2
Anderson Rd E9 . . . .17 C2
Andersons Sq N1 . . .86 B4
Anderson St SW3 . .144 C2
Anderton Cl SE5 . . . .63 C4
Andover Ho 5 N7 . . .5 B2
Andover Pl NW6 . . . .78 A1
Andover Rd N7 . . . . .5 B2
Andoversford Ct 7
SE15 . . . . .49 A4
Andre St E8 . . . . .16 C3
Andrew Borde St
WC2 . . . . .105 C2
Andrewes Ho EC2 . .109 A3
Andrew Ho
London SE4 . . . . .51 B1
Putney SW15 . . . . . .56 C2
Andrew Marvell Ho 12
N16 . . . . .16 A4
Andrew Pl SW8 . . . .171 C4
Andrew Reed Ho
SW18 . . . . .70 A4
Andrews Crosse
WC2 . . . . .107 B1
Andrew's Rd E8 . . . .25 A4
Andrew St E14 . . . . .34 B3
Andrews Wlk SE17 . .48 A4
Anfield Cl SW12 . . . .73 B4
Angel EC1 . . . . .86 A1

Angela Davis Ind Est 21
SW9 . . . . .63 A3
Angel Alley E1 . . . . .111 A2
Angel Ct EC2 . . . . . .109 C2
SW1 . . . . .119 A1
Angel Gate EC1 . . . .96 B4
Angel Ho N1 . . . . . . .85 C1
Angelina Ho 2
SE15 . . . . .49 C2
Angel La E15 . . . . . . .19 C2
Angell Park Gdns 8
SW9 . . . . .62 C4
Angell Rd SW9 . . . . .63 A4
Angel Mews N1 . . . .85 C1
Putney SW15 . . . . . .68 C4
Stepney E1 . . . . .32 A2
Angel Pas EC4 . . . . .123 B3
Angel Pl SE1 . . . . . .137 B4
Angel Prim Sch N1 .85 C2
Angel St EC1 . . . . . .108 C2
Angel Sta EC1 . . . . . .86 A1
Angel Wlk W6 . . . . . .39 B2
Angerstein Bsns Pk
SE10 . . . . .43 C2
Angerstein La SE3 . .53 B2
Anglebury 5 W2 . . . .31 C3
Anglers La NW5 . . . .13 A2
Anglesey Ho 7 E14 .33 C3
Anglia Ho 15 E14 . . .33 A3
Anglo American Laundry
SW17 . . . . .71 B1
Anglo Rd 20 E3 . . . .26 B3
Angrave Ct 4 E8 . . .24 B4
Angrave Pas 5 E8 . .24 B4
Angus Ho 12 SW12 . .72 C4
Angus St SE14 . . . . .51 A3
Anhalt Rd SW11 . . .158 B2
Anley Rd W14 . . . . . .39 C4
Annabel Cl E14 . . . . .34 A3
Anna Cl E8 . . . . .24 B4
Annandale Prim Sch
SE10 . . . . .43 B1
Annandale Rd SE10 .43 B1
London W4 . . . . .38 A1
Anne Goodman Ho 1
E1 . . . . .32 B3
Anne Kerr Ct 18
SW15 . . . . .57 C1
Anne's Ct NW8 . . . . .90 B1
Annesley Ho SW9 . .173 B4
Annesley Wlk N19 . . .4 B2
Annette Cres 9 N1 . .15 B1
Annette Ct N7 . . . . . .5 B1
Annette Rd N7 . . . . . .14 B4
Annie Besant Cl E3 .26 B4
Anning St E2 . . . . . . .98 B2
Annis Rd E9 . . . . .18 A2
Ann La SW10 . . . . . .157 C1
Ann Moss Way SE16 .40 B3
Ann's Cl SW1 . . . . . .131 B3
Ann's Pl E1 . . . . .110 C3
Ansdell Rd SE15 . . . .50 B1
Ansdell St W8 . . . . .128 B2
Ansdell Terr W8 . . . .128 B2
Ansell Ho E1 . . . . . . .32 B4
Ansell Rd SW17 . . . .72 B1
Anselm Rd SW6 . . . .155 B3
Ansleigh Pl W11 . . . .30 C2
Anslie Wlk 3 SW12 .73 A4
Anson Ho 5 E1 . . . . .26 A1
SW1 . . . . .160 C4
Anson Prim Sch NW2 .9 C3
Anson Rd London N7 .13 C4
London NW2 . . . . .9 B3
Anstey Ct 6 W3 . . . .37 A4
Anstey Ho 8 E9 . . . .25 B4
Anstey Rd SE15 . . . .64 C4

Anstice Cl W4 . . . . . .46 A3
Antenor Ho 11 E2 . . .25 A3
Anthony Cope Ct
N1 . . . . .97 C4
Anthony Ho NW8 . . .90 A1
Anthony St E1 . . . . . .32 A3
Antilles Bay 7 E14 .42 B4
Antill Rd E3 . . . . .26 A2
Antill Terr 8 E1 . . . .32 C3
Anton St E8 . . . . .16 C3
Antony Ho 4 SE14 . .50 C3
2 SE16 . . . . .40 B2
Antrim Gr NW3 . . . . .12 B2
Antrim Ho SW11 . . . .60 C4
Antrim Mans 12 B2
Antrim Rd NW3 . . . . .12 B2
Antrobus Rd W4 . . . .37 B3
Apex Ind Est NW10 .21 B1
Aphrodite Ct 2 E14 .41 C2
Apollo Bldg 2 E14 .41 C2
Apollo Ho 51 E2 . . . .25 A3
SW10 . . . . .157 B3
London N6 . . . . .3 B4
Apollo Ind Bsns Ctr 20
SE8 . . . . .50 C4
Apollo Pl SW10 . . . .157 B2
Apollo Studios 13
NW5 . . . . .13 C3
Apothecary St EC4 .108 A1
Appach Rd SW2 . . . .62 C1
Appleby Rd E16 . . . .35 C3
London E8 . . . . .16 C1
Appleby St E2 . . . . . .24 B3
Appledore Cl SW12,
SW17 . . . . .72 B2
Appleford 8 NW5 . . .13 B3
Appleford Ho
W10 . . . . .23 A1
Appleford Rd W10 . .23 A1
Applegarth Ho SE1 .136 B4
8 SE15 . . . . .49 C3
Applegarth Rd W14 .39 C3
Apple Mkt WC2 . . . .120 B4
Appleshaw Ho 4
SE5 . . . . .64 A4
Appletree Ct SE13 . .67 C3
Apple Tree Yd
SW1 . . . . .119 A2
Applewood Cl NW2 . .9 A4
Appold St EC2 . . . . .110 A4
Apollo Ct SW9 . . . . .173 B4
Apprentice Way 5
E5 . . . . .17 A4
Approach Cl N16 . . . .16 A4
Approach Rd E2 . . . .25 B3
Approach The 2 W3 .28 C3
April Ct 20 E2 . . . . . .24 C3
April St E8 . . . . .16 B4
Apsley Ho E1 . . . . . . .32 B4
Apsley Way W1 . . . .131 C4
Aquila St NW8 . . . . . .79 C2
Aquinas St SE1 . . . .121 C1
Arabella Ct NW8 . . . .79 A2
Arabella Dr SW15 . . .56 A3
Arabian Ho 3 E1 . . .26 A1
Arabin Rd SE4 . . . . . .66 B3
Aragon Twr SE8 . . . .41 B2
Arakan Ho 4 N16 . . .15 C4
Aral Ho 14 E1 . . . . . .25 C1
Arapiles Ho 6 E14 . .34 C3
Arbery Rd E3 . . . . . . .26 A3
Arbon Ct N1 . . . . .87 A3
Arbor Ct N16 . . . . .6 C2
Arborfield Ho 6
E14 . . . . .33 C2
Arbourfield Cl SW2 .74 B3
Arbour Ho 3 E1 . . . .32 C3
Arbour Sq E1 . . . . . .32 C3

Arbuthnot Rd SE14 .50 C1
Arbutus St E8 . . . . . .24 B4
Arcade The 4 EC2 . .110 A3
1 London N7 . . . . .14 A4
Arcadia St E14 . . . . .33 C3
Archangel St SE16 . .40 C4
**Archbishop Michael
Ramsey Tech Coll**
SE5 . . . . .48 A3
Archbishop's Pl 1
SW2 . . . . .74 B4
**Archbishop Sumner's CE
Prim Sch** SE11 . . . .149 C3
**Archbishop Tenison's
Sch** SE11 . . . . .163 A3
Archdale Ct W12 . . .30 A1
Archdale Ho SE1 . . .138 A2
Archdale Rd SE22 . . .64 B3
Archel Rd W14 . . . . .154 C4
Archer Ho 25 N1 . . . .24 A4
W11 . . . . .113 A4
London W13 . . . . . .167 C3
Archers Lo SE16 . . .153 C1
Archer Sq SE14 . . . .51 A4
Archer St W1 . . . . . .119 B4
Archery Cl W2 . . . . .102 B1
Archery Fields Ho
WC1 . . . . .95 B4
Archery Steps W2 . .116 B4
Arches The WC2 . . . .120 B2
Archibald Mews
W1 . . . . .118 A3
Archibald Rd N7 . . . .13 C4
Archibald St E3 . . . . .26 C2
Archway N19 . . . . .4 B2
Archway Bsns Ctr 9
N19 . . . . .4 C1
Archway Cl W10 . . . .30 C4
Archway Hts 5 N19 . .4 B3
Archway Mews
SW15 . . . . .58 A3
Archway Rd N6 . . . . .4 A4
Archway St SW13,
SW14 . . . . .56 A4
Archway Sta N19 . . . .4 B2
Arcola St E8 . . . . .16 B3
Arctic St NW5 . . . . . . .13 A3
Ardbeg Rd SE24 . . . .63 C2
Arden 17 SW19 . . . .69 C3
Arden Cres E14 . . . . .41 C2
Arden Ho 20 N1 . . . .24 A3
SE11 . . . . .148 C3
London SW9 . . . . . .172 B1
Ardent Ho 28 E3 . . . .26 A3
Ardilaun Rd N5 . . . . .15 B4
Ardleigh Rd N1 . . . . .16 A2
Ardlui Rd SE27 . . . . .75 B2
Ardmere Rd SE13 . . .67 C1
Ardshiel Cl SW15 . . .57 C4
Ardwell Rd SW2 . . . .74 A2
Ardwick Rd NW2 . . .10 C4
Ares Ct 8 E14 . . . . . .41 C2
Arethusa Ho 8 E14 .42 A2
Argon Mews SW6 . .155 C1
Argos Ct SW9 . . . . .173 B4
Argos Ho 8 E2 . . . . .25 A3
Argosy Ho SE8 . . . . .41 A2
W1 . . . . .92 B1
Argyle Ho E14 . . . . . .42 B3
Argyle Pl W6 . . . . . . .39 A2
Argyle Prim Sch
WC1 . . . . .94 A4
Argyle Rd E1 . . . . . . .25 C1
Argyle Sq WC1 . . . . .94 B4
Argyle St WC1 . . . . . .94 B4
Argyle Way SE16 . . .153 C1

Argyle Wlk WC1	94 B3
Argyll Cl SW9	62 B4
Argyll Ct 15 SW2	74 B4
Argyll Mans SW3	157 C4
W14	140 B4
Argyll Rd W8	127 C3
Argyll St W1	104 C1
Arica Ho SE16	40 A3
Arica Rd SE4	66 A4
Ariel Ct SE11	150 A3
London W12	38 C3
Ariel Ho NW6	10 C2
Ariel Way W12	30 B1
Aristotle Rd SW4	61 C4
Arkansas Ho 21 N19	4 C4
Arklow Ho SE17	48 C4
Arklow Rd SE14	51 B4
Arklow Road Trad Est SE14	51 B4
Arkwright Ho 12 SW2	74 A4
Arkwright Mans NW3	11 B3
Arkwright Rd NW3	11 B3
Arlesey Cl SW15	58 A1
Arlesford Rd SW9	62 A4
Arlingford Rd SW2	62 C2
Arlington Ave N1	87 A3
Arlington Gdns W4	37 B1
Arlington Ho EC1	95 C4
3 SE8	51 B4
London W12	30 A1
Arlington Lo SW2	62 B3
Arlington Park Mans 3 W4	37 B1
Arlington Pl 7 SE10	52 B3
Arlington Rd NW1	82 B3
Arlington Sq N1	87 A3
Arlington St SW1	118 C2
Arlington Way EC1	95 C4
Armada Ct SE8	51 C4
Armadale Rd SW6	155 B3
Armada St 10 SE8	51 C4
Armagh Rd E3	26 B4
Arminger Rd W12	30 A1
Armitage Ho NW1	102 A4
Armitage Rd SE10	43 B1
London NW11	1 B3
Armour Cl N7	14 B2
Armoury Rd SE8	52 A1
Armoury Way SW18	58 C2
Armsby Ho 16 E1	32 B4
Armstrong Ho 8 SW15	57 C1
Armstrong Rd SW7	129 B1
London W3	29 B1
Arncliffe NW6	78 B3
Arne Ho SE11	149 A2
Arne St WC2	106 B1
Arneway St SW1	133 C1
Arnewood Cl SW15	68 C3
Arnhem Pl E14	41 C3
Arnhem Way 7 SE22	64 A2
Arnhem Wharf E14	41 C3
Arnhem Wharf Prim Sch E14	41 C3
Arnold Cir E2	98 C3
Arnold Est SE1	139 A3
Arnold Ho SE17	150 B1
9 London N16	7 A1
Arnold House Sch NW8	79 B1
Arnold Rd E3	26 C2
Arnot Ho 27 SE5	48 B3
Arnott Cl W4	37 C2
Arnould Ave SE5	63 C3
Arnside Ho 2 SE17	48 C4
Arnside St SE17	48 C4
Arodene Rd SW2	62 B1
Arragon Rd SW18	70 C3
Arran Ho N16	7 B3
Arran Wlk N1	15 B1
Arrol Ho SE1	137 A1
Arrowe Ct 7 E5	17 A4
Arrow Ho 24 N1	24 A4
Arrow Rd E3	27 A2
Arrowsmith Ho SE11	148 C2
Arsenal Sta N5	5 C1
Artemis Ct 8 E14	41 C2
Artesian Rd W2	31 C3
Arthur Ct SW11	169 C3
10 London W10	30 C3
London W2	100 A2
Arthur Deakin Ho 8 E1	111 B4
Arthurdon Rd SE4	66 C2
Arthur Henderson Ho Fulham SW6	164 C2
9 London N19	4 C4
Arthur Newton Ho 20 SW11	59 C4
Arthur Rd N7	14 B4
Arthur St EC4	123 C4
Arthur Wade Ho 12 E2	99 A4
Artichoke Hill 3 E1	32 A2
Artichoke Mews 5 SE5	48 C2
Artichoke Pl SE5	48 C2
Artillery La E1	110 B3
London W12	29 C3
Artillery Pass E1	110 B3
Artillery Row SW1	133 B1
Artizan St E1	110 B2
Arton Wilson Ho 18 SW15	56 C2
Arts Educational Sch The W4	38 A2
Arundel Bldgs SE1	138 B1
Arundel Cl SW11	60 A2
Arundel Ct SW3	144 B2
Barnes SW13	47 A4
Putney SW15	57 C2
Arundel Gdns W11	31 B2 112 C4
Arundel Gr N16	16 A3
Arundel Ho N1	86 B4
3 London W3	37 A4
Arundel Mans SW6	165 A4
Barnes SW13	47 A4
Arundel Pl N1,N7	14 C2
Arundel Sq N7	14 C2
Arundel St WC2	121 A4
Arundel Terr SW13	47 A4
Arvon Rd N5	14 C3
Asaph Ho SE14	51 B2
Ascalon Ct 16 SW2	74 B4
Ascalon Ho SW8	160 C1
Ascalon St SW8	160 C1
Ascham St NW5	13 B3
Ascot Ct NW8	89 B3
8 London SW4	62 A3
Ascot Ho NW1	92 B4
1 W9	31 C4
6 London W4	37 B1
Ascot Lo NW6	78 B2
Ascot Par 9 SW4	62 A3
Ascott Ave W5	36 A4
Asfil Ho EC1	107 C3
Ashbourne Ct E5	18 A4
Ashbourne Gr London SE22	64 B3
London SE8	38 A1
Ashbridge St NW8	90 A1
Ashbrook Rd N19	4 C2
Ashburn Gdns SW7	142 C4
Ashburnham Com Sch SW10	157 B2
Ashburnham Gr SE10	52 A3
Ashburnham Pl SE10	52 A3
Ashburnham Rd SW10	157 A1
London NW10	22 B3
Ashburnham Retreat 6 SE10	52 A3
Ashburnham Twr SW10	157 B2
Ashburn Pl SW7	142 C3
Ashburton Gr N7	14 C4
Ashburton Mans SW10	157 A2
Ashburton Rd E16	35 C3
Ashbury Rd SW11	60 C4
Ashby Ct NW8	89 C2
Ashby Gr N1	15 B1
Ashby Ho 5 London N1	15 B1
London SW9	48 A1
Ashby Mews SE4	51 B1
Ashby Rd SE4	51 B1
Ashby St EC1	96 B3
Ashchurch Ct 2 W12	38 C3
Ashchurch Gr W12	38 C3
Ashchurch Park Villas W12	38 C3
Ashchurch Terr W12	38 C3
Ashcombe Ct 4 SW15	58 A2
Ashcombe Ho 30 E3	27 A2
Ashcombe St SW6	166 A1
Ashcroft Ho SW8	170 C4
Ashcroft Rd E3	26 A2
Ashcroft Sq W6	39 B2
Ash Ct SW1	102 C2
London N19	4 B4
London SE10	60 C2
Ashdale Ho N4	6 C4
Ashdene 8 SE15	50 A3
Ashdown Cres NW5	12 C3
Ashdown Ho 5 E5	7 C2
Ashdown Rd N10	21 B4
Ashdown Way SW17	72 C2
Ashdown Wlk 19 E14	41 C2
Ashenden SE17	151 A4
Ashenden Rd E5	18 A3
Ashen Gr SW19	70 C2
Ashentree Ct EC4	107 C1
Asher Way E1	125 C3
Ashfield Ho 5 N5	15 B3
Ashfield Rd W3	29 B1
Ashfield St E1	32 B4
Ashford Ct NW2	9 C4
Ashford Ho 11 SE8	51 B4
14 London SW9	63 A3
Ashford Rd NW2	9 C4
Ash Gr E8	25 A4
London NW2	10 A4
London W5	36 A3
Ashgrove Ct 2 W9	31 C4
Ashgrove Ho SW1	147 C2
Ash Ho 8 E14	42 B4
SE1	153 A3
Ashington 1 NW5	12 C2
Ashington Ho 16 E1	25 A1
Ashington Rd SW6	165 A3
Ashlake Rd SW16	74 A1
Ashleigh Ho SW14	56 A4
Ashleigh Rd SW14	56 A4
Ashley Cres SW11	60 C4
Ashley Ct 10 London N16	16 A4
London NW3	11 A3
Ashley Pl SW1	132 C1
Ashley Rd London N19	5 A4
Richmond TW9	54 B3
Ashlin Rd E15	19 C4
Ash Lo SW6	47 C2
Ashlone Rd SW15	57 C4
Ashmead Bsns Ctr E16	27 C1
Ashmead Ho E9	18 A3
Ashmead Prim Sch SE8	51 C1
Ashmead Rd SE8	51 C1
Ashmere Gr 11 SW2, SW4	62 A3
Ashmere Ho 10 SW2	62 A3
Ashmill St NW8	102 A4
Ashmole Prim Sch SW8	163 A3
Ashmole St SW8	163 A3
Ashmore NW1	13 C1
Ashmore Cl SE15	49 B3
Ashmore Ho W14	126 B2
Ashmore Rd W9	23 B2
Ashmount Prim Sch N6	4 B4
Ashmount Rd N19	4 C4
Ashness Rd SW11	60 B2
Ashpark Ho 4 E14	33 A3
Ashtead Ct 18 SW19	69 C3
Ashtead Rd E5	7 C4
Ashton Ho London N1	163 C1
Roehampton SW15	69 A4
Ashton Rd E15	19 C3
Ashton St E14	34 B2
Ashurst Lo 5 N5	15 A3
Ashwin St E8	16 B2
Ashworth Cl SE5	48 C1
Ashworth Mans W9	88 B3
Ashworth Rd W9	88 B3
Asker Ho N7	14 A4
Aske St N1	98 A4
Askew Cres W12	38 C4
Askew Mans 14 W12	38 C4
Askew Rd W12	38 C4
Askham Ct W12	29 C1
Askham Rd W12	29 C1
Askill Dr SW15	58 A2
Asland Rd E15	27 C4
Aslett St SW18	71 B4
Asmara Rd NW2	10 A3
Asolando Dr SE17	151 A3
Aspen Cl 10 London N19	4 B2
London W5	36 A4
Aspen Ct London E8	16 B2
Richmond TW9	44 C3
Aspen Gdns W6	39 A1
Aspen Ho 8 SE15	50 B4
4 London NW3	12 B2
Aspenlea Rd W6	47 C4
Aspen Way E14	34 B2
Aspern Gr NW3	12 A3
Aspinall Ho SW12	74 A3
Aspinall Rd SE4	65 C4
Aspinden Rd SE16	40 A2
Aspire Bld SW15	58 B2
Aspley Ho SW18	59 A2
Assam SE1	125 A1
Assam St E1	111 B2
Assata Mews N1	15 A2
Assembly Pas E1	32 B4
Assisi Ct SW12	72 B3
Astbury Ho SE11	135 B1
Astbury Rd SE15	50 B2
Astell St SW3	144 B2
Aste St E14	42 B4
Astey's Row 3 N1	15 B1
Astle St SW11	169 C2
Astley Ave NW2	9 B3
Astley Ho SE1	153 A2
10 London W2	31 C4
Aston Ho SW8	171 B3
W11	113 A4
Aston St E14	33 A3
Astonville St SW18	70 C3
Astor Ct SW6	156 C1
Astoria Mans 18 SW16	74 A1
Astoria Par SW16	74 A1
Astoria Wlk SW9	62 C4
Astra Ho 4 E3	26 B2
London N4	5 B4
Astrop Mews W6	39 B3
Astrop Terr W6	39 B4
Astwood Mews SW7	142 C4
Asylum Rd SE15	50 A3
Atalanta St SW6	154 A1
Atheldene Rd SW18	71 B3
Athelstan Gdns 3 NW6	10 A1
Athelstan Ho London E9	18 B3
London N16	16 A4
Athena Ct NW8	79 B2
Athenia Ho 7 E14	34 C3
Athenlay Rd SE15	65 C2
Athenoeum Ct N5	15 B4
Athens Gdns W9	23 C1
Atherden Rd E5	17 B4
Atherfield Ct SW18	59 A1
Atherfold Rd SW9	62 A4
Atherstone Ct W2	100 B4
Atherstone Mews SW7	143 A4
Atherton St SW13	46 C3
Atherton St SW11	168 B2
Athlone Ho 3 E1	32 B3
NW5	12 C2
Athlone Rd SW2	74 B4
Athlone St NW5	12 C2
Atholl Ho W9	88 C3
Athol Sq E14	34 B3
Atkins Ct 8 E3	26 B4
Atkinson Ho 12 E2	24 C3
SE17	151 C3
5 London SW11	169 B3
Atkins Rd SW4,SW12	73 C4
Atlantic Ct 6 E14	34 C2
Atlantic Ho 4 E1	33 A4

Atlantic Ho continued
4 Putney SW15 ....58 B2
Atlantic Rd SW2,
SW9,SE24 ....62 C3
Atlas Mews E8 ...16 B2
Atlas Rd NW10 ...21 A2
Atley Rd E3 ....26 C4
Atney Rd SW15 ...58 A3
Atterbury St SW1 .148 A3
Attilburgh Ho SE1 138 C2
Attneave St WC1 ..95 A3
Atwater Cl SW2 ...74 C3
Atwell Rd 8 SE15 .49 C1
Atwood Ave TW9 ..44 C1
Atwood Ho SE21 ..76 A1
Atwood Rd W6 ....39 A2
Aubert Ct N5 ......15 A4
Aubert Pk N5 ......15 A4
Aubert Rd N5 ......15 A4
Aubrey Beardsley Ho
SW1 ....147 A3
Aubrey Mans NW1 .102 A4
Aubrey Moore Point
E15 ....27 B3
Aubrey Pl NW8 ....78 C1
Aubrey Rd
W14 ......31 B1 113 A1
Aubrey Wlk
W14 ......31 B1 113 A1
Auburn Cl SE14 ...51 A3
Aubyn Sq SW15 ...56 C2
Auckland Ho 11
W12 ....30 A2
Auckland Rd SW11 .60 A3
Auckland St SE11 .148 C1
Auden Pl NW1 .....81 B4
Audley Cl 9 SW11 .60 C4
Audley Rd TW10 ..54 B2
Audley Sq W1 .....117 C2
Audrey St E2 ......24 C3
Augustas Cl W12 ..39 A3
Augustine Rd W14 .39 C3
Augustines Ct E9 ..17 B3
Augustus Ct
8 Putney SW19 ..70 C2
Streatham SW16 ..73 C2
Augustus Rd SW19 .70 A2
Augustus St NW1 ..92 B4
Aulton Pl SE11 ....149 C1
Auriga Mews N1 ...15 C3
Auriol Mans W14 ..140 A3
Auriol Rd W14 .....140 A3
Austen Ho 2 NW6 .23 C2
Austin Friars Sq
EC2 ....109 C2
Austin Friars Sq
EC2 ....109 C2
Austin Ho 1 SE14 .51 B3
8 London SW2 ....62 C1
Austin Rd SW11 ...169 B3
Austins Ct SE15 ...64 C4
Austin St E2 ....98 C3
Australia Rd W12 ..30 A2
Austral St SE11 ....150 A4
Autumn St E3 .....26 C4
Avalon Rd SW6 ...166 A4
Avebury Ct N1 .....87 B3
Avebury St N1 .....87 B3
Aveline St SE11 ...149 B1
Ave Maria La EC4 .108 B1
Avenell Mans N5 ..15 A4
Avenell Rd N5 .....6 A1
Avenfield Ho W1 ..117 A4
Avening Rd SW18 ..70 C4
Avening Terr SW18 .70 C4
Avenue Cl NW8 ...80 B3

Avenue Cres W3 ...37 A4
Avenue Ct SW3 ...144 C3
London NW2 ....1 A1
Avenue Gdns
London W3 ....37 A4
Mortlake SW14 ....56 A4
Avenue Ho NW8 ...80 A1
London NW6 ....7 C2
London N16 ....22 A3
Avenue Lo 12 NW8 .11 C1
Avenue Mans NW3 .11 A3
Avenue Park Rd
SE21,SE27 ....75 A2
Avenue Rd NW8 ...80 A4
London N6 ....4 C4
London NW10 .....21 B3
London W3 ....37 A4
Avenue Sch The
NW6 ....10 A1
Avenue The NW6 ..23 A4
SE10 ....52 C3
London W4 ....38 A3
Richmond TW9 ....54 B4
Wandsworth SW18,
SW12 ....72 B4
Averill St W6 ......47 C4
Avery Farm Row
SW1 ....146 A3
Avery Hill Coll (Mile End
Annexe) E2 ....26 B1
Avery Row W1 .....118 B4
Aviary Ct E16 .....35 B2
Avigdor (Jewish) Prim
Sch N16 ....6 C2
Avignon Rd SE4 ...65 C4
Avington Ct SE1 ...152 B3
Avis Sq E1 ....32 C3
Avocet Cl SE1 .....153 B2
Avon Ct
1 London W3 .....28 B3
11 Putney SW15 ..58 A2
Avondale Ct E16 ..35 A4
Avondale Ho SE1 ..153 A1
8 Mortlake SW14 .55 C4
Avondale Mans
SW6 ....164 C4
Avondale Park Gdns
W11 ......31 A2 112 A3
Avondale Park Prim Sch
W11 ......31 A2 112 A3
Avondale Park Rd
W11 ......31 A2 112 A3
Avondale Rd E16 ..35 A4
Mortlake SW14 ....55 C4
Avondale Rise SE15 .64 B4
Avondale Sq SE1 ..153 B1
Avon Ho W14 .....141 A3
14 London N16 ....15 C4
Avonhurst Ho NW6 .10 A1
Avonley Rd SE14 ..50 B3
Avonmore Gdns
W14 ....141 A3
Avonmore Pl W14 .140 B4
Avonmore Prim Sch
W14 ....140 B4
Avonmore Rd W14 .140 C4
Avonmouth St SE1 .136 C2
Avon Pl SE1 ....137 A3
Avon Rd SE4 ......66 C4
Avriol Ho W12 ....30 A1
Avro Ct E9 ....18 A3
Axford Ho SW2 ...75 A3
Axis Bsns Ctr E15 .27 A4
Axminster Rd N7 ..5 B1
Aybrook St W1 ...103 B3
Aycliffe Rd W12 ...29 C1

Aylesbury Ho 13
SE15 ....49 C4
Aylesbury Rd SE17 .151 C1
Aylesbury St EC1 ..96 A1
Aylesford Ho SE1 ..137 C3
Aylesford St SW1 ..147 B1
Aylesham Ctr The
SE15 ....49 C2
Aylestone Ave NW6 .22 C4
Aylmer Ho SE10 ...42 C1
Aylmer Rd W12 ...38 B4
Aylton Est 22 SE16 .40 B4
Aylward St E1 .....32 C3
Aylwin Est SE1 ....138 B2
Aylwin Girls Sch
SE1 ....153 A4
Aynhoe Mans W14 .39 C2
Aynhoe Rd W14 ...39 C3
Ayres St SE1 ......137 A4
Ayrsome Rd N16 ...7 A1
Ayrton Gould Ho 8
E2 ....25 C2
Ayrton Rd SW7 ...129 B2
Aysgarth Rd SE21 .76 A4
Ayston Ho 10 SE8 ..40 C2
Ayton Ho 55 ....48 C3
Aytoun Ct SW9 ...173 A1
Aytoun Pl SW9 ....173 A1
Aytoun Rd SW9 ...173 A1
Azalea Ho SE14 ...51 B3
Azenby Rd SE15 ...49 B1
Azof St SE10 ......43 A2
Azov Ho 9 E1 .....26 A1

B

Baalbec Rd N5 ....15 A3
Babington Ct WC1 .106 B3
Babington Ho SE1 .137 A4
Babmaes St SW1 ..119 A3
Bacchus Wlk 12 N1 .24 A3
Bache's St N1 .....97 C4
Back Church La
E1 ....111 B1
Back Hill EC1 ......95 C1
Backhouse Pl SE1 .152 B3
Back La NW3 .....11 B4
Bacon Gr SE1 .....138 C1
Bacon's Coll SE16 ..41 A4
Bacon's La N6 .....3 C3
Bacon St E2 .24 C1 99 A2
Bacton NW5 ......12 C3
Bacton St E2 ......25 B2
Baddeley Ho SE11 .149 A2
Baddow Wlk N1 ...87 A4
Baden Pl SE1 .....137 B4
Badminton Ct 9 N4 .6 B4
Badminton Ho SE22 .64 A3
Badminton Mews 6
E16 ....35 C1
Badminton Rd
SW12 ....60 C1
Badric Ct SW11 ...167 C1
Badsworth Rd 3
SE5 ....48 B2
Bagley's La SW6 ..166 B3
Bagnigge Ho WC1 .95 B3
Bagshot Ho NW1 ..92 B4
Bagshot St SE17 ..152 B1
Baildon 23 E2 .....25 B3
Baildon St SE8 ....51 B3
Bailey Cl 9 E17 ...10 C3
Bailey Mews W4 ..45 A4
Bainbridge St
WC1 ....105 C2
Bain Ho SW9 .....172 B2
Baird Ho 20 W12 ..30 A2

Baird St EC1 ......97 A2
Baizdon Rd SE3 ...53 A1
Baker Ho 10 E3 ...26 C2
11 W10 ....21 A4
Bakers Field N7 ...14 A4
Bakers Hall Ct EC3 .124 B3
Baker's Mews W1 ..103 B2
Bakers Rents E2 ..98 C3
Baker's Row EC1 ..95 B1
Baker St W1 ....103 A4
Baker St NW1 .....91 A1
Baker Street Sta
NW1 ....91 A1
Baker's Yd EC1 ...95 B1
Balaclava Rd SE1 .153 A3
Balchier Rd SE22 ..65 A1
Balcombe Ho NW1 .90 C2
3 Streatham SW2 .74 B3
Balcombe St NW1 .90 C1
Balcorne St E9 ....17 B1
Balderton Flats
W1 ....103 C1
Balderton St W1 ..103 C1
Baldock Ho 20 SE5 .48 B1
Baldock St E3 .....27 A3
Baldrey Ho 11 SE10 .43 B1
Baldwin Cres SE5 ..48 B2
Baldwin Ho 15 SW2 .74 C3
Baldwin's Gdns
EC1 ....107 B4
Baldwin St EC1 ...97 B3
Baldwin Terr N1 ...86 C2
Baldwins Gdns 3
EC1 ....107 B4
Bale Rd E1 ....33 A4
Bales Coll W10 ...22 C2
Balfern Gr W4 ....38 A1
Balfern St SW11 ..168 B2
Balfe St N1 ....84 B1
Balfour Ho W10 ...30 C4
Balfour Mews W1 ..117 C2
Balfour Pl W1 .....117 C3
Putney SW15 .....57 A3
Balfour Rd
London N5 ....15 B4
London N4 ....28 B4
Balfour St SE17 ...151 B4
Balfron Twr 2 E14 .34 B3
Balham Gr SW12 ..72 C4
Balham High Rd
SW12,SW17 ......72 C3
Balham Hill SW12 ..61 A1
Balham New Rd
SW12 ....73 A4
Balham Park Mans
SW12 ....72 B3
Balham Park Rd
SW12,SW17 ......72 C3
Balham Station Rd
SW12 ....73 A3
Balin Ho SE1 ......137 B4
Balkan Wlk 1 E1 ..32 A2
Balladier Wlk E14 .34 A4
Ballance Rd E9 ...18 A2
Ballantine St SW18 .59 B3
Ballantrae Ho NW2 .10 B4
Ballard Ho SE10 ..52 A4
Ballast Quay SE10 .42 C1
Ballater Rd SW2,
SW4 ....62 A3
Ball Ct EC3 ....109 C1
Ballin Ct 2 E14 ...42 B4
Ballingdon Rd
SW11 ....60 C1
Ballinger Point 10
E3 ....27 A2

Balliol Ho 11 SW15 .57 C1
Balliol Rd W10 ....30 C3
Ballogie Ave NW10 .8 A4
Ballow Cl 25 SE5 ..49 A3
Ball's Pond Pl 3
N1 ....15 C2
Ball's Pond Rd N1 .16 A2
Balman Ho 3 SE16 .40 C2
Balmer Rd E3 .....26 B3
Balmes Rd N1 ....87 C4
Balmoral Cl 1
SW15 ....57 C1
Balmoral Ct NW8 ..79 B2
2 SE16 ....32 C1
Balmoral Gr N7 ...14 B2
Balmoral Ho W14 ..140 A4
London N4 ....6 B3
Balmoral Mews
W12 ....38 B3
Balmoral Rd NW2 ..9 A2
Balmore St N19 ...4 A2
Balmuir Gdns SW15 .57 B3
Balnacraig Ave
NW10 ....8 A4
Balniel Gate SW1 .147 C2
Balsam Ho 8 E14 ..34 A2
Baltic Ho 7 SE5 ...48 B1
Baltic St E EC1 ...96 C1
Baltic St W EC1 ...96 C1
Baltimore Ho SE11 .149 B2
Balvaird Pl SW1 ...147 C1
Balvernie Gr SW18 .70 C4
Bamborough Gdns 11
W12 ....39 B4
Bamford Ct E15 ...19 A3
Banbury Ct WC2 ..120 A4
Banbury Ho 8 E9 ..17 C1
Banbury Rd E9 ...17 C1
Banbury St SW11 ..168 B2
Bancroft Ct SW8 ..172 A4
Bancroft Ho 10 E1 .25 B1
Bancroft Rd E1 ...25 C1
Banff Ho 1 NW3 ..12 A2
Banfield Rd SE15 ..65 A4
Bangabandhu Prim Sch
E2 ....25 B2
Bangalore St SW15 .57 C4
Banim St W6 ......39 A2
Banister Ho SW8 ..171 A4
London E9 ....17 C3
19 London W10 ...23 A2
Banister Rd W10 ..22 C2
Bank Ct SW11 ....170 A4
Bank End SE1 .....123 A2
Bank La SW15 ....56 A2
Bank of England*
EC2 ....109 B1
Banks Ho SE1 ....136 C1
Bankside SE1 .....122 C3
SE1 ....123 A2
Bankside Pier SE1 .122 C3
Bank Sta EC3 .....109 C1
Bank The N6 ......4 A3
Bankton Rd SW2 ..62 C3
Banner Ho EC1 ...97 A1
Bannerman Ho
SW8 ....162 C3
Banner St EC1 ....97 A2
Banning Ho 4
SW19 ....69 C3
Banning St SE10 ..43 A1
Bannister Cl SW2 ..74 C3
Bannister Ho 28
SE14 ....50 C4
Banqueting House*
SW1 ....120 A1
Banstead Ct N4 ...6 B3

Banstead St SE15 ....65 B4
Bantock Ho E4 W10 ..23 A2
Bantry Ho B1 E1 ....25 C1
Bantry St SE5 ......48 C3
Banyan Ho B1 NW3 ...11 A2
Banyard Rd SE16 ....40 A3
Baptist Gdns NW5 ...12 C2
Barandon Wlk B6
  W11 ....30 C2
Barbanel Ho E1 E1 ..25 B1
Barbara Brosnan Ct
  NW8 ....79 B1
Barbauld Rd N16 ....7 A1
Barber Beaumont Ho E1
  E1 ....25 C2
Barbers Rd E15 .....27 A3
Barbican* EC2 .....109 A3
Barbican Arts & Con Ctr
  EC2 ....109 A4
Barbican Sta EC1 ..108 C4
Barb Mews W6 ......39 B3
Barbon Cl WC1 .....106 C4
Barbrook Ho E9 ....17 B2
Barchard St SW18 ..59 A2
Barchester St E14 ..34 A4
Barclay Cl SW6 ....155 B1
Barclay Ho E2 E9 ...17 B1
Barclay Rd SW6 ...155 C1
Barcombe Ave SW2 .74 B2
Bardell Ho E2 E16 ..139 B3
Bardolph Rd
  London N7 ....14 A4
  Richmond TW9 ....54 B4
Bard Rd W10 ....30 C2
Bardsey Pl E3 E1 ...25 B1
Bardsey Wlk E2 N1 .15 B2
Bardsley Ho E5
  SE10 ....52 B4
Bardsley La SE10 ...52 B4
Barents Ho E1 E1 ...25 C1
Barfett St W10 .....23 B1
Barfleur Ho SE8 ....41 B2
Barford Ho E3 E3 ...26 B3
Barford St N1 ......85 C3
Barforth Rd SE15 ...65 A4
Barge House St
  SE1 ....121 C2
Barham Ho SE17 ...152 B2
Baring Ct N1 ....87 B3
Baring Ho E1 E14 ...33 C3
Baring St N1 ....87 B3
Barker Dr NW1 .....13 C1
Barker Ho SE17 ....152 A3
  Dulwich SE21 .....76 A1
Barker Mews SW4 ..61 A3
Barker St SW10 ....156 C4
Barker Wlk SW16 ...73 C1
Bark Pl W2 ....114 A4
Barkston Gdns
  SW5 ....142 A3
Barkway Ct N4 .....6 B2
Barkwith Ho E4
  SE14 ....50 C4
Barkworth Rd SE16 .40 B1
Barlborough St
  SE14 ....50 C3
Barlby Gdns W10 ...22 C1
Barlby Prim Sch
  W10 ....22 C1
Barlby Rd W10 .....30 C4
Barleycorn Way E14 33 B2
Barley Mow Pas
  EC1 ....108 B3
  London W4 ....37 C1
Barling E6 NW1 ....13 A1
Barling Ct SW4 ....172 A2
Barlings Ho E2 SE4 .65 C3

Barloch Ho SW11 ..169 B2
Barlow Ho N1 ......97 B4
E4 W16 ....40 A2
E6 SE16 ....40 A2
W11 ....112 A4
Barlow Pl W1 ......118 B3
Barlow Rd Acton W3 .28 A1
  London NW6 ......10 B2
Barlow St SE17 ....151 C3
Barmouth Ho E6 N7 .5 B2
Barmouth Rd SW18 .59 B1
Barnabas Ho EC1 ..96 C3
Barnabas Lo SW8 ..172 B4
Barnabas Rd E9 ....17 C3
Barnaby Pl SW7 ...143 B3
Barnard Ct SW16 ...74 B1
Barnard Ho E2 E2 ..25 A2
Barnard Lo E3 W9 ..31 C4
Barnard Mews
  SW11 ....60 A3
Barnardo Gdns E1
  E1 ....32 C2
Barnardo St E1 E1 ..32 C3
Barnard Rd SW11 ..60 A3
Barnbrough NW1 ...82 C3
Barnby St NW1 .....93 A4
Barn Cl E1 NW5 ....13 C3
Barnersbury Ho N7 .14 A4
Barnes Ave SW13 ..46 C3
Barnes Bridge Sta
  SW13 ....46 A1
Barnes Common
  SW13 ....56 C4
Barnes High St
  SW13 ....46 B1
Barnes Ct N1 ......85 C4
Barnes Hospl SW14 .56 A4
Barnes St E14 .....33 A3
Barnes Terr SE8 ...41 B1
Barnet Ho E2 24 C2 99 B3
Barnet Ho E6 SE5 ..48 B1
Barnett Ho E1 E1 ...110 C3
Barnfeld Pl E14 ...42 A2
Barn Field NW3 ....12 B3
Barnfield Cl
  London N4 ....5 A4
  Wandsworth SW17 .71 B1
Barnfield Pl E14 ...41 C2
Barnham St SE1 ...138 B4
Barnsbury Gr N7 ...14 B1
Barnsbury Pk N1 ...14 C1
Barnsbury Rd N1 ...85 B3
Barnsbury Sq N1 ..14 C1
Barnsbury St N1 ...14 C1
Barnsbury Terr N1 .14 B1
Barnsdale Ave E14 41 C2
Barnsdale Rd W9 ..23 B1
Barnsley St E1 .....25 A1
Barn St N16 ....7 A2
Barnstaple La SE13 .67 B3
Barnston Wlk N1 ...86 C4
Barnwell Ho E6 SE5 49 A2
Barnwell Rd SW2 ..62 C2
Barnwood Cl W9 ..88 B1
Baroness Rd E2 ....24 B2 99 A4
Baron's Court Mans
  W14 ....140 B1
Baron's Court Rd
  W14 ....140 B1

Barons Court Sta
  W14 ....140 A2
Barons Gate E6 W4 .37 B3
Barons Keep W14 ..140 A2
Barons Lo E1 E14 ..42 B2
Baronsmead Rd
  SW13 ....46 C2
Baron's Pl SE1 ....135 C3
Baron St N1 ....85 C2
Baron Wlk E16 .....35 B2
Barque Mews E6 ...51 C4
Barratt Ho E6 N1 ..15 A1
Barratt Ind Pk E3 ..27 B1
Barret Ho NW6 ....23 C4
Barrett's Gr N16 ...16 A3
Barrett's Green Rd
  NW10 ....20 C3
Barrett St W1 .....103 C1
Barrhill Rd SW2 ....74 A2
Barriedale SE14 ...51 A1
Barrie Ho NW8 ....80 B3
  Acton W3 ....37 B4
  E6 London N16 ....7 A3
Barrington Ct NW5 .12 C3
Barrington Ct
  London SW9 .....172 B1
Barrington Rd SW9 .63 A4
Barrowgate Ho W4 .37 C1
Barrowgate Rd W4 .37 C1
Barrow Hill Est
  NW8 ....80 A1
Barrow Hill Jun Sch
  NW8 ....80 A1
Barry Ho E6 SE16 ..40 A1
Barry Lo N4 ....5 B4
Barry Par SE22 ....64 C3
Barset Rd SE15 ...65 B4
Barston Rd SE27 ..75 B1
Barstow Cres SW2 .74 B3
Barston Way SE27 .62 C1
Barter St WC1 .....106 B3
Bartholomew Cl
  EC1 ....108 C3
  London SW18 .....59 B3
Bartholomew Ct
  EC1 ....97 A2
E6 Poplar E14 .....34 C2
Bartholomew Ho E6
  EC2 ....109 C1
Bartholomew La
  EC2 ....109 C1
Bartholomew Pas
  EC1 ....108 B3
Bartholomew Pl
  EC1 ....108 C3
Bartholomew Rd
  NW5 ....13 B2
Bartholomew Sq E6
  E1 ....25 A1
Bartholomew St
  SE1 ....137 C1
Bartholomew Villas
  NW5 ....13 B2
Bartle Rd W11 .....31 A3
Bartlett Cl E14 .....33 C3
Bartlett Ct EC4 ....107 C2
Bartok Ho W11 ....112 C3
Bartolomew Sq EC1 97 A2
Barton Ct London E9 .17 B1
  London SE15 ......65 A4
Barton Ho W14 ....140 B2

Barton Ct continued
  London SW4 .....172 A2
Barton Ho E8 E3 ...27 A2
  London N1 ....15 A1
  London SW6 ......59 A4
Barton Rd W14 ....140 B1
Barton St SW1 ....134 A2
Bartonway NW8 ...79 B2
Bartram Rd SE4 ...66 A1
Bartrip St E9 ......18 B2
Barville Cl SE4 ....66 A3
Barwell Ho E2 .....99 C2
Barwick Ho E7 W3 .37 B4
Bascome St SW2 ..62 C1
Basevi Way SE8 ....52 A4
Bashley Rd NW10 ..20 C1
Basil Ho E1 ....111 C2
Basil St SW3 ......130 C3
SW8 ....162 A2
Basil Mans E1 SW1 .130 C3
Basil St SW1 ....130 C3
SW1,SW3 ....130 C3
Basin App E2 E14 ..33 A3
Basing Ct E12 SE15 .49 B2
Basingdon Way SE5 .63 C3
Basinghall Ave
  EC2 ....109 B2
Basinghall St EC2 ..109 B2
Basing Hill NW11 ...1 B3
Basing House Yd
  E2 ....98 B4
Basing Pl E2 ....98 B4
Basing St W11 .....31 B3
Basire St N1 ....87 A4
Baskerville Gdns
  NW10 ....8 A4
Baskerville Rd
  SW18 ....72 A4
Baslow Wlk E5 .....17 C4
Basnett Rd E8 SW11 60 C4
Basque Ct E1 SE16 .40 C4
Bassano St SE22 ..64 B2
Bassein Park Rd
  W12 ....38 B4
Bassett Rd W10 ...30 C3
Bassett St NW5 ...12 C2
Bassingbourn Ho E6
  N1 ....15 A1
Bassingham Rd
  SW18 ....71 B4
Bassishaw Highwalk
  EC2 ....109 B3
Basswood Cl SE15 .65 A4
Basterfield Ho EC1 .96 C1
Bastwick St EC1 ...96 C2
Basuto Rd SW6 ...165 C3
Batavia Ho E1 SE14 .51 A3
Batavia Mews E3
  SE14 ....51 A3
Batavia Rd SE14 ..51 A3
Batchelor St N1 ...85 C3
Bateman Ho E6
  SE17 ....48 A4
Bateman's Bldgs
  W1 ....105 B1
Bateman's Row
  EC2 ....24 A1 98 B2
Bateman St W1 ....105 B1
Bath Cl SE15 ......50 A3
Bath Ct EC1 ....95 B1
  EC1 ....97 B3
E6 Forest Hill SE26 .76 C1
Bathgate Ho E8
  SW9 ....48 A2
Bathgate Rd SW19 .69 C1
Bath Gr E2 ....24 C3
Bath Ho E6 ....24 C1 99 C2

Ban – Bay 181

Bath Ho continued
  SE1 ....137 A2
Bath Pl EC2 ....98 A3
  London NW6 ......39 B1
Bath Rd W4 ....38 A2
Baths App SW6 ...155 A2
Bath St EC1 ....97 B3
Bath Terr SE1 .....136 C2
Bathurst Gdns
  NW10 ....22 A3
Bathurst Ho E6 W12 30 A2
Bathurst Mews
  W2 ....115 C4
Batley Pl E6 N16 ...7 B1
Batley Rd N16 .....7 B1
Batman Cl W12 ....30 A1
Batoum Gdns W6 ..39 B3
Batson Ho E1 E1 ...111 C1
Batson St W12 ....38 C4
Batten Ho
E7 London SW4 ...61 B2
E8 London W10 ...23 A2
Batten St SW11 ...60 A4
Battersea Bridge Rd
  SW11 ....158 A1
Battersea Church Rd
  SW8 ....160 B1
Battersea Dogs Home
  SW8 ....160 B1
Battersea Park*
  SW11 ....159 B1
Battersea Park Rd
  SW11,SW8 ....169 C3
Battersea Park Sta
  SW8 ....160 A1
Battersea Power
  Station(dis) SW8 ..160 B3
Battersea Rise
  SW11 ....60 A3
Battersea Sq
  SW11 ....167 C3
Battersea Tech Coll
  SW11 ....169 A3
Battishill St E6 N1 .15 A1
Battlebridge Ct
  NW1 ....84 B2
Battle Bridge Ctr
  NW1 ....84 A2
Battle Bridge La
  SE1 ....124 A1
Battle Bridge Rd
  NW1 ....84 A2
Battledean Rd N5 ..15 A3
Batty St E1 ....111 C2
Baty Ho SW2 ......74 B3
Baulk The SW18 ...70 C4
Bavaria Rd N19 ....5 A2
Bavent Rd SE5 ....48 B1
Bawdale Rd SE22 ..64 B2
Bawtree Rd SE14 ..51 A3
Baxendale St
  E2 ....24 C2 99 B4
Baxter Ho E6 E3 ...27 A2
Baxter Rd N1 .....15 C2
Baycliffe Ho E6 E9 .17 C2
Bay Ct E2 E1 ......25 C1
  London W5 ....36 A3
Bayer Ho EC1 .....96 C1
Bayes Ct NW3 ....12 B1
Bayfield Ho E6 SE4 .65 C3
Bayford Rd NW10 ..22 C2
Bayford St E6 E8 ..17 A1

Bayford St Ind Ctr 4
E8 ....17 A1
Bayham Pl NW1 ......83 A3
Bayham St NW4 .....37 C3
Bayham St NW1 ......82 C3
Bayhurst Lo N4 ....6 B4
Bayley St WC1 ......105 B3
Baylis Rd SE1 ....135 B3
Baynes Mews 2
NW3 ....11 C2
Baynes St NW1 ....13 B1
Bayon Ho 28 N19 .....4 C4
Bayonne Rd W6 .....154 A3
Bayston Rd N16 ....7 B1
Bayswater Rd W2 ..115 B3
Bayswater Sta W2 .114 B4
Baythorne St 3
E3 ....33 B4
Bayton Ct 2 E8 ......16 C1
Baytree Rd SW2 .....62 B3
Bazalgette Ho NW8 .89 C2
Bazeley Ho SE1 .....136 A3
Bazely St E14 ....34 B2
BBC Television Ctr
W12 ....30 B1
Beach Ho SW5 ......141 B2
Beachy Rd E3 ....18 C1
Beaconsfield Terrace Rd
W14 ....126 A1
Beacon Gate SE14 ..65 C4
Beacon Hill N7 ....14 A3
Beacon Ho 10 SE5 ...48 C3
SW8 ....171 B4
Beacon Rd SE13 .....67 C1
Beaconsfield Cl 3 SE3 53 C4
London W4 ....37 B1
Beaconsfield Rd
SE17 ....152 A1
Greenwich SE3 ......53 C3
London NW10 ....8 B2
London W4 ....37 B1
Beaconsfield Wlk
SW6 ....165 A3
Beadon Rd W6 ....39 B2
Beak St W1 ....119 A4
Beale Ho SW9 ....172 C1
Beale Pl E3 ....26 B3
Beale Rd E3 ....26 B4
Beames Ho SW8 ....171 B4
Beaminster Ho
SW8 ....162 C2
Beamish Ho 5
SE16 ....40 B2
Beanacre Ct E9 ......18 B2
Bear Alley EC4 ......108 A2
Bear Croft Ho
SW6 ....164 C1
Beardsley Way 3 W3 37 C4
Bear Gardens Mus
SE1 ....122 C2
Bear Gdns SE1 ......122 C2
Bear La SE1 ....122 B1
Bear St WC2 ....119 C4
Bearstead Rise SE4 .66 B2
Beaton Cl SE15 ......49 B2
Beatrice Ho
1 London SW2 .....62 B2
4 London W6 ....39 B1
Beatrice Pl W8 .....128 A1
Beatrice Rd SE1 ....153 C3
London N4 ....5 C4
2 Richmond TW10 ..54 B2
Beatrice Tate Sch
E2 ....25 A2
Beatrice Webb Ho 3
E3 ....26 A3

Beatrix Ho SW5 .....142 B2
Beatrix Potter Prim Sch
SW18 ....71 B3
Beattie Ho SW8 .....171 A4
Beatty Rd N16 ....16 A4
Beatty St NW1 ....82 C2
Beauchamp Cl 10
W4 ....37 B3
Beauchamp Pl
SW3 ....130 B1
Beauchamp Rd
SW11 ....60 B3
Beauchamp St EC1 .107 B3
Beauchamp Terr
SW15 ....57 A4
Beauclerc Rd W6 ....39 A3
Beauclerk Ho 10
SW16 ....74 A1
Beaufort Cl SW19 ...69 A4
Beaufort Gdns
SW3 ....130 B1
Beaufort Ho SW1 ...147 B1
SW3 ....157 C3
London SW11 ....168 A2
Beaufort Mans
SW3 ....157 C3
Beaufort Mews
SW6 ....155 A4
Beaufort St SW3 ....157 B4
Beaufoy Rd SW8 ....162 C2
3 West Norwood
SE27 ....75 A1
Beaufoy Wlk SE11 ..149 A3
Beaulieu Cl SE5 .....63 C4
Beaulieu Pl W4 ......37 B3
Beaumanor Mans
W2 ....114 B4
Beaumaris Twr 2
W3 ....37 A4
Beaumont W14 .....141 A3
Putney SW15 ....58 A1
Beaumont Ave
W14 ....140 C2
Richmond TW9 ....54 B4
Beaumont Bldgs
WC2 ....106 B1
Beaumont Cres
W14 ....140 C1
Beaumont Ct 10 W4 37 B1
Beaumont Gdns NW3 1 C1
Beaumont Gr E1 .....25 C1
Beaumont Ho
1 Streatham SW2 ..74 A3
Wimbledon SW19 ...70 C1
2 London W4 ....38 A2
Beaumont Pl NW1,
WC1,W1 ....93 A2
Beaumont Rd
London W4 ....37 B3
Putney SW15,SW19 .70 A4
Beaumont Rise N19 ..4 C3
Beaumont Sq E1 .....32 C4
Beaumont St W1 ...103 C4
Beaumont Wlk NW3 .12 B1
Beauvale 4 NW1 ....12 C1
Beauval Rd SE22 ....64 B1
Beavis Ho N16 ....7 A1
Beavor La W6 ....38 C1
Beccles St E14 ....33 B2
Beck Ct SE13 ....52 A2
Beckers The N16 ....16 C4
Becket Ho SE1 ......137 B3
Becket St SE1 ....137 B2
Beckett Cl
London NW10 ....8 A2
Streatham SW16 ....73 C2
Beckett Ho 12 E1 ....32 B4

Beckett Ho continued
London SW9 ....172 B1
Beckfoot NW1 ....83 A1
Beckford Cl W14 ....140 C3
Beckford Ho 10 N16 .16 A3
Beckford Prim Sch
NW6 ....10 B3
Beckham Ho SE11 .149 A3
Beck Ho N16 ....7 A1
Beckington 18 NW5 .12 C2
Beckley Ho 3 E3 .....26 B1
Becklow Mews 7
W12 ....38 C4
Becklow Rd W12 .....38 C4
Beck Rd E8 ....25 A4
Beckton Rd E16 ......35 B2
Beckway St SE17 ...152 A3
Beckwith Ho 22 E2 ..25 A3
Beckwith Rd SE24 ..63 C2
Bective Pl SW15 .....58 B3
Bective Rd SW15 ....58 B3
Bedale St SE1 ....123 B1
Bedefield WC1 ....94 B3
Bede Ho
London SE14 ....51 B2
5 Putney SW15 ....57 C1
Bedford Ave WC1 ..105 C3
Bedfordbury WC2 ..120 A3
Bedford Cl W4 ....46 B4
Bedford Cnr 3 W4 ..38 A2
Bedford Court Mans
WC1 ....105 C3
Bedford Ct WC2 ....120 A3
1 Richmond TW9 ....54 B3
Bedford Gardens Ho
W8 ....113 C1
Bedford Gdns
W8 ....31 C1 113 C1
Bedford Hill SW12 ..73 A2
Bedford Ho
7 London SW4 .....62 A3
2 London W4 ....38 A2
Bedford Park Cnr 8
W4 ....38 A2
Bedford Park Mans
W4 ....37 C2
Bedford Pas SW6 ..154 B2
Bedford Pl WC1 ....106 A4
Bedford Rd
London SW2,SW4 ..62 A3
London W4 ....38 A3
Bedford Row WC1 .107 A3
Bedford Sq WC1 ...105 C3
Bedford St WC2 ....120 B3
Bedford Way WC1 ...93 C1
Bedgebury Gdns
SW19 ....70 A2
Bedlow Cl NW8 ......89 B1
Bedser Cl SE11 .....163 A4
Bedser Ct SW4 .....172 A2
Bedwell Ho SW9 ...173 B1
Beech Ave W3 ....29 A1
Beech Cl SE8 ....51 B4
London SW15 ....68 C4
Beechcroft Ave
NW11 ....1 B4
Beechcroft Cl 3
NW11 ....1 B4
Beech Croft Ct N5 ..15 A4
Beechcroft Rd
Mortlake SW14 ......55 B4
Upper Tooting SW17 72 A2
Beechcroft Way N19 .4 C3
Beech St 1 W1 .....102 C2
London NW2 ....1 C1
London W2 ....31 C4
Beechdale Rd SW2 .62 B1

Beechdene 4 SE15 .50 A2
Beeches Rd SW17 ..72 B1
Beeches The 1 N19 ..5 A3
Beechey Ho 5 E1 ...32 A1
Beech Gdns W5 ......36 A3
Beech Ho SE16 ......40 B4
5 London N16 ....6 C2
6 London NW3 ......12 B2
Beechmore Rd
SW11 ....169 A3
Beech St EC2 ....109 A4
Beech Tree Cl N1 ...14 C1
Beechwood Ave
TW9 ....44 C2
Beechwood Ct
Chiswick W4 ....45 C4
London N16 ....7 A4
Beechwood Gr W3 ..29 A2
Beechwood Ho 22
E2 ....24 C3
Beechwood Rd E8 ..16 B2
Beechworth Cl NW3 .1 C2
Beecroft Rd SE4 ....66 A2
Beehive Cl E8 ....16 B1
Beehive Pl SW9 .....62 C4
Beeston Cl 5 E8 .....16 C3
Beeston Pl SW1 ....132 B2
Beeston's Ho SE15 .65 A4
Beethoven St W10 ..23 A2
Begbie Rd SE3 ....53 A2
Begonia Wlk W12 ...29 B3
Beira St SW12 ....73 A4
Beis Rachel D'Satmar
Girls Sch N16 ....7 A4
Bekesbourne St 1
E14 ....33 A3
Beldanes Lo NW10 ..8 C1
Belenoyd Ct SW16 .74 B1
Belfast Rd N16 ....7 B2
Belfont Wlk N7 ....14 A4
Belford Ho 7 E8 .....24 B4
Belfort Rd SE15 .....50 B1
Belfry Cl 13 SE16 ...40 A1
Belgrade Ho N16 ....16 A4
Belgrade Rd N16 ....16 A4
Belgrave Cl 11 W3 ..37 B4
Belgrave Ct SW8 ...160 C1
6 London E14 ....33 B2
Belgrave Gdns
NW8 ....78 C3
Belgrave Mews N
SW1 ....131 B3
Belgrave Mews S
SW1 ....131 C2
Belgrave Mews W
SW1 ....131 B2
Belgrave Pl SW1 ...131 C1
Belgrave Rd SW1 ...146 C3
Barnes SW13 ....46 B3
Belgrave Sq SW1 ..131 B2
Belgrave St E1 ....32 C3
Belgrave Yd SW1 ...132 A1
Belgravia Ho 11
SW4 ....61 C1
Belgrave St WC1 ...94 A4
Belham Wlk 15 SE5 .48 C2
Belinda Rd 8 SW9 ..63 A4
Belitha Villas N1 ....14 C1
Bellamy Cl E14 ......141 A1
Bellamy's Ct 18
SE16 ....32 C1
Bellamy St SW12 ...73 A4
Bellasis Ave SW2 ...74 A2
Bell Dr SW18 ....70 A4

Bellefields Rd SW9 .62 B4
Bellenden Rd SE15 .49 B1
Bellenden Rd Ret Pk
SE15 ....49 C2
Bellenden Sch SE15 49 B1
Bellerbys Coll SE15 56 C1
Belleville Prim Sch
SW11 ....60 B2
Belleville Rd SW11 .60 B2
Belle Vue Gdns
SW9 ....172 B1
Bellevue Pl E1 ....25 B1
Bellevue Rd
Barnes SW13 ....46 C1
Upper Tooting SW17 72 B3
Bellew St SW17 .....71 B1
Bellgate Mews NW5 .4 A1
Bell Ho SE10 ....52 B4
13 Streatham SW2 ..74 C4
Bellina Mews NW5 ..13 B4
Bell Ind Est 2 W4 ...37 B2
Bell Inn Yd EC3 ....109 C1
Bell La E1 ....110 C3
E16 ....35 C1
Bellmaker Ct 18 E3 .33 C4
Bell Moor NW3 ....2 B1
Bello Cl SE24,SE27 .75 A3
Bellot St SE10 ....43 A1
Bellot St NW1 ....102 A4
Bell Wharf La EC4 .123 A4
Bellwood Rd SE15 ..65 C3
Bell Yd WC2 ....107 B1
Belmont Cl SW4 .....61 B4
Belmont Ct
6 London N16 ....7 A3
London N5 ....15 B4
Belmont Gr
London SE13 ....67 C4
London W4 ....37 C2
Belmont Hall Ct
SE13 ....67 C4
Belmont Hill SE13 ..67 C4
Belmont Mews
SW19 ....69 C2
Belmont Prim Sch
W4 ....37 C2
Belmont Rd
London SW4 ....61 B4
London W4 ....37 C2
Belmont Terr W4 ....37 C2
Belmore Ho N7 ......13 C3
Belmore St SW8 ...171 B4
Beloe Cl SW15 ......56 C3
Belsham St E9 ....17 B2
Belsize Ave NW3 ...12 A3
Belsize Court Garages
1 NW3 ....11 C3
Belsize Cres NW3 ..11 C3
Belsize Ct NW3 .....11 C3
Belsize Gr NW3 .....12 A2
Belsize La NW3 .....11 C3
Belsize Mews NW3 .11 C2
Belsize Park Gdns
NW3 ....12 A2
Belsize Park Mews 1
NW3 ....11 C2
Belsize Park Sta
NW3 ....12 A3
Belsize Pk NW3 .....11 C2
Belsize Pl NW3 .....11 C3
Belsize Rd NW6 .....78 B4
Belsize Sq NW3 .....11 C2
Belsize Terr NW3 ...11 C2

Beltane Dr SW19 . . . . .69 C1
Belthorn Cres SW12 73 B4
Belton Rd NW2 . . . . . . .8 C2
Belton Way E3 . . . . . . .33 C4
Beltran Rd SW6 . . . . .166 A1
Belvedere Bldgs
SE1 . . . . .136 B3
Belvedere Ct
London NW2 . . . . .9 C2
7 London SW4 . . . . . .61 C1
Putney SW15 . . . . .57 B3
Belvedere Heights
NW8 . . . . .90 B1
Belvedere Mews
SE15 . . . . .65 B4
Belvedere Pl SE1 . .136 B3
18 London SW2 . . . . .62 B3
Belvedere Rd SE1 . .121 A1
Belvedere The
SW10 . . . . .167 A3
Belvoir Lo SE22 . . . . .76 C4
Belvoir Rd SE22 . . . . .76 C4
Bembridge Cl NW6 . .10 A1
Bembridge Ho
8 SE8 . . . . .41 B2
Wandsworth SW18 . . .59 A1
Bemerton St N1 . . . . .84 C4
Bemish Rd SW15 . . . .57 C4
Benabo Ct **6** E8 . . . .16 C3
Benbow Ho **13** 39 A3
Benbow Ho **12** SE8 . .51 C4
Benbow Rd W6 . . . . . .39 A3
Benbow St SE8 . . . . . .51 C4
Bence Ho **13** SE8 . . . .41 A2
Bendall Mews
NW1 . . . . .102 B4
Bendemeer Rd
SW15 . . . . .57 C4
Bendon Ho SE13 . . . .67 B2
Bendon Valley
SW18 . . . . .71 A4
Benedict Rd SW9 . . . .62 B4
Benenden Ho SE17 152 B2
Ben Ezra Ct SE17 . .151 A3
Benfleet Ct **6** E8 . . . .24 B4
Bengal Ct EC3 . . . . . .109 C1
Bengal Ho E1 . . . . . . .32 C4
Bengeworth Rd SE5 63 B4
Benham's Pl **6**
NW3 . . . . .11 B4
Benhill Rd SE5 . . . . . .48 C2
Benjamin Cl E8 . . . . . .24 C4
Benjamin St EC1 . . .108 A4
Ben Jonson Ct **8**
N1 . . . . .24 A3
Ben Jonson Prim Sch
E1 . . . . .26 A1
Ben Jonson Rd E1 . .33 A4
Benledi St E14 . . . . . .34 C3
Bennelong Cl W12 . .30 A3
Bennerley Rd SW11 . .60 B2
Bennet's Hill EC4 .122 B4
Bennett Ct London **5**
London NW6 . . . . .11 A2
1 London W3 . . . . . .37 A4
Bennett Gr SE13 . . . .52 A2
Bennett Ho NW1 . .147 C4
2 Streatham SW4 . .73 C4
Bennett St SW1 . . . .118 C2
London W4 . . . . .38 A1
Bennett's Yd SW1 .133 C1
Benn St E9 . . . . .18 A2
Benns Wlk **3** TW9 . .54 A3
Bensbury Cl SW15 . .69 B4
Ben Smith Way
SE16 . . . . .139 C2

Benson Ct SW8 . . . .172 A4
1 London N19 . . . . .13 B4
Benson Ho E2 . . . . . . .98 C2
Benson Quay E1 . . . . .32 B2
SE1 . . . . .121 C1
Benson Ho E2 . . . . . . .98 C2
Benthal Ho N16 . . . . . .7 C1
Benthal Prim Sch
N16 . . . . .7 C1
Benthal Rd N16 . . . . . .7 C1
Bentham Ct **10** N1 . .15 B1
Bentham Ho SE1 . .137 B1
Bentham Rd E9 . . . . . .17 C2
Bentinck Cl NW8 . . . .80 B1
Bentinck Ho **4**
W12 . . . . .30 A2
Bentinck Mans
W1 . . . . .103 C2
Bentinck Mews
W1 . . . . .103 C2
Bentley Cl SW19 . . . .70 C1
Bentley Ho
4 Bow E3 . . . . .26 C1
London SE5 . . . . .49 A2
Bentley Rd N1 . . . . . . .16 A2
Bentworth Ct **2** . . .99 B2
Bentworth Prim Sch
W12 . . . . .30 A3
Bentworth Rd W12 . .30 A3
Benville Ho SW8 . .163 A1
Benwell Rd N7 . . . . . .14 C3
Benwick Cl SE16 . . . .40 A2
Benworth St E3 . . . . . .26 B2
Benyon Ho EC1 . . . . . .95 C4
Benyon Rd N1 . . . . . . .87 C4
Beormund Prim Sch
SE1 . . . . .137 B3
Bequerel Ct SE10 . .43 B3
Berberis Ho **15** E3 . .33 C4
Berber Pl **15** E14 . . .33 C2
Berber Rd SW11 . . . . .60 B2
Berebinder Ho **17**
E3 . . . . .26 B3
Berenger Twr
SW10 . . . . .157 B2
Berenger Wlk
SW10 . . . . .157 B2
Berens Rd NW10 . . . .22 C2
Beresford Ct E9 . . . . .18 A3
Beresford Ho
Dulwich SE21 . . . . . . .76 A1
14 London SW4 . . . .62 A3
Beresford Rd N5 . . . .15 C3
Beresford Terr **3**
N5 . . . . .15 B3
Bere St E1 . . . . .32 C2
Berestede Rd **4**
W6 . . . . .38 B1
Bergen Ho **12** SE5 . .48 B1
Bergen Sq SE16 . . . . .41 A3
Berger Prim Sch E9 17 C2
Berger Rd E9 . . . . .17 C2
Berghem Mews
W14 . . . . .39 C3
Bergholt Cres N16 . . . .7 A4
Bergholt Mews **4**
NW1 . . . . .13 C1
Bering Sq E14 . . . . . . .41 C1
Berisford Mews
SW18 . . . . .59 B1
Berkeley Ct NW1 . . . .91 A1
1 London NW11 . . . . .1 B4
5 Streatham SW2 . .74 C3
Berkeley Gdns W8 113 C1
Berkeley Ho **4**
8 SE8 . . . . .41 B1

Berkeley Mews
W1 . . . . .103 A1
Berkeley Rd SW13 . .46 C2
Berkeley Sq W1 . . . .118 B3
Berkeley St W1 . . . . .118 B2
Berkeley Wlk **1** N7 . .5 B2
Berkeley's SW15 . . . .57 C2
Berkley Gr NW1 . . . . .12 C1
Berkley Rd NW1 . . . . .12 B1
Berkshire Rd E9 . . . . .18 B2
Berkeley Ct NW10 . . .22 A3
Bermans Way NW10 . .8 B4
Bermondsey Leather
Mkt SE1 . . . . .138 A3
Bermondsey Mkt* . . . . .
SE1 . . . . .138 B2
Bermondsey Sq
SE1 . . . . .138 B2
Bermondsey St
SE1 . . . . .138 A2
Bermondsey Sta
SE16 . . . . .40 B1
Bermondsey Trad Est
SE16 . . . . .40 B1
Bermondsey Wall E
SE16 . . . . .40 A4
Bermondsey Wall W
SE1,SE16 . . . . .139 B4
Bernard Angell Ho **1**
SE10 . . . . .52 C4
Bernard Cassidy St **2**
E16 . . . . .35 B2
Bernard Shaw Ct **3**
NW1 . . . . .13 B1
Bernard Shaw Ho **2**
NW10 . . . . .20 C4
Bernay's Gr SW9 . . . .62 B3
Bernays Cl NW10 . . . .8 C1
Berners Ho N1 . . . . . . .85 B2
Berners Mews W1 105 A3
Berners Pl W1 . . . . . .105 A2
Berners Rd N1 . . . . . . .86 A3
Berners St W1 . . . . . .105 A2
Berner Terr E1 . . . . .111 B2
Bernwood Ho **6** N4 . .6 C4
Berridge Mews
NW6 . . . . .10 C3
Berriman Rd N7 . . . . . .5 B1
Berry Cl NW10 . . . . . . .8 A1
Berryfield Rd SE17 150 B2
Berry Ho **22** E1 . . . . .25 A1
London SW11 . . . . . .169 A2
Berrymead Gdns
W3 . . . . .37 B4
Berrymede Inf Sch
W3 . . . . .37 A4
Berrymede Jun Sch
W3 . . . . .37 A4
Berry Pl EC1 . . . . .96 B3
Berry St EC1 . . . . .96 B1
Berry Way W5 . . . . . . .36 A3
Bertha Neuberg Ho **6**
SE5 . . . . .48 B2
Berthon St SE8 . . . . . .51 C4
Bertie Rd NW10 . . . . . .8 C2
Bertram St N19 . . . . . .4 A2
Bertrand Ho **11**
SW16 . . . . .74 A1
Bertrand St SE13 . . . .67 A4
Bertrum House Sch
SW17 . . . . .72 C2
Berwick St W1 . . . . .105 A1
Berwyn Ho **3** N16 . . .7 B3
Berwyn Rd
Mortlake SW14,TW10 55 A3

Berwyn Rd continued
Streatham SE24 . . . . .75 A3
Beryl Rd W6 . . . . .39 C1
Besant Cl NW2 . . . . . .1 A1
Besant Ct N1 . . . . .15 C3
Besant Ho NW8 . . . . .78 C3
Besant Rd NW2 . . . . .10 A4
Besant Wlk N7 . . . . . . .5 B2
Besford Ho **22** E2 . . .24 C3
Bessant Dr TW9 . . . . .45 A2
Bessborough Gdns
SW1 . . . . .147 C2
Bessborough Pl
SW1 . . . . .147 C2
Bessborough Rd
SW15 . . . . .68 C3
Bessborough St
SW1 . . . . .147 B2
Bessemer Ct **5**
NW1 . . . . .13 B1
Bessemer Grange Prim
Sch SE24 . . . . .64 A3
Bessemer Park Ind Est
3 SE24 . . . . .63 A3
Bessemer Rd SE5 . . .48 B1
Bessingham Wlk
SE4 . . . . .65 C2
Besson St SE14 . . . . .50 C2
Bessy St E2 . . . . .25 B2
Bestwood St SE8 . . . .40 C2
Beswick Mews **1**
NW6 . . . . .11 A2
Beta Pl **22** SW4 . . . .62 B3
Betchworth Ho **6**
N7 . . . . .13 C3
Bethersden Ho
SE17 . . . . .152 B2
Bethlehem Ho **13**
E14 . . . . .33 B2
Bethnal Green Mus of
Childhood* E2 . . . . . .25 B2
Bethnal Green Rd
E1 . . . . .24 B1 99 B1
Bethnal Green Sta
E1 . . . . .25 A1
Bethnal Green Sta
E2 . . . . .25 B2
Bethnal Green Tech Coll
E2 . . . . .99 B3
Bethune Rd
London N16 . . . . .7 A4
London NW10 . . . . . . .20 C1
Bethwin Rd SE5 . . . . .48 B3
Betsham Ho SE1 . . .137 B4
Betterton Ho WC2 .106 B1
Betterton St WC2 . .106 B1
Bettridge Rd SW6 .165 A1
Betts Ho E1 . . . . .32 A2
Betts St E1 . . . . .32 A2
Betty Layward Prim Sch
N16 . . . . .6 C1
Betty May Gray Ho **1**
E14 . . . . .42 B2
Bevan St N1 . . . . .87 A3
Bev Callender Cl **4**
SW8 . . . . .61 A4
Bevenden St N1 . . . . .97 C4
Beveridge Rd **1**
NW10 . . . . .8 A1
Beverley Cl
Barnes SW13 . . . . . . .46 C1
6 London SW11 . . . .59 C3
Beverley Cotts
SW15 . . . . .68 A1
Beverley Ct
London N5 . . . . .15 A2
London SE4 . . . . .66 B4
5 London W12 . . . . .38 A4

Beverley Ct continued
9 London W4 . . . . . .37 B1
Beverley Gdns
Barnes SW13 . . . . . . .56 B4
London NW11 . . . . .1 A4
Beverley Lo **6**
TW10 . . . . .54 A2
Beverley Path **9**
SW13 . . . . .46 B1
Beverley Rd
Barnes SW13 . . . . . . .56 B4
London W4 . . . . .38 B1
Beversbrook Rd N19 .4 C1
Beverstone Rd SW2 .62 B2
Beverston Mews
NW1 . . . . .102 C3
Bevin Cl SE16 . . . . . . .33 A1
Bevin Ct WC1 . . . . . . .95 A4
Bevington Prim Sch
W10 . . . . .31 A4
Bevington Rd W10 . .31 A4
Bevington St SE16 139 C3
Bevin Ho **22** E2 . . . .25 B2
7 E3 . . . . .26 C2
Bevin Sq SW17 . . . . . .72 B1
Bevin Way WC1 . . . . .95 B4
Bevis Marks EC3 . .110 B2
Bew Ct SE21 . . . . .76 C4
Bewdley Ho N4 . . . . . .6 B4
Bewdley St N1 . . . . . .14 C1
Bewick Mews SE15 . .50 A3
Bewick St SW8 . . . . .170 B1
Bewley Ct SW2 . . . . . .62 B1
Bewley Ho **2** E1 . . . .32 A2
Bewley St E1 . . . . .32 A2
Bexhill Rd
London SE4 . . . . .66 B1
Mortlake SW14 . . . . . .55 B4
Bexley Ho SE4 . . . . . .66 A3
BFI London Imax
Cinema SE1 . . . . .121 B1
Bianca Rd SE1,SE15 .49 C4
Bicester Rd TW9 . . . . .55 A4
Bickenhall Mans
W1 . . . . .103 A4
Bickenhall St W1 . . .103 A4
Bickerton Rd N19 . . . .4 B2
Bicknell Ho **3** E1 . . .111 C1
Bicknell Rd SE5 . . . . .63 B4
Bicknor Ho **2** E5 . . .17 A3
Bidborough St N1,
WC1 . . . . .94 A3
Biddenham Ho **10**
SE16 . . . . .40 C2
Bidder St E16 . . . . . . .35 A4
Biddesden Ho
SW3 . . . . .144 C3
Biddestone Rd N7 . .14 B4
Biddulph Mans W9 . .88 B3
Biddulph Rd W9 . . . . .88 B3
Bidwell St SE15 . . . . .50 A2
Big Ben* SW1 . . . . . .134 B3
Biggerstaff Rd E15 . .27 B4
Biggerstaff St N4 . . . .5 C2
Bigg's Row SW15 . . . .57 C4
Bigland Green Prim Sch
E1 . . . . .32 A3
Bigland St E1 . . . . .32 A3
Bilberry Ho **13** E3 . .33 C4
Billingford Cl SE4 . . .65 C3
Billing Ho **6** E1 . . . .32 C3
Billingley NW1 . . . . . .82 C3
Billing Pl SW10 . . . .156 B2
Billing Rd SW10 . . . .156 B2

Billingsgate Mkt E14 ...34 A1
Billing St SW10 ...156 B2
Billington Ho SW8 .171 C3
Billington Rd SE14 ..50 C3
Billiter Sq EC3 ...110 B1
Billiter St EC3 ...110 B1
Billson St E14 ...42 B2
Bilton Ho SW8 ...171 B3
Bilton Twrs W1 ...103 A1
Bina Gdns SW5 ...142 C3
Binbrook Ho W10 ...30 B4
Binden Rd W12 ...38 B3
Binfield Ct SE5 ...48 B1
Binfield Rd SW4 ...172 B3
Bingfield St N1 ...84 C4
Bingham Pl W1 ...103 B4
Bingham St N1 ...15 C2
Binley Ho SW15 ...56 B1
Binney St W1 ...103 C1
Binnie Ho SE1 ...136 C1
Binns Rd W4 ...38 A1
Binns Terr 3 W4 ...38 A1
Binstead Ho SW18 ..59 A1
Binyon Ho 8 N16 ..16 A4
Bircham Path SE4 ..65 C3
Birch Cl E16 ...35 A4
London N19 ...4 B2
London SE15 ...49 C1
Birchdown Ho 32 E3 ...27 A2
Birches The SE5 ...49 A1
Birchfield Ho 2 E14 ...33 C2
Birchfield St E14 ...33 C2
Birch Ho London SE14 ...51 B2
8 London SW2 ...62 C1
Birchington Ct NW6 78 A4
Birchington Ho 1 E5 ...17 A3
Birchington Rd NW6 ...23 C4
Birchin La EC3 ...109 C1
Birchlands Ave SW12 ...72 B4
Birchmere Lo 18 SE16 ...40 A1
Birchmere Row SE3 .53 B1
Birchmore Wlk N5 ...6 B1
Birch Vale Ct NW8 ..89 C2
Birchwood Dr NW3 ..2 A1
Birdcage Wlk SW1 .133 B3
Birdhurst Rd SW18 ..59 B2
Bird In Bush Rd SE15 ...49 C3
Bird In Hand Yd 14 NW3 ...11 B4
Birdsall Ho 5 SE5 ..64 A4
Birdsfield La E3 ...26 B4
Bird St W1 ...103 C1
Birkbeck Ave W3 ...28 B2
Birkbeck Coll W1 ..105 B2
Birkbeck Ct W3 ...28 C1
Birkbeck Gr W3 ...37 C4
Birkbeck Hill SE21 ..75 A3
Birkbeck Mews 5 E8 ...16 B3
Birkbeck Pl SE21 ...75 B2
Birkbeck Rd
London E8 ...16 B3
London W3 ...28 C1
Birkbeck St E2 ...25 A2
Birkdale Cl 30 SE16 .40 A1
Birkenhead Ho 11 N7 ...14 C3
Birkenhead St WC1 .94 B4
Birkwood Cl SW12 ..73 C4
Birley Lo NW8 ...79 C2
Birley St SW11 ...169 B1
Birnam Rd N4 ...5 B2
Birrell Ho SW9 ...172 C1
Birse Cres NW10 ...8 A4
Birtwhistle Ho 5 E3 ...26 B4
Biscay Ho 11 E1 ...25 C1
Biscay Rd W6 ...39 C1
Biscoe Way SE13 ...67 C4
Biscott Ho 3 E3 ...27 A1
Bisham Gdns N6 ...3 C3
Bishop Challoner Collegiate Sch
E1 ...125 C3
E1 ...32 B3
Bishop Ct 20 SW2 ...62 C1
Bishop Duppa's Almshouses 7 TW10 ...54 A2
Bishopgate 32 N1 ...24 A4
Bishop King's Rd W14 ...140 B4
Bishop's Ave SW6 .164 A2
Bishop's Bridge Rd W2 ...100 C2
Bishop's Cl N19 ...4 B1
Bishops Cl W4 ...37 B1
Bishop's Ct EC4 ...108 A2
WC2 ...107 B2
Bishops Ct W2 ...100 B2
Bishopsdale Ho 8 NW6 ...23 C4
Bishopsgate EC2 ..110 A2
Bishopsgate Arcade E1 ...110 B3
Bishopsgate Church Yd EC2 ...110 A2
Bishops Ho SW8 ..162 B1
Bishop's Mans SW6 .47 C1
Bishops Mead SE5 ..48 B3
Bishop's Park Rd SW6 ...47 C1
Bishops Rd SW6 ..164 C4
Bishop St N1 ...86 C4
Bishop's Terr SE11 .149 C4
Bishopstone Ho SW11 ...169 B2
Bishop's Way E2 ...25 B3
Bishopswood Rd N6 .3 B4
Bishop Way NW10 ...8 A1
Bishop Wilfred Wood Cl SE15 ...49 C1
Bisley Ho SW19 ...69 C2
Bissextile Ho SE13 ..52 A1
Bisson Rd E15 ...27 B3
Bittern Ct 8 SE8 ...51 C4
Bittern Ho SE1 ...136 C3
Bittern St SE1 ...136 C3
Blackall St EC2 ...98 A2
Blackburn Ct 21 SW2 ...62 C1
Blackburne's Mews W1 ...117 B3
Blackburn Rd NW6 .11 A2
Blackdown Ho E8 ..16 C4
Blackett St SW15 ...57 C4
Blackfriars Bridge EC4 ...122 A3
Blackfriars Ct EC4 .122 A4
Black Friars La EC4 ...108 A1
Blackfriars Pas EC4 ...122 A4
Blackfriars Pier EC4 ...122 A4
Blackfriars Rd SE1 122 A2
Blackfriars Sta EC4 ...122 A4
Blackfriars Underpass EC4 ...121 C4
Blackheath SE3 ...53 A2
Blackheath Ave SE3 .53 A3
Blackheath Bsns Est SE10 ...52 B2
Blackheath Gr SE3 ..53 B1
Blackheath High Sch SE3 ...53 C3
Blackheath High Sch (Girls) SE3 ...53 B1
Blackheath High Sch GPDST (Jun Dept) SE3 ...53 C1
Blackheath Hill SE10 ...52 B2
Blackheath Rd SE10 52 A2
Blackheath Rise SE13 ...52 B1
Blackheath Vale SE3 ...53 A1
Blackheath Village SE3 ...53 B1
Black Horse Ct SE1 ...137 C2
Blackhorse Rd SE8 .51 A4
Blacklands Terr SW3 ...145 A3
Black Lion La W6 ...38 C2
Black Lion Mews 4 W6 ...38 C2
Blackmore Ho N1 ..85 A3
2 London SW18 ...59 A2
Blackmore Twr 1 W3 ...37 B3
Blackpool Rd SE15 ..50 A1
Black Prince Rd SE1,SE11 ...149 A3
Black Roof Ho 9 SE5 ...48 A2
Black's Rd W6 ...39 B2
Blackstock Ho N5 ...6 A1
Blackstock Mews N4 .6 A1
Blackstock Rd N4,N5 .6 A2
Blackstone Ho SW1 ...146 C1
Dulwich SE21 ...76 A1
Blackstone Rd NW2 ..9 B4
Black Swan Yd SE1 ...138 A4
Blackthorn Ct 10 SE15 ...49 B3
4 London E15 ...19 C4
Blackthorn St E3 ...26 C1
Blacktree Mews 12 SW9 ...62 C4
Blackwall Sta E14 ...34 B2
Blackwall Trad Est E14 ...34 C4
Blackwall Tunnel E14,SE10 ...34 C1
Blackwall Tunnel App SE10 ...43 A4
Blackwall Tunnel Northern Approach E14,E3 ...27 B1
Blackwall Way E14 ..34 B2
Blackwater Ho NW8 ...101 C4
Blackwater St SE22 .64 B2
Blackwell Cl 10 E5 ..17 C4
Blackwell Ho 3 SW4 ...61 C1
Blackwood Ho 11 E1 ...25 A1
Blackwood St SE17 ...151 B2
Blade Mews SW15 ..58 B3
Bladen Ho 4 E1 ...32 C3
Blades Ct SW15 ...58 B3
Blades Ho SE11 ...163 B3
Blades Lo 16 SW2 ...62 C1
Blagdon Rd SE13 ...67 A1
Blagrove Rd 1 W10 31 B4
Blair Cl N1 ...15 B2
Blair Ct NW8 ...79 B4
Blairderry Rd SW2 ..74 A2
Blair Ho SW9 ...172 C2
Blair St E14 ...34 C3
Blake Ct 8 SE16 ...40 A1
London NW6 ...23 C2
Blake Gdns SW6 ...166 A4
Blake Ho SE1 ...135 B2
2 SE8 ...51 C4
14 London N16 ...16 A4
1 London N19 ...13 C3
Blake Mews 14 TW9 44 C2
Blakemore Rd SW16 ...74 A1
Blakeney Cl
4 London E8 ...16 C3
5 London NW1 ...13 C1
Blakenham Ct W12 .29 C1
Blaker Rd E15 ...27 B4
Blakes Cl W10 ...30 B4
Blake's Rd SE15 ...49 A3
Blanca Ho 16 N1 ...24 A3
Blanchard Way E8 ..16 C2
Blanch Cl SE15 ...50 B3
Blanchedowne SE5 .63 C3
Blanche Ho NW8 ...90 A1
Blandfield Rd SW12 .72 C4
Blandford Ct
6 London N1 ...16 A1
London NW6 ...10 A1
Blandford Ho SW8 .162 C2
Blandford Rd W4 ...38 A3
Blandford Sq NW1 ..90 B1
Blandford St W1 ..103 B3
Bland Ho SE11 ...149 A2
Blantyre St SW10 ..157 B2
Blantyre Twr SW10 ...157 B2
Blantyre Wlk SW10 ...157 B2
Blashford NW3 ...12 B1
Blasker Wlk E14 ...42 A1
Blaxland Ho 12 W12 30 A2
Blechynden Ho 17 W10 ...30 C3
Blechynden St W10 .30 C2
Bleeding Heart Yd EC1 ...107 C3
Blemundsbury WC1 ...106 C4
Blendworth Point 4 SW15 ...69 A3
Blenheim 26 SW19 ..69 C3
Blenheim Cres W11 ...31 A3 112 B4
Blenheim Ct
17 SE16 ...32 C1
London N19 ...5 A2
London N7 ...14 A2
Richmond TW9 ...54 B4
Blenheim Gdns
London NW2 ...9 B3
Blenheim Gdns *continued*
London SW2 ...62 B1
Blenheim Gr SE15 ..49 C1
Blenheim Pas NW8 .78 C2
Blenheim Rd NW8 ..79 A2
London W4 ...38 A3
Blenheim St W1 ...104 A1
Blenheim Terr NW8 .78 C2
Blenkarne Rd SW11 .60 B1
Blessed John Roche RC Sch The E14 ...33 C3
Blessed Sacrament RC Prim Sch N1 ...84 C3
Blessington Cl SE13 67 C4
Blessington Rd SE13 ...67 C3
Bletchley Ct N1 ...87 B1
Bletchley St N1 ...87 A1
Bletsoe Wlk N1 ...87 A2
Blick Ho 1 SE16 ...40 B3
Blincoe Cl SW19 ...69 C2
Blissett St SE10 ...52 B2
Bliss Mews 17 W10 .23 A2
Blisworth Ho 12 E2 .24 C4
Blithfield St W8 ...128 A1
Bloemfontein Ave W12 ...30 A1
Bloemfontein Rd W12 ...30 A2
Blomfield Ct SW11 167 C4
W9 ...89 A2
Blomfield Mans W12 ...30 B1
Blomfield Rd W9 ..100 C4
Blomfield St EC2 ..109 C3
Blomfield Villas W9 ...100 C4
Blondel St SW11 ...169 B2
Blondin St E3 ...26 C3
Bloomburg St SW1 ...147 A3
Bloomfield Ho E1 .111 B3
Bloomfield Pl W1 .118 B4
Bloomfield Terr SW1 ...145 C2
Bloom Gr SE27 ...75 A1
Bloom Park Rd SW6 ...154 C1
Bloomsbury Ct WC1 ...106 B3
Bloomsbury Ho 10 SW4 ...61 C1
Bloomsbury Pl WC1 ...106 B3
London SW18 ...59 B2
Bloomsbury Sq WC1 ...106 B3
Bloomsbury St WC1 ...105 C3
Bloomsbury Way WC1 ...106 B3
Blore Cl SW8 ...171 B3
Blore Ct W1 ...119 B4
Blossom Cl W5 ...36 A4
Blossom Pl E1 ...98 B1
Blossom St E1 ...24 A1 98 B1
Blount St E14 ...33 A3
Blucher Rd SE5 ...48 B3
Blue Anchor Alley 4 TW9 ...54 A3
Blue Anchor La SE16 ...40 A2
Blue Anchor Yd E1 ...125 B4
Blue Ball Yd SW1 ..118 C1
Bluebell Cl 16 E9 ...25 B4

Blue Gate Fields Jun &
Inf Schs E1 ...32 B2
Bluegate Mews E1 ..32 A2
Blundell St N7 ...14 A2
Blurton Rd E5 ...17 C4
Blyth Cl 4 E14 ...42 C2
Blythe Ho SE11 ...163 C4
Blythe Mews
W14 ...39 C3
Blythendale Ho 51
E2 ...24 C3
Blythe Rd W14 ...126 A1
Blythe St E2 ...25 A2
Blyth's Wharf E14 ...33 A2
Blythwood Rd N4 ...5 A4
Boadicea St N1 ...84 C3
Boadoak Ho NW6 ...78 B3
Boardwalk Pl E14 ...34 B1
Boarley Ho SE17 ...152 A3
Boathouse Ctr The
W10 ...22 C1
Boat Lifter Way 19
SE16 ...41 A2
Bobbin Cl 4 SW4 ...61 B3
Bobbington St WC1 ...106 B4
Bob Marley Way 6
SE24 ...62 C3
Bocking St E8 ...25 A4
Boddicott Cl SW19 ...70 A2
Boddington Ho
SE14 ...50 C4
Bodeney Ho 10 SE5 ...49 A2
Boden Ho 1 E1 ...111 B4
Bodington Ct 2
W12 ...39 C4
Bodley Manor Way
SE24 ...74 C4
Bodmin St SW18 ...70 C3
Bodney Mans 14 E8 ...17 A3
Bodney Rd E5,E8 ...17 A3
Bohemia Pl 1 E8 ...17 A2
Bohn Rd E1 ...33 A4
Boileau Rd SW13 ...47 A4
Boilerhouse SE1 ...124 C1
Boisseau Ho 22 E1 ...32 B4
Bolden St SE8 ...52 A1
Boldero Pl NW8 ...90 A1
Boleyn Rd N16 ...16 A3
Bolina Rd SE16 ...40 B1
Bolingbroke Gr
SW11 ...60 B1
Bolingbroke Hospl The
SW11 ...60 A2
Bolingbroke Rd
W14 ...39 C3
Bolingbroke Wlk
SW11 ...168 A4
Bollo Bridge Rd W3 ..37 B4
Bollo Ct 2 W3 ...37 B3
Bollo La W3 ...37 A4
Bolney Gate SW7 ...130 A3
Bolney St SW8 ...162 C1
Bolsover St W1 ...92 B1
Bolt Ct EC4 ...107 C1
Bolton Cres SE5 ...48 A3
Bolton Ct SW11 ...169 C3
Bolton Gdns SW5 ...142 B2
London NW10 ...22 C2
Bolton Gdns Mews
SW10 ...142 C2
Bolton Ho 4 SE10 ...43 A1
Chiswick W4 ...45 B3
London NW10 ...21 A4
Boltons Ct SW5 ...142 B2
Bolton St W1 ...118 B2
Boltons The SW10 .142 C2

Bolton Studios
SW10 ...143 A1
Bolton Wlk N7 ...5 B2
Bombay St SE16 ...40 A2
Bomore Rd
W11 ...31 A2 112 A4
Bonar Rd SE15 ...49 C3
Bonchurch Rd W10 ..31 A4
Bond Ct EC4 ...109 B1
Bond Ho 4 NW6 ...23 C3
Bonding Yard Wlk
SE16 ...41 A3
Bond Street Sta
W1 ...103 C1
Bondway SW8 ...162 B4
Bonfield Rd SE13 ...67 B3
Bonham Ho W11 ...112 C3
Bonham Rd SW2 ...62 B2
Bonheur Rd W4 ...37 C4
Bonhill St EC2 ...97 C1
Bonington Ho 1 ...84 C1
Bonita Mews SE15 ...65 C4
Bonner Ho 3 SW15 ..56 C2
Bonner Prim Sch
E2 ...25 B2
Bonner Rd E2 ...25 B3
Bonner St E2 ...25 B3
Bonneville Gdns
SW4 ...61 B1
Bonneville Prim Sch
SW4 ...61 B1
Bonnington Sq
SW8 ...162 C4
Bonny St NW1 ...13 B1
Bonsor Ho SW8 ...171 A4
Bonsor St SE5 ...49 A3
Benthron Ho SW15 ..57 A4
Booker Cl 15 E13 ...33 C4
Boord St SE10 ...43 A3
Boothby Rd N19 ...4 C2
Booth Cl 10 E9 ...25 A4
Booth Ho 2 SW2 ...74 C4
Booth La EC4 ...122 C4
Booth's Pl W1 ...105 A3
Boot St N1 ...98 A3
Bordon Wlk 5
SW15 ...68 C4
Boreas Wlk N1 ...86 B1
Boreham Ave E16 ...35 C3
Boreman Ho 10
SE10 ...52 B4
Borland Rd SE15 ...65 B3
Borneo St SW15 ...57 B4
Borough High St
SE1 ...123 B1
Borough Mkt* ...123 B1
Borough Rd SE1 ...136 B2
Borough Sq SE1 ...136 C3
Borough Sta SE1 ...136 C3
Borrett Cl SE17 ...150 C1
Borrodale Rd SW18 ..59 A1
Borrowdale NW1 ...92 C3
Borthwick St SE8 ...41 C1
Boscastle Rd NW5 ...4 A1
Boscobel Ho 4 E8 ...17 A2
Boscobel Pl SW1 ...145 C4
Boscobel St NW8 ...89 C1
Boscombe Cl E5 ...18 A3
Boscombe Rd W12 ..38 C4
Boss Ho SE1 ...138 C4
Boss St SE1 ...138 C4
Boston Gdns W4 ...46 A4
Boston Ho NW1 ...90 C2
8 London SE5 ...48 B1
Boston Pl NW1 ...90 C1

Bosun Cl 8 E14 ...41 C4
Boswell Ct WC1 ...106 B4
8 London W14 ...39 C3
Boswell Ho WC1 ...106 B4
Boswell St WC1 ...106 B4
Bosworth Ho 4
W10 ...23 A1
Bosworth Rd W10 ...23 A1
Bothwell Cl E16 ...35 C2
Bothwell St 6 W6 ...47 C4
Botolph Alley EC3 ...124 A4
Botolph La EC3 ...124 A4
Bott's Mews
W2 ...31 C3 113 A4
Boughton Ho SE1 ...137 B4
Boulcott St E1 ...32 C3
Boulevard The 4
SW17 ...72 C2
Boulogne Ho SE1 ...138 C2
Boulter Ho 8 SE14 ...50 B2
Boulton Ho 8 W4 ...36 A1
Boundaries Mans 3
SW12 ...72 C3
Boundaries Rd
SW12 ...72 C3
Boundary Ho 5 SE5 ..48 B3
Balham SW12 ...73 A3
Boundary La SE17 ...48 B4
Boundary Pas 2 ...98 C2
Boundary Rd NW8 ...79 A4
Boundary Road Est
NW8 ...78 C3
Boundary Row
SE1 ...136 A4
Boundary St
E2 ...24 B1 98 C2
Bourchier St 1 ...119 B4
Bourdon Pl W1 ...118 B4
Bourdon St W1 ...118 B3
Bourke Cl
London NW10 ...8 A2
London SW4 ...62 A1
Bourlet Cl W1 ...104 C3
Bourne Cl 4 ...104 C3
Bourne Ho 6 SW4 ...61 B3
Bourne Mews W1 ...103 C1
Bournemouth Cl
SE15 ...49 C1
Bournemouth Rd
SE15 ...49 C1
Bourne Pl W4 ...37 C1
Bourne St SW1 ...145 B3
Bourne Terr W2 ...100 B4
Bousfield Prim Sch
SW10 ...142 C2
Bousfield Rd SE14 ...50 C1
Boutcher CE Prim Sch
SE1 ...152 C4
Boutflower Rd
SW11 ...60 A3
Bouverie Mews N16 ..7 A2
Bouverie Pl W2 ...101 C2
Bouverie Rd N16 ...7 A2
Bouverie St EC4 ...107 C1
Bovingdon Cl 3 N19 ..4 B2
Bovingdon Rd
SW6 ...166 B3
Bowater Cl SW2 ...62 A1
Bowater Ho EC1 ...97 A1
Bow Brook The 20
E2 ...25 C3
Bow Church Sta E3 ..26 C2
Bow Churchyard
EC2,EC4 ...109 A1
Bow Common La
E3 ...26 B1
Bowden St 22 E3 ...27 A2

Bowden St SE11 ...149 C1
Bowditch SE8 ...41 B1
Bowen Dr SE21 ...76 A1
Bowen St E14 ...34 A3
Bower Ave SE3 ...53 A3
Bowerdean St
SW6 ...166 A3
Bower Ho SE14 ...50 C2
Bowerman Ave
SE14 ...51 A4
Bowerman Ct 1
N19 ...4 C2
Bower St E1 ...32 C3
Bowes Rd W3 ...29 A2
Bowfell Rd W6 ...47 B4
Bowhill Cl SW9 ...163 C2
Bowie Cl SW4 ...73 C4
Bow Ind Pk E15 ...18 C1
Bow La EC2,EC4 ...109 A1
Bowland Ho N4 ...6 B4
Bowland Rd SW4 ...61 C3
Bowland Yd SW1 ...131 A3
Bowl Ct EC2 ...98 B1
Bowles Rd 1 SE1 ...49 C4
Bowley Ho SE16 ...139 B2
Bowling Green Cl
SW19 ...69 A4
Bowling Green Ho
SW10 ...157 B2
Bowling Green La
EC1 ...95 C2
Bowling Green Pl
SE1 ...137 B4
Bowling Green St
SE11 ...163 B4
Bowling Green Wlk
N1 ...98 A4
Bowman Ave E16 ...35 B2
Bowman Mews E1 ...125 B4
Wandsworth SW18 ...70 B3
Bowman's Mews N7 ..5 A1
Bowman's Pl N7 ...5 A1
Bowmore Wlk NW1 ..13 C1
Bowness Cl 6 E8 ...16 B2
Bowness Ho SE15 ...50 B3
Bowood Rd SW11 ...60 C2
Bow Rd E3 ...26 C2
Bowry Ho 14 E14 ...33 B4
Bow Sch E3 ...26 C2
Bowsprit Point 5
E14 ...41 C3
Bow St WC2 ...106 B1
Bowstead Ct SW11 ..167 C3
Bowyer Ho 24 N1 ...24 A4
Wandsworth SW18 ...59 A3
Bowyer Pl SE5 ...48 B3
Bowyer St 15 SE5 ...48 B3
Boxall Rd SE21 ...64 A1
Boxley Ho 8 E5 ...17 A3
Boxmoor Ho 5
W11 ...30 C1
Box Tree Ho SE8 ...41 A2
Boxworth Gr N1 ...85 A4
Boyce Ho W10 ...23 B2
Boyce St SE1 ...121 B1
Boyd Ct SW15 ...57 B1
Boydell Ct NW8 ...11 C1
Boyd St E1 ...111 C1
Boyfield St SE1 ...136 B3
Boyle St W1 ...118 C4
Boyne Ct NW10 ...8 C1
Boyne Rd SE13 ...67 C4
Boyne Terr Mews
W11 ...31 B1 112 C2

Boyson Rd 10 SE17 ...48 C4
Boyton Cl E1 ...25 C1
Boyton Ho NW8 ...79 C2
SE11 ...149 B1
Brabazon St E14 ...34 A4
Brabner Ho 2 ...99 B4
Braburn Gr SE15 ...50 B1
Bracer Ho 1 N1 ...24 A3
Bracewell Rd W10 ...30 B4
Bracey St N4 ...5 A2
Bracken Ave SW12 ...72 C4
Brackenbury N4 ...5 B3
Brackenbury Gdns
W6 ...39 A3
Brackenbury Prim Sch
W6 ...39 A3
Brackenbury Rd
W6 ...39 A3
Bracken Gdns SW13 ..46 C1
Bracken Ho 14 E3 ...33 C4
Brackley Ct NW8 ...89 C2
Brackley Rd W4 ...38 A1
Brackley St EC1 ...109 A4
Brackley Terr 4
W4 ...38 A1
Bracklyn St N1 ...87 B2
Bracklyn St N1 ...87 B2
Bracknell Gate
NW3 ...11 A3
Bracknell Gdns
NW3 ...11 A3
Bracknell Way NW3 ..11 A3
Bradbeer Ho 22 E2 ..25 B2
Bradbourne
SW6 ...165 C3
Bradbury Ct 2 SE3 ...53 C3
Bradbury Ho E1 ...111 A2
Bradbury St 28 N16 ..16 A3
Bradby Ho NW8 ...78 B1
Braddon Rd TW9 ...54 B4
Braddyll St SE10 ...43 A1
Bradenham 11 SE17 ..48 C4
Bradenham Cl SE17 ..48 C4
Bradfield Ct 14
NW1 ...13 A1
Bradford Ho 4
W14 ...39 C3
Bradgate Rd SE6 ...67 A1
Brading Rd SW2 ...74 B4
Bradiston Rd W9 ...23 B2
Bradley Ho 7 ...14 B2
Bradley Ho 4 E3 ...22 A3
8 E3 ...27 A2
SE16 ...40 A2
Bradley Mews SW12 ..72 A3
Bradley's Cl N1 ...85 C2
Bradlord Ho E1 ...76 A1
Bradmead SW8 ...160 C1
Bradmore Park Rd
W6 ...39 A2
Brad St SE1 ...121 C1
Bradstock Ho E9 ...18 A1
Bradstock Rd E9 ...17 C2
Bradwell Ho NW6 ...78 A3
Brady Ho SW8 ...171 A4
London SW4 ...61 C2
Brady St E1 ...25 A1
Braefoot Ct SW15 ...57 C2
Braemar SW15 ...57 C1
Braemar Ave SW18,
SW19 ...70 C2

Braemar Ho W9 ...88 C3
Braemar Mans W8 128 B1
Braemore Ho 21
　SE15 ...49 C3
Braes St N1 ...15 A1
Braganza St SE17 .150 A1
Braham Ho SE11 .149 A1
Braham St E1 ...111 A2
Brahma Kumaris World
　Spiritual Univ NW10 8 A3
Braid Ave W3 ...29 A3
Braid Ho SE10 ...52 B2
Braidwood St SE1 .124 A1
Brailsford Rd SW2 ..62 C1
Braintree Ho 5 E1 .25 B1
Braintree St E2 ....25 B2
Braithwaite Ho EC1 .97 B2
　14 South Bromley
　E14 ...34 C3
Braithwaite Twr
　W2 ...101 B4
Bramah Gn SW9 .173 C4
Bramall Ct N7 ....14 B2
Bramber Ho 4
Bramber Ct TW8 ...36 A2
Bramber Rd W14 .154 C4
Brambledown 4 N4 .5 A4
Bramble Gdns W12 .29 B2
Bramble Ho 12 E3 .33 C4
Brambling Ct 25
　SE8 ...51 B4
Bramcote Gr SE16 .40 B1
Bramcote Rd SW15 .57 A3
Bramerton NW6 ....9 C1
Bramerton St SW3 158 B4
Bramfield Ct N4 ...6 B2
Bramfield Rd SW11 .60 B2
Bramford Rd SW18 .59 B3
Bramham Gdns
　SW5 ...142 B2
Bramham Ho SE22 .64 A3
Bramlands Cl SW11 .60 A4
Bramley Cres SW8 .162 A2
Bramley Ho
　10 London W10 .30 C3
　5 Roehampton
　SW15 ...56 B1
Bramley Rd W10 ...30 C3
Bramshaw Rd E9 ...17 C2
Bramshill Gdns NW5 .4 A1
Bramshill Rd NW10 .21 B3
Bramshurst 8 ...78 B3
Bramston Rd
　London NW10 ....21 C3
　Wandsworth SW17 .71 B1
Bramwell Ho SE1 .137 A1
Bramwell Mews N1 .85 A4

Brandrams Wharf
　SE16 ...40 B4
Brandreth Rd SW17 .73 A2
Brand St SE10 ...52 B3
Brangton Rd SE11 .149 A1
Brangwyn Cr SW4 .126 A1
Branksea St SW6 .154 A1
Branksome Ho
　SW8 ...162 C2
Branksome Rd SW2 .62 A2
Bransby Ct 4 N16 .16 A4
Branscombe St
　SE13 ...67 A4
Branscombe St
Branston Ho 2
　N7 ...14 B2
Branstone Rd TW9 .44 B2
Branston Ho N7 ...14 C3
Brantwood Ho 9
　SE5 ...48 B3
Brantwood Rd SE24 .63 B2
Brasenose Dr SW13 .47 B4
Brassey Ho 1 E14 .42 A2
Brassey Rd NW6 ...10 B2
Brassey Sq SW11 ..60 C4
Brassie Ave W3 ...29 A3
Brass Talley Alley 31
　SE16 ...40 C4
Brathay NW1 ...83 A1
Brathway Rd SW18 .70 C4
Bratley St E1 ...99 B1
Bravington Pl W9 .23 B1
Bravington Rd W9 .23 B2
Brawne Ho 12 SE17 .48 A4
Braxfield Rd SE4 ..66 B3
Bray NW3 ...12 A1
Brayard's Rd SE15 .50 A1
Braybrook St W12 .29 B3
Brayburne Ave
　SW4 ...171 A1
Bray Cres SE16 ....40 C4
Braydon Rd N16 ...7 C3
Bray Dr E16 ...35 B2
Brayfield Terr N1 ..14 C1
Brayford Sq 1 E1 .32 B3
Bray Pl SW3 ...144 C3
Bread St EC2,EC4 .109 A1
Breakspeare 21 ..76 B1
Breakspears Mews
　SE4 ...51 C1
Breakspears Rd SE4 66 C4
Breakwell Ct 18
　W10 ...23 A1
Bream's Bldgs EC4 .107 B2
Bream St E3 ...18 C1
Breasley Cl SW15 ..57 A3
Brechin Pl SW7 ...143 A3
Brecknock Prim Sch
　NW1 ...13 C2
Brecknock Rd N19 .13 C3
Brecon Ho W2 ...100 C2
　London N16 ...7 B3
　Wandsworth SW18 .70 C4
Brecon Rd W6 ...154 B3
Bredel Ho 1 E14 ..33 C4
Bredgar SE13 ...67 A2
Bredgar Rd N19 ....4 B2
Bredinghurst SE22 .76 C4
Bredinghurst Sch
　SE15 ...65 C3
Breer St SW6 ...59 A4
Breezer's Ct 1 E1 .125 C3
Breezer's Hill E1 ..125 C3
Bremans Row SW18 71 B2
Bremner Rd SW7 .129 A2

Brenchley Gdns
　SE15,SE22,SE23 ...65 C1
Brenda Rd SW17 ...72 B2
Brendon Ave NW10 .8 A4
Brendon Ho NW1 .103 B4
Brendon St W1 ...102 B2
Brenley Ho SE1 ...137 B4
Brent 5 W12 ...38 A3
Brentford Community
　Leisure Centre W4 36 C1
Brentham Ho SE1 .137 B4
Brenthouse Rd E9 .17 B2
Brenthouse Rd E9 .17 B2
Brent New Ent Ctr
　NW10 ...8 B2
Brenton Ct E9 ...18 A3
Brenton St E14 ...33 A3
Brent Rd E16 ...35 C4
Brent Trad Est NW10 8 A4
Brentwick Gdns
　TW8 ...36 A2
Brereton Ho 4
　SW2 ...74 C4
Bressenden Pl
　SW1 ...132 C2
Breton Ho EC2 ...97 A1
　2 ...138 C2
Brett Cl N16 ...7 A2
Brett Cres NW10 ..20 C4
Brettell St SE17 ...151 C1
Brett Ho SW15 ...69 C4
Brett House Ct 2
　SW15 ...69 C4
Brettinghurst SE1 .153 B1
Brett Manor E8 ...17 A3
Brett Pas E8 ...17 A3
Brett Pas 15 E8 ...17 A3
Brett Rd E8 ...17 A3
Brewer St W1 ...119 A4
Brewers Bldgs EC1 .96 A4
Brewers Ct W2 ...100 C2
Brewer's Gn SW1 .133 B2
Brewer's Ct W1 ...119 A4
Brewery Ind Est The
　N1 ...97 B4
Brewery Rd N7 ...14 A2
Brewery Sq SE1 ...124 C1
Brewhouse La E1 ..32 A1
Brewhouse La SW15 58 A4
Brewhouse St SW15 58 A4
Brewhouse Wlk
　SE16 ...33 A1
Brewhouse Yd EC1 .96 A2
Brewster Gdns W10 .30 B4
Brewster Ho E14 ...33 B2
　2 ...153 A4
Briant Ho SE1 ...135 A1
Briant St SE14 ...50 C3
Briar Ct E8 ...16 B1
Briardale SW19 ...70 B3
Briardale Gdns NW3 1 C1
Briardale Ho N16 ...7 A3
Briar Rd NW2 ...9 B4
Briar Wlk W10 ...23 A1
　Putney SW15 ...57 C2
Briarwood Rd SW4 .61 C2
Briary Cl NW3 ...12 A1
Brickbarn Cl SW10 157 A2
Brick Ct EC4 ...107 B1
Brick Farm Cl TW9 .45 A2
Brick La E1 ...99 A2
　E2 ...24 B2 99 A3
Bricklayers Arms
　SE1 ...137 C1
Brick St W1 ...118 A1
Brickwork Ho
　SW9 ...173 C4
Bridal Mews N1 ...85 B4
Brideale Cl SE15 ...49 B4

Bride Ct EC4 ...108 A1
Bride La EC4 ...108 A1
Bride St N7 ...14 B2
Bridewain St SE1 .138 C2
Bridewell Pl 20 E1 .32 A1
　EC4 ...108 A1
Bridford Mews W1 .92 B1
Bridge App NW3 ...12 C1
Bridge Ave W6 ...39 B1
Bridge Avenue Mans 7
　W6 ...39 B1
Bridge Cl 18 W10 .30 C3
Bridge Field Ho
　W2 ...100 A2
Bridgefoot SE1 ...148 B1
Bridge Ho London E9 17 C1
　1 London NW1 ...12 C1
　London SE4 ...66 B3
Bridge House Quay
　E14 ...34 B1
Bridge La SW11 ...168 B3
Bridgeland Rd E16 .35 C2
Bridgeman Ho E9 ..17 B1
Bridgeman Rd N1 ..14 B1
Bridgeman St NW8 .80 A1
Bridge Meadows
　SE14 ...50 C4
Bridgend Rd SW18 .59 B3
Bridgen Ho 6 E1 ..32 A3
Bridge Pk 7 SW18 .58 C2
Bridge Pl SW1 ...146 B4
Bridgeport Pl E1 ..125 C2
Bridge Rd E15 ...27 C4
　London NW10 ....8 A2
　London E9 ...17 C3
Bridges Ct SW11 ..167 B1
Bridges Ho 6 SE5 ..48 C3
Bridge St SW1 ...134 B3
　London W4 ...37 C2
Bridge Terr E15 ...19 C1
Bridgeview 2 W6 ..39 B1
Bridgewater Rd E15 27 C4
Bridgewater Sq
　EC2 ...108 C4
Bridgewater St
　EC2 ...108 C4
Bridgeway St NW1 .83 A1
Bridge Wharf 18 E2 25 C3
Bridge Yd SE1 ...123 C2
Bridgford St SW17,
Bridgman Rd W4 ..37 B3
Bridgnorth Ho 10
　SE15 ...49 C4
Bridgwater Ho W2 .100 C2
Bridle La W1 ...119 A4
Bridlington Ho
　SW18 ...59 B3
Bridport SE17 ...151 A1
Bridport Ho N1 ...87 C3
Bridport Pl N1 ...87 C3
Bridstow Pl W2 ...31 C3
Brief St SE5 ...48 A2
Brierfield NW1 ...82 C3
Brierley Rd
　London E11 ...19 C4
　Upper Tooting SW12 73 B2
Brierly Gdns E2 ...25 B3
Brigade St SE3 ...53 B1
Briggeford Cl 5 E5 .7 C2
Briggs Ho 2 ...99 A4
Brightling Rd SE4 ..66 B1
Brightlingsea Pl 5
　E14 ...33 B2
Brightman Rd SW18 71 C3
Brighton Bldgs
　SE1 ...138 A1

Brighton Ct SW15 ..58 B1
Brighton Gr SE14 ..51 A2
Brighton Ho 6 SE5 .48 C2
Brighton Rd N16 ...16 A4
Brighton Terr SW9 .62 B3
Brightside Rd SE13 .67 C1
Bright St E14 ...34 A4
Brightwell Ct N7 ...14 B3
Brightwells SE6 ...166 A2
Brig Mews SE8 ...51 C4
Brigstock Ho SE5 ..48 B1
Brill Pl NW1 ...83 C1
Brimsdown Ho E3 ..27 B1
Brindley Ho
　10 London W2 ...31 C4
　22 Streatham SW12 .74 A4
Brindley St SE14 ...51 B2
Brine Ho 10 E3 ...26 A3
Brinklow Ho W2 ...100 A3
Brinkworth Way E9 .18 B2
Brinsley Ho 11 E1 .32 B3
Brinsley St 20 E1 ..32 A3
Brinton Wlk SE1 ...122 A1
Brion Pl E14 ...34 B4
Brisbane Ho 2
　W12 ...30 A2
Brisbane St SE5 ...48 C3
Briset St EC1 ...96 A1
Briset Way N7 ...5 B2
Bristol Gdns SW9 ..88 B1
Bristol Ho SE11 ...135 B1
Bristol Mews W9 ..88 B1
Bristowe Cl 8 SW2 .62 C1
Britannia Gate 12
　E16 ...35 C1
Britannia Junc NW1 82 B4
Britannia Rd 11 E14 .41 C2
　London SW6 ...156 A1
Britannia Row N1 ..86 C4
Britannia St WC1 ..94 C4
Britannia Way
　NW10 ...20 A1
Britannia Wlk N1 ..97 B4
British Gr W4 ...38 B1
British Grove Pas 3
　W4 ...38 B1
British Grove S 3
　W4 ...38 B1
British Library The*
　WC1 ...93 C4
British Mus* WC1 .106 A3
British St E3 ...26 B2
British Wharf Ind Est
　SE14 ...50 C4
Brittany Ho SW15 ..57 B3
Brittany Point
　SE11 ...149 B3
Britten Cl NW11 ...2 A3
Britten Ho SW3 ...144 B2
Britten St SW3 ...144 A2
Britton St EC1 ...96 A1
Brixton Day Coll
　SW9 ...62 A4
Brixton Hill SW2 ..62 B1
Brixton Hill Ct 8
　SW2 ...62 B2
Brixton Hill Pl SW2 .74 A4
Brixton Oval 7
　SW2 ...62 C3
Brixton Rd SW9 ...173 B2
Brixton Sta SW9 ...62 C3
Brixton Station Rd
　SW9 ...62 C3
Brixton Water La
　SW2 ...62 B2

Broadbent Cl N6 ....4 A3
Broadbent St W1 ....**118** A4
Broad Bridge Cl
  SE3 ....53 C3
Broad Common Est
  N16 ....7 C3
Broad Ct WC2 ....**106** B1
Broadfield N6 ......**11** A2
Broadfield La NW1 ....4 C4
Broadfields Way
  NW10 ....8 B3
Bradford Ho **11** E1 .26 A1
Broadgate EC2 ...**110** A4
Broadgate Circ
  EC2 ....**110** A3
Broadgates Ct
  SE11 ....**149** C1
Broadgates Rd
  SW18 ....71 C3
Broadhinton Rd
  SW4 ....61 B4
Broadhurst Cl
  London NW6 .....11 A2
  6 Richmond TW10 .54 B2
Broadhurst Gdns
  NW6 ....11 A2
Broadhurst Mans
  NW6 ....11 A2
Broad La EC2 .....**110** A4
Broadlands N6 ......3 C4
Broadlands Ave
  SW16 ....74 A2
Broadlands Cl
  London N6 ....3 C4
  Streatham SW16 .74 A2
Broadlands Ct TW9 .44 C3
Broadlands Lo **6** N6 .3 B4
Broadlands Mans **2**
  SW16 ....74 A2
Broadlands Rd N6 ..3 C4
Broadley St NW8 ..**102** A4
Broadley Terr NW1 .90 B1
Broadmayne SE17 **151** B2
Broadmead W14 ..**140** A3
Broadoak Ct **3**
  SW9 ....62 C4
Broadoak Ho NW6 .78 B3
Broad Sanctuary
  SW1 ....**134** A3
Broad St Ave EC2 **110** A3
Broadstone Ho
  SW8 ....**162** C1
Broadstone Pl W1 **103** B3
Broad St PI EC2 .**109** C3
Broadwalk Ho
  SW7 ....**128** C3
Broadwalk La NW11 .1 B4
Broadwall SE1 ....**121** C2
Broadway SW1 ...**133** B2
  London E15 ....**19** C1
Broadway Arc **3**
  W6 ....39 B2
Broadway Ho **2** E8 .25 A4
Broadway Mans
  SW6 ....**155** C1
Broadway Market
  E8 ....25 A4
Broadway Market Mews
  2 E8 ....24 C4
Broadway Mews E5 .7 A4
Broadway The
  Barnes SW13 ......46 A1
  London W3 ....36 C4
  Broadwick St W1 ..**105** A1
Broad Wlk NW1 ...81 C1
  W1 ....**117** B2
  Richmond TW9 ....44 B3

Broad Wlk The W8 .**114** B1
Broadwood Terr
  W14 ....**141** A4
Broad Yd EC1 ......96 A1
Brocas Cl **3** NW3 .12 A1
Brockbridge Ho **11**
  SW15 ....56 B1
Brocket Ho SW8 .**171** B2
Brockham Dr SW2 .74 B4
Brockham Ho NW1 .83 A3
  11 Streatham SW2 .74 B4
Brockham St SE1 .**137** A2
Brock Ho WC1 ...**105** B4
Brockhurst Ho **11** .6 C4
Brockill Cres SE4 ..66 A3
Brocklebank Rd
  SW18 ....71 B4
Brocklebank Road Ind
  Est SE7 ....43 C2
Brocklehurst St
  SE14 ....50 C3
Brockley Cross SE4 .66 B4
Brockley Cross Bsns Ctr
  SE4 ....66 A4
Brockley Gdns SE4 .51 B1
Brockley Gr SE4 ....51 B1
Brockley Hall Rd
  SE4 ....66 A2
Brockley Ho SE17 **152** A2
Brockley Mews SE4 .66 A2
Brockley Prim Sch
  SE4 ....66 B2
Brockley Rd SE4 ...66 B2
Brockley Sta SE4 ..66 A4
Brockley Way SE4 ..66 A2
Brockmer Ho **6** E1 .32 A2
Brock PI E3 ....27 A1
Brock St SE15 .....65 B4
Brockweir **2** E2 ...25 B3
Brockwell Ct **2**
  SW2 ....62 C2
Brockwell Ho
  SE11 ....**163** A4
Brockwell Park
  SE24 ....63 A1
Brockwell Park Gdns
  SE24 ....75 A4
Broderick Ho SE21 .76 A1
Brodia Rd N16 .....7 A1
Brodick Ho **11** E3 ..26 B3
Brodie Ho SE1 ....**153** A2
Brodie St SE1 ....**153** A2
Brodlove La E1 ....32 C2
Brodrick Rd SW17 .72 A2
Broken Wharf EC4 **122** C4
Brokesley St E3 ...26 B2
Broke Wlk E8 ......24 B4
  1 E8 ....24 C4
Bromar Rd SE5 .....64 A4
Bromehead St **8**
  E1 ....32 B3
Bromell's Rd SW4 ..61 B3
Bromfelde Rd
  SW4 ....**171** C1
Bromfield St SE16 **139** C3
Bromfield St N1 ...**85** C2
Bromleigh Ho SE1 **138** C2
Bromley-by-Bow Sta
  E3 ....27 A2
Bromley SE13 .....67 C2
Bromley Hall Rd
  E14 ....34 B4
Bromley High St E3 .27 A2
Bromley Lo **2** W3 .28 B3
Bromley PI W1 ....**104** C4
Bromley St E1 .....32 C3
Brompton WC1 ...**106** C3

Brompton Arc
  SW1 ....**131** A3
Brompton Oratory
  SW3 ....**130** A1
Brompton Park Cres
  SW6 ....**156** A3
Brompton PI SW3 **130** B2
Brompton Rd SW3 **130** A2
Brompton Sq SW3 **130** A2
Bromstone Ho
  SW9 ....**173** B3
Bromwich Ave N6 ..3 C2
Bromwich Ho **3**
  TW10 ....54 A1
Bromyard Ave W3 .29 A2
Bromyard Ho **3**
  SE15 ....50 A3
Bron Ct NW6 .....23 C4
Brondesbury Coll for
  Boys NW6 ....9 C2
Brondesbury Ct NW2 .9 C1
Brondesbury Mews **11**
  NW6 ....10 C1
Brondesbury Park Sta
  NW6 ....23 A4
Brondesbury Pk NW2 .9 C1
Brondesbury Rd
  NW6 ....23 C3
Brondesbury Sta
  NW6 ....10 B1
Brondesbury Villas
  NW6 ....23 C3
Bronsart Rd SW6 .**154** A1
Bronte Ct **4** W14 .39 C3
Bronte Ho
  6 London N16 .16 A3
  London NW6 .....23 C2
Bronti Cl SE17 ...**151** A2
Bronwen Ct NW8 .89 B3
Bronze St SE8 .....51 C3
Brookbank Rd SE13 .67 A4
Brook Cl SW17 ....72 C2
Brook Ct London E15 .76 B3
  Mortlake SW14 ...56 A4
Brookdale Rd SE6 .67 A1
Brook Dr SE11 ...**150** A4
Brooke Ho **3** SE14 .51 A2
Brookes Mkt EC1 .**107** B4
Brooke's Mkt EC1 .**107** C3
Brooke St EC1 ...**107** B3
Brookfield N6 ......3 C1
  11 London N4 .....5 C2
Brookfield Pk NW5 .4 A1
Brookfield Prim Sch
  N19 ....4 A2
Brookfield Rd
  London E9 ....18 A2
  London W4 ....37 C4
Brook Gate W1 ...**117** A3
Brook Gdns SW13 .56 B4
Brook Gn W6 ......39 C2
Brook Green Flats **11**
  W14 ....39 C3
Brook Ho
  3 London SW4 ...61 B2
  London W3 ....36 C4
  4 London W6 .....39 B2
Brook Hos NW1 ...83 A1
Brooklands Ave
  SW18 ....71 A2
Brooklands Court
  Apartments **3**
  NW6 ....10 B1
Brooklands Ct **2**
  NW6 ....10 B1

Brooklyn Ct W12 ...30 B1
Brookmarsh Ind Est
  SE10 ....52 A3
Brook Mews N W2 **115** A4
Brookmill Rd SE8 ..51 C2
Brooksbank Ho **7**
  E9 ....17 B2
Brooksbank St **3**
  E9 ....17 B2
Brooksby Mews N1 .14 C1
Brooksby St N1 ....14 C1
Brooksby's Wlk E9 .17 C3
Brooks Ct SW8 ...**161** A2
  London SW4 .....**172** A2
Brookside Rd N19 ..4 B2
Brooks La W4 .....44 C4
Brook's Mews W1 .**118** A4
Brooks Rd W4 .....36 C1
Brook St W1 .....**118** A4
  W2 ....**115** C4
Brookstone Ct SE15 .65 A3
Brooksville Ave
  NW6 ....23 A4
Brookville Rd SW6 **154** C1
Brookwood Ave
  SW13 ....46 B1
Brookwood Ho
  SE1 ....**136** B3
Brookwood Rd
  SW18 ....70 C3
Broome Ct **3** TW9 .44 C2
Broome Ho **7** E5 ..17 A3
Broome Way SE5 ..48 C3
Broomfield **8** NW1 .12 C1
Broomfield Ho
  SE17 ....**152** A3
Broomfield House Sch
  TW9 ....44 B2
Broomfield Rd TW9 .44 B2
Broomfield St E14 .34 A4
Broomgrove Rd
  SW9 ....**173** A1
Broomhill Rd SW18 .58 C2
Broomhouse La
  SW6 ....**165** A2
Broomhouse Rd
  SW6 ....**165** B3
Broomsleigh St
  NW6 ....10 B3
Broomwood Hall Sch
  SW12 ....61 C2
Broomwood Rd
  SW11 ....60 C2
Brougham Rd E8 .24 C4
  London W3 ....28 B3
Brougham St
  SW11 ....**169** A2
Brough Cl SW8 ...**162** B1
Brough SW8 .....**162** B1
Broughton Dr **20**
  SW9 ....63 A3
Broughton Rd SW6 **166** B2
Broughton Road App
  SW6 ....**166** A2
Broughton St SW8 **170** A2
Broughton Street
  Arches Ind Area
  SW11 ....**170** A1
Brouncker Rd W3 ..37 B4
Browne Ho **13** SE8 .51 C3
Brownfield St E14 .34 A3
Brownflete Ho SE4 .66 A3
Brown Hart Gdns
  W1 ....**117** C4
Browning Cl W9 ...89 A1

Browning Ct W14 .**154** C4
Browning Ho
  10 London N16 ...16 A4
  London W12 .....30 B3
Browning Mews
  W1 ....**103** C3
Browning St SE17 **151** A3
Brownlow Ho SE16 **139** B3
Brownlow Mews
  WC1 ....**95** A1
Brownlow Rd E8 ..24 C4
  London NW10 .....8 A1
  London W1 SE1 .**107** A3
Brown's Bldgs EC3 **110** B1
Brown St W1 .....**102** C2
Brownswood Rd N4 .6 B2
Broxash Rd SW11 **60** C1
Broxbourne Ho **11**
  E3 ....27 A1
Broxholme Ho
  SW6 ....**166** A4
Broxholm Rd SE27 .74 C1
Broxwood Way
  NW8 ....80 B3
Bruce Cl W10 .....30 C4
Bruce Glasier Ho **13**
  N19 ....4 C4
Bruce Ho
  4 London SW4 ...61 C1
  London W10 .....30 C4
  Putney SW15 .....57 A2
Bruce Rd E3 ......27 A2
Bruckner St W10 ..23 B2
Bruges PI **8** NW1 .13 B1
Brune Ho E1 .....**110** C3
Brunei Ct NW10 ..21 C2
Brunel Est W2 ....31 C4
Brunel Ho E14 ....42 A1
  SW10 ....**157** C2
  4 London NW5 ..13 A4
  London W10 .....30 C3
  Putney SW15 .....57 C2
Brunel Rd SE16 ...32 B1
  London W3 ....29 A4
Brunel St E16 .....35 B1
Brunlees Ho SE1 .**137** A1
Brunswick Ct EC1 ..96 A3
  SE1 ....**138** B4
  SW1 ....**147** C3
Brunswick Gdns
  W8 ....31 C1 **113** C1
Brunswick Ho **4** E2 .24 B3
  London N1 ....**90** C2
Brunswick Mews
  W1 ....**103** A2
Brunswick Park Prim
  Sch SE5 ....48 C3
Brunswick Pk SE5 .49 A2
Brunswick Pl N1 ...**97** C3
Brunswick Quay
  SE16 ....40 C3
Brunswick Rd E14 .34 B3
Brunswick Sh Ctr
  WC1 ....94 B2
Brunswick Sq WC1 .94 B2
Brunswick Villas **2**
  SE5 ....49 A2
Bruntion PI E14 ...33 A3
Brushfield St E1 .**110** C4
Brushwood Ho **4**
  E14 ....34 A4
Brussels Rd SW11 .59 C3
Bruton La W1 ....**118** B3
Bruton PI W1 ....**118** B3

Bruton St W1 . . . . .118 B3
Bryan Ave NW10 . . . . .9 A1
Bryan Ct W1 . . . . .102 C2
Bryan Ho SE16 . . . . .41 B4
Bryan Rd SE16 . . . . .41 B4
Bryanston Ct W1 . . . . . . .102 C2
Bryanston Ho **11**
SE15 . . . . .49 B2
Bryanston Mans
W1 . . . . .102 C4
Bryanston Mews E
W1 . . . . .102 C3
Bryanston Mews W
W1 . . . . .102 C2
Bryanston Pl W1 . . . . . . .102 C3
Bryanston Sq W1 . . . . . .102 C2
Bryanston St W1 . . . . . . .103 A1
Bryant Ct E2 . . . . .24 B3
Bryantwood Rd N5,
N7 . . . . .14 C3
Bryce Ho **22** SE14 . . . . . .50 C4
Brydale Ho **2** SE16 . . . . .40 C2
Brydges Pl WC2 . . . . . . .120 A3
Brydges Rd E15 . . . . .19 C3
Brydon Wlk N1 . . . . .84 B4
Bryer Ct EC2 . . . . .108 C4
Bryett Rd N7 . . . . .5 A1
Bryher Ho W4 . . . . .37 B1
Brymay Cl E3 . . . . .26 C3
Brymon Ct W1 . . . . .103 A3
Brynmaer Ho
SW11 . . . . .169 A3
Brynmaer Rd
SW11 . . . . .169 A3
Bryony Rd W12 . . . . .29 C2
BT Telecom Twr★
W1 . . . . .104 C4
Buccleuch Ho E5 . . . . . . .7 C4
Buchanan Ct **16**
SE16 . . . . .40 C2
Buchanan Gdns
NW10 . . . . .22 A3
Buchanan Ho
Dulwich SE21 . . . . .76 A1
Wandsworth SW18 . . . .70 C4
Buchan Ho W3 . . . . .37 A4
Buchan Rd SE15 . . . . . . .65 B4
Bucharest Rd SW18 . . . .71 B4
Buckfast St
E2 . . . . .24 C2 99 C3
Buck Hill Wlk W2 . . . . . .115 C3
Buckhold Rd SW18 . . . . .58 C1
Buckhurst Ho **12** N7 . . . .13 C3
Buckhurst St E1 . . . . .25 A1
Buckingham Gate
SW1 . . . . .133 A2
Buckingham Ho
London N4 . . . . .6 B3
Richmond TW10 . . . . . .54 C2
Buckingham Mans
NW6 . . . . .11 A3
Buckingham Mews
SW1 . . . . .132 C2
17 London N1 . . . . .16 A2
London NW10 . . . . . . .21 B3
Buckingham Palace★
SW1 . . . . .132 C2
Buckingham Pl
SW1 . . . . .132 C2
Buckingham Rd
London N1 . . . . .16 A2
London NW10 . . . . . . .21 B3

Buckingham St
WC2 . . . . .120 B3
Buckingham Yd
NW10 . . . . .21 B3
Buckland Cres NW3 . . . .11 C2
Buckland Ct **3** N1 . . . . . .24 A3
Buckland St N1 . . . . .87 C1
Buckland Wlk **2**
W3 . . . . .37 B4
Buckler's Alley
SW6 . . . . .155 A2
Bucklersbury EC2,
EC4 . . . . .109 B1
Bucklers Ct E5 . . . . .111 A2
Buckley Ct **5** NW6 . . . . . .10 B1
Buckley Rd NW6 . . . . . . .10 B1
Buckley St SE1 . . . . .121 B1
Buckmaster Cl
SE17 . . . . .150 C2
1 London Sw9 . . . . . . .62 C4
Buckmaster Ho **1**
N7 . . . . .14 B4
Buckmaster Rd
SW11 . . . . .60 A3
Bucknall St WC1 . . . . . .106 A2
Bucknell Cl SW2 . . . . . . .62 B3
Buckner Rd SW2 . . . . . . .62 B3
Buckridge Bldg
EC1 . . . . .107 C3
Buckshead Ho **19**
W2 . . . . .31 C4
Buck St NW1 . . . . .13 A1
Buckstone Cl SE23 . . . . .65 B1
Buckters Rents
SE16 . . . . .33 A1
Buckthorne Rd SE4 . . . . .66 A1
Budge Row EC4 . . . . . . .109 B1
Budge's Wlk W2 . . . . . . .115 A2
Budleigh Ho **10**
SE15 . . . . .49 C3
Buer Rd SW6 . . . . .164 C1
Bugsbys Way SE10 . . . . .43 B2
Buick Ho **4** E3 . . . . .26 C1
Bulinca St SW1 . . . . .147 C3
Bullace Row SE5 . . . . . . .48 C2
Bullards Pl **16** E2 . . . . . . .25 C2
Bulleid Way SW1 . . . . . .146 B3
Bullen Ho **8** E1 . . . . .25 A1
Bullen St SW11 . . . . .168 B2
Buller Cl SE15 . . . . .49 C3
Buller Ho SE21 . . . . .22 C2
Bullfinch Ct **3** SE21 . . . .75 C2
Bullingham Mans
W8 . . . . .127 C4
Bull Inn Ct WC2 . . . . . . .120 B3
Bullivant St **2** E14 . . . . .34 B2
Bulls Alley SW14 . . . . . . .45 C1
Bull's Gdns SW3 . . . . . .144 B4
Bulls Head Pas
EC3 . . . . .110 A1
Bull Yd SE15 . . . . .49 C2
Bulmer Mews
W11 . . . . .31 C1 113 B2
Bulow Ct SW6 . . . . .166 B3
Bulstrode Pl W1 . . . . . . .103 C3
Bulstrode St W1 . . . . . . .103 C2
Bulwer St W12 . . . . .30 B1
Bunbury Ho SE15 . . . . . .49 C3
Bunhill Row EC1 . . . . . . .97 B1
Bunhouse Pl SW1 . . . . .145 C2
Bunkers Hill NW11 . . . . . .2 B4
Bunning Ho N7 . . . . .14 A4
Bunning Way N7 . . . . . . .14 B1
Bunsen Ho **3** E3 . . . . . . .26 A3
Bunsen St **2** E3 . . . . . . .26 A3
Bunyan Ct EC2 . . . . .108 C4

Buonaparte Mews
SW1 . . . . .147 B2
Burbage Cl SE1 . . . . .137 B1
Burbage Ho London N1 . .87 C3
16 SE14 . . . . .50 C4
Burbage Rd SE21,
SE24 . . . . .75 C1
Burcham St E14 . . . . .34 B3
Burchell Ho SE11 . . . . . .149 A2
Burchell Rd SE15 . . . . . .50 A2
Burcote Rd SW18 . . . . . .71 C4
Burden Ho SW8 . . . . . . .162 A1
Burdenshott Ave
TW10 . . . . .55 A3
Burder Cl N1 . . . . .16 A2
Burder Rd N1 . . . . .16 A2
Burdett Coutts &
Townshend CE Prim
Sch SW1 . . . . .147 C4
Burdett Mews **4**
W2 . . . . .100 A2
Burdett Rd E3 . . . . .33 B4
Richmond TW9 . . . . . . .54 B4
Burford Ho
2 Brentford TW8 . . . . .36 A1
London SW9 . . . . .173 A1
Burford Rd E15 . . . . .27 C4
Brentford TW8 . . . . . . .36 A1
Burford Wlk SW6 . . . . . .156 B1
Burgate Ct **10** SW9 . . . . .62 C4
Burges Gr SW13 . . . . . . .47 A3
Burgess Hill NW2 . . . . . .10 C4
Burgess Ho **8** SE5 . . . . . .48 B3
Burgess Ind Pk SE5 . . . . .48 C3
Burgess Park Mans
NW6 . . . . .10 C4
Burgess St E14 . . . . .33 C4
Burge St SE1 . . . . .137 C1
Burghley Hall Cl
SW19 . . . . .70 A3
Burghley Ho SW19 . . . . .70 A1
Burghley Rd NW5 . . . . . .13 A4
Burghley Twr W3 . . . . . . .29 B2
Burgh St N1 . . . . .86 B2
Burgon St EC4 . . . . .108 B1
Burgos Gr SE10 . . . . .52 A2
Burgoyne Rd SW9 . . . . . .62 B4
Burhan Uddin Ho
E1 . . . . .98 C1
Buriton Ho **9** SW15 . . . .69 A3
Burke Cl SW15 . . . . .56 A3
Burke Ho **1** SW11 . . . . . .59 C3
Burke St E16 . . . . .35 B2
Burland Rd SW11 . . . . . .60 B2
Burleigh Ho SW3 . . . . . .157 C3
London W10 . . . . .30 C4
Burleigh Pl SW15 . . . . . .57 C2
Burleigh St WC2 . . . . . . .120 C4
Burley Ho E1 . . . . .32 C3
Burlington Arc W1 . . . . .118 C3
Burlington Cl W9 . . . . . . .23 C1
Burlington Ct W4 . . . . . .45 B3
Burlington Danes Sch
W12 . . . . .30 A3
Burlington Gdns
W1 . . . . .118 C3
Fulham SW6 . . . . .164 B1
London W3 . . . . .28 B1
London W4 . . . . .37 B1
Burlington Ho NW3 . . . . .11 C3
Burlington La W4 . . . . . . .45 C3
Burlington Mews
London W3 . . . . .28 B1
1 Putney SW15 . . . . . .58 A2
Burlington Pl SW6 . . . . .164 B1

Burlington Rd
Fulham SW6 . . . . .164 B1
London W4 . . . . .37 B1
Burma Rd N16 . . . . .15 C4
Burmarsh **6** NW5 . . . . . .12 C2
Burmester Ho SW17 . . . .71 B1
Burmester Rd SW17 . . . .71 B1
Burnaby Cres W4 . . . . . . .45 B4
Burnaby Ct SE16 . . . . . .139 C3
Burnaby Gdns W4 . . . . . .45 A4
Burnaby St SW10 . . . . . .157 A1
Burnand Ho **3** W14 . . . . .39 C3
Burnaston Ho **5** E5 . . . . .7 C1
Burnbury Rd SW12 . . . . .73 B3
Burne Jones Ho
W14 . . . . .140 B3
Burnell Ho SW2 . . . . .74 C3
Burnell Wlk SE1 . . . . . . .153 A2
Burness Cl N7 . . . . .14 B2
Burne St NW1 . . . . .102 A4
Burnett Ct E9 . . . . .17 B3
Burnett Ho **6** SE13 . . . . .52 B1
Burney St SE10 . . . . .52 B3
Burnfoot Ave SW6 . . . . .164 B3
Burnham NW3 . . . . .12 A1
Burnham Cl SE1 . . . . . . .153 A3
Burnham Ct **2** W2 . . . . .114 B4
Burnham Est **8** E2 . . . . .25 B2
Burnham St E2 . . . . .25 B2
Burnhill Ho EC1 . . . . .96 C3
Burnley Rd
London SW9 . . . . .8 C3
London SW9 . . . . .172 C2
Burns Cl SW17 . . . . .144 B2
Burns Ho **10** E2 . . . . .25 B2
SE17 . . . . .150 B1
11 London N16 . . . . . .16 A4
London N7 . . . . .14 B2
Burn's Ho NW10 . . . . . . .21 A4
Burnside Cl SE16 . . . . . . .32 C1
Burns Rd SW11 . . . . . . .168 C2
Burns'd Rd NW10 . . . . . .21 B4
Burnthwaite Rd
SW6 . . . . .155 A1
Burntwood Cl SW18 . . . .72 A3
Burntwood Ct SW17 . . . .71 B1
Burntwood Grange Rd
SW18 . . . . .72 A3
Burntwood La
SW17 . . . . .71 C1
Burntwood Sch
SW17 . . . . .71 C2
Buross St E1 . . . . .32 A3
Burrage Ct **11** SE16 . . . .40 C2
Burrard Ho **2** E2 . . . . . . .25 B3
Burrard Rd NW6 . . . . . . .10 C4
Burr Cl E1 . . . . .125 B2
Burrell St SE1 . . . . .122 A2
Burrell's Wharf Sq
E14 . . . . .42 A1
Burrhill Ct SE16 . . . . .40 C3
Burrow Ho SW9 . . . . . . .173 A1
Burrow Rd SE22 . . . . .64 A3
Burrows Mews
SE1 . . . . .136 A4
Burrows Rd NW10 . . . . . .22 B2
Burrow Wlk SE21 . . . . . . .75 B4
Burr Rd SW18 . . . . .70 C4
Bursar St SE1 . . . . .124 A1
Burslem St **1** E1 . . . . . .111 B2
Burstock Rd SW15 . . . . .58 A3
Burston Rd SW15 . . . . . .57 C2
Burtley Cl N4 . . . . .6 B3
Burton Bank N1 . . . . .15 C1
Burton Ct SW3 . . . . .145 A2
Burton Gr SE17 . . . . .151 B1

Burton Ho **6** SE16 . . . . .40 A4
London SE5 . . . . .48 A2
London SE3 . . . . .58 B2
Burton Mews SW1 . . . . .145 C3
Burton Pl WC1 . . . . .93 C3
Burton Rd
London NW6 . . . . .10 B1
London SW9 . . . . .48 A1
London SW9 . . . . .173 B2
Burtons Ct E15 . . . . .19 C1
Burton St WC1 . . . . .93 C2
Burtonwood Ho N4 . . . . . .6 C4
Burtt Ho N1 . . . . .98 A4
Burwash Ho SE1 . . . . . .137 C3
Burwell Cl **22** E1 . . . . . . .32 A3
Burwell Wlk **3** E3 . . . . . .26 C1
Burwood Ho **11**
SW9 . . . . .63 A3
Burwood Pl W2 . . . . . . .102 B2
Bury Cl SE16 . . . . .32 C1
Bury Ct EC3 . . . . .110 B2
Bury Pl WC1 . . . . .106 B3
Bury St EC3 . . . . .110 B1
SW1 . . . . .119 A2
Bury Wlk SW3 . . . . .144 A2
Busbridge Ho
E14 . . . . .33 C4
Busby Pl NW5 . . . . .13 C2
Bushbaby Cl SE1 . . . . . .138 A1
Bushberry Rd E9 . . . . . . .18 A2
Bush Cotts **12** SW18 . . . .58 C2
Bush Ct **7** W12 . . . . .39 C4
Bushell Cl SW2 . . . . .74 B2
Bushell St **1** E1 . . . . . . .125 C1
Bushey Down SW12 . . . .73 A2
Bushey Hall SE5 . . . . . . .49 B2
Bushey Hill Rd SE5 . . . . .49 B2
Bushfield Ho N5 . . . . .15 B3
Bush Ind Est NW10 . . . . .20 C1
Bush La EC4 . . . . .123 B4
Bushnell Rd SW17 . . . . .73 A1
Bush Rd E8 . . . . .25 A4
SE8 . . . . .40 C2
Richmond TW9 . . . . . . .44 C4
Bushwood Dr SE1 . . . . .153 A3
Bushwood Rd TW9 . . . . .44 C4
Business Design Ctr★
N1 . . . . .85 C3
Buspace Studios **2**
W10 . . . . .23 A1
Butcher Row E1 . . . . .32 C3
Butchers Rd E16 . . . . . . .35 C3
Bute Gdns W6 . . . . .39 C2
Bute House Prep Sch
W6 . . . . .39 C2
Bute St SW7 . . . . .143 B4
Butfield Ho **6** E9 . . . . . . .17 B2
Butler Ho **15** E14 . . . . . .33 B3
20 E2 . . . . .25 B2
London SW9 . . . . .48 A2
Butler Pl SW1 . . . . .133 B2
Butler Rd NW10 . . . . .8 B1
Butler St **33** E2 . . . . .25 B2
Butler's Wharf W
SE1 . . . . .124 C1
Butley Ct **8** E3 . . . . .26 A3
Butterfield Cl **11**
SE16 . . . . .40 A4
Butterfly Wlk **2**
SE5 . . . . .48 C2
Buttermere NW1 . . . . . . .92 B4
Buttermere Cl SE1 . . . . .152 C3
London E11 . . . . .19 C4
Buttermere Ct NW8 . . . .79 B4
Buttermere Dr
SW15 . . . . .58 A2

Buttermere Ho 🔢
E3 . . . . 26 B2
Butterwick Wlk 🔢
E8 . . . . 16 B2
Butterwick W6 . . . . . .39 B2
Butterworth C
SW16 . . . . .74 A1
Buxhall Cres E9 . . . . .18 B2
Buxted Rd London SE8 16 B1
London SE22 . . . . .64 A3
Buxton Ct N1 . . . . .97 C4
Buxton Gdns W3 . . . . .28 A2
Buxton Ho 🔢 SW11 . . .59 C3
Buxton Rd N19 . . . . . . .4 C3
London NW2 . . . . .9 A2
Mortlake SW14 . . . . . .56 A4
Buxton St E1 . . .24 C1 99 B1
Byam Shaw Sch of Art
N19 . . . . .4 C2
Byam St SW6 . . . . . .166 C1
Byards Ct SE16 . . . . . .40 C3
Byas Ho 🔢 E3 . . . . . . .26 B2
Byefield Cl SE16 . . . . .41 A4
Byelands Cl 🔢 SE16 32 C1
Bye The W3 . . . . .29 A3
Byeway The SW14 . . . .55 B4
Byfeld Gdns SW13 . . .46 C2
Bygrove Prim Sch
E14 . . . . .34 A3
Bygrove St E14 . . . . . .34 A3
Byng Pl WC1 . . . . .93 B1
Byng St E14 . . . . .41 C4
Byrne Ho 🔢 SW2 . . . . .62 B2
Byrne Rd SW12 . . . . . .73 A2
Byron Cl E8 . . . . .24 C4
Byron Ct SW3 . . . . . .144 B3
W9 . . . . .23 C1
WC1 . . . . .94 C2
Dulwich SE21 . . . . .76 C3
🔢 London NW6 . . . . . . .11 B1
Byron Mews NW3 . . . .12 A4
Byron St E14 . . . . .34 B3
Bythorn St SW9 . . . . . .62 B3
Byward St EC3 . . . . .124 B3
Bywater Pl SE16 . . . . .33 A1
Bywater St SW3 . . . .144 C2
Bywell Pl W1 . . . . . . .104 C3
Byworth Wlk N19 . . . . .5 A3

C

Cabbell St NW1 . . . . .102 A3
Cabinet Off SW1 . . . .134 A4
Cabinet War Rooms★
SW1 . . . . .133 C4
Cable Ho WC1 . . . . . . .95 B4
Cable Pl SE10 . . . . . . .52 B2
Cable St E1 . . . . .32 A2
Cabot Ct SE16 . . . . . . .40 C3
Cabot Sq E14 . . . . . . .33 C1
Cabul Rd SW11 . . . . .168 B1
Cactus Cl SE5 . . . . . . .49 A1
Cactus Wlk W12 . . . . .29 B3
Cadbury Way SE16 . .153 B4
Caddington Rd NW2 . . .1 A1
Cadell Cl E2 . . . . .24 B3
Cadell Ho 🔢 E2 . . . . . .24 B3
Cade Rd SE10 . . . . . . .52 C2
Cader Rd SW18 . . . . . .59 B1
Cadet Dr SE1 . . . . . . .153 A2
Cade Tyler Ho 🔢
SE10 . . . . .52 B2
Cadiz St SE17 . . . . . .151 A1
Cadman Cl SW9 . . . . . .48 A3
Cadmore Ho 🔢 N1 . . .15 A1
Cadmus Cl 🔢 SW4 . . .61 C4

Cadmus Ct SW9 . . . . .173 B4
Cadnam Lo E14 . . . . . .42 C3
Cadnam Point 🔢
SW15 . . . . .69 A3
Cadogan Cl E9 . . . . . . .18 B1
Cadogan Ct SW3 . . . .144 C3
Cadogan Ct Gdns
SW1 . . . . .145 A3
Cadogan Gate
SW1 . . . . .145 A3
Cadogan Gdns
SW3 . . . . .145 A3
Cadogan Ho 🔢 SW3 .157 C3
Cadogan La SW1 . . . .131 B1
Cadogan Pl SW1 . . . .131 A1
Cadogan Sq SW1 . . . .131 A1
Cadogan St SW3 . . . .144 C3
Cadogan Terr E9 . . . . .18 B1
Caedmon Rd N7 . . . . .14 B4
Caernarvon Ho
W2 . . . . .100 C2
Caesar Ct 🔢 E2 . . . . . .25 C3
Cahill St EC1 . . . . .97 A1
Cahir St E14 . . . . .42 A2
Caine Ho W3 . . . . .37 A4
Caird St W10 . . . . .23 B2
Cairns Ho 🔢 N7 . . . . .14 B4
Cairns Rd SW11 . . . . . .60 A2
Caister Ho
🔢 Balham SW12 . . . . .73 A4
London N7 . . . . .14 B2
Caistor Mews SW12 . .73 A4
Caistor Rd SW12 . . . . .73 A4
Caithness Ho N1 . . . . .84 C4
Caithness Rd W14 . . . .39 C3
Calabria Rd N5 . . . . . .15 A3
Calais Gate SE5 . . . . . .48 A2
Calais St SE5 . . . . .48 A2
Calbourne Rd SW12 . .72 C4
Calcraft Ho 🔢 E2 . . . .25 B3
Caldecot Ct SE5 . . . . . .48 B1
Caldecot Rd SE5 . . . . .48 B1
Calder Ct SE16 . . . . . . .33 B1
Calderon Ho NW8 . . . .80 A2
Calderon Pl W10 . . . . .30 B4
Caldervale Rd SW4 . . .61 C2
Caldew St SE5 . . . . . . .48 C3
Caldwell St SW9 . . . .163 B1
Caldy Wlk 🔢 N1 . . . . .15 B2
Caleb St SE1 . . . . .137 A4
Caledonia Ho
E14 . . . . .33 A3
Caledonian Market
SE1 . . . . .138 B2
Caledonian Rd N1 . . . .84 C3
London N7 . . . . .14 B2
Caledonian Road &
Barnsbury Sta N7 . .14 B1
Caledonian Road Sta
N7 . . . . .14 B2
Caledonian Wharf Rd
E14 . . . . .42 C2
Caledonia St N1 . . . . .84 B1
Cale St SW3 . . . . .144 A2
Caletock Way SE10 . . .43 B1
Calgarth NW1 . . . . . . .83 A1
Calgary Ct 🔢 SE16 . . .40 B4
Caliban Twr 🔢 N1 . . . .24 A3
Calico Ho 🔢 SW11 . . .59 B4
Calico Row 🔢 SW11 . .59 B4
Calidore Cl SW2 . . . . .62 B1
Callaby Terr 🔢 N1 . . . .15 C2
Callahan Cotts 🔢
E1 . . . . .32 B4
Callcott Ct NW6 . . . . . .10 B1
Callcott Rd NW6 . . . . .10 B1
Callcott St W8 . . . . . .113 B2

Callendar Rd SW7 . . .129 B2
Callingham Cl 🔢
E14 . . . . .33 B4
Callingham Ho 🔢
SW4 . . . . .62 A4
Callow St SW3 . . . . . .157 B4
Calmington Rd SE5 . . .49 A4
Calshot Ho N1 . . . . . . .84 C2
Calshot St N1 . . . . .84 C1
Calstock NW1 . . . . .83 B3
Calstock Ho SE11 . . . .149 C2
Calthorpe St WC1 . . . .95 A2
Calton Ave SE21 . . . . .64 A1
Calver 🔢 NW5 . . . . . . .13 A4
Calverley Gr N19 . . . . . .4 C3
Calvert Ave E2 . . . . . . .98 C3
Calvert Ct
🔢 London N19 . . . . .4 B3
🔢 Richmond TW9 . . . .54 B4
Calvert Ho 🔢 W12 . . . .30 A2
Calverton SE5 . . . . . . .49 A4
Calvert Rd SE10 . . . . .43 B1
Calvert's Bldgs
SE1 . . . . .123 B1
Calvert St NW1 . . . . . .81 B4
Calvin St E1 . . .24 B1 98 C1
Calypso Cres 🔢
SE15 . . . . .49 B3
Calypso Way SE8,
SE16 . . . . .41 B2
Cambalt Ho 🔢
SW15 . . . . .57 C2
Cambalt Rd SW15 . . . .57 C2
Cambay Ho 🔢 E1 . . . .26 A1
Camber Ho 🔢 SE15 . . .50 B4
Camberley Ho NW1 . . .82 B1
Camberwell Church St
SE5 . . . . .48 C2
Camberwell Coll of Arts
SE5 . . . . .49 A2
London SE5 . . . . .48 C3
Camberwell Glebe
SE5 . . . . .49 A2
Camberwell Gn SE5 . .48 C2
Camberwell Gr SE5 . . .49 A1
Camberwell Green
SE5 . . . . .48 B2
Camberwell New Rd
SW9 . . . . .48 A3
Camberwell Rd SE5 . .48 B3
Camberwell Station Rd
SE5 . . . . .48 B2
Camberwell Trad Est
SE5 . . . . .48 B2
Camborne Rd SW18 . .70 C4
Cambourne Mews 🔢
W11 . . . . .31 A3
Cambray Rd SW12 . . .73 B3
Cambria Ho 🔢 E14 . . .33 A3
Cambria Rd SE5 . . . . . .63 B4
Cambria St SW6 . . . .156 B1
Cambrian Ave
NW6 . . . . .23 C3
Cambridge Cotts
TW9 . . . . .44 C4
Cambridge Cres 🔢
E2 . . . . .25 A3
Cambridge Ct 🔢 E2 . .25 A3
🔢 NW6 . . . . .23 C3
London N16 . . . . .7 A4
Cambridge Gate
NW1 . . . . .92 A2

Cambridge Gate Mews
NW1 . . . . .92 B2
Cambridge Gdns
NW6 . . . . .23 C3
W10 . . . . .31 A3
Cambridge Gr W6 . . . .39 A2
Cambridge Heath Rd
E1,E2 . . . . .25 A2
Cambridge Heath Sta
E2 . . . . .25 A3
🔢 London SE5 . . . . . . .58 A4
Cambridge Mans
SW11 . . . . .168 C3
Cambridge Pas 🔢
E9 . . . . .17 B1
Cambridge Pl W8 . . . .128 B3
Cambridge Rd N
W4 . . . . .37 A1
Cambridge Rd S 🔢
W4 . . . . .37 A1
Cambridge Sch W6 . . .39 A2
Cambridge Sq W2 . . .102 A2
Cambridge St SW1 . .146 C2
Cambridge Terr
NW1 . . . . .92 A3
Cambridge Terr Mews
NW1 . . . . .92 B3
Cambus Rd E16 . . . . . .35 C4
Cam Ct 🔢 SE15 . . . . . .49 B4
Camden Gdns NW1 . . .13 A1
Camden High St
NW1 . . . . .82 C3
Camden Ho 🔢 SE8 . . .41 B1
Camdenhurst St
E14 . . . . .33 A3
Camden Lock Pl
NW1 . . . . .13 A1
Camden Mews NW1 . .13 C2
Camden Mkt★ NW1 . . .82 C4
Camden Park Rd
NW1 . . . . .13 C2
Camden Pas N1 . . . . . .86 A3
Camden Rd NW1 . . . . .82 C4
Camden Road Sta
NW1 . . . . .13 B1
Camden Row SE3 . . . .53 A1
Camden Sch for Girls
The NW5 . . . . .13 B2
Camden Sq NW1 . . . . .13 C2
Camden St NW1 . . . . . .83 A4
Camden Studios
NW1 . . . . .83 A3
Camden Terr 🔢
NW1 . . . . .13 C2
Camden Town Sta
NW1 . . . . .82 B4
Camden Wlk N1 . . . . . .86 A3
Camdeford Ct 🔢
SW12 . . . . .74 A4
Camelford Ho 🔢
NW1 . . . . .83 A3
🔢 31 A3
Camelford Ct 🔢
W11 . . . . .31 A3
Camelford Wlk 🔢
W11 . . . . .31 A3
Camelia Ho SE8 . . . . .51 B3
Camellia St SW8 . . . .162 A1
Camelot Ho 🔢 NW1 . .13 C2
Camelot Prim Sch
SE15 . . . . .50 A4
Camera Pl SW10 . . . .157 B4
Cameret Ct 🔢 W11 . . .39 C4
Cameron 🔢
SW19 . . . . .70 A3
Cameron Ho NW8 . . . .80 A2

Cameron Ho continued
SE5 . . . . .48 B3
Cameron House Sch
SW10 . . . . .157 B3
Camerton Cl 🔢 E8 . . .16 B2
Camilla Rd SE16 . . . . .40 A2
Camlet St E2 . . . . .98 C2
Camley St NW1 . . . . . .83 C2
Camomile St EC3 . . .110 B2
Campaign Ct W9 . . . . .23 B1
Campana Rd SW6 . . .165 C4
Campbell Ct SW7 . . . .128 C1
🔢 Dulwich SE21 . . . . .76 C3
Campbell Gordon Way
NW2 . . . . .9 A4
Campbell Ho SW1 . . .146 C1
🔢 89 B1
🔢 London W12 . . . . . .30 A2
Campdale Rd N7 . . . . . .4 C1
Campden Gr 🔢 W8 . .127 C4
Campden Hill W8 . . . .127 B4
Campden Hill Ct 🔢
W8 . . . . .127 C4
Campden Hill Gate
W8 . . . . .127 B4
Campden Hill Gdns
W8 . . . . .113 B2
Campden Hill Mans
W8 . . . . .113 C2
Campden Hill Pl
W14 . . . . .113 A2
Campden Hill Rd
W8 . . . . .127 B4
Campden Hill Sq
W14 . . . . .31 B1 113 A2
Campden Ho 🔢 W8 . .113 C1
🔢 London NW6 . . . . . .11 C1
Campden Hos W8 . . .113 B1
Campden House Cl
W8 . . . . .127 C4
Campden St
W8 . . . . .31 C1 113 B1
Campen Ct SW19 . . . . .70 A2
Camperdown St
E1 . . . . .111 A1
Campion Ho 🔢 N16 . .16 A3
Campion Rd SW15 . . .57 B2
Camplin St SE14 . . . . .50 C3
Campshill Pl SE13 . . . .67 B2
Campshill Rd SE13 . . .67 B2
Compton Cl
SE1 . . . . .113 B2
Cam Rd E15 . . . . .27 C4
Camsey Ho 🔢 SW2 . .62 B2
Canada Cres W3 . . . . .20 B1
Canada Gdns SE13 . . .67 B2
Canada Rd W3 . . . . . . .28 B4
Canada Sq E14 . . . . . .34 A1
Canada St SE16 . . . . . .40 C4
Canada Way W12 . . . .30 A2
Canal App SE8 . . . . . . .51 A4
Canal Bldg N1 . . . . . . .86 C2
Canal Bridge SE15 . . .49 C4
Canal Cl E1 . . . . .26 A1
London W10 . . . . .22 C1
Canal Gr SE15 . . . . . . .50 A4
Canal Head Public Sq
SE15 . . . . .49 C2
Canal Path E2 . . . . . . .24 B4
Canalside Studios 🔢
N1 . . . . .24 A4
Canal St SE5 . . . . .48 C4
Canal Way W10 . . . . . .22 C1
Canal Wlk N1 . . . . .87 C4

Canary Wharf* E14 .34 A1
Canary Wharf Pier
(River Bus) E14 ...33 B1
Canary Wharf Sta
E14 ....34 A1
Canberra Prim Sch
W12 ....30 A2
Canbury Mews
SE26 ....76 C1
Cancell Rd SW9 .173 C4
Candahar Rd
SW11 ....168 B1
Candida Ct ■ NW1 .13 A1
Candishe Ho SE1 .138 C4
Candover St W1 ...104 C3
Candy St E3 ....26 B4
Canfield Gdns NW6 .11 A1
Canfield Pl NW6 ...11 B2
Canford Rd SW11 ..60 C2
Canham Rd W3 .....38 A4
Cann Ho W14 ......126 B2
Canning Cross SE5 .49 A1
Canning Ho ② W12 .30 A2
Canning Pas W8 ..128 C2
Canning Pl W8 ....128 C2
Canning Pl Mews
W8 ....128 C2
Canning Rd N5 ....6 A1
Cannington NW5 .12 C2
Canning Town E16 .35 A4
Canning Town Sta
E16 ....35 A4
Cannock Ho N4 ......6 C4
Cannon Dr E14 .....33 C2
Cannon Hill NW6 ...10 C3
Cannon Ho SE11 .149 A3
Cannon La NW3 ......2 C1
Cannon Pl NW3 ......2 C1
Cannon St EC4 ....123 A4
Cannon Street Rd
E1 ....32 A3
Cannon Street Sta
EC4 ....123 B4
Cannon Wharf Bsns Ctr
🖪 SE8 ....41 A2
Canon Barnett CE Prim
Sch L1 ....111 A2
Canon Beck Rd
SE16 ....40 B4
Canonbury Cres ⑯ N1 .15 B1
Canonbury Ct ② N1 .15 A1
Canonbury Gr N1 ...15 B1
Canonbury La N1 ...15 A1
Canonbury Pk N N1 .15 B2
Canonbury Pk S N1 .15 B2
Canonbury Prim Sch
N1 ....15 A2
Canonbury Rd N1 ..15 A1
Canonbury Sq N1 ..15 A1
Canonbury St N1 ...15 B1
Canonbury Sta N1,
N5 ....15 B3
Canonbury Villas
N1 ....15 A1
Canon Murnane Rd
SE1 ....138 C1
Canon Row SW1 ..134 A3
Canons Cl N2 ....2 C4
Canon St N1 ....86 C3
Canrobert St E2 ....25 A2
Cantelowes Rd
NW1 ....13 C2
Canterbury SE13 ...67 B2

Canterbury Cl ⑯
SE5 ....48 B1
Canterbury Cres
SW9 ....62 C4
Canterbury Ct NW6 .23 C3
London W3 ....29 A1
Canterbury Gr SE27,
SW16 ....74 C1
Canterbury Ho
⑥ E3 ....27 A2
SE1 ....135 A2
Canterbury Ind Pk ⑯
SE15 ....50 B4
Canterbury Mans
NW6 ....11 A2
Canterbury Pl
SE17 ....150 B3
Canterbury Rd NW6 .23 C3
Canterbury Terr
NW6 ....23 C3
Cantium Ret Pk SE1 .49 C4
Canton St E14 ......33 C3
Cantrell Rd E3 ......26 C1
Canute Ct SW16 ....74 C1
Canute Gdns SE16 .40 C2
Canvey St SE1 ....122 C2
Cape Henry Ct ⑦
E14 ....34 C2
Capel Ho ⑰ E9 .....17 B1
Capel Lo
⑥ Richmond TW9 .44 B2
⑫ Streatham SW2 .74 B4
Capener's Cl SW1 .131 B3
Capern Rd SW18 ...71 B3
Capital Interchange Way
TW8 ....36 C1
Capital Wharf ⑥ E1 .125 C1
Capland Ho NW8 ...89 C2
Capland St NW8 ....89 C2
Caple Ho SW10 ...157 A2
Caple Rd NW10 ....21 B3
Capper St WC1 .....93 A1
Capstan Ho ⑥ E14 .42 B2
Capstan Rd SE8 ....41 B2
Capstan Sq E14 ....42 B4
Capstan Way SE16 .33 A1
Capulet Mews ❶
E16 ....35 C1
Caradoc Cl W2 .....31 C3
Caradoc St SE10 ...43 A1
Caranday Villas ⑥
W11 ....30 C1
Caravel Cl E14 .....41 C3
Caravel Mews ⑭
SE8 ....51 C4
Caraway Hts E14 ...34 B2
Carbery Ave W3 ....36 B4
Carbis Rd E14 ......33 B3
Carbroke Ho ⑯ E9 .25 B4
Carburton St W1 ...92 B1
Cardale St ❶ E14 ..42 B3
Carden Rd SE15 ....65 A4
Cardiff Ho ⑥ SE15 .49 C4
Cardigan Rd E3 ....26 B3
Barnes SW13 ....46 C1
Richmond TW10 ......54 A1
Cardigan St SE11 .149 B2
Cardigan Wlk ❶ N1 .15 B1
Cardinal Bourne St
SE1 ....137 C1

Cardinal Pl SW15 ...57 C3
Cardinal Pole RC Sch
London E9 ....18 A3
London E9 ....17 C1
Cardinals Way N19 ..4 C3
Cardinal Vaughan
Memorial Sch
W14 ....126 A4
Cardine Mews SE15 .50 A3
Cardington St NW1 .93 A3
Cardozo Rd N7 .....14 A3
Cardross St ⑥ W6 .39 A3
Cardwell Rd N7 ....14 A4
Career Ct ⑰ SE16 .40 C4
Carew Cl N7 ....5 B2
Carew Ct ⑱ SE14 ..50 C4
Carew Ho SW16 ....74 C1
Carew St SE5 ....48 B1
Carey Ct ⑳ SE5 ....48 B3
Carey Gdns SW8 .171 B3
Carey La EC2 ......108 C2
Carey Pl SW1 .....147 B3
Carey St WC2 .....107 A1
Carfax Pl SW4 .....61 C3
Carfree Cl ⑥ N1 ...14 C1
Cargill Rd SW18 ...71 B3
Carinthia Ct ⑱ SE8 .41 A2
Carisbrook Ct ❶
SW16 ....74 B1
Carisbrooke Ho ⑦
SW3 ....37 B4
Carisbrooke Gdns
SE15 ....49 B3
Carisbrooke Ho
TW10 ....54 C2
Carleton Gdns N19 .13 B3
Carleton Rd N7 .....13 C4
Carlile Cl E3 ....26 B3
Carlile Ho SE1 ....137 C1
Carlingford Rd
NW3 ....2 C1
Carlisle Ave EC3 ..110 C1
London W3 ....29 A3
Carlisle La SE1 ....135 A2
Carlisle Pl SW1 ....132 C1
Carlisle Rd NW6 ...23 A4
London N4 ....5 C4
Carlisle St W1 .....105 B1
Carlisle Wlk ⑥ E8 .16 B2
Carlos Pl W1 ......118 A3
Carlow St NW1 .....82 C2
Carlton Cl NW3 ......1 C2
Carlton Ct SW9 ....48 A2
London NW2 ....9 B2
London SW9 ....48 A2
Carlton Dr SW15 ...58 A2
Carlton Gdns SW1 .119 B1
Carlton Gr ⑥ SE15 .50 A3
London SE15 ....50 A2
Carlton Hill NW8 ...78 C2
Carlton Ho NW6 ...23 C3
London W6 ....23 B3
W1 ....103 B2
Carlton House Terr
SW1 ....119 B1
Carlton Lo N4 ....5 C4
Carlton Mans W14 .126 B4
W9 ....88 B4
London N16 ....7 B3
⑦ London N6 ....4 A3
London SW9 ....62 C3
Carlton Prim Sch
NW5 ....12 C3
Carlton Rd London N4 .5 C4
London W4 ....37 C4
Mortlake SW14 ......55 B3
Carlton Sq E1 ......25 C1
Carlton St SW1 ...119 B3

Carltons The ⑤
SW15 ....58 A2
Carlton Tower Pl
SW1 ....131 A2
Carlton Vale NW6 ...23 C3
Carlton Vale Inf Sch
NW6 ....23 B2
Carlyle Cl ⑩ 20 C4
Carlyle Ct SW6 ...166 B3
Carlyle Ho ⑧ SE5 .48 B3
SW3 ....157 C2
⑦ London N16 ....7 A1
Carlyle Mans SW3 .158 A3
Carlyle Mews E1 ...25 C1
Carlyle Pl SW15 ...57 C3
Carlyle's Ho* SW3 .158 A3
Carlyle's Sq SW3 .143 C1
Carlyle Sq SW3 ...143 C1
Carmalt Gdns SW15 .57 B3
Carmarthen Ho ⑧
SW15 ....69 B4
Carmarthen Pl
SE1 ....138 A4
Carmel Ct W8 .....128 A4
Carmelite St EC4 ..121 C4
Carmen St E14 .....34 A3
Carmichael Cl ⑤
SW11 ....59 C4
Carmichael Ct ⑤
SW13 ....46 B1
Carmichael Ho ⑥
E14 ....34 B2
Carmichael Mews
SW18 ....71 C4
Carminia Rd SW17 .73 A2
Carnaby St* W1 ..104 C1
Carnac St SE21,SE27 .75 C1
Carnegie Ho NW3 ...2 C1
Carnegie Pl SW19 .69 C1
Carnegie St N1 .....85 A3
Carnicot Ho ⑨
SE15 ....50 A2
Carnoustie Dr N1 .14 B1
Carnwath Ho SW6 .59 A4
Carnwath Rd SW6 .59 A4
Caroline Cl W2 ...114 B3
Streatham SW16 .....74 B1
London W2 ....114 B3
⑳ London W6 ....39 B1
Caroline Gdns E2 ..98 B4
Caroline Ho W2 ...114 B3
London W6 ....39 B1
Caroline Martyn Ho ⑧
N19 ....4 C4
Caroline Pl W2 ...114 B3
London SW11 ....169 C1
Caroline Pl Mews
W2 ....114 B3
Caroline St E1 ......32 C3
Caroline Terr SW1 .145 B3
Caroline Wlk W6 ..154 A3
Carol St NW1 ....82 C4
Caronia Ct ④ SE16 .41 A2
Carpenter Ho
⑩ E14 ....33 C4
⑥ London N19 ......13 C4
Carpenters Bsns Pk
E15 ....19 A1
Carpenters Ct NW1 .82 C4
Carpenters' Pl SW4 .61 C3
Carpenters Prim Sch
E15 ....19 C4
Carpenter's Rd E15 .19 A1
Carpenter St W1 ..118 A3
Carrara Wharf SW6 .58 A4
Carrara Wlk ⑯ SW9 .63 A3
Carriage Dr E
SW11 ....159 C2
Carriage Drive E
SW11 ....159 B1

Carriage Drive N
SW11,SW8 ....159 C3
Carriage Dr N
SW11 ....158 C2
SW8,SW11 ....159 C3
Carriage Dr S
SW11 ....169 B4
Carriage Dr W
SW11 ....158 C1
Carrick Ho SE11 ...150 A2
London N7 ....14 B2
Carrick Mews SE8 .51 C4
Carrington Ct SW11 .60 A3
Carrington Ho W1 .118 A1
Carrington Lo ⑧
TW10 ....54 A2
Carrington St
TW10 ....54 C3
Carrington St W1 .118 A1
Carrol Cl NW5 ....13 A4
Carroll Ho W2 ....115 B4
Carron Cl E14 ......34 A3
Carroun Rd SW8 ..162 C2
Carr St ⑥ E14 ......33 A3
Carslake Rd SW15 .57 B1
Carson Rd E16 ......35 C4
Dulwich SE21 ....75 C2
Carter Ct EC4 .....108 B1
Carteret Ho ⑧ W12 .30 A2
Carteret St SW1 ..133 B3
Carteret Way SE8 ..41 A2
Carter Ho ❶
⑪ London SW2 ......62 C2
⑥ SE14 ....51 A4
Carter La EC4 .....108 B1
Carter Pl SE17 ....151 A1
Carters Cl ❶ NW5 .13 C2
Carter's Rd SE17 .150 C1
Carter's Yd SW18 .58 C2
Carthew Rd W6 ....39 A3
Carthew Villas W6 .39 A3
Carthusian St EC1 .108 C4
Cartier Circ E14 ...34 B1
Carting La WC2 ...120 B3
Cartmel NW1 ....92 C4
Carton Ho SE16 ..139 B2
⑫ London W11 ......30 C2
Cartwright Gdns
WC1 ....94 A3
Cartwright Ho SE1 .137 A1
Cartwright St E1 ..125 A3
Cartwright Way
SW13 ....47 A3
Carvel Ho E14 ......42 B1
Carver Cl ⑧ W4 ....37 B3
Carver Rd SE24 ....63 B1
Carville Cres TW8 .36 A2
Caryl Ho ⑧ SW19 .69 C3
Carysfort Rd N16 ..15 C4
Casby Ho SE16 ...139 B2
Casella Rd SE14 ...50 C3
Casey Cl NW8 ....90 B3
Casino Ave SE24 ..63 C2
Caspian Ho ⑦ E1 ..32 C4
Caspian St SE5 ....48 C3
Cassandra Ct NW2 ..9 B2
Cassel Ho SW9 ....172 B2
Casserley Ho W4 ..37 C3
Cass Ho ⑳ E9 ....17 C2
Cassidy Rd SW6 ..155 B1
Cassinghurst SE24 .63 C2
Cassland Rd E9 ....17 C2
Casson Ho E1 .....111 B4
Casson St E1 ......111 B3
Castalia Sq ⑥ E14 .42 B4
Castellain Mans W9 .88 B2
Castellain Rd W9 ..88 B2
Castell Ho ⑧ SE8 ..51 C3

Castello Ave SW15 ..57 B2
Castelnau SW13 ....47 A3
Casterbridge NW6 ..78 B4
 3 London W11 ....31 C3
Casterton St E8 ....17 A2
Castleacre W2 ......102 A1
Castle Baynard St
EC4 ....122 C4
Castlebrook CI
SE11 ....150 A4
Castle CI London E9 ..18 A3
 London W3 ....37 A4
Wimbledon SW19 ....69 C1
Castlecombe Dr
SW19 ....69 C4
Castle CI EC3 .....109 C1
Castleden Ho NW6 ..11 C1
Castleford Ct NW8 ..89 C2
Castlefrank Ho N1 ..98 B4
Castlegate TW9 ....54 B4
Castlehaven Rd
NW1 ....13 A1
Castle Ho SE1 .....150 C4
SW8 ....162 B2
Castle Ind Est
SE17 ....150 C4
Castle La SW1 .....132 C2
Castlemaine SW11 ..169 A2
Castle Mead SE5 ....48 B3
Castle Mews NW1 ..13 A2
Castlenau Gdns
SW13 ....47 A4
Castlenau Mans
SW13 ....47 A4
Castlenau Row
SW13 ....47 A4
Castle PI 8 W4 ....38 A2
Castle Rd NW1 ......13 A2
Castlereagh St W1 ..102 C2
Castleton Ho 2 E14 ..42 B2
Castletown Rd
W14 ....140 B1
Castleview CI N4 ....6 B2
Castle Way SW19 ..69 C1
Castle Yd SE1 .....122 B2
 London N6 ....3 C4
Castor La E14 ......34 A2
Caterham Rd SE13 ..67 C4
Catesby Ho 22 E9 ..17 B1
Catesby St SE17 ...151 C3
Cathay Ho SE16 ....40 A4
Cathay St 8 SE16 ..40 A4
Cathcart Hill N19 ....4 B1
Cathcart Rd SW10 ..156 C4
Cathcart St NW5 ....13 A2
Cathedral Ct EC4 ..108 B2
Cathedral Sch of St
Saviour & St Mary
Overie Prim Sch
SE1 ....137 A4
Cathedral St SE1 ..123 B2
Catherall Rd N5,N16 ..6 B1
Catherine Baird Ct 3
SW12 ....73 A4
Catherine Dr TW9 ..54 A3
Catherine Gr SE10 ..52 A2
Catherine Griffiths Ct
EC1 ....95 C2
Catherine Ho 16 N1 ..24 A4
Catherine PI SW1 ..132 C2
Catherine St WC2 ..120 C4
Cayford Ho 11 NW3 ..12 B3
Catherine Wheel Alley
E1 ....110 B3
Catherine Wheel Yd
SW1 ....118 C1
Catherwood Ct N1 ..87 B1
Cathles SW12 ......61 A1

Cathnor Rd W12 ....39 A4
Catlin St SE16 ......40 A1
Catman Ho N4 ......5 B3
Cato Rd SW4 ....61 C3
Cator St SE15 ......49 B3
SE15 ....49 B4
Cato St W1 ....102 B2
Catton St WC1 .....106 C3
Caughley Ho N11 ..135 B1
Caulfield Ct 12 NW1 13 B1
Caulfield Rd SE15 ..50 A1
Causeway The
SW18 ....59 A2
Causton Cotts 3
E14 ....33 A3
Causton Ho SE5 ....48 B3
Causton Rd N6 .....4 A4
Causton St SW1 ....147 C2
Cautley Ave SW4 ..61 B2
Cavalry Gdns SW15 58 B2
Cavaye Ho SW10 ..157 A4
Cavaye PI SW10 ...143 A1
Cavell Ho 8 N1 ....24 A4
Cavell St E1 ....32 A4
Cavendish Ave NW8 79 C1
Cavendish CI NW6 ..10 B2
 3 Putney SW15 ....58 A2
Cavendish Ct EC2 ..110 B2
Cavendish Gdns
SW4 ....61 B1
Cavendish Ho NW8 ..79 C1
SW8 ....172 A4
Cavendish Mans
EC1 ....95 B1
 London E5 ....17 B3
 5 London NW6 ....10 C3
 2 London SW12 ..61 B1
Cavendish Mews N
W1 ....104 B4
Cavendish Mews S
W1 ....104 B3
Cavendish Par 3
SW12 ....61 A1
Cavendish PI W1 ..104 B2
Cavendish Prim Sch
W4 ....46 A3
Cavendish Rd
Chiswick W4 ......45 B2
 London W6 ....10 B1
London SW12 ......61 B1
Cavendish Sch The
NW1 ....82 B4
Cavendish Sq W1 ..104 B2
Cavendish St N1 ....87 B1
Cavendish Terr 10
E3 ....26 B2
Caversham Ho 2
N15 ....7 A4
Caversham Ho
SE15 ....49 C4
Caversham Rd NW5 13 B2
Caversham St
SW3 ....158 C4
Caverswall St W12 ..30 B3
Cavour Ho SE17 ...150 B2
Caxton Gr E3 ......26 C2
Caxton Hall SW1 ..133 B2
Caxton Rd W12 ....39 C4
Caxton St SW1 ....133 B2
Caxton St N E16 ..35 B1

Cazenove Rd N16 ..7 C2
Cecil Ct SW10 .....156 C4
WC2 ....120 A3
London NW6 ....11 A1
Cecilia Rd E8 ......16 C3
Cecil Mans 2 SW17 72 C2
Cecil Rd
London NW10 .....21 A4
London W3 ....28 B4
Cecil Rhodes Ho
NW1 ....83 B2
Cedar Ct E1 Bow E3 ..26 B4
East Norwood SE27 75 B2
Cedar Ct W1 ......102 B2
London N1 ....15 B1
Mortlake SW14 .....55 B3
Wimbledon SW19 ..69 C1
Cedar Gr W5 ......36 A3
Cedar Ho 6 E14 ....42 B4
 16 SE16 ....40 C4
W8 ....128 A2
Cedar Lo NW2 ......10 B2
Cedar Lo SW6 .....47 C2
Cedarne Rd SW6 ..156 A1
Cedar Rd NW2 ......9 B4
Cedars CI SE13 ....67 C4
Cedars Ct SW15 ....56 C1
Cedars Ho 2 SW2 ..62 B3
Cedars Mews SW4 ..61 A3
Cedars Rd
Barnes SW13 ......46 C1
 London SW4 ......61 A3
London W4 ....38 A1
Cedar The E9 ......17 C1
Cedar Terr TW9 ....54 A3
Cedar Tree CI SE5 ..48 B2
Cedar Way NW1 ....83 B4
Cedra Ct N16 ......7 C3
Cedric Chambers
NW8 ....89 B2
Celadine CI E3,E14 33 C4
Celandine Dr E8 ...16 B1
Celbridge Mews
W2 ....100 B2
Celestial Gdns SE13 67 C3
Celia Ct 7 TW9 ....44 B2
Celia Ho 10 N1 ....24 A3
Celia Rd N19 ......13 B4
Celtic St E14 ......34 A4
Cenacle CI NW3 ....1 C1
Cenotaph* SW1 ...134 A4
Centaur Ct 3 TW8 ..36 A1
Centaur St SE1 ....135 A2
Central Ave SW11 ..159 A1
Central Bsns Ctr
NW10 ....8 A3
Central Criminal Court
(Old Bailey)*
EC4 ....108 B2
Central Foundation
Lower Sch E3 .....26 A2
Central Foundation Sch
EC2 ....97 C2
Central Foundation
Upper Sch E3 .....26 B2
Central Middlesex Hospl
NW10 ....20 B2
Central Par W3 ....37 A4
Central Sch of Speech &
Drama The SW3 ....11 C1
Central School of Ballet
EC1 ....95 C1
Central St EC1 .....96 C3

Central St Martins Coll
of Art & Design (The
London Inst)
WC1 ....106 C3
Central St Martin's Sch
of Art & Design
W1 ....105 C1
Central Way NW10 ..20 B2
Centre Ave
London NW10 .....22 B2
London W3 ....28 C1
Centre Bldg SE17 ..151 A4
Centre Hts 5 NW3 ..11 C1
Centre Point SE1 ..153 B2
Centre St E2 ....25 A3
Centurion CI N7 ....14 B1
Centurion La E3 ....26 B3
Century Ho SE13 ..52 A1
Cephas Av E1 ......25 B1
Cephas Ho 5 E1 ....25 B1
Cephas St E1 ......25 B1
Cerise Rd SE15 ....49 C2
Cerney Mews W2 ..115 B4
Cervantes Ct W2 ..100 B1
Ceylon Rd W14 ...126 A1
 6 London W14 ....39 C3
Chadacre Ho 10
SW9 ....63 A3
Chadbourn St E14 ..34 A4
Chadston Ho 11 N1 ..15 A1
Chadswell SE1 .....94 B3
Chadwick CI SW15 ..68 B4
Chadwick Rd
London NW10 .....21 B4
London SE15 ......49 B1
Chadwick St SW1 ..133 B1
Chadworth Ho EC1 ..96 C3
London N4 ....6 B3
Chagford Ho 31 E3 ..27 A2
 7 London NW1 ....90 C1
Chagford St NW1 ..91 A1
Chalbury Ho 2
SW9 ....62 B3
Chalbury Wlk N1 ...85 B2
Chalcot Cres NW1 ..81 A4
Chalcot Gdns NW3 ..12 B2
Chalcot Mews
SW16 ....74 A1
Chalcot Rd NW1 ....81 B4
Chalcot Sch NW1 ..13 A1
Chalcot Sq NW1 ...12 C1
Chaldon Rd SW6 ..154 B2
Chale Rd SW2 .....62 A1
Chalfont Ct NW1 ...91 A1
Chalfont Ho 2
SE16 ....40 A3
Chalford 7 NW3 ...11 B2
Chalford Ct 15
W14 ....140 C1
Chalkers Cnr TW9 ..55 A4
Chalk Farm Rd NW1 82 B4
Chalk Farm Sta
NW1 ....12 C1
Chalk Hill Rd W6 ..39 C2
Chalkwell Ho 9 E1 ..32 C3
Challenge CI NW10 21 A4
Challenger Ho 7
E14 ....33 A2
Challice Way SW2 ..74 B3
Challoner Cres
W14 ....140 C1
Challoner Mans
W14 ....140 C1
Challoner St W14 ..140 C1
Chalmers Ho 15
SW11 ....59 B4

Chalmers Wlk 24
SE17 ....48 A4
Chalner Ho SW2 ...74 C3
Chaloner Ct SE1 ...137 B4
Chalsey Rd SE4 ....66 B3
Chalton St NW1 ....83 B1
Chamberlain Cotts
SE5 ....48 C2
Chamberlain Ho 8
E1 ....32 B2
Chamberlain St 7
NW1 ....12 B1
Chamberlayne Mans 3
NW10 ....22 C2
Chamberlayne Rd
NW10 ....22 B4
Chambers La NW10 ..9 B1
Chambers Rd N7 ...14 A4
Chambers St SE16 139 C3
Chamber St E1 ....125 A4
Chambon PI 2 W6 ..38 C2
Chambord Ho 20
E2 ....99 A3
Chambord St E2 ...99 A3
Champion Gr SE5 ..63 C4
Champion Hill SE5 ..63 C4
Champion Pk SE5 ..48 C1
Champlain Ho 20
W12 ....30 A2
Chancel Ct W1 ....119 B4
Chancellor Gr SE21 75 B1
Chancellor Ho
 20 E1 ....32 A1
SW7 ....129 A2
Chancellors' Ct
WC1 ....106 C4
Chancellor's Rd W6 39 B1
Chancellors St W6 ..39 B1
Chancellors Wharf 21
W6 ....39 B1
Chancel St SE1 ....122 A1
Chancery Bldgs 18
E1 ....32 B2
Chancery La EC4 ..107 B2
Chancery Lane Sta
WC1 ....107 B3
Chance St E2 ....98 C2
Chandler Ave E16 ..35 C4
Chandlers Mews
E14 ....41 C4
Chandler St 1 E1 ..32 A1
Chandlers Way 11
SE24 ....63 C2
Chandler Way SE15 49 B3
Chandos PI WC2 ..120 A3
Chandos Rd
London E15 ....19 C3
London NW10 .....21 A1
London NW2 ....9 B3
Chandos St W1 ....104 B3
Chandos Way NW11 ..2 A3
Change Alley EC3 ..109 C1
Channel Ho E14 ...33 A4
Channelsea Bsns Ctr
E15 ....27 C3
Channing Sch N6 ..4 A3
Chantrey Rd SW9 ..62 B4
Chantry CI W9 .....23 B1
Chantry Cres NW10 ..8 B2
Chantry Sq W8 ....128 A1
Chantry St N1 .....86 B3
Chant Sq E15 ......19 C1
Chant St E15 ......19 C1
Chapel CI NW10 ....8 B2

Chapel Ct EC2 98 A3
SE1 137 B4
Chapel House St E14 42 A2
Chapel Market N1 85 B2
Chapel Pl EC2 98 A3
N1 85 C2
W1 104 A1
Chapel Side W2 114 A3
Chapel St NW1 102 A3
SW1 131 C3
Chapleton Ho SW2 62 C2
Chaplin Cl SE1 136 A4
Chaplin Ho 6 SW9 62 C3
Chaplin Rd NW2 8 C2
Chapman Ho 28 E1 32 A3
2 West Norwood SE27 75 A1
Chapman Rd E9 18 B2
Chapmans Park Ind Est NW10 8 B2
Chapman Sq SW19 69 C2
Chapman St E1 32 A2
Chapone Pl W1 105 B1
Chapter Cl 15 W4 37 B3
Chapter Rd SE17 150 B1
London NW2 8 C3
Chapter St SW1 147 B3
Chara Pl W4 45 C4
Charcot Ho 9 SW15 56 B1
Charcroft Ct 11 W14 39 C4
Chard Ho 7 N7 5 B2
Chardin Ho SW9 173 C4
Chardin Rd 11 W4 38 A2
Chardmore Rd N16 7 C3
Charecroft Way W12 39 C4
Charfield Ct W9 88 B1
Charford Rd E16 35 C4
Chargrove Cl 24 SE16 40 C4
Charing Cross SW1 120 A2
Charing Cross Hospl W6 39 C1
Charing Cross Rd WC2 105 C1
Charing Cross Sta WC2 120 B2
Charing Ho SE1 135 C4
Charlbert Ct NW8 80 A2
Charlbert St NW8 80 A2
Charles Allen Ho EC1 95 B4
Charles Auffray Ho 26 E1 32 B4
Charles Barry Cl SW4 61 B4
Charles Burton Ct E5 18 A4
Charles Coveney Rd 4 SE15 49 B2
Charles Darwin Ho 8 E2 25 A2
Charles Dickens Ho 1 E2 25 A2
Charles Dickens Prim Sch SE1 136 C3
Charles Edward Brooke Sch SW9 48 A2
Charles Haller St 25
... 74 C4
Charles Harrod Ct SW13 47 B4
Charles Hobson Ho NW10 8 A1
Charles Hocking Ho 8 W3 37 B4
Charles II Pl SW3 144 C1
Charles II St SW1 119 B2
Charles La NW8 80 A2
Charles Lamb Prim Sch N1 86 C4
Charles Mackenzie Ho SE16 153 C4
Charles Pl NW1 93 A3
Charles Rowan Ho WC1 95 B3
Charles Sq N1 97 C3
Charles St W1 118 A2
Barnes SW13 46 A1
Charleston St SE17 151 A3
Charles Townsend Ho EC1 96 A2
Charlesworth Ho 2 E14 33 C3
Charleville Ct SW5 140 C1
Charleville Mans W14 140 B1
Charleville Rd W14 140 C1
Charlotte Ho 12 W6 39 B1
Charlotte Mews W1 105 A4
W14 140 A4
London W10 30 C3
Charlotte Pl SW1 146 C3
W1 105 A3
Charlotte Rd EC2 24 A1 98 A2
Barnes SW13 46 B2
Charlotte Row SW4 61 B4
Charlotte Sharman Prim Sch SE11 136 A1
Charlotte Sq 5 TW10 54 B1
Charlotte St W1 105 A4
Charlotte Terr N1 85 A3
Charlow Cl SW6 166 C1
Charlton Ct 28 E2 24 B4
17 London N7 13 C3
Charlton Ho NW1 93 B4
5 Brentford TW8 44 A4
Charlton King's Rd NW5 13 C3
Charlton Pl N1 86 A2
Charlton Rd NW10 21 A4
Charlton Way SE10, SE3 53 A2
Charlwood Ho SW1 147 B3
1 Streatham SW2 74 B3
Charlwood Pl SW1 147 A3
Charlwood Rd SW15 57 C3
Charlwood St SW1 147 A2
Charlwood Terr 5 SW15 57 C3
Charman Ho SW8 162 A2
18 London SW2 62 C1
Charmian Ho 19 N1 24 A3
Charmouth Ct TW10 54 B2
Charmouth Ho SW8 162 C2
Charnock Ho 22 W12 30 A2
Charnwood Gdns E14 41 C2
Charrington St NW1 83 B2
Charter Ct W1 102 B3
London N4 5 C3
Charter Ho WC2 106 B1
Charterhouse Bldgs EC1 96 C1
Charterhouse Mews EC1 108 B4
Charterhouse Rd E8 16 C3
Charterhouse Sq EC1 108 B4
Charterhouse Square Prim Sch The EC1 108 A4
Charterhouse St EC1 108 A4
Charteris Rd NW6 23 B4
London N4 5 C3
Charter Nightingale Hospl The NW1 102 B4
Charter Sch The SE24 63 C2
Chartes Ho SE1 138 B2
Chartfield Ave SW15 57 B2
Chartfield Sch SW15 57 A2
Chartfield Sq SW15 57 C2
Chartham Ct 13 SW9 62 C4
Chartham Gr SE27 75 A1
Chartham Ho SE1 137 C2
Chartridge SE17 48 C4
Chart St N1 97 C4
Chartwell 23 SW19 69 C3
Chase Ct SW3 130 C1
Chase Ctr The NW10 20 C2
Chaseley Ct W4 37 A1
Chaseley St E14 33 A3
Chasemore Ho SW6 154 B2
Chase Rd NW10 20 C1
Chase Road Trad Est NW10 20 C1
Chase The SW4 61 A4
Chater Ho 6 E2 25 C2
Chatfield Rd SW11 59 B4
Chatham Ct SW11 60 B2
Chatham Ho 7 SE5 49 A1
Chatham Pl E9 17 B2
Chatham Rd SW11 60 B2
Chatham St SE17 151 C4
Chatsworth Ct W8 141 B4
London E5 17 C4
Chatsworth Est E5 17 C4
Chatsworth Gdns W3 28 A1
Chatsworth Lo 1 W4 37 C1
Chatsworth Rd
Chiswick W4 45 B4
London E5 17 C4
London NW2 9 C2
Chatsworth Way SE27 75 B1
Chattenden Ho 8 N4 6 C4
Chatterton Ct TW9 44 B1
Chatterton Rd N4 6 A1
Chatto Rd SW11 60 B2
Chaucer Ave TW9 44 C1
Chaucer Ct 17 N16 16 A4
Chaucer Dr SE1 153 A3
Chaucer Ho SW1 146 C1
Chaucer Rd
London SE24 63 A2
London W3 28 B1
Chaulden Ho EC1 97 C3
Cheadle Ct NW8 89 C2
Cheadle Ho 11 E14 33 B3
Cheam St 4 SE15 65 A4
Cheapside EC2 109 A1
Chearsley SE17 151 A4
Cheddington Ho 9 E2 24 C4
Chedworth Cl E16 35 B1
Chedworth Ho 2 E5 7 C2
Cheesemans Terr W14 140 C1
Chelmer Rd E9 17 C3
Chelmsford Cl W6 47 C4
Chelmsford Ho 5 N7 14 B4
Chelmsford Sq NW10 22 B4
Chelsea Barracks SW1 145 C1
Chelsea Bridge SW1 160 A4
Chelsea Bridge Rd SW1 145 C1
Chelsea Cl NW10 20 C4
Chelsea Cloisters SW3 144 B3
Chelsea Coll of Art & Design SW3 144 A1
London W12 39 B4
Chelsea Cres SW10 167 A3
Chelsea Ct SW3 159 B4
Chelsea Emb SW3 158 C3
Chelsea Est SW3 158 A3
Chelsea Farm Ho SW10 157 C3
Chelsea Gate SW1 145 C1
Chelsea Gdns SW1 145 C1
Chelsea Harbour Design Ctr SW10 167 A4
Chelsea Harbour Dr SW10 167 A4
Chelsea Harbour Pier SW10 167 B3
Chelsea Lo SW3 159 A4
SW6 166 A4
Chelsea Manor Ct SW3 158 B4
Chelsea Manor Gdns SW3 144 B1
Chelsea Manor St SW3 144 B1
Chelsea Manor Studios SW3 144 B1
Chelsea Park Gdns SW3 157 B4
Chelsea Physic Gdn* SW1 158 C4
Chelsea Reach Twr SW10 157 B2
Chelsea Sq SW3 143 C1
Chelsea Twrs SW3 158 B4
Chelsea & Westminster Hospl SW10 157 A3
Chelsfield Ho SE17 152 A3
Chelsfield Point 3 E9 17 C1
Chelsham Ho 1 SW4 61 C4
Chelsham Rd SW4 61 C4
Cheltenham Pl 1 W3 37 A4
Cheltenham Rd SE15 65 B2
Cheltenham Terr SW3 145 A2
Chelverton Ct SW15 57 C3
Chelverton Rd SW15 57 C3
Chelwood NW5 12 C3
Chelwood Ct SW11 167 C4
Chelwood Gdns TW9 44 C1
Chelwood Ho W2 101 C1
Chenies Ho W2 114 A4
Chenies Mews WC1 93 B1
Chenies Pl NW1 83 C2
Chenies St WC1 105 B4
Chenies The NW1 83 C2
Cheniston Gdns W8 128 A2
Chepstow Cl SW15 58 A2
Chepstow Cres W11 31 C2 113 B4
Chepstow Ct W11 113 B4
Chepstow Pl W2 31 C2 113 C4
Chepstow Rd W2 31 C3
Chepstow Villas W11 31 C2 113 B4
Chequers Ct EC1 97 C1
Chequers Ho NW8 90 A2
Chequer St EC1 97 A1
Cherbury Ct N1 87 C1
Cherbury St N1 87 C1
Cheriton Ho 9 E5 17 A3
Cheriton Sq SW17 72 C2
Cherry Cl 7 SW2 74 C4
Cherry Ct W3 29 A1
Cherry Garden Ho 5 SE16 40 A4
Cherry Garden Sch SE16 153 C4
Cherry Garden St SE16 40 A4
Cherry Laurel Wlk SW2 62 B1
Cherry Tree Cl 17 E9 25 B4
Cherry Tree Dr SW16 74 A1
Cherrytree Ho 8 W10 22 C2
Cherry Tree Ho SE14 51 B1
Cherry Trees Sch The E3 26 C2
Cherry Tree Terr SE1 138 B4
Cherry Tree Wlk EC1 97 A1
Cherrywood Cl E3 26 A2
Cherrywood Dr SW15 57 C2
Chertsey Ct SW14 55 A4
Chertsey Ho E2 98 C3
Cherwell Ho NW8 89 C1
Cheryls Cl SW6 166 B4
Chesham Cl SW1 131 B1
Chesham Ct SW18 71 C4
Chesham Flats W1 117 C4
Chesham Mews SW1 131 B2
Chesham Pl SW1 131 B1
Chesham St SW1 131 B1

Cheshire St
E2 . . . . .24 C1 99 B2
Chesholm Rd N16 . . . .7 A1
Cheshunt Ho NW6 . . .78 A3
Chesil Ct ⑪ E2 . . . . .25 B3
SW3 . . . . .158 B4
Chesilton Rd SW6 .164 C4
Chesney Ct W9 . . . . .23 C1
Chesney Ho SE13 . .67 C3
Chesney St SW11 . .169 B3
Chessington Ho
SW8 . . . . .171 B2
Chesson Rd W14 . . .155 A4
Chester Ave TW10 . .54 B1
Chester Cl SW1 . . . .132 A3
Barnes SW13 . . . . . .57 A4
⑪ Richmond TW10 . .54 B1
Chester Close N
NW1 . . . . .92 B4
Chester Close S
NW1 . . . . .92 B3
Chester Cres E8 . . . .16 B3
Chester Ct NW1 . . . .92 B3
④ SE5 . . . . .48 C3
SE8 . . . . .40 C1
London NW5 . . . . .4 B1
Chesterfield Gdns
SE10 . . . . .52 C3
W1 . . . . .118 A2
Chesterfield Gr
SE22 . . . . .64 B2
Chesterfield Hill
W1 . . . . .118 A3
Chesterfield Ho
W1 . . . . .117 C2
Chesterfield Rd W4 .45 B4
Chesterfield St
W1 . . . . .118 A2
Chesterfield Way
SE15 . . . . .50 B3
Chesterford Gdns
NW3 . . . . .11 A4
Chester Gate NW1 . .92 B3
Chester Ho ⑪ SE8 . .51 B4
London N19 . . . . .4 A2
Chesterman Ct W4 .46 A3
Chester Mews
SW1 . . . . .132 A2
Chester Pl NW1 . . . .92 A4
Chester Rd NW1 . . . .92 B4
London N19 . . . . .4 A2
Chester Row SW1 .145 C4
Chester Sq SW1 . .146 A4
Chester Sq Mews
SW1 . . . . .132 A1
Chester St E2 . . . . . .24 C4
E2 . . . . .24 C1 99 C2
SW1 . . . . .131 C2
Chester Terr NW1 . .92 A4
Chesterton Cl SW18 .58 C2
Chester Way SE11 .149 C3
Chesterton Ho
③ W10 . . . . .30 C2
㉑ London SW11 . . . .59 C4
Chesterton Prim Sch
SW11 . . . . .169 B3
Chesterton Rd W10 .31 A4
Chesterton Sq W8 .141 B3
Chester Way SE11 .149 C3
Chestnut Alley
SW6 . . . . .155 A3
Chestnut Ave ⑪
SW14 . . . . .55 C4
Chestnut Cl
⑪ London N16 . . . . .6 C2
SE6 . . . . .51 B2
Chestnut Ct SW6 . .155 A4
Chestnut Gr SW12 . .72 C3

Chestnut Grove Sch
SW12 . . . . .72 C3
Chestnut Ho
⑦ London NW3 . . . .12 B2
London SE7 . . . . .66 B4
⑪ London W4 . . . . . .38 A2
West Norwood SE27 .75 B1
Chestnuts The ⑪
N5 . . . . .15 A4
Chettle Cl SE1 . . . .137 B2
Chetwode Ho NW8 .90 A2
Chetwynd Rd NW5 . .4 A1
Chetwynd Rd NW5 . .4 A1
Cheval Ct SW15 . . . .57 A3
Cheval Pl SW7 . . . .130 B2
Cheval St E14 . . . . . .41 C3
Chevening Rd NW6 .23 A4
SE10 . . . . .43 B1
Cheverell Ho ⑤④ E2 .24 C3
Cheverton Rd N19 . . .4 C3
Chevet St E9 . . . . . . .18 A3
Chevington NW2 . . .10 B2
Cheviot Cl ⑪ SE14 . .50 B3
Cheviot Gate NW2 . . .1 A2
Cheviot Gdns NW2 . . .1 A2
Cheviot Ho N16 . . . . .7 B3
Chevron Cl E16 . . . . .35 C3
Cheylesmore Ho
SW1 . . . . .146 A2
Cheyne Gdns SW3 .158 B3
Cheyne Mews SW3 .158 B3
Cheyne Row SW3 . .158 A3
Cheyne Wlk SW10 .157 B2
Cheyney Ho ② E9 . .17 C2
Chichele Rd NW2 . . . .9 C3
Chicheley St SE1 . .135 A4
Chichester Ho NW6 .23 C3
Chichester Rd NW6 .23 C3
London W2 . . . . . . .100 B4
Chichester Rents
WC2 . . . . .107 B2
Chichester St SW1 .147 A1
Chichester Way E14 .42 C2
Chicksand St E1 . . .111 B3
Chicksand St E1 . . .111 B3
Chiddingstone SE13 .67 B2
Chiddingstone St
SW6 . . . . .165 C2
Chigwell Hill E1 . . . .32 A2
Chilam Ho ⑤ SE15 . .50 B4
Chilcombe Ho ⑥
SW15 . . . . .68 C4
Chilcot Cl ⑪ E14 . . .34 A3
Childebert Rd SW17 .73 A2
Childeric Prim Sch
SE14 . . . . .51 A3
Childeric Rd SE14 . .51 A3
Childerley St SW6 .164 A4
Childers St SE8 . . . .51 B4
Child La SE10 . . . . . .43 B3
Child's Hill Prim Sch
NW2 . . . . .1 A1
Child's Pl SW5 . . . .141 C3
Child's St SW5 . . . .141 C3
Child's Wlk SW5 . . .141 C3
Chilham Ct ⑭ SW9 .62 C4
Chilham Ho ⑪ SE1 .137 C2
Chillingworth Rd
N7 . . . . .14 C3
Chiltern Ct NW1 . . . .91 A1
⑱ SE14 . . . . .50 B3
Chiltern Ho SE17 . . .48 C4
④ W10 . . . . .31 A4
⑤ London N16 . . . . . .7 B3

Chiltern Rd E3 . . . . .26 C1
Chiltern St W1 . . . .103 B4
Chilton Gr SE8 . . . . .41 A2
Chilton Rd TW9 . . . .54 C4
Chilton St E2 . .24 B1 99 A2
Chilver St SE10 . . . . .43 B1
Chilworth Ct ⑧
SW19 . . . . .69 C3
Chilworth Mews
W2 . . . . .101 B1
Chilworth St W2 . . .101 A1
Chimney Ct ㉒ E1 . . .32 A1
China Ct ⑪ E1 . . . . .32 A2
China Mews ⑰ SW2 .74 B4
Chindit Ho ⑪ N1 . . .15 C2
Chinnocks Wharf
E14 . . . . .33 A2
Chipka St E14 . . . . . .42 B4
Chipley St SE14 . . . .51 A4
Chippendale Ho
SW1 . . . . .146 B1
Chippenham Gdns
NW6 . . . . .23 C2
Chippenham Mews
W9 . . . . .23 C1
Chip St SW4 . . . . . . .61 C3
Chipstead Ho ④
SW2 . . . . .74 C2
Chipstead St SW6 .165 C2
Chisenhale Prim Sch
E3 . . . . .26 A3
Chisenhale Rd E3 . .26 A3
Chisholm Ct W6 . . . .38 C1
Chisholm Rd ⑪
TW10 . . . . .54 B1
Chisledon Wlk E9 . .18 B2
Chislehurst Rd ⑪
TW10 . . . . .54 A2
Chislet ⑤ NW5 . . . .12 C2
Chiswell St EC1 . . .109 B4
Chiswick & Bedford
Park Prep Sch W4 .38 A2
Chiswick Common Rd
W4 . . . . .37 C2
Chiswick Com Sch
W4 . . . . .45 B3
Chiswick Green Studios
⑪ W4 . . . . .37 B2
Chiswick High Rd
W4 . . . . .38 A2
Chiswick High Road
(North Circular Rd)
W4 . . . . .36 C1
Chiswick Ho * W4 . .45 C4
Chiswick La W4 . . . .38 A1
Chiswick La S W4 . . .46 B4
Chiswick Mall W4 . .38 B1
Chiswick Maternity
Hospl W4 . . . . .38 B1
Chiswick Park Sta
W4 . . . . .37 A2
Chiswick Pier W4 . .46 B3
Chiswick Plaza W4 .45 B4
Chiswick Quay W4 .45 B2
Chiswick Rd W4 . . . .37 B2
Chiswick Rdbt W4 . .36 C1
Chiswick Sq W4 . . . .46 A4
Chiswick Staithe
W4 . . . . .45 B2
Chiswick Terr ⑥
W4 . . . . .37 B2
Chiswick Village
W4 . . . . .45 A4
Chiswick Wharf W4 .46 B4

Chitty St W1 . . . . . .105 A4
Chivalry Rd SW11 . .60 A2
Chivelston ㉗ SW19 .69 C3
Chobham Gdns
SW19 . . . . .69 C2
Chobham Rd E15 . . .19 C3
Cholmeley Cres N6 . .4 A4
Cholmeley Lo N6 . . . .4 A3
Cholmeley Pk N6 . . . .4 A4
Cholmley Gdns
NW6 . . . . .10 C3
Cholmondeley Ave
NW10 . . . . .21 C3
Chopin's Ct ⑯ E1 . . .32 A1
Chopwell Cl E15 . . . .19 C1
Choumert Gr SE15 . .49 C1
Choumert Mews
SE15 . . . . .49 C1
Choumert Rd SE15 .49 B1
Choumert Sq ⑦
SE15 . . . . .49 C1
Chow Sq ⑧ E8 . . . . .16 B3
Chrisp Ho SE10 . . . . .53 A4
Chrisp St E14 . . . . . .34 A3
Christchurch Ave
NW6 . . . . .10 A1
Christ Church Bentinck
CE Prim Sch NW1 102 B3
Christchurch CE Prim
Sch SW3 . . . . .158 C4
Christ Church CE Prim
Sch
SE10 . . . . .43 A1
London NW6 . . . . . . .10 B1
London SW11 . . . . . .60 B1
Christ Church CE Sch
E1 . . . . .110 C3
Christ Church Ct
London NW10 . . . . . .21 A4
London NW6 . . . . . . .10 A1
Christchurch Hill
NW3 . . . . .11 C4
Christchurch Ho ②
SW2 . . . . .74 A3
Christchurch Pas
NW3 . . . . .2 B1
Christ Church Prim Sch,
Hampstead NW3 . . . .2 C1
Christchurch Rd
SW14 . . . . .55 B2
Christ Church Sch
NW1 . . . . .92 B4
Christ Church Sq ④
E9 . . . . .25 B4
Christchurch St
SW3 . . . . .158 C4
Christ Church
Streatham CE Prim Sch
SW2 . . . . .74 B3
Christchurch Terr
SW3 . . . . .158 C4
Christchurch Way
SE10 . . . . .43 A1
Christian Ct SE16 . . .33 B1
Christian St E1 . . . .111 C1
Christie Ct
⑪ London N19 . . . . .5 A2
London NW3 . . . . . .12 A3
Christie Ho ② SE10 .43 B1
Christie Rd E9 . . . . . .18 A2
Christina Sq N4 . . . . .6 A3
Christina St EC2 . . . .98 A2
Christopher Boone's
Almshouses ⑦
SE13 . . . . .67 C3
Christopher Cl SE16 .40 C4
Christopher Hatton Prim
Sch EC1 . . . . .95 C1

Christopher Lo ② N6 .4 C4
Christopher Pl NW1 .93 C3
Christopher St EC2 . .97 C1
Christ's Coll SE3 . . . .53 C2
Christ's Sch (East Side)
TW10 . . . . .54 C2
Christ's Sch (West Side)
TW10 . . . . .54 B2
Christ the King RC Prim
Sch N4 . . . . .5 B2
Christ the King RC Sixth
Form Coll SE13 . . . .67 C4
Chryssell Rd SW9 .163 C1
Chubworthy St
SE14 . . . . .51 A4
Chudleigh Rd
London NW6 . . . . .9 C1
London SE4 . . . . .66 C2
Chudleigh St E1 . . . .32 C3
Chumleigh Gdns
SE5 . . . . .49 A4
Chumleigh St SE5 . .49 A4
Church App SE21 . . .75 C1
Church Ave NW1 . . .13 A2
Mortlake SW14 . . . . .55 C4
Church Cl W8 . . . . .128 A4
Church Cres E9 . . . .17 C1
Churchcroft Cl
SW12 . . . . .72 C4
Church Ct EC4 . . . .107 C1
Churchdale Ct
W4 . . . . .37 A1
Church Entry EC4 .108 B1
Church Estate
Almshouses ⑧
TW9 . . . . .54 B3
Churchfield Ho W2 .89 B1
Churchfield Mans
SW6 . . . . .165 A1
Churchfield Rd W3 .28 B1
Churchfields SE10 . .52 B4
Church Garth ⑧ N19 .4 C2
Church Gate SW6 . . .58 A4
Church Gn SW9 . . . .173 C2
Church Gr SE13 . . . .67 A2
Churchill Ct
London N4 . . . . .5 C4
London NW2 . . . . .9 A3
Churchill Gardens Prim
Sch SW1 . . . . .147 A1
Churchill Gdns
SW1 . . . . .160 C4
Churchill Gdns Rd
SW1 . . . . .160 B4
Churchill Pl E14 . . . .34 A1
Churchill Rd
London NW2 . . . . .9 A2
London NW5 . . . . . . .13 A4
Church Mead SE5 . .48 B3
Churchmead Rd
NW10 . . . . .8 C2
Church Path W4 . . . .37 B3
London SW1 . . . . . . .19 A3
Church Rd Acton W3 .37 B4
Barnes SW13 . . . . . .46 C2
⑫ London N1 . . . . . .15 A2
London NW10 . . . . . . .8 A1
Richmond TW10,TW9 .54 A2
Church Row NW3 . .11 B4
Church St NW8 . . . . .90 A1
Chiswick W4 . . . . . . .46 B4
Churchward Ho
SE17 . . . . .48 A4
SW5 . . . . .141 A1

Churchway WlK 93 C4

Church Wlk
  Barnes SW13 ....46 C2
  London N16 ....15 C4
  London NW2 ....1 B1

Churchyard Row
  SE11 ....150 B4
Churnfield ☑ N4 ....5 C2
Churston Cl ☑ SW2 ..74 C3
Churston Mans
  WC1 ....95 A1
Churton Pl SW1 .....147 A3
  Brentford W4 ....45 A4
Churton St SW1 .....147 A3
Chute Ho SW9 ....173 B1
Chuter Ede Ho
  SW6 ....155 A3
Cicada Ho SE18 .....59 B2
Cicely Ho NW8 ....79 C1
Cicely Rd SE15 ......49 C2
Cinnabar Wharf Central
  E1 ....125 C2
Cinnabar Wharf East
  E1 ....125 C2
Cinnabar Wharf West
  E1 ....125 C2
Cinnamon Cl ☑
  SE15 ....49 B3
Cinnamon Row ☑
  SW11 ....59 B4
Cinnamon St E1 .....32 A1
Cinnamon Wharf
  SE1 ....139 A4
Circle Ho ☑ E14 ....34 C3
Circle The SE1 .....139 A4
Circus Lo NW8 ....89 B4
Circus Mews w1 ....102 C4
Circus Pl EC2 ....109 C3
Circus Rd NW8 ....79 B1
Circus St SE10 ......52 B3
Cirencester St ☑ W2 100 A4
Cissbury Ho ☑
  SE26 ....76 C1
Citizen Ho N7 ....14 C4
Citizen Rd N7 ....14 C4
Citron Terr ☑ SE15 .65 A4
Citrus Ho ☑ SE8 ....41 B1
City Airport Pier
  E16 ....35 B1
City and Islington Coll
  EC1 ....96 A4
City Bsns Ctr ☒
  SE16 ....40 B4
City Central Est EC1 96 C3
City Forum EC1 ......96 C4
City Garden Row
  N1 ....86 B1
City Gate E1 ....25 B1
City & Guilds of London
  Art Sch The SE11 .149 C1
City Harbour E14 ...42 A3
City & Islington Coll
  N1 ....87 B4
  London N4 ....6 A2
City Literature Inst The
  WC2 ....106 B2
City of London Sch
  EC4 ....122 C4
City of London Sch for
  Girls EC2 ....109 A4
City of Westminster Coll
  NW1 ....102 A4
  W2 ....101 B4

City of Westminster
  Coll, Maida Vale Ctr
  W9 ....88 B3
City of Westminster
  Coll, Queens Park Ctr
  W9 ....23 C2
City Rd EC1 ....97 A4
City of London Coll
  EC1 ....108 A1
Civil Service Coll
  SW1 ....146 C3
Clabon Mews SW1 .144 C4
Clack St SE16 ....40 B4
Claire Ct NW2 ....10 A2
Claire Pl E14 ....41 C3
Clancarty Rd SW6 .165 C1
Clandon Cl W3 ....37 A4
Clandon St SE8 ......51 C1
Clanfield Ho ☑
  SW15 ....68 C3
Clanricarde Gdns
  W2 ....31 C2 113 C4
Clapham Common *
  SW4 ....61 A3
Clapham Common North
  Side SW4 ....61 B4
Clapham Common
  South Side SW4 .....61 B2
Clapham Common West
  Side
  London SW11 ....60 C2
  London SW4,SW11 .....60 B3
Clapham Court Terr ☑
  SW4 ....62 A2
Clapham Cres SW4 .61 C3
Clapham Ct ☑ SW4 62 A2
Clapham High St
  SW4 ....61 C3
Clapham High Street Sta
  SW4 ....61 C4
Clapham Junction Est
  SW11 ....60 A4
Clapham Junction Sta
  SW11 ....60 A3
Clapham Manor Ct ☑
  SW4 ....61 B4
Clapham Manor Prim
  Sch SW4 ....61 C4
Clapham Manor St
  SW4 ....61 C4
Clapham Mans SW4 61 B1
Clapham North Sta
  SW4 ....62 A4
Clapham Park Rd
  SW4 ....61 C3
Clapham Park Terr ☑
  SW2 ....62 A2
Clapham Rd SW9 .162 C4
Clapham South Sta
  SW4 ....61 A2
Clapton Comm E5 ....7 C4
Clapton Girls Tec Coll
  E5 ....17 B4
Clapton Pas E5 ......17 B3
Clapton Sq E5 ....17 B3
Clapton Terr E5 ......7 C3
Clapton Way E5 .....16 C4
Clara Grant Prim Sch
  The E3 ....26 C1
Clare Ct WC1 ....94 B3
Claredale Ho ☑ E2 .25 A3
Claredale St E2 .....24 C3
Clare Gdns W11 .....31 A3
Clare Grant Ho ☑
  E14 ....41 C3

Clare Ho ☑ E3 ....26 A4
SE1 ....153 A2
Clare La N1 ....15 B1
Clare Lawn Ave
  SW14 ....55 C2
Clare Mews SW6 ...156 A1
Clare Mkt WC2 .....107 A1
Claremont ☑ SW15 .58 A2
Claremont Cl N1 ....85 C1
  ☒ Streatham SW2 ...74 B3
Claremont Ct ☑ W9 .23 B2
Claremont Gr W4 ...46 A3
Claremont Rd
  London N6 ....4 B4
  London W9 ....23 B3
Claremont Sq N1 ....85 B1
Claremont St SE10 .52 A4
Clarence Ave SW4 ..61 C1
Clarence Ct ☒ W6 ..39 A2
Clarence Gate Gdns
  NW1 ....91 A1
Clarence Gdns NW1 92 B3
Clarence Ho SE17 ..48 B4
Clarence Ho ★
  SW1 ....119 C1
Clarence La SW15 ..56 B1
Clarence Mews
  ☑ SE16 ....32 C1
  Balham SW12 ....73 A4
  London E5 ....17 A3
Clarence Pl ☑ E5 ...17 A3
Clarence Rd
  London E5 ....17 A4
  London N16 ....10 B1
  London NW6 ....10 B1
  Richmond TW9 ....44 C2
Clarence St ☑ TW9 .54 A3
Clarence Terr NW1 ..91 A2
Clarence Way NW1 ..13 A1
Clarence Wlk SW4 .172 A2
Clarendon Cl ☑ W2 .116 A4
  ☒ Hackney E9 ....17 B1
Clarendon Cross
  W11 ....112 B3
Clarendon Ct W9 ....89 A2
  London NW2 ....9 B1
  ☑ Richmond TW9 ....44 C2
Clarendon Dr SW15 .57 B3
Clarendon Flats
  W1 ....103 C1
Clarendon Gdns
  W9 ....89 A1
Clarendon Gr NW1 ..93 B4
Clarendon Ho NW1 ..83 A1
Clarendon Mews
  W2 ....116 A4
Clarendon Pl W2 ...116 A4
Clarendon Rd
  W11 ....31 A1 112 B3
Clarendon Rise
  SE13 ....67 B3
Clarendon St SW1 .146 B2
Clarendon Terr W9 ..89 A2
Clarendon Wlk ☑
  W11 ....31 A3
Clare Pl SW15 ....68 B4
Clare Rd NW10 ......8 C1
  London SE14 ....51 B2
Clare St E2 ....25 A3
Clareville Ct SW7 ..143 A3
Clareville Gr SW7 ..143 A3
Clareville Grove Mews
  SW7 ....143 A3
Clareville St SW7 ..143 A3
Clarewood Ct W1 ..102 C3
Clarewood Wlk
  SW9 ....62 C3

Clarges Ho W1 .....118 B2
Clarges Mews W1 ..118 A2
Clarges St W1 ......118 B2
Claribel Rd SW9 ....48 A1
Claridge Ct SW6 ...164 C3
Clarissa Ho ☑ E14 .34 A3
Clarissa St E8 ....24 B4
Clarke Ho ☑ SW4 ..61 B4
Clarke Path N16 .....7 C3
Clarkes Mews W1 ..103 C4
Clark Lawrence Ct ☑
  SW11 ....59 C4
Clarkson Ho SW11 ..59 C3
Clarkson Rd E16 ....35 B3
Clarkson Row NW1 .82 C1
Clarkson St E2 ......25 A2
Clark's Pl EC2 ......110 A2
Clark St E1 ....32 B4
Classic Mans ☒ E9 .17 B1
Classinghall Ho ☑
  SW15 ....57 C1
Claude Rd SE15 .....50 A1
Claude St E14 ....41 C2
Claudia Jones Way
  SW2 ....62 A1
Claudia St SW19 ....70 A3
Clavell St ☑ SE10 ..52 B4
Claverdale Rd SW2 .74 C4
Clavering Ave SW13 47 A4
Clavering Ho SE13 ..67 C3
Claverton St ☑ SW1 147 A1
Clave St E1 ....32 B1
Claxton Gr W6 ......39 C1
Claybank Gr SE13 ..67 A4
Claybrook Rd W6 ....47 C4
Claydon SE17 ....150 C4
Clayhall Ct ☑ E3 ...26 B3
Claylands Pl SW8 .163 B2
Claylands Rd SW8 .163 A3
Claypole Rd E15 ....27 B3
Claypons Ave SW8 36 A2
Clayponds Hospl & Day
  Treatment Ctr
  W5 ....36 A2
Clayponds La TW8 ..36 A1
Clays Ct N16 ....7 B3
Clays La E15 ....19 A3
Clays Lane E15 ......19 A3
Clay St W1 ....103 A3
Clayton Ct N16 ......7 C4
Clayton Ho ☑ E9 ....17 B1
Clayton Rd SE15 ....49 C2
Clayton St SE11 ...163 B4
Clearbrook Way ☑
  E1 ....32 B3
Clearwater Ho ☑
  TW10 ....54 A2
Clearwater Terr ☑
  W11 ....39 C4
Clearwell Dr W9 .....88 B1
Cleaver Ho ☑ NW3 .12 B1
Cleaver Sq SE11 ...149 C1
Cleaver St SE11 ....149 C2
Cleeve Ho E2 ....98 B3
Cleeve Way SW15 ..68 B4
Clegg St ☑ E1 ......32 A1
Cleland Ho ☒ E2 ....25 B3
Clematis St W12 ....29 C2
Clem Attlee Ct
  SW6 ....155 A3
Clemence St E14 ....33 B4
Clement Attlee Ho
  NW10 ....8 B1
Clement Ave SW4 ..61 C3
Clement Cl
  London NW6 ....9 C1

Clement Cl continued
  London W4 ....37 C2
Clement Ho ☒ SE8 .40 C4
  London W10 ....30 B4
Clements Ave ☑
  E16 ....35 C2
Clements Inn WC2 .107 A1
Clements Inn Pas
  WC2 ....107 A1
Clement's La EC2,
  EC4 ....123 C4
Clement's Rd SE16 .40 A3
Clemson Ho ☑ E8 ..24 B4
Clenham St SE1 ....137 A4
Clenston Mews
  W1 ....102 C2
Clent Ho ☑ N16 ......7 B3
Cleopatra's Needle ★
  WC2 ....120 C3
Clephane Rd ☑ N1 .15 B2
Clephane Rd N N1 ..15 B2
Clephane Rd S N1 ..15 C2
Clere Pl EC2 ....97 C2
Clere St EC2 ....97 C2
Clerkenwell Cl EC1 .95 C1
Clerkenwell Gn EC1 .96 A1
Clerkenwell Parochial
  CE Prim Sch EC1 ...95 B4
Clerkenwell Rd EC1 .96 A1
Clermont Rd E9 .....25 B4
Clevedon Cl N16 .....7 B1
Clevedon Ct SW11 168 A4
  Dulwich SE21 ....75 C1
Clevedon Mans
  NW5 ....12 C4
Cleve Ho NW6 ......11 A1
Cleveland Ave W4 ..38 B2
Cleveland Gdns
  W2 ....100 C1
  Barnes SW13 ....46 B1
Cleveland Gr ☒ E1 .25 B1
Cleveland Mans
  SW9 ....163 B1
  W9 ....23 C1
  ☑ London NW6 ......10 B1
Cleveland Mews
  W1 ....104 C4
Cleveland Pl SW1 .119 A2
Cleveland Rd
  Barnes SW13 ....46 B1
  London N1 ....15 C1
  ☒ London W4 ....37 B3
Cleveland Row
  SW1 ....119 A1
Cleveland Sq W2 ..100 C1
Cleveland St W1 .....92 C1
Cleveland Terr W2 .101 A2
Cleveland Way E1 ..25 B1
Clevedon Cl N16 .....7 B1
Cleve Rd NW6 ......11 A1
Cleverly Cotts W12 .29 B1
Cleverly Est W12 ...29 C2
Cley Ho SE4 ....65 C3
Clichy Ho ☒ E1 .....32 B4
Clifden Rd E5 ....17 B3
Cliff Ct ☑ NW1 .....13 C2
Cliffe Ho ☑ SE10 ...43 B1
Clifford Ave SW14 ..45 B1
Clifford Ct
  London NW10 ....8 A4
  London W2 ....100 A3
  Wandsworth SW18 ...71 C4
Clifford Dr SW9 .....63 A3
Clifford Gdns NW10 22 B3
Clifford Haigh Ho
  SW6 ....47 C3
Clifford Ho W14 ....140 C3

Clifford's Inn Pas
EC4 .... **107** B1
Clifford St W1 .....**118** C3
Clifford Way NW10 ...8 B4
Cliff Rd NW1 ....13 C2
Cliffsend Ho SW9 **173** C3
Cliff Terr SE8 ....51 C1
Cliffview Rd SE13 ..66 C4
Cliff Villas NW1 .....13 C2
Cliff Wlk E16 ....35 B2
Clifton Ave N1 ....29 B1
Clifton Cres SE15 ..50 A3
Clifton Ct NW8 ......**89** B2
SE15 ....50 A3
London N4 ....5 C4
Putney SW15 ....57 C2
Clifton Gate SW10 **156** C4
Clifton Gdns W9 ...**88** C1
London W4 ....37 C2
Clifton Gr E8 ....16 C2
Clifton Hill NW8 ....**78** C3
Clifton Ho E2 ....**98** C2
Clifton Mans **4**
SW9 ....62 C3
Clifton Pl SE16 .....40 B4
W2 ....**101** C1
Clifton Rd E16 ......35 A4
W9 ....**89** A2
London NW10 .....21 C3
Clifton Rise SE14 ..51 A3
Clifton Terr N4 ......5 C2
Clifton Villas W9 ..**100** C4
Clifton Way SE15 ..50 B3
Climsland Ho SE1 **121** C2
Clinch Ct **II** E16 ...35 C4
Cline Ho SW15 .....56 C2
Clinger Ct N1 ....24 A4
Clink St SE1 ....**123** B2
Clinton Rd E3 ....26 A2
Clipper Cl **II** SE16 ..40 C4
Clipper Ho E14 .....42 B1
Clipper Way SE13 ..67 B3
Clipstone Ho **II**
SW15 ....56 C2
Clipstone Mews
W1 ....**104** C4
Clipstone St W1 ...**104** C4
Clissold Cres N16 ..15 C4
Clissold Ct N4 ....6 B2
Clissold Ho **II** N16 ...6 C2
Clitheroe Rd SW9 **172** B1
Clive Ct W9 ....**89** A2
Cliveden Pl SW1 ..**145** B4
Clive Ho SE10 .....52 B4
London SW8 .....**171** B2
Clive Rd SE21,SE27 ..75 C1
Cloak La EC4 ......**123** A4
Clochar Ct NW10 ..21 B4
Clock Ho N16 ....7 B4
Clockhouse Cl
SW19 ....69 B2
Clockhouse Pl
SW15 ....58 A1
Clockhouse The
SW19 ....69 B1
Clock Tower Mews
N1 ....**87** A3
Clock Tower Pl N7 ..14 A2
Cloister Rd
London NW2 ......1 B2
London W3 ....28 B4
Cloisters The N6 .....4 A3
Cloisters The SW9 **173** C3
Clonbrock Rd N16 ..16 A4
Cloncurry St SW6 ..47 C1

Clone Ct **4** W12 ...38 A3
Clonmel Rd SW6 ..**165** A4
Clonmore St SW18 ..70 B3
Clorane Gdns NW3 ..1 C1
Close The **II** SW19 ...70 A2
Close The Mews
N1 ....13 C1
Coborn Mews **3** E3 26 B2
Coborn Rd E3 ......26 B2
Coborn St E3 ....26 B2
Cobourg Prim Sch
SE5 ....49 B4
Cobourg Rd SE5 ...49 B4
Cobourg St NW1 ...**93** A3
Coburg Cl SW1 ....**147** A4
Coburg Cres SW2 ..74 C3
Coburg Dwellings **10**
E1 ....32 B2
Cochrane Cl NW8 ..**79** C1
Cochrane Mews
NW8 ....**79** C1
Cochrane St NW8 ..**79** C1
Coci Ho W14 ....**141** A3
Cockburn Ho NW1 **147** C1
Cock Hill E1 ....**110** B3
Cock La EC1 ....**108** B3
Cockpit Yd WC1 ...**107** A4
Cockspur Ct SW1 ..**119** C2
Cockspur St SW1 ..**119** C2
Code St E1 ....**24** B1 99 A1
Codicote Ho **28** SE8 .40 C2
Codicote Terr N4 ...6 B2
Codling Cl E1 ......**125** C2
Codrington Ct SE16 .33 A1
Codrington Ho **7**
E1 ....25 A1
Codrington Mews
W11 ....31 A3
Cody Rd E16 ....27 C1
Coffey St SE8 ......51 C3
Cohen Lo E5 ....18 A3
Coin St SE1 ....**121** B2
Coity Rd NW5 .....12 C2
Cokers La SE21 ....75 C3
Coke St E1 ....**111** C2
Colas Mews **7** NW6 23 C4
Colbeck Mews
SW5 ....**142** B3
Colberg Pl N16 .....7 B4
Colbert **II** SE5 .....49 B2
Colborne Ho **7** E14 33 C2
Colchester Ho
SW8 ....**171** B2
Colchester St E1 ..**111** A2
Coldbath Sq EC1 ..**95** B2
Coldbath St SE13 ..52 A1
Coldblow La SE14 ..50 C4
Coldharbour E14 ..34 B1
Coldharbour Ind Est
SE5 ....48 B3
Coldharbour La
SW9 ....63 A4
Coldharbour Pl SE5 48 C1
Coldstream Gdns
SW18 ....58 B1
Colebeck Mews N1 .15 A2
Colebert Ave E1 ...25 B1
Colebert Ho **20** E1 ..25 B1
Colebrook Cl SW19 69 C4
Colebrooke Ct SW3 **144** B3
Colebrooke Pl N1 ..**86** B4
Colebrooke Row
N1 ....**86** A2
Colebrooke Sch N1 **86** B2
Colebrook Ho E14 ..34 A3
Coleby Path **21** SE5 .48 C3

Cobden Ho E2 .....**99** C4
NW1 ....**82** C2
Cobham Cl SW11 ..60 A1
Cobham Mews **6**
NW1 ....13 C1
Coborn Mews **3** E3 26 B2
Cobham Ho E2

Colechurch Ho
SE1 ....**153** B1
Coleford Rd SW18 **59** B2
Colegrave Prim Sch
E15 ....19 C3
Colegrave Rd E15 ..19 C3
Colegrove Rd SE15 ..49 B4
Coleherne Ct
SW10 ....**142** B1
Coleherne Mans
SW5 ....**142** B2
Coleherne Mews
SW10 ....**142** A1
Coleherne Rd
SW10 ....**142** A1
Colehill Gdns SW6 **164** A3
Colehill La SW6 ...**164** B3
Cole Ho SE1 ....**135** C3
Coleman Ct SW18 ..70 C4
Coleman Fields N1 ..**87** A4
Coleman Mans N19 ..5 A4
Coleman Rd SE5 ...49 A3
Coleman St EC2 ..**109** B2
Coleman St Bldgs
EC2 ....**109** B2
Colenso Rd E5 .....17 B4
Coleraine Rd SE3 ..53 B4
Coleridge Cl SW8 **170** B1
Coleridge Ct **8**
W14 ....39 C3
Coleridge Gdns
NW6 ....11 B1
Coleridge Ho SE17 **151** A2
SW1 ....**147** A1
Coleridge Prim Sch
N8 ....4 C4
Coleridge Rd N4,N7 ..5 C2
London N8 ....4 C4
Coles Ct SW11 ....**167** C3
Coleshill Flats
SW1 ....**145** C3
Cole St SE1 ....**137** A3
Colestown St
SW11 ....**168** B2
Colet Gdns W14 ...39 C2
Colet Ho SE17 ....**150** B1
Colette Ct **6** SE16 ..40 C4
Coley St WC1 .....95 A1
Colfe & Hatchcliffe's
Glebe SE13 ......67 A2
Colgate Ho SE13 ..52 A1
Colin Blanchard Ho
SE4 ....51 C1
Colin Ct SW16 ....73 C2
Colinette Rd SW15 ..57 B3
Colin Rd NW10 ....8 C2
Colinsdale N1 .....**86** A3
Colin Winter Ho **37**
E1 ....25 B1
Coliston Pass SW18 70 C4
Coliston Rd SW18 ..70 C4
Collamore Ave
SW18 ....72 A3
Collard Pl NW1 ...13 A1
College App SE10 ..52 B4
College Cl E5 ......17 B3
College Cross N1 ..14 C1
College Ct SW3 ..**145** A1
London NW3 ....11 C2
II London W6 .....39 B1
College Gdns
Dulwich SE21 ....76 A3
Upper Tooting SW17 72 A2

College Park Sch
W2 ....**100** A1
College Pl NW1 ...**83** A3
SW10 ....**156** C2
College Rd
Dulwich SE19,SE21 ..76 A2
London NW10 ....22 B3
College St EC4 ...**123** A4
College Terr E3 ...26 B2
Collent Ho **II** E9 ..17 B2
Collent St E9 ......17 B2
Collerston Ho SE10 43 B1
Collette Ho N16 .....7 B3
Collett Rd SE16 ...**139** C2
Colley Ho **II** N7 ...13 C3
Collier St N1 ....**84** C1
Collingbourne Rd
W12 ....30 A1
Collingham Gdns
SW5 ....**142** B3
Collingham Pl
SW5 ....**142** B4
Collingham Rd
SW5 ....**142** B3
Collington St SE10 **42** C1
Collingwood Ho **II**
E1 ....25 A1
Collingwood St E1 ..25 A1
Collins Ct E8 ......16 C2
Collins Ho **4** E14 ..34 B2
6 SE10 ....43 B1
Collinson Ct SE1 **136** C3
Collinson Ho **12**
SE15 ....49 C3
Collinson St SE1 **136** C3
Collinson Wlk SE1 **136** C3
Collin's Yd N1 .....**86** A3
Collison Pl N16 ....7 A3
Collister Ho N16 ..86 A3
Coll of NW London
(Willesden Centre) The
NW10 ....**9** B3
Coll Sharp Ct E2 .**98** C3
Coll's Rd SE15 ....50 B2
Collyer Pl SE15 ...49 C2
Colmans Wharf **5**
E14 ....34 A4
Colmar Cl **3** E1 ..25 C1
Colmore Mews
SE15 ....50 A2
Colnbrook St SE1 **136** A2
Colne Ho NW8 ....**89** C1
Colne Rd E5 ......18 A4
Cologne Rd SW11 ..59 C3
Colombo St SE1 ..**122** A1
Colomb St SE10 ...43 A1
Colonades The **4**
SE5 ....48 C2
Colonial Dr W4 ...37 B2
Colonnade **II** WC1 ..94 B1
Colonnades The **6**
E8 ....17 A2
Colonnade The **II**
SE8 ....41 B2
Colstead Ho **22** E1 ..32 A3
Colston Rd SW14 ..55 B3
Colthurst Cres N4 ..6 B2
Coltman Ho **II** E14 33 A3
SE10 ....52 B4
Columba Ho SE14 ..51 B2
Columbas Dr NW3 ..2 C3
Columbia Ho **18** E3 26 C2
Columbia Point **7**
SE16 ....40 B3

Columbia Prim Sch
E2 ....98 C3
Columbia Rd
E2 ......24 B2 98 C4
Colverson Ho 11 E1 .32 B4
Colvestone Cres E8 .16 B3
Colvestone Prim Sch
E8 ....16 B3
Colville Gdns W11 .31 B3
Colville Ho 8 E2 ...25 B3
W11 ....31 B3
Colville Mews W11 .31 B3
W11 ....31 B3
Colville Prim Sch
W11 ....31 B3
Colville Rd W11 ...31 B3
London W3 ....37 A3
W11 ....31 B3
Colville Sq Mews 18
W11 ....31 B3
Colville Terr W11 .173 A1
Colwell Rd SE22 ...64 B2
Colwick Cl N6 .....4 C4
Colwith Rd W6 .....47 B4
Colworth Gr SE17 .151 A3
Colwyn Ho SE1 ....135 B1
Colyton Rd SE22 ...65 A2
Combe Ave SE3 ....53 B3
Combedale Rd SE10 43 C1
Combe Ho 20 W2 ...31 C4
Mortlake SW14 ....45 B1
Combemartin Rd
SW18 ....70 A3
Combe Mews 4
SE3 ....53 B3
Comber Gr SE5 ....48 B3
Comber Grove Prim Sch
SE5 ....48 B3
Comber Ho SE5 ....48 B3
Combermere Rd
SW9 ....62 B4
Combe The W1 .....92 B3
Comeragh Mews
W14 ....140 B1
Comeragh Rd W14 140 B1
Comerford Rd SE4 .66 B3
Comet PI SE8 ......51 C3
Comet St SE8 .....51 C3
Comins Ho SW4 ....61 B2
Commercial Rd
E1 ....32 B3 111 C2
Commercial St E1 .110 C4
Commercial Way
Wembley NW10 ....20 A3
SE15 ....49 C3
Commercial Pl SE10 43 B1
Commerell St SE10 .43 A1
Commodore Ct 8 .51 C2
Commodore Ho 7
E14 ....34 B2
Commodore St E1 ..26 A1
Commondale SW15 .57 B4
Common Rd SW13 ..56 C4
Common View
SW15 ....57 B4
Commonwealth Ave 7
W12 ....30 A2
Community Coll The
E9 ....25 C4
London 17 C3
Community Rd E15 .19 C3
Compania Bldg 11
E1 ....32 C2
Compass Ct SE1 ..124 C1

Compass Ho
London SE8 ....52 A1
London W2 ....100 A1
Compass Point 9
E14 ....33 C2
Compayne Gdns
NW6 ....11 A1
Compton Ave
London N1 ....15 A2
London N6 ....3 A4
Compton Cl NW1 ...92 B3
SE15 ....49 B3
Compton Cres W4 .45 B4
Compton Ho SW11 168 A4
Compton Pas EC1 ..96 B2
Compton Pl WC1 ...94 A2
Compton Rd
London N1 ....15 A2
London NW10 ......22 C2
London N1 ....21 A3
6 Richmond TW9 ..54 B2
Compton St EC1 ...96 B2
Compuasht St W2 ..102 C1
Comus Ho SE17 ...152 A3
Comus Pl SE17 ....152 A3
Comyn Rd SW11 ...60 A3
Comyns Cl E16 ....35 B2
Conant Ho SE11 ...48 A4
Conant Mews E1 ..125 B4
Concanon Rd SW2,
SW4 ....62 B3
Concert Hall App
SE1 ....121 A1
Concord Bsns Ctr
W3 ....28 A4
Concord Ctr W12 ..39 C4
Concord Rd W3 ...20 A1
Condell Rd SW8 ..171 A3
Conder St E14 ....33 A3
Condray Pl SW11 .158 A1
Conduit Ct WC2 ..120 A4
Conduit Ho SE10 ..52 C2
Conduit Mews W2 101 B1
Conduit Pas W2 ..101 B1
Conduit Pl W2 ...101 B1
Conduit St W1 ...118 C4
Conewood St N5 ...6 A1
Coney Acre SE21 ..75 B3
Coney Way SW8 ..163 A3
Congers Ho SE8 ..51 C3
Congreve Ho 16
N16 ....16 A3
Congreve St SE17 .152 A3
Conifer Ct 28 SW19 69 C3
Conifer Gdns SW16 .74 B1
Conifer Ho SE4 ...66 B3
Coniger Rd SW6 ..165 B2
Coningham Ct
SW10 ....157 A2
Coningham Mews
W12 ....29 C1
Coningham Rd W12 39 A4
Coningsby Rd N4 ...6 A4
Conington Rd SE13 52 B1
Conisborough NW1 .82 C3
Coniston NW1 .....92 C4
Coniston Cl
Barnes SW13 ....46 B3
Chiswick W4 ....45 B3
Coniston Ct 6 SE16 40 C4
W2 ....102 B1
Conistone Way N7 .14 A1
Coniston Ho 18 E3 .26 B2
18 SE5 ....48 B3
Coniston Wlk E9 ..17 B3
Conlan St W10 ....23 A1
Conley Rd NW10 ...8 A2

Conley St SE10 ....43 A1
Connaught Ave
SW14 ....55 B3
Connaught Cl W2 .102 B1
Connaught Ho W1 .118 A3
London NW10 ......22 A2
Connaught Lo N4 ..5 C4
Connaught Mans
SW1 ....168 B3
SW6 ....164 A4
12 London N16 ....15 C4
3 London N16 .....15 C4
London SW9 ....62 C3
Connaught Pl W2 .102 C1
Connaught Rd
London N4 ....5 C4
London NW10 ......21 A3
8 Richmond TW10 .54 B2
Connaught Sq W2 .102 C1
Connaught St W2 .102 B1
Connell Ct 3 SE14 .50 C4
Connett Ho 5 E2 ..25 A3
Connor Ct SW11 ..170 A3
Connor St E9 .....25 C4
Conrad Ho 9 E16 .33 A2
SW8 ....162 A2
12 London N16 ....16 A3
Consort Ho W2 ...114 B3
Consort Lo NW8 ..80 C3
Consort Rd SE15 ..50 A1
Cons St SE1 ......135 C4
Constable Ct 11
SE16 ....40 A1
Constable Ho NW3 .12 B1
Constable Wlk SE21 76 A1
Constant Ho 22 E14 .34 A2
Constantine Ho
SE17 ....75 A3
Constantine Rd
NW3 ....12 A4
Constitution Hill
SW1,W1 ....132 B4
Consul Ho 5 E3 ...26 C1
Content St SE17 ..151 B3
Convent Gdns W11 31 B3
Convent of Jesus &
Mary Language Coll
NW10 ....21 B4
Convent of Jesus &
Mary RC Inf Sch
NW2 ....9 B2
Conway Gr W3 ....28 C4
Conway Ho 5 E14 .42 A2
6 Streatham SW2 .74 A3
Conway Mews W1 .92 C1
Conway St W1 ....92 C1
Conybeare NW3 ...12 A1
Conyer St 10 E3 ..26 A3
Cookham Dene SE16 40 C4
Cookham Ho E2 ..98 C2
Cook's Rd E15 ....27 A3
SE17 ....48 A4
Coomassie Rd W9 .23 B1
Coombe Ho 12 N7 .13 C3
Coombe Rd W4 ...38 A1
Coombs St N1 .....86 B1
Coomer Mews
SW6 ....155 A3
Coomer Pl SW6 ..155 A3
Cooperage The
SE1 ....124 C1
Cooper Cl SE1 ...135 C3
Cooper Ct E15 ....76 B3
Cooper Ho NW8 ...89 B1
Cooper Rd NW10 ..8 C3
Coopersale Rd E9 .17 C3
Coopers Cl E1 ....25 B1

Coopers Ct E3 ....26 B1
9 London W3 ......28 B1
Coopers La NW1 ...83 C1
Cooper's Rd SE1 .153 A2
Cooper's Row E3 .124 C4
Cooper St 16 E16 .35 B2
Cope Ho EC1 .....97 A3
Copeland Dr E14 ..41 C2
Copeland Ho SE11 135 A1
Copeland Rd SE15 .50 A1
Copenhagen Gdns
W4 ....37 C4
Copenhagen Ho N1 .85 B3
Copenhagen Pl E14 33 B3
Copenhagen Prim Sch
N1 ....84 C3
Copenhagen St N1 .84 C3
Cope Pl W8 ......127 B1
Cope St SE16 .....40 C2
Cope Yd E1 ......125 C2
Copford Wlk N1 ..86 C4
Copleston Rd SE15 .64 B4
Copley Cl 6 SE17 .48 A4
Coppedhall 2 SE21 75 C2
Copperas St SE8 ..52 A4
Copper Beech N6 ..3 C4
Copperbeech Cl
NW3 ....11 C3
Copperfield Ho
SE1 ....139 B3
Copperfield Rd E3 .33 A4
Copperfields Ct W3 36 C4
Copperfield St
SE1 ....136 C4
Coppice Dr SW15 .57 A1
Coppin Ho SW2 ...75 A3
Coppock Cl SW11 168 A1
Copse Ct SW15 ...58 A2
Copthall Ave EC2 109 C2
Copthall Bldgs
EC2 ....109 C2
Copthall Cl EC2 ..109 B2
Copthorne Ave
SW12 ....73 C4
Coptic St WC1 ...106 A3
Copton Cl E3 .....33 C4
Coral Ho 6 E1 ....26 A1
Coral Row 14 SW11 59 B4
Coral St SE1 .....135 C3
Coram Ho WC1 ...94 A2
9 London W4 .....38 A1
Coram St WC1 ....94 A2
Corbden Cl SE15 ..49 B2
Corbet Ct EC3 ...109 C1
Corbet Ho N1 .....85 B3
Corbet Pl E1 .....110 C4
Corbett Ho SW10 156 C4
Corbett's La SE16 .40 B2
Corbidge Ct SE8 ..52 A4
Corbiere Ho 11 N1 24 A4
Corbin Ho 7 E3 ..27 A2
Corbridge Cres E2 .25 A3
Corbyn St N4,N19 ..5 A3
Corby Rd NW10 ...20 C3
Corby Way E3 ....26 C1
Cordelia Cl SE24 ..63 A3
Cordelia Ho 25 N1 24 A3
Cordelia St E14 ...34 A3
Cording St E14 ...34 A4
Cordwainers Coll
E8 ....17 A1
Cordwainers Ct 18
E9 ....17 B1
Cord Way 7 E14 ..41 C3
Corfe Ho SW8 ...162 C2

Corfe Lo SE21 ....75 C2
Corfe Twr 6 W3 ..37 B4
Corfield St E2 ....25 A2
Coriander Ave E14 .34 C3
Coriander Ct SE1 138 C2
Corinne Rd N19 ...13 B4
Cork Sq E1 ....32 A1
Cork St W1 ......118 C3
Cork St Mews W1 118 C3
Corlett St NW1 ..102 A4
Cormont Rd SE5 ..48 A2
Cormorant Ct
24 SE8 ....51 B4
12 Dulwich SE21 ..75 C2
Cornbury Ho 8 SE8 51 B4
Cornelia St N7 ...14 B2
Corner Fielde SE21 74 B3
Corner Gn SE3 ...53 C1
Corner House St
WC2 ....120 A2
Cornerways SW15 .56 C3
Corney Rd W4 ....46 A4
Corney Reach Way
W4 ....46 A3
Cornflower Terr
SE22 ....65 A1
Cornford Gr SW12 .73 A2
Cornhill EC3 .....109 C1
Cornick Ho 7 SE16 40 A3
Cornish Ho 7 SE17 48 A4
Brentford TW8 .....36 B1
Cornmill La SE13 ..67 B4
Cornmow Dr NW10 .8 C3
Cornwall Ave E2 ..25 B2
Cornwall Cres W11 31 A3
Cornwall Gdns
SW7 ....128 B1
London W2 ....9 A2
Cornwall Gdns Wlk
SW7 ....128 B1
Cornwall Gr W4 ..38 A1
Cornwall Ho NW1 .91 A1
3 Putney SW15 ...69 B4
Cornwall Mans
NW1 ....91 A1
SW10 ....157 A2
Cornwall Mews S
SW7 ....128 B1
Cornwall Mews W
SW7 ....128 B1
Cornwall Rd SE1 .135 C4
London N4 ....5 C4
Cornwall Sq SE11 150 B2
Cornwall St 4 E1 ..32 A2
Cornwall Terr NW1 91 A1
Cornwall Terr Mews
NW1 ....91 A1
Cornwood Dr E1 ..32 B3
Coronation Ave 11
N16 ....16 B4
Coronation Ct W10 30 B4
Coronet St N1 .....98 A3
Corporation Row
EC1 ....95 C2
Corporation St N7 .14 A3
Corpus Christi RC Prim
Sch SW2 ....62 B2
Corrance Rd SW2,
SW4 ....62 B3
Corringham Ct NW11 1 C4
Corringham Ho 10
E1 ....32 C3

Corringham Rd
NW11 ....1 C4
Corringway NW11 ....2 A4
Corry Dr SW9 ....63 A3
Corry Ho 4 E14 ....34 A2
Corsley Way E9 ....18 B2
Corsham St N1 ....97 C3
Corsica St N5 ....15 A2
Cortayne Rd SW6 ....164 C2
Cortis Rd SW15 ....57 A1
Cortis Terr SW15 ......57 A1
Corunna Rd SW8 .....171 A4
Corunna Terr SW8 ...170 C4
Corvette Sq 5 SE10 ...52 C4
Coryton Path W9 ......23 B1
Cosbycote Ave SE24 ..63 B2
Cosgrove Ho 1 E2 ....24 C4
Cosmo Pl WC1 ....106 B4
Cosmur Cl W12 ....38 B3
Cossall Wlk SE15 .....50 A2
Cossar Mews 10
...............................62 C2
Cosser St SE1 ....135 B2
Costa St SE15 ....49 C1
Coston Wlk 4 SE4 ....65 C3
Cosway Mans NW1 ..102 B4
Cosway St NW1 ......102 B3
Cotall St E14 ....33 C4
Cotes Ho NW8 ....90 A1
Cotham St SE17 ......151 A3
Cotherstone Rd
SW2 ....74 B3
Cotleigh Rd NW6 .....10 C1
Cotman Cl SW15 ......57 C2
Cotman Ho NW8 ....80 A2
Cotswold Ct EC1 ......96 C2
Cotswold Gate NW2 ...1 A3
Cotswold Ho N16 ....7 B3
Cotswold Mews
SW11 ....167 C3
Cottage Gn SE5 ....48 C3
Cottage Gr SW9 ....62 A4
Cottage Pl SW3 ....130 A1
Cottage St E14 ....34 A2
Cottage Wlk 2 N16 ...7 B1
Cottenham Ho 3
N19 ....5 A2
Cottesbrook St 8
SE14 ....51 A3
Cottesloe Ho NW8 ...90 A2
Cottesloe Mews
SE1 ....135 C2
Cottesmore Ct W8 ..128 B2
Cottesmore Gdns
W8 ....128 B2
Cottingham Rd
SW8 ....163 A2
Cottington St SE11 ..150 A2
Cotton Ave W3 ....28 C3
Cotton Ho
London W12 ....38 B4
18 Streatham SW2 ...74 A4
Cotton Row SW11 ....59 C4
Cotton's Gdn E2 ....98 B4
Cottons La SE1 ....123 C2
Cotton St E14 ....34 B2
Cottrell Ct SE10 ....43 B2
Couchman Ho 8
SW4 ....61 B1
Coulgate St SE4 ....66 A4
Coulsdon Ho 5
SW2 ....74 A4
Coulson St SW3 ......144 C2
Coulter Rd W6 ....39 A3
Coults Cres NW5 ....3 C1
Councillor St SE5 .....48 B3
Counters Ct W14 ....126 B2

Counter St SE1 ......124 A1
Countess Rd NW5 ...13 B3
Countisbury Ho
SE26 ....76 C1
County Gr SE5 ....48 B2
County Ho SW9 ......173 B4
County St SE1 ....137 A1
Courier Ho 10 SW2 ...74 C4
Courland Gr SW8 ...171 C3
Courland St SW8 ....171 C3
Courtauld Galleries★
WC2 ....120 C4
Courtauld Ho 11 E2 ...24 C3
Courtauld Inst of Art
W1 ....103 A2
Courtauld Rd N19 .....4 C3
Courtenay Ave N6 .....3 A4
Courtenay Sq SE11 ..149 B1
Courtenay St SE11 ..149 B2
Courtfield Gdns
SW5 ....142 B3
Courtfield Ho EC1 ...107 B4
Courtfield Mews
SW5 ....142 B3
Courtfield Rd SW7 ..142 C3
Courthill Rd SE13 .....67 B3
Courthope Ho
6 SE16 ....40 B3
London SW8 ....162 A1
Courthope Rd NW3 ..12 B4
Court La SE21 ....76 B4
Courtlands TW10 ......54 C2
Courtlands Ave
TW9 ....45 A1
Court Lane Gdns
SE21 ....76 A4
Court Mans 8 W6 ....38 C2
Courtmead Cl SE24 ..63 B1
Courtnell St W2 ....31 C3
Courtney Ct N7 ....14 C3
Courtney Ho W14 ...126 B2
Courtney Rd N7 ....14 C3
Courtrai Rd SE23 .....66 A1
Court Royal SW15 ....58 A2
Court St E1 ....32 A4
Courtville Ho 11
W10 ....23 A2
Court Way W3 ....28 B4
Courtyard The
Fulham SW6 ....164 A3
London N1 ....14 B1
12 London SE8 ....59 C3
Cousin La EC4 ....123 B3
Couzens Ho 9 E3 ....33 B4
Coval Gdns SW14 ....55 A3
Coval La SW14 ....55 A3
Coval Rd SW14 ....55 B3
Covell Ct 10 SE8 ......51 C3
Covent Garden Sta
WC2 ....120 B4
Covent Gdn★ WC2 ..120 B4
Coventry Cl NW6 .....23 C4
Coventry Rd E1 ....25 A1
Coventry St W1 ......119 B3
Coverdale Pl NW6 .....9 C1
Coverdale Rd
London NW2 ....10 A2
London W12 ....39 A4
Coverham Ho 5
SE4 ....65 C3
Coverley Cl E1 ....111 C4
Coverley Point
SE11 ....148 C3
Cowcross St EC1 ....108 A4
Cowdenbeath Path
N1 ....84 C4

Cowdray Hall Coll of
Nursing W1 ....104 A2
Cowdray Ho 22
SE22 ....64 A4
Cowdry Rd E9 ....18 B2
Cowley Rd
London SW9 ....173 C4
London W3 ....29 B1
Mortlake SW14 ....56 A4
Cowley St SW1 ......134 A1
Cowling Cl W11 ......112 A2
Cowper Ho SE17 ....151 A2
London SW1 ....147 C1
Cowper Rd
London N16 ....16 A4
London W3 ....28 C1
Cowper's Ct EC3 ....109 C1
Cowper Terr W10 .....30 C4
Cowthorpe Rd
SW8 ....171 C4
Cox Ho W6 ....154 A4
Cox's Ct E1 ....110 C3
Coxson Way SE1 ....138 C3
Coysh Ct 5 SW15 ....58 A2
Crabtree Cl E2 ....24 B3
Crabtree Hall SW6 ...47 A3
Crabtree La SW6 .....47 C3
Craddock St NW5 ...12 C2
Craigie Ho SE1 ......153 A3
Craigleith SW15 ....57 C1
Craignair Rd SW2 ....74 C4
Craig's Ct SW1 ......120 A2
Craik Ct NW6 ....23 B3
Crail Row SE17 ......151 C3
Cramer St W1 ....103 C3
Crammond Cl W6 ...154 A3
Crampton St
SE17 ....150 B2
Crampton St SE17 ..150 C2
Cranbourn Alley
WC2 ....119 C4
Cranbourne Ct
SW11 ....158 B2
Cranbourne Rd E15 ..76 B4
Cranbourn Ho 4
SE16 ....40 A4
Cranbourn St WC2 ..119 C4
Cranbrook NW1 ....83 A3
Cranbrook Ho 5
E5 ....17 A3
Cranbrook Rd
London SE8 ....51 C2
London W4 ....38 A1
Cranbrook St E2 ....25 C3
Cranbury Rd SW6 ..166 B1
Crandale Ho 8 E5 ....17 A3
Crandley Ct SE8 ....41 A2
Crane Ave W3 ....28 B2
Crane Ct EC4 ....107 C1
7 London W12 ....38 A4
Crane Gr N7 ....14 C2
Crane Ho 22 E3 ....26 A3
Crane Mead SE16 ....40 C2
Crane St SE10 ....42 C1
5 London SE15 ....49 B2
Cranfield Ho WC1 ..106 B4
Cranfield Rd SE4 .....66 B4
Cranford Cotts 8
E1 ....32 C2
Cranford Lo SW19 ...69 C2
Cranford St E1 ....32 C2
Cranhurst Rd NW2 ....9 B3
Cranleigh W11 ....112 C3

Cranleigh Ct
4 London N16 ....7 A3
Richmond TW9 ....54 C4
Cranleigh Hos NW1 ..83 A1
Cranleigh Mews
SW11 ....168 B1
Cranleigh St NW1 ....83 A1
Cranley Gdns SW7 ..143 B2
Cranley Mews
SW7 ....143 A2
Cranley Pl SW7 .....143 B3
Cranmer Ct SW3 ....144 B3
Cranmer Ho SW11 .168 A4
Cranmer Rd SW9 ...163 C2
Cranswick Rd SE16 ..40 A1
Cranwell Cl E3 ....27 A1
Cranwich Rd N16 ....7 A4
Cranwood Ct EC1 ....97 C3
Cranwood St EC1 .....97 C3
Cranworth Gdns
SW9 ....173 B4
Cranworth Ho 6
N7 ....14 B4
Craster Rd SW2 ....74 B4
Craston Ho 2 SE5 ....49 A1
Craven Cl N16 ....7 C4
Craven Cottage (Fulham
FC) Wks 47 C2
Craven Ct NW10 ......21 A4
Craven Hill W2 ......115 A4
Craven Hill Gdns
W2 ....114 C4
Craven Hill Mews
W2 ....115 A4
Craven Ho 2 SW14 ..55 C4
Craven Lo W2 ....115 A4
Fulham SW6 ....47 C2
Craven Park Mews
NW10 ....21 A4
Craven Park Rd
London NW10 ....21 A4
Craven Pas WC2 ....120 A2
Craven Pk NW10 .....21 A4
Craven Rd W2 ....101 A1
London NW10 ....20 C4
London WC2 ....120 A2
Craven St WC2 ......120 A2
Craven Terr W2 ....115 A4
Craven Wlk E5,N16 ...7 C4
Crawford Bldgs
NW1 ....102 B3
Crawford Mews
W1 ....102 C3
Crawford Pas EC1 ....95 C1
Crawford Pl W1 ......102 B3
Crawford Place
Dwellings W1 ....102 B3
Crawford Point 4
E16 ....35 B1
Crawford Prim Sch
SE5 ....48 B2
Crawford Rd SE5 .....48 B1
Crawford St W1 ......102 C3
Crawshay Ct SW9 ..173 C4
Crawshay Ho 7
N16 ....15 C4
Crawthew Gr SE22 ..64 B3
Crayford Ho SE1 ....137 C3
London N7 ....14 A4
Crayford Rd N7 ....14 A4
Crayle Ho EC1 ....96 B2
Crealock St SW18 ....59 A1
Creasy Est SE1 ......138 A1
Crebor St SE22 ....64 C1
Credenhill Ho 2
SE15 ....50 A3

Crediton Hill NW6 ...11 A3
Crediton Rd E16 ......35 C3
London NW10 ....22 C4
Creechurch La
EC3 ....110 B1
Creechurch Pl EC3 .110 B1
Creed Ho SE15 ....65 A4
Creed La EC4 ....108 B1
Creek Ho W14 ....126 B2
Creek Rd SE10,SE8 ..52 A4
Creekside SE8 ....52 A3
Crefeld Cl W6 ....154 A3
Creighton Cl W12 ....30 A2
Creighton Rd NW6 ..22 C3
Cremer Bsns Ctr 3
E2 ....24 B3
Cremer Ho 9 SE8 ....51 C3
Cremer St E2 ....24 B3
Cremorne Rd
SW10 ....157 B2
Creon Ct SW9 ....173 B4
Crescent EC3 ....124 C4
Crescent Ct SW4 .....61 C2
Crescent Gdns
SW19 ....70 C1
Crescent Gr SW4 .....61 B3
Crescent La SW4 .....61 C2
Crescent Mans
W11 ....112 B4
London N5 ....15 A3
Crescent Pl SW3 ....144 B4
Crescent Row EC1 ...96 C1
Crescent St N1 ....14 B1
Crescent Stables
SW15 ....58 A2
Crescent The
Barnes SW13 ....46 C1
London W3 ....29 A3
Wimbledon SW19 ....70 C1
Crescent Way SE4 ...66 C4
Crescent Wood Rd
SE21,SE26 ....76 C1
Cresford Rd SW6 ...166 A3
Cressage Ho 7
TW8 ....44 A4
Cressall Ho 8 E14 ...41 C3
Cresset Ho 8 E9 .....17 B2
Cresset Rd E9 ....17 B2
Cresset St SW4 ....61 C4
Cressfield Cl NW5 .....12 C3
Cressida Rd N19 ......4 C3
Cressingham Rd
SE13 ....67 B4
Cressington Cl 4
N16 ....16 A3
Cresswell Gdns
SW5 ....142 C2
Cresswell Pl SW10 .143 A2
Cressy Ct 6 E1 ....32 B4
London W6 ....39 A3
Cressy Ho SW13 ......57 A4
Cressy Hos 7 E1 .....32 B4
Cressy Pl E1 ....32 B4
Cressy Rd NW3 ....12 B4
Cresta Ho
7 Bow E3 ....26 C1
London NW6 ....11 C1
Crestfield St N1,
WC1 ....94 B4
Crestview NW5 ....4 A1
Crestway SW15 ....57 A1

Creswick Ct W3 .....28 A2
Creswick Rd W3 .....28 A2
Creswick Wlk 6 E3 .26 C2
Crewdson Rd SW9 .163 B1
Crewe Pl NW10 ....21 B2
Crewkerne Ct
SW11 ....167 C4
Crews St E14 ......41 C2
Crewys Rd
London NW2 ....1 B2
London SE15 ......50 A1
Crichton St SW8 .170 C2
Cricketers Mews 4
SW18 ....59 A2
Cricketfield Rd E5 ..17 A4
Cricklade Ave SW2 .74 B2
Cricklewood Broadway
NW2 ....9 C4
Cricklewood La NW2 1 B1
Cricklewood Sta
NW2 ....9 C4
Crieff Rd SW18 ....59 B1
Criffel Ave SW2 ....73 C3
Crimscott St SE1 .138 B1
Crimsworth Rd
SW8 ....161 C1
Crinan St N1 ......84 B2
Cringle St SW8 ...160 C2
Cripplegate St
EC1 ....109 A4
Crispe Ho N1 ......85 A3
Crispian Ct NW10 ...8 A4
Crispin Ct SE17 ..152 A3
Crispin St E1 .....110 C3
Crisp Rd W6 ....39 B1
Cristowe Rd SW6 ..165 A1
Criterion Mews N19 .4 C2
Crockerton Rd
SW17 ....72 B2
Croftdown Rd NW5 ..4 A1
Crofters Ct 6 SE8 .41 A2
Crofters Way NW1 .83 B4
Croft Ho
12 London W10 ....23 A2
Putney SW15 ......57 C1
Crofton Ave W4 ...45 C3
Crofton Gate Way
SE4 ....66 A2
Crofton L Ctr SE4 .66 C1
Crofton Park Rd
SE4 ....66 B1
Crofton Park Sta
SE4 ....66 B2
Crofton Rd SE5 ....49 A1
Crofton Sch SE4 ..66 C1
Crofton Terr
London E5 ....18 A3
Richmond TW9 .....54 B3
Crofts Ho 15 E2 ...24 C3
Crofts St E1 ......125 B3
Croft St SE8 ......41 A2
Croft The NW10 ...21 B3
Crogsland Rd NW1 .12 C1
Cromartie Rd N19 ...4 C4
Cromarty Ho 8 E1 .33 A4
Crombie Mews
SW11 ....168 B2
Cromdale Ct N16 ...7 B4
Cromer Ct
Streatham SW16 ..74 A1
Wandsworth SW18 .58 B1
Cromer St WC1 ....94 B3
Cromer Terr E8 ....16 C3
Cromer Villas Rd
SW18 ....58 B1

Cromford Path 1
E5 ....17 C4
Cromford Rd SW18 .58 C2
Crompton Ct SW3 .144 A4
Crompton Ho SE1 .137 A1
SW8 ....171 A3
W2 ....89 B1
Crompton St W2 ..89 B1
Cromwell Ave N6 ...4 A3
London W6 ....39 A2
Cromwell Cl
London W3 ....28 B1
2 London W4 ....37 A1
Cromwell Cres
SW5 ....141 B4
Cromwell Ctr NW10 .20 C2
Cromwell Gdns
SW7 ....129 C1
Cromwell Gr W6 ...39 B3
Cromwell Ho
SW11 ....169 C3
Putney SW15 .....56 C3
Cromwell Hospl
SW5 ....142 A4
Cromwell Lo 28 E1 .25 B1
Cromwell Mans
SW5 ....141 C4
Cromwell Mews
SW7 ....143 C4
Cromwell Pl N6 ....4 A3
SW7 ....143 C4
6 London W3 ...28 B1
Mortlake SW14 ...55 B4
Cromwell Rd SW7 .142 C4
London SW9 ......48 A2
Crondace Rd SW6 .165 C3
Crondall Ct 7 N1 ..24 A3
Crondall Ho SW15 .68 C3
Crondall Pl 11 N1 .24 A3
Crondall St N1 ....24 A3
Crone Ct 8 NW6 ..23 B3
Cronin St SE15 ....49 B3
Crooked Billet Yd
E2 ....98 B4
Crooke Rd SE8 ....41 A1
Crookham Rd SW6 164 C3
Croom's Hill SE10 .52 C3
Croom's Hill Gr
SE10 ....52 B3
Cropley Ct N1 .....87 B2
Cropley St N1 .....87 B2
Cropthorne Ct W9 .89 A3
Crosby Ct SE1 ...137 B4
Crosby Row SE1 .137 B4
Crosby Sq EC3 ...110 A2
Crosby Wlk
3 London E8 .....16 B2
Streatham SW2 ..74 C4
Crosfield Ct 3 W10 .30 C3
Crosfield Ho W11 .112 A3
Crosland Pl 5
SW11 ....60 C4
Crossbow Ho 15 N1 .24 A4
Cross Cl SE15 ....50 B1
Cross Ct SE5 .....63 C4
Crossfield Rd NW3 .11 C2
Crossfield St SE8 .51 C3
Crossford St SW9 .172 C1
Crossharbour & London
Arena Sta E14 ....42 A3
Cross Keys Cl W1 .103 C3
Cross La EC3 .....124 A3
Crossleigh Ct 3
SE14 ....51 B3
Crosslet St SE17 .151 C4
Crosslet Vale SE10 .52 A2

Crossley St N7 ....14 C2
Crossman Hos 19
SW12 ....74 A4
Crossmount Ho 13
SE5 ....48 B3
Cross Rd SE5 .....49 A1
Cross St N1 ....86 B4
Mortlake SW13 ...56 A4
Crossthwaite Ave
SE5,SE24 ....63 C3
Crosswall EC3 ...124 C4
Crossway E8,N16 .16 A3
Crossway Ct SE4 .51 A1
Croston St E8 .....24 C4
Crouch End Hill N8 ..4 C4
Crouch Hall Ct N19 ..5 A3
Crouch Hill N4,N8,
N19 ....5 A4
Crouchmans Cl
SE21,SE26 ....76 C1
Crowder St E1 ....32 A2
Crowfield Ho N5 ..15 B4
Crowfoot Cl E9 ...18 B3
Crowhurst Cl SW9 173 C2
Crowhurst Ho
SW9 ....173 A1
Crowland Ho NW8 .78 C3
Crowland Terr N1 .15 C1
Crowline Wlk 1 N1 .15 B2
Crown Cl E3 ......26 C4
NW6 ....11 A2
Crown Close Bsns Ctr
E3 ....26 C4
Crown Ct EC4 ....109 A1
NW8 ....90 B3
WC2 ....106 B1
4 Putney SW15 ..57 C3
Crowndale Ct NW1 .83 A2
Crowndale Rd NW1 .83 A2
Crownfield Rd E15 .19 C4
Crownhill Rd NW10 .21 B4
Crownleigh Ct SW2 .62 C2
Crown Lo SW3 ....144 B3
Crown Office Row
EC4 ....121 B4
Crown Pas SW1 ..119 A1
Crown Pl EC2 ....110 A3
London NW5 .....13 A2
Crown Reach SW1 147 C1
Crown St SE5 ....48 B3
Acton W3 ....28 B1
Crownstone Ct 1
SW2 ....62 C2
Crownstone Rd
SW2 ....62 C2
Crown Terr TW9 ..54 B3
Crows Rd E15 ....27 C2
Crowther Ave TW8 .36 A2
Crowther Cl SW6 154 C4
Crowthorne Cl
SW18 ....70 B3
Crowthorne Rd
W10 ....30 C3
Croxley Rd W9 ....23 B2
Croxted Cl SE21 ..75 B4
Croxted Mews SE24 .63 B1
Croxted Rd SE21,
SE24 ....75 C3
Croxteth Ho SW8 .171 B2
Croydon Ho SE1 ..135 C4
Crozier Ho SW8 ..162 C1
Crozier Terr E9 ...17 C3
Crucifix La SE1 ...138 A4
Cruden Ho 28 E3 .26 B3
11 SE17 ....48 A4
Cruden St N1 .....86 B3

Cruickshank St
WC1 ....95 B4
Cruikshank Ho NW8 80 B2
Crusoe House Sch
N1 ....97 B4
Crusoe Mews N16 .6 C2
Crutched Friars
EC3 ....124 B4
Crystal Palace Rd
SE22 ....64 C2
Cuba St E14 ......41 C4
Cubitt Ho 4 SW4 .61 B1
Cubitt St WC1 ....95 A3
Cubitt Terr SW4 ..61 B4
Cubitt Town Jun & Inf
Sch E14 ....42 B3
Cuddington SE17 .151 A4
Cudworth Ho SW8 171 A3
Cudworth St E1 ...25 A1
Cuffley Ho W10 ...30 B4
Cuff Point E2 .....98 C4
Culand Ho SE17 ..152 A3
Culford Gdns SW3 145 A3
Culford Mans SW3 145 A3
Culford Mews N1 .16 A2
Culford Rd N1 ....24 A4
London N1 ....16 A2
Culham Ho 2 .....98 C3
2 W2 ....31 C4
Cullen Ho W9 ....23 B3
Culling Rd SE16 ..40 B3
Cullingworth Rd
NW10 ....9 A3
Culloden Cl 16 ...153 C1
Culloden Prim Sch
E14 ....34 B3
Cullum St EC3 ...124 A4
Culmore Rd SE15 .50 B3
Culmstock Rd SW11 60 C2
Culpepper Ct SE11 149 B4
Culross Bldgs NW1 .84 A2
Culross St W1 ....117 B3
Culver Ct SW18 ..59 A1
Culverden Rd SW12 73 B2
Culverhouse WC1 .106 C3
Culverhouse Gdns
SW16 ....74 B1
Culvert Ct SW11 .169 B2
Culvert Pl SW11 .169 B1
Culvert Rd SW11 .169 A2
Culworth Ho NW8 .80 A2
Culworth St NW8 .80 A1
Cumber Ho SW18 .70 C3
Cumberland Ave
NW10 ....20 A2
Cumberland Bsns Pk
NW10 ....20 A2
Cumberland Cl E8 .16 B2
Cumberland Cres
W14 ....140 B4
Cumberland Ct
W1 ....103 A1
Cumberland Gate
W1 ....117 A4
Cumberland Gdns
WC1 ....95 B4
Cumberland Ho
SW15 ....69 B4
Cumberland Mans
W1 ....102 C2
7 London NW6 ...10 C3
Cumberland Market
NW1 ....92 B4
Cumberland Mills Sq
E14 ....42 C1

Cumberland Park Ind
Est NW10 ....21 C2
Cumberland Pk NW3 28 B2
Cumberland Pl
NW1 ....92 A4
Cumberland Rd
Barnes SW13 .....46 C2
London W3 ....28 B2
Richmond TW9 ...44 C3
Cumberland Sch
E16 ....35 B2
Cumberland St
SW1 ....146 B2
Cumberland Terr
NW1 ....82 A1
Cumberland Terrace
Mews NW1 ....82 A1
Cumberland Villas
W3 ....28 B2
Cumbria Ho 2
SW15 ....58 B2
Cumbrian Gdns NW2 1 A2
Cuming Mus SE17 .151 A3
Cumming St N1 ...85 A1
Cumnor Cl SW9 ..173 A2
Cunard Pl EC3 ...110 B1
Cunard Rd NW10 .20 C2
Cunard Wlk 3 SE16 41 A2
Cundy St SW1 ...145 C3
Cunningham Ct W2 89 B1
Cunningham Ho 16
SE5 ....48 C3
Cunningham Pl
NW8 ....89 B2
Cunnington St W4 .37 B2
Cupar Rd SW11 ..169 C4
Cureton St SW1 ..147 C3
Curlew Ho
6 London SE15 ..49 B2
London SE4 ......66 A3
Curlew St SE1 ...139 A4
Curran Ho SW3 ..144 A3
Curricle St W3 ...29 A1
Currie Ho 10 SW12 73 C4
Cursitor St EC4 ..107 B2
Curtain Pl EC2 ...98 B2
Curtain Rd
EC2 ....24 A1 98 B2
Curtis Dr W3 .....28 C3
Curtis Ho SE17 ..151 B2
Curtis St SE1 ....152 C4
Curtis Way SE1 ..152 C4
Curve The W12 ...29 C2
Curwen Rd W12 ..38 C4
Curzon Cres SW6 .154 B1
Curzon Gate W1 .117 C1
Curzon Pl W1 ....117 C1
Curzon St W1 ....118 A2
Custance Ho N1 ..87 B1
Custance St N1 ...97 B4
Custom House
EC3 ....124 A3
Custom House Reach
SE16 ....41 B3
Cutbush Ho N7 ...13 C3
Cutcombe Mans 22
SE5 ....48 B1
Cutcombe Rd SE5 .48 B1
Cuthbert Harrowing Ho
EC1 ....96 C1
Cuthbert Ho W2 ..101 B4
Cuthbert St W2 ...89 B1
Cuthill Wlk 3 SE5 .48 C2
Cutlers Gdns EC2 .110 B2
Cutlers Sq E14 ...41 C2
Cutler St EC2 ....110 B2
Cut The SE1 .....135 C4

Dee Rd TW9 . . . .54 B3
Deerdale Rd SE24 . . .63 B3
Deerhurst Ho **6**
SE15 . . . . .49 C4
Deerhurst Rd NW2 . .9 C2
Deer Lo SW6 . . . . .58 A4
Deeside Rd SW17 . .71 C1
Dee St E14 . . . . . . .34 B3
Defoe Ave TW9 . . . .44 C3
Defoe Ho EC2 . . .108 C4
6 London N16 . . . .7 A1
Defoe Pl EC2 . . . .108 C4
Defoe Rd SE16 . . . .41 B4
London N16 . . . . . . .7 A1
De Gama Pl E14 . . .41 C1
Dekker Ho **16** SE5 . .48 C3
Dekker Rd SE21 . . .64 A1
Delafield Ho E1 . . .111 C1
Delaford Rd SE16 . .40 A1
Delaford St SW6 . .154 B3
Delamere Ho **4** N4 . . .6 C4
Delamere Rd W5 . . .36 A4
Delamere St W2 . . .100 C3
Delamere Terr W2 .100 B4
Delancey Pas NW1 . .82 B3
Delancey St NW1 . . .82 B3
Delancey Studios
NW1 . . . . .82 B3
Delany Ho SE10 . . . .52 B4
Delarch Ho SE1 . . .136 A3
De Laune St SE17 .150 A1
Delaware Rd W9 . . .88 A2
Delawyk Cres SE24 .63 C1
Delft Way **2** SE22 . .64 A2
Delhi St N1 . . . . . . .84 B3
Delia St SW18 . . . . .71 A4
Delius Gr E15 . . . . .27 B3
Dellafield N4 . . . . . .5 C2
Dell Cl E15 . . . . . . .27 C4
Dellow Ho **3** E1 . . . .32 A2
Dellow St E1 . . . . . .32 A2
Dell's Mews SW1 . .147 A3
Deloraine Ho SE8 . .51 C2
Deloraine St SE8 . . .51 C2
Delorme St W6 . . . .47 C4
Delta Bldg **4** E14 . . .34 B3
Delta Ho N1 . . . . . .97 B4
Delta Pk SW18 . . . .59 A3
Delta St E2 . . . . . . .99 B4
Delverton Ho SE17 .150 B2
Delverton Rd SE17 .150 B1
Delvino Rd SW6 . . .165 C3
De Montfort Par **1**
SW16 . . . . .74 A1
De Montfort Rd
SW16 . . . . .74 A2
De Morgan Rd SW6 .59 A4
Dempster Rd SW18 .59 B2
Denbigh Cl
W11 . . . . .31 B2 113 A4
London NW10 . . . . .21 A4
Denbigh Gdns TW10 .54 B2
Denbigh Ho SW1 . .131 A2
W11 . . . . .31 B2 113 A4
7 W11 . . . . .31 B3
Denbigh Mews
SW1 . . . . .146 C3
Denbigh Pl SW1 . . .146 C2
Denbigh Rd
W11 . . . . .31 B2 113 A4
Denbigh St SW1 . . .147 A2
Denbigh Terr
W11 . . . . .31 B2 113 A4
Denbury Ho **48** E3 . .27 A2
Denby Ct SE11 . . . .149 A4

Dence Ho E2 . . . . . .99 B3
Denchworth Ho
SW9 . . . . .173 B1
Dendy St SW12 . . . .72 C3
Dene Cl SE4 . . . . . .66 A3
Denehurst Gdns
Acton W3 . . . . .28 A1
Richmond TW10 . . . .54 C3
Dene Mans NW6 . . .10 C2
Denesmead SE24 . . .63 B2
Denewood Rd N6 . . .3 B4
Dengie Wlk N1 . . . . .86 C4
Denham Ho **22** W12 .30 A2
Denham St SE10 . . .43 C1
Denholme Rd W9 . . .23 B2
Denland Ho SW8 . .163 A1
Denman Ho N16 . . . .7 A2
Denman Rd SE15 . . .49 B1
Denman St W1 . . . .119 B3
Denmark Gr N1 . . . .85 B2
Denmark Hill SE5 . . .48 C1
Denmark Hill Sta
SE5 . . . . .48 C1
Denmark Mans **14**
SE5 . . . . .48 B1
Denmark Pl WC2 . .105 C2
Denmark Rd NW6 . .23 B3
London SE5 . . . . . . .48 B1
Denmark St WC2 . .105 C2
Denmead Ho
SW15 . . . . .56 C2
Denne Terr E8 . . . . .24 B4
Dennett's Gr SE14 . .50 C1
Dennett's Rd SE14 . .50 B2
Denning Cl NW8 . . .89 A3
Denning Point E1 . .111 A2
Denning Rd NW3 . . .11 C4
Dennington Park Rd
NW6 . . . . .10 C2
Dennis Ho **3** E3 . . . .26 B3
Dennison Point E15 .19 B1
Dennis Way SW4 . . .61 C4
Denny Cres SE11 . .149 C2
Denny St SE11 . . . .149 C2
Densham Ho NW8 . . .79 C1
Denstone Ho **5**
SE15 . . . . .49 C4
Dent Ho SE17 . . . . .152 A3
Denton NW1 . . . . . .12 C2
Denton Ho N1 . . . . .15 A1
Denton St SW18 . . . .59 A1
Dents Rd SW11 . . . .60 B1
Denver Rd N16 . . . . .7 A4
Denyer Ho **1** NW5 . .13 A4
Denyer St SW3 . . . .144 B4
Denys Bldg EC1 . . .107 C3
Denzil Rd NW10 . . . .8 B3
Deodar Rd SW15 . . .58 A3
Depot App NW2 . . . .9 C4
Depot Rd W12 . . . . .30 B2
Depot St SE5 . . . . . .48 C4
Deptford Bridge
SE8 . . . . .51 C2
Deptford Bridge Sta
SE8 . . . . .51 C2
Deptford Broadway
SE8,SE14 . . . . .51 C2
Deptford Church St
SE8 . . . . .51 C3
Deptford Ferry Rd **7**
E14 . . . . .41 C2
Deptford Gn SE8 . . .51 C4
Deptford Green Sch
SE14 . . . . .51 B3
Deptford Green Sch
(Annexe) SE14 . . . .51 A3

Deptford High St
SE8 . . . . .51 C3
Deptford Park Prim Sch
SE8 . . . . .41 A1
Deptford Sta SE8 . . .51 C3
Deptford Trad Est
SE8 . . . . .51 A4
Deptford Wharf SE8 .41 B2
Dept of Transport &
Environment
SW1 . . . . .133 C2
De Quincey Mews **3**
E16 . . . . .35 C1
Derby Ct **8** E5 . . . .17 C4
Derby Gate SW1 . .134 A4
Derby Ho SE11 . . . .149 B4
Derby Rd E9 . . . . . .25 C4
Mortlake SW14 . . . .55 A3
Derbyshire St
E2 . . . . .24 C2 99 C3
Derby St W1 . . . . .117 C1
Dereham Ho **4** SE4 .65 C3
Dereham Pl EC2 . . .98 B2
Derek Walcott Cl
SE24 . . . . .63 A2
Dericote St E8 . . . . .25 A4
Dering St W1 . . . . .104 B1
Dermody Gdns
SE13 . . . . .67 C2
Dermody Rd SE13 . .67 C2
Deronda Rd SE24,
SW2 . . . . .75 A3
Derrick Ho **13** SW2 .74 C3
Derrycombe Ho
W11 . . . . .31 B4
10 W11 . . . . .31 C4
Derry St W8 . . . . . .128 A3
Dersingham Rd NW2 .1 A1
Derwent NW1 . . . . . .92 C3
Derwent Ct **15** SE16 .40 C4
8 London N16 . . . . .7 A3
Derwent Gr SE22 . . .64 B3
Derwent Ho E3 . . . .26 B1
SW7 . . . . .143 A4
Derwent St SE10 . . .43 A1
Derwentwater Mans **3**
W3 . . . . .28 B1
Derwentwater Prim Sch
W3 . . . . .28 B1
Derwentwater Rd
W3 . . . . .28 B1
Desborough Cl
W2 . . . . .100 B4
Desborough Ho
W14 . . . . .155 A4
Desenfans Rd SE21 .64 A1
Desmond St SE14 . .51 A4
Despard Ho SW2 . . .74 C2
Despard Rd N19 . . . .4 B3
Dethick Ct **3** E3 . . .26 A4
Detling Ho SE17 . . .152 A3
Devas St E3 . . . . . . .27 A1
Deventer Cres **3**
SE22 . . . . .64 A2
De Vere Cotts W8 .128 C2
De Vere Gdns W8 .128 C3
Deverell St SE1 . . .137 B1
De Vere Mews W8 .128 C2
Devereux Ct WC2 . .107 B1
Devereux Ho **3**
SW15 . . . . .56 C2
Devereux La SW13 . .47 A3
Devereux Rd SW11 .60 B1
Devitt Ho **3** E14 . . .34 A2
Devizes St N1 . . . . .87 C3
Devonhurst Pl **4**
W4 . . . . .37 C1

Devonia Rd N1 . . . . .86 B2
Devon Mans SE1 . .138 B4
Devonport **6**
W2 . . . . .102 A2
Devonport Ho **23**
W2 . . . . .31 C4
Devonport Rd W12 .39 A4
Devonport St E1 . . . .32 C3
Devonshire Cl W1 .104 A4
Devonshire Ct **6**
TW9 . . . . .44 B2
Devonshire Dr SE10 .52 A2
Devonshire Gdns
W4 . . . . .45 B3
Devonshire Gr SE15 .50 A4
Devonshire Hall **14**
E9 . . . . .17 B2
Devonshire Ho
SE1 . . . . .136 C2
SW1 . . . . .147 C2
W2 . . . . .101 C4
14 Balham SW12 . . .73 A4
London NW6 . . . . . .10 B2
2 Putney SW15 . . . .69 B4
Devonshire Hospl
W1 . . . . .103 C4
Devonshire House Prep
Sch NW3 . . . . .11 C3
Devonshire House Sch
NW3 . . . . .11 B3
Devonshire Mews **2**
W4 . . . . .38 A1
Devonshire Mews N
W1 . . . . .104 A4
Devonshire Mews S
W1 . . . . .104 A4
Devonshire Mews W
W1 . . . . .103 C4
Devonshire Pl NW2 . .1 C1
W1 . . . . .103 C4
W8 . . . . .128 A1
Devonshire Place Mews
W1 . . . . .103 C4
Devonshire Rd W4 . .38 A1
Devonshire Row
EC2 . . . . .110 B3
Devonshire Row Mews
W1 . . . . .92 B1
Devonshire Sq
EC2 . . . . .110 B2
Devonshire St W1 .104 A4
London W4 . . . . . . .38 A1
Devonshire Terr
W2 . . . . .101 A1
Devons Rd E3 . . . . .27 A1
Devons Road Sta
E3 . . . . .27 B1
Devon St SE15 . . . . .50 A4
De Walden Ho NW8 .80 A2
De Walden St W1 . .103 C3
Dewar St SE15 . . . . .64 C4
Dewberry St E14 . . .34 B4
Dewey Rd N1 . . . . . .85 B2
Dewhurst Rd W14 . .39 C3
Dewsbury Ct **1** W4 .37 B2
Dewsbury Rd NW10 . .8 C3
Dewsbury Terr NW1 .82 B4
D'eynsford Rd SE5 . .48 C2
Dhonau Ho SE1 . . .153 A3
Diadem Ct W1 . . . .105 B2
Dial Wlk The W8 . . .128 B4
Diamond Est SW17 .72 A1
Diamond Ho **20** E3 .26 A3
Diamond St SE15 . . .49 A3
Diamond Terr SE10 .52 B2
Diana Cl **45** SE8 . . .51 B4
Diana Ho **4** SW13 . .46 B2

Diana, Princess of
Wales Mml Wlk
W2 . . . . .114 C1
Dibden Ho **16** SE5 . .49 A3
Dibden St N1 . . . . . .86 C4
Dibdin Ho W9 . . . . .78 A1
Dicey Ave NW2 . . . . .9 B4
Dickens Ho NW8 . . .89 C2
SE17 . . . . .150 B1
WC1 . . . . .94 A2
London NW6 . . . . . .23 C2
Dickens House Mus
WC1 . . . . .95 A1
Dickenson Rd N8 . . .5 A4
Dickens Sq SE1 . . .137 A2
Dickinson Ho **3** E2 .99 B3
Dickinson Ho **2** E2 .99 B3
Dicksee Ho NW8 . . .89 B1
Dick Shepherd Ct **17**
SW2 . . . . .62 C1
Dickson Ho **13** E1 . .32 A3
Didbin Ho N7 . . . . . .5 B2
Digby Cres N4 . . . . .6 B2
Digby Mans W6 . . . .39 B1
Digby Rd E9 . . . . . .17 C2
Digby St E2 . . . . . . .25 B2
Digby Stuart Coll
SW15 . . . . .56 C2
Diggon St **1** E1 . . . .32 C4
Dighton Ct SE17 . . .48 B4
Dighton Rd SW18 . .59 B3
Dignum St N1 . . . . . .85 B2
Digswell St N7 . . . . .14 C2
Dilke St SW3 . . . . . .159 A4
Dilston Gr SE16 . . . .40 B2
Dimes Pl **6** W6 . . . .39 A2
Dimson Cres E3 . . . .26 C2
Dinerman Ct NW8 . . .79 B4
Dingle Gdns E14 . . .33 C2
Dingley La SW16 . . .73 C2
Dingley Pl EC1 . . . .97 A3
Dingley Rd EC1 . . . .96 C3
Dingwall Rd SW18 . .71 B4
Dinmont Ho **24** E2 . .24 C3
Dinmont St **1** E2 . . .25 A3
Dinmore Ho **8** E9 . .25 B4
Dinnington Ho **11**
E1 . . . . .25 A1
Dinsdale Rd SE3 . . .53 B4
Dinsmore Rd SW12 .73 A4
Dinton Ho NW8 . . . .90 A2
Dinwiddy Ho N1 . . . .84 C1
Disbrowe Rd W6 . .154 B3
Discovery Bsns Pk
SE16 . . . . .139 C1
Discovery Ho **1**
E14 . . . . .34 B2
Disney Pl SE1 . . . .137 A4
Disney St SE1 . . . .137 A4
Disraeli Cl W4 . . . . .37 C2
Disraeli Gdns SW15 .58 B3
Disraeli Rd
Acton NW10 . . . . . .20 C3
Putney SW15 . . . . . .58 A3
Distaff La EC4 . . . .122 C4
Distillery La W6 . . . .39 B1
Distillery Rd W6 . . . .39 B1
Distillery Wlk **14**
TW8 . . . . .44 A4
Distin St SE11 . . . .149 B3
Ditchburn St E14 . . .34 B2
Ditton Ho **10** E5 . . .17 A3
Divis Way SW15 . . . .57 A1
Dixon Clark Ct N1 . .15 A2

Dixon Rd SE14 .....51 A2
Dobree Ave NW10 ....9 A1
Dobson Cl NW1 .....11 C1
Dobson Ho 18 SE14 .50 C4
SE5 ....48 C3
Doby Ct EC4 ....123 A4
Dockers Tanner Rd 10
E14 ....41 C2
Dockhead SE1 ......139 A3
Dockhead Wharf
SE1 ....139 A4
Dock Hill Ave SE16 .40 C4
Docklands Heritage Mus
SE16 ....33 B1
Dockley Rd SE16 ...139 B1
Dockley Road Ind Est
SE16 ....139 B1
Dock Offices 12
SE16 ....40 B3
Dock St E1 ....125 B4
Doctor Spurstowe
Almshos 9 E8 ......17 A2
Docura Ho N7 ....5 B2
Docwra's Bldgs N1 .16 A2
Dodbrooke Rd SE27 .75 A1
Dodd Ho 10 SE16 ....40 A2
Doddington Gr
SE17 ....150 B1
Doddington Pl 4
SE17 ....48 A4
Dodson St SE1 .....135 C3
Dod St E14 ....33 C3
Dog Kennel Hill
SE22 ....64 A4
Dog Kennel Hill Sch
SE22 ....64 A4
Dog La NW10 ....8 A4
Dolben Ct SE8 ......51 B4
Dolben St SE1 .....122 B1
Dolby Rd SW6 ......164 C1
Dolland Ho SE11 ...149 A1
Dolland St SE11 ...149 A1
Dollar Bay E14 .....42 B4
Dollis Hill Sta NW2 ...8 C3
Dolman Cl W4 ......37 C2
Dolman St SW4 .....62 B3
Dolphin Ct 8 SE16 .40 C4
Dolphin Ct N7 ......13 C4
Dolphin La E14 .....34 A2
Dolphin Sch SW11 .60 B2
Dolphin Sq SW1 ...147 A1
Dolphin Twr 21 SE8 .51 B4
Dombey Ho SE1 ....139 A4
4 London W11 ......30 C1
Dombey St WC1 ....106 C4
Domelton Ho SW18 .59 A1
Domett Cl SE5 .....63 C3
Domfe Pl E5 ....17 B4
Domingo St EC1 ....96 C1
Dominion St
EC2 ....109 C4
Donaghue Cotts 1
E14 ....33 A4
Donaldson Rd NW6 .23 B4
Donegal Ho 2 E1 ...25 B1
Donegal St N1 .....85 A1
Doneraile Ho SW1 .146 A1
Doneraile St SW6 ..47 C2
Dongola Rd E1 .....33 A4
Donkey Alley SE22 .64 C1
Donkin Ho 9 SE16 .40 A2
Donne Ct SE24 .....63 B1
Donne Ho 7 E14 ....33 C3
14 SE14 ....50 C4
18 London N16 .....15 C4
Donnelly Ct SW6 ..154 B2
Donne Pl SW3 .....144 B4

Donnington Ct
London NW10 ....9 A1
11 London NW1 ....13 A1
Donnington Ct
NW8 ....171 B2
Donnington Prim Sch
NW10 ....22 A4
Donnington Rd
NW10 ....22 A4
Donovan Ct SW7 ..143 B1
Donovan Ho 3 E1 ..32 B2
Don Phelan Cl SE5 .48 C2
Doon St SE1 ....121 B2
Doradus Ct 20
SW19 ....69 C3
Dora Ho 1 E14 .....33 B3
11 London W11 ....30 C2
Doral Ct W12 ......30 A2
Doran Wlk E15 .....76 B1
Dora St E14 ....33 B3
Dorcas Ct 9 SW18 .59 C3
Dorchester Ct
SW1 ....131 A1
1 London N1 ....16 A1
London SE24 ....63 B2
5 Streatham SW16 .74 A2
Dorchester Dr SE24 .63 B2
Dorchester Gr W4 ..38 B1
Dordrecht Rd W3 ..29 A1
Doria Rd SW6 ......165 A2
Doric Ho 7 E2 ......25 C3
Doric Way NW1 ....93 B4
Doris Emmerton Ct
SW18 ....59 B3
Dorking Cl SE8 .....51 B4
Dorking Ho SE1 ...137 C2
Dorlcote Rd SW18 .72 A4
Dorleston Ct N1 ...87 C4
Dorman Way NW8 ..79 B4
Dormay St SW18 ..59 A2
Dormstone Ho
SE17 ....152 A3
Dornan Wlk E15 ...27 B4
Dornberg Ct SE3 ..53 C3
Dorncliffe Rd SW6 164 B2
Dorney NW3 ....12 A1
Dorney Ct SW6 ....58 A4
Dornfell St NW6 ....10 C3
Dornoch Ho 23 E3 .26 B3
Dornton Rd SW12,
SW17 ....73 B2
Dorothy Charrington Ho
1 SE22 ....64 C2
Dorothy Rd SW11 ..60 B4
Dorrien Wlk SW16 .73 C2
Dorrington Point 20
E3 ....27 A2
Dorrington St EC1 107 B4
Dorrit Ho 9 W11 ...30 C1
Dorrit St SE1 ......137 A4
Dorset Bldgs EC4 .108 A1
Dorset Cl NW1 ....102 C4
Dorset Ct 3 N1 ....16 A1
Dorset Mans 6 W6 47 C4
Dorset Mews SW1 132 A2
Dorset Pl E15 ......19 C2
Dorset Rd SW8 ....162 C2
Dorset Rise EC4 ..108 A1
Dorset Sq NW1 ....90 C1
Dorset St W1 ......103 A3
Dorton Cl 6 SE15 .49 A3
Dorville Cres W6 ..39 A3
Doughty Ct 11 E1 .32 A1
Doughty Mews WC1 94 C1
Doughty St WC1 ...94 C1
Douglas Bldgs SE1 137 A4
Douglas Ct 5 NW6 .10 C1

Douglas Gracey Ho
SW18 ....70 A4
Douglas Ho SW1 ...147 C2
Douglas Johnstone Ho
SW6 ....154 C3
Douglas Mews NW2 ..1 A1
Douglas Rd 5 E16 .35 C4
N6 ....23 B4
London N1 ....15 B1
Douglas Rd N N1 ..15 B2
Douglas Rd S N1 ..15 B2
Douglas St SW1 ...147 B3
Douglas Waite Ho
NW6 ....11 A1
Douglas Way SE8 .51 B3
Doulton Ho SE11 ..149 A4
Doulton Mews 4
NW6 ....11 A2
Dounesforth Gdns
SW18 ....71 A3
Douro Pl W8 ......128 B2
Douro St E3 ....26 C3
Douthwaite Sq 1 E1 125 C2
Dovecote Gdns 3
SW14 ....55 C4
Dovedale Cotts
SW11 ....168 C2
Dovedale Ho N16 ...6 C4
Dovedale Rd SE22 .65 A1
Dovehouse St
SW3 ....144 A1
Dove Mews SW7 ...143 A2
Dovercourt Rd SE22 64 B1
Dover Ct EC1 ....96 A2
London SE10 ....52 A2
Dove Rd N1 ....15 C2
Doverfield Rd SW2 .74 A4
Dover Flats SE1 ...152 B3
Dover Ho 11 SE15 .50 B4
Doveton Ho 8 E1 ..25 B1
Doveton St 5 E1 ...25 B1
Dove Wlk SW1 ....145 B2
Dowdeswell Cl
SW15 ....56 A3
Dowding Ho N6 .....3 C4
Dowell Ho SE21 ...76 B1
Dowes Ho 12 SW16 .74 A1
Dowgate Hill EC4 .123 B4
Dowland St W10 ...23 A2
Dowlas St SE5 .....49 A3
Downbarton Ho
SW9 ....173 B4
Downbury Mews 13
SW18 ....58 C2
Downend Ct 8
SE15 ....49 A4
Downer's Cotts SW4 61 B3
Downey Ho 5 E1 ...25 C1
Downfield Cl W9 ...88 A1
Downham Ct 4 N1 .15 C1
Downham Rd N1 ..15 C1
Downing Ho
2 London W10 ....30 C3
4 Putney SW15 ...56 C2
Downing St* SW1 134 A4
Down Pl W6 ....39 A1

Downs Ct 16 E8 ....17 A3
Downsell Jun & Inf Schs
E15 ....19 C4
Downsell Rd E15 ...19 C4
Downshire Hill
NW3 ....11 C4
Downside 2 SW15 .58 A2
Downside Cres
NW3 ....12 A3
Downs La 5 E5 .....17 A4
Downs Park Rd E5,
E8 ....16 C3
Downs Rd E5,N16 .16 C4
Downs Side JMI Sch
E5 ....16 C4
Down St W1 ....118 A1
Down St Mews
W1 ....118 A1
Downsview Sch E5 .17 A4
Downton Ave SW2 .74 B2
Downtown Rd SE16 .41 A4
Dowrey St N1 ......85 B4
Dowson Cl SE5 ....63 C3
Dowson Ct SE13 ...67 C4
Dowson Ho 7 E1 ..32 C3
Doyce St SE1 .....136 C4
Doyle Gdns NW10 .22 A4
Doyle Ho W3 ....37 A4
D'Oyley St SW1 ...145 B4
Doynton St N19 ....4 A2
Draco St SE17 ....48 B4
Dragon Rd SE15 ...49 A4
Dragon Yd WC1 ...106 B2
Dragoon Rd SE8 ..41 B1
Dragor Rd NW10 ..20 B1
Drake Cl 3 SE16 ..40 C4
Drake Croft N16 ...6 C2
Drake Ct 5 W12 ...39 A4
Drakefell Rd SE4,
SE14 ....65 C4
Drakefield Rd SW17 72 C1
Drake Ho 17 E1 ...32 B4
2 E14 ....33 A2
Drakeley Ct N5 ....15 A4
Drake Rd SE4 ......66 C4
Drakes Ctyd NW6 .10 B1
Drake St WC1 .....106 C3
Draldo Ho 9 SW15 58 A2
Draper Ho SE1 ...150 B4
Draper Pl N1 ....86 B4
Drapers Almshouses 4
E3 ....26 C2
Drapers Gdns EC2 109 C2
Drapers Rd E15 ...19 C4
Drappers Way
SE16 ....153 C4
Draycott Ave SW3 144 B3
Draycott Cl SW11 168 A4
Draycott Ho SW3 144 B3
Draycott Pl SW3 ..144 C3
Draycott Terr SW3 145 A3
Drayford Cl W9 ...23 B1
Dray Gdns SW2 ...62 B2
Draymans Ct 6
SW9 ....62 B4
Drayson Mews W8 127 C3
Drayton Ct SW10 143 A1
Drayton Gdns
SW10 ....143 A1
Drayton Ho 14 SE5 .48 C3
Drayton Park Prim Sch
N5 ....14 C3
Drayton Park Sta
N5 ....14 C3
Drayton Pk N5,N7 .14 C4
Drayton Rd NW10 .21 B4

Dreadnought St
SE10 ....43 A3
Dresden Cl NW6 ...11 A2
Dresden Ho SE11 .149 A4
London SW11 .....169 B2
Dresden Rd N19 ...4 C3
Dressington Ave
SE4 ....66 C1
Drewett Ho 2 E1 ..111 C1
Drew Ho 3 SW16 ..74 A1
Drewstead Rd
SW16 ....73 C2
Driffield Rd 3 E3 ..26 A3
Driftway Ho 15 E3 .26 B3
Drinkwater Ho 11
SE5 ....48 C3
Drive Mans SW6 ..164 B2
Drive The London N7 .14 B2
London NW10 .....21 B4
London NW11 ....1 A4
London W3 ....28 B3
Dr Johnson Ave
SW17 ....73 A1
Dr Johnson's Ho
EC4 ....107 C1
Droitwich Cl SE26 .76 C1
Dromore Rd SW15 .58 A1
Dron Ho E1 ....32 B4
Droop St W10 .....23 A1
Drovers Ct SE13 ..67 B4
Drovers Pl SE15 ..50 A3
Druce Rd SE21 ....64 A1
Druid St SE1 ......138 C3
Drummer Lo N7 ....5 B1
Drummond Cres
NW1 ....93 B4
Drummond Gate
SW1 ....147 C2
Drummond Ho 12
E2 ....24 C3
Drummond Rd SE16 40 A3
Drummonds Pl TW9 54 A3
Drummond St NW1 .92 C2
Drum St E1 ....111 A2
Drury Ho SW8 ....170 C4
Drury La WC2 .....106 B1
Dryad St SW15 ....57 C4
Dryburgh Ho SW1 146 B2
Dryburgh Mans
SW15 ....57 B4
Dryburgh Rd SW15 57 B4
Dryden Ct SE11 ...149 C3
Dryden Ho
10 London SE5 ....7 A1
6 London SE5 .....49 A2
Dryden St WC2 ...106 B1
Dryer's Bldgs EC1 107 B3
Dryfield Wlk 1 SE8 51 C4
Drysdale Flats 3
E8 ....16 B3
Drysdale Ho E2 ...98 B4
Drysdale Pl N1 ....98 B4
Drysdale St N1 ....98 B4
Dublin Ave E8 .....24 C4
Ducal St E2 ....99 A3
Ducane Cl W12 ...30 B3
Du Cane Ct SW12 .72 C3
Du Cane Rd W12 ..29 C3
Ducavel Ho SW2 ..74 B3
Duchess Mews W1 104 B3
Duchess of Bedford Ho
W8 ....127 B4
Duchess of Bedford's
Wlk W8 ....127 B4
Duchess St W1 ...104 B3

Duchy St SE1 ....**121** C2
Ducie Ho **2** SW15 ..**57** B2
Ducie St SW4 ....**62** B3
Duckett St E1 ......**33** A4
Duck La W1 ....**105** B1
Du Cros Rd W3 .....**29** A1
Dudden Hill La NW10 **8** B3
Dudley Ct W1 .....**102** C1
WC2 ....**106** A2
Dudley Ho W2 ....**101** B3
London SW9 ....**173** B2
Dudley Mews **14**
SW2 ....**62** C1
Dudley Rd NW6 ....**23** B3
Richmond TW9 .....**44** B1
Dudley St W2 ....**101** B3
Dudmaston Mews
SW3 ....**143** C2
Duffell Ho SE11 ..**149** A1
Dufferin Ave EC1 ..**97** B1
Dufferin Ct EC1 ....**97** B1
Dufferin St EC1 ....**97** A1
Duffield Ho N4 ......**6** B4
Duff St E14 ....**34** A3
Dufour's Pl W1 ...**105** A1
Dugdale Ho **10** N7 ..**13** C3
Duke Humphrey Rd
SE3 ....**53** A1
Duke of Wellington Pl
SW1,W1 ....**131** C4
Duke Of York's Sq
SW3 ....**144** C3
Duke of York St
SW1 ....**119** A2
Duke Rd W4 ....**37** C1
Duke's Ave W4 ....**37** C1
Dukes Ct
London SE13 ....**52** B1
London SE22 ....**65** A2
London SE28 ....**76** C2
Dukes Gate **4** W4 ..**37** B2
Dukes Head Yd N6 ..**4** A3
Duke's Ho SW1 ...**147** C4
Duke Shore Wharf
E14 ....**33** B2
Dukes La W8 ......**128** A4
Duke's Mews W1 .**103** C2
Duke's PI EC3 ....**110** B1
Dukes Point N6 ....**4** A3
Duke's Rd WC1 ....**93** C3
Duke St W1 ......**103** C1
Duke St Hill SE1 ..**123** C2
Duke St St Mans W1 **103** C1
Duke St St James's
SW1 ....**119** A2
Duke's Yd W1 ....**117** C4
Dulas St N4 ....**5** B3
Dulford St
W11 ....**31** A2 **112** A4
Dulka Rd SW11 ....**60** B2
Dulverton NW1 ....**83** A3
Dulverton Mans
WC1 ....**95** A1
Dulwich Coll (Endowed)
SE21 ....**76** A2
Dulwich Coll Picture
Gall SE21 ....**76** A4
Dulwich Coll Prep Sch
SE21 ....**76** A1
Dulwich Comm
SE21 ....**76** A3
Dulwich Hamlet Jun Sch
SE21 ....**63** C1
Dulwich High Sch for
Boys SE24 ....**63** C2

Dulwich Hospl SE22 **64** B4
Dulwich Mead SE24 **63** B1
Dulwich Mews **1**
SE22
Dulwich Oaks The
SE21 ....**76** B1
Dulwich Rd SE24 ..**63** A1
Dulwich Village
SE21 ....**64** A1
Dulwich Village CE Inf
Sch SE21 ....**64** A1
Du Maurier Ho **2**
NW3 ....**12** B3
Dumbarton Ct **18**
SW2 ....**74** A4
Dumbarton Rd SW2 **62** A1
Dumont Rd N16 .....**7** A1
Dumphreys Ho **5**
SW4 ....**73** C4
Dumpton PI NW1 ..**12** C1
Dunbar St SE27 ....**75** B1
Dunbar Wharf **50**
E14 ....**33** B2
Dunboyne Rd NW3 .**12** B3
Dunbridge Ho **7**
SW15 ....**56** B1
Dunbridge St E2 ..**25** A1
Duncan Ct **3** E14 ..**34** B4
Duncan Gr W3 ....**29** A3
Duncan Ho **8** NW3 **12** B1
Duncannon Ho
SW1 ....**147** C1
Duncannon St
WC2 ....**120** A3
Duncan Rd E8 .....**25** A4
Richmond TW9 .....**54** A3
Duncan St N1 ......**86** A2
Duncan Terr N1 ....**86** A2
Dunch St **30** E1 ....**32** A3
Duncombe Ho **7**
SW19 ....**69** C3
Duncombe Prim Sch
N19 ....**5** A3
Duncombe Rd N19 ..**4** C3
Duncrievie Rd SE13 **67** C1
Dundalk Ho **2** E1 ..**32** B3
Dundalk Rd SE4 ...**66** A4
Dundas Ho **12** E2 ..**25** B3
Dundas Rd SE15 ...**50** B1
Dundee Ct **30** E1 ..**32** A1
Dundee Ho W9 ....**88** C4
Dundee St E1 .....**32** A1
Dundee Wharf E14 **33** B2
Dundonald Rd
NW10 ....**22** C4
Dundry Ho **8** SE26 **76** C1
Dunelm Gr SE27 ..**75** B1
Dunelm St E1 .....**32** C3
Dunford Rd N7 ....**14** B4
Dungarvan Ave
SW15 ....**56** C3
Dungeness Ho
SW18 ....**59** B3
Dunhill Point **12**
SW15 ....**69** A3
Dunkeld Ho **15** E14 **34** C3
Dunlace Rd E5 .....**17** C4
Dunlin Ct **11** SE21 ..**75** C2
Dunlin Ho **6** SE16 ..**40** C2
Dunloe Ct **7** E2 ....**24** B3
Dunloe St E2 ......**24** B3
Dunlop PI SE16 ...**139** A1
Dunmore Point E2 ..**98** C4
Dunmore Rd NW6 ..**23** A4
Dunmow Ho SE11 .**149** A2
Dunmow Rd E15 ...**19** C4

Dunmow Wlk N1 ...**86** C4
Dunnage Cres SE16 **41** A2
Dunnet Ho **29** E3 ..**26** B3
Dunnico Ho SE17 .**152** A2
Dunn's Pas WC1 ..**106** B2
Dunn St E8 ....**16** B3
Dunollie PI NW5 ...**13** B3
Dunollie Rd NW5 ...**13** B3
Dunoon Ho N1 .....**84** C3
Dunraven Ho **12**
TW9 ....**44** B2
Dunraven Rd W12 ..**29** C1
Dunraven St W1 ..**117** A4
Dunraven Upper Sch
SW16 ....**74** B1
Dunsany Rd W14 ...**39** C3
Dunsdale Way
SE3 ....**74** B4
Dunsfold Way
SW15 ....**57** A1
Dunsmure Rd N16 ..**7** A3
Dunstable Ct **3**
SE3 ....**53** C3
Dunstable Mews
W1 ....**103** C4
Dunstable Rd TW10,
TW9 ....**54** A3
Dunstall Ho **9** SE15 **49** C2
Dunstan Ho SE4 ...**51** B1
Dunstan Hos **5** E1 ..**32** B4
Dunstan Rd NW11 ..**1** C3
Dunstan's Gr SE22 **65** A1
Dunstan's Rd SE22 **64** C1
Dunster Ct EC3 ...**124** B4
Dunster Gdns NW6 **10** B1
Dunsterville Way
SE1 ....**137** C3
Dunston Rd E8 ....**24** B4
London SW11 ......**169** C1
Dunston St E8 .....**24** B4
Dunton Ho **56** SW16 **74** A1
Dunton Rd SE1 ...**152** C3
Duntshill Rd SW18 .**71** A3
Dunworth Mews
W11 ....**31** B3
Duplex Ride SW1 .**131** A3
Durand Gdns SW9 **173** A3
Durand Prim Sch
SW9 ....**173** A3
Durant St E2 ......**24** C2
Durban Ho **32** W12 **30** A2
Durdans Ho **1** NW1 **13** B1
Durfey Ho SE5 ....**48** C3
Durford Cres SW15 **69** A3
Durham Ct **3** NW6 **23** C3
Durham Ho NW8 ...**90** B3
Durham House St
WC2 ....**120** B3
Durham PI SW3 ...**144** C1
Durham Rd N4,N7 ...**5** B2
Durham Row E1 ...**33** A4
Durham St SE11 ..**162** C4
Durham Terr W2 ..**100** A2
Durley Rd N16 .....**7** A4
Durlock Ho SW9 ..**173** B4
Durlston Rd E5 .....**7** C2
Durnford St **5** SE10 **52** B4
Durnsford Ave
SW18,SW19 ....**70** C2
Durnsford Rd SW18,
SW19 ....**71** C1
Durrell Rd SW6 ...**164** C3
Durrels Ho W14 ..**141** A4
Durrington Rd E5 ..**18** A4

Durrington Twr
SW8 ....**171** A2
Durrisdeer Ho NW2 **10** B4
Dursley Cl SE3 ....**53** D1
Durston NW5 ....**12** C3
Durward St E1 .....**32** A4
Durweston Mews
W1 ....**103** A3
Durweston St W1 .**103** A3
Dutch Yd SW18 ....**58** C2
Dutton Ho SW2 ....**75** A3
Dutton St SE10 ....**52** B2
Dwight Ct SW6 ...**164** B2
Dycer Ho **9** E9 ...**17** C2
Dye House La E3 ..**26** C4
Dyer's La SW15 ....**57** A3
Dykes Ct **11** SW2 ..**74** B3
Dylan Rd **2** SE24 ..**63** A3
Dylways SE5 ......**63** C3
Dymchurch Ho **12**
E5 ....**17** A3
Dymes Path SW19 .**69** C2
Dymock St SW6 ...**59** A4
Dyne Rd NW6 .....**10** B1
Dynevor Rd
London N16 ....**7** B1
Richmond TW10 ...**54** A2
Dynham Rd NW6 ..**10** C1
Dyott St WC1 ....**105** C2
WC1,WC2 ....**106** A2
Dysart St EC2 SA4 **98** A1
Dyson Ho **3** SE10 ..**43** B1

E

Eade Rd N4 ....**6** B4
Eagle Cl SE16 .....**40** B1
Eagle Ct EC1 .....**108** A4
Eagle Dwellings
EC1 ....**97** A4
Eagle Ho **22** E1 ...**25** A1
Eagle Hts **10** SW11 **60** A4
Eagle Lo NW11 .....**1** B4
Eagle Mans N16 ...**16** B3
Eagle Mews N1 ....**16** A2
Eagle PI SW1 .....**119** A3
SW7 ....**143** A2
Eagle St WC1 ....**106** C3
Eagle Wharf SE1 ..**124** C1
Eagle Wharf Rd N1 **87** A2
Ealing,Hammersmith &
West London Coll
W14 ....**140** B2
Ealing Tertiary Coll
W3 ....**28** A1
Eamann Casey Ho
SW9 ....**173** C3
Eamont Ct NW8 ...**80** B2
Eamont St NW8 ...**80** B2
Eardley Cres SW5 **141** C1
Earldom Rd SW15 .**57** B3
Earle Ho SW1 ....**146** A1
Earl Ho NW1 ......**90** B1
Earlom Ho WC1 ...**95** B3
Earl Rd SW14 .....**55** B3
Earl's Court Ex Ctr*
SW5 ....**141** B2
Earl's Court Gdns
SW5 ....**142** A3
Earl's Court Rd
SW5,W8 ....**141** C4
Earl's Court Sq
SW5 ....**142** A2
Earl's Court Sta
SW5 ....**141** C3
Earlsferry Way N1 ..**14** A1

Earlsfield Prim Sch
SW18 ....**71** B2
Earlsfield Rd SW18 **71** B3
Earlsfield Sta SW18 **71** B3
Earlsmead Rd NW10 **22** B2
Earl St EC2 ....**110** A4
Earls Terr W8 ....**127** A1
Earlsthorpe Mews **3**
SW12 ....**60** C1
Earlston Gr E9 ....**25** A4
Earlston Gr E9 ....**96** A4
Earlston St E12 ...**126** A4
Earls Wlk W8 ....**127** B1
Earlswood Cl **10**
SE10 ....**43** A1
Earlswood Ho **2**
SW2 ....**74** B3
Earlswood St SE10 .**43** A1
Early Mews NW1 ..**82** B4
Earnshaw St WC1,
WC2 ....**105** C2
Earsby St W14 ...**140** B4
Eashing Point **5**
SW15 ....**69** A3
Easleys Mews W1 **103** C2
East Acton Arc W3 .**29** B3
East Acton La W3 ..**29** A2
East Acton Prim Sch
W3 ....**29** A2
East Acton Sta W12 **29** B3
East Arbour St E1 ..**32** C3
East Bank N16 ......**7** A4
East Block **5** E1 ...**32** C2
Eastbourne Av W3 **28** C3
Eastbourne Gdns
SW14 ....**55** B4
Eastbourne Mews
W2 ....**101** A2
Eastbourne Rd W4 **45** B4
Eastbourne Terr
W2 ....**101** A2
Eastbury Gr W4 ...**38** A1
Eastbury Terr E1 ..**25** C1
Eastcastle St W1 .**105** A2
Eastcheap EC3 ...**124** A4
East Churchfield Rd
W3 ....**28** C1
Eastcote St SW9 .**172** C1
East Cross Ctr E15 **18** C2
East Cross Route
E3 ....**26** C4
London E9 ....**18** B3
Eastdown Ho E8 ..**16** C4
Eastdown Pk SE13 **67** C3
East Dulwich Gr
SE22 ....**64** A2
East Dulwich Rd
SE15,SE22 ....**64** B3
East Dulwich Sta
SE22 ....**64** A3
Eastern Rd SE4 ...**66** C3
East Ferry Rd E14 .**42** A2
Eastfields Rd W3 ..**28** B4
Eastfield St E14 ...**33** A4
East Harding St
EC4 ....**107** C2
East Heath Rd NW3 .**2** C1
East Hill SW18 ....**59** B2
East India Bldgs **9**
E14 ....**33** C2
East India Dock Basin
E14 ....**35** A1
East India Dock Rd *
E14 ....**34** A2
East India Dock Road
Tunnel **17** E14 ...**34** C3

East India Dock Wall Rd E14 ....34 C2
East India Sta E14 ....34 C2
East La SE16 ....139 B3
Eastlake Ho NW8 ....89 C1
Eastlake Rd SE5 ....48 B1
Eastlands Cres SE21 64 B1
Eastleigh Wlk 🔟 SW15 ....68 C4
East London Coll & Toynbee Theatre E1 ....111 A3
East London Stadium E3 ....33 B4
Eastman Dental Hospl WC1 ....94 C2
Eastman Ho 🔟 SW4 61 B1
Eastman Rd W3 ....37 C4
Eastmearn Rd SE21, SE27 ....75 B2
East Mount St E1 ....32 A4
East Parkside SE10 ....43 B3
Easton Ho 🔟 SE27 ....75 A1
Easton St WC1 ....95 B3
East Pas EC1 ....108 C4
East Point 🔟 SE1 ....153 B2
East Poultry Ave EC1 ....108 A3
East Putney Sta SW15 ....58 A2
East Rd N1 ....97 C4
East Row W10 ....23 A1
Eastry Ho SW8 ....162 A1
East Sheen Ave SW14 ....55 C3
East Sheen Prim Sch SW14 ....56 A3
East Smithfield E1 125 A3
East Surrey Gr SE15 49 B3
East Tenter St E1 ....111 A1
Eastvale W3 ....29 B1
East View NW3 ....2 C2
Eastway E3,E9 ....26 A4
London E9,E10 ....18 C4
Eastwell Ho SE1 ....137 C2
Eastwick Ct 🔟 SW19 ....69 C3
Eaton Cl SW1 ....145 B3
Eaton Dr SW9 ....63 A3
Eaton Gate SW1 ....145 B4
Eaton Ho SW11 ....167 C3
Eaton House The Manor Sch SW4 ....61 A3
Eaton La SW1 ....132 B1
Eaton Mans SW1 ....145 B3
Eaton Mews N SW1 ....131 C1
Eaton Mews S SW1 ....132 A1
Eaton Mews W SW1 ....145 C4
Eaton Pl SW1 ....131 C1
Eaton Row SW1 ....132 A1
Eaton Sq SW1 ....131 C1
Eaton Square Sch SW1 ....146 A3
Eaton Terr E1 ....26 A2
SW1 ....145 C4
Eaton Terr Mews SW1 ....145 B4
Eatonville Rd SW17 72 B2
Eatonville Villas SW17 ....72 B2
Ebbisham Dr SW8 ....162 C1
Ebbsfleet Rd NW2 ....10 A4

Ebenezer Ho SE11 ....150 A3
Ebenezer Mussel Ho 🔟 E2 ....25 B3
Ebenezer St N1 ....97 B4
Ebley Cl SE15 ....49 B4
Ebner St SW18 ....59 A2
Ebony Ho NW3 ....11 A2
Ebor Cotts SW15 ....68 A1
Ebor St E1,E2 ....98 C2
Eburne Rd N7 ....5 A1
Ebury Bridge Rd SW1 ....145 C1
Ebury Mews SW1 ....146 A4
Ebury Mews E SW1 ....132 A1
Ebury Sq SW1 ....145 C3
Ebury St SW1 ....146 A4
Ecclesbourne Prim Sch N1 ....15 B1
Ecclesbourne Rd N1 ....15 B1
Eccles Ct 🔟 SW2 ....62 C1
Eccleston Ho 🔟 SW2 ....62 C1
Eccleston Mews SW1 ....131 C1
Eccleston Pl SW1 ....146 A4
Eccleston Sq SW1 ....146 B3
Eccleston Sq Mews SW1 ....146 B3
Eccleston St SW1 ....146 A4
Eckersley St E2 ....99 A1
Eckford St N1 ....85 B2
Eckstein Rd SW11 ....60 A3
Edans Ct W12 ....38 B4
Edbrooke Rd W9 ....23 C1
Eddisbury Ho 🔟 SE26 ....76 C1
Eddiscombe Rd SW6 ....165 A2
Eddystone Rd SE4 ....66 A2
Eddystone Twr SE8 ....41 A1
Edenbridge Cl 28 SE16 ....40 A1
Edenbridge Rd E9 ....17 C1
Eden Cl W8 ....127 C2
London NW3 ....1 C2
Edendale W3 ....28 A2
Eden Gr N7 ....14 B3
Edenham Way W10 ....31 B4
Eden Ho NW8 ....90 A1
🔟 SE16 ....40 C4
Edenhurst Ave SW6 ....58 B4
Eden Lodge NW6 ....9 C1
Eden Mews SW17 ....71 B1
Edensmuir Ct SE3 ....53 C3
Edensor Gdns W4 ....46 A3
Edensor Rd W4 ....46 A3
Edenvale St SW6 ....166 C1
Edgar Ho NW8 ....162 A2
London E9 ....18 A3
Edgar Kail Way SE22 ....64 A3
Edgarley Terr SW6 ....164 A3
Edgar Rd E3 ....27 A2
Edgcott Ho W10 ....30 B4
Edgecombe Ho 🔟 SE5 ....49 A1
Putney SW19 ....70 A4
Edgecote Cl 🔟 W3 ....28 B1
Edgehill Ho 🔟 SW9 ....48 A1
Edgeley La SW4 ....61 C4
Edgeley Rd SW4 ....61 C4
Edgel St SW18 ....59 A3
Edge St W8 ....31 C1 113 C2
Edgeworth Ho NW8 ....78 C4
Edgson Ho 🔟 SW1 ....146 A2

Edgware Rd W1, W2,NW1,NW8 ....102 A3
Edgware Road Sta (Bakerloo) NW1 ....102 A3
Edgware Road Sta (Ham,Distr,Circle) NW1 ....102 B3
Edinburgh Cl 🔟 E2 ....25 B3
Edinburgh Ct 🔟 SE16 ....32 C1
Edinburgh Ho W9 ....88 B4
🔟 London W3 ....28 C3
Edington 20 NW5 ....12 C2
Edison Bldg 🔟 E14 ....41 C4
Edison Ct SE10 ....43 B3
Edison Ho SE1 ....151 B4
Editha Mans SW10 ....156 C3
Edith Cavell Cl 🔟 N19 ....5 A4
Edith Gr SW10 ....157 A2
Edith Ho 🔟 W6 ....39 B1
Edithna St SW9 ....62 A4
Edith Neville Prim Sch NW1 ....83 B1
Edith Ramsay Ho 🔟 E1 ....33 A4
Edith Rd W14 ....140 B3
London E15 ....19 C3
Edith Row SW6 ....166 B4
Edith St E2 ....24 C3
Edith Summerskill Ho 🔟 SW6 ....154 C2
Edith Terr SW10 ....156 C2
Edith Villas W14 ....140 C2
Edith Yd SW10 ....157 A2
Edmeston Cl E9 ....18 A2
Edmond Ct SE14 ....50 B2
Edmonton Ct 🔟 SE16 ....40 B3
Edmund Halley Way SE10 ....43 B4
Edmund Ho SE17 ....150 B1
London SE14 ....51 B2
Edmundsbury Ct Est 🔟 SW9 ....62 B3
Edmund St SE5 ....48 C3
Edmund Waller Prim Sch SE14 ....50 C1
Ednam Ho SE15 ....49 C4
Edna St SW11 ....168 A3
Edred Ho E9 ....18 A4
Edrich Ho SW4 ....172 A3
Edric Ho SW1 ....147 C4
Edric Rd SE14 ....50 C3
Edridge Ho 🔟 SE27 ....75 A1
Edward Alleyn Ho SE21 ....76 A4
Edward Cl 🔟 E16 ....35 C4
Edward Dodd Ct N1 ....97 C4
Edward Edwards Ho SE1 ....122 A1
Edwardes Sq W8 ....127 C1
Edward Friend Ho 🔟 N16 ....7 A1
Edward Ho SE11 ....149 A2
W2 ....89 B1
Edward Mann Cl 🔟 E1 ....32 C3
Edward Mews NW1 ....82 B1
Edward Pl SE8 ....51 B4
Edward Robinson Ho 🔟 SE14 ....50 C3
Edward's Cotts 🔟 N1 ....15 A1

Edward's La N16 ....7 A2
Edwards Mews W1 ....103 B1
London N1 ....14 C1
Edward Sq N1 ....84 C3
🔟 SE16 ....33 A1
Edward St SE14 ....51 A3
SE16 ....51 B4
Edward VII Mans NW10 ....22 C2
Edward Wilson Prim Sch W2 ....100 A4
Edwin Ho SE15 ....49 C3
Edwin's Mead E9 ....18 A4
Edwin St E1 ....25 B1
E16 ....35 C4
Edwy Ho E9 ....18 B4
Edwyn Ho SW18 ....59 A1
Effie Pl SW6 ....155 C1
Effie Rd SW6 ....155 C1
Effingham Ho 🔟 SW8 ....171 B1
Effra Ct SW2 ....62 B2
Effra Mans SW2 ....62 C2
Effra Par SW2 ....62 C2
Effra Rd SW2 ....62 C2
Effra Road Ret Pk SW2 ....62 C2
Egbert Ho E9 ....18 A3
Egbert St NW1 ....81 B4
Egbury Ho SW15 ....56 B1
Egerton Cres SW3 ....144 B4
Egerton Ct 🔟 TW10 ....54 A2
Egerton Dr SE10 ....52 A2
Egerton Gdns SW3 ....130 A1
Willesden NW10 ....22 B4
Egerton Gdns Mews SW3 ....130 B1
Egerton Pl SW3 ....130 B1
Egerton Rd W4 ....45 B4
London N16 ....7 B4
Egerton Terr SW3 ....130 B1
Egham Cl SW19 ....70 A2
Eglantine Rd SW18 ....59 B2
Eglington Ct SE17 ....48 B4
Egliston Mews SW15 ....57 B4
Egliston Rd SW15 ....57 B4
Egmont St SE14 ....50 C3
Egremont Ho SE13 ....52 A1
Egremont Rd SE27 ....74 C1
Egret Ho 🔟 SE16 ....40 C2
Eider Ct 🔟 SE8 ....51 B4
Ekarra Ho SW8 ....172 B4
Elaine Ct 🔟 NW3 ....12 B2
Elaine Gr NW5 ....12 C3
Elaine Ho N4 ....5 A3
Elam Cl SE5 ....48 A1
Elam St SE5 ....48 A1
Elan Ct E1 ....32 A4
Eland Rd SW11 ....60 B4
Elba Pl SE17 ....151 A4
Elbe St SW6 ....166 C2
Elborough St SW18 ....70 C3
Elbury Dr E16 ....35 C3
Elcho St SW11 ....158 B1
Elcot Ave SE15 ....50 A3
Elderberry Rd W5 ....36 A4
Elderfield Ho 🔟 E14 ....33 C2
Elderfield Rd E5 ....17 C4
Elder St E1 ....24 B1 98 C1
Elder Wlk N1 ....86 B4
Eldon Ct NW6 ....23 C4
Eldon Gr NW3 ....11 C3
Eldon Ho SW9 ....63 A4
Eldon Rd W8 ....128 B1
Eldon St EC2 ....109 C3
Eldon Way NW10 ....20 A3

Eldridge Ct SE16 ....139 B1
Eleanor Cl SE16 ....40 C4
Eleanor Ct 🔟 E2 ....24 C4
Eleanor Gr SW13 ....56 A4
Eleanor Ho 🔟 London NW5 ....13 B3
🔟 London W6 ....39 B1
Eleanor Palmer Prim Sch NW5 ....13 B4
Eleanor Rathbone Ho 🔟 N6 ....4 C4
Eleanor St E3 ....26 C2
Electric Ave SW9 ....62 C3
Electric Ho 🔟 E3 ....26 C2
Electric La 🔟 SW9 ....62 C3
Electric Mans 🔟 SW9 ....62 C3
Elephant & Castle SE1 ....136 B1
SE1 ....150 B4
Elephant & Castle Sta SE1 ....136 B1
SE17 ....150 C4
Elephant La SE16 ....40 B4
Elephant Rd SE17 ....150 C4
Elfindale Rd SE24 ....63 B2
Elfort Rd N5 ....14 C4
Elf Row E1 ....32 B2
Elgar Ave W5 ....36 A4
Elgar Cl SE8 ....51 C3
Elgar Ct W14 ....126 A1
Elgar Ho NW6 ....146 B1
London NW6 ....11 B1
Elgar St SE16 ....41 A3
Elgin Ave W9 ....88 B4
London W12 ....39 A3
Elgin Cres W11 ....31 A2 112 B4
Elgin Ct W9 ....88 A2
Elgin Ho 🔟 E14 ....34 A3
Elgin Mans W9 ....88 A3
Elgin Mews W11 ....31 A3
Elgin Mews N W9 ....88 B4
Elgin Mews S W9 ....88 B4
Elgood Ho NW8 ....79 C1
Elham Ho 🔟 E5 ....17 A3
Elia Mews N1 ....86 A1
Elias Pl SW8 ....163 B3
Elia St N1 ....86 A1
Elim Est SE1 ....138 A2
Elim St SE1 ....138 A2
Eliot Ct SW18 ....59 A1
Eliot Gdns SW15 ....56 C3
Eliot Hill SE13 ....52 B1
Eliot Ho 🔟 TW10 ....54 B1
Eliot Mews NW8 ....78 C1
Eliot Pk SE13 ....52 B1
Eliot Pl SE3 ....53 A1
Eliot Vale SE3 ....52 C1
Elizabeth Ave N1 ....87 A4
Elizabeth Barnes Ct SW6 ....166 B2
Elizabeth Cl 🔟 E14 ....34 A3
W9 ....89 A1
Elizabeth Cotts 🔟 TW9 ....44 C2
Elizabeth Ct SW1 ....133 C1
SW10 ....157 C3
SW1 ....133 C1
Elizabeth Finn Ho W12 ....38 C3
Elizabeth Garrett Anderson Hospl NW1 ....92 C1

Elizabeth Garrett
Anderson Language
Coll N1 .... 84 C2
Elizabeth Gdns W3 .29 B1
Elizabeth Ho 48 E3 .27 A2
SE11 .... 149 C3
15 London N6 ......39 B1
Elizabeth Ind Est
SE14 ....50 C4
Elizabeth Kenny Ho
N1 ....15 B2
Elizabeth Mews
NW3 .... 12 B2
Elizabeth Selby Inf Sch
E2 ....24 C2 99 C4
Elizabeth Sq 13
SE16 ....33 A2
Elizabeth St SW1 .145 C4
Elkington Point
SE11 .... 149 B3
Elkstone Rd W10 ..31 B4
Ellacombe Ho 1
SW2 ....74 C4
Ellaline Rd W6 .....47 C4
Ella Mews NW3 ....12 B4
Elland Ho 12 E14 ..33 B3
Elland Rd SE15 ....65 B3
Ella Rd N4,N8 ......5 A4
Ellenborough Ho 5
W12 ....30 A2
Ellenborough Pl
SW15 ....56 C3
Ellen St E1 ....111 C1
Ellen Wilkinson Ho
7 E2 ....25 C2
SW6 .... 155 A3
Ellerby St SW6 .....47 C2
Ellerdale Cl 22 NW3 11 B4
Ellerdale Rd NW3 ..11 B3
Ellerdale St SE13 ..67 A4
Ellerker Gdns TW10 54 A1
Ellerslie Gdns
NW10 ....21 C4
Ellerslie Ind Est
SW2 ....62 A2
Ellerslie Rd W12 ..30 A1
Ellerton St E3 ......33 A4
Ellerton Rd
Barnes SW13 ......46 C2
Wandsworth SW17,
SW18 ....71 C2
Ellery Ho SE17 ....151 C3
Ellery St SE15 ......50 A1
Ellesmere Ct W4 ...45 C4
Ellesmere Rd E3 ...26 A3
Chiswick W4 ....45 C4
London NW10 ......8 C3
Ellesmere St E14 ..34 A3
Ellingfort Rd E8 ....17 A1
Ellingham Rd
London E15 ....19 C4
London W12 ....38 C4
Ellington Ho SE1 .137 A1
Ellington St N7 ....14 C2
Elliot Rd SW9 ......48 A3
Elliott Rd
London SW9 ....48 A2
London W4 ....38 A2
Elliott Sch SW15 ..57 B1
Elliott's Pl N1 ......86 B3
Elliott Sq NW3 .....12 A1
Elliott's Row SE11 150 B4
Ellis Cl NW10 ....9 B2
Ellisfield Dr SW15 .68 C4

Ellis Franklin Ct
NW8 ....78 C2
Ellis Ho SE17 .....151 B2
Ellison Ho 1 SE13 .52 B1
Ellison Rd SW13 ...46 B1
Ellis St SW1 ....145 B4
Ellsworth St E2 ....25 A2
Ellwood Ct W9 .....88 B1
Elm Bank Gdns
SW13 ....46 A1
Elm Bank Mans
SW13 ....46 A1
Elmbourne Rd
SW17 ....73 A1
Elmbridge Wlk E8 .16 C1
Elm Cl N19 ....4 B2
Elmcourt Rd SE21,
SE27 ....75 A2
Elm Court Sch SE27 75 A2
Elm Cres W5 ....36 A4
Elmcroft N6 ....4 B4
Elmcroft Ave NW11 .1 B4
Elmcroft Cres NW11 1 A4
Elmcroft St E5 .....17 B4
Elm Ct EC4 ....107 B1
London SE13 ......67 C4
6 London W2 ......31 C4
Elmer Cl SW6 .....164 A4
Elmer Ho NW1 ....102 A4
Elmfield Ho W9 ...23 C1
6 London N5 .....15 B3
Elmfield Mans 5
SW17 ....72 C2
Elmfield Rd SW17 .73 A2
Elmfield Way W9 ..31 C4
Elm Friars Wlk
NW1 ....13 C1
Elm Gn W3 ....29 A3
Elm Gr NW2 ....9 C4
London SE15 ....49 C1
Elm Grove Rd
Barnes SW13 ......46 C1
London W5 ....36 A4
Elm Ho 4 E14 ......42 B4
Elmhurst Mans
SW4 ....61 C4
Elmhurst St SW4 ..61 C4
Elmhurst Villas
SE15 ....65 B3
Elmington Rd SE5 .48 C3
Elmira St SE13 .....67 A4
Elm Lo SW6 ....47 C2
Elmore Ho SW9 ...48 A1
Elmore St N1 ....15 C1
Elm Park Gdns
SW10 ....143 B1
Elm Park Ho SW10 143 B1
Elm Park La SW3 .143 B1
Elm Park Mans
SW10 ....157 A4
Elm Pk SW2 ....62 B1
Elm Park Rd SW3 .157 B4
Elm Quay SW8 ....161 B3
Elm Rd SW14 .....55 B3
Elm Row NW3 ......2 B1
Elms Cres SW4 ....61 C1
Elmshaw Rd SW15 .56 C2
Elmslie Point 2 E3 .33 B4
Elms Mews W2 ....115 B4
Elms Rd SW4 ......61 B2
Elm St WC1 ....95 A1
Elms The
Barnes SW13 ......56 A4
London NW10 .....21 A3
Elmstone Rd SW6 .165 B4

Elm Terr NW2 ....1 C1
Elmton Ct NW8 ....89 B2
Elmton Way E5 ......7 C1
Elm Tree Cl NW8 ..89 B4
Elm Tree Ct NW8 ..89 B4
5 London SE5 ....48 B2
Elm Tree Rd NW8 .89 B4
Elm Way NW10 .....8 A4
Elm Wlk NW3 ....1 C2
Elmwood Ct SW11 170 A4
Elm Wood Prim Sch
SE27 ....75 C1
Elmwood Rd
Chiswick W4 ......45 B4
London SE24 ......63 C2
Elmworth Gr SE21 .75 C2
Elnathan Mews W9 .88 B1
Elphinstone St N5 .15 A4
Elrington Rd E8 ....16 C2
Elsa St E1 ....33 A4
Elsdale St E9 ......17 B2
Elsden Mews E2 ...25 B3
Elsenham St SW18,
SW19 ....70 B2
Elsfield NW5 ....13 A3
Elsham Rd W14 ...126 A3
Elsham Terr W14 ..126 A3
Elsie Lane Ct W2 .100 A4
Elsiemaud Rd SE4 .66 B2
Elsie Rd SE22 ......64 B3
Elsinore Gdns NW2 .1 A1
Elsinore Ho N1 ....85 B3
12 London SE5 ...48 B1
Elsinore Way TW9 .55 A4
Elsley Rd SW11 ....60 C4
Elsley Sch SW11 ..60 C4
Elspeth Rd SW11 ..60 B3
Elstead Ho 9 SW2 .74 B4
Elsted St SE17 ....151 C3
Elstow Grange NW6 .9 C1
Elswick Rd SE13 ...52 A1
Elswick St SW6 ...166 C2
Elsworthy Rd NW3 .80 A4
Elsworthy Rise NW3 12 B1
Elsworthy Terr NW3 12 A1
Elsynge Rd SW18 .59 C2
Elsynge Road Mans
SW18 ....59 C2
Elthiron Rd SW6 ..165 C3
Elthorne Rd N19 ...4 C2
Elthruda Rd SE13 .67 C1
Elton Ho 3 E3 .....26 B4
Elton Pl N16 ....16 A3
Elton St 11 N16 ...16 A3
Eltringham St SW18 59 B3
Elvaston Mews
SW7 ....129 A2
Elvaston Pl SW7 ..129 A1
Elveden Ho 17 SW9 63 A3
Elver Gdns E2 .....24 C2
Elverson Rd SE8 ...52 A1
Elverson Rd Sta
SE8 ....52 A1
Everton St SE17 ..147 B4
Elvin Ho 2 E9 .....17 B2
Elvis Rd NW2 ....9 B2
Elwin St E2 ..24 C2 99 B4
Elwood Ho N5 ......6 A1
Elworth Ho SW8 ..163 A1
Ely Cottages SW8 .162 C1
Ely Court Flats
SW6 ....164 A3
Ely Ho 22 SE15 ...49 C3
Ely Pl EC1 ....107 C3
Elysium Gate SW6 164 C2
Elysium Pl SW6 ...164 C1

Elysium St SW6 ...164 C1
Elystan Pl SW3 ...144 C2
Elystan St SW3 ...144 B3
Elystan Wlk N1 ....85 B3
Elyston Ct SW15 ..57 A2
Emanuel Ave W3 ..28 B3
Emanuel Ct W3 ....28 C3
Emanuel Sch SW11 60 A2
Embankment SW15 47 C1
Embankment Gdns
SW3 ....159 A4
Embankment Pier
WC2 ....120 B2
Embankment Pl
WC2 ....120 B2
Embankment Sta
WC2 ....120 B2
Embassy Ct NW8 .79 C1
Embassy Ho 2
NW6 ....10 C1
Emba St SE16 .....139 C3
Ember Ct 8 W12 ...38 A3
Emberton SE5 .....49 A4
Emberton Ct EC1 ..96 A3
Embleton Rd SE13 67 A3
Embley Point 5 E5 .17 A4
Emden St SW6 ....166 A4
Emerald St WC1 ...106 C4
Emerson Ho N16 ..16 A3
Emerson St SE1 ..122 C2
Emery Hill St SW1 133 A1
Emery St SE1 .....135 C2
Emily Ho 11 W10 ..31 A4
Emily St 7 E16 .....35 B1
Emlyn Gdns 5 W12 38 A4
Emlyn Rd W12 ......38 A4
Emmanuel CE Prim Sch
NW6 ....10 C3
Emmanuel Ho
SE1 ....149 B3
Dulwich SE21 .....75 C1
Emmanuel Rd SW12 73 C3
Emma St E2 ....25 A3
Emminster NW6 ...78 A4
Emmott Cl E1 ......26 A1
Emperor's Gate
SW7 ....142 C4
Empingham Ho 50
SE8 ....40 C2
Empire Ho SW3 ..130 A1
Empire Sq N19 ....5 A1
Empire Wharf E3 ..26 A4
Empire Wharf Rd
E14 ....42 C2
Empress Mews 37
SE5 ....48 B1
Empress Pl SW5 ..141 B1
Empress St SE17 ..48 B4
Empson St E3 .....27 A1
Emsworth St SW2 .74 B2
Emu Rd SW8 .....170 A1
Enard Ho 27 E3 ...26 B3
Enbrook St W10 ...23 A2
Enclave Ct EC1 ....96 A2
Endell St WC2 .....106 A1
Enderby St SE10 ..43 A1
Endlesham Ct 2
SW12 ....72 C4
Endlesham Rd
SW12 ....72 C4
Endsleigh Gdns
WC1 ....93 B2
Endsleigh Mans 4
SW16 ....74 A1
Endsleigh Pl WC1 .93 C2
Endsleigh St WC1 .93 C2
Endwell Rd SE4 ...51 A1

Endymion Rd
London N4 ....6 A4
London SW2 ....62 B1
Energen Cl
London NW10 ......8 A4
London NW10 ......8 A2
Enfield Cloisters
N1 ....98 A4
Enfield Ho 5 SW9 172 B2
Enfield Rd
London E8,N1 .....16 A1
London N1 ....37 A4
Enford St W1 .....102 C4
Engadine St SW18 .70 C3
Engate St SE13 ...67 B3
England's La NW3 .12 B2
Englefield NW1 .....92 C3
Englefield Rd N1 ..16 A1
Englewood Rd
SW12 ....61 B1
English Gardening Sch
The SW3 ....158 C4
English Grounds
SE1 ....124 A1
English Martyrs RC Prim
Sch E1 ....110 C1
English St E3 ....26 B1
Enid St SE16 ......139 A2
Enid Stacy Ho 11
N19 ....5 A4
Enmore Ct SW14 ..55 C2
Enmore Gdns SW14 55 C2
Enmore Rd SW15 ..57 B2
Ennerdale Ho 3 N4 6 A4
Ennerdale Rd TW9 .44 B1
Ennersdale Prim Sch
SE13 ....67 C2
Ennersdale Rd SE13 67 C2
Ennis Ho 10 E14 ...34 A3
Ennismore Ave W4 .38 B2
Ennismore Gdns
SW7 ....130 A3
Ennismore Gdns Mews
SW7 ....130 A2
Ennismore Mews
SW7 ....130 A2
Ennismore St SW7 130 A2
Ennis Rd N4 ....5 C3
Ensbury Ho SW8 .162 C2
Ensign Cl E1 ......125 C3
Ensign St E1 ......125 B4
Ensor Mews SW7 .143 B2
Enterprise Way
London NW10 .....21 C2
London SW18 .....58 C3
Enterprize Way SE8 41 B2
Epirus Mews SW6 .155 B2
Epirus Rd SW6 ...155 A2
Epping Cl E14 .....41 C2
Epping Ho 15 ....7 C2
Epping Pl N1 ......14 C2
Epple Rd SW6 ....165 A4
Epworth St EC2 ...97 C1
Equity Sq E2 ....99 A3
Erasmus St SW1 ..147 C3
Erconwald St W12 .29 B3
Eresby Ho SW7 ...130 B3
Eresby Pl NW6 ....10 C1
Erica Ct SW4 ......172 B3
Erica Ho SE4 ......66 B4
Erica St W12 ......29 C2
Ericcson Cl SW18 .58 C2
Eric Fletcher Ct 7
N1 ....15 B1
Eric Macdonald Ho
SW6 ....165 C3
Eric Rd NW10 ....8 B2

Ericson Ho
London N16 . . . . 7 B3
London SE13 . . . . 67 C3
Eric St E3 . . . . 26 B1
Eric Wilkins Ho
SE1 . . . . 153 B1
Eridge Ho SE22 . . . . . . 64 B4
Eridge Rd W4 . . . . 37 C3
Erlanger Rd SE14 . . . . . 50 C1
Ermine Rd SE13 . . . . . . 67 A3
Ernest Bevin Coll
SW17 . . . . 72 A2
Ernest Gdns W4 . . . . . . 45 A4
Ernest Simmonds Ho
SE14 . . . . 50 B1
Ernest St E1 . . . . 25 C1
Ernshaw Pl SW15 . . . . . 58 A2
Eros (Shaftesbury
Meml) W1 . . . . 119 B3
Erpingham Rd
SW15 . . . . 57 B4
Errington Rd W9 . . . . . 23 B1
Errol St EC1 . . . . 97 A1
Erskine Ho SW1 . . . . . 146 C1
Erskine Rd NW3 . . . . . 12 B1
Escuan Lo N5 . . . . 15 B3
Esher Gdns SW19 . . . . . 69 C2
Esher Ho SW8 . . . . . . 171 C2
Eskdale NW1 . . . . 82 C1
Esk Ho E3 . . . . 26 B1
Esme Ho SW15 . . . . . . 56 B3
Esmeralda Rd SE1 . . . 153 C3
Esmond Ct W8 . . . . . . 128 B2
Esmond Gdns W4 . . . . . 37 C2
Esmond Rd NW6 . . . . . 23 B4
London W4 . . . . 37 C3
Esmond St SW15 . . . . . 58 A3
Esparto St SW18 . . . . . 71 A4
Essendine Mans
W9 . . . . 23 C2
Essendine Prim Sch
W9 . . . . 23 C2
Essendine Rd W9 . . . . . 23 C2
Essex Ct EC4 . . . . 107 B1
Barnes SW13 . . . . 46 B1
London W6 . . . . 39 B3
Essex Park Mews
W3 . . . . 29 A1
Essex Pl W4 . . . . 37 B2
Essex Place Sq W4 . . . . 37 C2
Essex Rd N1 . . . . 86 B4
London NW10 . . . . 8 A1
London N13 . . . . 28 B2
London W4 . . . . 37 C2
Essex Road Sta N1 . . . 15 B1
Essex St WC2 . . . . . . 121 B4
Essex Villas W8 . . . . . 127 B3
Essian St E1 . . . . 33 A4
Essington St SW11 . . . . 58 A1
Estcourt Rd SW6 . . . . 154 C2
Estella Ho W11 . . . . . . 30 C2
Estelle Rd NW3 . . . . . . 12 B4
Esterbrooke St
SW1 . . . . 147 B3
Este Rd SW11 . . . . 60 A4
Estoria Cl ☲ SW2 . . . . 74 C4
Etal Ho N1 . . . . 15 A1
Etchingham Rd E15 . . . 76 B4
Ethelbert Ho E9 . . . . . 18 A4
Ethelbert St SW12 . . . . 73 A3
Ethelburga St
SW11 . . . . 168 B4
Ethelburga Twr
SW11 . . . . 168 B4
Ethelden Rd W12 . . . . . 30 A1

Ethel Rankin Ct
SW6 . . . . 164 C2
Ethel St SE17 . . . . 151 A3
Ethelworth Ct ☐
SW2 . . . . 74 C3
Etherow St SE22 . . . . . 76 C4
Ethnard Rd SE15 . . . . . 50 A4
Eton Ave NW3 . . . . . . 12 A1
Eton Cl SW18 . . . . 71 A4
Eton College Rd
NW3 . . . . 12 B2
Eton Ct NW3 . . . . 11 C1
Eton Garages ☲
NW3 . . . . 12 A2
Eton Hall NW3 . . . . . . 12 B2
Eton Ho N5 . . . . 15 A4
Eton Pl NW1 . . . . 12 C1
Eton Rd NW3 . . . . 12 B2
Eton Rise NW3 . . . . . . 12 B2
Eton St TW10 . . . . 54 A2
Eton Villas NW3 . . . . . 12 B2
Etta St SE8 . . . . 51 A4
Ettrick St E14 . . . . 34 B3
Eugene Cotter Ho
SE17 . . . . 151 C3
Eugenia Rd SE16 . . . . . 40 B2
Euro Cl NW10 . . . . 8 C2
Eurolink Bsns Ctr
SW2 . . . . 62 C2
Europa Pl EC1 . . . . 96 C3
Eustace Ho SE11 . . . . 148 C4
Eustace Rd SW6 . . . . . 155 B2
Euston Rd NW1 . . . . . . 93 A2
Euston Sq NW1 . . . . . . 93 B3
Euston Square Sta
WC1 . . . . 93 A2
Euston St NW1 . . . . . . 93 A3
Euston Sta NW1 . . . . . 93 B3
Euston Underpass
NW1 . . . . 92 C2
Evandale Rd SW9 . . . . 173 C2
Evangelist Rd NW5 . . . 13 A4
Evans Cl E8 . . . . 16 B2
Evans Ho SW8 . . . . . . 161 C1
☲ London W12 . . . . . 30 A2
Evelina Mans ☲
SE5 . . . . 48 C3
Evelina Rd SE15 . . . . . 50 B1
Eveline Lowe Prim Sch
SE1 . . . . 153 C1
Evelyn Ct N1 . . . . 87 B1
W1 . . . . 102 C1
London E8 . . . . 16 C4
Evelyn Denington Ct ☐
N1 . . . . 15 A1
Evelyn Fox Ct W10 . . . 30 B4
Evelyn Gdns SW7 . . . 143 B1
Richmond TW9 . . . . . . 54 A3
Evelyn Ho
☲ London SW2 . . . . . 62 B2
London W12 . . . . 38 B4
Evelyn Rd
London W4 . . . . 37 C3
Richmond TW9 . . . . . . 54 A4
Evelyn St SE8 . . . . 41 A1
Evelyn Terr SW14 . . . . 54 A4
Evelyn Wlk N1 . . . . 87 B1
Evelyn Yd W1 . . . . 105 B2
Evenwood Cl SW15 . . . 58 A2
Everard Ho ☐ E1 . . . . 111 C1
Everatt Cl SW18 . . . . . 58 B2
Everdon Rd SW13 . . . . 46 C4
Everest Pl E14 . . . . 34 B4
Everett Ho SE17 . . . . . 151 B2
London N7 . . . . 14 C4
Evergreen Sq ☲ E8 . . . 16 B1
Everilda St N1 . . . . 85 A3

Evering Rd E5,N16 . . . . 7 C1
Everington St W6 . . . . 47 C4
Everitt Rd NW10 . . . . . 20 C2
Everleigh St N4 . . . . . . 5 B3
Eversfield Rd TW9 . . . . 44 B1
Evershed Ho E1 . . . . . 111 A2
Evershed Wlk W4 . . . . 37 C2
Evershott St NW1 . . . . 83 A1
Evershot Rd N4 . . . . . . 5 B3
Eversleigh Rd
London SW11 . . . . . . 169 B1
Eversley Ho E2 . . . . . . 99 B3
Everthorpe Rd SE15 . . . 64 B4
Everton Bldgs NW1 . . . 92 C3
Evesham Ct ☲
TW10 . . . . 54 B1
Evesham Ho ☲ E2 . . . . 25 B3
☲ NW8 . . . . 78 C3
SW1 . . . . 146 B2
Evesham St W11 . . . . . 30 C2
Evesham Way SW11 . . 60 C4
Evesham Wlk
London SE5 . . . . 48 C1
London SW9 . . . . 173 B2
Ewald Rd SW6 . . . . . . 164 C1
Ewart Pl ☲ E3 . . . . 26 B3
Ewe Cl N7 . . . . 14 A2
Ewen Cres SW2 . . . . . . 74 C4
Ewen Ho N1 . . . . 84 C3
Ewer St SE1 . . . . 122 C1
Ewhurst ☲ SW15 . . . . . 57 C1
Ewhurst Cl E1 . . . . 32 B4
Ewhurst Rd SE4 . . . . . 66 B1
Exbury Ho London E9 . . 17 B2
☲ London SW9 . . . . . 62 B3
Excel Ct WC2 . . . . 119 C3
Excelsior Gdns SE13 . . 52 B1
Excelsior Ind Est
SE16 . . . . 50 B4
Exchange Arc EC2 . . . 110 B4
Exchange Ct WC2 . . . . 120 B3
Exchange Mans ☲
NW11 . . . . 1 B4
Exchange Pl EC2 . . . . 110 A4
Exeter Ct NW6 . . . . . . 23 C3
Exeter Ho ☲ SE15 . . . . 49 C4
W2 . . . . 100 C2
Exeter Mans NW2 . . . . 10 A2
Exeter Mews SW6 . . . 155 B2
London E16 . . . . 35 C4
London NW2 . . . . 10 A2
London SE2 . . . . 120 C4
Exeter St WC2 . . . . . . 120 C4
Exeter Way ☲ SE14 . . . 51 B3
☲ London SW9 . . . . . 48 A1
Exford Ct SE1 . . . . . . 167 C4
Exhibition Cl W12 . . . . 30 B2
Exhibition Rd SW7 . . . 129 C2
Exmoor Ho ☲ E3 . . . . . 26 A3
Exmoor St W10 . . . . . . 30 C4
Exmouth Ho ☲ E14 . . . 42 A2
Exmouth Market
EC1 . . . . 95 C2
Exmouth Mews
NW1 . . . . 93 A3
Exmouth Pl E8 . . . . . . 17 A1
Exmouth St E1 . . . . . . 32 B3
Exonbury NW8 . . . . . . 78 B3
Exon St SE17 . . . . 152 A3
Eynella Rd SE21 . . . . . 76 B4
Eynham Rd W12 . . . . . 30 B3
Eynsford Ho SE1 . . . . 137 B4
☲ SE15 . . . . 50 B4
SE17 . . . . 152 A3
Eyot Gdns W6 . . . . 38 B1
Eyot Gn W4 . . . . 38 B1
Eyre Ct NW8 . . . . 79 B2

Eyre St Hill EC1 . . . . . 95 B1
Eythorne Rd SW9 . . . . 173 C3
Ezra St E2 . . . . 99 A4

F

Fabian Rd SW6 . . . . . . 155 A2
Fabyc Ho TW9 . . . . 44 C3
Fairacres SW15 . . . . . . 56 C3
Fairbairn Gn ☐
SW9 . . . . 48 A2
Fairbridge Rd N19 . . . . 4 C2
Fairburn Ct SW15 . . . . 58 A2
Fairburn Ho SW5 . . . . 141 A1
☲ London N16 . . . . . . 7 A3
Fairby Ho SE1 . . . . . . 153 A4
Fairchild Cl SW11 . . . . 167 C1
Fairchild Ho ☐
London E9 . . . . 17 B1
☲ London N1 . . . . . . 87 B4
London N16 . . . . 7 A3
Fairchild Pl EC2 . . . . . 98 B1
Fairchild St EC2 . . . . . 98 B1
Fairclough St E1 . . . . . 111 C1
Faircourt NW3 . . . . . . 12 B2
Faircroft N16 . . . . 6 C3
Fairdale Gdns SW15 . . 57 A3
Fairdene Ct N7 . . . . . . 14 A3
Fairfax Ho
☲ London SW9 . . . . 173 C1
London NW6 . . . . 11 B1
London W4 . . . . 38 A3
Fairfax Mews SW15 . . . 57 B3
Fairfax Pl NW6 . . . . . . 11 B1
London NW6 . . . . 11 A2
Fairfax Rd
London NW6 . . . . 11 B1
London W4 . . . . 38 A3
Fairfield ☐ E1 . . . . 32 B4
Fairfield Ct
London NW10 . . . . . . 21 C4
☲ London SW18 . . . . 59 A2
Fairfield Dr SW18 . . . . 59 A2
Fairfield Rd E3 . . . . . . 26 C3
Fairfield St SW18 . . . . 59 A2
Fairfoot Rd E3 . . . . . . 26 C1
Fairford Ho SE11 . . . . 149 C3
Fairhazel Gdns
London NW6 . . . . 11 B1
☲ London SW18 . . . . 59 A2
Fairheathe SW15 . . . . . 57 C1
Fairholme Rd W14 . . . 140 B1
Fairholt Cl N16 . . . . . . 7 A3
Fairholt Rd N16 . . . . . . 6 C3
Fairholt St SW7 . . . . . 130 B2
Fairhurst ☲ NW6 . . . . . 11 B2
Fairlawn Ave W4 . . . . . 37 B2
Fairlawn Ct ☲ W4 . . . . 37 B2
Fairlawn Gr W4 . . . . . . 37 B2
Fairlawn Mans SE14 . . 50 C2
Fairlawns SW15 . . . . . . 57 C2
Fairley House Sch
SW1 . . . . 147 B3
Fairlie Ct ☲ E3 . . . . . . 27 A2
☐ London N7 . . . . . . 13 C3
Fairlight Ave NW10 . . . 21 A3
Fairlight Ct NW10 . . . . 21 A3
Fairlop Pl NW8 . . . . . . 89 C3
Fairmead Ho E9 . . . . . 18 A4
Fairmead Rd N19 . . . . . 5 A1
Fairmont Ho ☲ E3 . . . . 26 C1
Fairmount Rd SW2 . . . 62 B1
Fair St SE1 . . . . 138 C4
Fairstead Wlk N1 . . . . . 86 C4
Fairthorn Rd SE7,
SE10 . . . . 43 C1
Fairview Ho ☲ SW2 . . . 74 B4
Fairview Pl SW2 . . . . . 74 B4

Fairwall Ho ☲ SE5 . . . . 49 A2
Fairway Cl NW11 . . . . . 2 B4
Fairway Ct ☲ SE16 . . . 40 C4
Fairway The W3 . . . . . . 29 A3
Fairweather Ho N7 . . . 14 A4
Faith Ct NW2 . . . . 9 A2
Faithfull Ho N5 . . . . . . 15 B3
Fakruddin St
E1 . . . . 24 C1
Falconberg Ct W1 . . . 105 C2
Falconberg Mews
W1 . . . . 105 C2
Falconbrook Inf Sch
SW11 . . . . 59 C4
Falcon Ct SE1 . . . . . . 122 B2
Chiswick W4 . . . . 45 B4
☲ London EC4 . . . . . 107 B1
London N1 . . . . 86 B1
☲ Dulwich SE21 . . . . 75 C2
Falconer Wlk ☐ N7 . . . 5 B2
Falcon Gr SW11 . . . . . 60 A4
Falcon Ho ☲ SE15 . . . . 49 B2
Falcon La SW11 . . . . . 60 A4
Falcon Lo ☲ W9 . . . . . 31 C4
Falcon Pk Ind Est
NW10 . . . . 8 A3
Falcon Point SE1 . . . . 122 B3
Falcon Rd SW11 . . . . . 60 A4
Falcon Terr SW11 . . . . 60 A4
Falcon Way E14 . . . . . . 42 A2
Falconwood Ct SE3 . . . 53 B1
Falkener Ct
SW11 . . . . 169 C3
Falkirk Ct ☲ SE16 . . . . 32 C1
Falkirk Ho W9 . . . . 24 A3
Falkirk St N1 . . . . 24 A3
Falkland Ho W14 . . . . 140 C2
London W8 . . . . 128 A1
Falkland Pl ☲ NW5 . . . 13 B3
Falkland Rd NW5 . . . . 13 B3
Falladon Ho W11 . . . . . 31 B4
Fallodon Ho SW8 . . . . 171 C2
Fallow Ct SE16 . . . . . . 153 C1
Falmouth Ho SE11 . . . 149 C2
W2 . . . . 116 A4
Falmouth Rd SE1 . . . . 137 A1
Falmouth St E15 . . . . . 19 C3
Falstaff Ct SE11 . . . . . 150 A3
Falstaff Ho ☲ N1 . . . . . 24 A3
Fane St W14 . . . . 155 A4
Fann St EC1 . . . . 97 A1
Fanshaw St N1 . . . . . . 97 C4
Fanthorpe St SW15 . . . 57 B4
Faraday Cl N7 . . . . 14 B2
Faraday Ho ☲ SE1 . . . . 33 A2
London W10 . . . . 31 A4
☲ Balham SW12 . . . . 73 A4
☲ London NW5 . . . . . 13 A4
London SE10 . . . . 43 B3
London W3 . . . . 28 B2
Fareham Ho ☲
SW15 . . . . 68 C3
Fareham St W1 . . . . . 105 B2
Farjeon Ho NW6 . . . . . 11 C1
Farleigh Pl N16 . . . . . . 16 B4
Farleigh Rd N16 . . . . . 16 B4
Farley Ct NW1 . . . . 91 B1
W14 . . . . 126 C2
Farlington Pl SW15 . . . 69 A4
Farlow Rd SW15 . . . . . 57 C4
Farlton Rd SW18 . . . . . 71 A4
Farm Ave NW2 . . . . 1 B1
Farm Cl SW6 . . . . 155 C2

Farmdale Rd SE10 . . . .43 C1
Farmer Ho 4 SE16 . . . .40 A3
Farmers Rd SE5 . . . . . .48 A3
Farmer St W8 . . . . . . .113 B2
Farm La SW6 . . . . .155 C3

Farmleigh Ho SW9 . . . .63 A2
Farm Pl W8 . . . . .113 B2
Farm Rd NW10 . . . . . . .20 C4
Farm St W1 . . . . .118 A3
Farnaby Ho 4 W10 . .23 B2
Farnborough Ho 1
SW15 . . . . .68 C3
Farnborough Way 10
SE15 . . . . .49 A3
Farncombe St
SE16 . . . . .139 C3
Farndale Ho NW6 . . . .78 A4
Farnell Mews SW5 . . .142 A2
Farnell PI W3 . . . . . . .28 A2
Farnfield Ho 12
SW2 . . . . .74 A4
Farnham Ct 2 N16 . . .7 A3
Farnham Ho NW1 . . . .90 B1
SE1 . . . . .122 C1
Farnham PI SE1 . . . .122 B1
Farnham Royal
SE11 . . . . .149 A1
Farnhurst Ho
SW11 . . . . .169 B2
Farningham Ho 9
N4 . . . . .6 C4
Farnley Ho SW8 . . . .171 B2
Farnworth Ho 5
E14 . . . . .42 C2
Faroe Rd W14 . . . . . . .39 C3
Farquhar Rd SW19 . .70 C1
Farrance St E14 . . . . .33 C3
Farrant Ho 10 SW11 . .59 C4
Farrell Ho E1 . . . . .32 B3
Farrer Ho SE8 . . . . . . .51 C3
Farrier Mews SE15 . . .65 B4
Farrier St NW1 . . . . . .13 B1
Farrier Wlk SW10 . . .156 C4
Farringdon La EC1 . . .95 C1
Farringdon Rd EC1 . . .95 C1
Farringdon St EC4 . .108 A2
Farringdon Sta
EC1 . . . . .108 A4
Farrins Rents SE16 . . .33 A1
Farrow La SE14 . . . . .50 B3
Farrow PI SE16 . . . . . .41 A3
Farthingale Wlk
E15 . . . . .19 C1
Farthing Alley 1 SE1 139 B3
Farthing Fields 8
E1 . . . . .32 A1
Fashion & Design
Museum The ★
SE1 . . . . .138 A4
Fashion St E1 . . . . . .111 A3
Fassett Rd E8 . . . . . . .16 C2
Fassett Sq E8 . . . . . . .16 C2
Fauconberg Ct W4 . . .45 B4
Fauconberg Rd W4 . . .45 B4
Faulkner Ho SW15 . . .47 C1
Faulkner's Alley
EC1 . . . . .108 A4
Faulkner St SE14 . . . .50 B2
Faunce Ho 5 SE17 . .48 A4
Faunce St SE17 . . . . .150 A1
Favart Rd SW6 . . . . . .165 C4
Faversham Ho NW1 . .83 A3
SE17 . . . . .152 A1

Fawcett CI SW11 . . . .167 C1
Fawcett Est E5 . . . . . . .7 C3
Fawcett Ho SW9 . . . .172 B2
Fawcett Rd NW10 . . . . .8 B1
Fawcett St SW10 . . . .156 C4
Fawe Park Rd SW15 . .58 B3
Fawe St E14 . . . . .34 A4
Fawkham Ho SE1 . . . .153 A3
Fawley Ct SE27 . . . . . .75 A2
Fawley Lo 2 E14 . . . .42 C2
Fawley Rd NW6 . . . . . .11 A3
Fawnbrake Ave
SE24 . . . . .63 B2
Fayetville Ho 20 N19 .4 C4
Faygate Rd SW2 . . . . .74 B2
Fazerley Ct 48 W2 . . .31 C4
Fearnley Ho SE5 . . . . .49 A1
Fearon St SE10 . . . . . .43 C1
Feathers PI SE10 . . . .52 C4
Featherstone St
EC1 . . . . .97 B2
Featley Rd SW9 . . . . .63 A4
Felbridge Ho 22
SE22 . . . . .64 A4
Felday Rd SE13 . . . . . .67 A1
Felden St SW6 . . . . . .164 C3
Feldman CI N16 . . . . . .7 C3
Felgate Mews 8
W6 . . . . .39 A2
Felix 10 E2 . . . . .25 A3
Felix St 8 E2 . . . . .25 A3
Felixstowe Rd
NW10 . . . . .22 A2
Fellbrigg Rd SE22 . . . .64 B2
Fellbrigg St 21 E1 . . .25 A1
Fellows Ct 2 . . . . .24 B3
Fellows Rd NW3 . . . . .12 A1
Fells Haugh 6 W3 . . .28 B3
Felltram Way SE7 . . . .43 C1
Felmersham CI 2
SW4 . . . . .61 C3
Felsberg Rd SW2 . . . .74 A4
Felsham Ho SW15 . . .57 C4
Felsham Rd SW15 . . .57 C4
Felstead St E9 . . . . . . .18 B2
Felstead Wharf E14 . .42 B1
Felton Ho N1 . . . . .87 C3
Felton St N1 . . . . .87 C3
Fenchurch Ave
EC3 . . . . .110 A1
Fenchurch Bldgs
EC3 . . . . .110 B1
Fenchurch PI EC3 . . .124 B4
Fenchurch St EC3 . . .124 B4
Fenchurch Street Sta
EC3 . . . . .124 B4
Fen Ct EC3 . . . . .124 A4
Fendall St SE1 . . . . . .138 B1
Fender Ct SW4 . . . . . .172 A2
Fendt CI 8 E16 . . . . . .35 B1
Fenelon PI W14 . . . . .141 A3
Fenham Rd SE15 . . . . .50 A3
Fenner CI SE16 . . . . . .40 A2
Fenner Sq 10 SW11 . .59 C4
Fenning St SE1 . . . . .138 A4
Fenn St E9 . . . . .17 B3
Fen St E16 . . . . .35 B2
Fenstanton Prim Sch
SW2 . . . . .74 C3
Fentiman Rd SW8 . . .162 C2
Fenton CI London E8 .16 B2
London SW9 . . . . . . .172 C1
Fenton Ho SE14 . . . . .51 A4
Fentons SE3 . . . . .53 B3
Fenton St E1 . . . . .32 A3
Fenwick Gr SE15 . . . .64 C4

Fenwick PI SW9 . . . . .62 A4
Fenwick Rd SE15 . . . .64 C4
Ferdinand Ho 1
NW1 . . . . .13 A1
Ferdinand PI NW1 . . .12 C1
Ferdinand St NW1 . . .12 C1
Ferguson Dr W3 . . . . .28 C3
Ferguson Ho SE10 . . .52 B2
Ferguson's CI E14 . . .41 C2
Fergus Rd N5 . . . . .15 A3
Fermain Ct E N1 . . . .24 A4
Fermain Ct N N1 . . . .24 A4
Fermain Ct W N1 . . . .24 A4
Fermoy Rd W9 . . . . . . .23 B1
Fernbank Mews
SW12 . . . . .61 B1
Fern CI 3 N1 . . . . .24 A3
Ferncliff Rd E8 . . . . . . .16 C3
Ferncroft Ave NW3 . . .10 C4
Fern Ct SE14 . . . . .50 C1
Ferndale 3 SE3 . . . . .53 B3
Ferndale Ho N16 . . . . .6 C3
Ferndale Rd SW4,
SW9 . . . . .62 B3
Ferndene Rd SE24 . . .63 B3
Ferndown Lo 14 E14 .42 B3
Fernhead Rd W9 . . . . .23 B2
Fernhill Ho E5 . . . . .7 C2
Fernholme Rd SE15 . .65 C2
Fernhurst Rd SW6 . . .164 B4
Fernie Ho SE22 . . . . . .64 B4
Fernlea Rd SW12 . . . .73 A3
Fernleigh CI W9 . . . . .23 B2
Fernsbury St WC1 . . . .95 B3
Fernshaw Mans
SW10 . . . . .156 C3
Fernshaw Rd
SW10 . . . . .156 C3
Fernside Rd SW12 . . .72 C4
Fern St E3 . . . . .26 C1
Fernthorpe Rd SW16 .73 C1
Fern Wlk SE16 . . . . . .153 C1
Fernwood SW19 . . . . .70 B3
Ferrey Mews SW9 . . .173 B1
Ferriby CI N1 . . . . .14 C1
Ferrier Ind Est
SW18 . . . . .59 A3
Ferrier Point 6
E16 . . . . .35 C4
Ferrier St SW18 . . . . .59 A3
Ferrings SE21 . . . . . . .76 A1
Ferris Rd SE22 . . . . . .64 C3
Ferrybridge Ho
SE11 . . . . .135 A1
Ferry La
Barnes SW13 . . . . . .46 B4
Brentford TW8 . . . . . .44 A4
Richmond TW9 . . . . .44 C3
Ferry Rd SW13 . . . . . .46 C2
Ferry Sq 1 TW8 . . . . .44 A4
Ferry St E14 . . . . .42 B1
Festing Rd SW15 . . . .57 C4
Festival Pier SE1 . . . .120 C2
Festival Pleasure Gdns
SW11 . . . . .158 C1
Fetter La EC4 . . . . . . .107 C2
Fettes Ho NW8 . . . . . .79 C1
Ffinch St SE8 . . . . .51 C3
Field Ct WC1 . . . . . . .107 A3
London N7 . . . . .14 A3
London NW3 . . . . . . .11 B3
Wimbledon SW19 . . .70 C1
Fieldgate Mans 1 . . .111 C3
Fieldgate St E1 . . . . .111 C3
Fieldhouse Rd
SW12 . . . . .73 B3
Fielding Ho NW8 . . . . .78 C4

Fielding Ho continued
Chiswick W4 . . . . . . .46 A4
3 London NW6 . . . . .23 C2
Fielding Mews
SW13 . . . . .47 A4
Fielding Rd
London W14 . . . . . . .39 C3
London W4 . . . . .38 A3
Fielding St SE17 . . . . .48 B4
Field Rd W6 . . . . .154 A4
Fields Est E8 . . . . .16 C1
Field St WC1 . . . . .94 C4
Fieldsway Ho N5 . . . . .14 C3
Fieldview SW17,
SW18 . . . . .71 C3
Fieldview Ct N5 . . . . .15 A3
Fieldway Cres N5,
N7 . . . . .14 C3
Fieldwick Ho 14 E9 . .17 C2
Fife Rd E16 . . . . .35 C4
Mortlake SW14 . . . . .55 B2
Fife Terr N1 . . . . .85 A2
Fifth Ave W10 . . . . . . .23 A2
Fig Tree CI NW10 . . . .21 A4
Filey Ave N16 . . . . .7 C3
Filey Ho SW18 . . . . . .59 B3
Filigree Ct SE16 . . . . .33 B1
Filmer Ho SW6 . . . . . .164 B4
Filmer Rd SW6 . . . . . .154 C1
Filmer Road Studios
SW6 . . . . .164 B4
Filton Ct 14 SE14 . . .50 B3
Finborough Ho
SW10 . . . . .156 C4
Finborough Rd
SW10 . . . . .156 B4
Finchdean Ho SW15 .68 B4
Finch Ho 1 SE8 . . . . .52 A3
Finch La EC2,EC3 . . .109 C1
Finchley PI NW8 . . . . .79 B2
Finchley Rd NW8 . . . . .11 C1
London NW3 . . . . . . .11 B2
Finchley Road & Frognal
Sta NW3 . . . . .11 B3
Finchley Road Sta
NW3 . . . . .11 B2
Finch Lo 13 W9 . . . . .31 C4
Finch Mews 13 SE15 .49 B2
Finch's Ct 9 E14 . . . .34 A2
Findhorn St E14 . . . . .34 B3
Findon CI SW18 . . . . .58 C1
Findon Rd W12 . . . . . .38 C4
Fineran Ct 11 SW11 .59 C3
Fingal St SE10 . . . . . .43 B1
Fingest Ho NW8 . . . . .90 A2
Finland Rd SE4 . . . . . .66 A4
Finland St SE16 . . . . .41 A3
Finlay St SW6 . . . . . . .47 C2
Finley Ct 21 SE5 . . . .48 B3
Finmere Ho N4 . . . . . . .6 B4
Finnemore Ho N1 . . . .86 C4
Finn Ho N1 . . . . .97 C4
Finnis St E2 . . . . .25 A1
Finsbury Ave EC2 . . .109 C3
Finsbury Cir EC2 . . . .109 C3
Finsbury Ct EC2 . . . .109 B4
Finsbury Market
EC2 . . . . .110 A4
Finsbury Park N4, . . .6 A2
Finsbury Park Rd N4,
N5 . . . . .6 A2
Finsbury Park Sta
N4 . . . . .6 A2
Finsbury Pavement
EC2 . . . . .109 C4
Finsbury Sq EC2 . . . .109 C4
Finsbury St EC2 . . . .109 B4

Finsen Rd SE5 . . . . . .63 B4
Finstock Rd W10 . . . . .30 C3
Finton House Sch
SW17 . . . . .72 B2
Finucane Ct TW9 . . . .54 B4
Finwhale Ho E14 . . . . .42 A3
Fiona Ct 9 NW6 . . . . .23 B3
Firbank Rd SE15 . . . . .50 A1
Fircroft N1 . . . . .86 B4
Fircroft Prim Sch
SW17 . . . . .72 B1
Fircroft Rd SW17 . . . .72 B1
Fire Brigade Pier
SE1 . . . . .148 B4
Firecrest Dr NW3 . . . . .2 A1
Firle Ho W10 . . . . .30 B4
Fir Lo SW15 . . . . .57 A3
Firmston Ho 9
SW14 . . . . .55 C4
Firs Ave SW14 . . . . . .55 B3
Firsby Rd N16 . . . . .7 C3
First Ave W10 . . . . . . .23 B1
London W3 . . . . .29 B1
Mortlake SW14 . . . . .56 A4
First St SW3 . . . . .144 B4
Firth Gdns SW6 . . . . .164 A3
Fir Tree Ho 11 SE14 .50 B3
Fir Trees CI SE16 . . . .33 A1
Fisher Ho 8 E1 . . . . .32 B2
N1 . . . . .85 B3
2 N19 . . . . .4 B1
Fishermans Dr SE16 .40 C4
Fisherman's Wlk
E14 . . . . .33 C1
Fishers Ct SW16 . . . .73 C1
Fishers La W4 . . . . . . .37 C2
Fisher St E16 . . . . . . .35 C4
WC1 . . . . .106 C3
Fisherton St NW8 . . . .89 C1
Fisherton Street Est
NW8 . . . . .89 C1
Fishlock Ct SW4 . . . .172 A2
Fish St Hill EC3 . . . . .123 C3
Fitch Ct SW2 . . . . . . .62 C2
Fitzalan St SE11 . . . .149 B4
Fitzclarence Ho
W11 . . . . .126 B4
Fitz-George Ave
W14 . . . . .140 A3
Fitzgerald Ave
SW14 . . . . .56 A4
Fitzgerald Ho
14 E14 . . . . .34 A3
London SW9 . . . . . . .173 B1
Fitzgerald Rd SW14 .55 C4
Fitzhardinge Ho
W1 . . . . .103 B2
Fitzhardinge St
W1 . . . . .103 B2
Fitzherbert Ho 11
TW10 . . . . .54 B1
Fitzhugh Gr SW18 . . .59 C1
Fitzjames Ave
W14 . . . . .140 B3
Fitzjohn's Ave NW3 . .11 C3
Fitzjohns Mans
NW3 . . . . .11 B2
Fitzjohns Prim Sch
NW3 . . . . .11 C3
Fitzmaurice Ho 16
SE16 . . . . .40 A2
Fitzmaurice PI W1 . .118 B2
Fitzneal St W12 . . . . .29 B3
Fitzroy CI N6 . . . . .3 B3
Fitzroy Cres W4 . . . . .45 C3
Fitzroy Ct W1 . . . . . . .93 A1

Fitzroy Ho 14 E14 . . . .33 B3
SE1 . . . . .153 A2
Fitzroy Mews W1 . . .92 C1
Fitzroy Pk N6 . . . . . . .3 B3
Fitzroy Rd NW1 . . . .81 B4
Fitzroy Sq W1 . . . . .92 C1
Fitzroy St W1 . . . . . .92 C1
Fitzroy Yd NW1 . . . .81 B4
Fitzsimmons Ct 1
NW10 . . . . .20 C4
Fitzwarren Gdns N19 .4 B3
Fitzwilliam Ave
TW9 . . . . .44 B1
Fitzwilliam Mews
E16 . . . . .35 C1
Fitzwilliam Rd SW4 .61 B4
Fives Ct SE11 . . . . .136 A1
Fiveways Rd SW9 . .173 C1
Flamborough Ho 11
SE15 . . . . .49 C2
Flamborough St
E14 . . . . .33 A3
Flamingo Ct 2 SE8 .51 C3
Flamsteed Ho SE10 .52 C3
Flanchford Rd W12 .38 B3
Flanders Mans 1
W4 . . . . .38 B2
Flanders Rd W4 . . . .38 A2
Flanders Way E17 . .17 C2
Flank St 1 . . . . . . .125 B4
Flansham Ho 2
E14 . . . . .33 B3
Flask Wlk NW3 . . . .11 C4
Flavell Mews SE10 . .43 A1
Flaxman Ct W1 . . . .105 B1
Flaxman Ho 5
4 London W4 . . . . . .38 A1
Flaxman Rd SE5 . . . .48 A1
Flaxman Terr WC1 . .93 C3
Flecker Ho 5 SE5 . .48 C3
Fleece Wlk N7 . . . . .14 A2
Fleet Ct 1 W12 . . . .38 A3
Fleetfield WC1 . . . . .94 B4
Fleet Ho 4 E14 . . . .33 A2
6 London SW2 . . . . .62 C2
Fleet Pl EC4 . . . . . .108 A2
Fleet Prim Sch NW3 12 B3
Fleet Rd NW3 . . . . .12 B3
Fleet Sq WC1 . . . . . .95 A3
Fleet St EC4 . . . . . .107 C1
Fleet Street Hill 1 .99 B1
Fleetway W1 . . . . . .94 B4
Fleet Wood 5 N16 . .7 B2
Fleetwood Rd NW10 .8 C3
Fleetwood St N16 . . .7 A2
Fleming Ct 3 W2 . .101 B4
Fleming Ct 1 . . . . . .101 B4
Fleming Ho 5 SE16 .139 B3
London N4 . . . . .6 B3
Fleming Rd SE17 . . .48 A4
Fletcher Bldgs
WC2 . . . . .106 B1
Fletcher Ct 6 NW5 .13 A4
Fletcher Ho 1 N1 . .24 A4
16 London N16 . . . . .16 A4
Fletcher Path 7
SE8 . . . . .51 C3
Fletcher Rd W4 . . . .37 B3
Fletcher St E1 . . . . .125 C4
Fleur Gates 7
SW19 . . . . .69 C4
Flinders Ho 28 E1 . .32 A1
Flinton St SE17 . . . .152 B2
Flint St SE17 . . . . . .151 C3
Flitcroft St WC2 . . .105 C1
Flitton Ho 7 N1 . . . .15 A1
Flock Mill Pl SW18 . .71 A3

Flodden Rd SE5 . . . .48 B2
Flood St SW3 . . . . .158 B4
Flood Wlk SW3 . . . .158 B4
Flora Cl E14 . . . . . . .34 A3
Flora Gardens Prim Sch
W6 . . . . .39 A2
Flora Gdns 2 W6 . . .39 A2
Floral St WC2 . . . . .120 A4
Florence Ct W9 . . . .89 A3
4 London SE5 . . . . . .7 C1
Florence Gdns W4 . .45 B4
Florence Ho
20 SE16 . . . . .40 A1
3 London SW18 . . . .59 C3
2 London SW2 . . . . .62 B2
11 London W11 . . . .30 C2
Florence Mans
SW6 . . . . .164 C4
1 N1 . . . . .15 B2
Florence Nightingale
Mus SE1 . . . . .135 A3
Florence Nightingale
Ho 1 N4 . . . . .5 C4
London SE14 . . . . . .51 B2
London W4 . . . . . . .37 C3
Florence Rd
London N4 . . . . .5 C4
London SE14 . . . . . .51 B2
London W4 . . . . . . .37 C3
Florence St N1 . . . . .15 A1
Florence Terr
Kingston u T SW15 . .68 A1
London SE14 . . . . . .51 B2
Florence Way SW12 .72 B3
Flores Ho 10 E1 . . . .32 C4
Florfield Rd E8 . . . . .17 A2
Florian SE5 . . . . .49 A2
Florian Rd SW15 . . .58 A3
Florida St E2 . .24 C2 99 C3
Florin Ct SE1 . . . . . .138 C2
Floris Pl 3 SW4 . . . .61 B4
Florys Ct 7 SW19 . .70 A3
Floss St SW15 . . . . .47 B1
Flower & Dean Wlk
E1 . . . . .111 A3
Flowersmead SW17 .72 C2
Flowers Mews 2
N19 . . . . .4 B2
Flower Wlk The
SW7 . . . . .129 A4
Fluer De Lis St E1 . . .98 C1
Flynn Ct 15 E14 . . . .33 C2
Foley Ho 11 E1 . . . .32 B3
Foley St W1 . . . . . .104 C3
Folgate St E1 . . . . .110 C4
Foliot Ho N1 . . . . . . .84 C2
Foliot St W12 . . . . . .29 B3
Follett Ho SW10 . . .157 B2
Follett St E14 . . . . . .34 B3
Folly Wall E14 . . . . .42 B4
Fontarabia Rd
SW11 . . . . .60 C3
Fontenelle SE5 . . . . .49 A2
Fontenoy Ho SE11 .150 A3
Fontenoy Rd SW12,
SW17 . . . . .73 B2
Fonthill Ho SW1 . . .146 B2
W14 . . . . .126 B2
Fonthill Mews N4 . . .5 B2
Fonthill Rd N4 . . . . . .5 C2
Fontley Way SW15 . .68 C4
Footpath The SW15 .56 C2
Forber Ho 2 E2 . . . .25 B2
Forbes Ho 2 W4 . . .36 C1
Forbes St E1 . . . . . .111 C1
Forburg Rd N16 . . . . .7 C3
Ford Cl 13 E3 . . . . . .26 A3
Fordcombe 13 NW5 .12 C2
Fordham St E1 . . . . .111 C2
Fordingley Rd W9 . .23 B2

Ford Rd E3 . . . . .26 B3
Fords Park Rd E16 . .35 C3
Ford Sq E1 . . . . .32 A4
Ford St E16 . . . . . . .35 B1
3 . . . . .26 A3
Fordwych Ct NW2 . . .10 A2
Fordwych Rd NW2 . .10 A3
Fordyce Rd SE13 . . .67 B2
Foreign, Commonwealth
& Home Offices
SW1 . . . . .134 A4
Foreland Ho W11 . .112 A4
Foreshore SE8 . . . . .41 B2
Fore St EC2 . . . . . . .109 B3
Fore St Ave EC2 . . .109 B3
Forest Gr E8 . . . . . .16 B1
Forest Hill Rd SE22 .65 A1
Forest Rd London E8 .16 B2
Richmond TW9 . . . . .44 C3
Forest Way 6 N19 . . .4 B2
Forge Pl NW1 . . . . . .12 C2
Forman Ho SE4 . . . .65 C3
Forman Pl N16 . . . . .16 B4
Formby Ct 6 N7 . . . .14 C3
Formosa Ho 1 E1 . . .26 A1
Formosa St W9 . . . . .88 B1
Formunt Cl E16 . . . . .35 B2
Forrest Ct N7 . . . . . .14 C2
Forrest Ho SW15 . . .47 B1
Forset Ct W1 . . . . . .102 B2
Forset St W1 . . . . . .102 B2
Forster Rd SW2 . . . .74 A4
Forston St N1 . . . . . .87 A2
Forstic Wlk E1 . . . . .111 A3
Forsyth Gdns SE17 . .48 A4
Forsyth Ho 6 E9 . . . .17 B1
14 London E9 . . . . .17 B1
Forsythia Ho SE4 . . .66 A4
Fortescue Ave 1
E8 . . . . .17 A1
Fortess Gr NW5 . . . .13 B3
Fortess Rd NW5 . . . .13 B3
Fortess Wlk NW5 . . .13 A3
Forthbridge Rd
SW11 . . . . .60 C3
Forth Ho 26 E3 . . . . .26 B3
Forties The 3 NW5 .13 B3
Fortior Ct N6 . . . . . . .4 B4
Fortnam Rd N19 . . . . .4 C2
Fort Rd SE1 . . . . . . .153 A3
Fortrose Gdns
SW12,SW2 . . . . . . .74 A3
Fort St E1 . . . . .110 B3
Fortuna Cl N7 . . . . . .14 B2
Fortune Gate Rd
NW10 . . . . .21 A4
Fortune Green Rd
NW6 . . . . .10 C4
Fortune Ho EC1 . . . .97 A1
SE11 . . . . .149 B3
Fortune St EC1 . . . . .97 A1
Fortune Way NW10 .22 A2
Forty Acre La E16 . .35 C4
Forward Bsns Ctr The
E16 . . . . .27 C1
Fosbroke Ho SW8 . .162 A1
Fosbury Ho 7 SW9 .62 B3
Fosbury Mews W2 . .114 B3
Foscote Mews W9 . .31 C4
Foskett Rd SW6 . . .165 A1
Fosse Ho SE13 . . . . .66 C4
Fossil Rd SE13 . . . . .66 C4
Foster Ct E16 . . . . . .35 B2
4 London NW1 . . . . .13 B1
Foster Ho SE14 . . . .51 B2
Foster La EC2 . . . . .108 C2

Foster Rd
London W3 . . . . .29 A1
London W4 . . . . .37 C1
Foubert's Pl W1 . . .104 C1
Foulden Rd N16 . . . .16 B4
Foulden Terr N16 . . .16 B4
Foulis Terr SW7 . . .143 C2
Foulser Rd SW17 . . .72 C1
Foundary Ho 5 E14 .34 A4
Founders Ho SW1 . .147 B2
Founders St SW1 . . .147 B2
Foundling Ct WC1 . . .94 A2
Foundry Cl SE16 . . . .33 A1
Foundry Mews NW1 .93 A3
Foundry Pl E1 . . . . . .32 B4
Fountain Ct EC4 . . .121 B4
SW1 . . . . .146 A3
Fountain Green Sq
SE16 . . . . .139 C3
Fountain Ho SE16 . .139 C3
W1 . . . . .117 B2
1 London NW6 . . . .23 C4
Fountain Mews
1 London N5 . . . . . .15 B4
London NW3 . . . . . .12 B2
Fountain Pl SW9 . . .173 C3
Fountayne Rd N16 . . .7 C2
Fount St SW8 . . . . .161 C1
Fournier St E1 . . . . .111 A4
Four Seasons Cl E3 .26 C3
Fourth Ave W10 . . . .23 A2
Fovant Ct SW8 . . . .170 C1
Fowey Cl E1 . . . . . . .32 A1
Fowey Ho SE11 . . . .149 C2
Fowler Cl SW11 . . . .59 C4
Fowler Ho N1 . . . . . .86 B4
SW8 . . . . .171 C3
Fowler Rd N1 . . . . . .86 B4
Fownes St SW11 . . . .60 A4
Foxberry Ct SE4 . . . .66 B3
Foxberry Rd SE4 . . . .66 B3
Foxborough Gdns
SE4 . . . . .66 C2
Foxbourne Rd
SW17 . . . . .72 C2
Fox Cl E1 . . . . .25 B1
E16 . . . . .35 C4
Foxcombe Rd 3
SW15 . . . . .68 C3
Foxcote SE5 . . . . . .152 B1
Foxcroft N1 . . . . .85 A2
Foxglove St W12 . . .29 B2
Foxham Rd N19 . . . . .4 C1
Fox Ho 2 SW11 . . . .59 C3
Fox & Knot St EC1 .108 B4
Foxley Cl E8 . . . . . . .16 C3
Foxley Ho 4 E3 . . . .27 A2
Foxley Rd SW9 . . . .48 A3
Foxley Sq 3 SW9 . .48 A2
Foxmore St SW11 . .168 C3
Fox Prim Sch
W8 . . . . .31 C1 113 B1
Fox Rd E16 . . . . .35 B2
Fox's Yd E2 . . . . . . .99 A2
Foxwell Mews SE4 . .66 A4
Foxwell St SE4 . . . . .66 A4
Foyle Rd SE3 . . . . . .53 B4
Fradel Lo N16 . . . . . .6 C1
Framfield Rd N5 . . . .15 A3
Frampton NW1 . . . . .13 C1
Frampton Ct 3 W3 .37 B4
Frampton Ho NW8 . . .89 C1
Frampton Park Rd
E9 . . . . .17 B1
Frampton St NW8 . . .89 C1
Francemary Rd SE4 .66 C2

Frances Grey Ho 13
E1 . . . . .32 C4
Franche Court Rd
SW17 . . . . .71 B1
Francis Chichester Way
SW11 . . . . .169 C3
Francis Ct 12 SE14 . .42 C2
Francis Ct 15 SE14 . .51 A4
Francis Ho 1 N1 . . . .24 A4
London NW10 . . . . . .21 B4
Francis Holland Sch
NW1 90
SW1 . . . . .145 C3
Francis Snary Lo 1
SW18 . . . . .58 C2
Francis St 1 SW1 . . .147 A4
Francis Terr N19 . . . .4 B1
Francis Wlk N1 . . . . .84 C4
Franconia Rd SW4 . .61 C2
Frank Barnes Prim Sch
for Deaf Children
NW3 . . . . .11 C1
Frank Beswick Ho
SW6 . . . . .155 A3
Frank Dixon Cl
SE21 . . . . .76 A3
Frank Dixon Way
SE21 . . . . .76 A3
Frank Douglas Ct
W6 . . . . .38 C2
Frankfurt Rd SE24 . .63 B2
Frankham Ho 6
SE8 . . . . .51 C3
Frankham St SE8 . . .51 C3
Frank Ho SW8 . . . . .162 A2
Frankland Cl SE16 . .40 A2
Frankland Ho 4
SW12 . . . . .73 A4
Frankland Rd SW7 .129 B1
Franklin Bldg 3
E14 . . . . .41 C4
Franklin Cl
London SE13 . . . . . .52 A2
West Norwood SE27 . .75 A1
Franklin Ho 26 E1 . . .32 A1
Franklin Sq 3 . . . . .141 A1
Franklin's Row
SW3 . . . . .145 A2
Franklin St 15 E3 . . .27 A2
Franklyn Rd NW10 . . .8 B2
Frank Soskice Ho
SW6 . . . . .155 A3
Frank Whymark Ho 4
SE16 . . . . .40 B4
Frans Hals Ct E14 . .42 C3
Fraserburgh Ho 28
E3 . . . . .26 B3
Fraser Ct SW11 . . . .168 A4
Brentford TW8 . . . . .36 B1
London SW9 . . . . . .171 B1
Fraser Ho
Brentford TW8 . . . . .36 B1
London SW8 . . . . . .171 B1
Fraser Regnart Ct 7
NW5 . . . . .12 B3
Fraser St W4 . . . . . .38 A1
Frazier St SE1 . . . . .135 B3
Frean St SE16 . . . . .139 B2
Frearson Ho WC1 . . .95 A4
Freda Corbett Cl 9
SE15 . . . . .49 C3
Frederica St 4 N7 . .14 B1
Frederick Cl W2 . . . .116 C4
Frederick Charrington
Ho 3 E1 . . . . .25 B1
Frederick Cres SW9 .48 A3

Frederick Ct SW6 ....58 A4
Frederick's Pl EC2 .109 B1
Frederick Sq **11**
SE16 ....33 A2
Frederick's Row
EC1 ....96 A4
Frederick St WC1 ...94 C3
Frederic Terr E8 ...16 B1
Frederic Mews
SW1 ....131 B3
Freedom St SW11 .169 A2
Freegrove Rd N7 ...14 A3
Freeling St N1 .....79 B4
Freeling St **7** N1 ..14 B1
Freeman Ho **13**
SW2 ....74 A4
Freemantle St
SE17 ....152 A2
Freemens Hos **1**
SW9 ....62 B3
Freke Rd SW11 .....60 C4
Fremantle Ho **14** E1 .25 A1
Fremont St E9 ......25 B4
French Ordinary Ct
EC3 ....124 B4
French Pl E1 ....98 B2
Frendsbury Rd SE4 .66 A3
Frensham Ct N5 ....15 B3
Frensham Dr SW15 .68 C2
Frensham St SE15 ..49 C4
Frere St SW11 .....168 B2
Freshfield Ave E8 ..16 B1
Freshfield Cl SE13 .67 C3
Freshford St SW17,
SW18 ....71 B1
Freston Rd W10,
W11 ....30 C2
Freswick Ho **8** SE8 .41 A2
Freud Mus The
NW3 ....11 B2
Frewell Bldg EC1 ..107 C3
Frewin Rd SW18 ....71 C3
Friar Mews SE27 ...75 A1
Friars Ave SW15 ...68 B1
Friars Cl SE1 .....122 B1
Friars Gdns W3 ....28 C3
Friars Mead E14 ...42 B3
Friars Place La W3 .28 C2
Friars Prim Sch
SE1 ....136 B3
Friars Stile Pl **7**
TW10 ....54 A1
Friars Stile Rd
TW10 ....54 A1
Friar St EC4 ......108 B1
Friars Way W3 .....28 C3
Friary Park W3 ....28 B3
Friary Rd SE15 ....49 C3
London W3 ....28 C3
Friday St EC4 .....122 C4
Frideswide Pl NW5 .13 B3
Friendly Pl SE13 ..52 A2
Friendly St SE8 ...51 C2
Friendly Street Mews
SE8 ....51 C1
Friend St EC1 ......96 A4
Friern Rd SE22 ....64 C1
Frigate Ho **6** E14 ..42 B2
Frigate Mews SE8 ..51 C4
Frimley Cl SW19 ...70 A2
Frimley Way E1 ....25 C1
Frinstead Ho **1**
W10 ....30 C2
Friston St SW6 ...166 A1
Frith Ho E2 ....24 C2 99 B3

Frith Ho continued
NW8 ....89 C1
Frith Rd E11 ......19 C4
Frith St W1 ....105 B1
Frithville Ct W12 ..30 B1
Frithville Gdns W12 .30 B1
Frobisher Ct
11 SE10 ....52 C4
3 London SE10 ...39 B4
Frobisher Ho **7** E1 ..32 A1
Frobisher Pas E14 .34 A1
Frobisher Pl SE14 .51 A3
Frobisher St SE10 .53 A4
Froebel Coll SW15 .56 B1
Frogley Rd SE22 ...64 B3
Frogmore SW18 ....58 C2
Frogmore Est NW10 .20 B2
Frogmore Ind Est
N5 ....15 B4
Frognal NW3 ....11 B3
Frognal Cl NW3 ....11 B3
Frognal Gdns NW3 .11 B4
Frognal La NW3 ....11 A3
Frognal Par NW3 ...11 B3
Frognal Rise NW3 ..11 B4
Frognal Way NW3 ..11 B4
Frome Ho SE15 ....65 B3
Frome St N1 ....86 C2
Fronteñac W10 .....9 C7
Froude St SW8 ....170 B1
Frye Ct E3 ....26 B2
Frying Pan Alley
E1 ....110 C3
Fry Rd NW10 ......21 B4
Fulbeck Ho N7 ....14 B2
Fulbourne St E1 ...32 A4
Fulbrook Rd N19 ...13 B4
Fulcher Ho **10** N1 ..24 A4
18 SE8 ....41 B1
Fulford Mans N19 ..5 A1
Fulford St SE16 ...40 A4
Fulham Broadway
SW6 ....155 C1
Fulham Broadway Sta
SW6 ....155 C2
Fulham Cross Sec Sch
SW6 ....154 B2
Fulham Ct SW6 ...165 B4
Fulham High St
SW6 ....164 B1
Fulham Palace*
SW6 ....164 A1
Fulham Palace Rd
SW6 ......47 C3 164 A3
Fulham Park Gdns
SW6 ....164 C1
Fulham Park Rd
SW6 ....164 C1
Fulham Prep Sch
SW6 ....155 B3
Fulham Rd SW10 ..157 A4
Fulham SW6 ....165 A4
Fuller Cl E2 ....99 B2
Fullers Ho **5** SW18 .58 C2
Fullerton Rd SW18 .59 B2
Fullwood's Mews
N1 ....97 C4
Fulmar Ct **5** SE21 .175 C2
Fulmar Ho NW8 ...90 B1
8 SE16 ....40 C2
Fulmead St SW6 ..166 B3
Fulneck **1** E1 .....32 B4
Fulthorp Rd SE3 ..53 C1
Fulton Mews W2 ..114 C4

Fulwood Pl WC1 ...107 A3
Fulwood Wlk SW19 .70 A3
Furber St W6 ......39 A3
Furley Ho **2** SE15 .49 C3
Furley Rd SE15 ...49 C3
Furlong Rd N7 ....14 C2
Furmage St SW18 .71 A4
Furness Ho SW1 ..146 A2
Furness Lo **6** SW14 .55 A3
Furness Rd
London NW10 ....21 C3
London SW6 ....166 B2
Furnival St EC4 ...107 B2
Furrow La E9 ......17 B3
Fursecroft W1 ....102 C2
Furze St E3 ....33 C4
Fyfield N4 ....5 C2
Fyfield Rd **6** SW9 .62 C4
Fynes St SW1 .....147 B4

G

Gable Ho **12** W4 ...38 A2
Gables Cl SE5 .....49 A2
Gables The
London NW3 ....2 C1
3 London SW4 ...61 C3
Gabriel Ho SE11 ..148 C4
Gabrielle Ct NW3 .11 C2
Gabriel's Wharf
SE1 ....121 B2
Gaddesden Ho EC1 .97 C3
Gadsden Ho **8** W10 .23 A1
8 London E9 ......17 C2
Gagarin Ho SW11 ..59 C4
Gage Rd E16 ......35 A4
Gage St WC1 ......106 B4
Gainford Ho **11** E2 .25 A2
Gainford St N1 ....85 B4
Gainsborough Ct
5 E14 ....33 A2
SW1 ....147 C3
London N4 ....5 B4
3 London NW3 ...11 B4
Gainsborough Prim Sch
E9 ....18 C2
Gainsborough Gdns
London NW11 ....1 B4
London NW3 ....2 C1
Gainsborough Ho
5 E14 ....33 A2
SW1 ....147 C3
London N4 ....5 B4
3 London NW3 ...11 B4
Gainsborough Rd
London W4 ....38 B2
Richmond TW9 ......54 B4
Gainsford St SE1 .139 A4
Gairloch Ho **2**
NW1 ....13 C1
Gairloch Rd SE5 ..49 A1
Gaisford St NW5 ..13 B2
Gaitskell Ct SW11 .168 A2
Gaitskell Ho SE17 .48 C4
Galata Rd SW13 ...46 C3
Galatea Sq SE15 ..65 A4
Galbraith St E14 ..42 B3
Gale Ho **10** SW2 ...62 B2
Galena Ho **6** W6 ..39 A2
Galena Rd W6 .....39 A2
Galen Pl WC1 .....106 B3
Galesbury Rd SW18 .59 B1
Galgate Cl **4** SW19 .70 A3
Galleon Cl SE16 ...40 C4
Galleon Ho **7** E14 .42 B2
Gallery Ct SW10 ..156 C3

Gallery Rd SE21 ...75 C3
Galleywall Prim Sch
SE16 ....40 A2
Galleywall Rd SE16 .40 A2
Galleywall Road Trad
Est **22** SE16 ....40 A2
Galleywood Ho W10 .30 B4
Gallia Rd N5 ......15 A3
Galloons Rd SE7 ..43 C2
Galloway Rd W12 .29 C1
Galsworthy Ave E14 .33 A4
Galsworthy Ho **4**
W11 ....31 A3
Galsworthy Rd NW2 .10 A4
Galton St W10 ....23 A2
Galveston Ho **2** E1 .26 A1
Galveston Rd SW15 .58 B2
Galway Cl **28** SE16 .40 A1
Galway Ho **6** E1 ...25 C1
EC1 ....97 A3
Galway St EC1 ....97 A3
Gambetta St SW8 .170 B1
Gambia St SE1 ....122 B1
Gambier Ho **5** EC1 .97 A3
Gamlen Rd SW15 ..57 C4
Gandolfi St **5** SE15 .49 A4
Ganley Ct **19** SW11 .59 C4
Gannet Ct **5** SE21 .75 C2
Gannet Ho SE15 ...49 B2
Ganton St W1 .....105 A1
Garbett Ho **2** SE17 .48 A4
Garbutt Pl W1 ....103 C3
Garden Ct EC4 ....121 B4
NW8 ....89 B4
12 London W4 ....37 B3
4 Richmond TW9 ..44 B2
Garden Flats SW16 .74 A1
Garden Ho SW9 ...172 B2
Garden La SW2 ....74 B3
Garden Mews W2 .113 C3
Garden Pl **1** E8 ...24 B4
Garden Rd NW8 ...89 A1
Richmond TW9 .....54 C4
Garden Row SE1 ..136 A2
Garden Royal **16**
SW15 ....57 C1
Garden St E1 ......32 C4
Gardens The
London N16 ....7 B4
London SE22 ......64 C3
Garden Terr SW1 .147 B2
2 London SW7 ...130 B3
Garden Wlk
EC2 ....24 A2 98 A2
Gardiner Ave NW2 .9 B3
Gardiner Ct NW10 .20 C4
Gardiner Ho SW11 .168 A4
Gardner Ct N5 ....15 B4
Gardners La EC4 ..123 A4
Gardnor Mans **10**
NW3 ....11 B4
Gardnor Rd NW3 ..11 C4
Gard St EC1 ....96 B4
Gareth Ct SW16 ...73 C1
Garfield Rd SW11 .60 C4
Garford St E14 ...33 C2
Garland Ho N16 ....6 C1
Garlick Hill EC4 ..123 A4
Garlinge Ho **9** SW9 .173 B4
Garlinge Rd NW2 ..10 B2
Garnault Mews EC1 .95 C3
Garnault Pl EC1 ...95 C3
Garner St E2 ......24 C3
Garnet Rd NW10 ...8 A2
Garnet St E1 ......32 B2
Garnett Ho **3** NW3 .12 B3

Garnett Rd NW3 ...12 B3
Garnham Cl **2** N16 .7 B2
Garnham St **1** N16 .7 B2
Garnies Cl SE15 ...49 B3
Garrad's Rd SW16 .73 C1
Garratt Wlk NW10 .8 A2
Garratt Ho **8** N16 ..7 A3
Garrat La SW18 ...71 A3
Garratt Park Sch
SW18 ....71 A2
Garraway Ct SW13 .47 B3
Garraway Ho SE21 .76 B1
Garrett Cl W3 .....28 C4
Garrett Ho W12 ...30 A3
Garrett St EC1 ....97 A2
Garrick Cl SW18 ..59 B3
Garrick Ho W1 ...118 A1
Chiswick W4 ......46 A4
Garrick Rd TW9 ...44 C1
Garrick St WC2 ...120 A4
Gasdale Terr
SW5 ....140 C2
Garsington Mews
SE4 ....66 B4
Garson Ho W2 ....115 B4
Garston Ho **5** N1 ..15 A1
Garter Way SE16 ..40 C4
Garth Cl W4 ....45 C4
Garth Ho NW2 .....1 B2
Garth Rd London NW2 .1 B2
8 London W4 .....37 C1
Gartmoor Gdns
SW19 ....70 B3
Garton Ho **6** N6 ...4 C4
Garton Pl SW18 ...59 B1
Gartons Way SW11 .59 B4
Garway Rd W2 ....100 A1
Gascoigne Pl E2 ...98 C3
Gascony Ave NW6 .10 C1
Gascoyne Ho **2** E9 .17 C1
Gascoyne Rd E9 ..17 C1
Gaselee St E14 ....34 B2
Gasholder Pl SE11 .149 A1
Gaskarth Rd SW12 .61 A1
Gaskell St SW4 ...172 A2
Gaskin Ho N16 .....6 C1
Gaspar Cl SW7 ...142 B4
Gaspar Mews SW5 .142 B4
Gasson Ho **24** SE14 .50 C4
Gastein Rd W6 ....47 C4
Gastigny Ho EC1 ..97 A3
Gaston Bell Cl TW9 .54 B4
Gaston Gate **6** SW8 .172 C4
Gataker Ho **5** SE16 .40 A3
Gataker St **6** SE16 .40 A3
Gatcliff Cl SW1 ...145 C1
Gatcombe Ho **20**
SE22 ....64 A4
Gatcombe Rd
8 E16 ....35 C1
London N19 ....4 C1
Gatebeck Ho **21**
SE22 ....64 A4
Gatefield Ct SE15 .64 C4
Gateforth St NW8 .90 A1
Gate Hill Ct W11 .113 A2
Gatehouse Sch E2 .25 C3
Gatehouse Sq SE1 .123 A2
Gateley Ho **6** SE4 .65 C3
Gateley Rd SW9 ..62 B4
Gate Mews SW7 ..130 B3
Gatesborough St
EC2 ....98 A2
Gates Ct SE17 ....150 C2
Gatesden WC1 .....94 B3

Gateside Rd SW17 . . . .72 B1
Gate St WC2 . . . . .106 C2
Gateway SE17 . . . . .48 B4
Gateway Mews 4
E8 . . . . .16 B3
Gateway Prim Sch
NW8 . . . . .89 C2
Gateways The
SW3 . . . . .144 B3
Gateway Trad Est
NW10 . . . . .21 B2
Gathorne St 16 E2 . . . .25 B3
Gatliff Rd SW1 . . . . . .146 A1
Gatonby St SE15 . . . . . .49 B2
Gatwick Ho 8 E14 . . . .33 B3
Gatwick Rd SW18 . . . . .70 B4
Gauden Cl SW4 . . . . . . .61 C4
Gauden Rd SW4 . . . . . .61 C4
Gaugin 13 SE16 . . . . . .40 A1
Gaunt St SE1 . . . . .136 C2
Gautrey Rd SE15 . . . . . .50 B1
Gavel St SE17 . . . . . . .151 C4
Gaviller Pl 4 E5 . . . . .17 A4
Gavrelle Ho EC1 . . . . . .97 B1
Gawber St E2 . . . . .25 B2
Gawthorne Ct E3 . . . . .26 C3
Gay Cl NW2 . . . . .9 A3
Gaydon Ho W2 . . . . . .100 A4
Gayfere St SW1 . . . . . .134 A1
Gayford Rd W12 . . . . . .38 B4
Gay Ho N16 . . . . .16 A3
Gayhurst SE17 . . . . . . .48 C4
Gayhurst Ho NW8 . . . . .90 B2
Gayhurst Rd E8 . . . . . . .16 C1
Gayhurst Sch E8 . . . . . .16 C1
Gaymead NW8 . . . . . . .78 B3
Gay Rd E15 . . . . .27 C3
Gaysley Ho SE11 . . . . .149 B3
Gay St SW15 . . . . .57 C4
Gayton Cres NW3 . . . . .11 C4
Gayton Ho E3 . . . . .26 C1
Gayton Rd NW3 . . . . . .11 C4
Gayville Rd SW11 . . . . .60 B1
Gaywood Cl SW2 . . . . . .74 C3
Gaywood St SE1 . . . . .136 B1
Gaza St SE17 . . . . .150 A1
Gaze Ho 10 E14 . . . . . .34 C3
Gean Ct 3 E11 . . . . . . .19 C4
Geary Ho N7 . . . . .14 B3
Geary Rd NW10 . . . . . . .8 C3
Geary St N7 . . . . .14 B3
Gedling Ho SE22 . . . . . .64 B4
Gedling Pl SE1 . . . . . .139 A2
Gees Ct W1 . . . . .103 C1
Gee St EC1 . . . . .96 C2
Geffrye Ct N1 . . . . .24 A3
Geffrye Mus* E2 . . . . .24 B3
Geffrye St E2 . . . . .24 B3
Geldart Rd SE15 . . . . . .50 A3
Geldeston Rd E5 . . . . . . .7 C2
Gellatly Rd SE14 . . . . . .50 C1
Gemini Bsns Ctr
E16 . . . . .27 C1
Gemini Ho SW15 . . . . . .57 C3
General Wolfe Rd
SE10 . . . . .52 C2
Geneva Ct 6 London N16 .6 C3
■ Putney SW15 . . . . . . .57 C2
Geneva Dr SW9 . . . . . . .62 C3
Genoa Ave SW15 . . . . . .57 B2
Genoa Ho 19 E1 . . . . . .25 C1
Geoffrey Chaucer Tech
Coll SE1 . . . . .137 B1
Geoffrey Cl SE5 . . . . . .48 B1
Geoffrey Ct SE4 . . . . . .66 B4
Geoffrey Ho SE1 . . . . .137 C2

Geoffrey Jones Ct
NW10 . . . . .21 C4
Geoffrey Rd SE4 . . . . . .66 B4
Geological Mus
SW7 . . . . .129 C1
George Beard Rd 10
SE8 . . . . .41 B2
George Beare Lo 9
SW4 . . . . .61 B2
George Belt Ho 8
E2 . . . . .25 C2
George Ct WC2 . . . . . .120 B3
George Downing Est
N16 . . . . .7 B2
George Eliot Ho
SW1 . . . . .147 A3
George Eliot Jun & Inf
Sch NW8 . . . . .79 B4
George Elliot Ho
SE17 . . . . .150 C2
George Eliston Ho
SE1 . . . . .153 B1
George Eyre Ho
NW8 . . . . .79 C1
George Green's Sec Sch
E14 . . . . .42 B1
George Inn Yd SE1 . . .123 B1
George La SE13 . . . . . . .67 B1
George Lansbury Ho
■ E3 . . . . .26 B2
London NW10 . . . . .8 A1
George Lashwood Ct 13
SW9 . . . . .62 B3
George Leybourne Ho
E1 . . . . .125 C4
George Lindgren Ho
SW6 . . . . .155 A2
George Loveless Ho
B E2 . . . . .24 B2 B3
George Mews NW1 . . . .92 C3
George Orwell Sch
N4 . . . . .5 B3
George Peabody Ct
NW1 . . . . .102 A4
George Row SE16 . . . .139 B3
George's Rd N7 . . . . . . .14 B3
George's Sq SW6 . . . . .155 A4
George St 8 E16 . . . . . .35 B1
W1 . . . . .103 A2
George Tingle Ho
SE1 . . . . .139 A2
Georgette Pl SE10 . . . . .52 B3
George Vale Ho 52
E2 . . . . .24 C3
George Walter Ho 7
SE16 . . . . .40 B2
George Wyver Cl
SW18 . . . . .70 A4
George Yd EC3 . . . . . .109 C1
W1 . . . . .117 C4
Georgiana St NW1 . . . . .83 A4
Georgian Ct 18 E9 . . . . .25 B4
Georgina Gdns 2 E2 . .99 A4
Geraldine Rd
Brentford W4 . . . . .44 C4
London SW18 . . . . .59 B2
Geraldine St SE11 . . . .136 A1
Gerald Mews SW1 . . . .145 C4
Gerald Rd SW1 . . . . . .145 C4
Gerard Ct NW2 . . . . .9 C3
Gerard Rd SW13 . . . . . .46 B2
Gerards Cl SE16 . . . . . .40 B1
Gernigan Ho SW18 . . . .59 C1
Gernon Rd E3 . . . . .26 A3
Gerrard Ho 5 SE14 . . . .50 C3
Gerrard Pl W1 . . . . . . .119 C4
Gerrard Rd N1 . . . . .86 B2

Gerrard St W1 . . . . . . .119 C4
Gerridge Ct SE1 . . . . . .135 C2
Gerridge St SE1 . . . . . .135 C2
Gerry Raffles Sq
E15 . . . . .19 C2
Gertrude St SW10 . . . .157 A3
Gervase St SE15 . . . . . .50 A3
Ghent Way E8 . . . . .16 B2
Giant Arches Rd
SE24 . . . . .63 B1
Gibbings Ho SE1 . . . . .136 B3
Gibbins Rd E15 . . . . . . .76 B1
Gibbon Ho NW8 . . . . . . .89 C1
Gibbon Rd
London SE15 . . . . .50 B1
London W3 . . . . .29 A2
Gibbons Rd NW10 . . . . . .8 A2
Gibbon's Rents
SE1 . . . . .124 A1
Gibbon Wlk SW15 . . . . .56 C3
Gibbs Gn SW14 . . . . . .141 A2
Gibbs Green Sch
W14 . . . . .141 A2
Gibbs Ho 6 SW12 . . . . .73 A4
Gibraltar Ho NW10 . . . .21 A3
Gibraltar Wlk E2 . . . . . .99 A3
Gibson Cl E1 . . . . .25 B1
Gibson Gdns N16 . . . . . .7 B2
Gibson Rd SE11 . . . . . .149 A3
Gibson Sq N1 . . . . .85 C4
Gibson St SE10 . . . . . . .43 A1
Gideon Rd SW11 . . . . . .60 C4
Giesbach Rd N19 . . . . . .4 C2
Giffen Square Mkt
SE8 . . . . .51 C3
Giffin St SE8 . . . . .51 C3
Gifford Ho SE10 . . . . . .42 C1
5 London SW4 . . . . .61 C3
Gifford St N1 . . . . .14 A1
Gilbert Ho 5 E2 . . . . . . .25 C2
EC2 . . . . .109 A3
SE8 . . . . .51 C4
SW1 . . . . .146 B1
SW8 . . . . .162 A2
Gilbert Pl WC1 . . . . . . .106 A3
Gilbert Rd SE11 . . . . . .149 C4
Gilbert Sheldon Ho
W2 . . . . .101 C4
Gilbert St
E14 . . . . .41 C3
W1 . . . . .103 C1
Gilbeys Yd NW1 . . . . . . .12 C1
Gilby Ho 6 E9 . . . . .17 C2
Gilda Cres N16 . . . . .7 C3
Gildea St W1 . . . . .104 B3
Gilden Cres NW5 . . . . . .12 C3
Giles Ho SE16 . . . . . . .139 B2
London W11 . . . . .31 C3
Gilesmead SE5 . . . . . . .48 C2
Gilkes Cres SE21 . . . . . .64 A1
Gilkes Pl SE21 . . . . .64 A1
Gillam Ho 2 SE16 . . . . .40 B2
Gill Ave E16 . . . . .35 C3
Gillender St E3 . . . . . . .27 B1
Gillespie Prim Sch
N5 . . . . .6 A1
Gillespie Rd N4,N5 . . . . .6 A1
Gillett Pl 21 E8 . . . . .16 A3
Gillett St E8,N16 . . . . . .16 A3
Gillfoot NW1 . . . . .82 C1
Gillian St SE13 . . . . . . .67 A2
Gillies Ho NW6 . . . . .1 C1
Gilling Ct 5 NW3 . . . . . .12 A2
Gillingham Mews
SW1 . . . . .146 C4
Gillingham Rd NW2 . . . .1 A1

Gillingham Row
SW1 . . . . .146 C4
Gillingham St SW1 . . . .146 C4
Gillison Wlk SE16 . . . . .139 C2
Gilman Ho 22 E2 . . . . . .24 C3
Gilray Ho SW10 . . . . . .157 B3
Gill St E14 . . . . .33 B2
Gilmore Rd SW4 . . . . . .60 B3
Gilmore Rd SE13 . . . . . .67 C3
Gilpin Ave SW14 . . . . . .55 C3
Gilpin Cl W2 . . . . .101 A3
Gilpin Rd E5 . . . . .18 A4
Gilray Ho W2 . . . . .115 B4
Gilstead Rd SW6 . . . . .166 B2
Gilston Rd SW10 . . . . . .143 A1
Giltspur St EC1 . . . . . .108 B2
Gilwell Ct 8 E5 . . . . . . .17 A4
Gipsy Cnr W3 . . . . .28 C4
Gipsy La SW15 . . . . . . .57 A4
Gipsy Moth IV SE10 . . . .52 C4
Giraud St E14 . . . . .34 A3
Girdlers Rd W14 . . . . . .39 C2
Girdlestone Wlk N19 . . . .4 B2
Girdwood Rd SW18,
SW19 . . . . .70 A4
Girling Ho 9 N1 . . . . . . .24 A4
Gironde Rd SW6 . . . . . .155 A1
Girton Ho SW15 . . . . . . .57 C1
Girton Villas 6 W10 . . .30 C3
Gissing Wlk N1 . . . . . . .14 C1
Gladding Terr N16 . . . . . .7 B1
Gladsmuir Rd N19 . . . . . .4 B3
Gladstone Ct SW1 . . . .147 C3
London NW10 . . . . .9 A3
Gladstone Ho 14
E14 . . . . .33 C3
Gladstone Park Sch
NW10 . . . . .9 A3
Gladstone St SE1 . . . . .136 A2
Gladstone Terr
SW8 . . . . .170 B4
Gladwin Ho NW1 . . . . . .83 A1
Gladwyn Rd SW15 . . . . .57 C4
Gladys Rd NW6 . . . . . . .10 C1
Glaisher St 2 SE10 . . . .52 B3
SE8 . . . . .52 A4
Glamis Ct W3 . . . . .37 A4
Glamis Est 3 E1 . . . . . .32 C2
Glamis Pl E1 . . . . .32 B2
Glamis Rd E1 . . . . .32 B2
Glanville Ho 3
SW12 . . . . .73 B4
Glanville Rd SW2 . . . . . .62 A2
Glasbrook Rd SW9 . . . .172 B1
Glaserton Rd N16 . . . . . . .7 A4
Glasgow Ho W9 . . . . . . .78 B1
Glasgow Terr SW1 . . . .146 C1
Glasshill St SE1 . . . . . .136 B4
Glasshouse Fields
E1 . . . . .32 C2
Glasshouse St W1 . . . .119 A3
Glasshouse Wlk
SE11 . . . . .148 C2
Glasshouse Yd EC1 . . . .96 C1
Glass St 6 E2 . . . . .25 A1
Glastonbury Ct 18
SE14 . . . . .50 B3
Glastonbury Ho
SW1 . . . . .146 A2
Glastonbury Pl 20
E1 . . . . .32 B3
Glastonbury St NW6 . . . .10 B3
Glaucus St E3 . . . . .34 A4
Glazbury Rd W14 . . . . .140 B2
Glazebrook Cl SE21 . . . .75 C2
Glebe Cl 1 W4 . . . . .38 A1

Glebe Ho 8 SE16 . . . . . .40 A3
Glebelands Cl SE5 . . . . .64 A4
Glebe Pl SW3 . . . . .158 A4
Glebe Rd
Barnes SW13 . . . . .46 C1
London E8 . . . . .16 B1
London NW10 . . . . .8 C2
Glebe St W4 . . . . .38 A1
Glebe Terr 13 E3 . . . . . .27 A2
Gledhow Gdns
SW5 . . . . .142 C3
Gledstanes Rd
W14 . . . . .140 B1
Glegg Pl 3 SW15 . . . . . .57 C3
Glenaffric Ave E14 . . . . .42 C2
Glen Albyn Rd
SW19 . . . . .69 C2
Glenalmond Ho 3
SW15 . . . . .57 C1
Glenarm Rd E5 . . . . . . .17 C4
Glenbrook Inf Sch
SW4 . . . . .61 C1
Glenbrook Jun Sch
SW4 . . . . .61 C1
Glenbrook Rd NW6 . . . . .10 C3
Glenburnie Rd
SW17 . . . . .72 B1
Glencoe Mans
SW9 . . . . .163 B1
Glendall St SW9 . . . . . .62 B3
Glendarvon St
SW15 . . . . .57 C4
Glendower Gdns 10
SW14 . . . . .55 C4
Glendower Pl SW7 . . . .143 B4
Glendower Prep Sch
SW7 . . . . .143 B3
Glendower Rd
SW14 . . . . .55 C4
Glendown Ho 2 E8 . . . .16 C3
Glendun Ct W3 . . . . . . .29 A2
Glendun Rd W3 . . . . . . .29 A2
Gleneagles Cl 17
SE16 . . . . .40 A1
Glenelg Rd SW2 . . . . . .62 A2
Glenfield Rd SW12 . . . . .73 B3
Glenfinlas Way SE5 . . . .48 A3
Glenforth St SE10 . . . . .43 B1
Glengall Gr E14 . . . . . . .42 B3
Glengall Pass 2
NW6 . . . . .23 C4
Glengall Rd NW6 . . . . . .23 B4
Glengall Terr SE15 . . . .49 B4
Glengarnock Ave
E14 . . . . .42 B2
Glengarry Rd SE22 . . . .64 B2
Glenhurst Ave NW5 . . . .12 C4
Glenilla Rd NW3 . . . . . . .12 A2
Glenister Rd SE10 . . . . .43 B1
Glenloch Rd 3 NW3 . . .12 A3
Glenluce Rd SE3 . . . . . .53 C4
Glenmore SW15 . . . . . . .57 C1
Glenmore Ho 6
SW15 . . . . .57 A1
Glenmore Rd NW3 . . . . .12 A2
Glennie Ct SE21 . . . . . . .76 C3
Glennie Ho SE10 . . . . . .52 B2
Glennie Rd SE27,
SE16 . . . . .74 C1
Glenridding NW1 . . . . . .83 A1
Glenrosa St SW6 . . . . .166 C2
Glenroy St W12 . . . . . . .30 B3

Glensdale Rd SE4 ....66 B4
Glenshaw Mans
SW9 ....163 B1
Glentanner Way
SW17 ....71 C1
Glen Terr E14 ....42 B4
Glentham Gdns
SW13 ....47 A4
Glentham Rd SW13 .....47 A4
Glenthorne Mews
W6 ....39 A2
Glenthorne Rd W6 ......39 A2
Glenthorpe SW15 ....56 C3
Glentworth St NW1 .....91 A1
Glenville Gr SE8 ....51 B3
Glenville Mews
SW18 ....71 A4
Glenworth Ave E14 .....42 C2
Gliddon Rd W14 ....140 A2
Glifford Ho W1 ....146 C1
Globe Pond Rd
SE16 ....33 A1
Globe Prim Sch E2 .....25 B2
Globe Rd E1,E2 ....25 B1
Globe St SE1 ....137 B3
Globe Terr ⊠ E2 ....25 B2
Globe Theatre The *
SE1 ....122 C3
Globe View EC4 ....122 C3
Globe Yd W1 ....104 A1
Gloucester W14 ....140 C4
Gloucester Ave
NW1 ....81 C4
Gloucester Cir SE10 ....52 B3
Gloucester Cres
NW1 ....82 A4
Gloucester Ct EC3 .....124 B3
SE1 ....137 A2
London NW11 ....1 B4
London SE22 ....76 C3
Richmond TW9 ....44 C3
Gloucester Dr N4 ....6 A2
Gloucester Gate
NW1 ....82 A2
Gloucester Gate Mews
NW1 ....82 A2
Gloucester Gdns
W2 ....100 C2
London NW11 ....1 B4
Gloucester Ho NW6 ...23 C3
Richmond TW10 ....54 C2
Gloucester Mews
W2 ....101 A1
Gloucester Mews W
W2 ....101 A1
Gloucester Pk
SW7 ....142 C4
Gloucester Pl W1 ......103 A4
Gloucester Pl Mews
W1 ....103 A3
Gloucester Prim Sch
SE15 ....49 A3
Gloucester Rd
SW7 ....142 C4
Acton W3 ....37 B4
Richmond TW9 ....44 C3
Gloucester Road Sta
SW7 ....142 C4
Gloucester Sq
⊠ E2 ....24 C4
W2 ....101 C1
Gloucester St SW1 .....146 C1
Gloucester Terr
W2 ....101 A1

Gloucester Way
EC1 ....95 C3
Gloucester Wlk
W8 ....127 C4
Glover Ho
London NW6 ....11 B1
London SE15 ....65 A3
Glycena Rd SW11 ......60 B4
Glyn Cl SE27 ....74 C1
Glynde Mews SW3 .....130 B1
Glynde Reach WC1 .....94 B3
Glynde St SE4 ....66 B1
Glynfield Rd NW10 .....8 A1
Glyn Mans W14 ....140 B4
Glyn Rd E5 ....17 C4
Glyn St SE11 ....148 C1
Goater's Alley
SW6 ....155 A1
Goat Wharf TW8 ....44 A4
Godalming Rd E14 .....34 A4
Goddard Ho SW19 .....69 C2
Goddard Pl N19 ....4 B1
Godfrey Ho EC1 ....97 B3
Godfrey St E15 ....27 B3
SW3 ....144 B2
Goding St SE11 ....148 B1
Godley Rd SW18 ....71 C3
Godliman St EC4 ......122 C4
Godman Rd SE15 ....50 A1
Godolphin Ho
London NW3 ....12 A1
⊠ Streatham SW2 ......74 C3
Godolphin & Latymer
Sch W6 ....39 A2
Godolphin Pl W3 ....28 C2
Godolphin Rd W12 .....39 A4
Godson St N1 ....85 C2
Godstone Ct ⊠ N16 ....7 A3
Godstone Ho SE1 .....137 C2
Godwin Cl N1 ....87 A2
Godwin Ct NW1 ....83 A2
Godwin Ho ⊠ E2 ....24 B3
NW6 ....78 A2
Goffers Ho SE3 ....53 A1
Goffers Rd SE3,SE13 ...53 A1
Goffton Ho SW9 ......173 A1
Golborne Gdns W10 ...23 B1
⊠ W10 ....23 A1
Golborne Mews ⊠
W10 ....31 A4
Golborne Rd W10 ......31 A4
Golden Cross Mews ⊠
W11 ....31 B3
Golden Hind Pl ⊠
SE8 ....41 B2
Golden La EC1 ....97 A1
Golden Plover Cl ⊠
E16 ....35 C3
Golden Sq W1 ....119 A4
Golders Ct NW11 ....1 B4
Golders Gdns NW11 ...1 B4
Golders Green Coll
NW11 ....1 B3
Golders Green Cres
NW11 ....1 C4
Golders Green Rd
NW11 ....1 A4
Golders Green Sta
NW11 ....1 C3
Golders Hill Sch
NW11 ....1 C4
Golderslea NW11 ....1 C3
Golders Park Cl
NW11 ....1 C3
Golders Way NW11 .....1 B4
Goldhawk Ind Est The
W6 ....39 A3

Goldhawk Mews ⊠
W12 ....39 A4
Goldhawk Rd
W12 ....38 C3
Goldhawk Road Sta
W12 ....39 B4
Goldhurst Terr NW6 ...11 B1
Goldie Ho N19 ....4 C4
Golding St E1 ....111 C1
Golding Terr E1 ....111 C2
Goldington Cres
NW1 ....83 B2
Goldington Ct NW1 .....83 B3
Goldington St NW1 .....83 B2
Goldman Cl
⊠ E2 ....24 C1
Goldney Rd W9 ....23 C1
Goldsboro Rd SW8 ...161 C1
Goldsborough Ho
SW8 ....171 C3
Goldsmith Ave W3 .....28 C2
Goldsmith Ct WC1 ....106 B2
Goldsmith Rd
London SE15 ....49 C2
London W3 ....28 C1
Goldsmiths Bldgs
W3 ....28 C1
Goldsmiths Cl W3 ......28 C1
Goldsmith's Coll, Univ of
London SE14 ....51 A2
Goldsmith's Pl NW6 ...78 A3
Goldsmith's Row ⊠ E2 .24 C3
Goldsmith's Sq ⊞
E2 ....24 C3
Goldsmith St EC2 ....109 A2
Goldsworthy Gdns
SE16 ....40 B2
Goldthorpe NW1 ....82 C3
Goldwell Ho SE22 .....64 A3
Goldwin Cl SE14 ....50 B2
Goldwing Cl E16 ....35 C3
Gomm Rd SE16 ....40 B3
Gondar Gdns NW6 .....10 B3
Gondar Mans NW6 .....10 B3
Gonson St SE8 ....52 A4
Gonston Cl SW19 ......70 A2
Gonville Ho ⊞
SW15 ....58 A4
Gonville St SW6 ......58 A4
Gooch Ho EC1 ....107 B4
Goodall Ho ⊞ SE4 .....65 C3
Goodfaith Ho ⊞
E14 ....34 A2
Goodge Pl W1 ....105 A3
Goodge St W1 ....105 A3
Goodge Street Sta
W1 ....105 B4
Goodhall St NW10 .....21 B2
Good Hart Pl E14 ......33 A2
Goodhope Ho ⊞
E14 ....34 A2
Gooding Cl N7 ....14 A2
Goodinge Rd N7 ....14 A2
Goodman Cres SW2 ...73 C2
Goodman's Stile
E1 ....111 B2
Goodman's Yd E1,
EC3 ....124 C4
Goodrich Com Sch
SE22 ....64 C1
Goodrich Ct ⊞ W10 ...30 C3
Goodrich Ho ⊠ E2 .....25 B3
London N16 ....7 A4
Goodrich Rd SE22 .....64 C1
Good Shepherd RC Prim
Sch The W12 ....38 B4
Goodson Rd NW10 .....8 A1

Goodsway NW1 ....84 A2
Goodway Gdns E14 ....34 C3
Goodwill Ho ⊞ E14 ....34 A2
Goodwin Cl SE16 .....139 A1
Goodwin Ho ⊠
SE15 ....65 A4
Goodwin Rd W12 ......38 C4
Goodwins Ct WC2 ....120 A4
Goodwin St N4 ....5 C2
Goodwood Ct W1 .....104 B4
Goodwood Ho ⊞
W4 ....37 B1
Goodwood Mans
SW9 ....62 C4
Goosander Ct SE14 ....51 A3
Goose Green Trad Est
SE22 ....64 C3
Gophir La EC4 ....123 B4
Gopsall St N1 ....87 C3
Gordon Ave SW14 .....56 A3
Gordonbrock Prim Sch
SE4 ....66 C2
Gordonbrock Rd
SE4 ....66 C2
Gordon Ct ⊠ W12 .....30 B3
Gordondale Rd
SW18,SW19 ....70 C2
Gordon Gr SE5 ....48 A1
Gordon Ho ⊞ E1 ....32 B2
⊞ SE10 ....52 B4
Gordon Hospl The
SW1 ....147 B3
Gordon House Rd
NW5 ....12 C4
Gordon Lo N16 ....6 C3
Gordon Pl W8 ....127 C4
Gordon Rd
Chiswick W4 ....45 A4
London E15 ....76 B4
London SE15 ....50 A1
Richmond TW9 ....44 B1
Gordon Sq WC1 ....93 C2
Gordon St WC1 ....93 B2
Gorefield Ho NW6 .....23 C3
Gorefield Pl NW6 ......23 C3
Gore Rd E9 ....25 B4
Gore St SW7 ....129 A2
Gorham Ho ⊞ SW4 ...61 B1
Gorham Pl W11 ....112 A3
Goring Ct EC3 ....110 B2
Gorleston St W14 ....140 B4
Gorse Cl E16 ....35 C3
Gorsefield Ho ⊞
E14 ....33 C2
Gorst Rd
London NW10 ....20 C1
London SW11 ....60 B1
Gorsuch Pl ⊠ E2 .....98 C4
Gorsuch St E2 ....98 C4
Gosberton Rd SW12 ..72 C3
Gosfield St W1 ....104 C3
Gosford St ⊞ E2 ......26 B3
Goslett Yd WC2 ......105 C2
Gosling Ho ⊞ E1 ......32 B2
Gosling Way SW9 ....173 B4
Gospel Oak Prim Sch
NW5 ....12 C4
Gospel Oak Sta
NW5 ....12 C4
Gosport Ho ⊞
SW15 ....68 C3
Gosset St E2 ...24 C2 99 B4
Gosterwood St SE8 ....51 A4
Goswell Pl EC1 ....96 B3
Goswell Rd EC1 ....96 B3
Gothic Ct ⊞ SE5 ......48 B3

Gottfried Mews
NW5 ....13 B4
Gough Ho N1 ....86 B4
Gough Sq EC4 ....107 C2
Gough St WC1 ....95 A1
Gough Wlk ⊞ E14 .....33 C3
Goulden Ho SW11 ....168 A2
Gouldman Ho ⊠ E1 ...25 B1
Gould Terr ⊠ E8 ......17 A3
Goulston St E1 ....110 C2
Goulton Rd E5 ....17 A4
Govan St E2 ....24 C4
Gover Ct SW4 ....172 B2
Gowan Ave SW6 ......164 A4
Gowan Ho E2 ....99 A3
Gowan Rd NW10 ....9 A2
Gower Cl SW4 ....61 B1
Gower Ct WC1 ....93 B2
Gower Ho SE17 ....151 A2
Gower Mews WC1 ....105 C4
Gower Pl NW1,WC1 ...93 B2
Gower St WC1 ....93 B1
Gower's Wlk E1 ......111 B1
Gowlett Rd SE15 ......64 C4
Gowrie Rd SW11 ......60 C4
Gracechurch St
EC3 ....109 C1
Gracefield Gdns
SW16 ....74 A1
Gracehill ⊠ E1 ....32 B4
Grace Ho SE11 ....163 A4
Grace Jones Cl E8 .....16 C2
Grace Pl E3 ....27 A2
Graces Mews NW8 ....79 A1
Grace's Mews SE5 ....49 A1
Grace's Rd SE5 ....49 A1
Grace St E3 ....27 A2
Graemesdyke Ave
SW14 ....55 A3
Grafton Cres NW1 .....13 A2
Grafton Ct ⊞ E8 ......16 C3
Grafton Ho ⊞ E3 .....26 C2
⊞ SE8 ....41 B1
Grafton Mews W1 ....92 C1
Grafton Pl NW1 ....93 C3
Grafton Prim Sch N7 ..5 A1
Grafton Rd
London NW5 ....12 C3
London W3 ....28 B2
Grafton Sq SW4 ......61 B4
Grafton St W1 ....118 B3
Grafton Terr NW5 .....12 C3
Grafton Way W1 ....93 A1
Graham Yd NW5 ......13 A2
Graham St SE14 ....50 C4
Graham Ho
⊞ Balham SW12 ......73 A4
London N19 ....13 C4
Graham Mans ⊠ E8 ..17 A2
Graham Rd
London E8 ....16 C2
London W4 ....37 C3
Graham St N1 ....86 B1
Graham Terr SW1 ....145 C3
Grainger Ct ⊠ SE5 ....48 B3
Grampian Gdns NW2 ..1 A3
Grampians The ⊞
W14 ....39 C4
Granard Ave SW15 ....57 A2
Granard Ho ⊠ E9 .....17 C2
Granard Prim Sch
SW15 ....57 A1
Granard Rd SW11,
SW12 ....72 B4
Granary Rd E1 ....25 A1
Granary St NW1 ....83 B3
Granby Pl SE1 ....135 B3

Granby St E1 ....99 B2
Granby Terr NW1 ......82 C1
Grand Ave EC1 ....108 B4
Grandfield Ct W4 ....45 C4
Grandison Rd SW11 ...60 B2
Grand Junction Wharf
N1 ....86 C1
Grand Par SW14 ....55 B3
Grand Union Ind Est
NW10 ....20 A3
Grand Union Cres
E8 ....24 C4
Grand Union Ind Est
NW10 ....20 A3
Grand Vitesse Ind Est
SE1 ....122 B1
Granfield St SW11 ....167 C3
Grangecourt Rd N16 ...7 A3
Grange Ct WC2 ....107 A1
London SE15 ....49 B1
Grangefield NW1 ....14 A1
Grange Gdns NW3 ....2 A1
Grange Gr N1 ....15 B2
Grange Ho SE1 ....138 C1
London NW10 ....21 A3
Grange La SE21 ....76 B2
Grangemill 11 NW5 ....13 A4
Grange Mills SW12 ....73 B3
Grange Mus of
Community History The
NW10 ....8 A4
Grange Pl NW6 ....10 C1
Grange Prim Sch
SE1 ....138 A1
Grange Rd SE1 ....138 C1
Barnes SW13 ....46 C2
London NW10 ....9 A2
London W4 ....37 A1
Grange St N1 ....87 C3
Grange The SE1 ....138 C1
W14 ....140 C3
London NW2 ....1 B2
London W12 ....38 A3
London W3 ....37 A4
7 London SW4 ....37 A1
Grangeway NW6 ....10 C1
Grange Wlk SE1 ....138 C1
Grange Yd SE1 ....138 C1
Gransden Ave E8 ....17 A1
Gransden Ho 11 SE8 ..41 B1
Gransden Rd W12 ......38 B4
Grantbridge St N1 .....86 B2
Grantham Ct 9
SE16 ....40 C4
Grantham Ho 12
SE15 ....49 C4
Grantham Pl W1 ......118 A1
Grantham Rd
Chiswick W4 ....46 A3
London SW9 ....172 B1
Grant Ho SW8 ....171 B1
Grantley Ho
2 SE14 ....50 C4
5 Putney SW15 ....69 C3
Grantley St E1 ....25 C1
Grant Rd SW11 ....60 A4
Grantully Rd W9 ....88 A3
Granville Ct N1 ....87 C4
8 SE14 ....51 B3
Granville Gr SE13 ......67 B4
Granville Ho 13 E14 ...33 C3
Granville Mans
WC1 ....94 A2
6 London W12 ....39 B4
Granville Pk SE13 ......67 C3
Granville Pl SW6 ......156 A1
W1 ....103 B1

Granville Point NW2 ...1 B2
Granville Rd NW6 ......23 C3
London NW2 ....1 B2
Wandsworth SW18 ...70 B4
Granville Sq
8 SE15 ....49 A3
WC1 ....95 A3
Granville St WC1 ....95 A3
Grape St WC2 ....106 A2
Grasmere 11 NW1 ......92 B3
Grasmere Ave W3 ......28 C2
Grasmere Ct SW13 ....46 C4
Grasmere Ho 19
N16 ....15 C4
Grasmere JMI Sch
N16 ....15 C4
Grasmere Point 2
SE15 ....50 B3
Grately Ho 10 SW15 ...69 A3
Gratton Rd W14 ....126 A1
Graveley Ho 7 SE8 ....41 A2
Gravel La E1 ....110 C2
Gravesend Rd W12 ....29 C2
Grayfriars Pas EC1 ...108 B2
Gray Ho SE17 ....151 A2
Grayland Ct WC1 ....94 C3
Grayling Ho N16 ....6 C2
Grayling Sq
E2 ....24 C2 99 C4
Grayshott Rd SW11 ...60 C4
Gray's Inn Pl WC1 ....107 A3
Gray's Inn Rd WC1 ....95 A2
Gray's Inn Sq WC1 ...107 B3
Grayson Ho EC1 ....97 A3
Gray St SE1 ....135 C3
Grayswood Point 14
SW15 ....68 C3
Gray's Yd W1 ....103 C2
Grazebrook Prim Sch
N16 ....7 A2
Grazebrook Rd N16 .....6 C2
Great Arthur Ho
EC1 ....96 C1
Great Bell Alley
EC2 ....109 B2
Great Castle St
W1 ....104 C2
Great Central St
NW1 ....102 C4
Great Chapel St
W1 ....105 B2
Great Chertsey Rd
SW14,W4 ....45 C2
Great Church La
W6 ....39 C1
Great College St
SW1 ....134 A2
Great Croft WC1 ....94 B3
Great Cumberland Mews
W1 ....102 C1
Great Cumberland Pl
W1 ....103 A1
Great Dover St
SE1 ....137 B2
Great Eastern Bldgs 16
E8 ....17 A2
Great Eastern Ent Ctr
E14 ....42 A4
Great Eastern Pier
E14 ....41 C1
Great Eastern St
EC2 ....24 A1 98 A2
Great Eastern Wharf
SW11 ....158 B1

Great Field 7 NW5 ....13 B3
Greatfield Cl
4 London N19 ....13 B4
London SE4 ....66 C3
Great George St
SW1 ....134 A3
Great Guildford Bsns Sq
SE1 ....122 C1
Great Guildford St
SE1 ....122 C1
Greatham Wlk 8
SW15 ....68 C3
Great James St
WC1 ....106 C4
Great Marlborough St
W1 ....104 C1
Great Mathers Rd
SE11 ....150 A4
Great Maze Pond
SE1 ....137 C4
Great Newport St
WC2 ....120 A4
Great New St EC4 ....107 C2
Greatorex Ho 11 E1 ...111 B4
Greatorex St E1 ....111 B4
Great Ormond St
WC1 ....94 C1
Great Ormond St Hospl
for Children WC1 .....94 C1
Great Percy St WC1 ...95 B4
Great Peter St
SW1 ....133 C1
Great Portland St
W1 ....104 B4
Great Portland Street
Sta W1 ....92 B1
Great Pulteney St
W1 ....119 A4
Great Queen St
WC2 ....106 B2
Great Russell St
WC1 ....106 A3
Great Scotland Yd
SW1,WC2 ....120 A2
Great Smith St
SW1 ....133 C2
Great Spilmans
SE22 ....64 A2
Great St Helen's
EC3 ....110 A2
Great St Thomas
Apostle EC4 ....123 A4
Great Suffolk St
SE1 ....122 B1
Great Sutton St EC1 ...96 B1
Great Swan Alley
EC2 ....109 B2
Great Titchfield St
W1 ....104 C3
Great Tower St
EC3 ....124 A4
Great Trinity La
EC4 ....123 A4
Great Turnstile
WC2 ....107 A3
Great Western Rd
W2,W9 ....31 B4
Great West Rd W4,
W6 ....45 C4
Great West Road Cedars
Rd W4 ....45 A4
Great West Road
Hogarth La W4 ....46 A4
Great Winchester St
EC2 ....109 C2
Great Windmill St
W1 ....119 B4

Great Yd SE1 ....138 B4
Greaves Cotts 12
E14 ....33 A4
Greaves Twr SW10 ...157 A2
Grebe Ct 11 E14 ....42 B4
Greek Ct W1 ....105 C1
Greek St W1 ....105 C1
Greenacre Ct E8 ....16 C3
Greenacre Sq 28
SE16 ....40 C4
Green Arbour Ct
EC1 ....108 A2
Greenaway Gdns
NW3 ....11 A4
Greenaway Ho 8 NW8 ..78 C4
Green Bank E1 ....32 A1
Greenberry St NW8 ...80 A1
Green Cl NW11 ....2 B4
Greencoat Pl SW1 ....147 A4
Greencoat Row
SW1 ....133 A1
Greencourt Ho 1 E1 ...25 C1
Greencroft Gdns
NW6 ....11 B1
Green Dale SE22 ....64 A2
Greendale SE22 ....64 A2
Green Dragon Ct
SE1 ....123 B1
Green Dragon Ho
WC1 ....106 B2
Green Dragon Jun & Inf
Sch TW8 ....44 A4
Green Dragon La
TW8 ....36 B1
Green Dragon Yd
E1 ....111 B3
Greene Ct 20 SE14 ....50 C4
Greenend Rd W4 ....38 A4
Greener Ho 3 SW4 ....61 C4
Greenfell Mans SE8 ...52 A4
Greenfield Gdns
NW2 ....1 A1
Greenfield Ho 2
SW19 ....69 C3
Greenfield Rd E1 ......111 C2
Greenham Cl SE1 .....135 B3
Greenham Ho 6 E9 ...25 B4
Greenheath Bsns Ctr 3
E2 ....25 A1
Greenhill NW3 ....11 C4
Greenhill Pk NW10 ...21 A4
Greenhill's Rents
EC1 ....108 A4
Greenhills Terr 18
N1 ....15 C2
Green Ho The 5
SW19 ....70 A3
Green Hundred Rd
SE15 ....49 C4
Greenland Ho 4 E1 ...26 A1
Greenland Mews
SE8 ....40 C1
Greenland Pl NW1 .....82 B4
Greenland Quay
SE16 ....40 C2
Greenland Rd NW1 ...82 C4
Green Lanes N4,N8,
N15 ....6 A4
Greenleaf Cl 6
SW2 ....74 C4
Greenman St N1 ....86 C4

Greenmead Sch
SW15 ....57 A2
Greenock Rd 11 W3 ...37 B3
Green Park SW1,
W1 ....132 B4
Green Park Sta
SW1 ....118 C2
Greens Ct 11 W11 ....119 B4
Green's Ct W11 ....112 C1
Greenside Prim Sch
W12 ....38 C4
Greenside Rd W12 ....38 C4
Green St W1 ....117 B4
Greenstead Gdns
SW15 ....57 A2
Greenstreet Hill
SE4 ....65 C4
Green Terr EC1 ....95 C3
Green The W3 ....29 A3
Greenview Cl W3 ......29 A1
Greenway Cl N4 ....6 B2
Greenwell St W1 ....92 B1
Greenwich Academy
SE10 ....52 A2
Greenwich Bsns Ctr
SE10 ....52 A3
Greenwich Bsns Pk
SE10 ....52 A3
Greenwich Church St
SE10 ....52 B4
Greenwich Ct 18 E1 ...32 A3
Greenwich District
Hospl SE10 ....43 B1
Greenwich High Rd
SE10 ....52 A3
Greenwich Ind Est
SE10 ....52 A3
Greenwich Mkt 1
SE10 ....52 B4
Greenwich Park
SE10 ....53 A3
Greenwich Park St
SE10 ....52 B3
Greenwich Park Sch
SE10 ....52 C4
Greenwich South St
SE10 ....52 A2
Greenwich Sta SE10 ...52 A3
Greenwich View
E14 ....42 A3
Green Wlk SE1 ....138 A1
Greenwood 6
SW19 ....69 C4
Green Wood NW5 .....13 B3
Greenwood Ho
London SW9 ....95 B3
8 London SE4 ....65 C4
Greenwood Pl NW5 ...13 A3
Greenwood Rd E8 .....16 C2
Greenwood Terr
NW10 ....20 C3
Green Yd WC1 ....95 A2
Greet Ho SE1 ....135 C3
Greet St SE1 ....121 C1
Gregor Mews SE3 ......53 C3
Gregory Pl W8 ....128 A4
Greig Terr SE17 ....48 A4
Grenada Ho 18 E14 ...33 B2
Grenade St E14 ....33 B2
Grena Gdns TW9 ....54 B3
Grena Rd TW10,TW9 ..54 B3
Grendon Cl SE15 ....49 C3
Grendon Ho N1 ....84 C2
25 London E9 ....17 B1

Grendon St NW8 90 A2
Grenfell Ho SE5 48 B3
Grenfell Rd W11 30 C2
Grenfell Twr 5 W11 30 C2
Grenfell Wlk 4 W11 30 C2
Grenville Ho 24 E3 26 A3
4 SE8 51 C4
Grenville Lo N6 4 B4
Grenville Mews SW7 143 A3
Grenville Pl SW7 142 C4
Grenville Rd N19 5 A3
Grenville St WC1 94 B1
Gresham Almshouses 3 SW9 62 B3
Gresham Coll EC1 107 C3
Gresham Gdns NW11 1 A3
Gresham Rd SW9 62 C4
Gresham St EC2 109 A2
Gresham Way SW19 70 C1
Gresham Way Est SW19 71 A1
Gresley Ho SW8 171 C4
Gresley Rd N19 4 B4
Gressenhall Rd SW18 70 B4
Gresse St W1 105 B2
Greswell St SW6 47 C2
Gretton Ho 2 E2 25 B2
Greville Hall NW6 78 B2
Greville Ho SW1 131 B2
Putney SW15 57 C4
Greville Lo W2 100 A2
Greville Mews NW6 78 A3
Greville Pl W9 78 B3
Greville Rd NW6 78 B2
Richmond TW10 54 B1
Greville St EC1 107 C4
Grey Coat Hospital CE Sch The SW1 133 B1
Grey Coat Hospital St Michaels The SW1 147 B3
Greycoat Pl SW1 133 B1
Greycoat St SW1 133 B1
Grey Eagle St E1 24 B1 99 A1
Greyfriars 16 SE26 76 C1
Greyfriars Ho SE3 53 B4
Grey Ho 27 W12 30 A2
Greyhound Ct WC2 121 B4
Greyhound Rd W6 154 A4
London NW10 22 A2
Greyladies Gdns SE10 52 B1
Greystoke Ho SE15 49 C4
Greystoke Pl EC4 107 C2
Grey Turner Ho W12 29 C3
Grice Ct N1 15 B2
Griffin Cl NW10 9 A3
Griffin Ct
8 Brentford TW8 44 A4
London W12 30 A1
London W4 38 B1
Griffin Gate SW15 57 C4
Grifton Ho 3 SW11 60 A4
Grigg's Pl SE1 138 B1
Grimaldi Ho N1 84 C2
Grimsby St E2 99 A2
Grimsel Path SE5 48 A3
Grimshaw Cl N6 3 C4
Grimston Rd SW6 164 C1
Grimthorpe Ho EC1 96 A2
Grimwade Cl SE15 65 B4
Grindall Ho 26 E1 25 A1
Grindal St SE1 135 B3
Grindley Ho 3 E3 33 B4
Grinling Gibbons Prim Sch SE8 51 B4
Grinling Pl SE8 51 C4
Grinstead Rd SE8 41 A1
Grisedale NW1 92 C4
Grittleton Rd W9 23 C1
Grocers' Hall Ct EC2 109 B1
Groombridge Rd E9 17 C1
Groom Cres SW18 71 C4
Groome Ho SE11 149 A3
Groom Pl SW1 131 C2
Grosse Way SW15 57 A1
Grosvenor Ave
London N5 15 B3
Mortlake SW14 56 A4
Richmond TW10 54 A2
Grosvenor Bridge SW1 160 B4
Grosvenor Cotts SW1 145 B4
Grosvenor Cres SW1 131 C3
Grosvenor Cres Mews SW1 131 B3
Grosvenor Ct
London NW6 22 C4
London W4 37 A1
Putney SW15 58 A2
Grosvenor Ct Mans W2 102 C1
Grosvenor Gdns
SW1 132 B1
London NW2 9 B3
Mortlake SW14 56 A4
Grosvenor Gdns Mews E SW1 132 B2
Grosvenor Gdns Mews N SW1 132 A1
Grosvenor Gdns Mews S SW1 132 B1
Grosvenor Hill W1 118 A4
Grosvenor Hill Ct W1 118 A4
Grosvenor Ho E5 7 C3
Grosvenor Park SE5 48 B3
Grosvenor Pier SW1 161 B4
Grosvenor Pk SE5 48 B4
Grosvenor Pl SW1 132 A3
Grosvenor Rd SW1 161 A4
London W4 37 B1
Richmond TW10 54 A2
Grosvenor Residences 1 W14 39 C3
Grosvenor Sq W1 117 C4
Grosvenor St W1 118 A4
Grosvenor Terr SE5 48 B4
Grosvenor The NW11 2 A4
Grosvernor Wharf Rd E14 42 C2
Grote's Bldgs SE3 53 A1
Grote's Pl SE3 53 A1
Groton Rd SW18 71 A2
Grotto Ct SE1 136 C4
Grotto Pas W1 103 C4
Grove Crescent Rd E15 19 C2
Grove Ct NW8 89 B4
SW10 143 A1
London SE5 49 A1
London SW4 61 B4
Grovedale Rd N19 4 C2
Grove Dwellings E1 32 B4
Grove End NW5 13 A4
Grove End Gdns NW8 79 A1
Grove End Ho NW8 89 B3
Grove End Rd NW8 89 B3
Grove Gdns NW8 90 B3
Grove Hall Ct E3 26 C3
NW8 89 A4
Grove Hill Rd SE5 64 A4
Grove Ho SW3 158 B4
London SE3 53 B1
Grove La SE5 64 A4
Groveland Ct EC4 109 A1
Grovelands Cl SE5 49 A1
Grove Lane Terr SE5 48 C1
Groveley Ho 7 N4 6 B4
Grove Lo SW4 61 B3
Grove Mans
3 London N16 7 C3
London SW4 60 B3
2 London W6 39 B4
Grove Mews W6 39 B3
Grove Park Bridge W4 45 B3
Grove Park Gdns W4 45 B3
Grove Park Mews W4 45 B3
Grove Park Prim Sch W4 45 B4
Grove Park Rd W4 45 A3
Grove Park Terr W4 45 A4
Grove Pk SE5 49 A1
Grove Pl
Balham SW12 61 A1
London NW3 2 C1
London W3 28 B1
Grover Ct SE13 52 A1
Grove Rd E3 26 A3
Barnes SW13 46 B1
London NW2 9 B2
London W3 28 B1
Richmond TW10 54 B1
Grover Ho SE11 149 A1
4 London SW4 61 B2
Groveside Ct SW11 167 B2
Grove St SE8 41 B1
Grove Terr NW5 13 A4
Grove The N6 3 C3
Dulwich SE21 76 C3
London N4 5 B4
London NW11 1 A4
Grove Vale SE22 64 B3
Grove Vale Prim Sch SE22 64 B3
Groveway SW9 173 A3
Grovewood 9 TW9 44 C2
Grovewood Ho NW2 1 B2
Grummant Rd SE15 49 B2
Grundy St E14 34 A3
Guardian Angels RC Prim Sch E3 26 A2
Guards Mus The SW1 133 A3
Gubyon Ave SE24 63 A2
Guerin Sq E3 26 B2
Guernsey Gr SE24 75 B4
Guernsey Ho 9 N1 15 B2
Guernsey Rd 8 N1 15 B2
Guildford Gr SE10 52 A2
Guildford Ho 24 SE5 48 B1
Guildford Rd SW8 172 B4
Guild Hall★ EC2 109 A2
Guildhall Bldgs EC2 109 B2
Guildhall Sch Music & Drama EC2 109 A4
Guildhall Yd EC2 109 A2
Guildhouse St SW1 146 C3
Guilford Pl WC1 94 C1
Guilford St WC1 94 B1
Guillemot Ct 23 SE8 51 B4
Guilsborough Cl NW10 8 A1
Guinness Cl E9 18 A1
Guinness Ct E1 111 A1
EC1 97 A3
NW8 80 B3
SW3 144 C3
Guinness Sq SE1 152 A4
Guinness Trust Bldgs
7 E2 24 C3
SE1 138 A4
SE11 150 A2
SW3 144 C3
London W6 39 B1
Guion Rd SW6 165 A2
Gujarat Ho 1 N16 7 A1
Gulland Wlk 20 N1 15 B2
Gullane Ho 22 E3 26 B3
Gulliver St SE16 41 B3
Gulston Wlk SW3 145 A3
Gunmakers La E3 26 A4
Gunnersbury Avenue (North Circular Rd) W3 36 C3
Gunnersbury Cl 8 W4 37 A1
Gunnersbury Cres W3 36 C4
Gunnersbury Ct 8 W3 37 A4
Gunnersbury Dr W5 36 B4
Gunnersbury Gdns W3 36 C4
Gunnersbury La W3 36 C4
Gunnersbury Mews 6 W4 37 A1
Gunnersbury Park W3 36 C3
Gunnersbury Park Mus W3 36 C3
Gunnersbury Sta W4 37 A1
Gunners Rd SW18 71 C2
Gunpowder Sq EC4 107 C2
Gun St E1 110 C3
Gunstor Rd N16 16 A4
Gunter Gr SW6 156 C2
Gunterstone Rd W14 140 B2
Gunthorpe St E1 111 A2
Gunwhale Cl SE16 32 C1
Gun Wharf E1 32 B1
E3 26 A4
Gurdon Ho 3 E14 33 C3
Gurdon Rd SE7 43 C1
Gurney Ho 14 E2 24 C3
London W2 100 A2
Gurney Rd SW6 59 B4
Guthrie Ct SE1 135 C3
Guthrie St SW3 144 A2
Gutter La EC2 108 C2
Guyscliff Rd SE13 67 B2
Guy's Hospl SE1 137 C4
Guy's Hospl Sch SE1 123 B1
Guy St SE1 137 C4
Gwalior Rd SW15 57 C4
Gwendolen Ave SW15 57 C2
Gwendolen Cl SW15 57 C2
Gwendwr Rd W14 140 B2
Gwent Ct 13 SE16 32 C1
Gwilym Maries Ho 11 E2 25 A2
Gwyn Cl SW6 156 C1
Gwynne Cl W4 46 B4
Gwynne Ho WC1 95 B3
6 Streatham SW2 74 B3
Gwynne Pl WC1 95 A3
Gwynne Rd SW11 167 C2
Gye Ho 2 SW4 62 A3
Gylcote Cl SE5 63 C3

H

Haarlem Rd 12 W14 39 C3
Haberdasher Pl N1 98 A4
Haberdasher St N1 97 C4
Habington Ho 9 SE5 48 C3
Hackett Cl SE8 41 B2
Hackford Rd SW9 173 A4
Hackford Wlk SW9 173 B3
Hackney Central Sta E8 17 A2
Hackney Coll (Poplar Ctr) E3 27 A1
Hackney Com Coll N1 98 B4
London N4 6 B4
Hackney Downs Sch E5,E8 16 C3
Hackney Downs Sta E8 17 A3
Hackney Free & Parochial CE Sch (Secondary) E9 17 B2
Hackney Gr E8 17 A2
Hackney Hospl E9 18 A3
Hackney Rd E2 24 C3
Hackney Wick E9 18 B2
Hackney Wick Sta E9 18 C2
Hackworth Point 24 E3 27 A2
Haddington Ct 4 SE10 52 A3
Haddo Ho SE10 52 A4
London NW5 13 A4
Haddon Ct W3 29 B2
Haddo St SE10 52 B4
Haden Ct N4 5 C2
Hadfield Ho E1 111 C1
Hadleigh Cl 18 E1 25 B1
Hadleigh Ho 15 E1 25 B1
Hadleigh St E2 25 B2
Hadley Ct N16 7 C3
Hadley Gdns W4 37 C1
Hadley St NW1 13 A2
Hadlow Ho SE17 152 B2
Hadrian Ct SE4 66 C4
Hadrian Est 30 E2 24 C3
Hadrian St SE10 43 A1
Hadstock Ho NW1 93 C4
Hadyn Park Ct 13 W12 38 C4
Hadyn Park Rd W12 38 C4
Hafer Rd SW11 60 B3
Haggerston Rd E8 24 B4
Haggerston Sch E2 24 B3
Hague Prim Sch E2 25 A1
Hague St E2 99 C3

Haig Ho 4 E2 ....24 C3
Hailsham Ave SW2 ..74 B2
Hailsham Ho NW8 ..90 A1
Hainford CI SE4 ....65 C3
Haining CI 3 W4 ....36 C1
Hainton CI E1 ......32 A3
Halcomb St N1 .....24 A4
Halcrow St E1 ......32 A4
Halcyon Wharf E1 ..125 C2
Haldane PI SW18 ...71 A3
Haldane Rd SW6 ...155 A3
Haldon Rd SW18 ....58 B1
Hale Ho SW1 ....147 C2
Hales Ho 3 SW12 ..73 A4
Hales Prior N1 .....84 C1
Hales St SE8 ....51 C3
Hale St E14 ....34 A2
Halesworth Rd
SE13 ....67 A4
Half Moon Ct EC1 ..108 C3
Half Moon La SE24 ..63 B1
Halfmoon Pas E1 ...111 A1
Half Moon St W1 ...118 B1
Halford Ho 2
SW15 ....57 C2
Halford Rd SW6 ....155 B3
Richmond TW10 .....54 A2
Haliday Ho N1 ......15 C2
Haliday Wlk 4 N1 ..15 C2
Halidon CI E9 ......17 B3
Haliwell Ho NW6 ...78 A3
Halkett Ho 1 E2 ...25 B4
Halkin Arc SW1 ....131 A2
Halkin Mews SW1 ..131 B2
Halkin PI SW1 ......131 B2
Halkin St SW1 ......131 C3
Hallam Ct W1 ......104 B4
Hallam Ho SW1 .....147 A1
London SW9 ....173 B4
Hallam Mews W1 ...104 B4
Hallam St SW13 ....57 A4
Hallam St W1 ......104 B4
Halley Gdns SE13 ..67 C3
Halley Ho 15 E2 ...24 C3
5 SE10 ....43 B1
Halley Prim Sch
E14 ....33 A4
Halley St E14 ......33 A4
Hallfield Jun & Inf Schs
W2 ....100 A2
Hall Gate NW8 ......89 A4
Halliday Ho 5
London E1 ....111 C1
Halliford St N1 .....15 C1
Halling Ho SE1 .....137 C3
Halliwell Ct 4 SE22 .64 C2
Halliwell Rd SW2 ...62 B1
Hall Oak Wlk NW6 ..10 B2
Hall PI W2 ....89 B1
Hall Rd NW8 ....89 A4
London E15 ....19 C4
Hall Sch The NW3 ..11 C2
Hall Sch Wimbledon
SW15 ....68 C1
Hall St EC1 ....96 B4
Hallsville Prim Sch
E16 ....35 C3
Hallsville Rd E16 ..35 B3
Hall Twr W2 ....101 C4
Halpin PI SE17 .....151 C3
Halsbury Ho 4 N7 ..14 B4
Halsbury Rd W12 ..30 A1
Halsey St SW3 .....144 C4
Halsmere Rd SE5 ..48 A2
Halstead Ct N1 .....87 C1
Halston CI SW11 ...60 B1
Halstow 12 NW5 ...12 C2

Halstow Prim Sch
SE10 ....43 C1
Halstow Rd
SE3,SE10 ....43 C1
London NW10 ....22 C2
Halton Cross St N1 ..86 B4
Haltone Ho SW4 ...171 C1
Halton Ho 22 N1 ...15 A1
Halton Mans N1 ....15 A1
Halton PI N1 ....86 C4
Halton Rd N1 ....86 B4
Halyard Ho E14 ....42 B3
Hambalt Rd SW4 ...61 B2
Hambledon SE17 ...48 C4
Hambledon Chase
N4 ....5 A4
Hambledon Ho E5 ..17 A4
Hambledon PI SE21 .76 B3
Hambledon Rd
SW18 ....70 B4
Hamble St SW6 ....59 A4
Hambley Ho 5
SE16 ....40 A2
Hamblyn Ct N16 ....7 B4
Hambridge Way
SW2 ....74 C4
Hambrook Ct 12
NW5 ....13 A4
Hamburg Rd SW8 ..162 B3
Hamilton CI NW8 ...89 B3
London SE16 ....41 A4
Hamilton Gdns
NW8 ....89 A4
Hamilton Hall NW8 ..78 C1
Hamilton Ho 1 E14 ..33 B2
10 E3 ....26 B2
5 NW8 ....89 B4
W8 ....128 A4
Chiswick W4 ....46 A4
Putney SW15 ....56 C2
16 Richmond TW9 ..44 C2
Hamilton La N5 .....15 A4
Hamilton Lo 7 E1 ..25 B1
Hamilton Mews
W1 ....132 A4
Hamilton Pk N5 ....15 A4
Hamilton Pk W N5 ..15 A4
Hamilton PI W1 ....117 C1
Hamilton Rd
London NW10 ......8 C3
London NW11 ......1 A4
London W4 ....38 A4
Hamilton Sq SE1 ...137 C4
Hamilton St SE8 ...51 C4
Hamilton Terr NW8 ..89 A4
Hamlet (Day) Hospl The
TW9 ....54 A4
Hamlet Gdns W6 ...38 C2
Hamlet Ind Est E9 ..18 C1
Hamlets Way E3 ...26 B1
Hamlet Sq NW2 ....1 A1
Hamlet Way SE1 ...137 C4
Hammelton Gn 2
SW9 ....48 A2
Hammersley Ho 3
SE14 ....50 B3
Hammersmith Bridge Rd
W6,SW13 ....39 B1
Hammersmith Broadway
5 W6 ....39 B2
Hammersmith Flyover
W6 ....39 B1

Hammersmith Gr
W6 ....39 B3
Hammersmith Hospl
W12 ....30 A3
Hammersmith Rd
W14 ....140 B4
London W6 ....39 C2
Hammersmith Sta
W6 ....39 B2
Hammersmith Terr
6 W6 ....38 C1
Hammett St EC3 ...124 C4
Hammond Ho E14 ..42 A3
10 SE14 ....50 B3
Hammond Lo 6
W12 ....31 C4
Hammond St NW5 ..13 B2
Hamond Sq N1 .....24 A3
Hampden CE
Prim Sch NW1 .....102 B2
Hampden Gurney St
W1 ....102 C1
Hampden Ho SW9 ..173 C1
Hampden Rd N19 ..4 C2
Hampshire Ct 6
SW13 ....46 B1
Hampshire Hog La 1
W6 ....39 A2
Hampshire Sch The
SW7 ....130 A3
Hampshire St 13 C2
Hampson Way
SW8 ....172 C4
Hampstead Gate
NW3 ....11 B3
Hampstead Gn NW3 ..12 A3
Hampstead Gr NW3 ..2 B1
Hampstead Heath*
NW3 ....2 C3
Hampstead Heath Sta
NW3 ....12 A4
Hampstead High St
NW3 ....11 C4
Hampstead Hill Gdns
NW3 ....12 A4
Hampstead Hill Sch
NW3 ....12 A3
Hampstead La N6 ..3 A4
Hampstead Parochial CE
Prim Sch NW3 .....11 B4
Hampstead Rd NW1 ..92 C4
Hampstead Sch
NW2 ....10 A4
Hampstead Sq NW3 ..2 C1
11 Hampstead West 1
NW6 ....10 C2
Hampstead Wlk 1
E3 ....26 B4
Hampton Ct 5 N1 ..15 A2
Hampton Ct
16 SE16 ....32 C1
London N1 ....15 A2
Hampton St SE1 ...150 B3
11 SE1 W1 ....150 C3
Hamstead St 12 SE16 ..35 C1
Hana Mews E5 .....17 A4
Hanbury Ho 1 E1 ..111 B4
Hanbury Rd W3 ....37 A4
Hanbury St E1 .....111 B4
Hancock Nunn Ho 1
NW3 ....12 B1
Hancock Rd E3 ....27 B2
Handa Wlk 3 N1 ...15 B2
Hand Ct WC1 ......107 A3

Handel Mans SW13 ..47 B3
Handel St WC1 .....94 B2
Handforth Rd SW9 ..163 B2
Handley Rd E9 ......25 B4
Hands Wlk E16 .....35 C3
Hanford Cl SW18 ...70 C3
Hankey Pl SE1 .....137 C3
Hanley Gdns N4 ...5 B3
Hanley Rd N4,N19 ..5 B3
Hanmer Wlk N7 ....5 B2
Hannah Mary Way
SE1 ....153 C3
Hannay La N8 ......4 C4
Hannay Wlk SW16 ..73 C2
Hannell Rd SW6 ...154 B2
Hannen Ho SE5 ....64 A4
Hannen Rd SE27 ...75 A1
Hannibal Rd E1 ....32 B4
Hannington Rd
SW4 ....61 A4
Hanover Ave E16 ...35 C1
Hanover Cl TW9 ...44 C3
Hanover Ct
London SE19 ....75 C1
London W12 ....29 C1
Hanover Gate Mans
NW1 ....90 B2
Hanover Gdns
SE11 ....163 B3
Hanover Ho 80 A1
Hanover Mans 5
SW2 ....62 C2
Hanover Pk SE15 ..49 C2
Hanover Pl 1 E3 ...26 B2
WC2 ....106 B1
Hanover Prim Sch
N1 ....86 C2
Hanover Rd NW10 ..22 B4
Hanover Sq W1 ....104 B1
Hanover St W1 ....104 B1
Hanover Steps W2 ..102 B1
Hanover Terr NW1 ..90 C3
Hanover Terr Mews
NW1 ....90 B3
Hanover West Ind Est
NW10 ....20 C2
Hanover Yd N1 ....86 C2
Hansard Mews W14 ..39 C4
Hanscomb Mews 3
SW4 ....61 B3
Hans Cres SW1 ....130 C2
Hansler Rd SE22 ...64 B2
Hanson Cl
Balham SW12 ......73 A4
Mortlake SW14 .....55 B4
Hanson Ho 1 E1 ...125 C4
Hanson St W1 .....104 C4
Hans Pl SW1 ....130 C2
Hans Rd SW3 ......130 C2
Hans St SW1 ....131 A1
Hanway Ho 1 SW9 ..173 C4
Hanway Pl W1 .....105 B2
Hanway St W1 .....105 B2
Hanwell Ho 2 W2 ..31 C4
Hanworth Ho SE5 ..48 A3
Harben Rd NW6 ....11 B1
Harberson Rd SW12 ..73 A3
Harberton Rd N19 ..4 B3
Harbet Rd W2 .....101 C3
Harbinger Prim Sch
E14 ....42 A2
Harbinger Rd E14 ..42 A2
Harbin Ho 5 SW2 ..74 C3
Harbledown Ho
SE1 ....137 B3
Harbledown Rd
SW6 ....165 B4

Harbord Cl SE5 ....48 C1
Harbord Ho 5 SE16 ..40 C2
Harbord St SW6 ...47 C2
Harborough Sch N19 ..4 C2
Harbour Ave SW10 ..167 A3
Harbour Exchange Sq
E14 ....42 A4
Harbour Rd SE5 ...63 B4
Harbridge Ave
SW15 ....68 C4
Harbut Rd SW11 ...59 C3
Harcombe Rd N16 ..7 A1
Harcourt Ho W1 ...104 A2
London SW8 ....171 B2
Harcourt Rd SE4 ...66 B4
Harcourt St W1 ....102 B3
Harcourt Terr
SW10 ....142 B1
Hardcastle Ho 8
SE15 ....49 C2
Hardel Rise SW2 ...75 A3
Hardel Wlk SW2,
SW2 ....74 C4
Harden Ho SE5 ....49 A1
Harders Rd SE15 ..50 A1
Hardess St SE24 ..63 B4
Hardham Ho 5
SW2 ....62 C1
Harding Cl SE17 ...48 B4
Hardinge Rd NW10 ..22 B4
Hardinge St E1 ....32 B3
Harding Ho SW13 ..47 A4
Hardington 2 NW1 ..12 C1
Hardwicke Ho 14
E3 ....27 A2
Hardwicke Mews
WC1 ....95 A3
Hardwicke Rd W4 ..37 C2
Hardwick Ho NW8 ..90 B2
London SW8 ....171 B2
Hardwick St EC1 ...95 C3
Hardwick's Way
SW18 ....58 C2
Hardwidge St SE1 ..138 A4
Hardy Ave E16 ....35 C1
Hardy Cl SE16 .....40 C4
Hardy Cotts 2 SE10 ..52 C4
Hardy Rd SE3 .....53 B4
Hardy Rd SE3 .....53 B4
Hare & Billet Rd
SE3 ....52 C1
Harecourt Rd N1 ..15 B2
Hare Ct EC4 ....107 B1
Haredale Ho 2 SE16 ..139 B3
Haredale Rd SE24 ..63 B3
Harefield Mews SE4 ..66 B4
Harefield Rd SE4 ..66 B4
Hare Marsh
E2 ....24 C1 99 B2
Hare PI EC4 ....107 C1
Hare Row E2 ......25 A3
Hare Wlk N1 ......24 A3
Harewood Ave NW1 ..90 B1
Harewood PI W1 ..104 B1
Harewood Row
NW1 ....102 B3
Harfield Gdns 1
SE5 ....64 A4
Harfleur Ct SE11 ..150 A3
Harford Ho SE5 ...48 B4
W11 ....31 B4
Harford St E1 .....26 A1
Hargrave Mans 2
N19 ....4 C2

Hargrave Park Prim Sch
N19 ....4 B2
Hargrave Pl N19 ....4 B2
Hargrave Rd N19 ....1 C3
Hargrave Rd N19 ....4 B2
Hargraves Ho **14**
W12 ....30 A2
Hargwyne St SW9 ...62 B4
Harkness Ho E1 ......111 C1
Harlech Twr **5** W3 ...37 A4
Harlescott Rd SE15 ..65 C3
Harlesden Gdns
NW10 ....21 B4
Harlesden Plaza **4**
NW10 ....21 B3
Harlesden Prim Sch
NW10 ....21 A3
Harlesden Rd NW10 ..21 C4
Harlesden Sta
NW10 ....21 B3
Harleyford Ct SW8 ..162 C4
Harleyford Manor **6**
W3 ....28 B1
Harleyford Rd
SE11 ....162 C4
Harleyford St SE11 ..163 B3
Harley Gdns SW10 ..143 A1
Harley Gr E3 ....26 B2
Harley Ho NW1 ....91 C1
Harley Pl W1 ....104 A3
Harley Rd
London NW10 ....11 C4
London NW3 ....11 C1
Harley St W1 ....104 A3
Harley Villas W1 ....21 A3
Harling Ct SW11 .....168 C2
Harlowe Ho **18** E8 ...24 B4
Harlynwood **15** SE5 .48 B3
Harman Cl SE1 ....153 B1
London NW2 ....1 A1
Harman Dr NW2 ....10 A4
Harmon Ho **6** SE8 ..41 B2
Harmood Gr NW1 .....13 A1
Harmood Ho **7**
NW1 ....13 A1
Harmood St NW1 ......13 A1
Harmsworth St
SE17 ....150 A1
Harold Ct **14** SE16 .40 C4
Harold Est SE1 ....138 B1
Harold Ho **10** E2 ...25 C3
Harold Laski Ho
EC1 ....96 B3
Harold Maddison Ho
SE17 ....150 B2
Harold Pl SE11 ......149 B1
Harold Rd NW10 ......20 C2
Harold Wilson Ho
SW6 ....155 A3
Harp Alley EC4 ....108 A2
Harpenden Rd SE27,
SW16 ....75 A2
Harpenmead Point
NW2 ....1 B2
Harper Ho **3** SW9 ..63 A4
Harper Mews SW17 ..71 B1
Harper Rd SE1 ....137 A2
Harp La EC3 ....124 A3
Harpley Sq E1 ....25 C1
Harpsden St SW11 ..169 B3
Harpur Mews WC1 ..106 C4
Harpur St WC1 ....106 C4
Harrier Ho **9** SW11 .60 A4
Harriet Cl E8 ....24 C4
Harriet Ho SW6 .....156 B1

Harriet St SW1 ....131 A3
Harriet Tubman Cl **21**
SW2 ....74 C4
Harriet Wlk SW1 ....131 A3
Harrington Ct
SW7 ....143 C4
W10 ....23 B2
Harrington Gdns
SW7 ....142 C3
Harrington Ho NW1 ..92 C4
SW1 ....147 C2
Harrington Rd
SW7 ....143 B4
Harrington Sq NW1 ..82 C1
Harrington St NW1 ...92 C4
Harriott Cl SE10 ......43 B2
Harriott Ho **11** E1 ..32 B3
Harris Ho **10** E3 ....26 C2
8 London SW9 .....62 C4
Harrison Ho SE17 ...151 B2
Harrisons Ct **1**
SE14 ....50 C4
Harrison St WC1 ......94 B3
Harris St SE5 ....48 C3
Harrodian Sch The
SW13 ....46 B3
Harrogate Ct **2**
SE26 ....76 C1
Harrold Ho **1** NW3 .11 B1
Harroway Rd
SW11 ....167 C2
Harrowby St W1 .....102 B2
Harrowgate Ho **22**
E9 ....17 C2
Harrowgate Rd E9 ...18 A2
Harrow La E14 ....34 B2
Harrow Pl E1 ....110 B2
Harrow Rd W2 ....101 B3
W2,W9 ....23 C1
Harrow St NW1 ......102 A4
Harry Gosling Prim Sch
E1 ....111 B2
Harry Hinkins Ho
SE17 ....151 A1
Harry Lambourn Ho **10**
SE15 ....50 A3
Hartfield Terr **3** 26 C3
Hartham Cl N7 ....14 A3
Hartham Rd N7 ....14 A3
Hart Ho SW2 ....74 C3
Hartington Ct SW8 .172 A4
Chiswick W4 ....45 B3
Hartington Rd
SW8 ....162 A1
Chiswick W4 ....45 B3
Hartismere Rd
SW6 ....155 A2
Hartlake Rd E9 ....18 A2
Hartland NW1 ....83 A3
Hartland Rd NW6 .....23 B4
London NW1 ....13 A1
Hartley Ho SE1 ......153 A4
Putney SW15 ....56 C2
Hartley St E2 ....25 B2
Hartnoll Ho **4** N7 ..14 C3
Hartnoll St N7 ....14 B3
Harton Lo **8** N7 .....14 B4
Harton St SE8 ....51 C2
Hartopp Ct N4 ....6 C4
Hartopp Point
SW6 ....154 B2
Hartshorn Alley
EC3 ....110 B1
Hart's La SE14 ....51 A2
Hart St EC3 ....124 B4
Hartswood Ho **10**
SW2 ....74 A3

Hartswood Rd W12 ..38 B3
Hartwell St E8 ....16 B2
Harvard Ct NW6 ......11 A3
Harvard Hill W4 ....45 A4
Harvard Ho **3** SE17 .48 A4
Putney SW15 ....57 C1
Harvard Mans **18**
SW11 ....59 C3
Harvard Rd
London SE13 ....67 B2
London W4 ....37 A1
11 London W4 .....37 B1
Brentford TW8 ....36 A1
Harvey Ct SW1 ....168 B4
Harvey Ho **10** E1 ...25 A1
1 London N1 ....15 A1
SW1 ....147 C1
Harvey Lo **6** W9 ...31 C4
Harvey Point **1** E16 .35 C4
Harvey Rd **15** SE5 ..48 C2
Harvey St N1 ....87 C3
Harvington Wlk E8 ..16 C1
Harvist Rd NW6 ......23 A3
Harwood Cl N11 ......87 C3
Harwood Ct **6**
SE16 ....40 C4
Harwood Rd SW6 ...156 A1
Harwood Terr
SW6 ....166 A4
Hascombe Ho **11**
SW15 ....69 A3
Hascombe Terr **2**
SE5 ....49 A1
Haselrigge Rd SW4 .61 C3
Hasker St SW3 ......144 B4
Haslam Cl N1 ....14 C1
Haslam Ho **11** N1 ..15 B1
Haslam St SE15 ......49 B2
Haslemere Ave
SW18 ....71 A2
Haslemere Ct **1**
SW18 ....71 A2
Haslemere Ind Est
SW18 ....71 A2
Haslemere Rd N8 .....5 A4
Hassard St E2 ....24 B3
Hassett Rd E9 ....18 A2
Hassop Rd NW2 ....9 C4
Hastings Cl **18** SE15 .49 C3
Hastings Ho **12** W12 .30 A2
Hastings Hos WC1 ...94 A3
Hastings St WC1 .....94 A3
Hatcham Mews Bsns Ctr
SE14 ....50 C2
Hatcham Park Mews
SE14 ....50 C2
Hatcham Park Rd
SE14 ....50 C2
Hatchard Rd N19 ......5 A2
Hatcliffe Almshouses **3**
SE10 ....43 A1
Hatcliffe St SE10 .....43 B1
Hatfield Cl SE14 ......50 C3
Hatfield Ct SE3 ....53 C3
Hatfield Ho EC1 ......96 C1
Hatfield Rd W4 ......37 C4
Hatfields SE1 ....121 C2
Hathaway Ho **5** N1 .24 A3
Hatherley Ct W2 ....100 A2
Hatherley Gr W2 ....100 A2
Hatherley Rd TW9 ...44 B2
Hatherley St SW1 ..147 A3
Hathersage Ct N1 ...15 C3
Hathersley Ho **3**
SW2 ....74 C4

Hathorne Cl **3**
SE15 ....50 A1
Hathway Ho **3**
SE15 ....50 B1
Hathway St **4** SE15 .50 B1
Hatley Rd N4,N7 ......5 B2
Hat & Mitre Ct EC1 ..96 B1
Hatteraick St **8**
SE16 ....40 B4
Hatton Gdn EC1 ....107 C4
Hatton Ho E1 ....125 C4
Hatton Pl EC1 ....107 C4
Hatton Row NW8 .....89 C1
Hatton St NW8 ....89 C1
Hatton Wall EC1 ....107 C4
Haunch of Venison Yd
W1 ....104 A1
Hauteville Court Gdns **2**
W6 ....38 B3
Havana Rd SW18,
SW19 ....70 C2
Havannah St E14 ....41 C4
Havelock Cl **16** W12 .30 A2
Havelock St N1 ....84 B4
Havelock Terr
SW8 ....160 B1
Haven Cl SW19 ....69 C1
Havenpool NW8 ......78 B3
Haven St **1** NW1 ...13 A1
Haven The TW9 ......54 C4
Havercourt **3** NW3 .12 A2
Haverfield Gdns
TW9 ....44 C3
Haverfield Rd E3 .....26 A2
Haverhill Rd SW12 ..73 B3
Havering **8** NW1 ...13 A1
Havering Ho N4 ....6 B4
Havering St E1 ....32 C3
Haversham Lo NW2 ..9 C3
Haversham Pl N6 .....3 B2
Haverstock Hill
NW3 ....12 B2
Haverstock Rd NW5 .12 C3
Haverstock Sch
NW1 ....12 C2
Haverstock St N1 .....86 B1
Havil St SE5 ....49 A2
Havisham Ho SE16 .139 B3
Hawarden Gr SE24 ..75 B4
Hawberry Ho N7 .....14 A2
Hawes St N1 ....15 A1
Hawgood St E3 ....33 C4
Hawke Ho E1 ....25 C1
Hawke Pl **2** SE16 ..40 C4
Hawkesbury Rd
SW15 ....57 A2
Hawkesworth Ho **5**
SW4 ....61 B1
Hawke Twr **4** SE14 .51 A4
Hawk Ho **7** SW11 ..60 A4
Hawkins Ho **3** SE8 ..51 C4
Hawkley Gdns SE27 ..75 A2
Hawkridge **1** NW5 ..12 C2
Hawkshead NW1 ......92 C4
Hawkshead Rd
London NW10 ....8 B1
London W4 ....38 A4
Hawkslade Rd SE15 ..65 C2
Hawksley Rd N16 .....7 A1
Hawks Mews **1**
SE10 ....52 B3
Hawksmoor Mews
E1 ....32 A2
Hawksmoor St **5**
W6 ....47 C4
Hawkstone Rd SE16 .40 B2
Hawkwell Wlk N1 ....87 A4

Hawley Cres NW1 ....13 A1
Hawley Inf Sch
NW1 ....13 A1
Hawley Mews **4**
NW1 ....13 A1
Hawley Rd **3** NW1 ..13 A1
Hawley St NW1 ....13 A1
Haworth Ct E15 ......76 B3
Haworth Ho **7** SW2 .62 C1
Hawstead Rd SE6 ...67 A1
Hawthorn Ave E3 ....26 B4
Hawthorn Ct
Putney SW15 ....57 A4
Richmond TW9 ....45 A2
Hawthorne Cl N1 .....16 A2
Hawthorne Ho
SW1 ....147 A1
Hawthorn Rd NW10 ..8 C1
Hawthorn Wlk W10 ..23 A1
Hawtrey Rd NW3 .....12 A1
Haycroft Gdns
NW10 ....22 A4
Haycroft Mans
NW10 ....21 C4
Haycroft Rd SW2 .....62 A2
Hay Currie St E14 ....34 A3
Hayday Rd E16 ....35 C4
Hayden's Pl W11 .....31 B3
Haydon St E1,EC3 ..124 C4
Haydon Way SW11 ..59 C3
Hayes Ct **22** SE5 ...48 B3
Streatham SW12 ......74 A3
Hayes Pl NW1 ....90 B1
Hayfield Pas E1 ....25 B1
Hay Hill W1 ....118 B3
Hayles Bldgs SE11 .150 B4
Hayles St SE11 ......150 B4
Hayling Ct **20** N16 .16 A3
Haymans Point
SE11 ....148 C2
Haymarket SW1 .....119 B3
Haymerle Ho **4**
SE15 ....49 C3
Haymerle Rd SE15 ..49 C4
Haymerle Sch SE15 .49 C4
Hayne Ho W11 ......112 A2
Haynes Ho **3** E9 ...17 C2
Hayne St EC1 ....108 B4
Hay's Galleria SE1 ..124 A2
Hay's La SE1 ....124 A2
Hay's Mews W1 .....118 A2
Hay St E2 ....24 C4
Hayter Ho W12 ....29 C2
Hayter Rd SW2 ....62 B2
Haythorn Ho SW11 .167 C3
Hayton Cl **1** E8 .....16 B2
Hayward Ct SW4 ....172 B2
Hayward Gallery*
SE1 ....121 A2
Hayward Gdns
SW15 ....57 B1
Hayward Ho N1 ....85 B2
Haywards PI EC1 .....96 A2
Haywood Lo **2** N7 ..13 C3
Hazelbourne Rd
SW12 ....61 A1
Hazel Cl London N19 ..4 B2
London SE15 ....49 C1
Hazeldon Rd SE4 ....66 A2
Hazel Ho
12 London NW3 ..12 B2
London SE4 ....66 B4
Hazellville Rd N19 ....4 C3
Hazelmere Ct **10**
SW2 ....74 B3
Hazelmere Rd NW6 .23 B4

Hazel Rd NW10 ....22 B2
Hazel Way SE1 ....152 C4
Hazelwood Cl W5 ...36 A4
Hazelwood Ho 11
SE8 ....41 A2
Hazelwood Mans
SW6 ....164 C4
Hazlebury Rd SW6 .166 B2
Hazledene Rd W4 ...45 B4
Hazlewell Rd SW15 .57 B2
Hazlewood Cres
W10 ....23 A1
Hazlitt Mews W14 .126 A1
Hazlitt Rd W14 ....126 A1
Headbourne Ho
SE1 ....137 C2
Headcorn 10 NW5 ..12 C2
Headfort Pl SW1 ..131 C3
Headington Rd
SW18 ....71 B2
Headlam Rd SW4 ..73 C4
Headlam St E1 ....25 A1
Heads Mews W11 .31 C3
Head St E1 ....32 C3
Heald St SE8,SE14 ..51 C2
Healey St NW1 ....13 A2
Healy Ho 7
E3 ....26 C1 163 C1
Heanor Ct 4 E5 ...17 C4
Hearne Rd W4 ....44 C4
Hearn's Bldgs
SE17 ....151 C3
Hearn St EC2 ..24 A1 98 B1
Hearnville Rd SW12 .72 C3
Heart Hospl The
W1 ....103 B3
Heathbrook Prim Sch
SW4 ....170 C1
Heath Brow NW3 ...2 B1
Heath Cl NW11 ....2 A4
Heathcote St WC1 ..94 C3
Heathcroft NW11 ....2 A3
Heathcroft 2
2 London NW3 ...11 B2
Heather Cl SW8 ...61 A4
Heather Ct SW4 ..172 B3
Heather Ho 7 E14 .34 B3
Heatherley Ct N16 ..7 C1
Heatherley Sch of Fine
Art SW10 ....157 A1
Heather Lo N16 ....7 A3
Heather Wlk W10 ..23 A1
Heathfield Ave
SW18 ....71 C4
Heathfield Ct
5 London W4 ....37 C1
Wandsworth SW18 ..71 C4
Heathfield Gdns
London SW18 ....59 C1
London W4 ....37 B1
Heathfield Ho SE3 .53 A1
Heathfield Pk NW2 ..9 B2
Heathfield Rd
London SW18 ....59 C1
London W3 ....37 A4
Heathfield Sq SW18 .71 C4
Heathfield Terr W4 .37 C1
Heathgate Pl NW3 .12 B4
Heath Hurst Rd
NW3 ....12 A4
Heath La SE3 ....52 C1
Heathland Rd N16 ..7 A3
Heathland Sch
SW19 ....69 C1

Heath Mans
4 London NW3 ...11 B4
Putney SW15 ....57 C1
Heathman's Rd
SW6 ....165 A3
Heath Mead SW19 .69 C1
Heathmere Prim Sch
SW15 ....68 C3
Heath Park Gdns
NW3 ....2 A1
Heathpool Ct 8 E1 .25 A1
Heath Rd SW8 ....170 B1
Heath Rise SW15 ..57 C1
Heath Royal SW15 .57 C1
Heathshott 8 TW10 .54 A1
Heathside NW3 ....11 C4
Heathstan Rd W12 .29 C3
Heath View NW5 ..12 C4
Heathview Ct SW19 .69 C2
Heathview Gdns
SW15 ....69 B4
Heathville Rd N4,N19 .5 A4
Heathwall St SW11 .60 B4
Heathway 6 SE3 ...53 B3
Greenwich SE3 ....53 C3
Heathway Ct NW3 ..1 C2
Heathwood Ct
SW12 ....73 B3
Heaton Ho SW10 ..157 A4
Heaton Rd SE15 ...50 A1
Heaver Rd 2 SW11 .59 C4
Hebden Ct 2 E2 ...24 B4
Hebdon Rd SW17 ..72 A1
Heber Prim Sch
SE22 ....64 B1
Heber Rd NW2 ....9 C4
London SE22 ....64 B1
Hebron Rd W6 ....39 A3
Heckfield Pl SW6 .155 B1
Heckford St E1 ....32 C2
Hector Ct
London SW9 ....173 B4
Putney SW15 ....57 C2
Hector Ho 14 E2 ...25 A3
Heddington Gr N7 ..14 B3
Heddon St W1 ....118 C4
Hedger's Gr E9 ....18 A2
Hedger St SE11 ...150 A4
Hedingham Cl 6
N1 ....15 B1
Hedley Ct SW15 ...57 C1
Hedley Ho E14 ....42 B3
Hedley Row N5,N16 ..7 C1
Hedsor Ho E2 ....98 C2
Heidegger Cres
SW13 ....47 A3
Heights The NW3 ..11 B4
Heiron St SE17 ...48 A4
Helby Rd SW4 ....61 C1
Heldar Ct SE1 ....137 C3
Helena Rd NW10 ...9 A3
Helena Sq 15 SE16 .33 A2
Helen Gladstone Ho
SE1 ....136 A4
Helen Ho 9 E2 ....25 A3
Helen Mackay Ho 11
E14 ....34 C3
Helen Peele Cotts 10
SE16 ....40 B3
Helenslea Ave NW11 .1 C3
Helen's Pl E2 ....25 B2
Helen Taylor Ho 2
SE16 ....153 B4

Heliport Est The
SW11 ....167 B1
Helios Rd SW2 ....62 B1
Helix Rd SW2 ....62 B1
Hellenic Coll of London
SW1 ....130 C1
Hellings St E1 ....125 C1
Helmet Row EC1 ..97 A2
Helmore Ho N6 ..78 A1
Helmsdale Ho NW6 .78 A1
Helmsley Pl E8 ...17 A1
Helmsley St 7 E8 ..17 A1
Helperby Rd NW10 ..8 A1
Helsby Ct NW8 ....89 B2
Helsinki Sq SE16 ..41 A3
Helston NW1 ....83 A2
Helston Ho SE11 ..149 C2
Hemans Est SW8 ..161 C1
Hemans St SW8 ..161 C1
Hemberton Rd SW9 .62 A4
Hemingford Rd N1 .85 A4
Hemlock Rd W12 ..29 B2
Hemming St
E1 ....24 C1 99 C1
Hemp Wlk SE17 ...151 C4
Hemstal Rd NW6 ..10 C1
Hemsworth Ct N1 ..24 A3
Hemsworth St N1 ..24 A3
Hemus Pl SW3 ....144 B1
Henchman St W12 .29 B3
Henderson Ct
2 SE14 ....50 C4
London NW3 ....11 C3
Henderson Dr NW8 .89 B2
Henderson Rd
SW18 ....72 A4
Hendham Rd SW17 .72 B2
Hendre Ho SE1 ...152 B3
Hendre Rd SE1 ...152 B3
Hendrick Ave SW12 .72 B4
Heneage La EC3 ..110 B1
Heneage Pl EC3 ...110 B1
Heneage St E1 ....111 A4
Henfield Cl N19 ....4 B3
Henfield Cl SE16 ..40 B4
Henley Ct
London NW2 ....9 C2
London SE15 ....64 C4
Henley Dr SE1 ...153 A4
Henley Ho E2 ....99 A2
Henley Prior N1 ...84 C1
Henley Rd NW10 ..22 B4
Henley St SW11 ..169 C2
Henniker Mews
SW3 ....157 B4
Henniker Rd E15 ..19 C3
Henning St SW11 .168 A3
Henrietta Cl SE8 ..51 C4
Henrietta Ho 11
W6 ....39 B1
Henrietta Mews
WC1 ....94 B2
Henrietta Pl W1 ..104 A2
Henrietta St WC2 .120 B4
London E15 ....76 B3
Henriques St E1 ...111 C1
Henry Cavendish Prim
Sch SW12 ....73 B3
Henry Compton Sec Sch
SW6 ....164 A4
Henry Dent Cl SE5 .63 C4
Henry Dickens Ct
W11 ....112 A2
Henry Fawcett Prim Sch
SE11 ....163 B4
Henry Ho NW8 ....80 A2
SW8 ....162 A2
SE1 ....121 C1
Henry Jackson Ho

Henry Jackson Ho
SW15 ....57 C4
Henry Jackson Rd
SW15 ....57 C4
Henry Rd N4 ....6 B3
Henryson Rd SE4 ..66 C2
Henry Wise Ho
SW1 ....147 A3
Henshall Point 19
E3 ....27 A2
Henshall St N1 ....15 C2
Henshaw St SE17 .151 B4
Henslowe Rd SE22 .64 C2
Henslow Ho 1
SE15 ....49 C3
Henson Ave NW2 ...9 B3
Henson Ct 8 N5 ...15 B4
Henty Cl SW11 ...168 B4
Henty Wlk SW15 ..57 A2
Hepburn Mews
SW11 ....60 B2
Hepplestone Cl
SW15 ....57 A1
Hepscott Rd E9 ...18 C1
Hepworth Ct N1 ...86 B4
Hera Ct 7 E14 ....41 C2
Heralds Pl SE11 ..150 A4
Herald St 6 E2 ...25 A1
Herbal Hill EC1 ...95 C1
Herbert Chapman Ct
N5 ....15 A4
Herbert Cres SW1 .131 A2
Herbert Gdns
Chiswick W4 ....45 A4
London NW10 ...22 A3
Herbert Ho E1 ...110 C2
Herbert Mews 5
SW2 ....62 C1
Herbert Morrison Ho
SW6 ....154 C3
Herbert Morrison Prim
Sch SW8 ....162 A1
Herbert St NW5 ...12 C2
Herbrand Est WC1 .94 A2
Herbrand St WC1 ..94 A2
Hercules Ct 7 ....5 A1
Hercules Pl N7 ...5 A1
Hercules Rd SE1 .135 A1
Hercules St N7 ...5 A1
Hereford Bldgs
SW3 ....157 C4
Hereford Ho NW6 ..23 C3
SW10 ....156 B2
SW3 ....130 B2
20 London SE5 ...48 B3
5 London SW2 ...62 C3
Hereford Mans 10
W2 ....31 C3
Hereford Mews 11
W2 ....31 C3
Hereford Pl SE14 ..51 B3
Hereford Rd
W2 ....31 C3 113 C4
London W3 ....28 B2
Hereford Retreat 5
SE15 ....49 C3
Hereford Sq SW7 .143 A3
Hereford St E2 ..24 C1 99 B2
Hereward House Sch
NW3 ....11 C2
Heritage Cl SW9 ..63 A4
Heritage Ct SE8 ...40 C1
Heritage Ho 22
SW19 ....69 C3
Hermes Cl 4 W9 ..23 C1
Hermes Ct SW9 ..173 B4
Hermes St N1 ....85 B1
Herm Ho 10 N1 ...15 B2

Hermitage Ct E1 ..125 C1
2 NW2 ....1 C1
Hermitage Gdns
NW2 ....1 C1
Hermitage La NW2 ..1 C1
Hermitage Prim Sch
E1 ....125 C2
Hermitage Row 9
E8 ....16 C3
Hermitage St W2 .101 B3
Hermitage The
Barnes SW13 ....46 B2
Richmond TW10 ...54 A2
Hermitage Wall
E1 ....125 C1
Hermit Pl NW6 ....78 A3
Hermit St EC1 ....96 A4
Herndon Rd SW18 .59 B2
Herne Cl NW10 ....8 A3
Herne Hill SE24 ...63 B2
Herne Hill Ho SE24 .63 A1
Herne Hill Mans
SE24 ....63 B1
Herne Hill Rd SE24 .63 B3
Herne Hill Sta SE24 .63 A2
Herne Hill Stad
SE24 ....63 C2
Herne Pl SE24 ....63 A2
Heron Cl NW10 ....8 A2
Heron Ct 14 E14 ..42 A3
6 Dulwich SE21 ..75 C2
Herondale Ave
SW18 ....72 A3
Heron Dr N4 ....6 B2
Herongate N1 ....87 A4
Heron Ho NW8 ....80 A1
SW11 ....168 B4
London SE15 ....49 B2
Heron Ind Est E15 .27 A3
W1 ....103 C2
Heron Pl SE16 ....33 A1
Heron Quays E14 ..33 C1
Heron Quays Sta
E14 ....33 C1
Heron Rd SE24 ....63 B3
Heron Trad Est W3 .28 A4
Herrick Ho 15 SE5 .48 C3
17 London N16 ...15 C4
Herrick Rd N5 ....6 B1
Herrick St SW1 ..147 C3
Herries St W10 ...23 A3
Hersant Cl NW10 ..21 C4
Herschell's Mews
SE5 ....63 B4
Hersham Cl SW15 .68 C4
Hershell Ct 1
SW14 ....55 A3
Hertford Ave SW14 .56 A3
Hertford Ct 18
SW11 ....60 A4
Hertford Lo 10
SW19 ....70 A3
Hertford Pl W1 ....93 A1
Hertford Rd N1 ...24 A4
Hertford St W1 ...118 A1
Hertmitage The 4
SE13 ....52 B1
Herslet Rd N7 ....5 B1
Hertsmere Rd E14 .33 C2
Hesewall Cl SW4 ..171 A1
Hesketh Pl W11 ..112 A3
Heslop Ct 1 SW12 .72 C3
Heslop Rd SW12 ..72 B3
Hesper Mews SW5 .142 B3
Hesperus Cres E14 .42 A2
Hessel St E1 ....32 A3

Hestercombe Ave
SW6 ....164 B3
Hester Rd SW11 .158 A1
Hester Terr TW9 ...54 C4
Heston Ho
  5 London SE8 ....51 C2
  London W4 ....37 A1
Heston St SE14 ....51 C2
Hetherington Rd
  SW2,SW4 ....62 A3
Hethpool Ho W2 ..89 B1
Hetley Rd W12 .....39 A4
Hevelius Cl SE10 ..43 B1
Hever Ho SE15 ....50 B4
Hewer Ho 6 SW4 ..61 B2
Hewer St W10 .....30 C4
Hewett St
  EC2 ....24 A1 98 B1
Hewison St E3 .....26 B3
Hewlett Rd E3 .....26 A3
Hewling Ho 1 N16 ..16 A4
Hewtt Rd SW15 ....47 B1
Hexagon The N6 ...3 B3
Hexham Rd SE27 ...75 B2
Hey Bridge 8 NW1 ..13 A2
Heydon Ho SE14 ....50 B2
Heyford Ave SW8 .162 B2
Heygate St SE17 .151 A4
Heylyn Sq E3 ......26 B2
Heysham La NW3 ....2 A1
Heythorp St SW18 ..70 B2
Heywood
  1 SE14 ....50 C4
  6 London SW2 ....62 C1
Heyworth Rd E5 ...17 A4
  London SE15 ......65 B4
Hibbert St SW11 ...59 C4
Hichisson Rd SE15 ..65 B3
Hickes Ho 6 NW6 ..11 C1
Hickey's Almshouses 7
  TW9 ....54 B3
Hickin St 2 E14 ...42 B3
Hickleton NW1 .....83 A3
Hickling Ho 10 SE16 .40 A3
Hickmore Wlk SW4 ..61 B4
Hicks Cl SW11 .....60 A4
Hicks St SE8 ......41 A1
Hide Pl SW1 ......147 B3
Hide Twr SW1 .....147 B3
Hieover SE21 ......75 B2
Higgins Ho 7 N1 ...24 A4
Higginson Ho 2
  NW3 ....11 B1
Higgs Ind Est 9
  SE24 ....63 A4
Highbridge Ct 13
  SE14 ....50 B3
High Bridge Wharf
  SE10 ....42 C1
Highbury (Arsenal FC)
  N5 ....6 A1
Highbury Cnr N5 ...15 A2
Highbury Corner
  N5 ....15 A2
Highbury Cres N5 ..14 C3
Highbury Fields Sch
  N5 ....15 A3
Highbury Gr N5 ....15 A3
Highbury Grange
  N5 ....15 B4
Highbury Grove Ct
  N5 ....15 A3
Highbury Grove Sch
  N5 ....15 B3
Highbury Hill N5 ...15 A4

Highbury & Islington Sta
  N1 ....15 A2
Highbury New Pk
  N5 ....15 B4
Highbury Pk N5 ....15 A4
Highbury Quadrant
  N5 ....6 B1
Highbury Quadrant Prim
  Sch N5 ....15 B4
Highbury Station Rd
  N1 ....14 C2
Highbury Terr N5 ..15 A3
Highbury Terrace Mews
  N5 ....15 A3
Highcliffe Dr SW15 .56 B1
Highcroft Rd N19 ...5 A4
Highcross Way 4
  SW15 ....68 C3
Highdown Rd SW15 .57 A1
Highfield Ave NW11 ..1 A4
Highfield Cl SE13 ...67 C1
Highfield Gr N6 ....3 B3
Highfield Rd W3 ...28 B4
Highfield Sch SW18 .72 A4
Highgate Archway
  N6 ....4 B3
Highgate Ave N6 ....4 A4
Highgate Cemetery*
  N19 ....4 A2
Highgate Cl N6 ....3 C4
Highgate High St N6 .4 B3
Highgate Hill N19 ...4 B3
Highgate Ho 11
  SE26 ....76 C1
Highgate Jun Sch N6 .3 B4
Highgate Rd NW5 ..13 A4
Highgate Sch N6 ....3 C4
Highgate West Hill
  N6 ....3 C2
Highgrove Point 3
  NW3 ....11 B4
High Holborn WC1 106 C3
Highlands Ave W3 ..28 B2
Highlands Cl N4 ....5 A4
Highlands Heath
  SW15 ....69 B4
Highlever Rd W10 ..30 B4
High London 8 N6 ..4 C4
Highmore Rd SE3 ..53 A3
High Park Ave TW9 .44 C2
High Park Rd TW9 ..44 C2
High Par The SW16 .74 A1
High Point N6 ......3 C4
High Rd NW10 ......8 C2
Highshore Rd SE15 .49 B1
Highshore Sch SE15 .49 B2
High St E15 ....27 B4
  Acton W3 ....28 A1
  Brentford TW8 .....44 A4
High Street Harlesden
  NW10 ....21 B3
High Street Kensington
  Sta W8 ....128 A3
High The SW16 ....74 A1
High Timber St
  EC4 ....122 C4
High Trees SW2 ....74 C3
Hightrees Ho SW12 .60 C1
Highview N8 ....5 A4
Highview Ct 2
  SW19 ....70 A3
High View Prim Sch
  SW11 ....59 B3
Highway Bsns Pk The 7
  E1 ....32 C2

Highway The E1 ....32 B2
Highway Trad Ctr The 6
  E1 ....32 C2
Highwood Rd N19 ..5 A1
Highworth St NW1 102 B4
Hilary Cl SW6 .....156 A2
Hilary Rd W12 .....29 B2
Hilborough Ct 1
  E8 ....24 B4
Hilborough Rd 1
  E8 ....16 B1
Hilda Terr SW9 ....173 C2
Hilditch Ho 7
  TW10 ....54 B1
Hildred Ho SW1 ...146 A4
Hildreth St 2 SW12 73 A3
Hildreth Street Mews 8
  SW12 ....73 A3
Hildyard Rd SW6 .155 C4
Riley Rd SE1 ......138 C2
Hilgrove Rd NW6 ..11 B1
Hillary Ho E14 .....34 B4
Hillbeck Cl SE15 ...50 B3
  SE15 ....50 B3
Hillbrow 7 TW10 ..54 A1
Hillbury Rd SW17 ..73 A1
Hillcourt Rd SE22 ..65 A1
Hillcrest W11 ......112 C3
  London N6 ....3 C4
  London SE24 ......63 C3
Hillcrest Ct NW2 ..10 A3
Hillcrest Rd W3 ...28 A1
Hill Ct London NW3 12 A4
  Putney SW15 ......57 C2
Hilldrop Cres N7 ..13 C3
Hilldrop Est N7 ....13 C3
Hilldrop La N7 .....13 C3
Hilldrop Rd N7 ....13 C3
Hillersdon Ave
  SW13 ....46 C1
Hillersdon Ho
  SW1 ....146 A2
Hillery Cl SE17 ....151 C3
Hill Farm Rd W10 ..30 C4
Hillfield Ct NW3 ...12 A3
Hillfield Ho N5 ....15 B3
Hillfield Mans NW3 .11 C3
Hillfield Rd NW6 ..10 C3
Hillgate Pl
  W8 ....31 C1 113 B2
  Balham SW12 ......73 A4
Hillgate St W8 ....113 B2
Hill House Sch
  SW1 ....130 C2
Hilliard Ho 15 E1 ..32 A1
Hilliard's Ct E1 ....32 B1
Hillier Ho 11 NW1 .13 C1
Hillier Rd SW11 ...60 B1
Hillingdon St SE17 .48 A4
Hill Lo SW11 ......59 C3
Hillman St E8 ......17 A2
Hillmarton Rd N7 ..14 A3
Hillmead Dr SW9 ..63 A3
Hill Mead Prim Sch
  SW9 ....63 A3
Hillmore Ct SE13 ..67 C4
Hill Rd NW8 ....79 A1
Hillrise Mans N19 ..5 A4
Hillrise Rd N19 ....5 A4
Hillsboro Rd SE22 .64 A2
Hillsborough Ct
  NW6 ....78 A3
Hillside NW10 .....20 C4
Hillside Cl NW8 ...78 B2
Hillside Ct NW3 ...11 A3
Hillside Gdns SW2 .74 C2
Hillside Rd SW2 ...74 C2

Hillsleigh Rd
  W14 .....31 B1 113 A2
Hills Pl W1 ....104 C1
Hill St W1 ....118 A2
Hillstone Ct 5 E3 ..27 A1
Hilltop Ct
  London NW8 ......11 B1
  12 London SW11 ..59 C3
Hilltop Ho 7 N6 ...4 C4
Hilltop Rd NW6 ....10 C1
Hillway N6 ....3 C2
Hill Wood Ho NW1 83 B1
Hillworth Rd SW2 .74 C4
Hillyard St SW9 ...173 B3
Hillfield Cl E9 .....18 A3
Hilsea Point 7
  SW15 ....69 A3
Hilsea St E5 ....17 B4
Hilton Ho London N7 14 A4
  London SE4 ....65 C3
Hilversum Cres 10
  SE22 ....64 A2
Hinckley Rd SE15 ..64 C3
Hind Ct EC4 ....107 C1
Hinde Mews W1 ...103 C2
Hinde St W1 ....103 C2
Hind Gr E14 ....33 C3
Hindhead Point 6
  SW15 ....69 A3
Hind Ho London N7 14 C4
Hindle Ho E8 ......16 B3
Hindley Ho N7 ....5 B1
Hindlip Ho SW8 ...171 B3
Hindmans Rd SE22 .64 C2
Hindmarsh Cl E1 ..125 C4
Hindrey Rd E5 .....17 A3
Hinstock NW6 .....78 A4
Hinton Rd SE24 ...63 A4
Hippodrome Mews
  W11 ....112 A3
Hippodrome Pl
  W11 ....112 B3
Hitchin Sq E3 .....26 A3
Hitherfield Prim Sch
  SW2 ....74 C2
Hitherfield Rd
  SW16,SW27 ....74 C1
Hither Green La
  SE13 ....67 C1
Hither Green Prim Sch
  SE13 ....67 C1
Hitherlands SW12 ..73 A2
HM Prison Wormwood
  Scrubs W12 ....29 C3
HMS Belfast* SE1 .124 B2
Hoadly Rd SW16 ...73 C2
Hobart Pl SW1 ....132 A2
Hobbes Wlk SW15 .57 A2
Hobb's Ct SE1 .....139 A4
Hobbs' Pl N1 ......24 A4
Hobday St E14 .....34 A3
Hobsons Pl E1 .....111 B4
Hoburn St SW10 ..157 B3
Hocker St E2 ......98 C3
Hockley Ho 4 E9 ..17 B2
Hockliffe Ho W10 ..30 B4
Hockney Ct 1 SE16 40 A1
Hockworth Ho 7
  N16 ....7 A3
Hocroft Ave NW2 ..1 B1
Hocroft Ct NW2 ...1 B1
Hocroft Rd NW2 ...1 B1
Hocroft Wlk NW2 ..1 B1

Hodister Cl 20 SE5 .48 B3
Hodnet Gr SE16 ...40 C2
Hoffman Sq N1 ....97 C3
Hofland Rd W14 ...140 B4
Hogan Mews W2 ..101 B4
Hogan Way E5 .....7 C2
Hogarth Bsns Pk
  W4 ....46 A4
Hogarth Ct E1 .....111 C1
  EC3 ....124 B4
  6 London NW1 ....13 B1
Hogarth Ho SW1 ..147 C3
Hogarth Ind Est
  NW10 ....21 C1
Hogarth La W4 ....46 A4
Hogarth Pl SW5 ...142 A3
Hogarth Prim Sch
  W4 ....38 A1
Hogarth Rd SW5 ..142 A3
Hogarth Roundabout
  W4 ....46 A4
Holbeach Mews 1
  SW12 ....73 A3
Holbeck Row SE15 .49 C3
Holbein Mews
  SW1 ....145 B2
Holbein Pl SW1 ...145 B3
Holberton Gdns
  NW10 ....22 A2
Holborn EC1 ....107 C3
Holborn Cir EC1 ...107 C3
Holborn PO WC1 ..106 C3
Holborn Sta WC1 ..106 C3
Holbrook Cl N19 ...4 A3
Holbrooke Ct N7 ..14 A4
Holbrook Ho
  London W3 ....28 C4
  5 Streatham SW2 ..74 B3
Holburn 33 N1 ....24 A4
Holburn Viaduct
  EC1 ....108 A3
Holcombe Ho SW9 .62 A4
Holcombe St W6 ..39 A2
Holcroft Ct W1 ....104 C4
Holcroft Ho
  London SE10 ......52 B2
  London SW11 .....59 C4
Holcroft Rd E9 ....17 B1
Holdenby Rd SE4 ..66 A2
Holden Ho N1 .....86 C3
  12 SE8 ....51 C3
Holden St SW11 ...169 B1
Holdernesse Rd 8
  SW17 ....72 C2
Holderness Ho SE5 64 A4
Holdsworth Ho 5
  SW2 ....74 C4
Holford Ho 6 SE16 40 A2
  WC1 ....95 A4
Holford Pl WC1 ...95 A4
Holford Rd NW3 ...2 B1
Holford St WC1 ...95 A4
Holgate Ave SW11 .59 C4
Holland Gdns W14 126 B2
Holland Gr SW9 ..163 C1
Holland Park
  W11 .....31 B1 112 C1
Holland Park Ave
  W11 .....31 B1 112 B1
Holland Park Ct
  W14 ....126 B4
Holland Park Gdns
  W14 ....126 A4
Holland Park Mews
  W11 .....31 B1 112 C1

Holland Park Rd
W14 . . . . 127 A1
Holland Park Rdbt
W12 . . . . .39 C4
Holland Park Sch
W8 . . . . 127 A4
Holland Park Sta
W11 . . . . . . .31 B1 112 C1
Holland Pl W8 . . . . . 128 A4
Holland Rd W14 . . . 126 B2
London NW10 . . . . . .22 A3
Holland Rise Ho
SW9 . . . . 163 A1
Holland St SE1 . . . . 122 B2
W8 . . . . 127 C4
Holland Villas Rd
W14 . . . . 126 A3
Holland Wlk N19 . . . .4 C3
W14 . . . . 127 A3
Hollar Rd N16 . . . . . . .7 B1
Hollen St W1 . . . . . 105 B2
Holles Ho SW9 . . . . 173 B2
Holles St W1 . . . . . 104 B2
Holley Rd W3 . . . . . .38 A4
Holliday Sq 7
SW11 . . . . .59 C4
Hollies Way 1
SW12 . . . . .72 C4
Hollingbourne Rd
SE24 . . . . .63 B2
Hollins Ho N7 . . . . . .14 A4
Hollisfield WC1 . . . . .94 B3
Holloway Rd
London N19 . . . . .4 C2
London N7 . . . . .14 B4
Holloway Road Sta
N7 . . . . .14 B3
Holloway Sch N7 . . .13 C3
Holly Berry La 6
NW3 . . . . .11 B4
Hollybush Gdns E2 . .25 A2
Holly Bush Hill 23
NW3 . . . . .11 B4
Hollybush Ho 21 E2 . .25 A2
Hollybush Pl E2 . . . . .25 A2
Holly Bush Vale 9
NW3 . . . . .11 B4
Holly Cl NW10 . . . . . .8 A1
Hollycroft Ave NW3 . .1 C1
Holly Dale Prim Sch
SE15 . . . . .50 B1
Hollydale Rd SE15 . .50 B1
Hollydene
London SE13 . . . . . . .67 C1
5 London SE15 . . . . .50 A2
Holly Gr SE15 . . . . . .49 C1
Holly Hedge Terr
SE13 . . . . .67 C2
Holly Hill NW3 . . . . .11 B4
Holly Lo SE13 . . . . . .67 C2
Holly Lodge Gdns N6 .3 C3
Holly Lodge Mans
N6 . . . . .3 C2
Holly Mews SW10 . . 143 A1
Holly Pk N4 . . . . .5 B4
Holly Pl NW3 . . . . . .11 B4
Holly Rd W4 . . . . . . .37 C2
Holly St E8 . . . . .16 B1
Holly Terr N6 . . . . . . .3 C3
Hollytree Cl SW19 . . .69 C3
Holly Tree Ho SE4 . .66 B4
Holly Village N6 . . . . .4 A2

Hollywell Row
EC2 . . . . .24 A1 98 A1
Hollywood Mews
SW10 . . . . 156 C4
Hollywood Rd
SW10 . . . . 156 C4
Holman Ho 2 E2 . . . .25 C3
Holman Hunt Ho
W14 . . . . 140 A1
Holman Rd SW11 . . 167 B1
Holmbrook NW1 . . . .82 C2
Holmbury Ct SW17 . .72 B1
Holmbury Ho SW9 . .63 A2
Holmbush Rd SW15 . .58 A1
Holmcote Gdns N5 . .15 B3
Holmdale Rd NW6 . .10 C3
Holmdene Ave SE24 .63 B2
Holmead Rd SW6 . . 156 B1
Holmefield Ho W10 . .23 A1
Holmes Ct
5 London SW4 . . . . 172 A2
17 London W4 . . . . .37 B3
Holmesdale Ave
SW14 . . . . .55 A3
Holmesdale Ho 10
NW6 . . . . .23 C4
Holmesdale Rd
London N6 . . . . .4 A4
Richmond TW9 . . . . .44 B2
Holmesley Rd SE23 . .66 A1
Holmes Pl SW10 . . . 157 A4
Holmes Rd NW5 . . . .13 A3
Holmes Terr 135 B4
Holmewood Gdns
SW2 . . . . .74 B4
Holmewood Rd
SW2 . . . . .74 B4
Holmfield Ct 4
NW3 . . . . .12 A2
Holmhurst SE13 . . . .67 C1
Holmleigh Prim Sch
N16 . . . . .7 A3
Holmleigh Rd N16 . . .7 A3
Holm Oak Cl SW15 . .58 B1
Holmsbury Ho 6
N7 . . . . .13 C3
Holmsdale Ho 2
E14 . . . . .34 A2
Holmside Ct SW12 . .60 C1
Holmside Rd SW12 . .60 C1
Holmsley Ho SW15 . .68 B4
Holm Wlk SE3 . . . . .53 C1
Holmwood Ct 3 N16 .7 B4
Holocaust Meml Gdn
W2 . . . . 130 C2
Holroyd Rd SW15 . . .57 B2
Holsgrove Ct W3 . . . .29 A1
Holst Mans SW13 . . .47 B3
Holsworthy Ho 4
E3 . . . . .27 A2
Holt Ct E15 . . . . . . .76 B3
Holt Ho SW2 . . . . . .62 C1
Holton St E1 . . . . . . .25 C1
Holwood Pl 7 SW4 . .61 C3
Holybourne Ave
SW15 . . . . .68 C4
Holy Cross RC Sch
SW6 . . . . 165 B3
Holy Family RC Prim
Sch E14 . . . . .33 C3
Holy Ghost RC Prim Sch
SW12 . . . . .72 C4
Holyhead Cl E3 . . . . .26 C2
Holyoake Ct SE16 . . .41 B4
Holyoak Rd SE11 . . 150 B3
Holyport Rd SW6 . . .47 C3

Holyrood Ho N4 . . . . .6 A3
Holyrood Mews 11
E16 . . . . .35 C1
Holyrood St SE1 . . . 124 A1
Holy Trinity CE Inf Sch
SW17 . . . . .72 B2
Holy Trinity CE JMI Sch
E8 . . . . .16 B2
Holy Trinity CE Jun Sch
TW10 . . . . .54 C3
Holy Trinity CE Prim Sch
SW1 . . . . 145 A4
SW1 . . . . 145 B4
London NW3 . . . . . . .11 B2
Streatham SW2 . . . . .74 C2
Holy Trinity & St Silas
CE Prim Sch NW1 . .13 A1
Holywell Cl 6 SE16 . .40 A1
3 SE3 . . . . .53 C4
Holywell La EC2 . . . .98 B2
Homan Ho 6 SW4 . . .73 C4
Homefield Rd W4 . . .38 B2
Homefield St 14 N1 . .24 A3
Homeleigh Ct 8
SW16 . . . . .74 A1
Homeleigh Rd SE15 . .65 C2
Homemead SW12 . . .73 A2
Home Office SW1 . . 133 C2
Home Park Rd
SW19 . . . . .70 B1
Home Rd SW11 . . . 168 A2
Homer Dr E14 . . . . . .41 C2
Homer Rd E9 . . . . . .18 A2
Homer Row W1 . . . 102 B3
Homer St W1 . . . . . 102 B3
Homerton Coll of
Technology E9 . . . . .17 B3
Homerton Gr E9 . . . .17 C3
Homerton High St
E9 . . . . .17 C3
Homerton Hospl E9 .17 C3
Homerton Rd E9 . . . .18 B3
Homerton Row E9 . . .17 B3
Homerton Sta E9 . . . .17 C2
Homerton Terr E9 . . .17 B2
Homestall Rd SE22 . .65 B2
Homestead Rd
SW6 . . . . 155 A1
Homewoods 3
SW12 . . . . .73 B4
Homildon Ho 10
SE26 . . . . .76 C1
Honduras St EC1 . . . .96 C2
Honeybourne Rd
NW6 . . . . .11 A3
Honeybrook Rd
SW12,SW4 . . . . .73 B4
Honeyfield N4 . . . . . . .5 C2
Honey La EC2 . . . . . 109 A1
Honeyman Cl NW6 . . .9 C1
Honeywell Jun & Inf
Schs SW11 . . . . .60 B1
Honeywell Rd SW11 .60 B1
Honeywood Ho 6
SE15 . . . . .49 C2
Honiton Gdns 1
SE15 . . . . .50 B1
Honiton Ho 3 SE5 . .48 B1
Honiton Rd NW6 . . . .23 B3
Honor Oak Park Sta
SE23 . . . . .65 C1
Honor Oak Pk SE23 .65 C1
Honor Oak Rise
SE23 . . . . .65 B1
Honwell Ho 2 W2 . . .31 C4

Hood Ave SW14 . . . .55 B2
Hood Ct N7 . . . . .5 B1
Hood Ho 7 SE5 . . . . .48 C3
Hooke Ct SE10 . . . . .52 B2
Hooke Ho 30 E3 . . . .26 A3
Hookham Ct SW8 . . 171 B4
Hooks Cl SE15 . . . . .50 A2
Hooper Ho 3 SW18 . .58 B4
Hooper Rd E16 . . . . .35 C3
Hooper's Ct SW1 . . 130 C3
Hooper's Mews 4
W3 . . . . .28 B1
Hooper St E1 . . . . . 111 B1
Hoop La NW11 . . . . . .1 C4
Hope Cl
2 Brentford TW8 . . . .36 A1
London N1 . . . . .15 B2
Hopefield Ave NW6 . .23 A3
Hope St SW11 . . . . . .59 C4
Hopetown St E1 . . . 111 A3
Hopewell St SE5 . . . .48 C3
Hop Gdns WC2 . . . . 120 A3
Hopgood St W12 . . . .30 B1
Hopkins Ho 12 E14 . .33 C3
Hopkinson Ho
SW11 . . . . 169 B2
Hopkinson's Pl NW1 .81 B4
Hopkins St W1 . . . . 105 B1
Hopping La N1 . . . . . .15 A2
Hop St SE10 . . . . . . .43 B3
Hopton Ho 5 SW9 . . .48 A1
Hopton's Gdns SE1 . 122 B2
Hopton St SE1 . . . . . 122 B2
Hopwood Cl SW17 . .71 B1
Hopwood Rd SE17 . . .48 C4
Hopwood Wlk E8 . . . .16 C1
Horatio Ho 10 E2 . . .24 B3
Horatio Pl E14 . . . . . .34 B1
Horatio St 1 E2 . . . . .24 B3
Horbury Cres
W11 . . . . . . .31 C2 113 B3
Horbury Mews
W11 . . . . . . .31 C2 113 A3
Horder Rd SW6 . . . . 164 B3
Hordle Prom E 14
SE15 . . . . .49 B3
Hordle Prom N 9
SE15 . . . . .49 B3
Hordle Prom S 7
SE15 . . . . .49 B3
Hordle Prom W 13
SE15 . . . . .49 A3
Horizon Bldg 14
E14 . . . . .33 C2
Horizon Sch N16 . . . .16 A4
Horle Wlk SE5 . . . . . .48 A1
Hormead Rd W9 . . . .23 B1
Hornbeam Cl SE11 . 149 B4
Hornbeam Ho 2
NW3 . . . . .12 B2
Hornblower Cl 2
SE16 . . . . .41 A2
Hornby Cl NW3 . . . . .11 C1
Hornby Ho 6 SE11 . . 163 C4
Horndean Cl 3
SW15 . . . . .68 C3
Horner Hos 22 N1 . . .24 A4
Horne Way SW15 . . .47 B1
Horn La SE10 . . . . . .43 C2
London W3 . . . . .28 B3
Hornsby House Sch
SW12 . . . . .72 C3
Hornsey La N6 . . . . . .4 B4
Hornsey Lane Gdns
N6 . . . . .4 B4
Hornsey Rd N7,N19 . .5 B2

Hornsey Rise Gdns
N19 . . . . .5 A4
Hornsey St N7 . . . . . .14 B3
Hornshay St SE15 . . .50 B4
Hornton Ct W8 . . . . 127 C3
Hornton Pl W8 . . . . 127 C3
Hornton St W8 . . . . 127 C4
Horrocks Ho SW15 . .57 A2
Horse & Dolphin Yd
W1 . . . . 119 C4
Horseferry Pl SE10 . .52 B4
Horseferry Rd E14 . . .33 A2
SW1 . . . . 147 C4
Horseferry Rd Est
SW1 . . . . 133 B1
Horseguards Ave
SW1 . . . . 120 A1
Horse Guards Par★
SW1 . . . . 119 C1
Horse Guards Rd
SW1 . . . . 133 C4
Horsell Rd N5 . . . . . .14 C3
Horselydown La
SE1 . . . . 124 C1
Horselydown Mans
SE1 . . . . 138 C4
Horseman Ho 11
N7 . . . . .13 C3
Horseshoe Cl E14 . . .42 B1
Horse Shoe Yd W1 . 118 B4
Horse Yd N1 . . . . . . .86 B4
Horsfield Ho 2 N1 . .15 B1
Horsford Rd SW2 . . .62 B2
Horsley Ho 11 SE4 . .65 C3
Horsley St 3 SE17 . . .48 C4
Horsman Ho SE5 . . . .48 B4
Horsman St SE5 . . . .48 B4
Horsmonden Rd
SE4 . . . . .66 B1
Horston Ho N4 . . . . . .6 B4
Hortensia Ho
SW10 . . . . 156 C2
Hortensia Rd
SW10 . . . . 156 C2
Horticultural Pl 6
W4 . . . . .37 C1
Horton Ave NW2 . . . .10 A4
Horton Ho 11 SE15 . .50 B4
SW8 . . . . 162 C2
W14 . . . . 140 A1
Horton Rd E8 . . . . . .17 A2
Horton St SE13 . . . . .67 A4
Horwood Ho 22 E2 . .25 A2
NW8 . . . . .90 B2
Hosack Rd SW12,
SW17 . . . . .72 C2
Hosier La EC1 . . . . . 108 B3
Hoskins St SE10 . . . .42 C1
Hospl for Tropical
Diseases NW1 . . . . .83 B3
Hospl of St John and St
Elizabeth NW8 . . . . .79 B1
Hotham Prim Sch
SW15 . . . . .57 B4
Hotham Rd SW15 . . .57 B4
Hothfield Pl SE16 . . .40 B3
Hotspur St SE11 . . . 149 B2
Houblon Rd TW10 . . .54 A2
Houghton Cl 10 E8 . .16 B2
Houghton St WC2 . . 107 A1
Houndsditch EC3 . . . 110 B2
Houseman Way 20
SE5 . . . . .48 C3
Houses of Parliament★
SW1 . . . . 134 B2

Hoveden Rd NW2 ....10 A3
Howard Cl Acton W3 .28 A3
  London NW2 ....9 C4
Howard Ct SE15 ......64 C4
Howard Ho 14 SE8 ..51 B4
W1 ....92 B1
  7 London SW9 ......62 C4
Howard Rd NW2 ....9 C2
  London N16 ....15 C4
Howard's La SW15 ..57 B3
Howbury Rd SE15 ..65 B4
Howcroft Ho 3 E3 ..26 B2
Howden St SE15 ......64 C4
Howell Ho 6 N7 ......13 C3
Howell Wlk SE1 ....150 B3
Howgate Rd SW14 ..55 C4
Howick Pl SW1 ......133 A1
Howie St SW11 ......158 A1
Howitt Cl 6 NW3 ....12 A2
Howitt Rd NW3 ......12 A2
Howland Ho 9
  SW16 ....74 A1
Howland Mews E
  W1 ....105 A4
Howland St W1 ......105 A4
Howland Way SE16 ..41 A4
Howletts Rd SE24 ..63 B1
Howley Pl W2 ....101 A4
Howsman Rd SW13 ..46 C4
Howson Rd SE4 ......66 A3
Howson Terr TW10 ..54 A1
How's St E2 ....24 B3
Hoxton Mkt N1 ....98 A3
Hoxton Point N1 ....98 A4
Hoxton Sq N1 ....98 A3
Hoxton St N1 ....24 A3
Hoylake Rd W3 ......29 A3
Hoyland Cl 4 SE15 ..50 A3
Hoy St E16 ....35 B1
Hub Buildings The 4
  SW12 ....73 A3
Huberd Ho SE1 ......137 C2
Hubert Gr SW9 ......62 A4
Hubert Ho NW8 ......90 A1
Hucknall Ct NW8 ....89 B2
Huddart St 3 E3 ....33 B4
Huddleston Cl E2 ..25 B3
Huddlestone Rd NW2 .9 A2
Huddleston Rd N7 ..13 B4
Hudson Cl 15 W12 ..30 A2
Hudson Ct 3 E14 ....41 C1
Hudson Ho SW10 ..156 C2
  5 W11 ....31 A3
Hudsons Ho N1 ......97 C3
Hudson's Pl SW1 ..146 C4
Huggin Ct EC4 ......123 A4
Huggin Hill EC4 ....123 A4
Huggins Ho 6 E3 ..26 C2
Huggins Pl SW2 ....74 B3
Hughan Rd E15 ......19 C3
Hugh Astor Ct SE1 .136 B2
Hughendon Terr
  E15 ....76 B4
Hughes Ho 26 E2 ....25 B2
  SE17 ....150 B3
  15 SE5 ....51 C4
  London SE5 ....48 B2
Hughes Mans
  E1 ....24 C1 99 C1
Hughes Terr 8 E16 ..35 B2
Hugh Gaitskell Cl
  SW6 ....154 C3
Hugh Gaitskell Ho
  London N16 ....7 B2
  London NW10 ....8 B1

Hugh Mews SW1 ....146 B3
Hugh Morgan Ho 5
  SW4 ....61 C4
Hugh Myddelton Prim
  Sch EC1 ....95 C3
Hugh Platt Ho 29
  E2 ....25 A3
Hugh St SW1 ....146 B3
Hugo Ho SW1 ......131 A2
Hugon Rd SW6 ......59 A4
Hugo Rd N19 ....13 B4
Huguenot Pl SW18 ..59 B2
Huguenot Sq SE15 ..65 A4
Hullbridge Mews
  N1 ....87 B4
Hull Cl SE16 ....32 C1
Hull Ct SE5 ....48 C1
Hull St EC1 ....96 C3
Hulme Pl SE1 ......137 A3
Humber Dr W10 ....22 C1
Humber Rd SE3 ....53 B4
Humberton Cl E9 ..18 A3
Humbolt Rd W6 ....154 A3
Hume Ct N1 ....15 A1
Hume Ho 14 W11 ..30 C1
Humphrey Ct
  SW11 ....167 C3
Humphrey St SE1 ..152 C2
Humphry Ho 10
  SW15 ....57 C2
Hungerford Bridge
  SE1 ....120 C2
Hungerford Ho
  SW1 ....161 A4
Hungerford Inf Sch
  N7 ....14 A2
Hungerford Jun & Inf
  Sch N7 ....13 C2
Hungerford La
  WC2 ....120 C2
Hungerford Prim Sch
  N7 ....14 A2
Hungerford Rd
  7 London N7 ....14 A2
  4 London N7 ....13 C2
Hungerford St 24
  E1 ....32 A3
Hunsdon Rd SE14 ..50 C3
Hunslett St 22 E2 ..25 B3
Hunstanton Ho
  NW1 ....102 B4
Hunter Cl SE1 ......137 C1
  8 London SW12 ....72 C3
Hunter Ho N19 ......4 B1
  SE1 ....136 B3
  SW5 ....141 C1
  SW8 ....161 C1
  WC1 ....94 B2
Hunter Lo 9 W9 ....31 C4
Hunter St WC1 ......94 B2
Huntingdon Ct
  SW14 ....55 B4
Huntingdon Gdns
  W4 ....45 B3
Huntingdon Ho
  SW5 ....141 C4
Huntingdon St
  London N1 ....14 B1
  E16 ....35 B1
Huntingfield Rd
  SW15 ....56 C2
Huntingford Ho
  SW15 ....47 B1
Huntley St WC1 ....93 B1
Hunton St E1 ......111 B4

Hunts Cl SE3 ....53 C1
Hunt's Ct WC2 ....119 C3
Huntshaw Ho 37 E3 .27 A2
Hunt's La E15 ......27 B3
Huntsman St SE17 ..152 A3
Huntspill St SW17 ..71 B1
Hunts Slip Rd SE21 .76 A2
Huntsworth Mews
  NW1 ....90 C1
Hurdwick Ho NW1 ..82 C2
Hurleston Ho 11
  SE8 ....41 B1
Hurley Cres SE16 ..40 C4
Hurley Ho E2 ....98 C3
  SE11 ....149 C3
Hurlingham Bsns Pk
  SW6 ....58 C4
Hurlingham & Chelsea
  Sec Sch SW6 ......58 C4
Hurlingham Court Mans
  SW6 ....165 B1
Hurlingham Sch SW6 .58 B4
Hurlingham Gdns
  SW6 ....58 B4
Hurlingham Rd
  SW6 ....165 A1
Hurlock Ho N5 ......6 A1
Hurlock St N5 ......6 A1
Huron Rd SW17 ....72 C1
Hurstbourne Ho 12
  SW15 ....56 B1
Hurstdene Gdns N15 ..7 A4
Hurst Ho N1 ....85 A1
Hurst St SE24 ......63 A1
Hurstway Wlk 4
  W11 ....30 C2
Husbourne Ho 8
  SE8 ....41 A2
Huson Cl NW3 ......12 A1
Hutching's St E14 ..41 C4
Hutchins Cl E15 ....76 B1
Hutchins Ho 3
  SW4 ....73 C4
Hutchinson Ho 9
  SE14 ....50 B3
Hutton Cl 8 N4 ......5 B3
Hutton Ho E2 ....99 B3
Hutton St EC4 ......107 C1
Huxbear St SE4 ....66 B2
Huxley Ho NW8 ....89 C1
  London SW9 ....172 C2
Huxley St W10 ......23 A2
Hyacinth Rd SW15 ..68 C3
Hyde Farm Mews
  SW12 ....73 C3
Hyde La SW11 ......168 A4
Hyde Park 6 W2 ..116 C2
Hyde Park Cnr
  SW1 ....131 C4
Hyde Park Corner Sta
  SW1 ....131 C4
Hyde Park Cres
  W2 ....102 A1
Hyde Park Gate Mews
  SW7 ....129 A3
Hyde Park Gdns
  W2 ....115 C4
Hyde Park Gdns Mews
  W2 ....116 A4
Hyde Park Mans
  NW1 ....102 A3
Hyde Park Pl W2 ..116 B4
Hyde Park Sq W2 ..102 A1

Hyde Park Square Mews
  W2 ....102 B1
Hyde Park St W2 ..102 A1
Hyde Park Twrs
  W2 ....114 C3
Hyde Rd N1 ....24 A4
Hyde's Pl 19 N1 ....15 A1
Hyde St SE8 ....51 C4
Hydethorpe Rd
  SW12 ....73 B3
Hyde Vale SE10 ....52 B3
Hylda Ct NW5 ......3 C1
Hyndman Ho 5
  N19 ....13 C4
Hyndman St SE15 ..50 A4
Hyperion Ho 22 E3 ..26 A3
  Streatham SW2 ....74 B4
Hyson Rd SE16 ......40 A1
Hythe Ho 7 SE16 ..40 B4
Hythe Rd NW10 ....21 C1
Hythe Road Ind Est
  NW10 ....21 C1

I

Ian Hamilton Ho
  NW1 ....93 C4
Ibberton Ho SW8 ..162 C2
  W14 ....126 B2
Ibbotson Ave E16 ..35 B1
Ibbott St 22 E1 ....25 B1
Iberia Ho 17 N19 ....4 C4
Ibis Ct SE8 ....51 B4
Ibis La W4 ....45 B2
Ibsley Gdns SW15 ..68 C3
Ibstock Place Sch
  SW15 ....56 B2
Icarus Ho 5 E3 ......26 B2
Iceland Rd E3 ....26 C4
Iceland Wharf SE16 ..41 A2
Ice Wharf NW1 ......84 B1
Ida St E14 ....34 B3
Idmiston Rd SE21,
  SE27 ....75 B2
Idol La EC3 ....124 A3
Idonia St SE8 ....51 C3
Iffley Ho E2 ....99 A3
Iffley Rd W6 ....39 A3
Ifield Ho SE17 ......152 B2
Ifield Rd SW10 ......156 B4
Ifor Evans Pl E1 ....25 C1
Ightham Ho SE17 ..152 A3
Ilbert St W10 ....23 A2
Ilchester Gdns W2 ..114 A4
Ilchester Mans W8 ..127 B2
Ilchester Pl W14 ..127 A2
Ildersly Gr SE21 ....75 C2
Ilderton Prim Sch
  SE16 ....40 B1
Ilderton Rd SE15,
  SE16 ....50 B4
Ilex Rd NW10 ....8 B2
Ilford Ho 10 N1 ....15 C2
Iliffe St SE17 ......150 B2
Iliffe Yd SE17 ......150 B2
Ilkeston Ct 7 E5 ..17 C4
Ilminster Gdns
  SW11 ....60 A3
Ilsley Ct SW8 ......170 C1
Imber St N1 ....87 A3
Imperial Ave 5 N16 ..16 A4
Imperial College Rd
  SW7 ....129 B2
Imperial Coll of Science,
Technology & Medicine
  SW7 ....129 B1

Imperial Ct NW8 ....80 B2
Imperial Ho 2 E14 ..33 B2
  E3 ....26 A2
Imperial Rd SW6 ..166 B3
Imperial Sq SW6 ..166 B4
Imperial St E3 ......27 B2
Imperial Twrs 3
  NW3 ....11 B2
Imperial War Mus*
  SE1,SE11 ....135 C1
Imre Cl W12 ....30 A1
Independant Pl E8 ..16 B3
Indescon Ct E14 ....42 A4
India St EC3 ....110 C1
India Way W12 ......30 A2
Indigo Mews N16 ..6 C1
Indus Ct 15 SE15 ..49 B3
Ingate Pl SW8 ......170 B3
Ingelow Ho W8 ....128 A4
Ingelow St SW8 ..170 A1
Ingersoll Rd W12 ..30 A1
Ingestre Pl W1 ....105 A1
Ingestre Rd NW5 ..13 A4
Ingham Rd NW6 ....10 C4
Inglebert St EC1 ....95 B4
Ingleborough St
  SW9 ....173 B2
Ingleby Rd N7 ....5 A1
Inglefield Sq 11 E1 ..32 A1
Ingle Ho 3 SW12 ..73 C3
Ingleshaw Wlk E9 ..18 B1
Ingleside Gr SE3 ..53 B4
Inglethorpe Ho 6 E5 ..7 C2
Inglethorpe St SW6 .47 C2
Ingleton St SW9 ..173 B2
Inglewood Cl E14 ..41 C2
Inglewood Mans 11
  NW6 ....10 C3
Inglewood Rd NW6 ..10 C3
Inglis Ho 11 SW15 ..57 B2
Inglis St SE5 ....48 A2
Ingram Ave NW11 ..2 B4
Ingram Cl SE11 ....149 A4
Ingram Ho E3 ....26 A4
Ingram Lo 5 SW4 ..61 C1
Ingrave St SW11 ..60 A4
Ingrebourne Ho
  NW8 ....101 C4
Ingress St 4 W4 ....38 A1
Inigo Pl WC2 ......120 A4
Inkerman Rd NW5 ..13 A2
Inkerman Terr W8 ..127 C1
Inkster Ho 9 SW11 ..60 A4
Inman Rd
  London NW10 ......21 A4
  Wandsworth SW18 ..71 B4
Inner Circ NW1 ......91 B3
Inner Park Rd SW19 .69 C2
Inner Temple La
  EC4 ....107 B1
Innes Gdns SW15 ..57 A1
Innis Ho SE17 ......152 A2
Insley Ho 8 E3 ......27 A2
Inst for Child Health
  WC1 ....94 C1
Institute Pl 3 E8 ..17 A3
Instituto Espanol
Vicente Canada Blanch
  W10 ....31 A4
Inst of Ophthalmology
  EC1 ....97 C2
Interchange The
  NW5 ....13 A3
International Sch of
  London W3 ....36 C2
Inveagh Cl E9 ......25 C4

Inver Ct W2 . . . . .100 B1
Inverforth Cl NW3 . . .2 B2
Inverforth Ho NW3 . .2 B2
Invergarry Ho NW6 . .78 A1
Inverness Gdns
W8 . . . . .114 A1
Inverness Mews
W2 . . . . .114 A4
Inverness Pl W2 . . . .114 B4
Inverness St NW1 . . .82 B4
Inverness Terr W2 . .114 B4
Inverton Rd SE15 . . .65 C3
Invicta Cl 19 E3 . . . .33 C4
Invicta Plaza SE1 . . .122 A2
Invicta Prim Sch
SE3 . . . . .53 C3
Invicta Rd SE3,SE7 . .53 C4
Inville Rd SE17 . . . .151 C1
Inwen Ct SE8 . . . . . . .41 A1
Inwood Ct 10 NW1 . .13 B1
Inwood Ho 15 SE22 . .64 A4
Inworth St SW11 . . .168 B2
Inworth Wlk N1 . . . .86 C4
Ion Ct 8 E2 . . . . .24 C3
Ionian Bldg 10 E14 . .33 A2
Ionian Ho 22 E1 . . . . .25 C1
Ipsden Bldgs SE1 . . .135 C4
Ipswich Ho SE4 . . . . .65 C2
Irby Ho SW2 . . . . .62 C1
Ireland Yd EC4 . . . . .108 B1
Irene Rd SW6 . . . . . .165 C3
Ireton Ho SW9 . . . . .173 C1
Ireton St 2 E3 . . . . . .26 C1
Iroko Ho 7 NW3 . . . .11 A2
Iron Bridge Cl NW10 .8 A3
Iron Bridge Ho NW3 . .12 B2
Iron Mill Pl SW18 . . .59 A1
Iron Mill Rd SW18 . . .59 A1
Ironmonger La
EC2 . . . . .109 B1
Ironmonger Pas
EC1 . . . . .97 A3
Ironmonger Row
EC1 . . . . .97 A3
Ironmonger's Pl 15
E14 . . . . .41 C2
Ironside Cl 16 SE16 . .40 C4
Ironside Ho E9 . . . . .18 A4
Irvine Ct W1 . . . . . . .93 A1
Irvine Ho 2 E14 . . . . .34 A4
London N7 . . . . .14 B2
Irving Gr SW9 . . . . .172 C1
Irving Ho SE17 . . . . .150 A1
Irving Mews N1 . . . . .15 B2
Irving Rd W14 . . . . . .39 C3
Irving St WC2 . . . . .119 C3
Irwell Est 20 SE16 . . .40 B4
Irwin Gdns NW10 . . . .22 A4
Isabella Ct 8 TW10 . .54 B1
Isabella Ho SE11 . . .150 A2
10 London W6 . . . . . .39 B1
Isabella Rd E9 . . . . . .17 B3
Isabella St SE1 . . . . .122 A1
Isabel St SW9 . . . . . .173 A4
Isambard Mews E14 . .42 B3
Isambard Pl SE16 . . . .32 B1
Iseldon Ct N7 . . . . . . .14 A4
Isel Way 4 SE22 . . . . .64 A2
Isis Cl SW15 . . . . .57 B3
Isis Ct W4 . . . . .45 A3
Isis Ho NW8 . . . . .89 C1
Isis St SW18 . . . . .71 B2
Islamia Girls' High Sch
NW6 . . . . .23 A4
Islamia Prim Sch
NW6 . . . . .23 A4

Islamic Coll for
Advanced Studies
NW10 . . . . .9 A2
Island Gardens Sta
E14 . . . . .42 B1
Island Row E14 . . . . .33 B3
Isledon Ho N1 . . . . . .86 C4
Isledon Rd N4,N7 . . . .5 C1
Islington Gn N1 . . . . .86 A3
Islington Green Sch
N1 . . . . .86 C3
Islington High St
N1 . . . . .86 A2
Islington Park Mews 1
N1 . . . . .15 A1
Islington Park St
N1 . . . . .14 C1
Islington Sixth Form Ctr
N7 . . . . .14 C4
Islip St NW5 . . . . .13 B3
Isokon Flats 5
NW3 . . . . .12 B3
Ivanhoe Ho 22 E3 . . .26 A3
Ivanhoe Ho SW12 . . .73 A4
Ivanhoe Rd SE5 . . . . .64 B4
Ivatt Pl W14 . . . . . . .141 A1
Iveagh Cl E9 . . . . . . .110 C1
Iveagh Ho SW10 . . . .157 A2
2 London SW9 . . . . . .48 A1
Ivebury Ct W10 . . . . .30 B3
Iveley Rd SW4 . . . . .170 C1
Iver Ct N1 . . . . .15 B2
Iverna Ct W8 . . . . . .127 C2
Iverna Gdns W8 . . . .127 C2
Iverson Rd NW6 . . . . .10 C2
Ives Rd E16 . . . . .35 A4
Ives St SW3 . . . . .144 B4
Ivimey St 2 E2 .24 C2 99 C4
Ivinghoe Ho N7 . . . . .13 C3
Ivor Ct NW1 . . . . .90 C2
Ivor Pl NW1 . . . . .90 C1
Ivor St NW1 . . . . .13 B1
Ivory Ho E1 . . . . .125 A2
9 London SW11 . . . . .59 B4
Ivybridge Ho 18
SE22 . . . . .64 A4
Ivybridge La WC2 . . .120 B3
Ivy Church La SE1,
SE17 . . . . .152 C2
Ivy Cres W4 . . . . .37 B2
Ivy Ct SE16 . . . . .153 C1
Ivydale Prim Sch
SE15 . . . . .65 C3
Ivydale Rd SE15 . . . . .65 C3
Ivyday Gr SW16 . . . . .74 B1
Ivy Lo W8 . . . . .113 B2
Ivymount Rd SE27 . . .74 C1
Ivy Rd E16 . . . . .35 C3
London E17 . . . . .19 A4
NW2 . . . . .9 B4
London SE4 . . . . .66 C3
Ivy St N1 . . . . .24 A3
Ixworth Pl SW3 . . . .144 A3

J

Jacaranda Gr 5 E8 . . .16 B1
Jackman Ho 20 E1 . . .32 A1
Jackman St E8 . . . . . .25 A4
Jackson Cl E9 . . . . . . .17 C1
Jackson Ho 16
SW11 . . . . .59 C4
Jackson Rd N7 . . . . . .14 B4
Jackson's La N6 . . . . . .4 A4

Jack Taylor Sch
NW8 . . . . .78 C4
Jack Tizard Sch
SW6 . . . . .47 C2
Jack Walker Ct N5 . . .15 A4
Jacobin Lo N7 . . . . . .14 A3
Jacob Mans 11 E1 . . .32 A3
Jacobson Ct SW11 . .168 B3
Jacobson Ho 1 E1 . . .110 C2
Jacob St SE1 . . . . . . .139 B4
Jacob's Well Mews
W1 . . . . .103 C2
Jacotts Ho W10 . . . . .22 B1
Jaggard Way SW12 . .72 B4
Jagger Ho SW11 . . . .168 C4
Jago Wlk 22 SE5 . . . .48 C3
Jamahirya Sch
SW3 . . . . .158 A4
Jamaica Rd SE1 . . . .139 B3
SE16 . . . . .40 A3
Jamaica St E1 . . . . . . .32 B4
James Allen's Girls' Sch
SE22 . . . . .64 A2
James Anderson Ct 20
E2 . . . . .24 A3
James Ave NW2 . . . . . .9 B3
James Brine Ho 17 E2 .99 A4
James Campbell Ho 2
E2 . . . . .25 B3
James Collins Cl
W9 . . . . .23 B1
James Docherty Ho 4
E2 . . . . .25 B3
James Hammett Ho 2
E2 . . . . .24 B3
James Ho 11 E1 . . . . .25 C1
16 SE16 . . . . .40 C4
James Joyes Wlk 7
SE5 . . . . .63 A3
James Leicester Hall of
Residence N7 . . . . .14 A2
James Lind Ho 6
SE8 . . . . .41 B2
James Middleton Ho 20
E2 . . . . .25 A2
Jameson Ct 6 E2 . . . .25 B3
Jameson Ho SE11 . . .148 C2
Jameson Pl 8 W3 . . . .37 B4
Jameson St W8 . . . . .113 C2
James St W1 . . . . . . .103 C1
WC2 . . . . .120 B4
James Stewart Ho
NW6 . . . . .10 B1
James Stroud Ho
SE17 . . . . .151 A1
Jamestown Rd NW1 .82 A4
Jamestown Way
E14 . . . . .34 C2
James Wolfe Prim Sch
SE10 . . . . .52 B3
Jamuna Cl E14 . . . . . .33 A4
Jane St E1 . . . . .32 A3
Janet St E14 . . . . .41 C3
Janeway Pl 2 SE16 . .40 A4
Janeway St SE16 . . . .139 C3
Jansen Wlk SW11 . . .59 C3
Japan Cres N4 . . . . . . .5 B3
Jardine Rd E1 . . . . . . .32 C2
Jarman Ho 15 E1 . . . .32 B4
SE16 . . . . .40 C2
Jarret Ho 11 E3 . . . . .26 C2
Jarrett Cl SW2 . . . . . .75 A3
Jarrow Rd SE16 . . . . .40 B1
Jarrow Way E9 . . . . . .18 A4
Jarvis Ct 2 SE10 . . . .52 B2
Jarvis Ho 3 SE15 . . . .49 C2
Jarvis Rd SE22 . . . . . .64 A3

Jasmin SE1 . . . . .125 A1
Jasmin Ho SE4 . . . . . .66 B4
Jasmin Lo 17 SE16 . . .40 A1
Jason Ct W1 . . . . . . .103 C2
London SW9 . . . . . . .173 B4
Jasper Wlk N1 . . . . . .97 B4
Java Wharf SE1 . . . . .139 A4
Jay Ho SW15 . . . . . . .47 B1
Jay Mews SW7 . . . . .129 A3
Jean Darling Ho
SW10 . . . . .157 B3
Jean Pardies Ho 21
E1 . . . . .32 B4
Jebb Ave SW2 . . . . . .62 A1
Jebb St E3 . . . . .26 C3
Jedburgh St SW11 . . .60 C3
Jedbo Mews W12 . . . .38 B4
Jeddo Rd W12 . . . . . .38 B4
Jefferson Bldg 3
E14 . . . . .41 C4
Jeffrey's Ct SW4 . . . .172 A2
Jeffrey's Pl NW1 . . . .13 B1
Jeffrey's Rd SW4 . . . .172 A2
Jeffrey's St NW1 . . . .13 B1
Jeger Ave E2 . . . . .24 B4
Jelf Rd SW2 . . . . .62 C2
Jellicoe Ho 17 E2 . . . .24 C3
4 Putney SW15 . . . . .57 C2
Jemotts Ct 10 SE14 . .50 C4
Jenkins Ho SW8 . . . .171 B4
Jenkinson Ho 15 E2 . .25 C2
Jenner Ave W3 . . . . . .28 C4
Jenner Ho SE3 . . . . . .53 A4
Jenner Pl SW13 . . . . .47 A4
Jenner Rd N16 . . . . . .7 B1
Jennifer Ho SE11 . . . .149 C3
Jennings Ho SE10 . . .42 C1
Jennings Rd SE22 . . . .64 B1
Jensen Ho 10 E3 . . . . .26 C1
Jephson Ct SW4 . . . .172 B1
Jephson Ho 8
SE17 . . . . .48 A4
Jephson St SE5 . . . . . .48 C2
Jephtha Rd SW18 . . . .58 C1
Jerdan Pl SW6 . . . . . .155 B2
Jeremiah St 11 E14 . .34 A3
Jeremy Bentham Ho
E2 . . . . .99 C3
Jermyn St SW1 . . . . .119 A2
Jerningham Ct
SE14 . . . . .51 A2
Jerningham Rd
SE14 . . . . .51 A2
Jerome Cres NW8 . . .90 A2
Jerome Ho NW1 . . . .102 B4
Jerome St E1 . .24 B1 98 C1
Jerrard Twr 3 W3 . . . .37 A4
Gerrard St SE13 . . . . .67 A4
Jerrold Lo SW15 . . . .57 B4
Jerrold St 24 N1 . . . . .24 A3
Jersey Ho 12 N1 . . . . .15 B2
Jersey Rd E16 . . . . . . .35 C3
Jersey St E2 . . . . .25 A2
Jerusalem Pas EC1 . . .96 A1
Jervis Bay Ho 8
E14 . . . . .34 C3
Jervis Ct W1 . . . . . . .104 B1
Jessel Ho SW1 . . . . .147 C4
WC1 . . . . .94 A3
Jessica Rd SW18 . . . .59 B2
Jessie Blythe La 2
N19 . . . . .5 A4
Jessie Duffett Ho 11
SE5 . . . . .48 B3
Jesson Ho SE17 . . . . .151 B3
Jessop Ct N1 . . . . .86 B1

Jessop Prim Sch
SE24 . . . . .63 B3
Jessop Sq E14 . . . . . .33 C1
Jeston Ho 10 SE27 . . .75 A1
Jethou Ho 18 N1 . . . .15 B2
Jevons Ho 8 NW8 . . . .11 C1
Jewell Ho 3 SW12 . . .73 B4
Jewish Prep Sch The
NW6 . . . . .78 A1
Jewry St EC3 . . . . . . .110 C1
Jews Row SW18 . . . . .59 B3
Jeymer Ave NW2 . . . . .9 B3
Jeypore Rd SW18 . . . .59 B1
Jim Griffiths Ho
SW6 . . . . .155 A3
Joanna Ho 7 W6 . . . .39 B1
Joan St SE1 . . . . .122 A1
Jocelin Ho N1 . . . . . . .85 A3
Jocelyn Rd TW9 . . . . .54 A4
Jocelyn St SE15 . . . . .49 C2
Jockey's Fields
WC1 . . . . .107 A4
Jodane St SE8 . . . . . . .41 B2
Jodrell Rd E3 . . . . . . .18 B1
Johanna Prim Sch
SE1 . . . . .135 B3
Johanna St SE1 . . . . .135 B3
John Adam St
WC2 . . . . .120 B3
John Aird Ct W2 . . . .101 A4
John Archer Way
SW18 . . . . .59 C1
John Ashby Cl SW2 . .62 A1
John Ball Prim Sch
SE3 . . . . .53 B1
John Barker Ct
NW6 . . . . .10 A1
John Betts' Ho W12 . .38 C3
John Betts Prim Sch
W6 . . . . .39 A3
John Bond Ho 2
E3 . . . . .26 B3
John Brent Ho 8
SE8 . . . . .40 C2
John Buck Ho
NW10 . . . . .21 B4
John Burns Prim Sch
SW11 . . . . .169 C1
John Campbell Rd 26
N16 . . . . .16 A3
John Carpenter St
EC4 . . . . .122 A4
John Cartwright Ho 7
E2 . . . . .25 A2
John Conwey Ho 23
SW2 . . . . .62 C1
John Dee Ho 3
SW14 . . . . .55 C4
John Donne Prim Sch
SE15 . . . . .50 A2
John Dwight Ho
SW6 . . . . .59 A4
John Felton Rd
SE16 . . . . .139 B3
John Fielden Ho 10
E2 . . . . .25 A2
John Fisher St E1 . . .125 B4
John F. Kennedy Specl
Sch E15 . . . . .27 C4
John Glynes Ct
SW15 . . . . .57 A3
John Harris Ho
SE15 . . . . .64 C4

John Harrison Way
SE10 ....43 B3
John Islip St SW1 .148 A3
John Keall Ho
SW15 ....57 C4
John Keble CE Prim Sch
NW10 ....21 B4
John Kennedy Ct 🄷
N1 ....15 C2
John Kennedy Ho 🄷
SE16 ....40 C2
John Kennedy Lo 🄿
N1 ....15 C2
John King Ct 🄸 N19 .4 C2
John Knight Lo
SW6 ....155 C3
John Maurice Cl
SE17 ....151 B4
John McDonald Ho 🄸
E14 ....42 B3
John McKenna Wlk
SE16 ....139 C2
John Milton Prim Sch
SW8 ....160 C1
John Nettleford Ho 🄵
E2 ....25 C2
John Orwell Sports Ctr
E1 ....32 A1
John Parker Sq 🄷
SW11 ....59 C4
John Parry Ct 🄿🄴
N1 ....24 A3
John Paul II Sch
SW19 ....69 C4
John Penn St SE13 .52 A2
John Perryn Prim Sch
W3 ....29 A3
John Prince's St
W1 ....104 B2
John Pritchard Ho 🄷
E1 ....99 C1
John Rennie Wlk 🄷
E1 ....32 B1
John Roan Sch The
SE3 ....53 A3
John Roll Way
SE16 ....139 C2
John Ruskin Prim Sch
SE5 ....48 B4
John Ruskin St SE5 .48 B4
John Scurr Ho 🄿🄾
E14 ....33 A3
John Scurr Prim Sch
E1 ....25 B1
John Silkin La 🄴🄰 SE8 .40 C1
John's Mews WC1 .95 A1
John Smith Ave
SW6 ....154 C2
Johnson Cl E8 ....24 C4
Johnson Ct 🄸🄾
SW18 ....59 C3
Johnson Ho E2 ....99 C3
NW1 ....83 A1
SW1 ....145 C3
SW8 ....161 C1
Johnson Lo 🄸 W9 .31 C4
Johnson Rd NW10 .20 C4
Johnsons Ct EC4 .107 C1
Johnson's Pl SW1 .146 C1
Johnson St E1 ....32 B3

Johnsons Way
NW10 ....20 A1
John Spencer Sq
N1 ....15 A2
John's Pl E1 ....32 A3
John St WC1 ....95 A1
John Stainer Com Prim
Sch SE4 ....66 A4
Johnston Cl SW9 .173 A3
Johnstone Ho SE13 .67 C4
John Strachey Ho
SW6 ....155 A3
John Trundle Ct
EC2 ....108 C4
John Tucker Ho 🄸
E14 ....41 C3
John Wesley's House &
Mus 🄴🄲 EC1 ....97 C2
John Wheatley Ho
SW6 ....155 A3
🄷 London N19 ....4 C4
John Williams Cl
SE14 ....50 C4
Johsen Ho 🄵 SW15 .56 C2
Joiners Arms Yd 🄷
SE5 ....48 C2
Joiner St SE1 ....123 C1
Jolles Ho 🄹 E3 ....27 A2
Jonathan Ct 🄾 W4 .38 A2
Jonathan St SE11 .148 C2
Jones Ho London N16 ....7 A3
🄼 South Bromley
E14 ....34 C3
Jones St W1 ....118 A3
Jones Wlk 🄸 TW10 .54 B1
Jonson Ho SE1 ....137 C1
🄵 London N16 ....16 A4
Jordan Ct SW15 .57 C3
Jordan ho N1 ....87 C3
🄸🄴 London SE4 .65 C3
Jordans Ho NW8 .90 A1
Joscoyne Ho 🄵 E1 .32 A3
Joseph Ave W3 ....28 C3
Joseph Conrad Ho
SW1 ....147 A3
Joseph Ct N16 .7 A4
Josephine Ave SW2 .62 B2
Joseph Irwin Ho 🄷
E14 ....33 B2
Joseph Lancaster Prim
Sch SE1 ....137 B1
Joseph Powell Cl 🄷
SW12 ....61 B1
Joseph Priestley Ho 🄸🄿
E2 ....25 A2
Joseph St E3 ....26 B1
Joshua St E14 ....34 B3
Joslings Cl W12 .29 C2
Josseline Cl 🄴 E3 .26 A3
Joubert Mans SW3 .144 B2
Joubert St SW11 .169 A2
Jowett Ho SW9 .172 B1
Jowett St SE15 .49 B3
Jubet Ho 🄸 N16 .15 C4
Jubilee Bldgs NW8 .79 B2
Jubilee Cl NW10 .21 A3
Jubilee Mans 🄸🄾 E1 .32 B3
Jubilee Market WC2 .120 B4
Jubilee Pl SW3 .144 B2
Jubilee Prim Sch
London N16 ....7 C2
London SW2 ....62 C1
Jubilee The 🄸 SE10 .52 A3

Jubilee Yd SE1 ....138 C4
Judd St WC1 ....94 A3
Jude St E16 ....35 B1
Judges' Wlk NW3 ....2 B1
Juer St SW11 ....158 B1
Julian Ave W3 ....28 A2
Julian Pl E14 ....42 A1
Julia St NW5 ....12 C3
Juliet Ho 🄸 N1 ....24 A3
Julius Ct TW8 ....44 A3
Julius Nyerere Cl
N1 ....84 C4
Junction App
London SE13 ....67 B4
London SW11 ....60 A4
Junction Mews
W2 ....102 A2
Junction Pl W2 ....101 C2
Junction Rd N19 ....4 C1
Juniper Cres NW1 ....12 C1
Juniper Ct N16 ....7 A3
Juniper Ho 🄸 SE14 ....51 A3
SE15 ....50 B3
Juno Ct SW9 ....163 C1
Juno Way SE14 ....50 C4
Juno Way Ind Est
SE14 ....50 C4
Jupiter Ct SW9 ....163 C2
Jupiter Way N7 ....14 B2
Jupp Rd E15 ....19 C1
Jupp Rd W E15 ....27 C4
Jura Ho SE16 ....41 A2
Jurston Ct SE1 ....135 C3
Justice Wlk SW3 ....158 A3
Jutland Cl N19 ....5 A3
Jutland Ho 🄵 SE5 .48 B1
Juxon St SE11 ....149 A4

K

Kambala Rd SW11 ....59 C4
Kara Way NW2 ....9 C4
Karen Ct 🄷 SE5 ....64 A4
Karen Ho 🄼 N16 .15 C4
Kasmin Ct NW10 ....8 C1
Kassala Rd SW11 .169 A3
Katherine Cl 🄷
SE16 ....32 C1
Katherine Ho 🄸🄸
W10 ....23 A1
Katherine Sq W11 .112 A2
Kathleen Ave W3 .28 B4
Kathleen Rd SW11 .60 B4
Kay Rd SW9 ....172 C1
Kay St E2 ....24 C3
Kean Ho 🄵 SE17 .48 A4
Kean St WC2 ....106 C1
Keates Est N16 ....7 B2
Keats Cl SE1 ....152 C3
London NW3 ....12 A4
Keats Gr NW3 ....12 A4
Keats Ho 🄴 E2 ....25 B2
🄲🄴 SE5 ....48 B3
SW1 ....161 A4
Keats House Mus *
NW3 ....12 A4
Keats Pl EC2 ....109 B3
Keble Ho 🄸 SW15 .57 C1
Keble Pl SW13 ....47 A4
Kedge Ho 🄸🄾 E14 .41 C3
Kedleston Ct E5 ....18 A4
Kedleston Wlk 🄱🄸
E2 ....25 A2
Keel Cl SE16 ....32 C1
Keeley St WC2 ....106 C1
Keen's Yd N1 ....15 A2
Keeper Wharf *E1 ....32 C2

Keepier Wharf 🄸🄾
E1 ....32 C2
Keep The SE3 ....53 C1
Keeton's Rd SE16 ....40 A3
Keevil Dr SW19 ....70 A4
Keighley Cl N7 ....14 A4
Keildon Rd SW11 .60 B3
Keir Hardie Ho
🄷 London N19 ....4 C4
London NW10 ....8 B1
London W6 ....47 C4
Keith Connor Cl 🄵
SW8 ....61 A4
Keith Gr W12 ....29 C1
Keith Ho NW6 ....78 A1
Kelby Ho N7 ....14 B2
Kelfield Ct 🄸 W10 .30 C3
Kelfield Gdns W10 .30 C3
Kelfield Mews W10 .30 C3
Kellett Ho N1 ....87 C3
Kellett Rd SW2 ....62 C3
Kellow Ho SE1 ....137 B4
Kelly Ave SE15 ....49 B2
Kelly Ct 🄸 E14 ....33 C2
Kelly St NW1 ....13 A2
Kelman Cl SW4 .171 C1
Kelmore Gr SE22 .64 C3
Kelmscott Gdns
W12 ....38 C3
Kelmscott Rd SW11 .60 B2
Kelross Rd N5 ....15 B4
Kelsey St E2 .24 C1 99 B2
Kelshall Ct N4 ....6 B2
Kelson Ho E14 ....42 B3
Kelso Pl W8 ....128 B2
Kelvedon Ho SW8 .172 B4
Kelvedon Rd SW6 .155 A1
Kelvin Ct W11 ....113 B3
Chiswick W4 ....37 A1
Kelvington Rd SE15 .65 C2
Kelvin Rd N5 ....15 A4
Kelway Ho 🄾 SW2 .74 C3
Kember St N1 ....14 B1
Kemble Ho SW9 .63 A4
Kemble St WC2 .106 C1
Kemerton Rd SE5 .63 B4
Kemey's St E9 ....18 A3
Kemp Ct SW8 ....162 A1
Kempe Ho SE1 ....137 C1
Kempe Rd NW6 .22 C2
Kemp Ho 🄸 E2 ....25 C3
Kempis Way 🄷
SE22 ....64 A2
Kemplay Rd NW3 .11 C4
Kemp's Ct W1 ....105 B1
Kemps Dr E14 ....33 C2
Kempsford Gdns
SW5 ....141 C1
Kempsford Rd
SE11 ....149 C3
Kemps Gdns SE13 .67 B2
Kempson Rd SW6 .155 C1
Kempthorne Rd SE8 .41 B2
Kempton Ct E1 ....32 A4
Kempton Ho 🄸🄸 N1 .24 A4
Kemsford Rd SE11 .150 A3
Kemsing Ho SE1 .137 C3
Kemsing Rd SE10 .43 C1
Kemsley SE13 ....67 A2
Kenbrook Ho W14 .127 A1
🄸 London NW5 ....13 B3
Kenbury Gdns 🄸
SE5 ....48 B1
Kenbury Mans 🄸🄸
SE5 ....48 B1
Kenbury St SE5 ....48 B1

Kenchester Cl
SW8 ....162 B1
Kendal Ho 🄷 N1 ....92 B4
Kendal Ave W3 .28 A4
Kendal Cl SE5 ....48 A3
Kendal Ct NW2 ....10 A3
Kendal Ho N1 ....85 A2
🄾 London E9 ....17 B1
Kendall Ct 🄸 SW19 .20 C4
Kendall Pl W1 ....103 B3
Kendal Pl SW15 ....58 B2
Kendal Rd NW10 ....8 C4
Kendal St W2 ....102 B1
Kendal Steps W2 .102 B1
Kender Prim Sch
SE14 ....50 B2
Kender St SE14 ....50 B2
Kendoa Rd 🄸 SW4 .61 C3
Kendrick Ct 🄸🄸 SE15 .50 A2
Kendrick Mews
SW7 ....143 B3
Kendrick Pl SW7 .143 B3
Kenilford Rd SW12 .73 A4
Kenilworth Ave SW8 .58 A4
Kenilworth Rd E3 .26 A3
NW6 ....23 B4
Kenley Wlk W11 .112 A3
Kenmare Mans
NW6 ....10 B3
Kenmont Gdns
NW10 ....22 A2
Kenmont Prim Sch
NW10 ....22 A2
Kenmore Ct TW9 .44 C2
Kenmore Rd NW6 .10 C1
Kenmure Rd E8 .17 A3
Kenmure Yd E8 ....17 A3
Kennacraig Cl 🄷
E16 ....35 C1
Kennard Ho SW11 .169 C3
Kennard Rd E15 ....19 C1
Kennard St SW11 .169 B3
Kennedy Cox Ho 🄿
E16 ....35 B2
Kennedy Ho SE11 .148 C2
Kennedy Wlk SE17 .151 C3
Kennet Cl SW11 ....59 C3
Kennet Ct 🄸🄷 W2 .31 C4
Kenneth Campbell Ho
NW8 ....89 C2
Kenneth Cres NW2 ....9 A3
Kenneth Ct SE11 .149 C4
Kennet Ho NW8 ....89 C1
Kenneth Younger Ho
SW6 ....155 A3
Kennet Rd W9 ....23 B1
Kennet St E1 ....125 C2
Kennet Wharf La
EC4 ....123 A4
Kenning Ho 🄸 N1 .24 A4
Kenning St 🄸🄷 SE16 .40 B4
Kennings Way
SE11 ....149 C2
Kennington Gr 🄸
SE11 ....163 A4
Kennington La
SE11 ....149 B1
Kennington Oval
SE11 ....163 A3
Kennington Palace Ct
SE11 ....149 B2
Kennington Park Gdns
SE17 ....48 A4
Kennington Park Ho
SE11 ....149 C1
Kennington Park Pl
SE11 ....48 A4

Kennington Park Rd
SE11 . . . . **150** A2
Kennington Rd
SE11 . . . . **149** B4
Kennington Sta
SE17 . . . . **150** A2
Kennoldes SE21 . . **75** C2
Kenrick Pl W1 . . . . **103** B3
Kensal Green Cemy (All
Souls)* NW10 . . . . **22** B2
Kensal Green Sta
. . . . **22** B2
Kensal Ho W10 . . **22** C1
Kensal Rd W10 . . . . **23** A1
Kensal Rise Prim Sch
NW6 . . . . **22** C3
Kensal Rise Sta
. . . . **22** C3
Kensington & Chelsea
Coll
SW10 . . . . **156** C2
W10 . . . . **31** A4
Kensington Church Ct
W8 . . . . **128** A3
Kensington Church St
W8 . . . . . . **31** C1 **113** C1
Kensington Church Wlk
W8 . . . . **128** A3
Kensington Court Mans
W8 . . . . **128** B3
Kensington Court Mews
W8 . . . . **128** B2
Kensington Court Pl
W8 . . . . **128** B2
Kensington Ct W8 **128** B3
Kensington Ct Gdns
W8 . . . . **128** B2
Kensington Gardens
W2 . . . . **115** A1
Kensington Gate
W8 . . . . **128** C2
Kensington Gdns Sq
W2 . . . . **114** A4
Kensington Gore
SW7 . . . . **129** B3
Kensington Hall Gdns
W14 . . . . **140** C2
Kensington High St
W8 . . . . **127** C2
Kensington Ho 🖪
NW5 . . . . **13** B3
Kensington Hts
W8 . . . . **113** B1
Kensington Mall
W8 . . . . **113** C2
Kensington Mans
SW5 . . . . **141** C2
Kensington Olympia Sta
W14 . . . . **126** A2
Kensington Palace*
W8 . . . . **114** B1
Kensington Palace Gdns
W8 . . . . **114** A2
Kensington Park Gdns
W11 . . . . **31** B2 **113** A3
Kensington Park Mews
W11 . . . . **31** B3
Kensington Park Rd
W11 . . . . **31** B2 **113** A4
Kensington Pl
W8 . . . . . . **31** C1 **113** B2
Kensington Prep Sch
SW6 . . . . **165** A4
Kensington Rd
SW7 . . . . **129** A3
W11 . . . . **112** A4

Kensington Sq W8 **128** A3
Kensington Village
W14 . . . . **141** A3
Kensington W
W14 . . . . **140** A4
Kensworth Ho EC1 **97** C3
Kent Ct 🖪 E2 . . . . . . **24** B3
Kent Ho SE1 . . . . . . **153** A1
SW1 . . . . **147** B1
🖪 London W4 . . . . **38** A1
Richmond TW10 . . **54** C2
Kentish Bldgs SE1 **123** B1
Kentish Town CE Prim
Sch NW5 . . . . **13** B3
Kentish Town Rd
NW1 . . . . **13** A2
Kentish Town Sta
NW5 . . . . **13** B3
Kentish Town West Sta
NW5 . . . . **13** A2
Kent Lo 🗓 SW19 . . **69** C3
Kentmere Ho SE15 . . **50** B4
Kenton Ct W14 . . **126** C1
Kenton Ho 🗓 E1 . . **25** B1
London N5 . . . . **5** C1
Kenton Rd E9 . . . . . . **17** C2
Kent Pas NW1 . . . . **90** C2
Kent Rd London W4 . . **37** B3
Richmond TW9 . . . . **44** C3
Kent St E2 . . . . **24** B3
Kent Terr NW1 . . . . **90** B3
Kentwell Cl SE4 . . . . **66** A3
Kentwode Gn SW13 . . **46** C3
Kent Yard SW7 . . **130** B3
Kenway Rd SW5 . . **142** A3
Ken Wilson Ho 🗓
. . . . **24** C3
Kenwood Cl NW3 . . . . **2** C3
Kenwood Ho* NW3 . . **3** A3
🗓 London SW9 . . . . **63** A3
Kenworthy Rd E9 . . **18** A2
Kenwrick Ho N1 . . . . **85** A3
Kenwyn Rd SW4 . . . . **61** C3
Kenyon St SW6 . . . . **47** C2
Kepler Ho 🗓 SE10 . . **43** B1
Kepler Rd SW2,SW4 . . **62** A3
Keppel Ho 🗓 SE8 . . **41** B1
SW3 . . . . **144** A3
Keppel Row SE1 . . **122** C1
Keppel St WC1 . . . . **105** C4
Kerbela St E2 . . . . . . **99** B2
Kerbey St E14 . . . . . . **34** A3
Kerfield Cres SE5 . . **48** C2
Kerfield Pl SE5 . . . . **48** C2
Kerridge Ct N1 . . . . **16** A2
Kerrier Ho SW10 **157** A1
Kerrington Ct 🗓
W12 . . . . **39** B4
Kerrin Point SE11 **149** B2
Kerrison Rd E15 . . . . **27** C4
London SW11 . . . . . . **60** A4
Kerry N7 . . . . **14** A2
Kerry Ho 🗓 E1 . . . . **32** B3
Kerry Path SE8 . . . . **51** B4
Kerry Rd SE8 . . . . . . **51** B4
Kerscott Ho 🗓 E3 . . **27** A2
Kersfield Ho SW15 . . **57** C1
Kersfield Rd SW15 . . **57** C1
Kershaw Cl SW18 . . **59** C1
Kershaw Ho 🖪
SE27 . . . . **75** A1
Kersley Mews
SW11 . . . . **168** C3
Kersley Rd N16 . . . . . . **7** A1
Kersley St SW11 . . **168** C2

Kerwick Cl 🗓 N7 . . . . **14** B1
Keslake Mans
NW10 . . . . **22** C3
Keslake Rd NW6 . . . . **22** C3
Keston Ho SE15 . . . . **64** C4
Keston Rd SE15 . . . . **64** C4
Kestrel Ho EC1 . . . . . . **96** C4
Kestrel Ave SE24 . . . . **63** B2
Keswick Broadway 🗓
SW15 . . . . **58** B2
Keswick Ct 🗓 SE22 . . **64** C2
Keswick Ho 🖪 SE5 . . **48** B2
Keswick Hts 🖪
SW15 . . . . **58** A2
Keswick Lo E8 . . . . . . **16** B2
Keswick Rd SW15 . . **58** A2
Kett Gdns SW2 . . . . **62** B2
Kettleby Ho SW9 . . . . **63** A4
Kevan Ho SE5 . . . . . . **48** B3
Kevin Ho N16 . . . . **6** C2
Kew Bridge TW8 . . **36** B1
Kew Bridge Ct 🗓
W4 . . . . **36** C1
Kew Bridge Distribution
Ctr TW8 . . . . **36** B2
Kew Bridge Rd TW8 . . **36** B1
Kew Bridge Sta
TW8 . . . . **36** B1
Kew Bridge Steam Mus
* TW8 . . . . **36** B1
Kew Foot Rd TW9 . . **54** A4
Kew Gardens Rd
TW9 . . . . **44** C2
Kew Gardens(Royal
Botanic)* TW9 . . **44** A2
Kew Gardens Sta
TW9 . . . . **44** C2
Kew Gn TW9 . . . . . . **44** B4
Kew Green TW9 . . . . **44** C4
Kew Lo 🖪 TW9 . . . . **44** B2
Kew Palace* TW9 . . **44** A3
Kew Pier TW9 . . . . . . **44** C4
Kew Ret Pk TW9,W4 . . **45** A2
Key Cl E1 . . . . **25** A1
Keyes Rd NW2 . . . . . . **9** C3
Keyham Ho 🗓 W2 . . **31** C4
Key Ho SE11 . . . . . . **163** B4
Keymer Rd SW2 . . . . **74** B2
Keynsham Ho 🗓 N4 . . **6** B4
Keyse Rd SE1 . . . . . . **138** C1
Keystone Cres N1 . . **84** B1
Keyworth Cl E5 . . . . **18** A4
Keyworth Pl SE1 . . **136** B2
Keyworth Prim Sch
SE17 . . . . **150** B2
Keyworth St SE1 . . **136** B2
Kezia St SE8 . . . . **41** A1
Khyber Rd SW11 . . **168** A1
Kibworth St SW8 . . **162** C1
Kidbrooke Gdns
SE3 . . . . **53** C2
Kidderpore Ave
NW3 . . . . **10** C4
Kidderpore Gdns
NW3 . . . . **10** C4
Kiffen St EC2 . . . . . . **97** C2
Kilbrennan Ho 🖪
E14 . . . . **34** B3
Kilburn Bridge 🗓
NW6 . . . . **23** C4
Kilburn High Rd
NW6 . . . . **23** C4
Kilburn High Road Sta
NW6 . . . . **78** A3

Kilburn Ho 🗓 W9 . . **23** B2
Kilburn La W10 . . . . **23** A2
Kilburn Park Jun Sch
NW6 . . . . **23** B3
Kilburn Park Rd
NW6 . . . . **23** C2
Kilburn Park Sta
NW6 . . . . **23** C3
Kilburn Pl NW6 . . . . **23** C4
Kilburn Priory NW6 . . **78** A3
Kilburn Sq NW6 . . . . **23** C4
Kilburn Sta NW2 . . . . **10** B2
Kilburn Vale NW6 . . **78** A3
Kilburn Vale Est 🗓
NW6 . . . . **23** C4
Kildare Ct
W2 . . . . . . **31** C3 **113** A4
Kildare Gdns
W2 . . . . . . **31** C3 **113** A4
Kildare Rd E16 . . . . . . **35** C4
Kildare Terr
W2 . . . . . . **31** C3 **113** A4
Kildare Wlk E14 . . . . **33** C3
Kildoran Rd SW2 . . . . **62** A2
Kilgour Rd SE23 . . . . **66** A1
Kilkie St SW6 . . . . . . **166** C1
Killarney Rd SW18 . . **59** B1
Killick St N1 . . . . **84** C1
Killieser Ave SW2 . . . . **74** A2
Killip Cl E16 . . . . **35** B1
Killowen Rd E9 . . . . . . **17** C2
Killyon Rd SW8 . . . . **171** B1
Kilmaine Rd SW6 . . **154** B1
Kilmarsh Rd W6 . . . . **39** B2
Kilmington Rd
SW13 . . . . **46** C4
Kilmore Ho 🗓 E14 . . **34** A3
Kilmuir Ho SW1 . . **145** C3
Kiln Ct E14 . . . . **33** B2
Kilner Ho SE11 . . . . **163** B4
Kilner St E14 . . . . **33** C4
Kiln Pl NW5 . . . . **12** C3
Kiloh Ct 🗓 SW11 . . . . **60** A4
Kilpatrick Ct N16 . . . . **7** B3
Kilpeck Ho 🖪 N4 . . . . **6** B4
Kilravock St W3 . . . . **23** B2
Kimbell Gdns SW6 **164** A3
Kimber Ctr The
SW18 . . . . **58** C1
Kimberley Ave SE15 . . **65** B4
Kimberley Ho 🗓
E14 . . . . **42** B3
Kimberley Rd NW6 . . **23** A4
London SW9 . . . . **62** A4
Kimber Rd SW18 . . . . **71** A4
Kimble Ho NW8 . . . . **90** B2
🗓 London N7 . . . . . . **14** A3
Kimbolton Row
SW3 . . . . **144** A3
Kimpton Ct 🗓 SE5 . . **48** C2
Kimpton Ho SW15 . . **68** C4
Kimpton Rd SE5 . . . . **48** C2
Kinburn St SE16 . . . . **40** C4
Kincaid Rd SE15 . . . . **50** A3
Kincardine Gdns
W9 . . . . **23** C1
Kindell Ho 🖪 SW14 . . **55** C4
Kinder Ho N1 . . . . . . **87** C2
Kindersley Ho 🗓 E1 **111** C1
Kinder St 🗓 E1 . . . . . . **32** A3
Kinefold Ho N7 . . . . . . **14** A2
Kinfauns Rd SW2 . . . . **74** C2
King Alfred Sch
NW11 . . . . **2** C3
King Arthur Cl SE15 . . **50** B3

King Charles Ho
SW6 . . . . **156** B2
King Charles St
SW1 . . . . **134** A4
King Charles Wlk 🖪
SW19 . . . . **70** A3
King David La E1 . . . . **32** B2
Kingdon Ho 🖪 E14 . . **42** B3
Kingdon Rd NW6 . . . . **10** C2
King Edward Mans 🗓
E8 . . . . **25** A4
King Edward Mews
SW13 . . . . **46** C2
King Edwards Mans 🗓
SW6 . . . . **155** B1
King Edward's Rd
E9 . . . . **25** B4
King Edward St
EC1 . . . . **108** C2
King Edward The Third
Mews 🖪 SE16 . . . . **40** A4
King Edward Wlk
SE1 . . . . **135** C2
King Fahed Acad
W3 . . . . **29** B2
Kingfield St E14 . . . . **42** B2
Kingfisher Ct
🖪 E14 . . . . **42** C4
🗓 London SW11 . . . . **60** A4
Putney SW19 . . . . . . **70** A2
Kingfisher Ho
W14 . . . . **126** C2
London SE15 . . . . . . **49** B2
Kingfisher Mews
SE13 . . . . **67** A2
Kingfisher Sq 🗓
SE8 . . . . **51** B4
King Frederick IX Ct
SE16 . . . . **41** B3
King George Sq
TW10 . . . . **54** B1
King George St
SE10 . . . . **52** B3
Kingham Cl
🗓 London W11 . . . . **39** C4
Wandsworth SW18 . . **71** B4
King Henry's Rd
NW3 . . . . **12** A1
King Henry's Reach
W6 . . . . **47** B4
King Henry St N16 . . **16** A3
King Henry's Wlk
N1 . . . . **16** A2
King Henry's Yd 🖪
N16 . . . . **16** A3
King Ho W12 . . . . . . **30** A3
Kinghorn St EC1 . . **108** C3
King James Ct SE1 **136** B3
King John Ct EC2 . . . . **98** B2
King John St E1 . . . . . . **32** C4
Kinglake St SE17 . . **152** B2
Kingly Ct W1 . . . . . . **119** A4
Kingly St W1 . . . . . . **118** C4
King & Queen St
SE17 . . . . **151** A2
King's Arms Ct E1 **111** B3
King's Arms Yd
EC2 . . . . **109** B2
Kings Ave SW4 . . . . . . **62** A2
Kings Avenue Sch
SW4 . . . . **62** A3
King's Bench St
SE1 . . . . **136** B4
King's Bench Wlk
EC4 . . . . **107** C1

Kingsbridge Ho N1 .....6 C3
Kingsbridge Ave
W3 .....29 A1
Kingsbridge Ct E14 .41 C2
Kingsbridge Rd
W10 .....30 B3
Kingsbury Rd N1 .....16 A2
Kingsbury Terr N1 ..16 A2
Kingsclere Cl SW15 .68 C4
Kingscliffe Gdns
SW19 .....70 B3
King's Coll WC2 ...121 A4
London SE24 .....63 C1
Kings College Ct
NW3 .....12 A1
King's College Hospl
SE5 .....48 C1
King's College London
NW3 .....10 C4
Kings College Ct
NW3 .....11 C1
Kings Coll London
W8 .....127 B4
Kings Coll London
(Chelsea Campus)
SW3 .....144 A1
Kingscote NW11 .....1 B3
Kingscote Rd W4 ....37 C3
Kingscote St EC4 .122 A4
King's Court N
SW3 .....144 A1
Kingscourt Rd
SW16 .....74 A1
King's Court S
SW3 .....144 A1
King's Cres N4,N5 ....6 B1
Kingscroft SW4 .....62 A1
Kingscroft Rd NW2 .10 B2
Kings Cross WC1 ....94 B4
King's Cross Bridge
WC1 .....94 B4
King's Cross Rd
WC1 .....95 A3
Kingscroft Rd SW2 .74 C2
Kingsmead Way E5 .18 A4
Kingsmere Cl SW15 .57 C4
Kingsmere Pl N16 ....6 C3
Kingsmere Rd
SW19 .....69 C2
King's Mews WC1 ...95 A1
1 London SE4 .....66 A2
Kingsmill NW8 .....79 C2
Kingsmill Terr NW8 .79 C2
Kingsnorth Ho 12
W10 .....30 C3
King's Par
London W12 .....38 C3
Willesden NW10 .....22 B4
King's Pas E9 .....17 B2
King's Pl SE1 .....136 C3
Kings Pl W4 .....37 B2
King Sq EC1 .....96 C3
King's Quay SW10 .167 A4
King's Rd SW1 .....156 B1
SW3 .....144 A1
Kings Rd
Richmond NW10,TW9 .54 B2
King's Rd SW14 .....55 C4
Kings Ride Gate
TW10 .....54 C3
Kingsridge SW19 ....70 A2

Kingsgate Prim Sch
NW6 .....10 C1
Kingsgate Rd NW6 .10 C1
King's Gdns 6 NW6 .10 C1
King's Gr SE15 .....50 A3
London SE15 .....50 A2
Kings Hall Mews
SE13 .....67 B4
King's Head Yd
SE1 .....123 B1
Kingshill SE17 .....151 A4
Kings Ho 10 E14 ...33 B2
Kingshold Rd E9 ...17 B1
King's House Jun Sch
TW10 .....54 B2
King's House Prep Sch
TW10 .....54 A2
King's Keep 6
SW15 .....57 C2
Kingsland NW8 .....80 B3
Kingsland Gn 1 E8,
N1 .....16 A2
Kingsland High St
E8 .....16 A3
Kingsland Pas 2
E8 .....16 A2
Kingsland Rd E2 ...24 A3
London SE8 .....51 B4
Kingsland Sh Ctr 18 E8 .16 B2
Kingslawn Cl SW15 .57 A2
Kingsley Ct NW2 ....9 A2
Kingsley Flats SE1 .152 B3
Kingsley Ho SW3 .157 C3
London SW4 .....171 C2
Kingsley Mews
W8 .....128 B1
Kingsley Pl N6 .....3 C4
Kingsley Rd NW6 ..23 B4
Kingsley St SW11 ..60 B4
Kings Mall W6 .....39 B2
King's Mans SW3 .158 A3
Kingsmead TW10 ..54 B1
Kingsmead Ct N6 ....4 C4
Kingsmead Ho E9 ...18 A4
Kingsmead Prim Sch
E9 .....18 A4
Kingsmead Rd SW2 .74 C2
Kingsmead Way E5 .18 A4

King's Scholars' Pas
SW1 .....146 C4
King St EC2 .....109 A1
London W3 .....28 B1
London W6 .....38 C2
King Stairs Cl SE16 .40 A4
King's Terr NW1 ....82 C3
Kingston Ho 7
NW6 .....10 A1
Kingston Ho E
SW7 .....130 A3
Kingston Ho N
SW7 .....130 A3
Kingston Ho S
SW7 .....130 A3
Kingston Rd SW15,
SW19 .....69 A3
Kingston Univ
Roehampton Vale Ctr
SW15 .....68 B1
Kingston Vale SW15 .68 B1
Kingstown St NW1 .81 B4
King Street Cloisters 7
W6 .....39 A2
King Street Coll
London W1 .....39 B4
London W6 .....39 B2
Kingsway WC2 .....106 C2
Mortlake SW14,TW9 .55 A4
Kingsway Coll NW5 .13 A2
Kingsway Pl EC1 ....96 A2
Kingswear Rd NW5 ..4 A1
Kingswood 32 E2 ..25 B3
Kingswood Cl SW8 .162 B1
Kingswood Ct 7
TW10 .....54 B2
Kings Wood Ct 4
NW6 .....10 C1
Kingswood Rd
London W4 .....37 B3
Streatham SW2 .....74 A4
Kingswood Terr W4 .37 B3
Kings Yd E15 .....18 C2
Kington Ho NW6 ...78 B3
Kingward Ho E1 ...111 B4
King William La 3
SE10 .....43 A1
King William St
EC4 .....123 C4
King William Wlk
SE10 .....52 B4
Kingwood Rd SW6 .154 A1
Kinloch St N7 .....5 B1
Kinnaird Ave W4 ..45 B3
Kinnear Rd W12 ...38 B4
Kinnerton Pl N
SW1 .....131 A3
Kinnerton Pl S
SW1 .....131 A3
Kinnerton St SW1 .131 B3
Kinnerton Yd SW1 .131 B3
Kinnoull Mans 10
E5 .....17 A4
Kinnoull Rd W6 ...154 A4
Kinross Ho N1 .....84 C4
Kinsale Rd SE15 ...64 C4
Kinsham Ho 12
E2 .....99 C2
Kintore Way SE1 ..152 C4
Kintyre Ct 17 SW2 .74 A4
Kinver Ho N4 .....6 C4
Kipling Ho 28 SE5 .48 B3

Kipling St SE1 .....137 C4
Kipling Twr 3 W3 ..37 B3
Kirby Est SE16 .....40 A3
Kirby Gr SE1 .....138 A4
Kirby St EC1 .....107 C4
Kirkeby Bldg EC1 .107 C3
Kirkley Ho N16 .....7 A3
Kirkman Pl W1 ....105 B3
Kirkmichael Rd E14 .34 B3
Kirkside Rd SE3 ...53 C4
Kirk's Pl E3 .....33 B4
Kirkstall Gdns SW2 .74 A3
Kirkstall Ho SW1 ..146 A2
Kirkstall Rd SW2 ..74 A3
Kirkstead Ct E5 ...18 A4
Kirkstone NW1 .....92 C4
Kirkton Lo SW18 ..59 A1
Kirkwall Pl E2 .....25 B2
Kirkwood Rd SE15 .50 A1
Kirtley Ho SW8 ...171 A4
Kirtling St SW8 ...160 C2
Kirton Cl W4 .....37 C2
Kirwin Way SE5 ...48 A3
Kitcat Terr E3 .....26 C2
Kite Ho 5 SW11 ...60 A4
Kitson Rd SE5 .....48 B3
Barnes SW13 .....46 C2
Kittiwake Ct 20 SE8 .51 B4
Kitto Rd SE14 .....50 C1
Kiver Rd N19 .....5 A2
Klea Ave SW4 .....61 B1
Kleffens Ct 2 SE3 .53 B3
Knapp Cl NW10 .....8 A2
Knapp Rd E3 .....26 C1
Knaresborough Dr
SW18 .....71 A3
Knaresborough Ho 4
N4 .....6 B4
Knaresborough Pl
SW5 .....142 A4
Knatchbull Rd
London NW10 .....20 C4
London SE5 .....48 A2
Knebworth Ho
SW8 .....171 C3
2 London N16 .....16 A4
Knebworth Rd 3
N16 .....16 A4
Kneller Ho SW8 ...171 C2
Kneller Rd SE4 ....66 A3
Knighten St E1 ....32 A1
Knighthead Point
E14 .....41 C4
Knight Ho SE17 ...152 A3
Knightleas Ct NW2 ..9 B2
Knightrider Ct EC4 .122 C4
Knightrider St EC4 .122 B4
Knights Arc SW1 ..130 C3
Knights Cl E9 .....17 B3
Knights Ho SE1 ...138 C4
SW10 .....140 C2
SW8 .....162 B2
Knight's Ho SW10 .156 C2
Knights Rd E16 ....35 C1
Knight's Wlk SE11 .150 A3
Knightswood Ct N6 ..4 C4
Knivet Rd SW6 ....155 B3
Knobs Hill Rd E15 .27 A4
Knoll Ho NW8 .....78 C2

Knoll Rd SW18 .....59 B2
Knolly's Cl SE27,
SW16 .....74 C1
Knolly's Rd SE27,
SW16 .....74 C1
Knot Ho SE1 .....124 C1
Knottisford St E2 ..25 B2
Knowlden Ho 4 E1 .32 B2
Knowle Cl SW9 ....62 C4
Knowles Hill Cres
SE13 .....67 C2
Knowles Ho
London NW10 .....21 C4
Wandsworth SW18 ..59 A1
Knowles Wlk SW4 .61 B4
Knowlton Ho SW9 .173 C4
Knowsley Rd
SW11 .....168 C1
Knox Ct SW4 .....172 B2
Knox Ho SW15 ....47 B1
Knox St W1 .....102 C4
Knoyle Ho W14 ...126 B2
Knoyle St SE14 ....51 A4
Kobi Nazrul Prim Sch
E1 .....111 C2
Kossuth St SE10 ...43 A1
Kotree Way SE1 ...153 C4
Kramer Mews
SW5 .....142 A1
Kreedman Wlk 8
E8 .....16 C3
Kreisel Wlk TW9 ..44 B4
Kylemore Ct 4
W12 .....38 C4
Kylemore Rd NW6 .10 C1
Kylestrome Ho
SW1 .....145 C3
Kynance Mews
SW7 .....128 B1
Kynance Pl SW7 ..128 C1
Kynaston Ho 7
SW2 .....74 B3
Kynaston Rd N16 ...7 A1
Kyrle Rd SW11 ....60 C1
Kyverdale Rd N16 ..7 B3

L

Laburnham Cl 5
SE15 .....50 B3
Laburnham Ct NW2 ..1 B2
Laburnham Ho SE4 .51 B1
Laburnum Ct 20 E2 .24 B4
Laburnum Ho 4 N16 ..6 C2
Laburnum JMI Sch
E2 .....24 B4
Laburnum St E2 ...24 B4
Lacey Ho 6 SE13 ..52 B1
Lacey Wlk E3 .....26 C3
Lacine Ct 20 SE16 .40 C4
Lackington St EC2 .109 C4
Lackland Ho SE1 ..153 A2
Lacland Ho SW10 .157 B2
Lacon Rd SE22 ....64 C3
Lacy Rd SW15 ....57 C3
Ladbroke Cres 1 W11 .31 A3
Ladbroke Gdns
W11 .....31 B2 112 C4
Ladbroke Gr W10 ..31 A4
W11 .....31 B2 112 C4
Ladbroke Grove Ho 6
W11 .....112 C4
Ladbroke Grove Sta
W10 .....31 A3
Ladbroke Mews
W11 .....112 B1

Ladbroke Rd
W11 ....31 B1 112 C2
Ladbroke Sq
W11 ....31 B2 113 A3
Ladbroke Terr
W11 ....31 B1 113 A2
Ladbroke Wlk
W11 ....31 B1 113 A2
Ladlands SE22 ......76 C4
Ladybower Ct 6 SE5 .17 C4
Ladycroft Rd SE13 ...67 A4
Lady Elizabeth Ho
SW14 ....55 B4
Lady Florence Ctyd 14
SE8 ....51 C3
Lady Margaret Rd
NW5 ....13 B3
Lady Margaret Sch
SW6 ....165 B3
Lady Somerset Rd
NW5 ....13 A4
Ladywell Cl SE4 ....66 C3
Ladywell Hts SE4 ...66 C1
Ladywell Rd SE13 ...67 A2
Ladywell Sta SE13 ..67 A2
Ladywell Water Twr
SE4 ....66 C2
Lafitte Ho 20 N19 ..4 C4
Lafone Ho 11 SW2 ..74 A4
Lafone St SE1 .....138 C4
Lagado Mews SE16 .32 C1
Lagonda Ho 11 E3 ..26 C1
Lagonier Rd EC1 ....97 A3
Laindon Ho 6 N16 ..7 B3
Laing Ho SE5 ....48 B3
Lainson St SW18 ....70 C4
Lairdale Cl SE21 ....75 B4
Laird Ho SE5 ....48 B3
Lairs Cl N7 ....14 A2
Laitwood Rd SW12 ..73 A3
Lakanal 14 SE5 ....49 A2
Lake Ho SE1 ....136 C3
Laker Ct SW4 ......172 B2
Laker Pl SW15 .....58 A1
Lakeside Ct N4 ......6 B3
Lakeside Rd W14 ....39 C3
Lakeview 23 E3 .....25 C3
Lake View Ct SW1 ..132 B2
Lakis Cl NW3 ....11 B4
Laleham Ho E2 .....98 C2
Lamb Ct 18 E14 .....33 A2
Lamberhurst Ho 14
SE15 ....50 B4
Lambert Ave TW9 ...55 A4
Lambert Ho
10 London N19 ....4 C4
London SW9 ....173 B1
Lambert Rd SW2 ....62 B2
Lambert St N1 ......14 C1
Lambeth Coll (Brixton Ctr) SW2 ......62 B2
Lambeth Coll (Clapham Ctr) SW4 ......61 B2
Lambeth Coll (Tower Bridge Ctr) SE1 ..124 B1
Lambeth Coll (Vauxhall Ctr) SW8 .....171 B4
Lambeth Ct 8
SW18 ....58 C2
Lambeth High St
SE1 ....148 C4
Lambeth Hill EC4 ...122 C4
Lambeth Hospl SW9 62 B4
Lambeth Inst Strand Ctr
SW2 ....74 B4
Lambeth North Sta
SE1 ....135 B2

Lambeth Palace★
SE1 ....134 C1
Lambeth Palace Rd
SE1 ....134 C2
Lambeth Pier SE1 ..134 B1
Lambeth Rd SE1 ....135 B1
Lambeth Twrs
SE11 ....149 A4
Lambfold Ho N7 ....14 A2
Lamble St NW5 .....12 C4
Lambolle Pl NW3 ....12 A2
Lambolle Rd NW3 ...12 A2
Lambourn Cl 9
NW5 ....13 B4
Lambourne Ho
NW8 ....101 C4
SE16 ....40 C2
Lambrook Ho 12
SE15 ....49 C2
Lambrook Terr
SW6 ....164 A4
Lamb's Bldgs EC1 ...97 B1
Lamb's Conduit Pas
WC1 ....106 C4
Lamb's Conduit St
WC1 ....94 C1
Lamb's Mews N1 ....86 A3
Lamb's Pas EC1 .....97 B1
Lamb St E1 ....110 C4
Lambton Ct 2 N19 ..5 A3
Lambton Pl W11 ....113 A4
Lambton Rd N19 .....5 A3
Lamb Wlk SE1 ......138 A3
Lamerton Lo 10
TW9 ....44 B2
Lamerton St 9 SE8 ..51 C4
Lamington St 8
W6 ....39 A2
Lamlash St SE11 ...150 A4
Lamley Ho SE10 .....52 A3
Lammas Rd E9 ......17 C1
Lammermoor Rd
SW12 ....73 A4
Lamont Rd SW10 ...157 B3
Lamont Rd Pas
SW10 ....157 B3
Lampard Gr N16 .....7 B3
Lampern Sq 22 E2 ..99 C4
Lampeter Sq W6 ....154 A3
Lamplighter Cl 31
E1 ....25 B1
Lampson Ho 8 N19 ..13 B4
Lanark Ho SE1 .....153 B1
Lanark Mans W9 ....89 A2
6 London W12 ......39 B4
Lanark Pl W9 ....89 A2
Lanark Rd W9 ....88 C3
Lanark Sq E14 ......42 A3
Lanbury Rd SE15 ....65 C3
Lancashire Ct W1 ..118 B4
Lancaster Ave SE21,
SE27 ....75 B2
Lancaster Cl W2 ....114 A3
9 London N1 ....16 A1
Lancaster Cotts 1
TW10 ....54 A1
Lancaster Ct SW6 ..155 A1
W2 ....115 A4
West Norwood SE27 ..75 A2
Lancaster Dr E14 ....34 B1
London NW3 ....12 A2

Lancaster Gate
W2 ....115 A4
Lancaster Gate Sta
W2 ....115 A4
Lancaster Gr NW3 ...12 A2
Lancaster Hall 1
E16 ....35 C1
Lancaster Lo 2
W11 ....31 A3
Lancaster Mews
3 London SW18 .....59 A2
2 Richmond TW10 ...54 A1
Lancaster Pk TW10 ..54 A2
Lancaster Pl WC2 ...120 C3
Lancaster Rd N4 .....5 B4
London N4 ....5 C4
London NW10 ....8 C3
Lancaster St SE1 ...136 B3
Lancaster Stables 12
NW3 ....12 A2
Lancaster Terr W2 ..115 B4
Lancaster Wlk W2 ..115 A2
Lancefield Ct 11
N4 ....23 A3
Lancefield Ho SE15 .65 A4
Lancefield St W10 ...23 B2
Lancell St N16 ....7 A2
Lancelot Pl SW7 ....130 C3
Lancer Sq 21 W8 ...128 A4
Lanchester Ct W2 ...102 C1
Lancing St NW1 .....93 B3
Lancresse Ct N1 ....24 A4
Landale Ho 13 SE16 .40 B3
Landcroft Rd SE22 ..64 B1
Landells Rd SE22 ....64 C1
Landford Rd SW15 ...57 B4
Landin Ho 4 E14 ....33 C3
Landleys Field 21
N7 ....13 C3
Landmann Ho 16
SE16 ....40 A2
Landmann Way
SE14 ....50 C4
Landon Pl SW1 .....130 C2
Landons Cl E14 .....34 B1
Landon Wlk 11 E14 ..34 A2
Landor Ct N16 ....16 A3
Landor Ho 7 SE5 ....48 C3
Landor Rd SW9 .....62 A4
Landor Wlk 11 W12 ..38 C4
Landrake NW1 ....83 A3
Landridge Rd SW6 ..164 C2
Landseer Ho NW8 ....89 C2
SW1 ....147 C3
London SW11 ....169 C3
Landseer Rd N19 .....5 A2
Landulph Ho SE11 ..149 C2
Landward Ct W1 ....102 B2
Lane Ct SW11 ......72 B4
Lanercost Cl SW2 ...74 C2
Lanercost Rd SW2 ...74 C2
Lane The NW8 ......78 C1
Laneway SW15 ......57 A2
Laney Bldg EC1 .....107 C3
Lanfranc Rd E3 .....26 A3
Lanfrey Pl W14 .....140 C1
Langbourne Ave N6 ..3 C2
Langbourne Ho 7
SE21 ....76 A1
Langbourne Mans
N6 ....3 C2
Langbourne Pl E14 ..42 A1
Langbourne Prim Sch
SE21 ....76 A1
Langdale NW1 ......92 C4

Langdale Cl SE17 ....48 B4
Mortlake SW14 ......55 A3
Langdale Ho SW1 ..146 C1
Langdale Rd SE10 ...52 B3
Langdale St 3 E1 ...32 A3
Langdon Ct EC1 .....86 B1
London NW10 ....21 A4
Langdon Ho 3 E14 ..34 B3
Langdon Park N6 ....4 B4
Langdon Park Sec Sch
E14 ....34 B3
Langdon Pl SW14 ...55 B4
Langdon Way SE1 ..153 C3
Langford Cl NW8 ....79 A2
London E8 ....16 C3
Langford Ct NW8 ....79 A1
Langford Gn SE5 ....64 A4
Langford Ho 5 SE8 ..51 C4
Langford Pl NW8 ....79 A2
Langford Prim Sch
SW6 ....166 B2
Langford Rd SW6 ...166 B2
Langham Ct 4
SW15 ....57 C2
Langham Ho SW4 ....61 B2
Langham Mans
SW5 ....142 A1
Langham Pl W1 ....104 B3
Chiswick W4 ....46 A4
Langham St W1 ....104 B3
Lang Ho 3 N19 .....4 B1
SW8 ....162 A1
Langholm Cl SW12 ..73 C4
Langhorne Ct 10
NW8 ....11 C1
Langhurst Ho
SW11 ....169 B2
Langland Gdns
NW3 ....11 A3
Langland Ho 10 SE5 .48 C3
Langland Mans
NW3 ....11 A3
Langler Rd NW10 ....22 B3
Langley Ct SW9 ....172 A4
WC2 ....120 A4
Langley Dr W3 ....37 A4
Langley Ho
11 London E5 ....17 A3
22 London W2 ....31 C4
Langley La SW8 ....162 B4
Langley Mans SW8 ..162 B4
Langley St WC2 ....106 A1
Langmead Ho 34 E3 .27 A2
Langmore Ho 11 .....111 C1
Langport Ho
SW9 ....48 A1
Langridge 18 NW5 ..12 C2
Langroyd Rd SW17 ..72 B2
Langside Ave SW15 ..56 C3
Langston Hughes Cl 8
SE24 ....63 A3
Langthorn Ct EC2 ..109 C2
Langthorne Lo 20
SW2 ....74 C4
Langthorne St SW6 ..47 C2
Langton Cl WC1 .....95 A2
Langton Ho SE11 ...149 A4
Langton Pl SW18 ....70 C3
Langton Rd SW9 ....48 A3
Langton St SW10 ...157 A3
Langton Way SE3 ...53 C3
Langtry Pl SW6 .....155 C4
Langtry Rd NW8 ....78 B3
Langtry Wlk NW8 ....78 C4
Lanhill Rd W9 ....23 C1
Lanier Rd SE13 .....67 C1
Lanner Ho 2 SW11 ..60 A4

Lannoy Point SW6 ..154 B2
Lanrick Rd E14 ......35 A3
Lansbury Gdns 11
E14 ....34 C3
Lanscombe Wlk
SW8 ....162 A1
Lansdowne Cres
W11 ....31 A2 112 C3
Lansdowne Dr E8 ...16 C1
Lansdowne Gdns
SW8 ....172 A4
Lansdowne Gr NW10 .8 A4
Lansdowne Hill
SE27 ....75 A1
Lansdowne Ho
W11 ....112 C3
Lansdowne Mews
W11 ....112 C3
Lansdowne Pl SE1 ..137 C2
Lansdowne Rd
W11 ....31 A2 112 B3
London E8 ....16 C2
Lansdowne Rise
W11 ....31 A2 112 B3
Lansdowne Row
W1 ....118 B2
Lansdowne Sch
SW9 ....62 B4
Lansdowne Terr
WC1 ....94 B1
Lansdowne Way
SW4,SW8 ....172 B3
Lansdowne Wlk
W11 ....31 A2 112 C3
Lansdowne Wood Cl 11
SE27 ....75 A1
Lansdown Ho 28
SE5 ....48 B1
Lantern Cl SW15 ....56 C3
Lantern Ho E14 .....41 C4
Lanterns Ct E14 .....41 C3
Lant Ho SE1 ....136 C3
Lant St SE1 ....28 A1
Lantry Ct 3 W3 .....28 A1
Lanvanor Rd SE15 ..50 B1
Lanyard Ho 3 SE8 ...41 B2
Lapford Cl W9 ......23 B1
Lapsang SE1 ....125 A1
Lapwing Twr 51 SE8 .51 B4
Lapworth Ct W2 ....100 B4
Lara Cl SE13 ....67 B1
Larch Ave W3 ....29 A1
Larch Cl 16 E8 ......25 B1
Balham SW12 ....73 A2
7 London N19 ....4 B2
Larch Ct 19 W2 .....23 A1
Larches Ave SW14 ..55 C3
Larchfield Ho 2 N5 .15 B3
Larch Ho 18 SE16 ...40 B4
London W10 ....23 A1
Larchmore Ct N19 ...5 A2
Larch Rd NW2 ....9 B4
Larcom St SE17 ....151 A3
Larden Rd W3 ....38 A4
La Retraite RC Girls Sch
SW12 ....73 B4
Larissa St SE17 ....151 C3
Larix Ct NW10 ......21 C4
Larkfield Rd TW9 ...54 A3
Lark Hall Inf Sch
SW4 ....172 A1
Lark Hall Jun Sch
SW4 ....172 B1
Larkhall La SW4 ....172 A3
Larkhall Rise SW4 ..171 B1
Lark Row E2 ....25 B4

Larmenier & Sacred
Heart RC Prim Sch
　W6 ....39 C2
Larnaca Ho SE1 ....138 C2
Larnach Rd N6 ....47 C4
Larpent Ave SW15 ....57 B2
La Saint Union RC Sec
　Sch NW5 ....3 C1
Lascelles Ho NW1 ......90 B1
Lassell St SE10 ....42 C1
Lasseter Pl SE3 ....53 B4
Latchmere Rd
　SW11 ....168 C2
Latchmere St
　SW11 ....168 C2
Latham Ho E1 ....32 C3
Latimer SE17 ....152 A1
Latimer Ho W10 ......113 A3
　🚇 London E9 ....17 C2
Latimer Pl W10 ....30 B3
Latimer Rd W10 ....30 B3
Latimer Road Sta
　W10 ....30 B3
Latona Rd SE15 ....49 C4
Lattimer Pl W4 ....46 A4
Latymer Ct W6 ....39 C2
Latymer Upper Sch
　W6 ....38 C1
Lauderdale Mans
　W9 ....88 B3
Lauderdale Rd W9 ....88 C3
Lauderdale Twr
　EC2 ....108 C4
Laud St SE11 ....148 C2
Laughton Ho 🔟
　SW2 ....62 C1
Launcelot St SE1 ....135 B3
Launceston Pl W8 ....128 C1
Launch St E14 ....42 B3
Laundress La N16 ......7 C1
Laundry La 🔟 N1 ......15 B1
Laundry Rd W6 ....154 A3
Laura Pl E5 ....17 B4
Laurel Bank Gdns
　SW6 ....165 A2
Laurel Cl 🔟 N19 ....4 B2
Laurel Ct London E8 ..16 B2
　🔁 Putney SW15 ......57 C2
Laurel Rd SW13 ......46 C1
Laurel St E8 ....16 B2
Laurence Mews 🔟
　W12 ....38 C4
Laurence Pountney Hill
　EC4 ....123 C4
Laurence Pountney La
　EC4 ....123 C4
Laurie Gr SE14 ....51 A2
Laurie Ho SE1 ....136 B1
　W8 ....31 C1 113 B1
Laurier Rd NW5 ....4 A1
Lauriston Lo NW6 ....10 B2
Lauriston Rd E9 ....17 C1
　Lauriston Sch E9 ....25 C4
Lausanne Rd SE15 ....50 B2
Lavell St N16 ....15 C4
Lavender Cl SW3 ....157 C3
Lavender Ct SW4 ....172 B3
Lavender Gdns
　SW11 ....60 B3
Lavender Gr E8 ....16 C1
Lavender Hill SW11 ..60 C4
Lavender Ho 🔟
　SE16 ....32 C1

Lavender Rd SE16 ....33 A1
　London SW11 ....59 C4
Lavender Sweep
　SW11 ....60 B3
Lavender Terr 🔟
　SW11 ....60 A4
Lavender Wlk SW11 ..60 B3
Lavendon Ho NW8 ....90 B2
Lavengro Rd SE27 ....75 B2
Lavenham Rd SW18 ..70 C3
Lavers Rd N16 ....7 A1
Laverstoke Gdns
　SW15 ....68 C4
Laverton Mews
　SW5 ....142 B3
Laverton Pl SW5 ....142 B3
Lavina Gr N1 ....84 C2
Lavington Cl E9 ....18 B2
Lavington St SE1 ....122 B1
Lawdale Jun Sch
　E2 ....24 C2 99 C4
Lawford Rd
　Chiswick W4 ....45 B3
　London N1 ....16 A1
　London NW5 ....13 B2
Lawfords Wharf 🔟
　NW1 ....13 B1
Lawless Ho 🔟 E14 ....34 B2
Lawless St 🔟 E14 ....34 A2
Lawley St E5 ....17 B4
Lawman Ct 🔟 TW9 ..44 B2
Lawn Cres TW9 ....44 C1
Lawnfield NW6 ....9 C1
Lawn House Cl E14 ..42 B4
Lawn La SW8 ....162 C4
Lawn Rd NW3 ....12 B3
Lawns The N16 ....16 A3
Lawrence Cl E3 ....26 C3
　🔟 London W12 ....30 A2
Lawrence Ct
　London N16 ....7 B1
　London W3 ....37 B3
Lawrence Ho 🔟
　SW1 ....147 C3
Lawrence La EC2 ....109 A2
Lawrence Mans
　SW3 ....158 A3
Lawrence Pl N1 ....84 B4
Lawrence's Bldgs 🔟
　　.................................7 B1
Lawrence St E16 ......35 B2
　SW3 ....158 A3
Lawrence Trad Est
　SE10 ....43 A2
Lawson Cl SW19 ......69 C1
Lawson Ct 🔟 N4 ......5 B3
Lawson Ho 🔟 W12 ..30 A2
Law St SE1 ....137 C2
Laxton Rd E3 ....26 A2
Laxfield Ct E8 ....24 C4
Laxley Cl SE5 ....48 A3
Laxton Path 🔟 SE4 ..65 C3
Laxton Pl NW1 ....92 B2
Layard Rd SE16 ....40 A2
Layard Sq SE16 ....40 A2
Laycock Prim Sch
　N1 ....15 A2
Laycock St N1 ....14 C2
Layfield Ho 🔟 SE10 ..43 C1
Laystall Ct EC1 ....95 B1
Laystall St EC1 ....95 B1
Layton Pl TW9 ....44 C2
Lazar Wlk 🔟 N7 ....5 B2
Leabank Sq E9 ....18 C2
Leabourne Rd N16 ....7 B4
Leacroft Ave SW12 ..72 B4
Lea Ct 🔟 W12 ....38 A4

Leadenhall Mkt
　EC3 ....110 A1
Leadenhall Pl EC3 ..110 A1
Leadenhall St EC3 ..110 A1
Leadenham Ct 🔟
　　.................................26 C1
Lea Ho NW8 ....90 A1
Lea Int E9 ....18 C3
Leake St SE1 ....135 A4 135 B3
Leamington Ct
　🔟 Forest Hill SE26 ..76 C1
　London W3 ....28 C4
Leamington Ho 🔟
　W11 ....31 B4
Leamington Pk W3 ..28 C4
Leamington Rd Villas
　W11 ....31 B4
Leamore St W6 ....39 B2
Leamouth Rd E14 ....34 C3
Leander Ct
　🔟 London E17 ....17 B1
　London SE8 ....51 C2
Leander Rd SW2 ......62 C1
Leary Ho SE11 ....149 A1
Leatherdale St 🔟
　E1 ....25 B1
Leatherhead Cl N16 ..7 B3
Leather La EC1 ....107 C4
Leathermarket Ct
　SE1 ....138 A3
Leathermarket St
　SE1 ....138 A3
Leathwaite Rd
　SW11 ....60 B2
Leathwell Rd SE8 ....52 A1
Lebanon Gdns
　SW18 ....58 C1
Lebanon Rd SW18 ....58 C2
Lebus Ho NW8 ....80 A1
Lechmere Rd NW2 ....9 A2
Leckford Rd SW18 ....71 B3
Leckhampton Pl 🔟
　SW2 ....74 C4
Lecky St SW7 ....143 B2
L'Ecole des Petits Sch
　SW6 ....166 B2
Leconfield Ave
　SW13,SW15 ....56 B4
Leconfield Ho SE5 ....64 A4
Leconfield Rd N5 ....15 C4
Leda Ct SW9 ....163 B1
Ledam Bldg EC1 ....107 C3
Ledbury Ho 🔟 SE22 ..64 A4
Ledbury Mews N
　W11 ....31 C2 113 B4
Ledbury Mews W
　W11 ....113 B4
Ledbury Rd
　W11 ....31 C3 113 B4
Ledbury St SE15 ......49 C3
Ledo Ho 🔟 N16 ......15 C4
Lee Conservancy Rd
　E9 ....18 B3
Leeds Ct EC1 ....96 A2
Lee Ho 🔟 N19 ....13 C3
Leeke St WC1 ....94 C4
Leeland Way NW10 ..8 B4
Leerdam Dr E14 ......42 B3
Lees Ct W1 ....117 B4
Leeson Rd 🔟 SE24 ..62 C3
Lees Pl W1 ....117 B4
Lee St E8 ....24 B4
Leet Ct N16 ....15 C4
Lee Valley Tp Ctr
　E15 ....19 A4

Leeve Ho 🔟 W9 ......23 B2
Leeward Ct E1 ....125 C2
Leeway SE8 ....41 B1
Lefevre Wlk E3 ....26 B4
Leffern Rd W12 ....38 C4
Leff Ho 🔟 NW6 ....10 A1
Lefroy Ho SE1 ....136 C3
Lefroy Rd W12 ....38 B4
Legard Rd N5 ....6 A1
Leggatt Rd E15 ....27 B3
Legge St SE13 ....67 B2
Leghorn Rd NW10 ..21 C3
Legion Cl N1 ....14 C1
Legion Terr E3 ....26 C4
Leicester Ct WC2 ....119 C4
　🔟 London W3 ....31 C4
Leicester Ho
　🔟 London SW9 ......63 A4
　🔁 Putney SW15 ....69 B4
Leicester Pl WC2 ....119 C4
Leicester Sq*
　WC2 ....119 C4
Leicester Square Sta
　WC2 ....119 C4
Leicester St WC2 ....119 C4
Leigham Ave SW16 ..74 A1
Leigham Hall 🔟
　SW16 ....74 A1
Leigham Hall Par 🔟
　SW16 ....74 A1
Leigham Vale SE27,
　SW16,SW2 ....74 C2
Leigh Ct 🔁 SW2 ......62 C1
Leighfield Ho 🔟 N4 ..6 A4
Leigh Gdns NW10 ..22 B3
Leigh Ho 🔁 SW15 ....56 C2
Leigh Orchard Cl
　SW16 ....74 B1
Leigh Pl EC1 ....107 B4
Leigh Rd N5 ....15 A4
Leigh St WC1 ....94 A3
Leighton Cres NW5 ..13 B3
Leighton Gdns
　NW10 ....22 B3
Leighton Gr NW5 ....13 B3
Leighton House (Art
　Gall & Mus) W14 ..127 A2
Leighton Pl NW5 ....13 B3
Leighton Rd NW5 ..13 B3
Leinster Ave SW14 ..55 B3
Leinster Ct NW6 ......23 C2
Leinster Gdns W2 ..114 C4
Leinster Mews W2 ..114 C4
Leinster Pl W2 ....100 C1
Leinster Sq W2 ......100 A1
Leinster Terr W2 ....114 C4
Leitch Ho 🔟 NW8 ....11 C1
Leithcote Path
　SW16 ....74 B1
Leith Ho
　🔟 London N7 ....13 C3
　🔟 Streatham SW2 ..74 A4
Leith Mans W9 ....88 A3
Leith Yd 🔟 NW6 ......10 C1
Lelitia Cl E8 ....24 C4
Leman St E1 ....111 A1
Lemmon Rd SE10 ....53 A4
Le Moal Ho 🔟 E1 ....32 B4
Lemsford Ct N4 ....6 B2
Lena Gardens Prim Sch
　W6 ....39 B3
Lena Gdns W6 ....39 B3
Lendal Terr 🔟 SW4 ..61 C4
Len Freeman Pl
　SW6 ....154 C3
Lenham 🔟 NW5 ......12 C2
Lenham Ho SE1 ......137 C3

Lennon Rd NW2 ....9 B2
Lennox Gdns SW1 ..130 C1
　London NW10 ....8 B4
Lennox Gdns Mews
　SW1 ....144 C4
Lennox Ho 🔟 E9 ......17 B2
Lennox Rd N4,N7 ......5 C2
Lenthall Ho SW1 ....147 A1
Lenthall Rd E8 ....16 C1
Lenthorp Rd SE10 ..43 B2
Lenton Rise TW9 ......54 A4
Len Williams Ct
　NW6 ....23 C3
Leonard Ct W8 ......127 B2
　WC1 ....94 A2
Leonard Day Ho 🔟
　NW5 ....13 A2
Leonard Pl 🔟 N16 ..16 A4
Leonard St EC2 ....97 C2
Leonora Ho W9 ....88 C2
Leontine Cl SE15 ......49 C3
Leopards Ct EC1 ....107 B4
Leopold Bldgs 🔟 E2 ..98 C4
Leopold Mews 🔟 E9 ..25 B4
Leopold Prim Sch
　NW10 ....8 B1
Leopold Rd NW10 ....8 A1
Leopold St E3 ....33 B4
Leopold Wlk SE11 ..148 C1
Leo St SE15 ....50 A3
Leo Yd EC1 ....96 B1
Leppoc Rd SW4 ....61 C2
Leroy St SE1 ....152 A4
Lerry Cl W14 ....154 C4
Lerwick Ho SW18 ....59 B3
Leslie Rd E11 ....19 C4
Lessar Ave SW4 ....61 B1
Lessar Ct SW4 ....61 B1
Lester Ct 🔟 E3 ....27 A2
Leston Pl N16 ....7 B1
Leswin Rd N16 ....7 B1
Letchford Gdns
　NW10 ....21 C2
Letchford Mews
　NW10 ....21 C2
Letchmore Ho W10 ..22 B1
Lethaby Ho 🔟 SW4 ..62 A3
Lethbridge Cl SE13 ..52 B1
Letterstone Rd
　SW6 ....154 C1
Lettice St SW6 ......165 A3
Lett Rd E15 ....19 C1
Lettsom St SE5 ....49 A1
Levana Cl SW19 ......70 A3
Levant Ho 🔟 E1 ......25 C1
Levehurst Way
　SW4,SW9 ....172 B2
Leven Rd E14 ....34 C3
Lever Ct 🔟 E9 ....17 C2
Leverett St SW3 ....144 B4
Leverington Pl N1 ....97 C3
Lever St EC1 ....96 C3
Leverstock Ho
　SW3 ....144 B2
Leverton Pl NW5 ....13 B3
Leverton St NW5 ....13 B3
Levison Way 🔁 N19 ..4 C3
Levita Ho NW1 ....93 C4
Levyne Ct EC1 ....95 B2
Lewesdon Cl 🔟
　SW19 ....69 C3
Lewes Ho SE1 ....138 B4
　SE15 ....49 C4
Leweston Pl N16 ......7 B4
Lewey Ho E3 ....26 B1
Lewin Rd SW14 ......55 C4
Lewis Ct 🔟 SE16 ....40 A1

Lewis Gr SE13 ......67 B4
Lewisham Bridge Prim
  Sch SE13 ....67 A4
Lewisham Bsns Ctr
  SE14 ....50 C4
Lewisham Coll Sch
  SE14 ....51 C1
Lewisham Ctr SE13 ...67 B3
Lewisham High St
  SE13 ....67 A2
Lewisham Hill SE13 .52 B1
Lewisham Hospl
  SE13 ....67 A2
Lewisham Pk SE13 ...67 B2
Lewisham Rd SE13 ...52 B1
Lewisham St SW1 ...133 C3
Lewisham Sta SE13 ...67 A2
Lewisham Way SE4,
  SE14 ....51 B2
Lewis Pl E8 ....16 C3
Lewis Silkin Ho �
  SE15 ....50 B4
Lewis St NW1 ....13 A2
Lexden Rd W3 ....28 A1
Lexfield Ho N5 ......15 B4
Lexham Gardens Mews
  W8 ....128 B1
Lexham Gdns W8 ...142 A4
Lexham Mews W8 ..141 C4
Lexham Wlk W8 ....128 B1
Lexington St W1 ....119 A4
Lexton Gdns SW12 ...73 C3
Leybourne Ho ﬂ E14 .44 C2
Leybourne Ho 🟔
  🟕ﬗ E14 ....33 B3
  🟖 SE15 ....50 B4
Leybourne Rd 🟗
  NW1 ....13 A1
Leybourne St 🟘
  NW1 ....13 A1
Leyden Mews 🟙 N19 ..5 A4
Leyden St E1 ....110 C3
Leydon Cl SE16 .....32 C1
Ley Ho 🟚 SE1 ......136 A3
Leyland Ho 🟛 E14 ..34 A2
Leylands SW18 ....58 B1
Leylang Rd SE14 .....50 C3
Leys Ct SW9 ....173 B1
Leysdown 🟜 NW5 ...12 C2
Leysdown Ho SE17 .152 B2
Leysfield Rd W12 ....38 C4
Leythe Rd W3 ....37 B4
Leyton Rd E15 ....19 C2
Liardet St SE14 .....51 A4
Liberia Rd N5 ....15 A2
Liberty Mews SW12 ..61 A1
Liberty Pl E1 ....125 C3
Liberty St SW9 .....173 A4
Libra Rd 🟝 E3 ......26 B3
Library Mans 🟞
  W12 ....39 B4
Library Par NW10 ....21 A4
Library Pl E1 ....32 A2
Library St SE1 ......136 B3
Lichfield Ct TW9 ....54 A3
Lichfield Gdns
  TW10,TW9 ....54 A2
Lichfield Ho 🟟 SE5 .48 B1
Lichfield Rd E3 .....26 A2
  London NW2 ....10 A4
  Richmond TW9 .....44 C1
Lichfield Terr 🟠
  TW9 ....54 A2
Lichport Ct N4 ....6 A3
Lickey Ho W14 .....155 A4
Lidcote Gdns SW9 ..173 A1
Liddell Gdns NW10 ..22 B3
Liddell Rd NW6 .....10 C2

Lidfield Rd N16 .....15 C4
Lidgate Rd 🟡 SE15 .49 B3
Lidiard Rd SW18 .....71 B2
Lidlington Pl NW1 ...83 A1
Lidyard Rd N19 ....4 B3
Liffey Ct NW10 ......8 C1
Liffords Pl SW13 ....46 B1
Lifford St SW15 .....57 C3
Ligatrer Cl 🟢 SE16 ..41 A2
Lighterman Mews 🟣
  E1 ....32 C3
Lighterman's Rd
  E14 ....42 A4
Lighterman's Wlk
  SW18 ....58 C3
Ligonier St 🟤 E2 ...98 C2
Lilac Ho SE4 ....66 B4
Lilac Pl SE11 ....148 C3
Lilac St W12 ....29 C2
Lilburn St SW15 .....57 C4
Lilestone Est NW8 ..89 C1
Lilestone Ho NW8 ...89 C2
Lilestone St NW8 ....90 A2
Liford Rd 🟥 SE5 ....48 B1
Liford Rd SE5 ....48 A1
Lilian Baylis Ho N1 .15 B2
Lilian Baylis Sch
  🟦 SE11 ....148 C2
Lilley Cl E1 ....125 C1
Lillian Ave W3 ....36 C4
Lillian Cl 🟧 N16 .....7 A1
Lillie Ho N5 ....14 C3
Lillie Rd SW6 ......154 C3
Lillieshall Rd SW4 ..61 B4
Lillie Yd SW6 ......155 B4
Lillington Ho N7 ....14 C4
Lily Cl W14 ....39 C2
Lily Pl EC1 ....107 C4
Lilyville Rd SW6 ...164 C4
Limberg Ho SE8 .....41 B2
Limborough Ho 🟨
  E14 ....33 C4
Limburg Rd SW11 ...60 A3
Limeharbour E14 ....42 A4
Limehouse Cswy
  E14 ....33 B2
Limehouse Cut 🟩
  E14 ....34 A4
Limehouse Fields Est
  E14 ....33 A4
Limehouse Link
  (Tunnel) E14 ......33 B2
Limehouse Sta E14 ..33 A3
Limekiln Wharf 🟪
  E14 ....33 B2
Limerston St SW10 .157 A3
Limes Ave
  Barnes SW13 ......46 B1
  London NW11 ....1 C4
Lime St EC3 ....9 C1
Limesford Rd SE15 ..65 C3
Limes Gdns SW18 ...58 C1
Lime St Pas EC3 ....110 A1
Limes The W2 ......113 C3

Limes The continued
  London SE5 ....64 A4
Lime St Pas EC3 ...124 A4
Limes Wlk SE15 .....65 B3
Limetree Cl SW2 .....74 B3
Limpsfield Ave
  SW19 ....69 C2
Limscott Ho 🟫 E3 ..27 A2
Linacre Cl SE15 .....65 A4
Linacre Ct W6 ....39 C1
Linacre Rd NW2 .....9 A2
Linale Ho N1 ....87 B1
Linberry Wlk 🟬 SE8 .41 B2
Lincoln Ave SW19 ...69 C1
Lincoln Ct N16 ......6 C4
Lincoln Ho SW1 ....130 C3
  🟭 Putney SW15 ....58 A2
Lincoln Mews NW6 ..23 B4
Lincoln's Inn★
  WC2 ....107 A2
Lincoln's Inn Fields
  WC2 ....107 A2
Lincoln St SW3 .....144 C3
Lindale SW19 ....70 A2
Lindal Rd SE4 ....66 B2
Linden Ave NW10 ...22 C3
Linden Ct
  🟮 London SE15 ....59 C3
  London W12 ....30 B1
Linden Gdns
  W2 ....31 C2 113 C3
  London W4 ....37 C1
Linden Gr SE15 .....65 B4
  🟯 London SE15 ....50 A1
Linden Lodge Sch
  SW19 ....70 A3
Linden Mans N6 .....4 A3
Linden Mews 🟰 113 C3
  London N1 ....15 C3
Lindens The W4 .....45 B2
Lindfield Gdns NW3 .11 B3
Lindfield Hts NW3 ..11 B3
Lindfield St E14 .....33 C3
Lindisfarne Way E9 ..18 A4
Lindley Ho 🟱 SE1 ..153 C3
Lindley Pl TW9 ......44 C2
Lindley St E1 ....32 B4
Lindore Rd SW11 ....60 B3
Lindo St SE15 ....50 B1
Lindrop St SW6 ....166 C2
Lindsay Ct SW11 ...167 C3
Lindsay Sq SW1 ....147 C2
Lindsell St 🟲 SE10 .52 B2
Lindsey Ho 🟳 SW10 157 C2
Lindsey Mews 🟴 15

Lindsey St EC1 .....108 B4
Linford Ho 🟵 E2 ....24 C4
Linford St SW8 .....170 C3
Lingard Ho 🟶 E14 ..42 B3
Lingards Rd SE13 ...67 B3
Lingfield Ho 🟷
  🟸 London W4 .....37 B1
Lingham St SW9 ....172 C1
Ling Rd E16 ....35 C4
Ling's Coppice SE21 .75 C2
Lingwell Rd SW17 ...72 A1
Lingwood Rd E5 .....7 C4
Linhope St NW1 .....90 C1
Linkenholt Mans 🟹
  W6 ....38 B2
Link St E9 ....17 B2
Links Yd 🟺 E1 .....111 A4
Link The W3 ....28 A3

Linkway N4 ....6 B4
Linkwood Wlk NW1 ..13 C1
Linnell Ho E1 ......110 C4
  NW8 ....78 C4
Linnell Rd SE5 .....49 A1
Linnet Mews SW12 ..72 C4
Linom Rd SW4 ......62 A3
Linscott Rd E5 ......17 B4
Linsey St SE16 .....139 C1
  SE16 ....153 B4
Linslade Ho 🟻 E2 ..24 C4
  NW8 ....90 B2
Linstead St 🟼 NW6 .10 C1
Linstead Way SW18,
  SW19 ....70 A4
Lintaine Cl W6 .....154 B3
Linthorpe Rd N16 ...7 A4
Linton Ho 🟽 E3 ....33 C4
Linton St N1 ....87 A3
Linver Rd SW6 .....166 A2
Linwood Cl SE5 .....49 B1
Lion Cl SE4 ....66 C1
Lionel Ho 🟾 W10 ...31 A4
Lionel Mans 🟿 14
  W14 ....39 C3
Lionel Mews W10 ...31 A4
Lionel Rd 🅰 Jun & Inf
  Sch TW8 ....36 A2
Lionel Road N TW8 ..36 B2
Lionel Road S TW8 ..36 B1
Lion Gate Gdns
  TW9 ....54 B4
Lion Gate Mews
  SW18 ....70 C4
Lion St N7 ....14 A2
Lion Yd SW4 ....61 C3
Lipton Rd 🅱 E1 .....32 C3
Lisburne Rd NW3 ....12 B4
Lisford St SE15 .....49 B2
Lisgar Terr W14 ....140 C4
Liskeard Gdns SE3 ..53 C3
Liskeard Ho SE11 ..149 C2
Lisle Ct NW2 ....1 A1
Lisle St WC2 ....119 C4
Lismore Wlk 🅲 N1 ..15 B2
Lissenden Gdns
  NW5 ....12 C4
Lissenden Mans
  NW5 ....12 C4
Lisson Cotts NW1 ..102 B4
Lisson Gr NW1,NW8 .90 A2
Lisson Ho NW1 .....102 A4
Lisson St NW1 .....102 A4
Lister Cl W3 ....28 C4
Lister Ct N16 ....7 A2
Lister Ho E1 ....111 C4
  SE3 ....53 A4
Lister Hospl SW1 ..146 A1
Lister Mews N7 .....14 B4
Liston Rd SW4 ......61 B4
Listowel Cl SW9 ...163 C2
Listria Lo N16 ....7 B2
Listria Pk N16 ....7 B2
Litcham Ho 🅳 E1 ...25 C2
Lithgow's Rd
  NW10 ....8 C2
Lithos Rd NW3 .....11 B2
Little Albany St
  NW1 ....92 B2
Little Argyll St 🅴 W1 104 C1
Little Boltons The
  SW10 ....142 B1
Little Britain EC1 ..108 B3
Littlebury Rd SW4 ..61 C4
Little Chelsea Ho
  SW10 ....157 A3

Little Chester St
  SW1 ....132 A2
Little College St
  SW1 ....134 A2
Little Combe Cl 🅵
  SW15 ....57 C1
Littlecote Cl SW19 ..70 A4
Little Dimocks
  SW12 ....73 A2
Little Dorrit Ct
  SE1 ....137 A4
Little Edward St
  NW1 ....92 B4
Little Essex St
  WC2 ....121 B4
Littlefield Cl N19 ...13 B4
Little George St
  SW1 ....134 A3
Little Green St NW5 .13 A4
Little Marlborough St
  W1 ....104 C1
Little Newport St
  WC2 ....119 C4
Little New St EC4 ..107 C2
Little Portland St
  W1 ....104 C2
Little Road Mans
  SW6 ....154 B3
Little Russell St
  WC1 ....106 A3
Little Sanctuary
  SW1 ....134 A3
Little Smith St
  SW1 ....133 C2
Little Somerset St
  E1 ....110 C1
Little St James's St
  SW1 ....118 C1
Little St Leonards
  SW14 ....55 B4
Little Titchfield St
  W1 ....104 C3
Littleton St SW18 ...71 B2
Little Trinity La
  EC4 ....123 A4
Little Venice* W9 ..100 C4
Littlewood SE13 ....67 B1
Livermere Ct 🅶 E8 ..24 B4
Livermere Rd E8 ....24 B4
Liverpool Gr SE17 ..151 B1
Liverpool Ho N7 ....14 C2
Liverpool Rd E16 ...35 A4
  N1 ....85 C3
  N1,N7 ....14 C1
Liverpool St EC2 ...110 A3
Liverpool Street Sta
  EC2 ....110 A3
Livesey Mus SE15 ..50 A4
Livesey Pl SE15 .....49 C4
Livingstone Ho 🅷
  SE5 ....48 B3
Livingstone Lo 🅸
  W9 ....31 C4
Livingstone Pl E14 .42 B1
Livingstone Rd E15 .27 B4
  London SW11 ......59 C4
Livity Sch The SW2 .62 A2
Livonia St W1 .....105 A1
Lizard St EC1 ....97 A3
Llandovery Ho 🅹
  E14 ....42 B4
Llanelly Rd NW2 ...1 B2
Llanvanor Rd NW2 ..1 B2
Llewellyn St SE16 .139 C3
Lloyd Baker St WC1 .95 B3

Lloyd Ct London SE13 .67 A2
6 West Norwood
SE27 .... .75 A1
Lloyd Ho N16 .... .6 C1
Lloyd's Ave EC3 .... .110 B1
Lloyd's Bldg★ EC3 ...... .110 B1
Lloyd's Pl SE3 .... .53 A1
Lloyd Sq WC1 .... .95 B4
Lloyd's Row EC1 ...... .96 A3
Lloyd St WC1 .... .95 B4
Lloyd Villas SE4 ...... .51 C1
Loampit Hill SE13 .... .52 A1
Loampit Vale SE13 .... .67 B4
Loanda Cl **17** E8 .... .24 B4
Loanda Ho SE15 ...... .65 B4
Loats Rd SW2 .... .62 A2
Locarno Rd **8** W3 ..28 B1
Lochaline St W6 ...... .47 B4
Lochbie N4 .... .5 A4
Lochinvar St SW12 .... .73 A4
Lochmore Ho SW1 .... .145 C3
Lochnagar St E14 .... .34 B4
Lockbridge Ct 8
W9 .... .31 C4
Locke Ho SW8 .... .170 C4
Lockesfield Pl E14 .... .42 A1
Lockgate Cl E9 .... .18 B3
Lockhart Cl N7 .... .14 B2
Lockhart St E3 .... .26 B1
Lock Ho N16 .... .7 C3
Lockhurst St E5 ...... .17 C4
Lockington Rd
SW8 .... .170 A4
Lockmead Rd SE13 .... .67 B4
Lockside E14 .... .33 A2
Locksley St E14 ...... .33 B4
Lock View Ct 9
E14 .... .33 A2
Lockwood Ho
SE11 .... .163 B3
Lockwood Sq SE16 .... .40 A3
Lockyer Est SE1 ...... .137 C3
Lockyer Ho 7 SE10 .43 B1
SW8 .... .162 A2
Putney SW15 .... .57 C2
Lockyer St SE1 .... .137 C3
Locton Gn **4** E3 ..... .26 B4
Loddiges Ho **9** E9 ..17 B1
Loddiges Rd E9 ...... .17 B1
Loddon Ho NW8 ...... .89 C1
Loder St SE15 .... .50 B3
Lodge Rd NW8 .... .90 A3
Lodore St E14 .... .34 B3
Lodsworth Ho
SW11 .... .169 B3
Loftie St SE16 .... .139 C3
Lofting Rd N1 .... .14 C1
Lofts on the Park 7
E9 .... .17 C2
Loftus Rd W12 .... .30 A1
Loftus Rd (Queens Park
Rangers FC) W12 ....30 A1
Logan Mews W8 ...... .141 B4
Logan Pl W8 .... .141 B4
Loggetts SE21 .... .76 A2
Lohmann Ho 1 SE11 .163 B4
Lolesworth Cl E1 ..... .111 A3
Lollard St SE11 .... .149 B3
Loman St SE1 .... .136 B4
Lomas St E1 .... .111 C4
Lombard Ct EC3 ...... .123 C4
Lombard Ho 4
SE10 .... .52 B3
Lombard La EC4 ...... .107 C1
Lombard Rd SW11 ... .167 B2

Lombard St EC3 ...... .109 C1
Lombardy Pl W2 ...... .114 B3
Lomley Ho **10** SW2 .62 C1
Lomond Gr SE5 ...... .48 C3
Lomond Ho **10** SE5 ..48 C2
Loncroft Rd SE5 ..... .49 A4
Londale Ct SE10 ..... .52 B2
Londesborough Ho 1
N16 .... .16 A4
Londesborough Rd
N16 .... .16 A4
London Aquarium★
SE1 .... .134 C3
London Bridge
EC4,SE1 .... .123 C2
London Bridge City Pier
SE1 .... .124 A2
London Bridge Hospl
SE1 .... .123 C2
London Bridge St
SE1 .... .123 C1
London Bridge Sta
SE1 .... .123 C1
London Business Sch
NW1 .... .90 C2
London Canal Mus
N1 .... .84 B2
London Central
Mosque★ NW8 ..... .90 B3
London Chest Hospl
E2 .... .25 B3
London Clinic NW1 .91 C1
London Coll of Fashion
EC2 .... .24 A1 **98** B2
London Coll of Fashion
The W1 .... .103 C1
London Coll of
International Business
Studies WC1 ...... .106 B3
London Coll of Printing
SE11 .... .136 C1
London Ct 8 SW18 .58 C2
London Docklands
Visitor Ctr E14 ..... .42 B4
London Dungeon The★
SE1 .... .123 C2
London Eye (Millennium
Wheel)★ SE1 .... .134 C4
London Fields East Side
E8 .... .17 A1
London Fields Prim Sch
E8 .... .25 A4
London Fields Sta
E8 .... .17 A1
London Fields West Side
E8 .... .16 C1
London Foot Hospl
W1 .... .92 C1
London Gas Mus The
E3,E16 .... .27 C1
London Ho NW8 .... .80 B2
London Hospital Dental
Inst E1 .... .32 A4
London Independent
Hospl The E1 .... .32 C4
London Inst The
W1 .... .104 A1
London International
Film Sch W2 .... .106 B2
London La E8 ...... .17 A1
London Metropolitan
Univ E1 .... .110 C1
London Metropolitan
Univ (Carleton Grange
Hall) **2** N7 .... .13 C4

London Metropolitan
Univ (Central Ho)
E1 .... .111 B2
London Metropolitan
Univ (Coll of Tech &
Design) E1 .... .111 B2
London Metropolitan
Univ Coll **12** SE10 .53 B4
London Metropolitan
Univ (Commercial Rd)
E1 .... .111 B2
London Metropolitan
Univ (Ladbrook Ho)
N5 .... .15 A3
London Metropolitan
Univ (Moorgate)
EC2 .... .109 C3
London Metropolitan
Univ (North London
Campus) N7 .... .14 C3
London Metropolitan
Univ (Tufnel Park Hall)
N7 .... .4 B1
London Metropolitan
Univ (Spring Ho)
N7 .... .14 C2
London Mews W2 .. .101 C2
London Nautical Sch
The SE1 .... .121 C2
London Oratory Sch The
SW6 .... .155 C2
London Peace Pagoda★
SW3 .... .159 A2
London Rd SE1 ...... .136 B2
London Stile **5** W4 .36 C1
London Terr **1** E2 ..24 C3
London Toy & Model
Mus W2 .... .114 C4
London Transport Mus★
WC2 .... .120 B4
London Wall EC2 ... .109 A3
London Wharf 4
E2 .... .25 A4
London Zoo★ NW1 .81 B2
Long Acre WC2 ..... .106 B1
Longbeach Rd
SW11 .... .60 B4
Longberrys NW2 .... .1 B1
Longbow Ho **20** N1 .24 A4
Longbridge Way
SE13 .... .67 B2
Longcliffe Ho SW18 .59 A2
Longdale Sq N1 ..... .85 B4
Long Dr W3 .... .29 A3
Longfellow Way
SE1 .... .152 C4
Longfield Dr SW14 .55 A2
Longfield Est SE1 ... .153 A3
Longfield St SW18 ..70 C4
Longford Ct
2 London E5 ...... .17 C4
1 London W12 .... .38 A4
Longford Ho **7** E1 ..32 B3
Longford Wlk **7** W2 .62 C1
SW2 .... .74 C4
Longhope Cl SE15 ..49 B4
Longhurst Ho **8**
W9 .... .23 B2
Long La EC1 .... .108 B4
SE1 .... .137 C3
Longland Ct SE1 ... .153 B2
London E9 .... .18 A3
Longlands Ct W11 .113 A4

Longleat Ho SW1 ... .147 B2
Longleigh Ho **8**
SE5 .... .49 A2
Longlents Ho **3**
NW10 .... .20 C4
Longley Ho **5** N19 .13 B4
Longley St SE1 ...... .153 B4
Longman Ho **9** E2 ..25 C3
10 E8 .... .24 B4
Long Meadow **20**
N7 .... .14 C3
Longmoor Point 14
SW15 .... .69 A3
Longmore St SW1 ..146 C3
Longnor Rd E1 ...... .25 C2
Long Pond Rd SE3 ..53 A2
Long Rd SW4 .... .61 B3
Longridge Ho SE1 ..137 A1
Longridge Rd SW5 .141 C3
Long's Ct WC1 ...... .119 C3
Longs Ct **2** TW9 ...54 B3
Longshore SE8 ..... .41 B2
Long St E2 .... .98 C4
Longstaff Cres
SW18 .... .70 C4
Longstaff Rd SW18 .58 C1
Longstone Ave
NW10 .... .21 B4
Longthorne Ho **20**
E3 .... .26 B2
Longville Rd SE11 ..150 B4
Long Wlk SE1 ...... .138 B2
Longwood Dr SW15 .56 C1
Long Yd WC1 .... .94 C1
Lonsdale Ho
6 London N4 ..... .6 B4
London SW6 .... .58 C4
Lonsdale Mews
4 Richmond TW9 .44 C2
London SW7 .... .129 C1
Lonsdale Pl N1 .... .14 C1
Lonsdale Rd NW6 ..23 C3
W11 .... .31 B3
Barnes SW13 ...... .46 B3
London W4 .... .38 B2
Lonsdell Ho **9** SW7 .62 A4
Lopez Ho **3** SW9 ..62 A4
Loraine Rd
Chiswick W4 .... .45 A4
London N7 .... .14 B4
Lord David Pitt Ho 3
SE24 .... .62 C3
Lorden Wlk **23**
E2 .... .24 C2 **99** B3
Lord Hills Rd W2 ....100 B4
Lord Holland La
SW9 .... .173 C2
Lord Napier Pl W6 ..38 C1
Lord North St SW1 .134 A1
Lord Roberts Mews
SW6 .... .156 A1
Lords Cl SE21 .... .75 B2
Lord's Cricket Mus
NW8 .... .89 C3
Lord's Ct
4 London SE13 .. .67 B4
Lord's Indoor Cricket
Sch
NW8 .... .89 C4
NW8 .... .90 B3

Lord's (MCC &
Middlesex Cty Cricket
Ground)★ NW8 .... .89 C4
Lord's View NW8 .... .89 C3
Loreburn Ho **2** N7 .14 B4
Lorenzo St N1,WC1 .94 C4
Loris Rd W6 .... .39 B3
Lorn Ct SW9 .... .173 B2
Lorne CI NW8 .... .90 B3
Lorne Ct SW15 ..... .57 C1
Lorne Gdns **5** W11 .39 C4
Lorne Ho **7** E1 ..... .33 A4
Lorne Rd London N4 ..5 B3
3 Richmond TW10 .54 B2
Lorn Rd SW9 .... .173 B2
Lorraine Ct **10** NW1 .13 A1
Lorrimore Rd SE17 ..48 A4
Lorrimore Sq SE17 ..48 A4
Lorton Ho **8** NW6 ..23 C4
Lostock Ho **8** SW8 .171 B2
Lothair Rd S N4 ..... .6 A4
Lothbury EC2 .... .109 B2
Lothian Rd SW9 .... .48 A2
Lothrop St W10 ..... .23 A2
Lots Rd SW10 ...... .157 A1
Loudoun Rd NW8 ... .79 A3
Loughborough Ct 7
SW9 .... .63 A4
Loughborough Junction
Sta SW9 .... .63 A4
Loughborough Pk
SW9 .... .63 A3
Loughborough Prim Sch
SW9 .... .63 A4
Loughborough Rd
SE5,SW9 .... .48 A1
Loughborough St
SE11 .... .149 A1
Lough Rd N7 .... .14 B2
Louisa Cl E9 .... .25 C4
Louisa Gdns E1 .... .25 C1
Louisa Ho SW15 ... .56 B3
Louisa St E1 .... .25 C1
Louise Bennett Cl 9
SE24 .... .63 A3
Louise De Marillac Ho
10 E1 .... .32 B4
Louise White Ho 1
N19 .... .4 C3
Louisville Rd SW17 .72 C1
Louvaine Rd SW11 .59 C3
Lovat La EC3 .... .124 A3
Lovatt Ct SW12 .... .73 A3
Loveday Ho **2** SW2 .74 C3
Lovegrove St SE1 ..49 C4
Lovegrove Wlk E14 .34 B1
Love La EC2 .... .109 A2
Lovelace Ho **12** E8 .24 B4
Lovelace Rd SE21 ..75 B3
Lovelinch Cl SE15 ..50 B4
Lovell Ho E8 .... .24 C4
Lovell Pl SE16 ...... .41 A3
Loveridge Mews
NW6 .... .10 B2
Loveridge Rd NW6 .10 B2
Lover's Wlk W1 ..... .117 B1
Lovette Ho **3** E3 ...26 C2
Love Wlk SE5 ...... .48 C1
Low Cross Wood La
SE21 .... .76 B1
Lowden Rd SE24 ... .63 A3
Lowder Ho **6** E1 ... .32 A1
Lowe Ave E16 ...... .35 C4
Lowell Ho **10** SE5 ..48 B3
Lowell St E14 ...... .33 A3
Lower Addison Gdns
W14 .... .126 A3

Lower Belgrave St
SW1 ...132 A1
Lower Clapton Rd
E5 ...17 B4
Lower Clarendon Wlk [7] W11 ...31 A3
Lower Common S
SW15 ...57 A4
Lower Grosvenor Pl
SW1 ...132 B2
Lower Grove Rd
TW10 ...54 B2
Lower James St
W1 ...119 A4
Lower John St W1 ...119 A4
Lower Lea Crossing
E14,E16 ...35 A1
Lower Mall W6 ...39 A1
Lower Marsh SE1 ...135 B3
Lower Merton Rise
NW3 ...12 A1
Lower Mortlake Rd
TW9 ...54 B4
Lower Pk [5] SW15 ...57 C2
Lower Place Bsns Ctr
NW10 ...20 B3
Lower Rd SE16 ...40 B4
Lower Richmond Rd
Mortlake,TW9 ...55 A4
Putney SW15 ...57 B4
Lower Robert St
WC2 ...120 B3
Lower Sloane St
SW1 ...145 B2
Lower Terr NW3 ...2 B1
Lower Thames St
EC3 ...124 A3
Lowerwood Ct W11 ...31 A3
Loweswater Ho E3 ...26 B1
Lowfield Rd
London NW6 ...10 C1
London W3 ...28 B3
Lowlands NW3 ...12 A2
Lowman Rd N7 ...14 B4
Lowndes Cl SW1 ...131 C1
Lowndes Ct
London W1 ...104 B1
London W12 ...39 A4
Lowndes Lo [14] NW8 ...79 B2
Lowndes Pl SW1 ...131 B1
Lowndes Sq SW1 ...131 A1
Lowndes St SW1 ...131 B2
Lowood [11] E1 ...32 B2
Lowood St E1 ...32 A3
Lowry Ct [9] SE16 ...40 A1
Lowther Ho
[11] E8 ...24 B4
SW1 ...147 A1
Lowther Prim Sch
SW13 ...46 C4
Lowther Rd
Barnes SW13 ...46 B2
London N7 ...14 C3
Lowth Rd SE5 ...48 B1
Loxford Ho SW1 ...145 C3
Loxham St WC1 ...94 B3
Loxley Rd SW18 ...71 C3
Lubbock Ho [18] E14 ...34 A2
Lubbock St SE14 ...50 B3
Lucan Ho N1 ...87 C3
Lucan Pl SW3 ...144 B3
Lucas Ct SW11 ...169 C3
Lucas Ho SW8 ...171 A2
Lucas St SE4,SE8 ...51 C2
Lucas Vale Prim Sch
SE8 ...51 C2
Lucerne Mews W8 ...113 C2
Lucerne Rd N5 ...15 A4
Lucey Rd SE16 ...139 B1
Lucey Way SE16 ...153 C4
Lucien Rd SW18 ...71 A2

Lucraft Ho [12] SW2 ...74 A4
Lucy Ashe Ho SE17 ...150 B3
Lucy Brown Ho
SE1 ...123 A1
Lucy Cres W3 ...20 B1
Ludgate Broadway
EC4 ...108 B1
Ludgate Cir EC4 ...108 A1
Ludgate Hill EC4 ...108 B1
Ludgate Sq EC4 ...108 B1
Ludham NW5 ...12 B3
Ludlow St EC1 ...96 C2
Ludovick Wlk SW15 ...56 A3
Ludwell Ho W14 ...126 B2
Ludwick Mews
SE14 ...51 A3
Lugard Ho [2] W12 ...30 A1
Lugard Rd SE15 ...50 A2
Luke Ho [2] E1 ...32 A3
Luke St EC2 ...24 A1 98 A2
Lukin St E1 ...32 B3
Lullingstone Ho [20]
SE15 ...50 B4
Lullingstone La
SE13 ...67 C1
Lulot Gdns N19 ...4 A2
Lulworth SE17 ...151 B2
London NW1 ...13 C1
Lulworth Ho SW8 ...162 C1
Lulworth Rd SE15 ...50 A1
Lumiere Ct [17] SW17 ...72 C2
Lumley Ct [20] WC2 ...120 B3
Lumley Flats SW1 ...145 B2
Lumley St W1 ...103 C1
Lumsdon Ho [1] ...78 B3
Lunan Ho [20] E3 ...26 B3
Lund Point E15 ...27 B4
Lupin Cl SW2 ...75 A2
Lupino Ct SE11 ...148 C3
Lupin Point SE1 ...139 A3
Lupton St NW5 ...13 B4
Lupus St SW1 ...147 A1
Luralda Gdns E14 ...42 C1
Lurgan Ave W6 ...47 C4
Lurline Gdns
SW11 ...169 C4
Luscombe Ho SW18 ...58 B2
Luscombe Way
SW8 ...162 A2
Lusher Ho SW15 ...57 C1
Lushington Rd
NW10 ...22 A3
Lushington Terr [11]
E8 ...16 C3
Luton Pl SE10 ...52 B3
Luton St NW8 ...89 C1
Luttrell Ave SW15 ...57 A2
Lutyens Ho [1] SW1 ...146 C1
Luxborough Ho
W1 ...103 B4
Luxborough St W1 ...103 B4
Luxborough Twr
W1 ...103 B4
Luxemburg Gdns
W6 ...39 C2
Luxford St SE16 ...40 C2
Luxmore St SE4 ...51 B2
Luxor St SE5 ...63 B4
Lyall Mews W1 ...131 B1
Lyall Mews W SW1 ...131 B1
Lyall St SW1 ...131 B1
Lyal Rd E3 ...26 A3
Lycée Français Charles
de Gaulle (French Univ
Coll) SW7 ...143 B4
Lycée The SW11 ...149 C1

Lycett Ho [10] SW2 ...74 A4
Lycett Pl [3] W12 ...38 C4
Lydden Gr SW18 ...71 A4
Lydden Rd SW18 ...71 A4
Lydford NW1 ...83 A3
Lydford Rd NW2 ...9 B2
Lydford Rd W9 ...23 B1
London NW2 ...9 C2
Lydgate Ho [8] N16 ...16 A4
Lydhurst Ave SW2 ...74 B2
Lydney Cl SE15 ...49 A3
Lydon Rd SW4 ...61 B4
Lydwell Ho SW8 ...171 B1
Lyford Rd SW18 ...72 A3
Lygon Ho [6] N6 ...4 C4
Lygon Ho E2 ...99 B4
Lygon Pl SW1 ...132 A1
Lyham Cl SW2 ...62 A1
Lyham Rd SW2 ...62 A1
Lyly Ho SE1 ...137 C1
Lyme Gr E9 ...17 B1
Lyme Grove Ho [2]
E9 ...17 B1
Lyme St NW1 ...82 C4
Lyminge Gdns
SW17,SW18 ...72 A3
Lymington Mans
NW6 ...11 A2
Lymington Rd NW6 ...11 A2
Lympstone Gdns
SE15 ...49 C3
Lynch Cl SE3 ...53 B3
Lynch Wlk [2] SE8 ...51 B4
Lyncott Cres SW4 ...61 A3
Lyncourt SE3 ...52 C1
Lyncroft Gdns NW6 ...10 C3
Lyncroft Mans [6]
NW6 ...10 C3
Lyndale NW2 ...1 B1
Lyndale Ave NW2 ...1 B2
Lyndale Cl SE3 ...53 B4
Lynde Ho [4] SW4 ...61 C4
Lynden Gate SW15 ...69 A3
Lyndhurst Gdns
NW3 ...11 C3
Lyndhurst Gr SE5,
SE15 ...49 B1
Lyndhurst Ho [2]
SW15 ...68 C4
Lyndhurst House Prep
Sch NW3 ...11 C3
Lyndhurst Lo [3]
E14 ...42 C2
Lyndhurst Rd NW3 ...11 C3
Lyndhurst Sch SE5 ...49 B2
Lyndhurst Sq SE15 ...49 B2
Lyndhurst Terr
NW3 ...11 C3
Lyndhurst Way SE15 ...49 B1
Lynette Ave SW4 ...61 B1
Lynford French Ho
SE17 ...150 C2
Lynmouth Rd N16 ...7 B3
Lynne Ct NW6 ...11 A1
Lynnett Ct E9 ...18 A3
Lynne Way NW10 ...8 A2
Lynn Ho SE15 ...49 C4
Lynn Rd SW12 ...73 A4
Lynton Cl NW10 ...8 A3
Lynton Est [1] SE1 ...153 B3
Lynton Ho [1] W2 ...100 B1
Lynton Lo N5 ...15 A3
Lynton Mans SE1 ...135 B2
Lynton Rd NW6 ...23 B3

Lynton Rd continued
SE1 ...153 A2
Acton W3 ...28 A3
Lynton Terr [4] W3 ...28 B3
Lyon Ho NW8 ...90 A1
Lyons Pl NW8 ...89 B1
Lyon St N1 ...14 B1
Lyons Wlk W14 ...140 A4
Lyric Rd SW13 ...46 B2
Lysander Gr N19 ...4 C3
Lysander Ho [10] E2 ...25 A3
Lysia Ct SW6 ...47 C3
Lysias Rd SW12 ...61 A1
Lysia St SW6 ...47 C3
Lysons Wlk SW15 ...56 C2
Lytcott Gr SE22 ...64 B2
Lytham St SE17 ...151 B1
Lyttelton Cl NW3 ...12 A1
Lytten Ct [8] W12 ...38 C4
Lyttleton Ho [10] E9 ...17 B1
Lytton Ct WC1 ...106 B3
Lytton Gr SW15 ...58 A1

M

Mabel Thornton Ho [1]
N16 ...15 C4
Mablethorpe Rd
SW6 ...154 A1
Mabley St E9 ...18 A3
MacArthur Ho [6]
SW2 ...74 A4
Macaulay CE Prim Sch
[2] SW4 ...61 A3
Macaulay Ct SW4 ...61 A4
Macaulay Ho
[10] London N16 ...7 A1
[1] SW4 ...61 A3
Macaulay Rd SW4 ...61 A4
Macaulay Sq SW4 ...61 A3
McAuley Cl SE1 ...135 B2
Macbeth Ho [4] N1 ...24 A3
Macbeth St W6 ...39 A1
McBride Ho [5] E3 ...26 B3
McCall Cl SW4 ...172 A2
McCall Ho N7 ...14 A4
Mccarthy Ct SW11 ...168 B3
Macclesfield Rd
EC1 ...96 C4
Macclesfield St
W1 ...119 C4
McCoid Way SE1 ...136 C3
McConnell Ho
SW8 ...171 B3
McCormick Ho [9]
SW2 ...74 C3
McCrone Mews [3]
NW3 ...11 C2
McCullum Rd E3 ...26 B4
McDermott Cl
SW11 ...60 A4
McDermott Rd SE15 ...64 C4
Macdonald Ho [5]
SW11 ...169 B2
McDougall Ct TW9 ...44 C1
McDowall Cl E16 ...35 B2
McDowall Rd SE5 ...48 B2
Macduff Rd SW11 ...169 C4
Mace Cl E1 ...32 A1
Mace St E2 ...25 C3
McEwan Way E15 ...27 C4
Macey Ho [9] SE10 ...52 B4
Macfarlane Rd W12 ...30 B1

Magdala Ave N19 .....4 B2
Magdalene Cl 7
SE15 ....50 A1
Magdalene Ho 7
SW15 ....57 C1
Magdalen Pas E1 ....125 A4
Magdalen Rd SW18 ..71 C3
Magdalen St SE1 ....124 A1
Magee St SE11 ......163 B4
Magellan Ho 4 E1 ...25 C1
Magellan Pl 10 E14 ..41 C2
Magnin Cl 8 E8 .....24 C4
Magnolia Ct
London SW11 ....60 B1
Richmond TW9 ....45 A2
Magnolia Ho 13 SE8 ..51 B4
Magnolia Pl SW4 .....62 A2
Magnolia Rd W4 .....45 A4
Magnolia Wharf
W4 ....45 A4
Magpie Ho 7 E3 .....26 B4
Magpie Pl SE14 ......51 A4
Maguire St SE1 .....139 A4
Mahatma Ganhi Ind Est
1 SE24 ....63 A3
Mahogany Cl SE16 ....33 A1
Mahoney Ho SE14 ....51 B2
Maida Ave W2 ....88 C3
Maida Vale W9 ....88 C3
Maida Vale Psychiatric
Hospl W9 ....89 A2
Maida Vale Sta W9 ...88 B4
Maida La SE1 ......123 A2
WC2 ....120 B4
London NW1 ....13 C1
Maidenstone Hill
SE10 ....52 B2
Maidstone Bldgs
SE1 ....123 B1
Maidstone Ho 4
E14 ....34 A3
Mail Coach Yd 2 E2 ..98 B4
Main Yd E9 ....18 C2
Maismore St SE15 ....49 C4
Maitland Cl 5 SE10 ..52 A3
Maitland Ct W2 ......115 B4
Maitland Ho 17 E2 ..25 B3
SW1 ....160 C4
Maitland Park Rd
NW3 ....12 B2
Maitland Park Villas
NW3 ....12 B2
Maitland Pl E5 ......17 B4
London E15 ....19 C3
Majestic Ct N4 ....6 A3
Major Rd SE16 ......139 C2
London E15 ....19 C3
Makepeace Ave N6 ....3 C2
Makepeace Mans N6 ..3 C2
Makins St SW3 ......144 B3
Malabar Ct 20 W12 ...30 A2
Malabar St E14 ......41 C4
Malam Ct SE11 ......149 B3
Malam Gdns 2 E14 ...34 A2
Malay Ho 2 E1 ......32 B1
Malbrook Rd SW15 ...57 A3
Malcolm Gavin Cl
SW17 ....72 A2
Malcolm Ho 13 N1 ...24 A3
Malcolm Pl E2 ....25 B1
Malcolm Rd E1 ......25 B1
Malcolmson Ho
SW1 ....147 C1
Malden Cres NW1 ....12 C2
Malden Pl NW5 ......12 C3
Malden Rd NW5 ......12 C2

Maldon Cl N1 ....87 A4
London E15 ....19 C3
London SE5 ....64 A4
Maldon Rd W3 ....28 B2
Malet Pl WC1 ....93 B1
Malet St WC1 ....105 C4
Maley Ave SE27 ......75 A2
Malfort Rd SE5 ....64 A4
Mallams Mews 1
SW9 ....63 A4
Mallard Cl NW6 ......23 C4
London E9 ....18 B2
Mallard Ho NW8 .....80 A1
7 London SE15 ......49 B2
Mallard Point 8 E3 ..26 C2
Mallet Ho 10 SW15 ..56 C2
Mallet Rd SE13 ......67 C1
Malling SE13 ....67 A2
Mallinson Rd SW11 ..60 B2
Mallon Gdns 8 E1 ..111 A3
Mallord St SW3 .....157 C4
Mallory Bldgs EC1 ...96 A1
Mallory Cl SE4 ....66 A3
Mallory Ho E14 ......34 B4
Mallory St NW8 ......90 B2
Mallow St EC1 ....97 B2
Mall Rd W6 ....39 A1
Mall Studios 9
NW3 ....12 B3
Mall The SW1 ....119 B1
Mortlake SW14 ....55 B2
Malmesbury 2 E2 ...25 B3
Malmesbury Prim Sch
E2 ....25 B2
Malmesbury Rd E16 ..35 A4
E3 ....26 B2
Malmesbury Terr
E16 ....35 B2
Malmsey Ho E14 ....149 A2
Malmsmead Ho E9 ...18 A3
Malorees Jun & Inf Schs
NW6 ....9 C1
Malpas Rd
London E8 ....17 A2
London SE4 ....51 B1
Malta St EC1 ....96 B2
Maltby St SE1 ....138 C2
Malthouse Dr W4 ....46 B4
Malthouse Pas
SW13 ....46 A1
Malting Ho E14 ......33 B2
Maltings W4 ....36 C1
Maltings Cl SW13 ....46 A1
Maltings Lo W4 ......46 A3
Maltings Pl SE1 .....138 B4
SW6 ....166 B3
Malton Mews 1
W10 ....31 A3
Malton Rd W10 ......31 A3
Maltravers St WC2 ..121 B4
Malt St SE1 ....49 C4
Malva Cl SW18 ......59 A2
Malvern Cl W10 ......31 B4
Malvern Ct 7 SW7 ..143 C4
Malvern Gdns NW2 ...1 A2
Malvern Ho N16 ......7 B3
Malvern Mews NW6 ..23 C2
Malvern Pl NW6 ......23 B2
Malvern Rd N19 ......4 C3
London E8 ....16 C1
London NW6 ....23 C2
Malvern Terr N1 .....85 B4
Malwood Rd SW12 ...61 A1
Malyons Rd SE13 ....67 A2
Malyons Terr SE13 ...67 A2
Managers St E14 ....34 B1

Manaton Cl SE15 .....65 A4
Manbre Rd W6 ....47 B4
Manchester Dr W10 ..23 A1
Manchester Gr E14 ..42 B1
Manchester Ho
SE17 ....151 A2
Manchester Mans
N19 ....4 C4
Manchester Mews
W1 ....103 B3
Manchester Rd E14 ..42 B3
Manchester Sq
W1 ....103 C2
Manchester St W1 ..103 B3
Manchuria Rd
SW11 ....60 C1
Manciple St SE1 ....137 C2
Mandalay Ho 6
N16 ....7 A3
Mandalay Rd SW4 ...61 B2
Mandarin Ct 1 SE8 ..51 C4
Mandela Cl 30 W12 ..30 A2
Mandela Ho 4 ......98 C4
Mandela Rd E16 .....35 C3
Mandela St NW1 .....83 A4
SW9 ....163 B1
Mandela Way SE1 ..152 B4
Manderville Ho
SE1 ....153 A2
Mandeville Cl 5
SE3 ....53 B3
Mandeville Ct E3 ....26 A4
Mandeville Ctyd
SW11 ....169 B3
Mandeville Ho 6
SE5 ....61 B2
Mandeville Pl W1 ...104 A2
Mandrake Rd SW17 ..72 B1
Mandrell Rd SW2 ....62 A2
Manette St W1 ......105 C1
Manfred Ct 5
SW15 ....58 B2
Manfred Rd SW15 ...58 B2
Manger Rd N7 ....14 A2
Manilla St E14 ....41 C4
Manitoba Ct 23
SE16 ....40 B4
Manley Ct N16 ....7 B1
Manley Ho SE11 ....149 B2
Manley St NW1 ......81 B4
Mannebury Prior
N1 ....85 A1
Mannering Ho 18
SW2 ....62 A2
Manningford Cl EC1 ..96 A4
Manning Ho 3
W11 ....31 A3
Manning Pl TW10 ....54 B1
Manningtree Cl
SW19 ....70 A3
Manningtree St E1 ..111 B2
Manny Shinwell Ho
SW6 ....155 A3
Manor Ave SE4 ......51 A1
Manor Circus TW9 ...54 C4
Manor Ct London SE5 .49 B2
7 London SW2 ....62 B2
London W3 ....36 C2
Streatham SW16 .....74 A1
Manorfield Cl 3
N19 ....13 B4
Manorfield Prim Sch
E14 ....34 A3
Manor Gdns
London N7 ....5 A1
London SW4 ....171 A1

Manor Gdns *continued*
London W3 ....36 C2
8 London W4 ....38 B1
Richmond TW10,TW9 ..54 B3
Manor Gt SE1 ....58 A2
Manor Ho NW1 .....102 B4
Manor House Ct
W9 ....88 C1
Manor House Dr
NW6 ....9 C1
Manor Lodge NW3 ...9 C2
Manor Mans
7 London NW3 ....12 A2
London N7 ....5 A1
Manor Mews NW6 ...23 C3
London SE4 ....51 B1
Manor Oak Mans
SE22 ....65 A1
Manor Par N16 ....7 B2
Manor Park Rd
NW10 ....21 B4
Manor Pk TW9 ......54 B3
Manor Pl SE17 .....150 C2
Manor Rd London N16 ..7 A3
Richmond TW10,TW9 ..54 B3
Manor Sch NW10 ....22 B4
Manor Street Est
SW3 ....158 B4
Manor The 1 W1 ...118 A3
Manor Way W3 ......36 C2
Manresa Rd SW3 ...144 A1
Mansel Ct SW11 ....168 B3
Mansel St E1 ....111 A1
Mansell Rd W3 ....37 C4
Mansell St E1 ....110 C1
Manse Rd N16 ....7 B1
Mansfield Ct 27 E2 ..24 B4
Mansfield Ho SW15 ..57 C1
Mansfield Mews
W1 ....104 A3
Mansfield Pl 11
NW3 ....11 B4
Mansfield Rd
Acton W3 ....20 A1
London NW3 ....12 B4
Mansfield St W1 ...104 A3
Mansford St E2 .....24 C3
Mansion Cl SW9 ....173 C4
Mansion Gdns NW3 ..2 A1
Mansion House ★
EC4 ....109 B1
Mansion House Pl
EC3,EC4 ....109 B1
Mansion House St
EC2 ....109 B1
Mansion House Sta
EC4 ....123 A4
Mansions The NW6 ..10 B3
Manson Mews
SW7 ....143 B3
Manson Pl SW7 ....143 B3
Manstone Rd NW2 ..10 A3
Manston Ho W14 ...126 B2
Mantell Ho SW4 ....61 B2
Mantle Rd SE4 .....66 A4
Manton Ho N16 ......6 C1
Mantua St 2 SW11 ..59 C4
Mantus Cl E1 ....25 B1
Mantus Rd E1 ....25 B1
Manville Gdns
SW17 ....73 A1
Manville Rd SW17 ...73 A1
Manwood Rd SE4 ...66 B1
Many Gates 2 ......73 A2

Mapesbury Ct NW2 ..10 A3
Mapesbury Rd NW2 ..10 A2
Mapeshill Pl NW2 ....9 B2
Mapes Ho 6 NW6 ...10 A1
Mape St 1 ....25 A1
Maple Ave W3 ....29 A1
Maple Cl SW4 ....61 C1
Maple Ct NW2 ....9 C4
Mapledene Est E8 ...16 C1
Mapledene Rd E8 ....16 C1
Maple Ho 5 SE8 ....51 B3
11 London NW6 ......12 B2
Maple Leaf Sq 27
SE16 ....40 C4
Maple Mews NW6 ...78 A2
Maple Pl W1 ....93 A1
Maples Pl 1 E1 ......32 A4
Maple St 1 W1 ......92 C1
Maplestead Rd SW2 .74 B4
Mapleton Cres
SW18 ....59 A1
Mapleton Rd SW18 ..59 A1
Maple Wlk W10 ......22 C1
Maple St E3 ....26 B2
Marada Ho NW6 .....10 A1
Marais W4 ....45 B3
Marban Rd W9 ....23 B2
Marble Arch ★ W1 ..117 A4
Marble Arch Sta
W1 ....103 A1
Marble Cl W3 ....28 A1
Marbleford Ct 4 N6 ..4 C4
Marble Ho W9 ....23 B1
Marcella Rd SW9 ...173 B1
Marchant Ct SE1 ....153 A2
Marchant Ho 9
SW2 ....62 B2
Marchant St SE14 ...51 A4
Marchbank Rd
W14 ....155 A4
March Ct SW15 .....57 A3
Marchmont Rd
TW10 ....54 B2
Marchmont St WC1 ..94 A3
Marchwood Cl 17
SE5 ....49 A3
Marcia Rd SE1 .....152 B3
Marcilly Rd SW18 ..59 C2
Marcon Ct 22 E8 ....17 A3
Marcon Pl E8 ....17 A3
Marco Rd W6 ....39 B3
Marcus Ct TW8 .....44 A3
Marcus Garvey Mews
SE22 ....65 A2
Marcus Garvey Way 5
SE24 ....62 C3
Marcus Ho 8 SE15 ..49 B2
Marcus St SW18 ....59 A1
Marcus Terr SW18 ..59 A1
Marden Ho 8 E8 ....17 A3
Marden Sq SE16 ....40 A3
Mardyke Ho E17 ....151 C4
Maresfield Gdns
NW3 ....11 B2
Mare St London E8 ..17 A2
London E8 ....25 A4
Margaret Bondfield Ho
4 E3 ....26 A3
22 London N7 ....13 C3
Margaret Ct 16 W1 ..104 C2
Margaret Herbison Ho
SW6 ....155 A3
Margaret Ho 16 W6 ..39 B1
Margaret Ingram Cl
SW6 ....154 C3

Margaret Mcmillan Ho
10 N19 .... 4 C4
Margaret Rd N16 ....7 B3
Margaret's Ct SE1 .123 B1
Margaret St W1 ....104 C2
Margaretta Terr
SW3 ....158 B4
Margaret White Ho
NW1 ....93 C4
Margate Rd SW2 ...62 A2
Margery Fry Ct N7 ...5 A1
Margery St WC1 ...95 B3
Margravine Gdns
W14 ....140 A2
London W6 ....39 C1
Margravine Rd
W6 ....154 A4
Marham Gdns SW17,
SW18 ....72 A3
Maria Cl SE1 ......153 C4
Maria Fidelis RC
Convent Sch NW1 .93 C4
Marian Ct E9 ......17 B3
Marian Pl E2 ......25 A3
Marian Sq E2 ......25 A3
Marian St E2 ......25 A3
Marian Way NW10 ...8 B1
Maria Terr E1 ......25 C1
Marie Curie SE5 ...49 A2
Marie Lloyd Ct 13
SW9 ....62 B3
Marie Lloyd Ho 1
N19 ....5 A4
Marie Lloyd Ho N1 .87 B1
Marigold St SE16 ...40 A4
Marina Ct 11 E3 ...26 C2
Marinefield Rd
SW6 ....166 B2
Marinel Ho 26 SE5 .48 B3
Mariners Mews E14 .42 C2
Marine St SE16 ....139 B2
Marine Twr 28 SE8 .51 B4
Marion Richardson Prim
Sch E1 ....32 C3
Marischal Rd SE13 .67 C4
Maritime Ho 8
SW4 ....61 B4
Maritime Quay 6
E14 ....41 C1
Maritime St E3 ....26 B1
Marius Mans 3
SW17 ....72 C2
Marius Rd SW17 ...72 C2
Marjorie Gr SW11 ...60 B3
Market Ct W1 ....104 C2
Market Mews W1 ...118 A1
Market Pl 1 SE16 ...40 A2
1 ....104 C2
3 London W3 ......28 B1
Market Rd
London N7 ....14 A2
Richmond TW9 ....54 C4
Market Sq E14 ....34 A3
Market Way E14 ...34 A3
Market Yd Mews
SE1 ....138 A1
Markham Pl SW3 ..144 C2
Markham Sq SW3 ..144 C2
Markham St SW3 ..144 B2
Mark Ho 3 E2 ....25 C3
Mark La EC3 ......124 B4
Markland Ho W10 ...30 C2
Mark Mans W12 ...38 C3
Marksbury Ave TW9 54 C4
Mark Sq EC2 ......98 A2
Mark St EC2 ......98 A2

Markstone Ho SE1 .136 A3
Markyate Ho W10 ...22 B1
Marland Ho SW1 ..131 A2
Marlborough W9 ...88 C4
11 Putney SW19 ...69 C3
Marlborough Ave 3
E8 ....24 C4
Marlborough Cl
SE17 ....150 B3
Marlborough Cres
W4 ....38 A3
Marlborough Ct
W8 ....141 B4
Marlborough Day Hospl
NW8 ....78 C2
Marlborough Flats
SW3 ....144 B4
Marlborough Gr
SE1 ....153 B1
Marlborough Hill
NW8 ....78 C1
Marlborough Ho
NW8 ....78 C1
London N4 ....6 B3
Richmond TW10 ...54 C2
Wimbledon SW19 ...69 C1
Marlborough House
SW1 ....119 A1
Marlborough Mans 5
NW6 ....10 C3
Marlborough Mews
SW2 ....62 B3
Marlborough Pl
NW8 ....79 A2
Marlborough Prim Sch
SW3 ....144 B3
Marlborough Rd
SW1 ....119 A1
London N19 ....5 A2
London W4 ....37 B1
Richmond TW10 ...54 B1
Marlborough St
SW3 ....144 B3
Marlborough Trad Est
TW9 ....45 A2
Marlborough Yd N19 .4 C2
Marlbury NW8 ......78 B3
Marley Ho 14 W11 ...30 C2
Marley Wlk NW2 ...9 B3
Marlin Ho SW15 ...58 A2
Marloes Rd W8 ....128 A1
Marlow Ct NW6 ....9 C1
Marlowe Bsns Ctr 2
SE14 ....51 A3
Marlowe Ct SW3 ..144 B3
Marlowe Ho SE8 ...41 B1
18 London N16 ....16 A4
Marlowes The NW8 .79 B4
Marlow Ho E2 ....98 C3
SE1 ....138 C2
London W2 ....100 B1
Marlow Studio
Workshops 2 E2 .98 C3
Marlow Way SE16 ...40 C4
Marl Rd SW18 ......59 B3
Marlton St SE10 ...43 B1
Marmion Ho 13
SW12 ....73 A4
Marmion Mews 4
SW11 ....60 C4
Marmion Rd SW11 .60 C3
Marmont Rd SE15 ..49 C3
Marmora Ho E1 ...33 A4
Marmora Rd SE22 .65 B1
Marner Prim Sch
E3 ....27 A1

Marne St W10 ......23 A2
Marney Rd SW11 ...60 C3
Marnfield Cres SW2 74 B3
Marnham Ave NW2 ..10 A4
Marnock Ho SE1 ..137 C2
Marnock Rd SE4 ...66 B2
Maroon St E14 ......33 A4
Marquess Rd N1 ...15 C2
Marquess Rd N N1 .15 C2
Marquess Rd S 17
N1 ....15 C2
Marquis Ct N4 ......5 B3
Marquis Rd
London N4 ....5 C3
London NW1 ......13 C2
Marrayat Sq SW6 .164 A4
Marrick Cl SW15 ...56 C3
Marrick Ho NW6 ...78 B3
Marriott Rd N4 ......5 B3
Marryat Ho 12 SW1 146 C1
Marryat Rd SW19 ...69 C1
Marsala Rd SE13 ...67 A3
Marsalis Ho 2 E3 .26 C2
Marsden Rd SE15 ...64 B4
Marsden St NW5 ...12 C2
Marshall Cl SW18 ...59 B1
Marshall Ct SW4 ..172 B3
Marshall Ho N1 ....87 C2
NW6 ....23 B3
SE17 ....151 B2
Marshall Rd E10 ...19 A4
Marshall's Pl SE16 .139 A1
Marshall St W1 ....105 A1
Marshalsea Rd
SE1 ....137 A4
Marsham Ct SW1 ..147 C4
19 Putney SW19 ...69 C3
Marsham St SW1 ..147 C4
Marsh Ct E8 ......16 C2
Marshfield St E14 ...42 B3
Marshgate Bsns Ctr
E15 ....27 B3
Marshgate Ctr The
E15 ....27 A4
Marshgate La E15 ...19 A1
Marsh Hill E9 ......18 A3
Marsh St SW1 ....147 C1
Marsh St E14 ......42 A2
Marsh Wall E14 ...42 A4
Marshwood Ho 10
NW6 ....23 C4
Marsland Cl SE17 .150 B1
Marsom Ho N1 ....87 B1
Marston Cl NW6 ...11 B1
Marston Ho SW9 ...173 C1
Marsworth Ho 8
E2 ....24 C4
Martaban Rd N16 ...7 B2
Martello St E8 ......17 A1
Martello Terr E8 ...17 A1
Martell Rd SE21 ...75 C1
Martel Pl E8 ......16 B2
Martha's Bldgs EC1 .97 C1
Martha St E1 ......32 B3
Martin Ct 10 E14 ...42 B4
Martindale SW14 ...55 B2
Martindale Ave 2
E16 ....35 C2
Martindale Ho 13
E14 ....34 A2
Martindale Rd
SW12 ....73 A4
Martineau Ho SW1 146 C1
Martineau Mews
N5 ....15 A4

Martineau Rd N5 ...15 A4
Martin Ho SE1 ....137 A1
SW8 ....162 A2
Martin La EC4 ....123 C4
Martlett Ct WC2 ...106 B1
Martlett Lo NW3 ...11 A4
Martley Ho SW8 ..171 A4
Martock Ct 10 SE15 .50 A2
Marton Rd 2 N16 ...7 A1
Marvel Ho 5 SE5 ...48 C3
Marville Rd SW18 ...59 C1
Marvin St 3 E8 ....17 A2
Mary Adelaide Cl
SW15 ....68 A1
Mary Adelaide Ho
W2 ....101 B4
Mary Ann Bldgs
SE8 ....51 C4
Mary Batchelor Sch
(Girls) SE5 ....48 C2
Mary Datchelor Cl
SE5 ....48 C2
Mary Dine Ct SW8 .163 A1
Mary Ho 5 NW6 ...78 B4
Mary Ho
London W6 ....39 B1
Mary James Ho 3
E2 ....24 C3
Mary Jones Ho 13
E14 ....33 C2
Maryland Rd W9 ...23 C1
London E15 ....19 C3
Marylands Rd W9 ...88 A1
Maryland Wlk N1 ...86 C4
Mary Lawrenson Pl 1
SE3 ....53 C3
Marylebone Flyover
NW1 ....102 A3
Marylebone High St
W1 ....103 C4
Marylebone La
W1 ....103 C2
Marylebone Pas
W1 ....105 A2
Marylebone Rd
NW1 ....103 B4
Marylebone St W1 ..103 C3
Marylebone Sta
NW1 ....90 C1
Marylee Way SE11 .149 A3
Mary Macarthur Ho
E2 ....25 C2
W14 ....154 A4
London N19 ....4 C4
Maryon Mews NW3 .12 A4
Mary Pl
W11 ....31 A2 112 A3
Mary Secole Cl 21
E8 ....24 B4
Mary St 5 E16 ....35 B2
London N1 ....87 A3
Mary Terr NW1 ....82 C3
Mary Wharrie Ho 4
NW3 ....12 B1
Masbro' Rd W14 ...39 C3
Mascotte Rd 2
SW15 ....57 C3
Masefield Ct N5 ...15 C3
Masefield Ho 1
NW6 ....23 C2
Mashie Rd W3 ......29 A3

Maskall Cl SW2 ....74 C1
Maskall Rd SW17 ...71 B1
Maskelyne Cl
SW11 ....168 B4
Mason Cl E16 ......35 C2
SE16 ....153 C2
Mason Ho SE1 ....153 C3
10 London E9 ......17 B1
Mason's Arms Mews
W1 ....118 B4
Mason's Ave EC2 ..109 B2
Mason's Pl EC1 ....96 C4
Mason St SE17 ....151 C4
Mason's Yd SW1 ..119 A2
Massie Rd E8 ......16 C2
Massinger St SE1,
SE17 ....152 A3
Massingham St E1 .25 C1
Mast Ct 17 SE16 ...41 A2
Masterman Ho 5
SE5 ....48 C3
Masters Dr SE16 ...40 A1
Masters Lo 22 E1 ...32 B3
Master's St 4 E1 ...32 C4
Mast House Terr
E14 ....41 C2
Mastin Ho SW18 ...70 C3
Mastmaker Rd E14 .41 C4
Matching Ct 13 E3 .26 C2
Matham Gr SE22 ...64 B3
Matheson Lang Ho
SE1 ....135 B3
Matheson Rd W14 .140 C3
Mathews Ct SE11 ...136 B3
Matilda Ho E1 ....125 B2
Matilda St N1 ......85 A4
Matlock Cl SE24 ...63 B3
Matlock Ct NW8 ...78 C2
7 London SE5 ....63 C3
Matlock St E14 ...33 A3
Maton Ho SW6 ...154 C2
Matson Ho 9 SE16 .40 A3
London E9 ....17 C2
Matthew Cl W10 ...22 C1
Matthew Parker St
SW1 ....133 C3
Matthews Ct N5 ...15 B4
Matthews Ho 3
..........33 C4
Matthews St SW11 168 C2
Matthias Ct 12
..........54 A1
Matthias Ho 2 N16 .16 A3
Matthias Rd N16 ...16 A3
Mattingly Way 4
SE15 ....49 B3
Maude Ho 3 E2 ...24 C3
Maude Rd SE5 ....49 A2
Maudlins Gn E1 ..125 B2
Maudsley Ho TW8 .36 A1
Maudsley Hospl The
SE5 ....48 C1
Maud Rd E10 ......35 B2
Maugham Ct 8 W3 37 B3
Mauleverer Rd SW2 62 A2
Maundeby Wlk NW10 8 A2
Maunsel St SW1 ..147 B4
Mauretania Bldg 1
E1 ....32 C2
Maurice Ho SW9 ...172 C2
Maurice St W12 ...30 A3
Mauritius Rd SE10 .43 A2
Maury Rd N16 ......7 C2
Maverton Rd E3 ...26 C4
Mavor Ho N1 ......85 A3

Mawbey Ho SE1 .....153 A1
Mawbey Pl SE1 ....153 A1
Mawbey Rd SE1 ......153 A1
Mawbey St SW8 ......162 A1
Mawdley Ho SE1 .....135 C2
Mawson Ho EC1 ......107 B4
Mawson La W4 ....46 B4
Maxden Ct SE16 ....64 A4
Maxted Rd SE15 ....64 B4
Maxwell Ct SE21 ....76 C3
Maxwell Rd SW6 .....156 B1
Maya Cl SE15 ....50 A1
Mayall Rd SE24 ....63 A2
Maybury Ct W1 ....103 C3
Maybury Gdns NW10 ..9 A2
Maybury Mews N6 ......4 B4
Maydew Ho SE16 ......40 B2
Maydwell Ho **6**
  E14 ....33 C4
Mayers Ct E8 ....16 C4
Mayfair Pl W1 ....118 B2
Mayfield Ave W4 ....38 A2
Mayfield Cl
  London E8 ....16 C3
  London SW4 ....61 C2
Mayfield Ho **20** E2 ..25 A3
Mayfield Mans
  SW15 ....58 B2
Mayfield Rd
  Acton W3 ....28 A2
  London E8 ....16 B1
  London W12 ....38 A4
Mayflower Cl SE16 ....40 C2
Mayflower Prim Sch
  E14 ....34 A3
Mayflower Rd SW9 ....62 A4
Mayflower St **1**
  SE16 ....40 B4
Mayford NW1 ....83 A2
Mayford Cl SW12 ......72 B4
Mayford Rd SW12 .....72 C4
Maygood Ho N1 ....85 B2
Maygood St N1 ....85 B2
Maygrove Rd NW6 ....10 B2
Mayhew Ct **2** SE5 ...63 C3
Maylands Ho SW3 ...144 B3
Maynard Cl SW6 .....156 B1
Maynard Ho E1 ....26 A2
Maynards Quay E1 ....32 B2
Mayola Rd E5 ....17 B4
Mayo Rd NW10 ....8 A2
May's Buildings Mews
  SE10 ....52 C3
Mays Ct WC2 ....120 A3
May's Ct SE10 ....52 C3
Maysoule Rd SW11 ...59 C3
Mayston Mews **3**
  SE10 ....43 C1
Maythorne Cotts
  SE13 ....67 C1
Mayton St N7 ....5 B1
May Tree Ho SE4 ......66 B4
Maytree Wlk SW2 .....74 C2
Mayward Ho **7** SE5 ..49 A2
Maze Hill SE10,SE3 ...53 A4
Maze Hill Lo **8**
  SE10 ....52 C4
Maze Hill Specl Sch
  SE10 ....52 C4
Maze Hill Sta SE10 ...53 A4
Mazenod Ave NW6 ...10 C1
Maze Rd TW9 ....44 C3
Meacod Cl **3** NW1 ..12 C1
Meadcroft Rd SE17 ...48 A4

Meade Cl W4 ....44 C4
Meader Ct SE14 ....50 C3
Mead Ho W11 ....112 C3
Mead Lo W4 ....37 C4
Meadowbank NW3 ...12 B1
Meadow Bank **7**
  SW15 ....58 B2
Meadowbank Cl
  SW6 ....47 B3
Meadow Cl E9 ....18 B3
Meadowcroft **9**
  W4 ....45 A4
Meadowgate Sch
  SE4 ....66 A4
Meadow Mews
  SW8 ....162 C3
Meadow Pl SW8 .....162 B2
Chiswick W4 ....46 A3
Meadow Rd SW8 .....162 C2
Meadow Row SE1 ...136 C1
Mead Pl E9 ....17 B2
Mead Row SE1 ....135 B2
Meadway The SE3 ....52 C1
Meakin Est SE1 ......138 A2
Meakin Ho N7 ....14 B3
Meard St W1 ....105 B1
Meath Ho SE24 ....63 A1
Meath St SW11 ......170 A4
Mecklenburgh Pl
  WC1 ....94 C2
Mecklenburgh Sq
  WC1 ....94 C2
Medburn St NW1 ......83 B2
Medcroft Gdns
  SW14 ....55 B3
Medfield St SW15 .....69 A4
Medhurst Cl **17** E3 ..26 A3
Median Rd E5 ....17 B3
Medical Coll of St
  Bartholomew's Hospl
  The EC1 ....96 B1
Medina Ct N7 ....5 C1
Medina Gr N7 ....5 C1
Medina Ho SE15 ....65 B3
Medina Rd N7 ....5 C1
Medley Rd NW6 ....10 C2
Medora Rd SW2 ....74 B4
Medresco Ho NW3 ....11 C3
Medusa Rd SE6,SE12 .67 A1
Medway Bldgs E3 .....26 A3
Medway Ct WC1 ....94 A3
Medway Ho NW8 ....102 A4
  SE1 ....137 C3
  London N16 ....15 C4
Medway Mews **18**
  E3 ....26 A3
Medway Rd E3 ....26 A3
Medway St SW1 .....133 C1
Medwin St SW4 ....62 B3
Meecham Ct SW11 .168 A2
Meeson St E5 ....18 A4
Meeting House Alley **7**
  E1 ....32 A1
Meeting House La
  SE15 ....50 A3
Mehetabel Rd E9 .....17 B3
Melba Ct E9 ....16 B3
Melbourne Ct W9 .....89 A2
  London E5 ....17 C4
Melbourne Gr SE22 ..64 B3
Melbourne Ho W8 ...113 B1
Melbourne Mews
  SW9 ....173 B3
Melbourne Pl WC2 ..107 A1
Melbourne Sq
  SW9 ....173 B3

Melbrook Ho **11**
  SE22 ....64 A4
Melbury Ct W8 ....127 A2
Melbury Dr SE5 ....49 A3
Melbury Ho SW8 ....162 C2
Melbury Rd W14 .....127 A2
Melchester **8** W11 ..31 B3
Melchester Ho **1**
  N19 ....4 C1
Melcombe Ct NW1 ..102 C4
Melcombe Ho
  SW8 ....162 C1
Melcombe Pl NW1 ..102 C4
Melcombe Prim Sch
  W6 ....47 C4
Melcombe St NW1 ...91 A1
Meldon Cl SW6 ......166 B4
Melford Ct SE22 ....76 C4
Melford Rd SE21,
  SE22 ....76 C3
Melgund Rd N5 ....14 C3
Melina Ct NW8 ....89 B3
  Putney SW15 ....56 C4
Melina Pl NW8 ....89 B3
Melina Rd W12 ....39 A4
Melior Pl SE1 ....138 A4
Melior St SE1 ....138 A4
Melisa Ct N6 ....4 C4
Mellington St **2** N16 ..7 C1
Mellis Ave TW9 ....45 A2
Mellish Ho **12** E1 ...32 A3
Mellish St E14 ....41 C3
Mellitus St W12 ....29 B3
Mell St **6** SE10 ....43 A1
Melody La N5 ....15 B3
Melody Rd SW18 ......59 B2
Melon Pl W8 ....127 C4
Melon Rd SE15 ....49 C2
Melrose Ave
  London NW2 ....9 B3
  Wimbledon SW19 .....70 C1
Melrose Cl SE12 ....83 B4
Melrose Gdns W6 .....39 B3
Melrose Ho NW6 .....146 B2
  London NW6 ....23 C2
Melrose Rd
  1 Barnes SW13 ....46 B1
  Wandsworth SW18 ...58 B1
Melrose Terr W6 ......39 B3
Melton Ct SW7 ....143 C3
Melton Ho E5 ....7 C2
Melton St NW1 ....93 B3
Melville Court Flats
  W12 ....39 A4
Melville Ct SE8 ....41 A2
  4 London W4 ....36 C1
Melville Ho SE10 .....52 B2
Melville Pl **4** N1 ....15 B1
Melville Rd SW13 .....46 C2
Melville Villas Rd
  W3 ....28 C1
Melvin Ct **11** TW9 ...44 C2
Melwood Ho **22** E1 ..32 A3
Melyn Cl N7 ....13 B4
Memel Ct EC1 ....96 C1
Memel St EC1 ....96 C1
Mendham Ho SE1 ...138 A2
Mendip Ct SE14 ......50 A4
  8 London SW11 ...59 B4
Mendip Dr NW2,
  NW11 ....1 A1
Mendip Ho **2** N4 .....6 C4
Mendip Hos **15** E2 ..25 B2
Mendip Rd SW11 .....59 B4
Mendora Rd SW6 ....154 C2
Menelik Rd NW2 ....10 A4
Menorah Gram Sch
  NW11 ....1 A4

Menorah Prim Sch
  NW11 ....1 A4
Menotti St E2 ....99 C2
Menteath Ho **5**
  E14 ....33 C3
Mentmore Terr E8 ....17 A1
Mentone Ct SW8 ....172 B4
Meon Rd W3 ....37 B4
Mepham St SE1 ......121 B1
Merbury Cl SE13 ......67 B2
Mercator Pl E14 ....41 C1
Mercator Rd SE13 ...67 C3
Merceron Ho **3** E2 ..25 B2
Merceron St E1 ....25 A1
Mercers Cl SE10 ......43 B2
Mercer's Cotts **8**
  E3 ....33 A3
Mercers Ho N19 ....4 C1
Mercers Mews N19 ...4 C1
Mercer St WC2 ......106 A1
Merchant Ct E1 ....32 B1
Merchant St E3 ....26 B2
Merchant Taylors Hall
  EC3 ....109 C1
Merchon Ho N7 ....13 B4
Mercia Gr **7** SE13 ...67 B3
Mercia Ho **2** SE5 ...48 B1
Mercier Rd SW15 .....58 A2
Mercury Ct **3** E14 ..41 C2
  London SW9 ....173 B4
Mercury Way SE14 ...50 C4
Mercy Terr SE13 ......67 A2
Mere Cl SW15,SW19 ..69 C4
Meredith Ave NW2 ....9 B3
Meredith Ho **11** N16 ..16 A3
Meredith Mews SE4 ..66 B3
Meredith St EC1 ....96 A3
Meredith Twr W3 ......37 A3
Meretone Cl SE4 ......66 A3
Mereworth Ho **3**
  SE15 ....50 B4
Merganser Ct **17**
  SE8 ....41 B1
Meridan St SE13 ......67 C3
Meriden Ct SW3 .....144 A1
Meriden Ho **20** N1 ..24 A4
Meridian Building
  SE10 ....52 C3
Meridian Ho SE10 ....43 A2
Meridian Pl E14 ....42 B4
Meridian Prim Sch
  SE10 ....52 C4
Meridian Sq E15 ......19 C1
Merivale Rd SW15 ...58 A3
Merlin Ho
  London NW3 ....11 C4
  3 London W4 ....37 C1
Merlins Ct WC1 ....95 B4
Merlin St EC1 ....95 B3
Mermaid Ct SE1 .....137 B4
  SE16 ....33 B1
Mermaid Ho **6** E14 ..34 B2
Mermaid Twr **22**
  SE8 ....51 B4
Meroe Ct N16 ....7 A2
Merredene St SW2 ...62 B1
Merricks Ct **5**
  SW14 ....55 A3
Merrick Sq SE1 ......137 B2
Merrington Rd
  SW6 ....155 C4
Merritt Rd SE4 ....66 B2
Merrivale NW1 ....83 A3
Merrow St SE17 ......151 B1
Merrow Wlk SE17 ....151 C2
Merryfield SE3 ....53 B1

Mersey Ho **10** N7 ...14 C3
Merstone Ho SW18 ...59 A1
Merthyr Terr SW13 ...47 A4
Merton Abbey Mills
  SW18 ....71 A3
Merton Ave W4 ....38 B2
Merton Ho SW18 .....70 C3
Merton La N6 ....3 B2
Merton Rd SW18 ......70 C4
Merton Rise NW3 .....12 A1
Merton Road Ind Est
  SW18 ....70 C4
Merttins Rd SE15 .....65 C2
Meru Cl NW5 ....12 C3
Mervan Rd SW2 ....62 C3
Messaline Ave W3 ....28 B3
Messina Ave NW6 ....10 C1
Messiter Ho N1 ....85 A3
Metcalfe Ho SW8 ...171 B2
Meteor St SW11 ....60 C3
Methley Ho **8** N7 .....5 B2
Methley St SE11 .....149 C1
Methodist Central Hall
  SW1 ....133 C3
Methwold Rd W10 ...22 C1
Metropolitan Benefit
  Societies Almshouses
  3 N1 ....16 A2
Metropolitan Ct **17**
  E14 ....33 C4
Mews St E1 ....125 B2
Mexborough NW1 ....82 C3
Mexfield Rd SW15 ...58 B2
Meyer Ho **1** SW12 ..73 A4
Meymott St SE1 .....122 A1
Meynell Cres E9 ......17 C1
Meynell Gdns E9 .....17 C1
Meynell Rd E9 ....17 C1
Meyrick Ho **5** E14 ..33 C4
Meyrick Rd
  London NW10 ....8 C2
  London SW11 ....59 C4
Miah Terr E1 ....125 C1
Micawber Ct N1 ....97 A4
Micawber Ho SE16 .139 C3
Micawber St N1 ....97 A4
Michael Cliffe Ho
  EC1 ....95 C3
Michael Faraday Ho
  SE17 ....151 C1
Michael Faraday Sch
  SE17 ....151 C1
Michael Rd SW6 ....166 B4
Michelangelo Ct **14**
  SE16 ....40 A1
Michelle Ct W3 ....28 C2
Michels Almshouses
  TW10 ....54 A2
Michelsdale Dr **3**
  TW9 ....54 A3
Michelson Ho
  SE11 ....149 A3
Michel's Row **2**
  TW9 ....54 A3
Michigan Ho E14 .....41 C3
Mickledore NW1 ....83 A1
Micklethwaite Rd
  SW6 ....155 C3
Mickleton Ho **2**
  W2 ....31 C4
Middlefield NW8 ....79 B4
Middle Row W10 ......23 A1
Middle Row Prim Sch
  W10 ....23 A1
Middlesex Ct **5** W4 ..38 B2
Middlesex Hospl
  W1 ....105 A3

Middlesex Hospl Annexe
W1 .... 105 A4
Middlesex Pas EC1 108 B3
Middlesex Pl 13 E9 .17 B2
Middlesex St E1 ....110 C2
Middle St EC1 .... 108 C4
Middle Temple
EC4 ....121 B4
Middle Temple La
EC4 ....121 B4
Middleton Bldgs
W1 ....104 C2
Middleton Dr SE16 .40 C4
Middleton Gr N7 ....14 A3
Middleton Ho SE1 137 B1
London E8 ....16 B1
Middleton Mews
N7 ....14 A3
Middleton Rd
London E8 ....16 B1
London NW11 ....1 C4
Middleton St E2 ....25 A2
Middleton Way
SE13 ....67 C3
Midford Pl W1 ....93 A1
Midhope Ho WC1 ..94 B3
Midhope St WC1 ....94 B3
Midhurst Ct N8 ......5 A4
Midhurst Ho E14 ..33 B3
Midhurst Way E5 ..16 C4
Midland Pl E14 ......42 B1
Midland Rd NW1 ..84 A1
Midland Terr NW10 .21 A1
Midlothian Rd E3 ..26 B1
Midmoor Rd SW12 .73 B3
Midship Cl SE16 ....32 C1
Midship Point E14 ..41 C4
Midstrath Rd NW10 .8 A4
Midway Ho EC1 ....96 B4
Milborne Gr
SW10 ....15 143 A1
Milborne Ho 9 E9 .17 B2
Milborne St E9 ......17 B2
Milcote St SE1 ......136 B3
Milday Gr N N1 .....15 C3
Mildmay Ave N1 ...15 C2
Mildmay Gr N N1 ..15 C3
Mildmay Ho 9
SW15 ....57 B2
Mildmay Mission Hospl
E2 ....98 C3
Mildmay Pk N1 .....15 C3
Mildmay Rd N1 .....16 A3
Mildmay St N1 ......15 C2
Mile End Pl E1 ......25 C1
Mile End Rd E1,E3 .25 C1
Mile End Sta E3 ....26 B2
Miles Bldgs NW1 ..102 A4
Miles Coverdale Prim
Sch W12 ....39 B4
Miles Ct E1 ....32 A3
Miles Ho 5 SE10 ..43 A1
Miles Lo E15 ....19 C3
Miles Pl NW8 ....101 C4
Miles St SW8 ....162 B3
Milestone Green
SW14 ....55 C3
Milfoil St W12 ....29 C2
Milford Cl 3 N16 ....7 A3
Milford La WC2 ....121 B4
Milford Mews SW16 .74 B1
Milk St EC2 ....109 A2
Milkwell Yd SE5 ....48 B2
Milkwood Rd SE24 .63 A3
Milk Yd E1 ....32 B2
Millais Rd E11 ......19 C4

Milland Ho 11 SW15 68 C3
Millard Cl 21 N16 ....16 A3
Millard Ho SE8 ......41 B1
Millbank SW1 ......148 A3
Millbank Prim Sch
SW1 ....147 C3
Millbrooke Ct 7
SW15 ....58 A2
Millbrook Ho 4
SE15 ....49 C4
Millbrook Rd SW9 .63 A4
Millender Wlk SE16 .40 B2
Millennium Bridge*
SE1,EC4 ....122 C3
Millennium Dome*
SE10 ....35 A1
Millennium Dr E14 .42 C2
Millennium Harbour
E14 ....41 C4
Millennium Pl 27
E2 ....25 A3
Millennium Prim Sch
SE10 ....43 B3
Millennium Sq
SE1 ....139 A4
Millennium Way
SE10 ....43 A3
Miller Ho 9 SW2 ..74 A4
Miller's Ave E8,N16 .16 B3
Miller's Ct 1 W4 ...38 B1
Miller St NW1 ....82 C2
Miller's Terr 1 E8 .16 B3
Miller's Way W6 ....39 B4
Millers Wharf Ho
E1 ....125 B1
Miller Wlk SE1 ....121 C1
Millfield La N6 ....3 B2
Millfield Pl N6 ....3 C2
Millfields Com Sch
E5 ....17 B4
Millgrove St SW11 169 B2
Millharbour E14 ....42 A4
Mill Hill SW13 ....56 C4
Mill Hill Rd W3 .....28 A1
Mill Hill Terr 9 W3 .28 A1
Milligan St E14 ......33 B2
Millington Ho N16 ..6 C1
Mill La NW6 ....10 B3
Millman Ct WC1 ....94 C1
Millman Mews WC1 .94 C1
Millman Pl WC1 ....95 A1
Millman St WC1 ....94 C1
Millmark Gr SE14 ..51 A1
Millner Ct SE4 ......51 B1
Mill Pl E14 ....33 A3
Mill Pond Cl SW8 .161 C2
Millpond Est SE16 .40 A4
Mill Row N1 ....24 A4
Mills Gr 1 E14 ....34 B4
Mills Ho SW8 ......171 A4
Millshot Cl SW6 ....47 B2
Mills Row W4 ....37 C2
Mill St SE1 ....139 A4
W1 ....118 C4
Millstream Rd SE1 138 C3
Mill Trad Est The
NW10 ....20 B2
Millwall Dock Rd
E14 ....41 C3
Millwood St 10 W10 31 A4
Mill Yd E1 ....125 B4
Milman Rd NW6 ....23 A3
Milman's Ho SE1 .157 B3

Milman's St SW10 .157 B3
Milner Ho 2 SW11 .59 C4
Milner Pl N1 ....85 C4
Milner Sq N1 ....15 A1
Milner St SW3 ......144 C4
Milnthorpe Rd W4 .45 C4
Milo Rd SE22 ....64 B1
Milroid Ho 11 E1 ....32 C4
Milroy Wlk SE1 ....122 A2
Milson Rd W14 ....126 A2
Milsted Ho 22 E5 ..17 A3
Milton Ave London N6 .4 B4
London NW10 ......20 C4
Milton Cl SE1 ....152 C3
Milton Court Rd
SE14 ....51 A4
Milton Ct EC2 ......109 B4
SE14 ....51 A4
Fulham SW6 ....58 A4
London SW18 ......58 C2
Milton Gr N16 ....16 A4
Milton Ho 19 E2 ....25 B2
2 SE5 ....48 C3
Milton House Mans
E8 ....16 B4
Milton Pk N6 ....4 B4
Milton Pl 3 N7 .....14 C3
Milton Rd London N6 .4 B4
London SE24 ....63 A2
London W3 ....28 C1
Mortlake SW14 ....55 C4
Milton St EC1,EC2 109 B4
Milverton NW5 ......12 C3
Milverton Rd NW6 ..9 B1
Milverton St SE11 149 C1
Milward St E1 ....32 A4
Mimosa St SW6 ....172 B3
Mimosa St SW6 ....164 C3
Mina Rd SE17 ......152 B2
Minchin Ho 8 E14 .33 C3
Mincing La EC3 ....124 A4
Minera Mews SW1 145 C4
Minerva Cl SW9 ...163 C2
Minerva Rd NW10 .20 C2
Minerva St E2 ....25 A3
Minerva Wlk EC1 ..108 B1
Minet Ave NW10 ...21 A3
Minet Gdns NW10 .21 A3
Minet Rd SE5,SW9 .48 A1
Minford Gdns W14 .39 C4
Mingard Wlk N7 ....5 B1
Ming St E14 ....33 C2
Minnow Wlk SE17 152 B3
Minories EC3 ....124 C4
Minshull St SW8 ..171 B3
Minson Rd E9 ....25 C4
Minstead Gdns
SW15 ....68 B4
Minster Rd NW2 ..10 A3
Mint Bsns Pk 13
E16 ....35 C4
Mintern St N1 ....87 C2
Minton Mews 3
NW6 ....11 A2
Mint St SE1 ....137 A4
Mirabel Rd SW6 ..155 A2
Miranda Cl 16 E1 ..32 B4
Miranda Ho 3 N1 ..24 A3
Miranda Rd N19 ....4 B3
Missenden SE17 ..151 C1
Missenden Ho NW8 .90 A2
Mission Pl SE15 ....49 C2
Mission Sq 13 TW8 .44 A4
Misterton Ct SW11 167 C4
Mistral SE5 ....49 A2
Mitali Pas E1 ....111 B3

Mitcham Ho 9 SE5 .48 B2
Mitcham Rd SW17 .72 B4
Mitchell Brook Prim Sch
NW10 ....8 A2
Mitchell Ho
51 London W12 ..30 A2
London W12 ....37 A1
Mitchell's Pl SE21 ..76 A4
Mitchell St EC1 ....97 A2
Mitchison Rd N1 ..15 C2
Mitford Rd N19 .....5 A2
Mitre Bridge Ind Pk
W10 ....22 A1
Mitre Ct EC2 ....109 A2
Mitre Rd SE1 ....135 C4
Mitre Sq EC3 ....110 B1
Mitre St EC3 ....110 B1
Mitre The 9 E14 ....33 B2
Mitre Way W10 ......22 A1
Moatfield Ho N6 ....10 A1
Moat Pl Acton W3 .28 A3
London SW9 ....62 B4
Moberly Rd SW4 ...73 C4
Mobey Ct SW4 .....172 A3
Mocatta Ho 6 E1 ..25 A1
Modbury Gdns NW5 12 C2
Modder Pl SW15 ...57 C3
Model Cotts SW14 .55 B4
Modling Ho 8 E2 ..25 C3
Moelwyn Hughes Ct
N7 ....13 C3
Moffat Ho 24 SE5 .48 B3
Mohawk Ho 31 E3 .26 A3
Moira Ct SW17 .....72 C2
Moira Ho 9 SW9 ..173 B4
Moland Mead SE16 .40 C1
Molasses Ho 1
SW11 ....59 B4
Molasses Row 2
SW11 ....59 B4
Mole Ct 2 W12 ....38 A4
Mole Ho NW8 ....89 C1
Molesey Ho 2 ......98 C2
Molesford Rd SW6 165 B3
Molesworth Ho 3
SE17 ....48 B4
Molesworth St SE13 67 B4
Molly Huggins Cl
SW12 ....73 B4
Molton Ho N1 ......85 A3
Molyneux St W1 ..102 B3
Mona Rd SE15 .....50 B1
Mona St E16 ....35 B2
Monck's Row SW18 58 B1
Monck St SW1 .....133 C1
Monclar Rd SE5 ...63 C3
Moncorvo Cl SW7 130 A3
Moncrieff St SE15 .49 C1
Mondragon Ho
SW8 ....172 B4
Moneyer Ho N1 ....97 B4
Monica Shaw Ct
NW1 ....83 C1
Monier Rd E3 ....18 C1
Monk Ct W12 ....29 C1
Monk Dr E16 ....35 C2
Monkridge 8 N8 ....4 C4
Monksfield N4 ....5 C2
Monkton Ct W14 ..126 C2
Monkton Ho
33 SE16 ....40 C4
22 London E5 .....17 A3
Monkton St SE11 ..149 C4
Monkwell Sq EC2 ..109 A3
Monmouth Cl W4 ..37 C3
Monmouth Gr TW8 .36 A2

Mon – Mon 231
Monmouth Ho
5 London NW5 .....13 A2
London SW18 ....58 C1
Monmouth Pl W2 100 A1
Monmouth Rd W2 .31 C3
Monmouth St WC2 106 A1
Monnery Rd N19 ....4 B1
Monner Rd SE1 ...153 B3
Monroe Dr SW14 ..55 A2
Monroe Ho NW8 ...90 B3
Monro Ho
4 London NW3 ....11 B4
4 London N19 ....4 C4
Monsal Ct E5 ....18 A4
Monsell Rd N4,N5 .6 A1
Monson Prim Sch
SE14 ....50 C3
Monson Rd SE14 ..50 C3
London NW10 ....22 A3
Montagu Ct W1 ..103 A3
Montague Ave SE4 .66 C3
Montague Cl SE1 123 B2
Montague Pl WC1 105 C4
Montague Rd
London E8 ....16 C3
Richmond TW10 ..54 A1
Montague Sq SE15 50 B3
Montague St EC1 108 C4
WC1 ....106 A4
Montagu Mans
W1 ....103 A3
Montagu Mews N
W1 ....103 A3
Montagu Mews S
W1 ....103 A3
Montagu Mews W
W1 ....103 A3
Montagu Pl W1 ...103 A3
Montagu Row W1 103 A3
Montagu Sq W1 ...103 A3
Montagu St W1 ...103 A2
Montana Rd SW17 .72 C1
Montcalm Ho E14 .41 C3
Montclare St
E2 ....24 B1 98 C2
Monteagle Ct 21 N1 24 A3
Monteagle Way
London E5 ....7 C1
London SE15 ......65 A4
Montefiore Ct 2 N16 7 B3
Montefiore St
SW8 ....170 B1
Montem Prim Sch
N7 ....5 B1
Montem St N4 ......5 B3
Montenotte Rd N8 .4 C4
Montesquieu Terr 3
E16 ....35 B1
Montford Pl SE11 .149 B1
Montfort Ho E14 ...42 B3
4 E2 ....25 B2
Montfort Pl SW19 .69 C3
Montgo Cl 10 SW2 .62 C3
Montgomery Ct W4 45 B4
Montgomery Ho 5
SW14 ....55 C4
Montgomery Lo 26
E1 ....25 B1
Montgomery Rd W4 37 B2
Montholme Rd
SW11 ....60 B1
Montolieu Gdns
SW15 ....57 A2
Montpelier Gr NW5 .13 B3

Montpelier Mews
SW7 .... **130** B2
Montpelier Pl 21 E1 **32** B3
SW7 .... **130** B2
Montpelier Rd SE15 ..**50** A2
Montpelier Rise
NW11 ....1 A4
Montpelier Row
SE3 ....53 B1
Montpelier Sq
SW7 .... **130** B3
Montpelier St 3 SW7 **130** B2
Montpelier Terr
SW7 .... **130** B3
Montpelier Vale
SE3 ....53 B1
Montpelier Way
NW11 ....1 A4
Montpelier Wlk
SW7 .... **130** B2
Montreal Pl WC2 .. **120** C4
Montrell Rd SW2 ....**74** A3
Montrose Ave NW6 ..**23** A3
Montrose St SW7 .. **129** C3
Montrose Ho E14 ....**41** C3
SW1 .... **131** C3
Montrose Pl SW1 .. **131** C3
Montrose Villas W6 ..**38** C1
Montserrat Rd
SW15 ....58 A3
Monument Gdns
SE13 ....67 B2
Monument St EC3 .. **124** A3
Monument Sta
EC3 .... **123** C4
Monument The*
EC3 .... **123** C4
Monza St E1 ....**32** B2
Moodkee St SE16 ....**40** B4
Moody Rd SE15 .....**49** B2
Moody St E1 ....**25** C2
Moon St N1 ....**86** A4
Moorcroft Rd SW16 **74** A1
Moore Cl SW14 ....**55** B4
Moore Ct N1 ....**86** B4
Moore Ho 6 E1 ....**32** B2
2 E2 ....**25** B2
5 SE10 ....**43** B1
Wandsworth SW17 ..**71** C1
Moore Park Ct
SW6 .... **156** B2
Moore Park Rd
SW6 .... **156** A1
Moore St SW3 .... **144** C4
Moorfields EC2 .. **109** B3
Moorfields Eye Hospl
EC2 ....97 B3
Moorfields Highwalk
EC2 .... **109** B3
Moorfields Prim Sch
EC1 ....97 B2
Moorgate EC2 .... **109** B3
Moorgate Pl EC2 **109** B2
Moorgate Sta EC2 **109** B3
Moorgreen Ho EC1 ..**96** A4
Moorhouse Rd W2 ..**31** C3
Moor La EC2 ...... **109** B4
Moorland Rd SW9 ..**63** A3
Moor Pl EC2 ...... **109** B3
Moor St W1 ...... **105** C1
Morant Ho SW9 .. **172** C2
Morant St E14 ....**33** C2
Mora Prim Sch NW2 ..**9** B4
Mora St EC1 ....**97** A3
Mora Rd NW2 ....9 B4

Morat St SW9 ..... **173** A4
Moravian Cl SW3 .. **157** C3
Moravian Pl SW10 **157** C3
Moravian St 10 E2 ..**25** B2
Moray Ho 8 E1 ....**26** A1
Moray Mews N4,N7 ..**5** B2
Moray Rd N4,N7 ....**5** B2
Mordaunt Ho
4 London NW10 ....**20** C4
London SW8 ...... **171** B1
Mordaunt Rd NW10 ..**20** C4
Mordaunt St SW9 ..**62** B4
Morden Hill SE13 ..**52** B1
Morden Ho 10 SW2 ..**62** C1
Morden La SE13 ....**52** B2
Morden Mount Prim Sch
SE13 ....52 A1
Morden Rd SE3 .... **53** C1
Morden Road Mews
SE3 ....53 C1
Morden St 3 SE13 ..**52** A2
Morden Wharf Rd
SE10 ....43 A3
Mordern Ho SW1 ....**90** B1
Morecambe Cl E1 ....**32** C4
Morecambe St
SE17 .... **151** A2
More Cl E16 ....**35** B1
W14 .... **140** A3
Moredown Ho 3
E8 ....16 C3
More House Sch
SW1 .... **131** A1
Moreland Ct 3 NW2 ..1 C1
Moreland Prim Sch
EC1 ....96 B3
Moreland St EC1 ....**96** B4
Morella Rd SW11,
SW12 ....84 B4
Morell Ho SW9 .. **172** C1
Moresby Wlk SW8 **170** B1
More's Gdn SW3 .. **157** C3
Moreton Ho SE16 ..**40** A3
Moreton Pl SW1 .. **147** A2
Moreton St SW1 .. **147** B2
Moreton Terr SW1 **147** A2
Moreton Terr Mews N
SW1 .... **147** A2
Moreton Terr Mews S
SW1 .... **147** A2
Moreton Twr 3 SW3 **28** A1
Morgan Ct SW11 .. **167** C2
Morgan Ho SW1 .. **147** A3
SW8 .... **171** A4
Morgan Rd W10 ....**31** B4
London N7 ....14 C3
Morgan St E16 .... **35** B2
E3 ....25 C2
Morgan's Wlk
SW11 .... **158** A1
Moriatry Cl N7 .....**14** A4
Morie St SW18 .....**59** A2
Morkyns Wlk SE21 ..**76** A1
Morland Cl NW11 ....2 A3
Morland Ct W12 ....**39** A4
Morland Est E8 .....**16** C1
Morland Ho NW1 .. **83** A1
NW6 ....23 C4
SW1 .... **148** A4
W11 ....31 A3
Morland Mews N1 ..**14** C1
Morley Coll SE1 .. **135** C2
Morley Ho
London N16 ....7 C2
Streatham SW2 .....**74** A4
Morley St SE13 ....**67** B3

Morley St SE1 .... **135** C3
Morna Rd SE5 .....**48** B1
Morning La E9 .....**17** B2
Morningside Prim Sch
E9 ....17 B2
Mornington Ave
W14 .... **140** C3
Mornington Avenue
Mans W14 .... **140** C3
Mornington Cres
NW1 ....82 C2
Mornington Crescent
Sta NW1 ....82 C2
Mornington Ct NW1 **82** C2
Mornington Gr E3 ..**26** C2
Mornington Mews 2
SE5 ....48 B2
Mornington Pl NW1 **82** C2
4 SE8 ....51 B3
Mornington Rd
SE14,SE8 ....51 B3
Mornington St NW1 **82** B2
Mornington Terr
NW1 ....82 B2
Morocco St SE1 .. **138** A3
Morpeth Gr E9 .....**25** C4
Morpeth Rd E9 .....**25** C4
Morpeth Sec Sch
E2 ....25 B2
Morpeth St E2 .....**25** C2
Morpeth Terr SW1 **146** C4
Morrel Ct 7 E2 .. **24** C3
Morris Blitz Ct 7
N16 ....16 B4
Morris Ct 3 SE5 .. **63** C3
Morris Gdns SW18 ..**70** C4
Morris Ho 7 E2 ....**25** B2
5 NW8 ....90 A1
10 London N19 .... **13** B4
4 London SW4 .....**62** A3
Morrish Rd SW2 ....**74** A4
Morrison Bldgs E1 **111** B2
Morrison Ho SW2 ..**74** C3
Morrison St SW11 ..**60** C4
Morris Pl N4 ....5 C2
Morris St E1 ....**32** A3
E14 ....34 A4
Morshead Mans W9 **23** C2
Morshead Rd W9 .. **23** C2
Mortain Ho 9 SE16 **40** A2
Morten Cl SW4 .....**61** C1
Mortimer Cl
1 London NW2 .....**1** A1
Streatham SW16 ....**73** C2
Mortimer Cres NW6 **78** B3
Mortimer Ct NW8 .. **79** A1
Mortimer Est NW6 **78** A3
Mortimer Ho W11 .. **30** C1
6 London W11 .... **30** C1
Mortimer Lo 11
SW19 ....70 A3
Mortimer Market
WC1 ....93 A1
Mortimer Pl NW6 .. **78** A3
Mortimer Rd
London N1 ....16 A1
London NW10 .....**22** B2
Mortimer Sq W11 ..**30** C2
Mortimer St W1 .. **105** A3
Mortimer Terr NW5 **13** A4
Mortlake High St
SW14 ....55 C4
Mortlake Rd SW14,
TW9 ....44 C2
Mortlake Sta SW14 **55** B4
Mortlock Cl SE15 ..**50** A2

Morton Ho SE17 ....**48** A4
Morton Mews
SW5 .... **142** A3
Morton Pl SE1 .... **135** B1
Morton Rd N1 ....**15** B1
Morval Rd SW2 ....**62** C2
Morven Rd SW17 ..**72** B1
Morville St E3 .....**26** C3
Morwell St WC1 .. **105** C3
Moscow Pl W2 .... **114** A4
Moscow Rd W2 .. **114** A4
Mosedale NW1 .... **92** B3
Moseley Way SE10 **43** B3
Mosque Terr E1 .. **111** B4
Mosque Tower E1 **111** B4
Moss Cl E1 .... **111** C4
Mossbury Rd SW11 **60** A4
Mossford St E3 ....**26** B1
Mossington Gdns
SE16 ....40 B2
Mossop St SW3 .. **144** B4
Mostyn Gdns NW10 **22** C3
Mostyn Gr E3 .....**26** C3
Mostyn Lo N5 ......**15** B4
Mostyn Rd SW9 .. **173** C3
Motcomb St SW1 **131** B2
Mothers Sq The 13
E5 ....17 A4
Motley Ave EC2 .....**98** A2
Motley St SW8 .. **170** C2
Moules Ct SE5 .....**48** B3
Moulins Rd E9 .....**17** B1
Moulsford Ho
32 W2 ....**31** C4
2 London N7 ......**14** A3
Mounsey Ho 10
W10 ....23 A2
Mount Adon Pk
SE21,SE22 .... **76** C4
Mountague Pl 2
E14 ....34 B2
Mountain Ho SE11 **148** C2
Mount Angelus Rd
SW15 ....68 B4
Mount Ararat Rd
TW10 ....54 A2
Mountbatten Ho N6 ..3 C4
Mountbatten Mews
SW18 ....71 B3
Mount Carmel RC Coll
N19 ....4 C3
Mount Carmel RC Sec
Sch N7 ....14 B3
Mounteagle Gdns
SW16,SW2 .... **74** B1
Mount Ephraim La
SW16 ....73 C1
Mount Ephraim Rd
SW16 ....73 C1
Mountfield NW2 .....1 B2
Mountfield Ct SE13 **67** C1
Mountford Ct E1 **111** B2
Mountfort Cres N1 **14** C1
Mountfort Terr 1
N1 ....14 C1
Mountgrove Rd N5 ..6 B1
Mountjoy Ho EC2 **108** C3
Mount Lodge SW4 ..**61** C3
Mount Mills EC1 ....**96** B3
Mount Nod Rd
SW16,SW2 .... **74** B1
Mount Pl 7 W3 ....**28** A1
Mount Pleasant
WC1 ....95 B1
Mount Pleasant Cres
N4 ....5 B4

Mount Pleasant Rd
London SE13 ....**67** B1
Willesden NW10 ....**22** B4
Mount Pleasant Villas
N4 ....5 B4
Mount Row SW18,
SW19 ....71 A2
Mount Row W1 .. **118** A3
Mounts Pond Rd
SE3,SE13 ....52 C1
Mount Sq The NW3 ..2 B1
Mount St W1 ..... **117** C3
Mount Terr E1 .... **32** A4
Mount Tyndal NW3 ..**2** C3
Mount Vernon NW3 **11** B4
Mountview 5 SW16 **74** B1
Mountview Cl NW11 ..**2** B3
Mount Villas SE27 ..**75** A1
Mourne Ho NW3 ....**11** B2
Mowatt Cl N19 ......**4** C3
Mowbray Rd NW6 ..**10** A1
Mowlem Prim Sch
E2 ....25 B3
Mowlem St E2 .....**25** A3
Mowll St SW9 .... **163** B1
Moxon St W1 .... **103** B3
Moye Cl 11 E2 ....**24** C3
Moylan Rd W6 .... **154** B3
Moyle Ho SW1 .. **161** A4
Moyne Ho 10 SW9 **63** A3
Mozart St W10 .....**23** B2
Mudchute Sta E14 ..**42** A2
Mudie Ho 3 SW2 ..**74** A4
Muirdown Ave
SW14 ....55 C3
Muirfield W3 ....**29** A3
Muirfield Cl 2
SE16 ....40 A1
Muirfield Cres E14 **42** A3
Muir Rd E5 ....7 C1
Mulberry Bsns Ctr
SE16 ....40 C4
Mulberry Cl SW3 **157** C3
London NW3 ....11 C4
London SE22 ....64 C1
Mulberry Ct E1 .....**96** B3
10 W9 ....23 B2
1 London EC1 .... **119** C4
London N5 ....15 A3
Mulberry Ho 1 E2 **25** B2
8 SE8 ....51 B4
Mulberry House Sch
NW2 ....10 A3
Mulberry Mews
4 SE14 ....51 B2
Mulberry Pl W6 ....**38** C1
London E8 ....16 B1
Mulberry Sch for Girls
E1 ....32 A3
Stepney E1 ....32 A2
Mulberry St E1 .. **111** B2
Mulberry Wlk SW3 **157** C4
Mulgrave Rd W14 **154** C4
London NW10 ....8 B2
Mulkern Rd N19 ....**4** C3
Mullard Ho WC1 .. **105** B4
Mullens Ho 7
SW15 ....57 B2
Mullen Twr EC1 ....**95** B1
Mullet Gdns E2 .....**24** C2
Mulletsfield WC1 ....**94** B3
Mull Ho 8 E3 .....**26** B3
Mullins Path SW14 **55** C4
Mulready St NW8 ..**90** A1

Multi Way W3 ......38 A4
Multon Ho E9 ......17 B1
Multon Rd SW18 ...71 C4
Mulvaney Way SE1 137 C3
Mumford Rd SE24 ...63 A2
Muncaster Rd SW11 60 C2
Mundania Ct SE22 ..65 A1
Mundania Rd SE22 ..65 B1
Munday Ho SE1 ....137 B1
Munday Rd E13 .....35 C4
Munden Ho ⑤ E3 ...27 A2
Munden St W14 ....140 A4
Mund St W14 ......141 A1
Mundy Ho ⑧ W10 ..23 A2
Mundy St N1 ......137 C4
Munro Ho SE1 .....135 B3
SE1 ....137 C3
Munro Mews W10 ..31 A4
Munster Ct SW6 ...164 C2
Munster Rd SW6 ..154 B1
Munster Residences
SW6 ....164 B4
Munster Sq NW1 ...92 B2
Munton Rd SE1,
SE17 ....151 A4
Murchison Ho ①
W10 ....31 A4
Murdoch Ho ④
SE16 ....40 B3
Murdock Cl E16 ....35 B1
Murdock St SE15 ...50 A4
Murfett Cl SW19 ...70 A2
Muriel St N1 ......85 A2
Murphy Ho SE1 ...136 B2
Murphy St SE1 ....135 B3
Murray Gr N1 .....87 B1
Murray Mews NW1 .13 C1
Murray St NW1 ....13 C1
Murray Terr NW3 ..11 C4
Musard Rd W6 ....154 B4
Musbury St E1 .....32 B3
Muscal W6 ....154 A4
Muscatel Pl SE5 ...49 A2
Muschamp Rd SE15 65 A4
Muscott Ho ⑱ E2 ..24 C4
Muscovy St EC3 ...124 B4
Museum Ho ⑦ E2 ..25 B2
Museum in Docklands*
E14 ....33 C2
Museum St WC1 ..106 A2
Musgrave Cres
SW6 ....165 C4
Musgrave Ct SW11 168 A4
Musgrove Ho ① E9 17 C2
Musgrove Rd SE14 .51 A2
Musical Rd
The TW8 ....44 A4
Musjid Rd SW11 ..167 C1
Mus of Garden History
SE1 ....134 C2
Mus of London* ...108 C3
Mustow Pl SW6 ...165 A2
Mutrix Rd NW6 ....23 C4
Mutton Pl NW1 ....12 C2
Myatt Ct ⑤ SE4 ...51 B1
Myatt Garden Prim Sch
SE4 ....51 B1
Myatt Ho SE5 .....48 A1
Myatt Rd SW9 .....48 A2
Myatts Field Ct SE5 48 B2
Mycenae Rd SE3 ...53 C4
Myddelton Pas EC1 95 C4
Myddelton Sq EC1 .95 C4
Myddelton St EC1 ..95 C3
Myddleton Ave N4 ..6 B2
Myers Ho ⑤ SE5 ...48 B3

Myers La SE14 ....50 C4
Mylius Cl SE14 ....50 B2
Mylne Cl W6 ....38 C1
Mylne St EC1 .....85 B1
Mymterne Ct ⑱
SW19 ....69 C3
Myrdle Ct E1 .....111 C2
Myrdle St E1 .....111 C2
Myron Pl SE13 ....67 B4
Myrtle Ho SE14 ...50 C2
Myrtle Rd W3 .....28 B1
Myrtle Wlk ⑳ N1 ..24 A3
Mysore Rd SW11 ..60 B3
Mytton Ho SW8 ..162 C1

N
N1 Shopping Ctr
N1 ....85 C1
Nags Head N7 .....14 B4
Nags Head Ct EC1 .97 A1
Nainby Rd SW11 ..169 B3
Nairn St E14 ......34 B4
Naish Ct N1 ....84 B4
Nalton Ho ⑩ NW6 ..11 B1
Nankin St E14 ....33 C3
Nansen Rd SW11 ..60 C4
Nant Ct NW2 ....1 B2
Nant Cl SW18 .....59 B3
Nant Rd NW2 ....1 B2
Nant St E2 ....25 A2
Naoroji St WC1 ....95 B3
Napier Ave E14 ...41 C1
SW6 ....58 B4
Napier Cl SE14,SE8 51 B3
W14 ....126 C2
Napier Ct N1 ......87 B2
SW6 ....58 B4
Napier Gr N1 ......87 A2
Napier Pl W14 ....126 C1
London NW10 ......22 A2
Napier Terr N1 ....15 A1
Narbonne Ave SW4 .61 B2
Narborough St
SW6 ....166 A1
Narcissus Rd NW6 ..10 C3
Narford Rd E5 ......7 C2
Narrow St E14 ....33 A2
⑧ Acton W3 ....28 A1
Nascot St W12 ....30 B3
Naseby Cl NW6 ....11 B1
Nashe Ho SE1 ....137 B1
Nash Ho NW1 ....146 B1
Nash Rd SE4 ......66 A2
Nash Street NW1 ..92 B4
Nasmyth St W6 ...39 A3
Nassau Rd SW13 ..46 B2
Nassau St W1 ....104 C3
Nassington Rd NW3 12 B4
Nathan Ho SE11 ..149 C3
Nathaniel Cl E1 ..111 A3
National Army Mus*
SW3 ....159 A4
National Fan Mus
SE10 ....52 B3
National Film Theatre
SE1 ....121 A2
National Gallery*
W1 ....119 C3
National Hospl The
WC1 ....94 B1
National Maritime
Mus* SE10 ....52 C4

National Portrait
Gallery* W1 .....119 C3
National Portrait Gallery
(Annexe)* SW1 ..119 C3
National Postal Mus
EC1 ....108 C2
National Theatre
SE1 ....121 A2
Natural History Mus*
SW7 ....129 B1
Nat West Twr*
EC2 ....95 B4
Nautilus Bldg The
E14 ....34 B2
Naval Row E14 ....34 B2
Navarino Gr E8 ....16 C2
Navarino Mans E8 ..16 C2
Navarino Rd E8 ....16 C2
Navarre St E2 .....98 C2
Navenby Wlk ⑱ E3 26 C1
Navy St SW4 ......61 C4
Naylor Ho SE17 ..151 C2
London SW8 .....171 B1
⑤ London W10 ....23 B2
Naylor Rd SE15 ....50 A3
Nazareth Cl SE15 ..50 A1
Nazrul St E2 ......98 C3
Neal St WC2 .....106 A1
Neal's Yd WC2 ...106 A1
Neasden Cl NW10 ..8 A3
Neasden Junc NW10 8 A4
Neasden La NW10 ..8 A3
Neasden Sta NW10 ..8 A3
Neate St SE5 ......49 B4
SE5 ....49 B4
Neathouse Pl SW1 146 C4
Nebraska St SE1 ..137 B3
Neckinger SE1 ...139 A2
Neckinger Est
SE16 ....139 A2
Neckinger St SE1 .139 A2
Nectarine Way SE13 52 A1
Nedahall Ct ④ NW11 1 B4
Needham Ho SE11 149 B3
Needham Rd W11 ..31 C3
Needleman St SE16 40 C4
Needwood Ho N4 ...6 B3
Neeld Cres NW4 ....9 A3
Neil Wates Cres ⑨
SW2 ....74 C3
Neldale Rd SE16 ...40 B2
Nell Gwynn Ho
SW3 ....144 B3
Nelson Cl ⑫ NW6 ..23 C2
Nelson Ct SE16 ....33 A1
Nelson Gdns
E2 ....24 C2 99 C4
Nelson Pas EC1 ...97 A4
Nelson Pl N1 .....86 B1
Nelson Rd SE10 ...52 B4
Nelson's Monument*
WC2 ....120 A2
Nelsons Row SW4 ..61 C3
Nelson St E1 ......32 A3
E16 ....35 B2
Nelson Terr N1 ....86 B1
Nemoure Rd W3 ..28 B2
Nepaul Rd ⑤ SW11 60 A4
Nepean St SW15 ..68 C4
Neptune Ct ⑤ E14 41 C2
Neptune Ho ⑥ SE16 40 B3
⑭ London N16 .....16 A3
Neptune St SE16 ..40 B3

Nesham Ho ⑭ N1 ..24 A4
Nesham St E1 ....125 B2
Ness St SE16 .....139 B2
Nestor Ho ⑱ E2 ...25 A3
Netheravon Rd W4 38 B1
Netheravon Rd S
W4 ....38 B1
Netherby Ho SW8 171 B1
Netherby Rd SE23 ..65 B1
Nethercombe Ho ④
SE3 ....53 C4
Nethercott Ho ⑰
E3 ....27 A2
Netherfield Rd
SW17 ....72 C1
Netherford Rd
SW4 ....171 A1
Netherhall Gdns
NW3 ....11 B3
Netherhall Way
NW3 ....11 B3
Netherleigh Cl N6 ..4 A3
Netherton Gr
SW10 ....157 A3
Netherwood Rd
W14 ....39 C4
Netherwood St
NW6 ....10 C2
Netley ⑤ SE5 .....49 A2
Netley Prim Sch
NW1 ....92 C3
Netley Rd TW8 ....44 A4
Netley St NW1 ....92 C3
Nettlecombe NW1 .13 C1
Nettleden Ho SW3 144 B3
Nettlefold Pl SE27 .75 A1
Nettleton Rd SE14 .50 C2
Nevada St SE10 ...52 B4
Nevena Ct ⑧ SW2 62 C2
Nevern Mans SW5 141 B2
Nevern Pl SW5 ...141 C3
Nevern Rd SW5 ..141 B3
Nevern Sq SW5 ..141 C3
Nevil Ho ⑦ SW9 ..48 A1
Nevill Ct SW10 ...156 C2
Neville Cl NW1 ....83 C1
SE15 ....49 C3
NW6 ....23 B3
Acton W3 ....37 B4
Neville Ct ⑩ SW12 73 B4
Neville Gill Cl SW18 59 A1
Neville Rd NW6 ...23 B3
Neville Terr SW7 .143 B2
Nevill Rd N16 .....7 A1
Nevinson Cl SW18 .59 C1
Nevis Rd SW17 ...72 C2
Nevitt Ho N1 ......87 C1
Newall Ho SE1 ...137 A2
Newark Cres NW10 20 C2
Newark Ho ⑤ SW9 48 A1
Newark St E1 .....32 A4
New Bentham Ct ⑪
N1 ....15 B1
Newbery Ho N1 ...15 B1
Newbold Cotts ④
E1 ....32 B3
Newbolt Ho SE17 151 B2
New Bond St W1 .118 B4
New Bridge St
EC4 ....108 A1
New Broad St EC2 110 A3
New Bsns Ctr The
NW10 ....21 B3
Newburgh Rd W3 ..28 B1
Newburgh St W1 .105 A1

New Burlington Mews
W1 ....118 C4
New Burlington Pl
W1 ....118 C4
New Burlington St
W1 ....118 C4
Newburn Ho SE11 149 A2
Newburn St SE11 149 A2
Newbury Ct E5 ....18 A3
Newbury Ho
London SW9 ....48 A1
London W2 ....100 B1
Newbury Mews
NW5 ....12 C2
Newbury St EC1 ..108 C4
New Butt La SE8 ...51 C3
Newby NW1 ....92 C4
Newby St SW8 ....61 A4
New Caledonian Wharf
SE16 ....41 B3
New Campden Ct ⑪
NW3 ....11 B4
Newcastle Cl EC4 108 A2
Newcastle Ct EC4 123 A4
Newcastle Ho W1 103 B4
Newcastle Pl W2 101 C4
Newcastle Row EC1 95 C1
New Cavendish St
W1 ....104 A3
New Change EC4 108 C1
New Charles St EC1 96 B4
New Church Rd SE5 48 C4
⑰ SE5 ....48 B3
New College Ct ⑥
NW3 ....11 B2
New College Mews ④
N1 ....14 C1
New College Par ①
NW3 ....11 C1
Newcombe Ho N5 .15 B3
Newcombe St W8 113 C2
Newcomen Ho ⑤
NW5 ....13 A4
Newcomen Rd
SW11 ....59 C4
Newcomen St SE1 137 B4
New Compton St
WC2 ....106 A1
New Concordia Wharf
SE1 ....139 A4
Newcourt Ho ⑳ E2 25 A2
Newcourt St NW8 80 A1
New Covent Garden
Flower Market
SW8 ....162 A3
New Covent Garden
Fruit & Vegetable Mkt
SW8 ....161 B1
New Crescent Yd ①
NW10 ....21 B3
New Cross SE14 ...51 B2
New Cross Gate
SE14 ....50 C2
New Cross Gate Sta
SE14 ....51 A3
New Cross Hospl
SE14 ....50 B4
New Cross Rd SE14 51 A2
New Cross Sta SE14 51 B3
New Ct EC4 ....107 B1
London N6 ....6 C3
⑬ London NW3 ...11 B4
New Den (Millwall FC)
The SE16 ....40 B1

Newdigate Ho **5**
E14 ....33 B3
Newell St E14 ....33 B3
New End NW3 ....2 B1
New End Prim Sch
NW3 ....1 B4
New End Sq NW3 ....11 C4
Newent Cl SE15 .....49 A3
New Fetter La EC4 .107 C2
Newfield Prim Sch
NW10 ....8 B1
New Furness Prim Sch
The NW10 ....21 C3
Newgate St EC1 ...108 B2
New Globe Wlk
SE1 ....122 C2
New Goulston St
E1 ....110 C2
Newham Sch of Nursing
E3 ....27 A1
Newham's Row
SE1 ....138 B3
Newhaven La **3**
E16 ....35 C4
Newington Barrow Way
N7 ....5 C1
Newington Butts
SE1,SE11 ....150 B3
Newington Cswy
SE1 ....136 C2
Newington Green Mans
N16 ....7 C3
Newington Green Prim
Sch N16 ....15 C3
Newington Green Rd
N1 ....7 B1
Newington Ind Est
SE17 ....150 C3
New Inn Broadway
EC2 ....98 B2
New Inn La WC2 ...107 A1
New Inn Sq EC2 .....98 B2
New Inn St EC2 ......98 B2
New Inn Yd
EC2 ....24 A1 98 B2
New James St SE15 65 A4
New Kent Rd SE1 ..151 A4
New King's Prim Sch
SW6 ....164 C2
New King's Rd
SW6 ....165 A3
New King St SE8 ....51 C4
Newland Ct E1 ....51 C1
Newland Ho **17**
SE14 ....50 C4
Newlands NW1 ......92 C4
Newlands Quay E1 .32 B2
New London St
EC3 ....124 B4
Newlyn NW1 ....83 A3
Newman Pas W1 ...105 A3
Newman's Ct EC3 ..109 C1
Newman's Row
WC2 ....107 A3
Newman St W1 .....105 A3
Newmill Ho E3 ....27 B1
Newmount NW3 ....11 C3
New Mount St E15 ..19 C1
Newnes Path SW15 .57 A3
Newnham Ho **9**
SW15 ....57 C1
Newnham Terr
SE1 ....135 B2
New North Pl EC2 ...98 A2
New North Rd N1 ...87 B3

New North Road Bridge
N1 ....87 B3
New North St WC1 .106 C4
Newnton Cl N4 ....6 C4
New Oxford St
WC1 ....106 A2
New Palace Yd
SW1 ....134 A3
New Park Ct **13**
SW2 ....74 A4
New Park Par **14** .....
New Park Rd SW2 ...74 A4
New Place Sq SE16 .40 A3
Newport Ave E14 ....34 C2
Newport Ct WC2 ...119 C4
Newport Ho E3 ....26 A2
Newport Rd SW13 ...46 C2
Newport St SE11 ...149 A4
New Priory Ct **8** ......
NW6 ....10 C1
Newquay Ho SE11 .149 B2
New Quebec St
W1 ....103 A1
New River St N5 .....15 C4
New River Way N4 ...6 C4
New Row WC2 ......120 A4
New Scotland Yard **★** .
SW1 ....133 B2
New Spring Gdns Wlk
SE11 ....148 B1
New Sq WC2 ....107 A2
New Sq Pas WC2 ...107 B2
New St EC2 ....110 B3
New St Sq EC4 .....107 C2
Newton Ave W3 .....37 B4
Newton Gr W4 ....38 A2
Newton Ho NW8 ....78 B4
London SW8 ....171 B2
1 Stepney E1 ......32 A2
Newton Pl E14 ....41 C2
Newton Point **1** ....
E16 ....35 C3
Newton Prep Sch
SW8 ....170 B4
Newton Rd
London E15 ....19 C3
London W2 ....100 A1
Newton St WC2 ....106 B2
Newton's Yd **14** ......
SW18 ....58 C2
New Tower Bldgs **21** ..
E1 ....32 A1
Newtown Ct SW11 .170 A3
London SW4 ....61 A2
New Union Cl E14 ...42 B3
New Union St EC2 .109 B3
New Wharf Rd N1 ...84 B2
Niagara Cl N1 ....87 A2
Niagara Ct **6** SE16 .40 B3
Nicholas Ct W4 .....46 A3
Nicholas Ho **2** ....
SW15 ....56 C2
Nicholas La EC2,
EC4 ....123 C4
Nicholas Pas EC3 .123 C4
Nicholas Rd E1 .....25 B1
Nicholay Rd N19 .....4 C3
Nicholl Ho N4 ....6 B3
Nicholl St E2 ....24 C4
Nichols Cl N4 ....5 C3
Nichols Ct E2 ....24 B3
Nicholson Ho SE17 151 B2
Nicholson St SE1 ..122 A1
Nickleby Ho SE1 ...139 B3

Nickleby Ho continued
7 London W11 .....30 C1
Nicoll Ct NW10 ......21 A4
Nicoll Rd NW10 .....21 A4
Nicosia Rd SW18 ...72 A4
Nigel Bldg EC1 ....107 C3
Nigel Playfair Ave
W6 ....39 A1
Nigel Rd SE15 ....64 C4
Nightingale Cl W4 ..45 B4
Nightingale Ct
12 E14 ....42 B3
SW6 ....166 B3
London N4 ....5 C4
Nightingale Gr SE13 67 C2
Nightingale Ho E1 .125 B2
21 E1 ....25 A2
London W12 ....30 B3
Nightingale La
SW11,SW12 ....60 C1
London N6 ....3 B4
W9 ....31 C4
Nightingale Mews
SE11 ....150 A3
Nightingale Pl
SW10 ....156 C4
Nightingale Rd
London W10 ....23 A2
London N1 ....15 B2
Nightingale Sch
SE17 ....72 A2
Nightingale Sq
SW12 ....72 C4
Nightingale Wlk
SW18,SW4 ....61 A1
Nile Cl N16 ....7 B1
Nile Ho N1 ....97 B4
Nile St N1 ....97 B4
Nile Terr SE1,SE15 .153 A1
Nimegem Way **9** .....
SE22 ....64 A2
Nimrod Pas **4** N1 ....16 A2
Nine Elms La SW8 .161 B3
Nisbet Ho E9 ....17 C3
Niton Rd TW9 ....54 C4
Niton St SW6 ....47 C3
Nobel Ho **8** SE5 .....48 B1
Noble Ct E1 ....32 A2
Noble St EC2 ....108 C2
Noel Coward Ho
SW1 ....147 A3
Noel Ho **3** NW3 ....11 C1
Noel Rd N1 ....86 B2
Acton W3 ....28 A3
Noel St W1 ....105 A1
Nolan Way E5 ....16 C4
Noll Ho N7 ....5 B2
Norbiton Rd E14 .....33 B3
Norbroke St W12 ...29 B2
Norburn St W10 .....31 A4
Norcombe Ho **2** N19 4 C1
Norcott Rd N16 ....7 C1
Norcroft Gdns SE22 76 C4
Norden Ho **28** E2 ....25 A2
Nore Ct NW10 ....8 C1
Norfolk Cres W2 ...102 B2
Norfolk Ho EC4 ....122 C4
SE3 ....53 A4
SW1 ....147 C4
London SE8 ....51 C2
4 Putney SW15 ...69 B4
Richmond TW10 ....54 C2
Norfolk House Rd
SW16 ....74 A1
Norfolk Mans
SW11 ....169 A3
16 London SW18 ...58 C2

Norfolk Mews
W10 ....31 A4
Norfolk Pl W2 ......101 C2
Norfolk Rd NW8 .....79 C3
London NW10 ....8 A1
Norfolk Row SE1,
SE11 ....148 C4
Norfolk Sq W2 .....101 C2
Norfolk Sq Mews
W2 ....101 C2
Norgrove St SW12 ..72 C4
Norland Ho **13** W11 .30 C1
Norland Pl
W11 ....31 A1 112 B1
Norland Place Sch
W11 ....31 A1 112 A1
Norland Rd W11 .....30 C1
Norland Sq
W11 ....31 A1 112 B1
Norley Vale SW15 ...68 C3
Norman Butler Ho **10**
W10 ....23 A1
Normanby Cl SE15 .58 B2
Normanby Rd NW10 .8 B4
Norman Ct NW10 .....8 C2
Dulwich SE22 ....76 C4
London N4 ....5 C4
Norman Gr E3 ......26 A3
Norman Ho **4** ....
SW2 ....74 B2
Norman Rd SE10 ...52 A3
Norman St EC1 ......97 A3
Normanton Ave
SW18,SW19 ....70 C2
Normanton Ho **6** .....
SW4 ....61 B1
Norman Way W3 ....28 A3
Norris Ho **22** E9 .....25 B4
12 N1 ....24 A4
Norris St SW1 ......119 B3
Norroy Rd SW15 ...57 C3
Norse Ho **18** SE5 .....48 B1
Norstead Pl SW15 ..68 C2
North Acton Rd
NW10 ....20 C2
North Acton Sta
W3 ....28 C4
Northampton Gr N1 15 C3
Northampton Pk
N1 ....15 C2
Northampton Rd
EC1 ....95 C2
Northampton Sq
EC1 ....96 A3
Northampton St N1 15 B1
North Audley St
W1 ....117 B4
North Ave **8** TW9 ...45 A2
Northaw Ho W10 ...22 B1
North Bank NW8 ....90 A3
North Block **18** E1 ..32 B2
Northbourne Ho **21** ..
E5 ....17 A3
Northbourne Rd
SW4 ....61 C2
North Branch Ave
NW10 ....22 B2
Northburgh St EC1 .96 B2
North Carriage Dr
W2 ....116 B2

Northchurch SE17 .151 C2
North Church Ho **19**
E2 ....24 C4
Northchurch Rd N1 .15 C1
Northchurch Terr
N1 ....16 A1
North Circular Rd
London NW10 ....8 A3
London NW2 ....8 A3
North Colonnade
E14 ....33 C1
Northcote Lodge Sch
SW11 ....60 B1
Northcote Rd
London SW11 ....60 B2
London SW11 ....60 B2
Northcourt W1 .....105 A4
North Cres E16 ......27 C1
WC1 ....105 B4
Northcroft Ct **8** ....
W12 ....38 C4
North Cross Rd
SE22 ....64 C2
North Ct SW1 ......134 A1
Northdown St N1 ...84 C1
North Dulwich Sta
SE21 ....63 C2
North End NW3 ....2 B2
North End Ave NW3 .2 B2
North End Cres
W14 ....140 C3
North End Ho W14 140 B3
North End Par
W14 ....140 B3
North End Rd W14 141 A1
London NW11 ....2 B3
North End Way NW3 .2 B2
Northern Hts N8 ......4 C4
Northesk Ho **6** E1 ..25 A1
North Eyot Gdns **5** ..
W6 ....38 B1
Northey St E14 ......33 A2
Northfield Hall N6 ....3 C4
Northfield Ho **3** ......
SE15 ....49 C4
Northfield Rd N16 ...7 A4
Northfields SW18 ...58 C3
Northfields Prospect
SW18 ....58 C3
Northfields Rd W3 ..28 B4
North Flower Wlk
W2 ....115 B3
North Gate NW8 ....80 A1
Northgate Ct **13** ......
SW9 ....62 C4
North Gower St
NW1 ....93 A3
North Gr N6 ....3 C4
North Greenwich Sta
SE10 ....43 A4
North Hill N6 ....3 B4
North Ho **3** SE8 .....41 B1
Northiam WC1 ....94 B3
Northiam St E9 ......25 A4
Northington St WC1 95 A1
Northlands St SE5 ..48 B1
Northleigh Ho **38** ....
E3 ....27 A2
North Lodge Cl
SW15 ....57 C2
North London Boys Sch
N16 ....7 C3
North Mews WC1 ...95 A1
Northolme Rd N5 ...15 B4
North Pas SW18 ....58 C2
North Pole Rd W10 .30 B4

Nor – Old 235

- Northport St N1 ...87 C3
- North Rd
  - Brentford TW8 ...44 A4
  - London N6 ...3 C4
  - London N7 ...14 A2
  - Richmond TW9 ...44 C1
- North Ride W2 ...116 A3
- North Rise W2 ...102 B1
- North Row W1 ...117 B4
- North Sheen Sta TW10 ...54 C3
- North Side Wandsworth Comm SW18 ...59 C2
- North St SW4 ...61 B4
- Northstead Rd SW2 .74 C2
- North Tenter St E1 ...111 A1
- North Terr SW3 ...130 A1
- Northumberland Alley EC3 ...110 B1
- Northumberland Ave WC2 ...120 A2
- Northumberland Ho NW5 ...13 B2
- Northumberland Mans E5 ...17 B4
- Northumberland Pl W2 ...31 C3
- Northumberland St WC2 ...120 A2
- Northumbria St E14 33 C3
- North Verbena Gdns W6 ...38 C1
- Northview 1 N7 ...5 A1
- Northview Cres NW10 ...8 B4
- Northview Prim Sch NW10 ...8 B3
- North Villas NW1 ...13 C2
- Northway Rd SE5 ...63 B4
- Northways Par 2 NW3 ...11 C1
- North Westminster Com Sch
  - W2 ...101 B4
  - W9 ...23 C1
- Northwest Pl N1 ...85 C2
- North Wharf Rd W2 ...101 B3
- Northwick Cl NW8 ..89 B2
- Northwick Ho NW8 .89 A2
- Northwick Terr NW8 ...89 B2
- North Wlk W2 ...114 C3
- Northwold Prim Sch E5 ...7 C2
- Northwold Rd E5,N16 .7 C2
- North Wood Lo NW3 ...11 A4
- Northwood Rd N6 ...4 A4
- North Worple Way SW14 ...55 C4
- Norton Folgate E1 .110 B4
- Norton Ho 33 E1 ...32 A3
  - 14 E2 ...25 C3
  - London SW9 ...173 A1
- Norval Gn SW9 ...173 C2
- Norvic Ho 5 SE5 ...48 B1
- Norway Gate SE16 .41 A3
- Norway Pl E14 ...33 B3
- Norway St SE10 ...52 A4
- Norwich Ho 6 E14 .34 A3
- Norwich St EC4 ...107 B2
- Norwood Ho 22 E14 34 A2
- Norwood Rd SE24, SE27 ...75 A3
- Notley St SE5 ...48 C3
- Notre Dame RC Girls Sch SE1 ...136 B2
- Notting Barn Rd W10 ...22 C1
- Nottingdale Sq W11 ...31 A1 112 A2
- Nottingham Ct WC2 ...106 A1
- Nottingham Ho
  - London N4 ...6 B3
  - 34 London SE5 ...48 B1
- Nottingham Pl W1 .103 B4
- Nottingham Rd SW17 ...72 B3
- Nottingham St W1 .103 B4
- Nottingham Terr NW1 ...91 B1
- Notting Hill Gate W11 ...31 C1 113 B2
- Notting Hill Gate Sta W11 ...31 C1 113 B2
- Nottingwood Ho W11 ...112 A4
- Nova Bldg 21 E14 ...41 C2
- Novello St SW6 ...165 B4
- Nowell Rd SW13 ...46 C4
- Noyna Rd SW17 ...72 B1
- Nuding Cl SE13 ...66 C4
- Nuffield Lo 14 W9 ...31 C4
- Nugent Rd N19 ...5 A3
- Nugent Terr NW8 ...79 A1
- Nun Ct EC2 ...109 B2
- Nunhead Cres SE15 .65 A4
- Nunhead Gr SE15 ...65 B4
- Nunhead La SE15 ...65 A4
- Nunhead Sta SE15 ...50 B1
- Nursery Cl
  - London SE4 ...51 B1
  - Putney SW15 ...57 C3
- Nursery La E2 ...24 B4
  - London W10 ...30 B4
- Nursery Rd
  - London E9 ...17 B2
  - London SW9 ...62 B3
- Nursery Row SE17 .151 C3
- Nutbourne St W10 ..23 A2
- Nutbrook St SE15 ...64 C4
- Nutcroft Rd SE15 ...50 A3
- Nutfield Rd
  - London E15 ...76 B4
  - London SE22 ...64 B3
- Nutford Pl W1 ...102 C2
- Nuthurst Ave SW2 ..74 B2
- Nutley Terr NW3 ...11 C2
- Nutmeg La E14 ...34 C3
- Nuttall St N1 ...24 A3
- Nutt St SE15 ...49 B3
- NW London Jewish Day Sch NW6 ...10 A1
- Nye Bevan Ho SW6 ...154 C2
- Nye's Wharf SE15 ...49 C4
- Nylands Ave TW9 ...44 C1
- Nynehead St SE14 ..51 A3
- Nyton Cl N19 ...5 A3

O

- Oakbank Gr SE24 ...63 B3
- Oakbury Rd SW6 ..166 B1
- Oakcourt 16 SE15 ...49 B3
- Oak Cres E16 ...35 A4
- Oakcroft Rd SE13 ...52 C1
- Oakdale Ct N19 ...5 A2
- Oakdale Rd SE15 ...65 B4
- Oakdene 3 SE15 ...50 A2
- Oakdene Ho N16 ...7 A3
- Oakden St SE11 ...149 C4
- Oake Ct SW15 ...58 A2
- Oakeford Ho W14 .126 B2
- Oakend Ho 10 N4 ...6 C4
- Oakeshott Ave N6 ...3 C2
- Oakey La SE1 ...135 B2
- Oakfield Ct London N8 5 A4
  - London SW4 ...62 A1
- Oakfield Prep Sch SE21 ...75 C3
- Oakfield Rd
  - London N4 ...5 C4
  - Wimbledon SW19 ...69 C1
- Oakfield St SW10 ..156 C4
- Oakford Rd NW5 ...13 B4
- Oak Gr NW2 ...10 A4
- Oakham Ho W10 ...22 B1
- Oakhill Ave NW3 ...11 A4
- Oakhill Ct
  - London SE23 ...65 B1
  - Putney SW15 ...58 B2
- Oak Hill Lo NW3 ...11 A4
- Oak Hill Park Mews NW3 ...11 B4
- Oak Hill Pk NW3 ...11 A4
- Oakhill Pl SW15 ...58 C2
- Oakhill Rd SW15 ...58 B2
- Oak Hill Way NW3 ..11 B4
- Oak Ho 8 E14 ...42 B4
  - London N16 ...6 C2
  - 8 London NW3 ...12 B2
- Oakhurst Gr SE22 ...64 C3
- Oakington Rd W9 ...23 C1
- Oakington Way N8 ...5 A4
- Oak La E14 ...33 B2
- Oaklands Ct NW10 ..21 A4
- Oaklands Gr W12 ...29 C1
- Oaklands Ho SE4 ...66 B4
- Oaklands Mews NW2 .9 C4
- Oaklands Pas NW2 ...9 C4
- Oaklands Pl 8 SW4 61 C3
- Oaklands Rd NW2 ...9 C4
  - Mortlake SW14 ...55 C4
- Oaklands Sec Sch E2 ...25 A2
- Oakley Cres EC1 ...86 B1
- Oakley Dr SE13 ...67 C1
- Oakley Gdns SW3 ..158 B4
- Oakley Ho SW1 ...145 A4
- Oakley Pl SE1 ...152 C1
- Oakley Rd N1 ...15 C1
- Oakley Sq NW1 ...83 A2
- Oakley St SW3 ...158 A4
- Oakley Wlk W6 ...47 C4
- Oak Lodge Sch SW12 ...72 C4
- Oakman Ho 29 SW19 ...69 C3
- Oakmead Rd SW12 .73 A3
- Oak Park Gdns SW19 ...69 C3
- Oak Park Mews N16 .7 B1
- Oakshaw Rd SW18 ..71 A4
- Oakshott Ct NW1 ...83 B1
- Oaks Sh Ctr The W3 ...28 B1
- Oaks The
  - London NW10 ...9 A1
  - London NW6 ...9 C1
- Oak Tree Ct
  - Acton W3 ...28 A2
  - 6 London SW4 ...62 A2
- Oak Tree Ho W9 ...88 A2
- Oak Tree Rd NW8 ...90 A3
- Oakview Lo NW11 ...1 B4
- Oak Village NW5 ...12 C4
- Oak Way W3 ...29 A1
- Oakwell Ho SW8 ..171 B1
- Oakwood Ct W14 ..126 C2
- Oakwood La W14 ..126 C2
- Oakworth Rd W10 ..30 C4
- Oast Ct 8 E14 ...33 B2
- Oast Lo W4 ...46 A3
- Oat La EC2 ...109 A2
- Oatlands Ct 3 SW19 ...69 C3
- Oatwell Ho SW3 ...144 B3
- Oban Ho E14 ...34 C3
- Oban St E14 ...34 C3
- Oberon Ho 5 N1 ...24 A3
- Oberstein Rd 15 SW11 ...59 C3
- Oborne Cl SE24 ...63 A2
- O'Brian Ho 10 E1 ...25 C2
- Observatory Gdns W8 ...127 C4
- Observatory Mews E14 ...42 C2
- Observatory Rd SW14 ...55 B3
- Occupation Rd SE17 ...150 C2
- Ocean St E1 ...32 C4
- Ocean Wharf E14 ...41 C4
- Ockbrook 3 E1 ...32 B4
- Ockendon Rd N1 ...15 C2
- Ockley Rd SW16 ...74 A1
- Octagon Arc EC2 ..110 A3
- Octagon The NW3 ..10 C4
- Octavia Ho W10 ...23 A1
- Octavia St SW11 ...168 B3
- Octavius St SE8 ...51 C3
- Odeon Ct 1 E16 ...35 C4
  - London NW10 ...21 A4
- Odessa Rd NW10 ...21 C3
- Odessa St SE16 ...41 B3
- Odette Duval Ho 24 E1 ...32 B4
- Odger St SW11 ...169 A2
- Odhams Wlk WC2 .106 B1
- Odin Ho 6 SE5 ...48 B1
- O'Donnell Ct WC1 ...94 B2
- O'Driscoll Ho W12 ..30 A3
- Offa's Mead E9 ...18 A4
- Offenbach Ho 12 E2 25 C3
- Offerton Rd SW4 ...61 B4
- Offham Ho SE17 ...152 A3
- Offley Ho 10 E9 ...17 C2
- Offley Rd SW9 ...163 B2
- Offord Rd N1 ...14 B1
- Offord St N1 ...14 B1
- Ogilvie Ho 11 E1 ...32 C3
- Oglander Rd SE15 ..64 B4
- Ogle St W1 ...104 C4
- O'Gorman Ho SW10 ...157 A2
- Oil Mill La W6 ...38 C1
- Okehampton Rd NW10 ...22 C4
- Okeover Manor SW4 ...61 A3
- Olaf St W11 ...30 C2
- Old Bailey EC4 ...108 B1
- Old Barrack Yd SW1 ...131 B3
- Old Bellgate Wharf E14 ...41 C3
- Old Bethnal Green Rd E2 ...25 A2
- Old Bldgs WC2 ...107 B2
- Old Bond St W1 ...118 C3
- Old Brewery Mews NW3 ...11 C4
- Old Broad St EC2 ..109 C2
- Old Brompton Rd SW5,SW7 ...143 A3
- Old Burlington St W1 ...118 C3
- Oldbury Ct E9 ...18 A3
- Oldbury Pl W1 ...103 C4
- Old Castle St E1 ...111 A2
- Old Cavendish St W1 ...104 A1
- Old Change Ct EC4 ...108 C1
- Old Chiswick Yd W4 ...46 A4
- Old Church Rd E1 ..32 C3
- Old Church St SW3 ...157 C4
- Old Compton St W1 ...105 B1
- Old County Hall SE1 ...134 C4
- Old Court Ho W8 ..128 A3
- Old Court Pl W8 ...128 A3
- Old Covent Garden WC2 ...120 B4
- Old Dairy Mews
  - 5 Balham SW12 ...72 C3
  - 4 London NW5 ...13 A2
- Old Deer Park Gdns TW9 ...54 A4
- Old Devonshire Rd SW12 ...73 A4
- Old Dock Cl TW9 ...44 C4
- Oldfield Gr SE16 ...40 C2
- Oldfield Ho 14 W4 ..38 A1
- Oldfield Mews N6 ...4 B4
- Oldfield Rd
  - London N16 ...7 A1
  - London NW10 ...8 B1
  - London W3,W12 ...38 B4
- Old Fish St Hill EC4 ...122 C4
- Old Fleet La EC4 ..108 A2
- Old Ford Prim Sch E3 ...26 B3
- Old Ford Rd E2,E3 ..25 C3
- Old Ford Trad Ctr E3 ...26 C4
- Old Forge Mews W12 ...39 A4
- Old Gloucester St WC1 ...106 B4
- Oldham Terr W3 ...28 B1
- Oldhill St N16 ...7 C3
- Old Hospital Cl SW12,SW17 ...72 B3
- Olding Ho 6 SW12 .73 B4
- Old Jamaica Bsns Est SE16 ...139 B1
- Old Jamaica Rd SE16 ...139 B2
- Old James St SE15 ..65 A4
- Old Jewry EC2 ...109 B1
- Old Kent Rd SE1 ...152 B2
  - SE1,SE15 ...50 B3
- Old Laundry The 14 SW18 ...59 C3
- Old Manor Yd SW5 ...142 A3
- Old Market Sq E2 ...99 A4
- Old Marylebone Rd NW1 ...102 B3
- Old Mitre Ct EC4 ..107 C1
- Old Montague St E1 ...111 B3

Old Nichol St
E2 .....24 B1 98 C2
Old North St WC1 .....106 C4
Old Oak Common La
NW10 .....21 A1
Old Oak La NW10 .....21 B2
Old Oak Prim Sch
W12 .....29 B3
Old Oak Rd W3 .....29 B2
Old Orch The NW3 .....12 B4
Old Palace Prim Sch
E3 .....27 A2
Old Paradise St
SE11 .....148 C4
Old Park Ave SW12 .....60 C1
Old Park La W1 .....118 A1
Old Pye St SW1 .....133 B2
Old Pye Street Est
SW1 .....133 B1
Old Quebec St W1 .....103 A1
Old Queen St SW1 .....133 C3
Oldridge Rd SW12 .....73 A4
Old Royal Free Pl
N1 .....85 C3
Old Royal Free Sq
N1 .....85 C3
Old Royal Observatory
Greenwich (National
Maritime Mus
Annexe)* SE10 .....52 C3
Old School Sq 🔲
E14 .....33 C3
Old School The
WC1 .....106 C4
Old Seacoal La
EC4 .....108 A1
Old South Lambeth Rd
SW8 .....162 B2
Old Spitalfields Mkt
E1 .....110 C3
Old Sq WC2 .....107 B2
Old St EC1 .....97 B2
Old Stable Mews N5 .....6 B1
Old Street Sta EC1 .....97 C2
Old Swan Wharf 🔲
SW11 .....167 C4
Old Theatre Ct
SE1 .....123 A2
Old Town SW4 .....61 B4
Old Woolwich Rd
SE10 .....42 C1
Old York Rd SW18 .....59 A2
O'Leary Sq E1 .....32 B4
Olga Prim Sch E3 .....26 A3
Olga St 🔲 E3 .....26 A3
Oliphant St W10 .....23 A2
Olive Blythe Ho 🔲
W10 .....23 A1
Oliver Bsns Pk
NW10 .....20 B3
Oliver Cl W4 .....45 A4
Olive Rd NW2 .....9 C4
Oliver Goldsmith Prim
Schs SE5 .....49 B2
Oliver Ho SE16 .....139 B3
SW8 .....162 A2
W11 .....112 A4
Oliver Mews SE15 .....49 C1
Oliver's Yd EC1 .....97 C2
Olive Tree Ho 🔲
SE15 .....50 B4
Olivette St 🔲 SW15 .....57 C3
Olive Waite Ho
NW6 .....11 A1

Ollerton Gn E3 .....26 B4
Ollgar Cl W12 .....29 B1
Olliffe St E14 .....42 B3
Olmar St SE1 .....49 C4
Olmar Wharf SE1 .....49 C4
Olney Ho NW8 .....90 B2
Olney Rd SE17 .....48 B4
Olympia Ex Ctr*
W14 .....126 B2
Olympian Ct 🔲 E14 .....41 C2
Olympia Way W14 .....126 B1
Olympia Yd W2 .....114 B3
Olympic Ho W10 .....30 B3
Olympus Sq E5 .....7 C1
Oman Ave NW2 .....9 B4
Oman Ct W4 .....9 A4
Ombersley Ho N4 .....6 B4
Omeara St SE1 .....123 A1
Omega Cl E14 .....42 A3
Omega Ho SW10 .....157 A2
Omega Pl N1 .....84 B1
Omega St SE14 .....51 C2
Ommaney Rd SE14 .....51 A2
Ondine Rd SE15 .....64 B3
Onedin Point E1 .....125 C3
Onega Gate SE16 .....41 A3
O'Neill Ho NW8 .....79 C1
One Tree Cl SE23 .....65 B1
Ongar Ho 🔲 N1 .....15 C2
Ongar Rd SW6 .....155 C4
Onslow Ave 🔲 E14 .....34 A2
Onslow Avenue Mans 🔲
TW10 .....54 A2
Onslow Ct SW10 .....143 A1
Onslow Gdns SW7 .....143 B2
Onslow Lo SW2 .....74 C4
Onslow Mews E
SW7 .....143 B3
Onslow Mews W
SW7 .....143 B3
Onslow Rd TW10 .....54 A1
Onslow Sq SW7 .....143 C3
Onslow St EC1 .....95 C1
Ontario St SE1 .....136 B2
Ontario Way E14 .....33 C2
Opal St SE11 .....150 A2
Open Air Theatre,
Regent's Park (30)
NW1 .....91 B3
Openview SW17,
SW18 .....71 C2
Operating Theatre Mus
& Herb Garret
SE1 .....123 C1
Ophelia Gdns NW2 .....1 A1
Ophir Terr SE15 .....49 C2
Opie Ho NW8 .....80 B2
Oppenheim Rd SE13 .....52 B1
Oppidans Rd NW3 .....12 B1
Orange Ct SE16 .....139 B3
Orange St WC2 .....119 C3
Orange Yd WC2 .....105 C1
Oratory La SW3 .....143 C2
Oratory RC Prim Sch
SW3 .....144 A2
Oratory The*
SW7 .....130 A1
Orbain Rd SW6 .....154 B1
Orbel St SW11 .....168 A3
Orb St SE17 .....151 B3
Orchard Cl N1 .....31 A4
London N1 .....15 B1
London SE23 .....65 B1
Orchard Ct W1 .....103 B2
Barnes SW13 .....56 B4
Orchard Dr SE3 .....53 A1
Orchard Hill SE13 .....52 A2

Orchard Ho 🔲 SE16 .....40 B3
London SE5 .....48 B2
London SW11 .....29 C2
Orchard Mead Ho
NW11 .....1 C1
Orchard Mews N1 .....15 C1
Orchard Pl E14 .....35 A1
Orchard Prim Sch
E9 .....17 B1
Orchard Rise TW9 .....54 C4
Orchard Rise TW10 .....55 A3
Richardson Ho
NW8 .....89 C1
Orchardson St NW8 .....89 C1
Orchard Sq W14 .....140 C1
Orchard St W1 .....103 B1
Orchard The
London SE3 .....52 C1
London N14 .....37 C2
Orchid Cl SE13 .....29 C2
Orchid St W12 .....29 C2
Orde Hall St WC1 .....106 C4
Orde Ho N16 .....15 C4
Ordell Ct 🔲 E3 .....26 B3
Ordell Rd E3 .....26 B3
Ordnance Cres
SE10 .....43 A4
Ordnance Hill NW8 .....79 C3
Ordnance Mews
NW8 .....79 C2
Ordnance Rd E16 .....35 B2
Oregano Dr E14 .....34 C3
Orestes Mews 🔲
NW6 .....10 C3
Orford Ct SE27 .....75 A2
Oriana Ho 🔲 E14 .....33 B2
Oriel Ct NW3 .....11 B4
Oriel Dr SW13 .....47 B4
Oriel Rd London E9 .....17 C2
London E9 .....18 A2
Orient St SE11 .....150 A4
Orion Bsns Ctr SE14 .....40 C1
Orion Ho 🔲 E1 .....25 A1
Orkney Ho N1 .....84 C4
Orkney St SW11 .....169 B2
Orlando Rd SW4 .....61 B4
Orleston Mews N7 .....14 C2
Orleston Rd N7 .....14 C2
Orlop St SE10 .....43 A1
Orme Ct W2 .....114 B3
Orme Ct Mews W2 .....114 B3
Orme Ho E8 .....24 B4
Orme La W2 .....114 B3
Ormeley Rd SW12 .....73 A3
Orme Sq W2 .....114 B3
Ormiston Gr W12 .....30 A1
Ormiston Rd SE10 .....43 C1
Ormond Cl WC1 .....106 B4
Ormonde Ct SW15 .....57 B3
Ormonde Gate
SW3 .....145 A1
Ormonde Pl SW1 .....145 C3
Ormonde Terr NW8 .....80 C3
Ormond Ho N16 .....6 C2
Ormond Mews WC1 .....94 B1
Ormond Rd N4,N19 .....5 A3
Ormond Yd SW1 .....119 A2
Ormrod Ct W11 .....31 B3
Ormsby Lo W4 .....38 A3
Ormsby Pl N16 .....7 B1
Ormsby St E2 .....24 B3
Ormside St SE15 .....50 B4
Ornan Rd NW3 .....12 A3
Oronsay Rd 🔲 N1 .....15 B2
Orpheus Ho 🔲 N19 .....4 C4

Orpheus St SE5 .....48 C2
Orsett Mews W2 .....100 C2
Orsett St SE11 .....149 B2
Orsett Terr W2 .....100 C2
Orsman Rd N1 .....24 A4
Orton St E1 .....125 B1
Orville Rd SW11 .....167 C2
Orwell Ct E8 .....24 C4
London N5 .....15 B4
Orwell Ho W12 .....29 C2
Osbaldeston Rd N16 .....7 C3
Osbert St SW1 .....147 B3
Osborn Cl E8 .....24 C4
Osborne Rd
London E9 .....18 B2
London N4 .....5 C3
London W3 .....37 A4
Osborn St E1 .....111 A3
Osbourne Ho TW10 .....54 C2
Oscar Faber Pl 🔲
N1 .....16 A1
Oscar St SE8 .....51 C2
Oseney Cres NW5 .....13 C2
O'Shea Gr E3 .....26 B4
Osier Ct E1 .....25 C1
Osier Mews W4 .....46 B4
Osiers Rd SW18 .....58 C3
Oslo Ct NW8 .....80 A1
Oslo Ho SE5 .....48 B1
Oslo Sq SE16 .....41 A3
Osman Prim Sch
E1 .....111 B4
Osman Rd W6 .....39 B3
Osmington Ho
SW8 .....163 A1
Osmund St W12 .....29 B4
Osnaburgh St NW1 .....92 B2
Osnaburgh Terr
NW1 .....92 B2
Osprey Ct NW3 .....11 A3
Osprey Ho 🔲 E14 .....33 A2
London SE15 .....49 B2
Ospringe Ho SE1 .....121 C1
Ospringe Rd NW5 .....13 B4
Osram Ct W6 .....39 B3
Ossian Rd N4 .....5 B4
Osric Path 🔲 N1 .....24 A3
Ossington Bldgs
W1 .....103 B3
Ossington Cl W2 .....113 C3
Ossington St W2 .....114 A4
Ossory Rd SE1 .....49 C4
Ossulston St NW1 .....93 C4
Ostade Rd SW2 .....74 B4
Osten Mews SW7 .....128 B1
Osterley Ho 🔲 E14 .....34 A3
Osterley Rd N16 .....16 A4
Oswald's Mead E9 .....18 A4
Osward Rd SW12,
SW17 .....72 B2
Oswell Ho 🔲 E1 .....32 A1
Oswin St SE11 .....150 B4
Oswyth Rd SE5 .....49 A1
Otford Cres SE4 .....66 B1
Otford Ho SE1 .....137 C3
SE15 .....50 B4
Otha Ho SW9 .....172 B2
Othello Cl SE11 .....150 A2
Otis St E3 .....27 B2
Otley Ho N5 .....6 A1
Ottaway Ct E5 .....7 C1
Ottaway St E5 .....7 C1
Otterburn Ho
SE5 .....48 B3
Otto St SE17 .....48 A4

Our Lady of Dolours RC
Prim Sch W2 .....100 A4
Our Lady of Lourdes RC
Prim Sch SE13 .....67 C4
Our Lady of Lourdes RC
Sch NW10 .....20 B4
Our Lady of the
Assumption RC Prim
Sch E2 .....25 B3
Our Lady of the Sacred
Heart RC Prim Sch
(Annexe) N7 .....14 B2
Our Lady of the Sacred
Heart RC Sch N7 .....14 B3
Our Lady of Victories RC
Prim Sch
SW7 .....143 A3
Putney SW15 .....57 C3
Our Lady Queen of
Heaven RC Sch
SW19 .....69 C4
Our Lady RC Prim Sch
E14 .....33 B3
NW1 .....82 C3
Our Lady's Convent High
Sch N15,N16 .....7 A4
Our Lady & St Joseph
RC Prim Sch N1 .....16 A2
Ouseley Rd SW12 .....72 B3
Outer Circ NW8 .....80 B1
Outgate Rd NW10 .....8 B1
Outram Pl N1 .....84 B4
Outwich St EC3 .....110 B2
Outwood Ho 🔲
SW2 .....74 B4
Oval Mans SE11 .....163 A4
Oval Pl SW8 .....163 A2
Oval Rd NW1 .....82 B4
Oval Sta SE11 .....163 B3
Oval The E2 .....25 A3
Oval The (Surrey Cnty
Crkt Gd) SE11 .....163 A4
Oval Way SE11 .....149 A1
Overbury Ho 🔲 E5 .....17 C4
Overbury St E5 .....17 C4
Overcliff Rd SE13 .....66 C4
Overhill Rd SE21,
SE22 .....76 C4
Overlea Rd E5 .....7 C4
Oversley Ho 🔲 W2 .....31 C4
Overstone Ho 🔲
E14 .....33 C3
Overstone Rd W6 .....39 B2
Overstrand Mans
SW11 .....169 B3
Overton Ho SW15 .....68 B4
Overton Rd SW9 .....173 C1
Overy Ho SE1 .....136 A3
Ovex Cl E14 .....42 B4
Ovington Ct SW3 .....130 B1
Ovington Gdns
SW3 .....130 B1
Ovington Mews
SW3 .....130 B1
Ovington Sq SW3 .....130 B1
Ovington St SW3 .....144 B4
Owen Ho N19 .....13 B4
Owen's Ct EC1 .....96 A4
Owen's Row EC1 .....96 A4
Owen St EC1 .....48 C3
Oxberry Ave SW6 .....164 B2
Oxbridge Ct W4 .....37 A1
Oxendon St SW1,
W1 .....119 B3
Oxenford St SE15 .....64 B4
Oxenham Ho 🔲 SE8 .....51 C4

Oxenholme NW1 ...83 A1
Oxestalls Rd SE8 ...41 A1
Oxford Ave NW10 ...22 B2
Oxford & Cambridge
  Mans NW1 ...102 B3
Oxford Cir W1 ...104 C1
Oxford Circus Ave
  W1 ...104 C1
Oxford Circus Sta
  W1 ...104 C1
Oxford Ct EC4 ...123 B4
  48 London W2 ...31 C4
  London W4 ...37 A1
Oxford Dr SE1 ...124 A1
Oxford Gardens Prim
  Sch W10 ...30 C3
Oxford Gate W6 ...39 C2
Oxford Gdns
  Brentford W4 ...44 C4
  London W10 ...30 C3
Oxford Rd NW6 ...23 C3
  London E15 ...19 C2
  London N4 ...5 C3
  Putney SW15 ...58 A3
Oxford Rd N W4 ...37 A1
Oxford Rd S W4 ...37 A1
Oxford Sq W2 ...102 B1
Oxford St W1 ...104 B1
Oxley Cl SE1 ...153 A2
Oxonian St SE22 ...64 B3
Oxo Tower SE1 ...121 C3
Oxo Tower Wharf
  SE1 ...121 C3
Oxted Ct N16 ...7 A3
Oyster Row E1 ...32 B3
Ozolins Way E16 ...35 C3

P

Pablo Neruda Cl 4
  SE24 ...63 A3
Pace Pl E1 ...32 A3
Pacific Ho 15 E1 ...25 C1
Pacific Rd E16 ...35 C3
Pacific Wharf SE16 ...32 C1
Packenham Ho 2 ...99 A4
  24 London N19 ...4 C4
Packington Ho
  SW9 ...172 B2
Packington Sq N1 ...86 C4
Packington St N1 ...86 B3
Padbury SE17 ...152 B1
Padbury Ct E2 ...99 A3
Padbury Ho NW8 ...90 B2
Paddenswick Ct
  W6 ...39 A3
Paddenswick Rd
  W6 ...38 C3
Paddington Com Hospl
  W9 ...31 C4
Paddington Gn
  W2 ...101 B4
Paddington Green Prim
  Sch NW8 ...89 B1
Paddington St W1 ...103 B4
Paddington Sta
  W2 ...101 B2
Paddock Cl SE3 ...53 C1
Paddock Sch SW15 ...56 B3
Padfield Rd SE5 ...63 B4
Padstow Ho 12 E14 ...33 B2
Pagden St SW8 ...170 B4
Pageant Cres SE16 ...33 B1
Pageantmaster Ct
  EC4 ...108 A1
Page Ho SE10 ...52 B4
Page St SW1 ...147 C4

Page's Wlk SE1 ...138 B1
Page's Yd W4 ...46 A4
Paget Ho 15 E2 ...25 B3
Paget Rd N16 ...6 C3
Paget St EC1 ...96 A4
Pagham Ho 10 W10 ...22 B1
Pagnell St SE14 ...51 B3
Pagoda Ave TW9 ...54 B4
Pagoda Gdns SE3 ...52 C1
Paine Ct SE3 ...53 B4
Painsthorpe Rd 3
  N16 ...7 A1
Painswick Ct 8
  SE15 ...49 B3
Painters Mews
  SE16 ...153 C4
Pakeman Ho SE1 ...136 B4
Pakeman Prim Sch
  N7 ...5 B1
Pakeman St N7 ...5 B1
Pakenham Cl SW12 ...72 C3
Pakenham St WC1 ...95 A2
Palace Ave W8 ...128 B4
Palace Ct W2 ...114 A3
  London NW3 ...11 A3
  Streatham SW2 ...74 C2
Palace Garden Mews
  W8 ...113 C2
Palace Gate W8 ...128 C3
Palace Gdns Mews
  W8 ...114 B1
Palace Gn W8 ...114 A1
Palace Mans W14 ...140 B4
Palace Mews SW1 ...145 C3
Palace Pl SW1 ...132 C2
Palace Rd SE27,
  SW16,SW2 ...74 C2
Palace St SW1 ...132 C2
Palamon Ct SE1 ...153 A2
Palatine Ave N16 ...16 A4
Palatine Rd N16 ...16 A4
Palemead Cl SW6 ...47 C2
Palermo Rd NW10 ...21 C3
Palewell Common Dr
  SW14 ...55 C2
Palewell Pk SW14 ...55 C2
Palfrey Pl SW8 ...163 A2
Palgrave Gdns NW1 ...90 B1
Palgrave Ho 7 SE5 ...48 B3
  4 London NW3 ...12 B3
Palgrave Rd W12 ...38 B3
Palissy St E2 ...98 C3
Pallant Ho SE1 ...137 C1
Palliser Ct W14 ...140 A1
Palliser Ho 2 E1 ...25 C1
  8 SE10 ...52 C4
Palliser Rd W14 ...140 A1
Pallister Terr SW15 ...68 B2
Pall Mall SW1 ...119 B1
Pall Mall E SW1 ...119 C2
Pall Mall Pl SW1 ...119 A1
Palm Ct 17 SE15 ...49 B3
  London N16 ...6 C2
Palmer Ct NW10 ...20 C4
Palmer Ho 5 N19 ...4 B1
  6 NW5 ...13 B4
  8 SE14 ...50 C3
Palmer Pl N7 ...14 C3
Palmers Rd E2 ...25 C3
  Mortlake SW14 ...55 B4
Palmer St SW1 ...133 B2
Palmerston Ct 22
  E3 ...25 C3
Palmerston Ho
  SW11 ...169 C3
  W8 ...113 B1

Palmerston Rd
  London NW6 ...10 B1
  London NW6 ...10 C1
  London W3 ...37 B3
  Mortlake SW14 ...55 B3
Palmerston Way
  SW8 ...160 B1
Palm Gr W5 ...36 A3
Palm Tree Ho 2
  SE14 ...50 C3
Pamela Ct NW10 ...8 C1
Pamela Ho 18 E8 ...24 B4
Pamlion Ct N4 ...5 A4
Panama Ho 6 E1 ...32 C4
Pancras La EC2 ...109 B1
Pancras Rd NW1 ...83 C2
Pandora Rd NW6 ...10 C2
Pangbourne NW1 ...92 C3
Pangbourne Ave
  W10 ...30 B4
Pangbourne Ho N7 ...14 A3
Pankhurst Cl 7
  SE14 ...50 C3
Panmure Cl N5 ...15 A4
Pansy Gdns W12 ...29 C2
Panton St SW1 ...119 B3
Panyer Alley EC2 ...108 C2
Paper Mill Wharf
  E14 ...33 A2
Papworth Gdns N7 ...14 B3
Papworth Way SW2 ...74 C4
Parade Mans 19
  SE5 ...48 B1
Parade Mews SE27,
  SW2 ...75 A2
Parade The SW11 ...159 A2
Paradise Pas N7 ...14 C3
Paradise Rd
  London SW4 ...172 A2
  Richmond TW10 ...54 A2
Paradise Row E2 ...25 A2
Paradise St SE16 ...40 A4
Paradise Wlk SW3 ...159 A4
Paragon Cl E16 ...35 C3
Paragon Mews
  SE1 ...151 C4
Paragon Pl SE3 ...53 B1
Paragon Rd E9 ...17 B2
Paragon The SE17 ...151 C3
Paragon The SE3 ...53 C1
Paramount Bldg
  EC1 ...96 A2
Paramount Ct WC1 ...93 A1
Parayhouse Sch
  W12 ...30 A1
Parbury Rd SE23 ...66 A1
Pardoner St SE1 ...137 C2
Pardon St EC1 ...96 B2
Parfett St E1 ...111 C2
Parfitt Cl NW3 ...2 B3
Parfrey St W6 ...47 B4
Paris Gdn SE1 ...122 A2
Paris Ho 12 E2 ...25 A3
Park Ave
  London NW11 ...2 A3
  London NW2 ...9 B2
  Mortlake SW14 ...55 C3
Park Ave N NW10 ...9 A3
Park Bsns Ctr 6
  NW6 ...23 C2
Park Cl 20 E9 ...25 B4
  SW1 ...130 C3
  W14 ...127 A2
Park Cres W1 ...92 A1
Park Cres Mews E
  W1 ...92 B1

Park Cres Mews W
  W1 ...92 A1
Park Ct SW11 ...170 A4
  Dulwich SE21 ...75 C1
  London SW4 ...61 C2
  Upper Tooting SW12 ...72 C3
Park Dr Acton W3 ...36 C3
  London NW11 ...2 A3
  Mortlake SW14 ...55 C2
Park Dwellings 7
  NW3 ...12 B3
Park End NW3 ...12 A4
Parker Ct N1 ...87 A4
Parke Rd SW13 ...46 C2
Parker Mews WC2 ...106 B2
Parkers Row SE1 ...139 B3
Parker's Row SE1 ...139 A3
Parker St WC2 ...106 B2
Parkfield Ind Est
  SW11 ...169 C2
Parkfield Rd
  London SE14 ...51 B2
Parkfields SW15 ...57 B3
Parkgate Gdns SW14 ...55 C2
Parkgate Ho 4
  SW11 ...60 C3
Parkgate House Sch
  SW11 ...60 C3
Parkgate Mews N6 ...4 B4
Parkgate Rd SW11 ...158 B1
Park Hall SE21 ...75 C1
Park Hall Road Trad Est
  SE21 ...75 C1
Parkham St SW11 ...168 A3
Park Hill
  London SW4 ...61 C2
  Richmond TW10 ...54 B1
Park Hill Ct SW17 ...72 B1
Parkhill Rd NW3 ...12 B3
Park Hill Wlk 10
  NW3 ...12 B3
Park Ho
  82 London E9 ...17 B1
  London N4 ...6 A2
  London SE5 ...48 C2
Parkholme Rd E8 ...16 C2
Parkhouse St SE5 ...48 C3
Parkhurst Ct N7 ...14 A4
Parkhurst Rd N7 ...14 A4
Parkinson Ct EC1 ...97 C3
  N1 ...97 C3
Parkinson Ho 9 E9 ...17 B1
Park La E15 ...27 C4
Parkland Gdns 12
  SW19 ...69 C3
Parklands London N6 ...4 A4
  London SE22 ...76 C4
Parklands Cl SW14 ...55 B2
Parkland Wlk N4,N8 ...5 B4
Park Lea E15 ...27 C4
Park Lo 10 E1 ...32 A1
  NW2 ...9 B2
  London NW8 ...11 C1
Park Lofts 3 SW4 ...62 A2
Park Lorne NW8 ...90 B3
Park Mans NW8 ...80 A1
  SW1 ...130 C3
  SW11 ...168 C3
  SW8 ...162 B2
  W6 ...38 B3

Parkmead SW15 ...57 A1
Park Mews W10 ...23 A3
Park Par Acton W3 ...36 C3
  London NW10 ...21 B3
Park Pl E14 ...33 C1
  SW1 ...118 C2
  London W3 ...36 C3
Park Place Dr W3 ...36 C3
Park Place Villas
  W2 ...101 A4
Park Rd NW1,NW8 ...90 B2
  Chiswick W4 ...45 C4
  London NW10 ...21 A4
  Richmond TW10 ...54 B1
Park Rd E W3 ...37 B4
Park Rd N
  London W3 ...37 A4
  London W4 ...37 C1
Park Row SE10 ...52 C4
Park Royal NW10 ...20 A4
Park Royal Bsns Ctr
  NW10 ...20 B1
Park Royal Metro Ctr
  NW10 ...20 A1
Park Royal Rd
  NW10,W3 ...20 B1
Park S SW11 ...169 B3
Park Sheen 5
  SW14 ...55 A3
Parkshot TW9 ...54 A3
Parkside SE3 ...53 B3
  London SW19 ...69 C1
Parkside Cres N7 ...5 C1
Parkside Est E9 ...25 C4
Parkside St SW11 ...169 B3
Park Sq E NW1 ...92 B2
Park Sq Mews NW1 ...92 A1
Park Sq W NW1 ...92 A1
Park St SE1 ...123 A2
  W1 ...117 B3
Parkstead Rd SW15 ...57 A2
Park Steps W2 ...116 B4
Park St James NW8 ...80 B3
Parkstone Rd 3
  SE15 ...49 C1
Park The NW11 ...2 A3
Parkthorne Rd
  SW12 ...73 C4
Park Twrs W1 ...118 A1
Park View London N5 ...15 B4
  London W3 ...28 B4
Parkview Ct SW6 ...164 B1
Park View Ct SW18 ...58 C1
Park View Ho SE24 ...63 A1
Park View Mews
  SW9 ...172 C2
Park View Rd NW10 ...8 B4
Park Village E NW1 ...82 B1
Park Village W
  NW1 ...82 A2
Park Vista SE10 ...52 C4
Park Walk Prim Sch
  SW10 ...157 B3
Parkway NW1 ...82 A3
Park Way W3 ...36 C2
Park West W2 ...102 B1
Park West Pl W2,
  W1 ...102 B2
Park Wlk SW10 ...157 B4
Parkwood Prim Sch
  N4 ...6 A2
Parliament Ct NW3 ...12 A4

Parliament Hill
NW3 ....12 A4
Parliament Hill Mans
NW5 ....12 C4
Parliament Hill Sch
NW5 ....12 C4
Parliament Mews
SW14 ....45 B1
Parliament Sq
SW1 ....134 A3
Parliament St
SW1 ....134 A4
Parliament View
Apartments SE1 ....134 B1
Parma Cres SW11 ...60 B3
Parminter Ind Est
E2 ....25 A3
Parmiter St E2 ......25 A3
Parmoor Ct EC1 ....96 C2
Parnell Cl W12 ......39 A3
Parnell Rd E3 ....26 B4
Parnham St E14 .....33 A3
Parolles Rd N19 .....4 B3
Parr Ct N1 ....87 B2
Parrington Ho **1**
SW4 ....61 C1
Parr Pl W4 ....38 B2
Parr St N1 ....87 B2
Parry Ho **27** E1 .....32 A1
Parry Rd W10 ....23 A2
Parry St SW8 ....162 B4
Parsifal Coll NW3 ...10 C4
Parsifal Ho NW3 ....10 C4
Parsifal Rd NW6 ....10 C3
Parsonage St E14 ...42 B2
Parson Ct SE13 .....67 A4
Parsons Gn SW6 ...165 B3
Parsons Green La
SW6 ....165 B3
Parsons Green Sta
SW6 ....165 B3
Parsons Ho W2 .....89 B1
1 Streatham SW12 ..74 A4
Parsons Lo NW6 ....11 A1
Parthenia Rd SW6 .165 C3
Partington Cl N19 ....4 C3
Partridge Ct EC1 ....96 A2
Partridge Ho **20** E3 .26 B3
Pascall Ho SE17 ....48 B4
Pascal St SW8 .....161 C2
Pascoe Rd SE13 ....67 C2
Pasley Cl SE17 .....150 C1
Passfield Dr E14 ....34 A4
Passfields W14 .....140 C1
Passing Alley EC1 ...96 B1
Passmore St SW1 ..145 B2
Pastor St SE1,SE11 107 A1
Patcham Terr SW8 .170 B4
Patent Ho E14 ......34 A4
Paternoster Row
EC2,EC4 ....108 C1
Paternoster Sq
EC4 ....108 B2
Pater St W8 ....127 B1
Patience Rd SW11 .168 A1
Patio Cl SW4 ....61 C1
Patmore Ho **9** N16 .16 A3
Patmore St SW8 ...171 A4
Paton Cl E3 ....26 C2
Paton Ho SW9 .....172 C2
Paton St EC1 ....96 C3
Patrick Coman Ho
EC1 ....96 A3
Patrick Connolly Gdns
1 E3 ....27 A2

Patriot Sq E2 ....25 A3
Patrol Pl SE6 ....67 A1
Pat Shaw Ho **2** E1 ..25 C1
Patshull Pl NW5 ....13 B2
Patshull Rd NW5 ...13 B2
Patten Ho N4 ....6 B3
Patten Rd SW18 ....72 A4
Patterdale NW1 .....92 B3
Patterdale Rd SE15 .50 B3
Pattina Wlk SE16 ...33 A1
Pattinson Point **10**
E16 ....35 C4
Pattison Ho **3** E1 ...32 C3
SE1 ....137 A4
Pattison Rd NW2 ....1 C1
Paul Ho **13** W10 ....23 A1
Paulet Rd SE5 ......48 A2
Paul Ho **13** W10 ....23 A1
Pauline Ho **1** E1 ..111 C4
Paul Julius Cl E14 ..34 C2
Paul's Ho E3 ....33 B4
Paul St EC2 ....24 A1 98 A2
Paultons Ho SW3 .157 C4
Paultons Sq SW3 ..157 C4
Paultons St SW3 ..157 C3
Pauntley Ho **8** N19 ..4 B3
Pauntley St **4** N19 ...4 B3
Pavan Ct **8** E2 .....25 B2
Paveley Dr SW11 ..158 A1
Paveley Ho
N1 ....84 C1
Paveley St NW8 ....90 B2
Pavement The
London SE27 ....75 B1
London W5 ....36 A4
Pavilion Ct **6** NW6 .23 C2
London NW3 ....11 B2
5 London NW3 ...11 B4
Pavilion Mans **10**
SW9 ....62 B3
Pavilion Rd SW1 ..131 A1
Pavilion St SW1 ...131 A1
Pavilion Terr W12 ...30 B3
Paxton Cl TW9 .....44 B1
Paxton Ho SE17 ...151 A2
Paxton Rd W4 ......46 A4
Paxton Terr SW1 ..160 B4
Payens Wlk W6 ...154 A3
Paymal Ho **22** E1 ...32 B4
Payne Ho N1 ....85 A4
Payne Rd E3 ....27 A3
Paynesfield Ave
SW14 ....55 C4
Payne St SE8 ....51 B4
Peabody Ave SW1 146 B3
Peabody Bldgs
SE17 ....151 A3
6 London SE5 ....48 C2
Peabody Cl SW1 ..160 B4
Peabody Ct EC1 ....97 A1
London SE5 ....48 C2
Peabody Est SE1 ..125 B4
4 E1 ....32 C2
12 E2 ....25 A3
EC1 ....95 C1
SE1 ....97 A1
SE1 ....121 C1
SW1 ....122 B3
SW1 ....147 A4
SW6 ....155 A4
W6 ....106 C1
London W10 ....23 A2
17 London W6 ....39 B1
Streatham SE24 ....75 B4
Peabody Hill SE21 .75 B3
Peabody Sq SE1 ..136 A3
Peabody Twr EC1 ...97 A1
Peabody Yd N1 .....86 C4

Peach Rd W10 .....23 A2
Peachum Rd SE3 ...53 B4
Peach Walk Mews **20**
E3 ....25 C3
Peacock St SE17 ..150 B3
Peacock Yd SE17 ..150 B3
Peak Ho N4 ....6 B3
Pearce Ho N19 ......4 B1
7 Streatham SW2 ..74 A4
Pear Cl SE14 ....51 A3
Pear Ct **2** SE15 ....49 B3
Peardon St SW8 ..170 B1
Pearfield Ho **1** N5 ..15 B3
Pearl St E1 ....32 A1
Pearman St SE1 ...135 C3
Pear Pl SE1 ....135 B4
Pearscroft Ct SW6 166 B3
Pearscroft Rd SW6 166 B3
Pearse St **3** SE5 ...49 A4
Pearson Cl **2** SE5 .48 B2
Pearson Ho SW15 ..47 B1
Pearson's Ave SE8,
SE14 ....51 C2
Pearson St E2 ......24 B3
Peartree Ave SW17 .71 B1
Pear Tree Cl **2** E2 ..24 B4
Pear Tree Cl EC1 ...95 C1
Putney SW15 ....57 A3
Pear Tree Ho SE4 ..66 B3
Peartree La E1 ......32 B2
Peartree St EC1 .....96 C2
Peary Pl **9** E2 ......25 B2
Peckarmans Wood
SE21,SE26 ....76 C1
Peckett Sq **3** N5 ...15 A4
Peckford Pl SW9 ..173 C1
Peckham Gr SE15 ..49 A3
Peckham High St
SE15 ....49 C2
Peckham Hill St
SE15 ....49 C3
Peckham Park Prim Sch
SE15 ....49 C3
Peckham Park Rd
SE15 ....49 C3
Peckham Rd SE5 ...49 A2
Peckham Rye
London SE22 ....64 C3
Peckham SE15,SE22 .65 A3
Peckham Rye Prim Sch
SE15 ....65 A4
Peckham Rye Sta
SE15 ....49 C1
Peckwater St NW5 .13 B3
Pedlars Wlk N7 ....14 A3
Pedley St E1 ...24 C1 99 B1
Pedro St E5 ....17 C4
Pedworth Gdns **4**
SE16 ....40 B2
Peel Gr E2 ....25 B3
Peel Pass W8 ......113 B1
Peel Prec NW6 .....23 C3
Peel Rd NW6 ....23 B2
Peel St W8 ...31 C1 113 B1
Peerless St EC1 ....97 B3
Pegasus Ct
Brentford TW8 .....36 B1
London NW10 ......22 C2
Pegasus Ho **9** E1 ...25 C1
Pegwell Ho **15** E5 ..17 A3
Pekin St E14 ....34 A3
Pekoe SE1 ....125 A1
Peldon Ct TW10 ....54 B2
Pelham Cl SE5 .....64 A4
Pelham Cres SW7 .144 A3
Pelham Ct SW3 ...144 A3
Pelham Pl SW7 ...144 A3

Pelham St SW7 ...143 C3
Pelican Ho **7** SE8 ..41 B2
Pelier St SE17 ......48 B4
Pella Rd SE11 .....149 A2
Pellant Rd SW6 ...154 B2
Pellatt Rd SE22 .....64 B2
Pellerin Rd N16 .....16 A3
Pellew Ho **1** E1 ....25 A1
Pelling St E14 ....33 C3
Pelter St E2 ....24 B2 98 C4
Pelton Rd SE10 .....43 A1
Pember Rd NW10 ..22 C2
Pemberton Ct **18**
E1 ....25 C2
Pemberton Gdns N19 .4 B1
Pemberton Pl **2** E8 .17 A1
Pemberton Row
EC4 ....107 C2
Pemberton Terr N19 .4 B1
Pembridge Cres
W11 ....31 C2 113 B4
Pembridge Gdns
W2 ....31 C2 113 B3
Pembridge Mews
W11 ....31 C2 113 B4
Pembridge Pl
W2 ....31 C2 113 C4
Pembridge Rd
W11 ....113 B3
Pembridge Sq
W2 ....31 C2 113 C3
Pembridge Villas
W11 ....31 C2 113 B4
Pembroke W14 ....140 C4
Pembroke Bldgs
NW10 ....21 C2
Pembroke Cl SW1 131 C3
Pembroke Gdns
W8 ....141 A4
Pembroke Gdns Cl
W8 ....127 B1
Pembroke Ho
Acton W3 ....37 B4
London W2 ....100 B1
Putney SW15 ....56 C2
Pembroke Mews
W8 ....127 B1
Pembroke Pl W8 ..127 B1
Pembroke Rd **4** N8 ..5 A4
Pembroke Rd W8 .141 B4
Pembroke Sq W8 .127 B1
Pembroke St N1 ....84 B4
Pembroke Studios
W8 ....127 A1
Pembroke Terr
NW8 ....79 B3
Pembroke Villas
W8 ....141 B4
Pembroke Wlk W8 141 B4
Pembrook Lo **2**
SW16 ....74 A1
Pembry Cl SW9 ...173 C3
Pembury Cl E5 ......17 A3
Pembury Ho SE5 ...49 A1
Pembury Pl **1** E5,
E8 ....17 A3
Pembury Rd E5 .....17 A3
Pemell Cl **27** E1 ...25 B1
Pemell Ho SE5 .....25 B1
Penally Pl N1 ....87 C4
Penang St E1 ....32 A1
Penarth St SE15 ...50 B4
Pencombe Mews
W11 ....113 A4
Pencraig Way SE15 .50 A4
Penda's Mead E9 ..18 A4
Pendennis Ho **15**
SE8 ....41 A2

Penderyn Way N7 ..13 C4
Pendle Ho **13** SE26 .76 C1
Pendley Ho **18** E2 ..24 C4
Pendrell Ho WC2 ..105 C1
Pendrell Rd SE4 ....51 A1
Penelope Ho SW9 173 B3
Penfield Lo **9** W9 ..31 C4
Penfields Ho N7 ....14 A2
Penfold Ct NW8 ....89 C1
Penfold Pl NW1 ...102 A4
Penfold St NW8 .....89 C1
Penford St SE5 .....48 A1
Penhurst Mans
SW6 ....164 C4
Peninsula Ct E14 ...42 A3
Peninsular Park Rd
SE7 ....43 C2
Penmayne Ho
SE11 ....149 C2
Pennack Rd SE15 ..49 B4
Penn Almshouse **1**
SE10 ....52 B2
Pennant Mews
W8 ....142 A4
Pennard Mans **1**
W12 ....39 B4
Pennard Rd W12 ...39 B4
Penner Cl SW19 ....70 A2
Pennethorne Cl E9 .25 B4
Pennethorne Ho
SW11 ....59 C4
Pennethorne Rd
SE15 ....50 A3
Penn Ho NW8 ....90 A1
Pennine La NW2 .....1 A2
Pennine Mans NW2 ..1 A2
Pennine Par NW2 ...1 A2
Pennington Ct **1** .125 C3
SE16 ....33 A1
Pennington St E1 ..32 A2
Penn Rd N7 ....14 A4
Penn St N1 ....87 C3
Penny Ct SW10 ...157 A4
Pennyfields E14 ....33 C2
Pennyford Ct NW8 .89 B2
Penny Mews SW12 .73 A4
Pennymore Wlk W9 .23 B1
Penny Rd NW10 ....20 A2
Penpoll Rd E8 ......17 A2
Penrhyn Cres SW14 .55 B3
Penrith Cl SW15 ....58 A2
Penrith Pl SE27 .....75 A2
Penrose Gr SE17 ..150 C1
Penrose Ho SE17 .150 C1
Penrose St SE17 ..150 C1
Penryn Ho SE11 ...150 A2
Penryn St NW1 .....83 B2
Penry St SE1 ....152 B3
Pensbury Pl SW8 .171 A2
Pensbury St SW8 .171 A2
Pensford Ave TW9 .44 C1
Penshurst **2** NW5 .12 C2
Penshurst Ho **1**
SE15 ....50 B4
Penshurst Rd E9 ...17 C1
Pentland Cl NW11 ...1 C2
Pentland Ho
17 NW5 ....12 C2
7 London N16 ......7 B3
Pentland Rd SW18 .59 B1
Pentlow St SW15 ...57 B4
Pentney Rd SW12 ..73 B3
Penton Gr N1 ....85 B1
Penton Ho N1 ....85 B1
Penton Pl SE17 ...150 B2
Penton Rise WC1 ...95 A4
Penton St N1 ....85 B1

Pentonville Rd N1 . . . . .85 A1
Pentridge St SE15 . . . . .49 B3
Penwith Rd SW18 . . . . .71 A2
Penwood Ho 4
SW15 . . . . .56 B1
Penywern Rd SW5 .141 C2
Penzance Ho SE11 .149 C2
Penzance Pl
W11 . . . . .31 A1 112 B2
Penzance St
W11 . . . . .31 A1 112 A2
Peony Gdns W12 . . .29 C2
Peperfield WC1 . . . . . .94 C3
Pepler Ho 17 W10 . . .23 A1
Pepler Mews SE1 .152 C1
Peploe Rd NW6 . . . . .22 C3
Peppermead Sq
SE13 . . . . .66 C2
Pepper St E14 . . . . . . .42 A3
SE1 . . . . .136 C4
Peppie Cl N16 . . . . . . .7 A2
Pepsi Trocadero
. . . . .119 C3
Pepys Cres 2 E16 . .35 C1
Pepys Ent Ctr 12
SE8 . . . . .41 B2
Pepys Ho E2 . . . . .25 B2
London SW4 . . . . .61 C2
Pepys Rd SE14 . . . . . .50 C1
Pepys St EC3 . . . . . .124 B4
Perceval Ave NW3 . .12 A3
Percheron Ct 3
SW9 . . . . .62 B4
Perch St E8 . . . . .16 B4
Percival Rd SW14 . .55 B3
Percival St EC1 . . . . . .96 B3
Percy Cir WC1 . . . . . . .95 A4
Percy Mews W1 . . . .105 B3
Percy Pas W1 . . . . . .105 B3
Percy Rd E16 . . . . .35 A4
London W12 . . . . .38 C4
Percy St W1 . . . . .105 B3
Peregrine Ho 4 EC1 . .96 B4
6 London SW11 . . . . .60 A4
Perham Rd W14 . . . .140 B1
Perifield SE21 . . . . . . .75 B3
Perkins Ho 15 E14 . .33 B4
Perkins Rents
SW1 . . . . .133 B1
Perkins Sq SE1 . . . . .123 A2
Perley Ho 16 E3 . . . . . .33 B4
Perotti Ho SW6 . . . . . .59 C4
Perran Rd SE24,SW2 .75 A2
Perren St NW5 . . . . . . .13 A2
Perrers Rd W6 . . . . . . .39 A2
Perring Est E3 . . . . . . .33 C4
Perrin's Ct 17 NW3 . .11 B4
Perrin's La NW3 . . . . .11 B4
Perrin's Wlk NW3 . . .11 B4
Perronet Ho SE1 . . .136 B1
Perry Ave W3 . . . . . . .28 C3
Perry Ct 5 E14 . . . . . .41 C1
Perry Ho 24 SW2 . . . .74 A4
Perrymead St SW6 .166 A3
Perryn Ho W3 . . . . . . .29 A2
Perryn Rd 1 SE16 . .40 A3
London W3 . . . . .28 C2
Perry's Pl W1 . . . . . .105 B2
Perrywood Ho 17
E5 . . . . .17 A3
Perseverance Pl
SW9 . . . . .163 B1
Perseverance Works
E2 . . . . .98 B4
Perth Ct 5 SE5 . . . . . .63 C3
Perth Ho N1 . . . . .14 B1
Perth Rd N4 . . . . .5 C3

Peter Ave NW10 . . . . . .9 A1
Peter Best Ho 6 E1 .32 A3
Peterboat Cl SE10 . .43 A2
Peterborough Ct
EC4 . . . . .107 C1
Peterborough Mews
SW6 . . . . .165 B2
Peterborough Prim Sch
SW6 . . . . .166 C1
Peterborough Rd
SW6 . . . . .58 C4
Peterborough Villas
SW6 . . . . .166 A4
Peter Butler Ho
SE1 . . . . .139 B3
Peterchurch Ho
SE15 . . . . .50 A4
Petergate SW11 . . . . .59 B3
Peter Hills Ho
SE16 . . . . .153 B4
Peter Hills with St
Mary's & St Paul's CE
Prim Sch SE16 . . . . . .32 C1
Peter Ho SW8 . . . . . .162 A2
Peterley Bsns Ctr 54
E2 . . . . .25 A3
Peters Ct W2 . . . . . .100 B2
Peter's Ct SW4 . . . . . .62 A1
Petersfield Rd W3 . .37 B4
Petersfield Rise
SW15 . . . . .69 A3
Petersham Ho
SW7 . . . . .143 B4
Petersham La
SW7 . . . . .128 C2
Petersham Mews
SW7 . . . . .129 A1
Petersham Pl SW7 .129 B2
Peter's La EC1 . . . . . .108 B4
Peterstow Cl SW19 . .70 A2
Petherton Ho NW10 .22 C4
Petherton Rd N4 . . . . .6 B3
Petherton Rd N5 . . . .15 B3
Petiver Cl 20 E9 . . . . .17 B1
Petley Rd W6 . . . . .47 C3
Peto Pl NW1 . . . . .92 B2
Peto St N E16 . . . . . . .35 B1
Petrel Ct 3 SE21 . . . .75 C2
Petrie Cl NW2 . . . . . . .10 A2
Petros Gdns 1
NW3 . . . . .11 B2
Petticoat Lane Mkt★
EC2 . . . . .110 C3
Petticoat Sq E1 . . . .110 C2
Petticoat Twr E1 . . .110 C2
Pettiward Cl SW15 . .57 B3
Petty France SW1 .133 B2
Petworth Ho 18
SE22 . . . . .64 A4
Petworth St SW11 .168 B4
Petyt Pl SW3 . . . . . . .158 A3
Petyward SW3 . . . . . .144 B3
Pevensey Ct
4 London W3 . . . . . . .37 A4
West Norwood SW16 .74 C1
Pevensey Ho 5 E1 . .33 A4
Peveril Ho SE1 . . . . .137 C1
Pewsham Ho N4 . . . . .6 B3
Peyton Pl SE10 . . . . . .52 B3
Pharamond NW2 . . . . .9 C2
Phelps Ho SW15 . . . . .57 C4
Phelp St SE17 . . . . . . .48 C4
Phene St SW3 . . . . . .158 B4
Philadelphia Ct
SW10 . . . . .157 A1

Philbeach Gdns
SW5 . . . . .141 B2
Phil Brown Pl 3
SW8 . . . . .61 A4
Philchurch Pl E1 . . . .111 C1
Philia Ho 2 NW1 . . . .13 B1
Philip Ct W2 . . . . . . .101 B4
Philip Ho NW6 . . . . . . .78 A3
Philip Rd SE15 . . . . . .65 A4
Philip Turner Est 20
E9 . . . . .17 B1
Philip Wlk SE15 . . . . .65 A4
Phillimore Ct W8 . . .127 C3
Phillimore Gardens Cl
W8 . . . . .127 B2
Phillimore Gdns
Willesden NW10 . . . . .22 B4
Phillimore Pl W8 . . .127 B3
Phillimore Terr
W8 . . . . .127 C2
Phillimore Wlk
W8 . . . . .127 C2
Phillip Ho E1 . . . . . . .111 A3
Phillipp St N1 . . . . .24 A4
Philpot La EC3 . . . . . .124 A4
Philpot Sq SW6 . . . . .59 A4
Philpot St E1 . . . . .32 A3
Phipps Ho 11 W12 . .30 A2
Phipps Mews SW1 . .132 A2
Phoebeth Rd SE4 . . .66 C2
Phoenix Bsns Ctr 30
E3 . . . . .33 C4
Phoenix Cl 18 E8 . . . .24 B4
Phoenix Ct 7 E14 . . .41 C2
2 SE14 . . . . .51 A4
4 Brentford TW8 . . . .36 A1
Phoenix High Sch
W12 . . . . .29 C3
Phoenix Lodge Mans 1
W6 . . . . .39 B2
Phoenix Pl WC1 . . . . .95 A2
Phoenix Rd NW1 . . . .93 B4
Phoenix Sch SE13 . .26 B2
Phoenix Sch The
NW3 . . . . .11 B2
Phoenix St WC2 . . . .105 C1
Phoenix Wharf Rd
SE1 . . . . .139 A3
Phyllis Hodges Ho
NW1 . . . . .83 B1
Physic Pl SW3 . . . . . .158 C4
Piccadilly W1 . . . . . .118 C2
Piccadilly Arc
SW1 . . . . .118 C2
Piccadilly Cir★
W1 . . . . .119 B3
Piccadilly Circus Sta
. . . . .119 B3
Piccadilly Pl W1 . . . .119 A3
Pickard St EC1 . . . . . .96 B4
Pickering Ho
London N4 . . . . .6 C4
London W2 . . . . .100 C2
Pickering Mews
W2 . . . . .100 A2
Pickering Pl SW1 . . .119 A1
Pickering St N1 . . . . . .86 B4
Pickets St SW12 . . . . .73 A4
Pickfords Wharf N1 . .87 A1
3 London SE1 . . . . . .139 A4
Pickwick Ho
1 London SE16 . . . . .139 B3
2 London W11 . . . . . .30 C1
Pickwick Rd SE21 . . .76 A4
Pickwick St SE1 . . . .136 C3
Pickworth Cl SW8 . .162 B1
Picton Ho 1 SW4 . . .74 A4
Picton Pl W1 . . . . . . .103 C1

Picton St SE5 . . . . . . .48 C3
Pied Bull Ct WC1 . . .106 B3
Pied Bull Yd WC1 . . .106 B3
Pierhead Wharf 47
E1 . . . . .32 A1
Pier Ho SW3 . . . . . . .158 B3
Piermont Rd SE22 . .65 A2
Pierpoint Bldg 5
E14 . . . . .41 C4
Pierrepoint Rd W3 . .28 A2
Pier St E14 . . . . .42 B2
Pier Terr SW18 . . . . . .59 B3
Piggott Ho 2 E2 . . . .25 C3
Pigott St E14 . . . . .33 C3
Pilgrimage St SE1 . .137 B3
Pilgrim Ho SE1 . . . . .137 C1
Pilgrims Cloisters 18
SE5 . . . . .49 A3
Pilgrims Ct SE3 . . . . .53 C2
Pilgrim's La NW3 . . . .11 C4
Pilgrims Mews 4 E14 .34 C2
Pilgrim St EC4 . . . . . .108 A1
Pilgrims Way N19 . . . .4 C3
Pilgrims Way Prim Sch
SE15 . . . . .50 B4
Pilkington Rd 4
London SE15 . . . . .50 A1
Pilsden Cl SW19 . . . . .69 C3
Pilton Pl SE17 . . . . . .151 A2
Pimlico Sta SW1 . . . .147 B2
Pimlico Rd SW1 . . . .145 C2
Pimlico Sch SW1 . . .147 A1
Pimlico Wlk N1 . . . . . .98 A4
Pinchin St E1 . . . . . . .125 C4
Pincombe Ho 20 SE17 .48 C4
Pincott Pl SE4 . . . . . .65 C4
Pindar St EC2 . . . . . . .110 A4
Pindock Mews W9 . . .88 B1
Pine Apple Ct
SW1 . . . . .132 C2
Pine Ave E15 . . . . .19 C3
Pine Cl 8 N19 . . . . . . .4 B2
Pinedene 2 SE15 . . . .50 A2
Pinefield Cl E14 . . . . .33 C2
Pine Gr N4,N19 . . . . . . .5 B2
Pine Ho 16 SE16 . . . .40 B4
16 London W10 . . . . .23 A2
Pinelands Cl 7 SE3 . .53 B3
Pine Lo SW15 . . . . . . .58 A1
Pine Rd NW2 . . . . .9 C4
Pines Ct 8 SW19 . . . .69 C3
Pine St EC1 . . . . .95 B2
Pine Tree Ho SE14 . .50 C3
Pinewood Ct SW4 . . .61 C1
Pinkham Mans W4 . .36 C1
Pinnacle Ho EC4 . . .123 A4
Pintail Ct 40 SE8 . . . .51 B4
Pinter Ho SW9 . . . . .172 B1
Pioneer Cl W12 . . . . .30 A3
Pioneer St SE15 . . . . .49 C2
Pioneer Way W12 . . .30 B3
Piper Cl N7 . . . . .14 B2
Pirbright Rd SW18 . .70 C3
Pitcairn Ho 1 E9 . . . .17 B1
Pitfield Ho N5 . . . . . . .15 B3
Pitfield St N1 . . . . .24 A3
Pitman Ho 4 SE8 . . .51 C2
Pitman St SE5 . . . . . . .48 B3
Pitmaston Ho 2
SE13 . . . . .52 B1
Pitsea Pl E1 . . . . .32 C3
Pitsea St E1 . . . . .32 C3
Pitt Ho 4 SW11 . . . . .59 C3

Pitt's Head Mews
W1 . . . . .117 C1
Pitt St W8 . . . . .127 C4
Pixley St E14 . . . . .33 B3
Planetarium The★
NW1 . . . . .91 B1
Plane Tree Ho SE8 . .51 A4
Plane Tree Wlk SE21 .75 C2
Plantain Pl SE1 . . . . .137 B4
Plantation The SE3 . .53 C1
Platina St EC2 . . . . . .97 C2
Plato Pl SW6 . . . . . . .165 A2
Plato Rd SW2 . . . . . . .62 A3
Platt's La NW3 . . . . . . .1 C1
Platt St NW1 . . . . .83 B2
Plaxdale Ho SE17 . . .152 A3
Playfair St W6 . . . . . . .39 B1
Playfield Cres SE22 . .64 B2
Playford Rd
London N4 . . . . .5 B2
London N4 . . . . .5 C2
Playhouse Yd EC4 . .108 A1
Pleasance Rd SW15 .57 A2
Pleasance The
SW15 . . . . .57 A3
Pleasant Pl N1 . . . . . .15 A1
Pleasant Row NW1 . .82 B3
Plender Ct NW1 . . . . .83 A3
Plender St NW1 . . . . .83 A3
Pleshey Rd N7 . . . . . .13 C4
Plevna St E14 . . . . . . .42 B3
Pleydell Ave SE16 . . .38 B2
Pleydell Ct EC4 . . . . .107 C1
Pleydell St EC4 . . . . .107 C1
Plimsoll Cl E14 . . . . . .34 A3
Plimsoll Rd N4 . . . . . . .6 A1
Plough Ct EC3 . . . . . .123 C4
Plough La SE22 . . . . .64 B1
Ploughmans Cl
NW1 . . . . .83 B4
Plough Pl EC4 . . . . . .107 C2
Plough Rd SW11 . . . .59 C3
Plough St 1
E1 . . . . .111 B2
Plough Terr SW11 . . .59 C3
Plough Way SE16 . . .41 A2
Plough Yd EC2 . . . . . .98 B1
Plover Ho SW9 . . . . .163 B2
Plover Way SE16 . . . .41 A3
Plowman Ho SW19 . .69 C2
Plumbers Row E1 . . .111 C2
Plumbridge St 3
SE10 . . . . .52 B2
Plume Ho SE10 . . . . .52 A4
Plummer Ct SE13 . . .67 A1
Plummer Rd SW4 . . .73 C4
Plumtree Ct EC4 . . . .108 A2
Plymouth Ho 25 E14 .36 C3
Plymouth Wharf
E14 . . . . .42 C2
Plympton Ave NW6 . .10 B1
Plympton Pl NW1 . . .90 A1
Plympton Rd NW6 . .10 B1
Plympton St NW8 . . .90 A1
Pocklington Ct
SW15 . . . . .68 C3
Pocock St SE1 . . . . . .136 B4
Podmore Rd SW18 . .59 B3
Poets Corner SW1 . .134 A2
Poet's Rd N5 . . . . .15 C3
Point Cl SE10 . . . . . . .52 B2
Pointer Sch The
SE3 . . . . .53 C3
Pointers Cl E14 . . . . .42 A1
Point Hill SE10 . . . . . .52 B2

Point Pleasant
SW18 . . . . .58 C3
Poland St W1 . . . . .105 A1
Polesworth Ho **16**
W2 . . . . .31 C4
Polish Univ Abroad
W6 . . . . .38 C2
Pollard Cl E16 . . . . . .35 C2
London N7 . . . . .84 C1
Pollard Ho N1 . . . . . .84 C1
Pollard Row
E2 . . . . .24 C2 99 C4
Pollard St E2 . .24 C2 99 C4
Pollen St W1 . . . . . .104 B1
Pollitt Dr NW8 . . . . . .89 C2
Pollock Ho W10 . . . . .23 A1
Polperro Mans **3**
NW6 . . . . .10 C3
Polperro Mews
SE11 . . . . .150 A3
Polygon Rd NW1 . . . .83 B1
Polygon The NW8 . . . .79 C4
1 London SW4 . . . . . .61 B3
Pomell Way E1 . . . .111 A2
Pomeroy Ct W11 . . . .31 A3
Pomeroy Ho **6** E2 . . .25 C3
Pomeroy St SE14 . . . .50 B2
Pomfret Rd SE5 . . . . .63 A4
Pomoja La N19 . . . . . .5 A2
Pomona Ho **10** SE8 . . .41 A2
Pond Cl SE3 . . . . .53 C1
Pond Cotts SE21 . . . . .76 A3
Ponder St **5** N7 . . . . .14 B1
Pondfield Ho **4** N5 . .15 B3
Pond Ho SW3 . . . . . .144 A3
Pond Mead SE21 . . . . .63 C1
Pond Pl SW3 . . . . . .144 A3
Pond Rd SE3 . . . . .53 B1
Pond Sq N6 . . . . .3 C3
Pond St NW3 . . . . . . .12 A3
Ponler St E1 . . . . .32 A3
Ponsard Rd NW10 . . . .22 A2
Ponsford St E9 . . . . .17 B2
Ponsonby Ho **13** E2 .25 B3
Ponsonby Pl SW1 . .147 C2
Ponsonby Rd SW15 .69 A4
Ponsonby Terr
SW1 . . . . .147 C2
Ponton Ho SW2 . . . . .74 C3
Ponton Rd SW8 . . . .161 C3
Pont St SW1 . . . . . . .131 A1
Pont St Mews
SW1 . . . . .130 C1
Pontypool Pl SE1 . .136 A4
Poole Ho SE11 . . . . .135 A1
Poole Rd E9 . . . . .17 C2
Pooles Bldgs EC1 . . . .95 B1
Pooles La SW10 . . . .156 C1
Pooles Park Prim Sch
N4 . . . . .5 B2
Pooles St N1 . . . . .87 B3
Pool Ho NW8 . . . . . .101 C4
Poolmans St SE16 . . . .40 C4
Poonah St E1 . . . . . . .32 B3
Pope Ho **5** SE16 . . . .40 A2
3 SE5 . . . . .48 C3
Pope John RC Prim Sch
W12 . . . . .30 A2
Pope's Head Alley
EC3 . . . . .109 C1
Pope's La W5 . . . . . . .36 A3
Pope's Rd SW9 . . . . . .62 C4
Pope St SE1 . . . . . . .138 B3

Popham Ct N16 . . . . . .7 A1
Popham Gdns TW9 . . .55 A4
Popham Rd N1 . . . . . .86 C4
Popham St N1 . . . . . .86 B4
N1 . . . . .86 C4
Poplar Bath St **10**
E14 . . . . .34 A2
Poplar Bsns Pk E14 .34 B2
Poplar Cl E9 . . . . .18 B3
Poplar Ct **4** SW16 . .74 B1
Poplar Gr W6 . . . . . . .39 B4
Poplar High St E14 . . .34 A2
Poplar Ho **10** SE16 . .40 C4
London SE4 . . . . .66 B3
Poplar Mews **2** .30 B1
Poplar Pl W2 . . . . . .114 B4
Poplar Rd SE24 . . . . . .63 B3
Poplars The NW5 . . . .13 B3
Poplars The SW24 . . . .63 A3
Poppins Ct EC4 . . . . .108 A1
Porchester Ct W2 . .114 B4
Porchester Gate
W2 . . . . .114 C3
Porchester Gdn Mews
W2 . . . . .100 B1
Porchester Gdns
W2 . . . . .114 B4
Porchester Mews
W2 . . . . .100 B2
Porchester Pl W2 . . .102 B1
Porchester Rd W2 . .100 B2
Porchester Sq W2 . .100 B2
Porchester Terr
W2 . . . . .114 C4
Porchester Terr N
W2 . . . . .100 B2
Porden Rd SW2 . . . . .62 B3
Porland Ct SE1 . . . .137 B1
Porlock Ho **5** SE26 .76 C1
Porlock St SE1 . . . . .137 C4
Portal Cl SE27 . . . . . .74 C1
Portbury Cl **10** SE15 .49 C2
Portchester Cl SE24 .63 C3
Portelet Ct **1** N1 . . .24 A4
Portelet Rd E1 . . . . . .25 C2
Porten Hos W14 . . . .126 A1
Porten Rd W14 . . . . .126 A1
Porter Sq N19 . . . . . . .5 A3
Porter St SE1 . . . . . .123 A2
W1 . . . . .103 A4
Porteus Rd W2 . . . . .101 A4
Portgate Cl W9 . . . . . .23 B1
Port Ho **6** SW11 . . . .59 B4
Portia Way E3 . . . . . . .26 B1
Porticos The SW3 . .157 B3
Portinscale Rd
SW15 . . . . .58 B2
Portishead Ho **26**
W2 . . . . .31 C4
Portland Ave N16 . . . . .7 B4
Portland Ct **1** SE14 .51 A4
7 London N1 . . . . . .16 A1
Portland Gr SW8 . . .172 C4
Portland Ho **20** SW2 .74 C3
Portland Hospl for
Women & Children The
W1 . . . . .92 B1
Portland Mews
W1 . . . . .105 A1
Portland Pl W11 . . . .104 B3
Portland Rd W11 . . .112 A3
W11 . . . . . . .31 A1 112 B2
Portland Rise N4 . . . . .6 B3
Portland Sq **4** E1 . . .32 A1
Portland St SE17 . . .151 B1

Portland Village
W6 . . . . .39 B3
Portman Ave SW14 . . .55 C4
Portman Cl W1 . . . . .103 B2
Portman Gate NW1 . . .90 B1
Portman Hts **1** NW3 . .1 C1
Portman Mews S
W1 . . . . .103 B1
Portman Pl E2 . . . . . . .25 B2
Portman Sq W1 . . . .103 B2
Portman St W1 . . . . .103 B1
Portman The NW11 . . .1 C4
Portman Twrs W1 . . .103 A2
Portnall Rd W9 . . . . . .23 B2
Portobello Ct Est
W11 . . . . .31 B3
Portobello Mews
W11 . . . . .113 B3
Portobello Rd
W11 . . . . . .31 A4 113 A4
W10 . . . . .31 A4
Portobello Road Mkt*
W10 . . . . .31 A4
Portpool La EC1 . . . .107 B4
Portree St E14 . . . . . . .34 C3
Port Royal Pl **3**
N16 . . . . .16 A3
Portsea Hall W2 . . . .102 B1
Portsea Ho **4**
SW15 . . . . .69 A3
Portsea Mews W2 . . .102 B1
Portsea Pl W2 . . . . .102 B1
Portslade Rd SW8 . .170 C2
Portsmouth Rd
SW15 . . . . .69 B4
Portsmouth St
WC2 . . . . .107 A1
Portsoken St E1,
EC3 . . . . .124 C4
Portswood Pl **10**
SW15 . . . . .56 B1
Portugal St WC2 . . . .107 A1
Poseidon Ct **4** E14 .41 C2
Postern The EC2 . . . .109 A3
Post Office Way
SW8 . . . . .161 B2
Potier St SE1 . . . . . .137 C1
Potterne Cl **5**
SW19 . . . . .69 C4
Potters Fields SE1 . .124 B1
Potters La E14 . . . . . . .42 B1
Potters Rd SW6 . . . .166 C1
Pottery La
W11 . . . . . . .31 A1 112 B2
Pottery Rd TW8 . . . . .44 A4
Pottery St SE16 . . . . . .40 A4
Pott St E2 . . . . .25 A2
Poullett Ho SW2 . . . . .75 A3
Poulton Cl E8 . . . . . . .17 A2
Poultry EC2 . . . . .109 B1
Pound La NW10 . . . . . .8 C2
Pountney Rd SW11 . . .60 C4
Povey Ho SE17 . . . . .152 A3
London SW2 . . . . .62 C1
Powell's Wlk W4 . . . .46 B4
Powergate Bsns Pk
NW10 . . . . .20 C2
Power Ho **17** TW9 . . .44 C2
Power Ho The W4 . . .38 B2
Power Rd W4 . . . . . . .36 C2
Powerscroft Rd E5 . . .17 B4
Powis Gdns W11 . . . . .31 B3
London NW11 . . . . .1 B4
Powis Ho WC2 . . . . .106 B2
Powis Mews W11 . . . .31 B3
Powis Pl WC1 . . . . . . .94 B1
Powis Rd E3 . . . . .27 A2
Powis Sq W11 . . . . . . .31 B3

Powis Terr W11 . . . . . .31 B3
Powlesland Ct **23**
E14 . . . . .33 A3
Powlett Ho NW1 . . . .13 A2
Pownall Pl NW1 . . . . .13 A1
Pownall Rd E8 . . . . . . .24 C4
Powrie Ho SW11 . . . .167 C2
Poynder Ct **3** N7 . . .14 A3
Poynders Ct **3** SW4 .61 B1
Poynders Gdns
SW12 . . . . .73 B4
Poynders Rd SW12,
SW4 . . . . .73 C4
Poynings Rd N19 . . . . .4 B1
Poynter Ho NW8 . . . .89 B2
10 London W11 . . . .30 C1
Poyntz Rd SW11 . . . .168 C1
Poyser St E2 . . . . .25 A3
Praed Mews W2 . . . .101 C2
Praed St W2 . . . . . . .101 C2
Prague Pl SW2 . . . . . .62 A2
Prah Rd N4 . . . . .5 C2
Prairie St SW8 . . . . .170 A1
Pratt Mews NW1 . . . . .82 C3
Pratt St NW1 . . . . .82 C4
Pratt Wlk SE1,SE11 .149 A4
Prebend Gdns W4,
W6 . . . . .38 B2
Prebend Mans **1**
W4 . . . . .38 B2
Prebend St N1 . . . . . .86 C4
Precinct The N1 . . . . .86 C3
London N5 . . . . .15 A3
Preedy Ho N1 . . . . . . .85 A2
Premier Park Rd
NW10 . . . . .20 A3
Premier Pl E14 . . . . . .33 C2
Prendergast Ho **7**
SW4 . . . . .73 C4
Prendergast Sch
SE4 . . . . .66 C3
Prescot St E1 . . . . . .125 A4
Prescott Ho **13**
SE17 . . . . .48 A4
Prescott Pl SW4 . . . . .61 C3
Presentation Mews
SW2 . . . . .74 B3
President Dr E1 . . . . . .32 A1
President Ho EC1 . . . .96 B3
President St EC1 . . . . .96 C4
Prestage Way E14 . . .34 B2
Prested Rd SW11 . . . .60 A3
Preston Cl SE1 . . . . .152 A4
Preston Gdns NW10 . .8 A2
Preston Ho SE1 . . . .138 C2
SE1 . . . . .152 A4
Preston Pl
London NW2 . . . . .8 C2
Richmond TW10 . . . . .54 A2
Preston's Rd E14 . . . .34 B1
Prestwich Terr SW4 .61 C2
Prestwood Ho **3**
SE16 . . . . .40 A3
Prestwood St N1 . . . .87 A1
Priam Ho **2** E2 . . . . .25 A3
Price Cl SW17 . . . . . . .72 B1
Price Ho N1 . . . . .86 C3
Prices Ct SW11 . . . . . .59 C4
Price's St SE1 . . . . . .122 B2
Price's Yd N1 . . . . . . .85 A3
Prichard Ct SW11 . .167 C3
London N7 . . . . .14 B3
Prideaux Ho WC1 . . . .95 A4
Prideaux Pl WC1 . . . . .95 A4
London W3 . . . . .28 C2
Prideaux Rd SW9 . . . .62 A4
Priestley Cl N16 . . . . . .7 B4

Priestley Ho EC1 . . . . .97 A2
2 London NW5 . . . .13 A2
Priestman Point **25**
E3 . . . . .27 A2
Priests Bridge
SW14 . . . . .56 A4
Priest's Ct EC2 . . . . .108 C2
Prima Rd SW9 . . . . .163 B2
Primrose Ct **11**
SW12 . . . . .73 C4
Primrose Gdns
NW3 . . . . .12 A2
Primrose Hill EC4 . . .107 C1
Primrose Hill Ct
NW3 . . . . .12 B1
Primrose Hill Rd
NW3 . . . . .12 B1
NW1,NW3 . . . . .80 C4
Primrose Hill Sch
NW1 . . . . .81 B3
Primrose Hill Sta
NW1 . . . . .12 C1
Primrose Hill Studios
NW1 . . . . .81 B4
Primrose Ho
7 London SE15 . . . .49 C2
1 Richmond TW9 . . .44 B2
Primrose Mans
SW11 . . . . .169 B4
Primrose Mews **2**
NW1 . . . . .12 B1
Primrose Sq E9 . . . . . .25 B4
Primrose St EC2 . . . .110 B4
Primrose Wlk **6** .51 A3
Primula St W12 . . . . . .29 C3
Prince Albert Ct
NW8 . . . . .80 C3
Prince Albert Rd
NW8 . . . . .80 C3
Prince Arthur Ct **18**
NW3 . . . . .11 B4
Prince Arthur Mews **20**
NW3 . . . . .11 B4
Prince Arthur Rd
NW3 . . . . .11 B3
Prince Charles Rd
SE3 . . . . .53 B2
Prince Consort Rd
SW7 . . . . .129 B2
Princedale Rd
W11 . . . . . . .31 A1 112 B2
Prince Edward Mans
W2 . . . . .113 C4
Prince Edward Rd
E9 . . . . .18 B2
Prince George Rd
N16 . . . . .16 A4
Princelet St E1 . . . . .111 A4
Prince of Orange La **3**
SE10 . . . . .52 B3
Prince of Wales Dr
SW11 . . . . .169 B4
Prince of Wales Mans
SW11 . . . . .169 C4
London SW4 . . . . .61 A2
Prince of Wales Pas
NW1 . . . . .92 C3
Prince Of Wales Rd
NW5 . . . . .12 C2
London SE3 . . . . .53 B2
Prince of Wales Terr
W8 . . . . .128 B3
London W4 . . . . .38 A1
Prince Regent Ct
SE16 . . . . .33 A1
Prince Regent Mews
NW1 . . . . .92 C3

Princes Arc SW1 .....119 A2
Princes Ave W3 ......36 C3
Princes Cir WC2 ....106 A2
Princes Cl N4 ....6 A3
Prince's Ct SE16 ....41 B3
Princes Ct
London NW2 ....10 A3
London NW3 ....11 C4
Stepney E1 ....32 A2
Princes Gate SW7 ..129 C3
Prince's Gate SW7 .130 A3
Princes Gate Ct
SW7 ....129 C3
Princes Gate Mews
SW7 ....129 C2
Princes Gdns SW7 ..129 C2
Princes Ho W11 ....113 B3
Prince's Mews W2 .114 A4
London W6 ....39 A1
Princes Pl SW1 ....119 A2
W11 ......31 A1 112 A2
Princes Rd
Richmond TW10 ....54 B2
Richmond TW9 .....44 B2
Prince's Rd SW11 ..55 C4
Princes Rise SE13 ..52 B1
Princes Riverside Rd **7**
SE16 ....32 C1
Princess Alexandra
School of Nursing The
E1 ....32 A4
Princess Alice Ho
W10 ....22 B1
Princess Beatrice Ho
SW10 ....142 A1
Princess Christian Coll
WC1 ....106 B4
Princess Cres N4 ....6 A2
Princess Ct W1 ....102 C3
W2 ....114 B4
London NW6 ......11 A1
Princess Frederica CE
Prim Sch NW10 ...22 B3
Princess Grace Hospl
The W1 ....91 B1
Princess Louise Cl
W2 ....101 B4
Princess Louise Hospl
W10 ....30 B4
Princess Mary Ho
SW1 ....147 C3
Princess May Prim Sch
N16 ....16 B4
Princess May Rd
N16 ....16 A4
Princess Mews
NW3 ....11 C2
Prince's Sq W2 ....114 A4
Prince's Rd NW1 ...81 C4
NW6 ....23 C3
Princes St SE1 ....136 B1
London W1 ....104 B1
Prince's St EC2 ...109 B1
Richmond TW10,TW9 .54 A2
London SE8 ....51 B4
Princes Way
Acton W3 ....36 C3
Putney SW15,SW19 .70 A3
Princes Yd W11 ...112 B3
Princethorpe Ho
W2 ....100 A4
Princeton Ct SW15 .57 C4
Princeton Mans
WC1 ....106 C3
Princeton St WC1 ..106 C4
Printers Mews E3 ..26 A4
Printer St EC4 .....107 C2

Printing House Yd
E2 ....98 B3
Printon Ho **12** E3 ..33 B4
Print Village Ind Est
SE15 ....49 B1
Prior Bolton St N1 .15 A2
Prioress Ho **2** E3 ..27 A2
Prioress Rd SE27 ..75 A1
Prioress St SE1 ...137 C1
Priors Lo **4** TW10 .54 A1
Prior St SE10 ......52 B3
Priority Ct SE15 ...65 B3
Prior Weston Prim Sch
EC1 ....97 A1
Priory Ave W4 .....38 A3
Priory Ct EC4 .....108 B1
London E9 ....17 C3
London SW8 ......171 C4
Putney SW15 ......57 B1
Roehampton SW15 .56 B3
Priory Gdns
Barnes SW13 ......56 B4
6 London W4 ...38 A2
Priory Gn N1 ......84 C2
Priory Gr SW8 ....172 A3
Priory Heights N1 ..84 C2
Priory Ho E1 .....110 C4
EC1 ....96 A2
SW1 ....147 B2
Priory Hospl The
SW15 ....56 B3
Priory La SW15 ....56 B2
Priory Lo **7** W4 ...36 C1
Priory Mans SW10 .143 A1
7 London NW3 ...12 B2
Priory Park
London NW6 ......11 A1
London W4 ....37 C3
Richmond TW9 ....44 C3
Priory St **6** E3 ...27 A2
Priory Terr NW6 ...78 A4
Priory The SE1 ....136 A3
Priory Wlk SW10 ..143 A1
Pritchard Ho **34** E2 .24 C3
Pritchard's Rd E2 ..24 C3
Priter Rd SE16 ....139 C1
SE16 ....139 C1
Probert Rd SW2 ...62 C2
Probyn Ho SW1 ...147 C4
Probyn Rd SW2 ....75 A2
Procter Ho **12** SE5 .48 C3
Procter St WC1 ...106 C3
Proctor Ho SE1 ...153 B1
Prome Ho **3** N16 ..15 C4
Promenade Approach
Rd W4 ....46 A3
Promenade The W4 .46 A2
Prospect Cotts
SW18 ....58 C3
Prospect Ho N1 ...85 B1
SE1 ....136 B1
1 London E8 ....16 B2
14 London W10 ..30 C3
Prospect House Sch
SW15 ....69 C4
Prospect Pl E1 ....32 B1
6 SE8 ....51 B4
4 London NW2 ...1 B1
London NW3 ......11 B4
2 London W4 ....37 C1
Prospect Quay
SW18 ....58 C3
Prospect Rd NW2 ..1 C1
Prospect St SE16 ..40 A4
Prospect Wharf E1 .32 B2

Prospero Rd N19 ...4 C3
Prothero Rd SW6 ..154 C2
Prout Gr NW10 ....8 B4
Provence St N1 ....86 C2
Providence Ct W1 .117 C4
Providence Ho **4** .25 C2
Providence Pl N1 ..86 A3
Providence Row N1 .84 C1
Providence Sq SE1 .139 B4
SE16 ....139 B4
Provost St N3 .....12 B2
Provost Rd NW3 ...12 B1
Provost St N1 .....97 B4
Prowse Pl NW1 ....13 B1
Prudent Pas EC2 ..109 A1
Prusom's Island **3**
E1 ....32 B1
Prusom St E1 .....32 A1
Pryors The NW3 ...2 C1
Public Record Office
EC4,WC2 ....107 B2
Richmond TW9 ....45 A3
Public Record Office
Mus EC4,WC2 ....107 B1
Pudding La EC3 ...123 C4
Pudding Mill La
E15 ....27 A4
Pudding Mill Lane Sta
E15 ....27 A4
Puddle Dock EC4 ..122 B4
Pugin Ct N1 ......14 C1
Pulborough Rd
SW18 ....70 B4
Pulham Ho SW8 ..162 C1
Pullman Ct SW2 ...74 B3
Pullman Gdns SW15 .57 B1
Pulross Rd SW9 ...62 B4
Pulteney Cl **3** E3 ..26 B4
Pulteney Terr N1 ..85 A4
Pulton Ho SE4 ....66 A3
Pulton Pl SW6 ....155 B1
Puma Ct E1 ....110 C4
Pump Ct EC4 .....107 B1
Pump House Cl
SE16 ....40 B4
Pumping Station Rd
W4 ....46 A4
Pump La SE14 .....50 B3
Punderson's Gdns
E2 ....25 A2
Purbeck Ho SW8 ..162 C1
Purbrook Est SE1 .138 B3
SW15 ....69 A3
Purbrook St SE1 ..138 B2
Purcell Cres SW6 ..154 A2
Purcell Ho SW10 ..157 B3
Purcell Mews NW10 .8 A1
Purcell St N1 .....24 A3
Purchese St NW1 ..83 C1
Purday Ho **4** W10 .23 B2
Purdon Ho **10** SE15 .49 C2
Purdy St E3 ....27 A1
Purley Ave NW2 ...1 A2
Purley Pl N1 ......15 A1
Purser Ho **3** SW2 .62 C1
Pursers Cross Rd
SW6 ....165 A4
Purves Rd NW10 ..22 B3
Pusey Ho **16** E14 ..33 C3
Puteaux Ho **6** E2 ..25 C3
Putney Bridge App
SW6 ....58 A4
Putney Bridge Rd
SW15 ....58 B3

Putney Bridge Sta
SW6 ....58 B4
Putney Comm SW15 .57 B4
Putney Heath SW15 .57 B1
Putney Heath La
SW15 ....57 C1
Putney High Sch
SW15 ....57 C2
Putney High St
SW15 ....58 A3
Putney Hill SW15 ..57 C2
Putney Hospl SW15 .57 B4
Putney Park Ave
SW15 ....56 C3
Putney Park La
SW15 ....57 A2
Putney Pier SW15 .58 A4
Putney School of Art &
Design SW15 .....58 A3
Putney Sta SW15 ..58 A3
Putney Wharf Twr
SW15 ....58 A4
Pylon Trad Est E16 .34 C4
Pymers Mead SE21 .75 B3
Pynfolds SE16 .....40 A4
Pynnersmead SE24 .63 B2
Pyrford Ho **19** SW9 .63 A3
Pyrland Rd
London N5 ....15 C3
London N19 ......54 B1
Pyrmont Gr SE27 ..75 A1
Pyrmont Rd W4 ...44 C4
Pytchley Rd SE22 ..64 A4

Q

Quadrande Cl SE1 .152 A4
Quadrangle The
SW10 ....157 A4
SW6 ....154 A1
W2 ....102 A2
London SE24 .....63 A1
London W12 ......30 B3
Quadrant Arc W1 .119 A3
Quadrant Gr NW5 ..12 B3
Quadrant The
NW6 ....23 A4
London W10 ......22 C2
Richmond TW9 ....54 A3
Quaker Ct EC1 ....97 A2
Quaker St E1 ..24 B1 98 C1
Quality Ct WC2 ...107 B2
Quantock Ho N16 ..7 B3
Quarrendon St
SW6 ....165 C2
Quarry Rd SW18 ..59 B1
Quarterdeck The
E14 ....41 C4
Quartermile La E10,
E15 ....19 A4
Quayside Ct **6**
SE16 ....32 C1
Quebec & Crown
Wharves E14 .....33 B3
Quebeck Ind Est
SE1 ....43 A1
Quebec Mews W1 .103 A1
Quebec Way SE16 ..41 A4
Quedgeley Ct **1**
SE15 ....49 B4
Queen Alexandra Mans
WC1 ....94 A3
Queen Anne Mews
W1 ....104 B3
Queen Anne Rd E9 .17 C2

Queen Anne's Gate
SW1 ....133 B3
Queen Anne's Gdns
London W4 ....38 A3
London W5 ....36 A4
Queen Anne's Gr
London W4 ....38 A3
London W5 ....36 A4
Queen Anne St
W1 ....104 A3
Queen Caroline St
W6 ....39 B1
Queen Charlottes &
Chelsea Hospl
W12 ....29 C3
Queen Elizabeth College
3 SE10 ....52 B3
Queen Elizabeth Hall &
Purcell Room
SE1 ....121 A2
Queen Elizabeth
Hospital for Children
The E2 ....24 C3
Queen Elizabeth II Con
Ctr SW1 ....133 C3
Queen Elizabeth II
Jubilee Sch W9 ..23 B1
Queen Elizabeth II Pier
SE10 ....35 B1
Queen Elizabeth's Cl
N16 ....6 C2
Queen Elizabeth's Ct
SE1 ....138 C2
Queen Elizabeth's Wlk
N16 ....6 C2
Queen Elizabeth Wlk
SW13 ....47 A2
Queenhithe EC4 ...123 A4
Queen Margaret Flats **22**
E2 ....25 A2
Queen Margarets Ct
N1 ....16 A3
Queen Margaret's Gr
N1 ....16 A3
Queen Mary's Gdns
NW1 ....91 B3
Queen Mary's Hospl
NW3 ....2 B1
Queen Mary's Univ
Hospl SW15 ......56 C1
Queen Mary, Univ of
London E1 ....26 A1
Queen of Denmark Ct
SE16 ....41 B3
Queensberry Mews W
SW7 ....143 B4
Queensberry Pl
SW7 ....143 B4
Queensberry Way
SW7 ....143 B4
Queensborough Mews
W2 ....114 C4
Queensborough Pas
W2 ....114 C4
Queensborough Terr
W2 ....114 B4
Queensbridge Ct **1**
E2 ....24 B3
Queensbridge Inf Sch
E8 ....16 B1
Queensbridge Rd
E2,E8 ....24 B3
London E8 ....16 B1
Queensbury St N1 ..15 B1

Queen's CE Prim Sch
The TW9 .... 44 C3
Queen's Cir SW11 160 A1
Queen's Club Gdns
W14 .... 154 B4
Queen's Club The
W14 .... 140 B1
Queen's Coll W1 ... 104 A3
Queen's Cres NW5 ... 12 C2
Queens Cres TW10 ... 54 A1
Queen's Ct 6 E14 ... 33 B2
SW11 .... 170 A4
Queen's Ct NW8 ... 79 B2
W2 .... 114 B3
Queens Ct SE5 ... 49 A1
Queen's Ct
Barnes SW13 .... 56 C4
8 Richmond TW10 ... 54 B2
Queensdale Cres
W11 .... 30 C1
Queensdale PI
W11 .... 112 A1
Queensdale Rd
W11 .... 31 A1 112 A1
Queensdale Wlk
W11 .... 112 A1
Queens Down Rd
E5 .... 17 A4
Queen's Elm Sq
SW3 .... 143 C1
Queen's Gallery The★
SW1 .... 132 B3
Queen's Gate SW7 129 A1
Queen's Gate Gdns
SW7 .... 129 A1
Queensgate Gdns
SW15 .... 57 A3
Queen's Gate Mews
SW7 .... 129 A2
Queen's Gate PI
SW7 .... 129 A1
Queensgate PI 10
NW6 .... 10 C1
Queen's Gate PI Mews
SW7 .... 129 A1
Queen's Gate Terr
SW7 .... 129 A2
Queens Gate Villas
E9 .... 18 A1
Queen's Gdns W2 114 C4
Queen's Gr NW8 ... 79 C3
Queen's Head Pas
EC2 .... 108 C2
Queen's Head St N1 86 B3
Queen's Head Yd
SE1 .... 123 B1
Queens Ho 9 SE17 48 C4
Queen's House The
SE10 .... 52 C4
Queensland PI N7 ... 14 C4
Queensland Rd N7 ... 14 C4
Queens Manor Prim Sch
SW6 .... 47 C3
Queens Mans NW6 ... 11 A3
Queen's Mans W6 .... 39 C2
Queensmead NW8 ... 79 C4
Queensmere CI
SW19 .... 69 C2
Queensmere Ct
SW13 .... 46 C4
Queensmere Rd
SW19 .... 69 C2
Queen's Mews W2 114 A4
Queensmill Rd SW6 47 C3

Queensmill Sch
SW6 .... 166 B1
Queens Par NW2 .... 9 B2
Queens Park Com Sch
NW6 .... 22 C4
Queens Park Ct 5
W10 .... 22 C2
Queen's Park Prim Sch
W10 .... 23 A1
Queens Park Sta
NW6 .... 23 B3
Queen Sq WC1 ... 106 B4
Queen Sq PI WC1 ... 94 B1
Queen's Quay EC4 123 A4
Queen's Rd
London SE14,SE15 ... 50 B2
Mortlake SW14 .... 55 C4
Richmond TW10 .... 54 B1
Queen's Ride SW13 57 A4
Queen's Rise TW10 54 B1
Queen's Road Sta
SE15 .... 50 B2
Queen's Row SE17 ... 48 C4
Queen St EC4 .... 123 A4
W1 .... 118 B2
Queens Terr NW8 ... 79 B2
Queenstown Rd
SW8 .... 170 B4
Queen St PI EC4 ... 123 A4
Queensville Rd
SW12,SW4 .... 73 C4
Queensway W2 ... 114 B4
Queensway Sta
W2 .... 114 B3
Queenswood Ct 6
SW4 .... 62 A2
Queen's Yd W1 .... 93 A1
Queens Yd E9 .... 18 C2
Queen Victoria Mon
SW1 .... 132 C4
Queen Victoria St
EC4 .... 122 C4
Quelch Ho 2 N19 ... 13 C3
Quemerford Rd N7 14 B3
Quendon Ho 10 N1 22 B1
Quenington Ct 5
SE15 .... 49 B4
Quennel Ho 7
SW12 .... 73 B4
Quentingdon Mans
SW6 .... 164 C4
Querrin St SW6 ... 166 C1
Quested Ct 27 E8 ... 17 A3
Quex Mews NW6 ... 23 C4
Quex Rd NW6 .... 23 C4
Quick Rd W4 .... 38 A1
Quick St N1 .... 86 B1
Quickswood W3 ... 12 A1
Quill La SW15 .... 57 C3
Quill St N4 .... 5 C1
Quilp St SE1 .... 136 C4
Quilter Ho 11 W9 ... 23 B2
Quilter St 2 24 C2 99 B4
Quilting Ct 23 SE16 40 C4
Quintin Ct W4 .... 45 B3
Quintock Ho 2
TW9 .... 44 C2
Quinton Ho SW8 ... 162 A2
Quinton Kynaston Sch
NW8 .... 79 B3
Quinton St SW18 ... 71 B2
Quixley St E14 .... 34 C2
Quorn Rd SE22 .... 64 A4

R

Rabbit Row W8 ... 113 C2
Rainsborough Ave
SE8 .... 41 A2
Rainsford Ct NW10 20 A3
Rainsford Ho 14
SW2 .... 62 B2
Rainsford Rd NW10 20 A3
Rainsford St W2 ... 102 A2
Rainton Rd SE7 ... 43 C1
Rainville Rd W6 ... 47 B4
Raleigh Ct 2 SE16 ... 32 C1
Raleigh Gdns SW2 62 B1
Raleigh Ho SW8 ... 171 B2
Raleigh Mews N1 ... 86 B3
Raleigh St N1 .... 86 B3
Ralph Ct W2 .... 100 B2
Ralston St SW3 ... 144 C1
Ramar Ho E1 .... 111 B4
Ramillies CI SW2 ... 62 A1
Ramillies PI W1 ... 104 C1
Ramillies Rd W4 ... 37 C3
Ramillies St W1 ... 104 C1
Rampart St E1 .... 32 A3
Rampayne St SW1 147 B2
Ramsay Ho NW8 ... 80 A2
Ramsay Rd W3 .... 37 B4
Ramsden Rd 11
SW15 .... 69 A3
Ramsden Rd SW12 72 C4
Ramsey Ho SW9 ... 163 C1
Ramsey St E2 24 C1 99 C2
Ramsfort Ho 4
SE16 .... 40 A2
Ramsgate St E8 ... 16 B2
Ram St SW18 .... 59 A2
Randal Cremer JMI Sch
E2 .... 24 B3
Randall CI SW11 ... 168 A4
Randall PI SE10 .... 52 B3
Randall Rd SE11 ... 148 C3
Randall Row SE11 148 C3
Randell's Rd N1 ... 84 B4
Randolph Ave W9 ... 88 C3
Randolph Cres W9 88 C2
Randolph Gdns
NW6 .... 78 A1
Randolph Mews W9 89 A1
Randolph Rd W9 ... 89 A1
Randolph St NW1 ... 13 B1
Ranelagh Ave
Barnes SW13 .... 46 C1
Fulham SW6 .... 58 B4
Ranelagh Gardens Mans
SW6 .... 58 A4
Ranelagh Gardens (site
of Chelsea Flower
Show) SW1 .... 145 C1
Ranelagh Gdns
Chiswick W4 .... 45 B3
Fulham SW6 .... 58 B4
8 London W6 .... 38 B3
Ranelagh Gr SW1 145 C2
Ranelagh Ho SW3 144 C2
Ranelagh Mans
SW6 .... 165 A2
Ranelagh Rd NW10 21 B3
London NW10 .... 21 B3
Rangdon St EC3 ... 110 C1
Rangers Sq SE10 ... 52 C2
Rangoon Ho 8 N16 15 C4
Rankine Ho SE1 ... 136 C1
Ranmere St SW12 73 A3
Rann Ho 1 SW14 ... 55 C4
Rannoch Rd W6 ... 47 C4
Ranston St NW1 ... 102 A4
Ranulf Rd NW2 .... 10 B4

Ranwell CI 11 E3 ... 26 B4
Ranwell Ho 10 E3 ... 26 B4
Raphael Ct 9 SE16 40 A1
Raphael St SW7 ... 130 C3
Rapley Ho 12 .... 99 B3
Rashleigh Ct 8
SW8 .... 61 A4
Rashleigh Ho 4 .... 94 A3
Rastell Ave SW12 ... 73 C3
Ratcliffe Cross St
E1 .... 32 C3
Ratcliffe Ho 10 E14 33 A3
Ratcliffe La 18 E14 33 A3
Ratcliffe Orch 5
E1 .... 32 C2
Rathbone Ho 6 E16 35 B1
SW6 .... 23 C4
Rathbone Mkt 4
E16 .... 35 B2
Rathbone PI W1 ... 105 B2
Rathbone Point E5 16 C4
Rathbone St E16 ... 35 B1
W1 .... 105 A3
Rathgar Rd SW9 ... 63 A4
Rathmell Dr SW4 ... 61 C1
Rattray Rd SW2 ... 62 C2
Raul Rd SE15 .... 49 C2
Raveley St NW5 ... 13 B4
Ravenet Ct SW11 170 A3
London SW8 .... 61 A2
Ravenet St SW11 170 A3
Ravenfield Rd SW17 72 B1
Raven Ho 10 SE16 ... 40 C2
Ravenna Rd SW15 57 C2
Raven Row E1 .... 32 A4
Ravensbourne Ho
NW8 .... 102 A4
Ravensbourne PI
SE13 .... 52 A1
Ravensbury Rd
SW18 .... 71 A2
Ravensbury Terr
SW18 .... 71 A2
Ravenscar NW1 ... 82 C3
Ravenscourt Ave
W6 .... 38 C2
Ravenscourt Gdns
W6 .... 38 C2
Ravenscourt Park Mans
W6 .... 39 A3
Ravenscourt Park Prep
Sch W6 .... 38 C2
Ravenscourt Park Sta
W6 .... 39 A3
Ravenscourt Pk W6 39 A2
Ravenscourt PI W6 39 A2
Ravenscourt Rd W6 39 A2
Ravenscourt Sq W6 38 C3
Ravenscourt Theatre
Sch W6 .... 39 A2
Ravenscroft Ave
NW11 .... 1 B4
Ravenscroft CI 4
E16 .... 35 C4
Ravenscroft Ct NW11 1 B4
Ravenscroft Rd E16 35 C4
Acton W4 .... 37 B2
Ravenscroft St E2 99 A4
Ravenshaw St NW6 10 B3
Ravenslea Rd SW11,
SW12 .... 72 B4
Ravensmede Way
W4 .... 38 B2
Ravenstone SE17 152 B1

Ravenstone Prim Sch
SW12 . . . . .72 C2
Ravenstone St
SW12 . . . . .72 C2
Ravenswood Rd
SW12 . . . . .73 A4
Ravensworth Ct
SW6 . . . . .155 B1
Ravensworth Rd
NW10 . . . . .22 A2
Raven Wharf SE1 .138 C4
Ravey St EC2 .24 A1 98 A2
Rav Pinter Ct N16 . . . .7 A4
Rawlings St SW3 .144 C4
Rawlinson Rd SE13 .67 C3
Rawlinson Point 8
E16 . . . . .35 B2
Rawreth Wlk N1 . . . . .87 A4
Rawson Ct SW11 .169 C3
Rawson St SW11 .170 A3
Rawstorne Pl EC1 . . .96 A4
Rawstorne St EC1 . . .96 A4
Rayburne Ct W14 .126 A2
Raydon St N19 . . . . . .4 A2
Ray Ho W10 . . . . . . .30 C3
Raymede Twr W10 .30 C4
Raymouth Rd SE16 .40 A2
Raynald Ho 15
SW16 . . . . .74 A1
Rayne Ct SE1 . . . . . .138 C4
Rayne Ho W9 . . . . . . .88 A2
◼ London SW12 . . . . .60 C1
Rayner Ct 10 W12 . . .39 B4
Rayner's Rd SW15 . .58 A2
Raynes Ct NW2 . . . . .10 A4
Raynham W2 . . . . . .102 A2
Raynham Ho 1 E1 . .25 C1
Raynham Rd W6 . . . .39 A2
Raynor Pl N1 . . . . . . .87 A4
Ray St EC1 . . . . .95 C1
Ray Wlk N7 . . . . .5 B2
Reachview Cl 14
NW1 . . . . .13 B1
Reade Ct 6 W3 . . . . .37 B3
Reade Ho 7 SE10 . .52 C4
Reade Wlk NW10 . . . .8 A1
Read Ho SE11 . . . . .163 B4
Reading Ho SE15 . . .49 C4
W2 . . . . .100 C1
Reading La E8 . . . . . .17 A2
Reapers Cl NW1 . . . . .83 B4
Reardon Ho 5 E1 . . .32 A1
Reardon Path 31 E1 .32 A1
Reardon St E1 . . . . . .32 A1
Reaston St SE14 . . . .50 C3
Reay Prim Sch
SW9 . . . . .163 A1
Reckitt Rd W4 . . . . . .38 A1
Record St SE16 . . . . .50 B4
Rector St N1 . . . . . . .86 C3
Rectory Gdns SW4 . .61 B4
Rectory Gr SW4 . . . .61 B4
Rectory Rd
Barnes SW13 . . . . . . .46 C1
London N16 . . . . .7 B1
◼ London W3 . . . . . . .28 B1
Rectory Road Sta
N16 . . . . .7 A1
Rectory Sq E1 . . . . . .32 C4
Reculver Ho 2
SE15 . . . . .50 B4
Reculver Rd SE16 . . .40 C1
Red Anchor Cl
SW3 . . . . .158 A3
Redan Pl W2 . . . . . .100 A1
Redan St W14 . . . . . .39 C3
Redan Terr SE5 . . . . .48 A1

Redbourne Ho 7
E14 . . . . .33 B3
Redburn Ho W10 . .22 B1
Redbridge Gdns
SE5 . . . . .49 A3
Redburn St SW3 .158 C4
Redcar St SE5 . . . . . .48 B3
Redcastle Cl E1 . . . . .32 B2
Redchurch St
E2 . . . . . . .24 B1 98 C2
Redcliffe Cl 5 SW5 .142 A1
Redcliffe Gdns
SW10 . . . . .156 B4
Chiswick W4 . . . . .45 A3
Redcliffe Mews
SW10 . . . . .142 B1
Redcliffe Pl SW10 .156 C3
Redcliffe Rd SW10 .157 A4
Redcliffe Sch
SW10 . . . . .156 C4
Redcliffe Sq SW10 .142 B1
Redcliffe St SW10 .156 B4
Redclyf Ho 2 E1 . . .25 B1
Redcroft 5 NW6 . . . .10 C2
Redcross Way SE1 .123 A1
Reddins Rd SE15 . . . .49 C4
Rede Pl W2 .31 A2 113 C4
Redesdale St SW3 .158 C4
Redfern Rd NW10 . . . .8 A1
Redfield La SW5 . . . .142 A4
Redfield Mews
SW5 . . . . .141 C4
Redhill Est SE16 . . . .43 B3
Redford Wlk N1 . . . . .86 C4
Redgate Terr SW15 .57 C1
Redgrave Rd SW15 .57 C4
Redhill Ct SW2 . . . . .74 C2
Redhill St NW1 . . . . .92 B4
Redington Gdns
NW3 . . . . .11 A4
Redington Ho N1 . . .85 A2
Redington Rd NW3 . .11 A4
Redlands Prim Sch
E1 . . . . .32 B4
Redlands Way SW2 .74 B4
Red Lion Cl 11 SE17 .48 C4
Red Lion Ct EC4 . . .107 C1
Red Lion Row SE17 .48 B4
Red Lion Sq WC1 . .106 C3
Red Lion St WC1 . . .106 C3
Red Lion Yd W1 . . . .117 C2
Redlynch Ct W14 .126 B3
Redlynch Ho SW9 .173 C4
Redman Bldg EC1 .107 C3
Redman Ho 1 SE1 .137 A3
Redman's Rd E1 . . . .32 B4
Redmayne Ho
SW9 . . . . .173 A2
Redmead La E1 . . . .125 B1
Redmill Ho 22 E1 . . .25 A1
Redmond Ho N1 . . . .85 A3
Redmore Rd W6 . . . .39 A2
Red Pl W1 . . . . .117 B4
Red Post Hill SE21,
SE24 . . . . .63 C2
Redriff Prim Sch
SE16 . . . . .41 A4
Redriff Rd SE16 . . . . .41 A3
Red Rover SW13 . . . .56 C4
Redrup Ho 27 SE14 .50 C4
Redruth Rd E9 . . . . . .25 B4
Red Sq The N16 . . . . .6 C1
Redstart Cl SE14 . . . .51 A3
Redvers St E2 . . . . . .98 B4
Redwood Cl SE16 . . .33 A1
Redwood Ct
London N19 . . . . .4 C4

Redwood Ct continued
London NW6 . . . . .10 A1
Redwood Mews 2
SW4 . . . . .61 A4
Redwoods SW15 . . . .68 C3
Reece Mews SW7 .143 B4
Reed Cl E16 . . . . .35 C4
Reedham St SE15 . . .64 C4
Reed Ho SW15 . . . . . .56 C1
Reedholm Villas
N16 . . . . .15 C4
Reed's Pl NW1 . . . . . .13 B1
Reedworth St
SE11 . . . . .149 C3
Reef Ho E14 . . . . .42 B3
Rees St N1 . . . . .87 A3
Reeves Ho SE1 . . . .135 B3
W1 . . . . .117 B3
Reeves Mews W1 .117 C3
Reeves Rd E3 . . . . . . .27 A1
Reform St SW11 . . . .169 A2
London SW11 . . . . . .168 C2
Regal Cl E1 . . . . .111 B4
Regal La NW1 . . . . . . .81 C3
Regal Pl 8 E3 . . . . . .26 B2
SW6 . . . . .156 B1
Regan Way N1 . . . . . .24 A3
Regatta Point SW8 . .44 B4
Regency Ct 2 E9 . . . .25 B4
Regency Lo NW3 . . . .11 C1
Regency Mews 1
NW10 . . . . .8 C2
Regency St SW1 . . .147 C3
Regent Ct N16 . . . . . .7 A4
SW9 . . . . .90 A3
London W14 . . . . . . .140 A4
Regent Lo 9 SW2 . . .74 B3
Regent Pl W1 . . . . . .119 A4
Regent Rd SE24 . . . . .63 A2
Regents Bridge Gdns
SW8 . . . . .162 B2
Regents Canal Ho 21
E14 . . . . .33 A3
Regent's Coll NW1 . .91 B2
Regents Ct E8 . . . . . .24 C4
Regents Gate Ho 20
E14 . . . . .33 A2
Regents Mews NW8 .79 A2
Regent's Park W1 . . .81 B1
Regent's Park Barracks
NW1 . . . . .82 B1
Regent's Park Rd
NW1 . . . . .81 B4
Regent's Park Sta
NW1 . . . . .92 A1
Regent's Pl SE3 . . . . .53 C1
Regent Sq 22 E3 . . . .27 A2
London WC1 . . . . .94 B3
Regents Row E8 . . . .24 C4
Regent St W1 . . . . . .118 C4
London W4 . . . . .36 C1
Regents Wharf
3 E2 . . . . .25 A4
N1 . . . . .84 C2
Reginald Pl 6 SE8 . .51 C3
Reginald Rd SE8 . . . .51 C3
Reginald Sq SE8 . . . .51 C3
Regina Point SE16 . .40 B3
Regina Rd N4 . . . . . . .5 B3
Regis Ct NW1 . . . . . .102 C4
Regis Pl 17 SW2 . . . .62 B3
Regis Rd NW5 . . . . . .13 A3

Regnart Bldgs NW1 . .93 A3
Reid Ct SW14 . . . . . . .45 B1
Reighton Rd E5 . . . . . .7 C2
Reizel Ct N16 . . . . . . .7 A3
Relay Rd W12 . . . . . .30 B1
Relf Rd SE15 . . . . .64 C4
Reliance Sq E2 . . . . . .98 B2
Relton Mews SW7 . .130 B2
Rembrandt Ct E14 . .42 C3
Rembrandt Ct 10
SE16 . . . . .40 A1
Remington St N1 . . . .86 B1
Remnant St WC2 . . .106 C2
Remsted Ho N6 . . . . .78 A3
Remus Rd E3 . . . . . . .18 C1
Renbold Ho 5 SE10 .52 B2
Rendlesham Ho 8
E5,N16 . . . . .7 C1
Rendlesham Rd E5 . . .7 C1
Renforth St SE16 . . . .40 B4
Renfrew Ho NW6 . . . .78 A1
Renfrew Rd SE11 . . .150 A3
Rennell Ho 18 E9 . . .17 C2
Rennell St SE13 . . . . .67 B4
Rennie Cotts 24 E1 .25 B1
Rennie Ct 1 SE1 . . .122 A2
Rennie Ho SE1 . . . . .136 C1
Rennie St SE1 . . . . . .122 A2
Renoir Ct 3 SE16 . . .40 A1
Renton Cl SW2 . . . . . .62 B1
Rephidim St SE1 . . .138 A1
Replingham Rd
SW18 . . . . .70 C3
Reporton Rd SW6 . .154 B1
Repton Ct 4 E8 . . . . .17 A3
Repton Ho 2 E14 . . .33 A3
SW1 . . . . .147 A3
Repton St E14 . . . . . .33 A3
Re Sassoon Ho
SE15 . . . . .50 B2
Reservoir Rd SE4 . . . .51 A1
Restell Cl SE3 . . . . . . .53 A4
Reston Ct 7 NW2 . .128 C3
Restoration Sq
SW11 . . . . .167 C3
Retcar Pl N19 . . . . . . .4 A2
Retford St 2 E2 . . . . .24 A3
Retreat Ho 5 E9 . . . .17 B2
Retreat Pl E9 . . . . . . .17 B2
Retreat The SW14 . .56 A4
Reunion Row E1 . . . .32 A2
Reveley Sq SE16 . . . .41 A4
Revelon Rd SE4 . . . . .66 A4
Revelstoke Rd
SW18,SW19 . . . . .70 C2
Reverdy Rd SE1 . . . .153 B3
Rewell St SW6 . . . . .156 C1
Rex Pl W1 . . . . .117 C2
Reynard Cl SE4 . . . . .66 A4
Reynard Pl SE14 . . . .51 A4
Reynolds Cl NW11 . . .2 A4
Reynolds Ho 18 E2 .25 B3
NW8 . . . . .79 C1
SW1 . . . . .147 C4
London N4 . . . . .5 A3
Reynolds Pl 12
TW10 . . . . .54 B1
Reynolds Rd
SE15 . . . . .65 B3
London W4 . . . . .37 B3
Rheidol Mews N1 . . . .86 C2
Rheidol Terr N1 . . . . .86 C3
Rhoda St E2 . .24 A1 99 A2
Rhodes Ho N1 . . . . . .97 B4
W12 . . . . .30 A1
Rhodesia Rd SW9 . .172 B1
Rhodes St N7 . . . . . .14 B3
Rhodeswell Rd E14 .33 A4

Rav – Ric 243

Rhondda Gr E3 . . . . .26 B2
Rhyl Prim Sch NW5 .12 C2
Rhyl St NW5 . . . . . . .12 C2
Ribbesdale Ho 11
NW6 . . . . .23 C4
Ribbon Dance Mews
SE5 . . . . .48 C2
Ribstone Ho 8 E9 . . .17 C2
Ricardo St E14 . . . . . .34 A3
Riceyman Ho WC1 . . .95 B3
Richard Anderson Ct 1
SE14 . . . . .50 C3
Richard Atkins Prim Sch
SW2 . . . . .74 A4
Richard Burbidge Mans
SW13 . . . . .47 B4
Richard Cloudesley Sch
EC1 . . . . .96 C1
Richard Cobden Prim
Sch NW1 . . . . .83 A3
Richard Fox Ho N4 . . .6 B1
Richard Ho 8 SE16 .40 B2
Richard Knight Ho
SW6 . . . . .165 C4
Richard Neale Ho 2
E1 . . . . .32 A2
Richardson Cl 18 E8 .24 B4
Richardson Ct
SW4 . . . . .172 B2
Richardson's Mews
W1 . . . . .92 C1
Richard's Pl SW3 . . .144 B4
Richard St 10 E1 . . . .32 A3
Richbell Pl WC1 . . . .106 C4
Richborne Terr
SW8 . . . . .163 A2
Richborough Ho
5 SE15 . . . . .50 B4
14 London E5 . . . . . .17 A4
Richborough Rd
NW2 . . . . .10 A4
Richford Gate W6 . . .39 B3
Richford St W6 . . . . . .39 B3
Rich La SW5 . . . . . . .142 A2
Richland Ho 7
SE15 . . . . .49 C2
Richman Ho 10 SE8 .41 B1
Richmond Ave N1 . . .85 A4
NW10 . . . . .9 B2
Richmond Bldgs
W1 . . . . .105 B1
Richmond Circus
TW9 . . . . .54 A3
Richmond Coll W8 .128 B2
Richmond Cres N1 . .85 B4
Richmond Ct SW1 . .131 A3
Richmond Gr N1 . . . .15 A1
Richmond Hill
TW10 . . . . .54 A1
Richmond Hill Ct 5
TW10 . . . . .54 A1
Richmond Ho NW1 . .82 B1
SE17 . . . . .151 B2
12 Forest Hill SE26 . .76 C1
Richmond International
Bsns Ctr 3 TW9 . . .54 B3
Richmond Mans
SW5 . . . . .142 A2
Putney SW15 . . . . . . .58 A3
Richmond Mews
W1 . . . . .105 B1
Richmond Park Rd
SW14 . . . . .55 C3
Richmond Rd
London E8 . . . . .16 C1

Richmond continued
London W5 ....36 A4
Richmond Sta TW9 .54 A3
Richmond Terr
SW1 ....19 B3
Richmond Way
W12,W14 ....39 C4
Rich St E14 ....33 B2
Rickard Cl SW2 ....74 C3
Rickett St SW6 ...155 C4
Rickman Ho 28 E2 ..25 B1
Rickman St 6 E1 ...25 B1
Rick Roberts Way
E15 ....27 C3
Rickthorne Rd 6
N19 ....5 A2
Riddell Ct SE1 ....152 C2
Ridgdale St E3 .....27 A3
Ridge Hill NW11 ....1 A3
Ridge Rd NW2 ......1 B1
Ridgeway 11 TW10 .54 A1
Ridgeway Dr W3 ...36 C3
Ridgeway Gdns N6 ..4 B4
Ridgeway The
Acton W3 ....36 C3
London NW11 ......1 B3
Ridgewell Cl N1 ....87 A4
Ridgmount Gdns
WC1 ....105 B4
Ridgmount Pl WC1 105 B4
Ridgmount Rd
SW18 ....59 A2
Ridgmount St WC1 105 B4
Ridgway Rd SW9 ...63 A4
Riding House St
W1 ....104 C3
Ridings Cl N6 ....4 A4
Riding The NW11 ...1 A4
Ridley Ho 14 SW11 .60 A4
Ridley Rd London E8 .16 B3
Ridley Road Mkt E8 16 B3
Riffel Rd NW2 ....9 B3
Rifle Ct SE11 ......163 C4
Rifle Pl W11 ....30 C1
Rifle St E14 ....34 A4
Rigault Rd SW6 ...164 B1
Rigden St E14 ......34 A3
Rigeley Rd NW10 ..21 C2
Rigge Pl SW4 ......61 C3
Rigg Ho 2 SW4 ....74 A4
Rignold Ho 6 SE5 ..49 A1
Rigo Ho 2 E1 ....32 C4
Riley Ho SW10 ....157 B3
    1 Bow E3 ....26 C1
    1 Streatham SW4 .73 C4
Riley Rd SE1 ......138 C2
Riley St SW10 ....157 B2
Rill Ho 24 SE5 .....49 A3
Rimini Ct SW12 ....72 B3
Rinaldo Rd SW12 ..73 A4
Ringcroft St N7 ....14 C3
Ring Cross Prim Sch
N7 ....14 B3
Ringford Ho SW18 .58 B1
Ringford Rd SW18 .58 C1
Ring Ho 14 E1 ......32 B2
Ringmer Ave SW6 .164 B3
Ringmer Gdns 2
N19 ....5 A2
Ringmer Ho 18
SE22 ....64 A4
Ringsfield Ho
SE17 ....151 A1

Ringwood Gdns
    11 E14 ....41 C2
    Roehampton SW15 ..68 C3
Ripley Gdns SW14 ..55 C4
Ripley Ho SW1 ....160 C4
    Mortlake SW14 ....56 A4
Riplington Ct SW15 .69 A4
Rippleside Gr N1 ...14 B1
Risborough 5
NW8 ....90 B2
Risborough St SE1 136 B4
Risdon Ho 20 SE16 .40 B4
Risdon St 19 SE16 ..40 B4
Riseholme Ho 14
SE22 ....64 A4
Riseldine Rd SE23 ..66 A1
Risinghill St N1 ....85 B2
Rising Sun Ct EC1 .108 B3
Risley Ho 7 E9 .....17 C2
Rita Rd SW8 ......162 C2
Ritchie Ho 8 SE16 ..40 B3
    London N19 ......5 A2
    11 South Bromley
    E14 ....34 C3
Ritchie St N1 ......85 C2
Ritherdon Rd SW17 .73 A2
Ritson Ho N1 ......84 C3
Ritson Rd E8 ....16 C2
Rivaz Pl E9 ....17 B2
Riven Ct W2 ......100 A2
Riverains The
SW11 ....167 B3
River Barge Cl E14 .42 B4
Rivercourt Rd W6 ..39 A1
River Ct SE1 ......122 A3
Riverdale Dr SW18 .71 A3
Riverfleet WC1 .....94 B4
Riverford Ho 28 W2 .31 C4
River Ho SW13 ....46 A1
Rivermead Ct SW6 ..58 B4
Rivermead Ho 19 E9 .18 A3
River Pl N1 ....15 B1
Riverside Prim Sch
SW8 ....70 C3
Riversdale Rd N5 ...6 B1
Riversdene N5 .....6 B1
Rivers Ho 11 TW8 ..36 C1
Riverside SW11 ...158 B2
    WC1 ....94 B4
    SW18 ....59 A1
Riverside Bsns Ctr
SW18 ....71 A3
Riverside Ct 6 SE1 .161 C4
Riverside Dr W4 ....46 A2
Riverside Gdns W6 .39 A1
Riverside Mans 4
E1 ....32 B1
Riverside Prim Sch
SE16 ....139 C3
Riverside Rd E15 ..27 B3
    SW17 ....71 B1
    Wandsworth SW17,
    SW19 ....71 B1
Riverside West
SW18 ....59 A3
Riverside Workshops
SE1 ....123 A2
River St EC1 ....95 B4
River Terr W6 ......39 B1
Riverton Cl W9 .....23 B2
Riverview Gdns
SW13 ....47 A4
Riverview W4 W4 ...45 A4
River View W4 W4 ..45 A4
River Way SE10 ....43 B3
Rivet Ho SE1 ......153 A2
Rivington Ct NW10 .21 C4

Rivington Pl EC2 ...98 B3
Rivington St EC2 ...98 A3
Rivington Wlk 4
    E8 ....24 C4
Rixon St N7 ....5 C1
Roach Rd E3 ....18 C1
Roach Works E3 ...18 C1
Roads Pl N19 ....5 A2
Roan St SE10 ......52 B4
Robert Adam St
W1 ....103 B2
Roberta St
E2 ....24 C2 99 C3
Robert Bell Ho
SE16 ....153 B4
Robert Blair Prim Sch
N7 ....14 A2
Robert Browning Prim
Sch SE17 ....151 B2
Robert Cl W9 ....89 A1
Robert Dashwood Way
SE17 ....150 C3
Robert Gentry Ho
W14 ....140 B1
Robert Jones Ho
SE16 ....153 B4
Robert Keen Cl 17
SE15 ....49 C2
Robert Lowe Cl
SE14 ....50 C3
Robert Owen Ho 22
E5 ....17 A4
Robert Owen Lo 5
E5 ....17 A4
Roberts Ct 8
SW1 ....131 B1
    21 London NW1 .....13 A1
Roberts Ho 5 SE27 .75 A1
Roberts Mews
SW1 ....131 B1
    WC2 ....120 B3
Robert Sutton Ho 20
E1 ....32 B3
Robeson St 8 E3 ...33 B4
Robin St E14 E14 ..42 B3
Robin Gr N6 ....3 C2
Robin Ho NW8 .....80 A1
Robin Hood SW15 ..68 A3
Robin Hood Gdns 15
E14 ....34 B2
Robin Hood La E14 .34 B2
Robinscroft Mews
SE10 ....52 A2
Robins Ct TW10 ...54 A1
Robin's Ct SW4 ....62 A1
Robinsfield Inf Sch
NW8 ....80 A2
Robinson Ct N1 ....86 B4
    8 Richmond TW9 ...54 B3
Robinson Ho 11 E14 .33 C4
    4 London W10 .....30 C3
Robinson Rd E2 ...25 B3
Robinson St SW3 .158 C4
Robsart St SW9 ..173 B2
Robson Ave NW10 .9 A1
Robson Rd SE27, ...
SE27 ....75 B1
Roby Ho EC1 ....96 C2
Rochdale Way 4
SE8 ....51 C3
Roche Ho 15 E14 ..33 B2
Rochelle Cl SW11 ..59 C3

Rochelle Ct 14 E1 ..32 B3
Rochelle Ct
SE13 ....98 C3
Rochemont Wlk 2
    E8 ....24 C4
Rochester Ct 1 E2 .25 A1
    7 London NW1 .....13 B1
Rochester Ho SE1 137 C3
    18 SE15 ....50 B4
Rochester Mews
NW1 ....13 B1
Rochester Pl NW1 .13 B2
Rochester Rd NW1 .13 B2
Rochester Row
SW1 ....147 A4
Rochester Sq NW1 .13 B1
Rochester St SW1 133 B1
Rochester Terr
NW1 ....13 B2
Rochester Wlk
SE1 ....123 B2
    8 Balham SW12 ....73 A4
Rochford Wlk 8 E8 16 C1
Rochfort Ho 8 SE8 41 B1
Rock Ave 13 SW14 .55 C4
Rockell's Pl SE22 ..65 A1
Rockfield Ho SE10 .52 B4
Rock Grove Way
SE16 ....153 C4
Rockhall Rd NW2 ..9 C4
Rockingham Cl
SW15 ....56 B3
Rockingham St
SE1 ....136 C1
Rockland Rd SW15 58 A3
Rockley Ct 9 W14 .39 C4
Rockley Rd W14 ...39 C4
Rocks La SW13 ....56 C4
Rock St N4 ....5 C2
Rockstraw Ho 5
NW3 ....12 B1
Rockwood Ct N16 ..7 C4
Rocliffe St N1 ......86 B1
Rocque Ho SW6 ..154 C2
Rodborough Rd
NW11 ....1 C3
Rodenhurst Ct SW4 .61 C1
Rodenhurst Rd SW4 61 C1
Roden St N7 ....5 B1
Roderick Ho 3
SE16 ....40 B2
Roderick Rd NW3 ..12 B4
Rodgers Ho 4 SW4 .73 C4
Roding Ct 8 W12 ..38 A4
Roding Ho N1 ......85 B3
Roding Mews E1 ..125 C2
Roding Rd E5 ......18 A3
Rodmarton St W1 103 A3
Rodmell WC1 ......94 B3
Rodmere St SE10 ..43 A1
Rodmill La SW2 ...74 A4
Rodney Ct NW8 ....89 A2
Rodney Ho E14 ...42 A2
    N1 ....85 A1
    11 London W11 ....113 B4
Rodney Pl SE17 ...151 A4
Rodney Rd SE17 ..151 B3
Rodney St N1 ......85 A1
Rodway Rd SW15 ..68 C4
Rodwell Rd SE22 ..64 B1
Roebuck Ho 1 SW1 .132 C2
Roedean Cres SW15 56 A2
Roehampton CE Prim
Sch SW15 ......69 A4
Roehampton Cl
SW15 ....56 C3
Roehampton Ct
SW13 ....56 C4

Roehampton Gate
SW15 ....56 A1
Roehampton High St
SW15 ....68 C4
Roehampton La
Putney SW15 .....56 C1
Roehampton SW15 .69 A3
Roehampton Vale
SW15 ....68 B2
Roger Dowley Ct 8
E2 ....25 B3
Roger's Almshouses 9
SW9 ....62 B3
Rogers Est 28 E2 ..25 B2
Rogers Ho SW1 ...147 C4
Rogers Rd E16 .....35 B1
Roger St WC1 ......95 A1
Rokeby Ho 8 ......94 C3
    8 Balham SW12 ....73 A4
Rokeby Rd SE4 ....51 B1
Rokeby Sch E15 ...19 C1
Rokeland Ho SE4 ..66 A3
Roland Gdns SW7 143 A2
Roland Mews 1 E1 .32 C4
Roland Way 1 E17 151 C1
    SW7 ....143 A2
Rollins St SE15 ....50 B4
Rollit Ho N7 ....14 C3
Rollit St N7 ....14 C3
Rolls Bldgs EC4 ..107 C2
Rollscourt Ave SE24 63 B2
Rolls Pas EC4 .....107 B2
Rolls Rd SE1 ......153 A2
Rolt St SE8 ....51 A4
Roman Cl W3 ......37 A4
Romanfield Rd SE24 .74 B4
Roman Rd E2,E3 ..25 C3
    E3 ....26 C4
    London N7 ....38 B2
Roman Square Mkt 8
E3 ....26 B3
Roman Way 4 SE15 50 B3
    London N7 ....14 B2
Roma Read Ct
SW15 ....69 A4
Romayne Ho SW4 .61 C4
Romberg Rd SW17 .72 C1
Romborough Gdns
SE13 ....67 B2
Romborough Way
SE13 ....67 B2
Romer Ho
    9 London SW2 .....62 B2
    12 London W10 ....23 B2
Romero Cl SW9 ...62 B4
Romey Mews W1 ..103 B4
Romeyn Rd SW16 ..74 B1
Romford Ho 17 N1 .15 C2
Romford St E1 .....32 A4
Romilly Rd N4 .....6 A2
Romilly St W1 .....119 C4
Romily Ct SW6 ...164 B2
Romney Cl 7 SE14 .50 B3
    London NW11 ......1 C3
Romney Ct
    9 London NW3 .....12 A2
    9 London W12 .....39 B4
Romney Rd SE10 ..52 C4
Romney St SW1 ..134 A1
Romola Rd SE24 ..
Romsey Ho 5
    SW11 ....59 C3
Ronald Ross Prim Sch
SW19 ....70 A4

Ronaldshay Rd N5 ....5 C3
Ronalds Rd N5 ....14 C3
Ronald St E1 ....32 B3
Rona Rd NW3 ....12 C4
Rona Wlk **7** N1 ....15 C2
Rondu Rd NW2 ....10 A3
Rood La EC3 ....123 C4
Rookery Rd SW4 ....61 B3
Rooke Way SE10 ....43 B1
Rookwood Rd N16 ....7 C4
Rootes Dr W10 ....30 C4
Ropemaker Rd
SE16 ....41 A3
Ropemaker's Fields **7**
E14 ....33 B2
Ropemaker St EC2 ....109 B4
Roper La SE1 ....**138** B3
Roper's Orchard
SW3 ....158 A3
Ropers Wlk **3** SE24 ....74 C4
Ropery St E3 ....26 B1
Rope St E3 ....41 A3
Ropewalk Gdns E1 ....111 C2
Ropley St **6** E2 ....24 C3
Rosa Alba Mews N5 ....15 B4
Rosalind Ho **25** N1 ....24 A3
Rosaline Rd SW6 ....154 B1
Rosaline Terr SW6 ....154 B1
Rosa Parks Ho
SW9 ....172 C1
Rosary Gdns SW7 ....143 A3
Rosary RC Prim Sch
NW3 ....12 A3
Rosaville Rd SW6 ....154 C1
Rosbury SW15 ....58 A1
Roscoe St EC1 ....97 A1
Roscommon Ho **3**
NW3 ....11 C3
Rose Alley EC2 ....110 B3
SE1 ....123 A2
Rosebank
London SW6 ....47 B3
2 London W3 ....28 C3
Rosebank Gdns E3 ....26 B3
1 London W3 ....28 C3
Rosebank Way W3 ....28 C3
Rosebank Wlk NW1 ....13 C1
Roseberry Pl E8 ....16 B2
Roseberry Ave EC1 ....95 C3
Rosebery C EC1 ....95 B2
W1 ....118 A2
Rosebery Ho **22** E2 ....25 B3
Rosebery Rd SW2 ....62 A1
Rosebery Sq EC1 ....95 B1
Rose Bruford Coll
SE8 ....51 C4
Rosebury Rd SW6 ....166 B1
Rose Bush Ct NW3 ....12 B3
Rosecroft Ave NW3 ....1 C1
Rose & Crown Ct
EC2 ....108 C2
Rose & Crown Yd
SW1 ....119 A1
Rose Ct E1 ....111 A3
N1 ....86 B4
Rosedale Ct N5 ....15 A4
Rosedale Ho N16 ....6 C3
Rosedale Rd TW9 ....54 A3
Rosedale Terr W6 ....39 A3
Rosedene Ave W 22 C4
Rosedene Ave
SW16 ....74 B1
Rosedew Rd W6 ....47 C4
Rosefield Gdns E14 ....33 C2
Rosehart Mews **8**
W11 ....31 C3

Rosehill Rd SW18 ....59 B2
Roseland Ho SW6 ....58 A4
Roseleigh Ave N5 ....15 A4
Rosemary Branch
Bridge N1 ....**87** B3
Rosemary Ct **13** SE8 ....51 B4
Rosemary Dr **16**
E14 ....34 C3
Rosemary Gdns
SW14 ....55 B4
Rosemary Ho N1 ....**87** C3
Rosemary La SW14 ....55 B4
Rosemary Mews N1 ....**87** C4
Rosemary Rd SE15 ....49 B3
Wandsworth SW17 ....71 B1
Rosemary Works Sch
N1 ....**87** B3
Rosemead Prep Sch
SE21 ....75 B2
Rosemont Mans **11**
NW3 ....11 A2
Rosemont Rd
Acton W3 ....28 A2
London NW3 ....11 B2
Richmond TW10 ....54 A1
Rosemoor St SW3 ....**144** C3
Rosemount Ct **2**
W3 ....28 A1
Rosemount Ho W3 ....28 A2
Rosenau Cres
SW11 ....168 C3
Rosenau Rd SW11 ....168 C4
Rosendale Prim Sch
SE21 ....75 B4
Rosendale Rd SE21,
SE24 ....75 B3
Roseneath Rd SW11 ....60 C1
Rosenthal Rd SE6 ....67 B1
Rosenthorpe Rd
SE15 ....65 C2
Roserton St E14 ....42 B4
Rose Sq SW7 ....143 C2
Rose St EC4 ....108 B1
WC2 ....120 A4
Rosethorn Cl SW12 ....73 C4
Rosetta Cl SW8 ....162 B1
Roseway SE21 ....63 C1
Rosewood Ct **2**
E11 ....19 C4
Rosewood Sq W12 ....29 C3
Rosher Cl E15 ....19 C1
Rosina St E9 ....17 C2
Roskell Rd SW15 ....57 C4
Roslin Ho **2** E1 ....32 C2
Roslin Rd W3 ....37 A3
Rosmead Rd
W11 ....31 A2 **112** A4
Rosoman Pl EC1 ....95 C2
Rose Ct **4** SW15 ....69 C4
Ross Rd SW18 ....72 A4
Rossdale Rd SW15 ....57 B3
Rossendale Way
NW1 ....83 A4
Rossetti Ct WC1 ....105 C3
Rossetti Ho SW1 ....147 C3
Rossetti Mews NW8 ....79 C3
Rossetti Rd SE16 ....40 A1
Ross Ho **18** E1 ....32 A1
Rossington St E5 ....7 C2
Rossiter Rd SW12 ....73 A3
Rosslyn Ave SW13 ....56 B4
Rosslyn Ct NW3 ....12 A3
Rosslyn Hill NW3 ....11 C3
Rosslyn Ho **5** TW9 ....44 B2
Rosslyn Mans NW6 ....11 B2

Rosslyn Park Mews
NW3 ....11 C3
Rossmore Ct NW1 ....90 C2
Rossmore Rd NW1 ....90 B2
Rostrevor Mans
SW6 ....164 C4
Rostrevor Rd SW6 ....164 C4
Rotary St SE1 ....136 B2
Rothay NW1 ....92 B4
Rothbury Rd E9 ....18 C1
Rotherfield Ct N1 ....**87** B4
N1 ....**87** A4
Rotherfield Prim Sch
N1 ....**87** A4
Rotherfield St N1 ....**87** A4
Rotherham Wlk
SE1 ....122 A1
Rotherhithe SE16 ....33 B1
Rotherhithe Holiday Inn
Pier SE16 ....33 A1
Rotherhithe New Rd
SE16 ....40 A1
Rotherhithe Old Rd
SE16 ....40 C2
Rotherhithe Prim Sch
SE16 ....40 C2
Rotherhithe St SE16 ....40 B4
10 SE16 ....40 A4
Rotherhithe Sta
SE16 ....40 B4
Rotherhithe Tunnel
SE16 ....32 C1
Rother Ho SE15 ....65 A3
Rotherwick Rd NW11 ....1 C4
Rotherwood Rd
SW15 ....57 C4
Rothery St N1 ....86 B4
Rothesay Ave SW14,
SW15 ....56 A3
Rothesay Ct SE11 ....163 B3
Rothsay St SE1 ....138 A1
Rothsay Wlk **15** E14 ....41 C2
Rothschild Rd W4 ....37 B3
Rothwell St NW1 ....81 A4
10 London NW1 ....12 B1
Rotten Row SW1 ....130 C4
Rotterdam Dr E14 ....42 B3
Rouel Rd SE16 ....139 B1
SE16 ....153 B4
Roundacre SW19 ....69 C2
Roundel Cl SE4 ....66 B3
Roundwood Rd
NW10 ....8 B1
Rounton Rd E3 ....26 C1
Roupell Rd SW2 ....74 B3
Roupell St SE1 ....121 C1
Rousden St NW1 ....13 B1
Routh Rd SW18 ....72 A4
Rover Ho **2** N1 ....24 A4
Rowallan Rd SW6 ....154 A1
Rowan Cl W5 ....36 A4
Rowan Ct **18** SE15 ....49 B3
London SW11 ....60 B1
Rowan Ho
5 London NW10 ....21 A1
3 London W6 ....39 C2
Rowan Rd W6 ....39 C2
Rowan Wlk W10 ....23 A1
Rowberry Cl SW6 ....47 B3
Rowcross St SE1 ....152 C3
Rowditch La SW11 ....169 B2
Rowdon Ave NW10 ....9 A1
Rowe La E9 ....17 B3

Rowena Cres
SW11 ....168 B1
Rowfant Rd SW12,
SW17 ....72 C2
Rowhill Mans **11** E5 ....17 A4
Rowhill Rd E5 ....17 A4
Rowington Cl W2 ....100 A4
Rowland Hill Ho
SE1 ....136 A4
Rowland Hill St
NW3 ....12 A3
Rowley Gdns N4 ....6 B4
Rowley Ho SE8 ....51 C4
Rowley Way NW8 ....78 B4
Rowntree Cl NW6 ....10 C2
Rowntree Cl E15 ....27 B4
Rowstock **1** NW5 ....13 C2
Rowstock Gdns N7 ....13 C3
Roxby Pl SW6 ....155 C4
Roxford Ho **2** E3 ....27 A1
Roxley Rd SE13 ....67 A1
Roxwell **10** NW1 ....13 A2
Roxwell Rd W12 ....38 C4
Royal Academy of
Dramatic Art★
WC1 ....105 C3
Royal Acad of Arts★
W1 ....118 C3
Royal Acad of Dance
SW11 ....167 C3
Royal Acad of Music
NW1 ....91 C1
Royal Albert Hall★
SW7 ....129 B3
Royal Arc W1 ....118 C3
Royal Army Medical Coll
SW1 ....148 A2
Royal Ave SW3 ....144 C2
Royal Avenue Ho
SW3 ....144 C2
Royal Ballet Sch The
WC2 ....106 B2
Royal Brompton Hospl
SW3 ....143 C2
SW3 ....144 A2
Royal Cir SE27 ....75 A1
Royal Cl SE8 ....51 B4
London N16 ....7 A3
Putney SW19 ....69 C2
Royal College St
NW1 ....83 A4
Royal Coll of
Anaesthetists
WC1 ....106 B3
Royal Coll of Art
SW7 ....129 B3
Royal Coll of Art
Sculpture Sch
SW11 ....158 A1
Royal Coll of Midwives
W1 ....104 A3
Royal Coll of Music
SW7 ....129 B2
Royal Coll of
Obstetricians &
Gynaecologists
NW1 ....90 C2
Royal Coll of Physicians
NW1 ....92 B2
Royal Coll of Science
SW7 ....129 B2
Royal Coll of Surgeons
WC2 ....107 A2
Royal Courts of Justice
WC2 ....107 B1
Royal Cres
W11 ....31 A1 **112** A1

Royal Crescent Mews
W11 ....30 C1
Royal Ct SE16 ....41 B3
Royal Duchess Mews
SW12 ....73 A4
Royal Exchange★
EC3 ....109 C1
Royal Exchange Ave
EC3 ....109 C1
Royal Exchange Bldgs
EC3 ....109 C1
Royal Festival Hall★
SE1 ....121 A1
Royal Free Hospl
NW3 ....12 A3
Royal Geographical
Society SW7 ....129 C3
Royal Hill SE10 ....52 B3
Royal Horticultural
Society (Lawrence Hall
& Conf Ctr) SW1 ....133 C1
Royal Horticultural
Society (Lindley Hall)
SW1 ....147 C3
Royal Hospital (Army
Pensioners) SW1 ....145 B1
Royal Hospital Rd
SW3 ....145 A1
Royal Hospl and Home
SW15 ....58 A1
Royal Langford
NW6 ....78 A2
Royal London Est The
NW10 ....20 C3
Royal London
Homeopathic Hospl
The WC1 ....106 B4
Royal London Hospl
(Mile End) The E2 ....25 C2
Royal London Hospl (St
Clements) The E3 ....26 B2
Royal London Hospl
(Whitechapel) The
E1 ....32 A4
Royal Marsden Hospl
SW3 ....143 C2
Royal Mews The
SW1 ....132 B2
Royal Mint Pl E1 ....125 A4
Royal Mint St E1 ....125 A4
Royal National TNE
Hospl The WC1 ....94 C4
Royal Naval Pl SE14 ....51 B3
Royal Oak Ct N1 ....98 A4
Royal Oak Pl SE22 ....65 A1
Royal Oak Rd **5** E8 ....17 A2
Royal Oak Sta W2 ....100 B3
Royal Opera Arc
SW1 ....119 B2
Royal Orchard Cl
SW18 ....70 A4
Royal Par SW6 ....154 A2
London SW3 ....53 B1
Royal Pl **11** SE10 ....52 B3
Royal Rd SE17 ....48 A4
Royal Sch Hampstead
The NW3 ....11 C4
Royal St SE1 ....135 A2
Royalty Mews W1 ....105 B1
Royalty Studios
W11 ....31 A3

Royal United Services
Mus SW1 ....**120** A1

Royal Veterinary Coll
NW1 ....**83** B3

Royal Victoria Sta
E16 ....**35** C2

Royal Victor Pl E3 ...**25** C3

Roycroft Cl SW2 .....**74** C3

Roydon Cl SW11 ....**168** C2

Roy Ho N1 ....**87** C3

Roy Ridley Ho 图
SW4 ....**61** C4

Roy Sq E14 ....**33** A2

Royston Ct 图 TW9 ..**44** B2

Royston Gdns SE15 .**49** C4

Royston Rd TW10 .....**54** A2

Royston St 图 E2 ....**25** B3

Rozel Ct 图 N1 ....**24** A4

Rozel Rd SW4 ....**61** B4

Rubens St SE6 ....**50** A4

Ruby Triangle SE15 ..**50** A4

Rucklidge Ave
NW10 ....**21** C3

Rudall Cres NW3 .....**11** C4

Rudbeck Ho 圆
SE15 ....**49** C3

Ruddington Cl E5 ....**18** A3

Rudge Ho SE16 ......**139** C2

Rudgwick Terr NW8 ..**80** B3

Rudhall Ho 图 SW2 ..**62** C1

Rudloe Rd SW12 ....**73** B4

Rudolf Pl SW8 ....**162** B3

Rudolph Rd NW6 .....**23** C3

Rudstone Ho 图 E3 ...**27** A2

Rudyard Ct SE1 .....**137** C3

Rufford St N1 ....**84** B4

Rufford Street Mews
N1 ....**84** B4

Rufford Twr 图 SW3 ..**28** A1

Rufus Bsns Ctr
SW18 ....**71** A2

Rufus St N1 ....**98** A3

Rugby Mans W14 ...**140** B4

Rugby Rd W4 ....**38** A4

Rugby St WC1 ....**94** C1

Rugg St E14 ....**33** C2

Rugless Ho 图 E14 ...**42** B4

Rugmere 图 NW1 ....**12** C1

Rumball Ho 图 SE5 ...**49** A3

Rumbold Rd SW6 ...**156** B1

Rum Cl E1 ....**32** B2

Rumford Ho SE1 ....**136** C1

Rumsey Rd SW9 .....**62** B4

Runacres Ct SE17 ...**150** C1

Runcorn Pl W11 .....**112** A4

Rundell Twr SW8 ...**172** C4

Running Horse Yd 图
TW8 ....**44** A4

Runnymede Ho
E9 ....**18** A4

Richmond TW10 ......**54** C2

Rupack St 图 SE16 ....**40** B4

Rupert Ct W1 ....**119** B4

Rupert Gdns SW9 ....**48** A1

Rupert Ho SE11 .....**149** C3

Rupert Rd NW6 ....**23** C3

London N19 ....**4** C2

London W4 ....**38** A3

Rupert St W1 ....**119** B4

Rusbridge Cl E8 ......**16** C3

Ruscoe Rd E16 ....**35** B1

Rusham Rd SW12 ....**72** B4

Rushbrook Ho
SW8 ....**171** B2

Rushby Ct SW4 ......**172** A3

Rush Common Mews 图
SW2 ....**74** B4

Rushcroft Rd SW2,
SW9 ....**62** C3

Rushcutters Ct 图
SE16 ....**41** A2

Rushey Mead SE4 ....**66** C2

Rushford Rd SE4 ......**66** B1

Rush Hill Mews 图
SW11 ....**60** C4

Rush Hill Rd SW11 ...**60** C4

Rushlake Ho SW11 .**169** B2

Rushmead 图 E2 ....**25** A2

Rushmere Ho 图
SW15 ....(not fully shown)

Rushmore Cres 圆
E5 ....**17** C4

Rushmore Ho N7 ....**13** C3

Rushmore Prim Sch
E5 ....**17** C4

Rushmore Rd
London E5 ....**17** C4

London E5 ....**18** A4

Rusholme Gr SE19 ..**58** A1

Rushton Ho SW8 ...**171** B1

Rushton St N1 ....**87** C2

Rushworth St SE1 ..**136** B3

Ruskin Ave TW9 ......**44** C3

Ruskin Ct SE5 ....**63** C4

Ruskin Ho SW1 .....**147** C3

Ruskin Park Ho SE5 .**63** C4

Ruskin Wlk SE24 ....**163** B2

Rusper Cl SW9 ....**172** B1

Russell Cl W4 ....**46** B4

Russell Ct SW1 ......**119** A1

图 London SE15 ......**50** A1

Russell Gdns 图
W14 ....**126** A2

Russell Gdns Mews
W14 ....**126** A2

Russell Gr 图 SW9 ..**173** C4

Russell Ho 图 E14 ...**33** C3

Russell Kerr Cl W4 ..**45** B3

Russell Lodge SE1 .**137** B1

Russell Mans 图
SW4 ....**62** A4

Russell Pickering Ho 图
SW4 ....**62** A4

Russell Pl SE16 ....**41** A3

London NW3 ....**12** A3

Russell Rd W14 .....**126** B1

Russell Sq WC1 ....**94** A1

Russell Square Mans
WC1 ....**106** B3

Russell Square Sta
WC1 ....**94** A1

Russell St WC2 .....**120** B4

Russell's Wharf 图
W9 ....**23** B1

Russell Wlk 图
TW10 ....**54** B1

Russet Cres N7 ....**14** B3

Russett Way SE13 ...**52** A1

Russia Ct EC2 ....**109** A2

Russia Dock Rd
SE16 ....**33** A1

Russia La E2 ....**25** B3

Russia Row EC2 ....**109** A1

Rusthall Ave W4 ......**37** C3

Rusthall Mans W4 ...**37** C2

Ruston Mews W11 ...**31** A3

Ruston St 图 E3 ....**26** B4

Rust Sq SE5 ....**48** C3

Ruth Ct 图 E3 ....**26** A3

Rutherford Ho 图
E1 ....**25** A1

Rutherford St SW1 .**147** B4

Ruth Ho W10 ....**23** A1

Ruthin Rd SE3 ....**53** C4

Ruthven St E9 ....**25** C4

Rutland Cl SW14 .....**55** B4

Rutland Ct SW7 .....**130** B3

London SE5 ....**63** B3

Rutland Gate 图
SW7 ....**130** B3

Rutland Gate Mews
SW7 ....**130** A3

Rutland Gdns SW7 .**130** B3

Rutland Gdns Mews
SW7 ....**130** B3

Rutland Gr W6 ....**39** A1

Rutland Ho W8 ......**128** A1

图 Putney SW15 ....**69** B4

Rutland Mews E
SW7 ....**130** A2

Rutland Mews S
SW7 ....**130** A2

Rutland Mews W
SW7 ....**130** A2

Rutland Park Gdns
NW2 ....**9** B2

Rutland Park Mans
NW2 ....**9** B2

Rutland Pk NW2 ....**9** B2

Rutland Pl EC1 ......**108** B4

Rutland Rd E9 ....**25** C4

Rutland St SW7 .....**130** B2

Rutland Studios
NW10 ....**21** C2

Rutley Cl SE11 ....**48** A4

Rutt's Terr SE14 ......**50** C2

Ruvigny Gdns SW15 .**57** C4

Ruvigny Mans SW15 .**57** C4

Rycott Path SE22 ....**76** C4

Rycuiff Sq SE3 ....**53** B1

Rydal Ho SW8 ......**171** B1

Rydal Water NW1 ...**92** C3

Ryde Ho 图 NW6 ......**23** C4

Ryder Ct SW1 ....**119** A2

Ryder Dr SE16 ....**40** A1

Ryder Ho 图 E1 ....**25** B1

Ryder St SW1 ....**119** A2

Ryder's Terr NW8 ....**78** C2

Ryder Yd SW1 ....**119** A2

Ryde Vale Rd SW12 .**73** B2

Rydon St N1 ....**87** A4

Rydston Cl 图 N7 ......**14** B1

Ryecotes Mead
SE21 ....**76** A3

Ryecroft Rd SE13 ....**67** B2

Ryecroft St SW6 ....**166** A3

Ryedale SE22 ....**65** A1

Ryefield Path 图
SW15 ....**68** C3

Ryegates 图 SE15 ....**50** A1

Rye Hill Pk SE15 .....**65** B3

Rye La SE15 ....**49** C1

Rye Rd SE15 ....**65** C3

Rye Wlk SW15 ....**57** C2

Ryfold Rd SW19 ......**70** C1

Ryland Rd NW5 ....**13** A2

Rylett Cres W12 ......**38** B3

Rylett Rd W12 ....**38** B3

Rylston Rd SW6 ....**154** C2

Rymer St SE24 ....**63** A1

Rysbrack St SW1 ...**130** C2

S

Saatchi Gallery★
SE1 ....**134** C3

Sabbarton St 图
E16 ....**35** B1

Sabella Ct E3 ....**26** B3

Sabine Rd SW11 ......**60** C4

Sable St N1 ....**15** A1

Sacketts Ho SW9 ...**173** C4

Sackville Ho 图
SW16 ....**74** A1

Sackville St W1 .....**119** A3

Sacred Heart High Sch
W6 ....**39** B2

Sacred Heart Jun Sch
W6 ....**39** C2

Sacred Heart Prim Sch,
Battersea SW11 ....**168** B2

Sacred Heart RC Prim
Sch SW15 ....**56** C2

Sacred Heart RC Sch
The SE5 ....**48** B2

Saddlers Mews
SW8 ....**172** B4

Sadler Ho 图 E3 ....**27** A2

EC1 ....**96** C4

Saffron Ave E14 ......**34** C2

Saffron Ct 图 N1 ....**15** C2

Saffron Hill EC1 ....**107** C4

Saffron St EC1 ....**107** C4

Saffron Wharf SE1 .**139** A4

Sage Mews SE22 ....**64** B2

Sage St E1 ....**32** B2

Sage Way WC1 ....**94** C3

Sailmakers Ct SW6 .**59** B4

Sail St SE11 ....**149** A4

Sainfoin Rd SW17 ...**72** C2

St Agnes Cl E9 ....**25** B4

St Agnes Pl SE11 ....**48** A4

St Agnes RC Prim Sch
E3 ....**27** A2

St Agnes RC Sch
NW2 ....**1** A1

St Aidan's Prim Sch
N4 ....**5** C4

St Aidan's Rd SE22 ..**65** A2

St Albans Ave W4 ...**37** C3

St Alban's CE Prim Sch
EC1 ....**107** B4

St Alban's Cl NW11 ...**1** C3

St Alban's Gr W8 ...**128** B2

St Albans La NW11 ...**1** C3

St Albans Mans
W8 ....**128** B2

St Alban's Pl N1 ......**86** A3

St Alban's Rd
London NW10 ....**21** A4

London NW5 ....**4** A1

St Alban's St SW1 ..**119** B3

St Albans Studios
W8 ....**128** B2

St Albans Terr W6 .**154** A4

St Alige Pas SE10 ...**52** B4

St Alige with St Peter's
CE Prim Sch SE10 ..**52** B4

St Aloysius RC Inf Sch
NW1 ....**93** C4

St Aloysius' RC Jun & Inf
Sch NW1 ....**93** C4

St Aloysius RC Jun Sch
NW1 ....**93** B4

St Alphage Gdn
EC2 ....**109** A3

St Alphage Highwalk
EC2 ....**109** A3

St Alphonsus Rd
SW4 ....**61** C3

St Andrew's CE Prim
Sch
N1 ....**85** A4

London SW9 ....**172** B1

St Andrew's Cl 图
SE16 ....**40** A1

St Andrew's Ct 图
SW18 ....**71** B2

St Andrew's Gr N16 ...**6** C3

St Andrew's Greek Sch
NW1 ....**13** B2

St Andrew's Hill
EC4 ....**108** B1

St Andrews Ho 图
SE16 ....**40** A3

St Andrew's Hospl
E3 ....**27** A1

St Andrew's Mans
W1 ....**103** B3

St Andrews Mews
Greenwich SE3 ....**53** C3

图 Streatham SW12 ..**73** C3

St Andrew's Mews
N16 ....**7** A3

St Andrew's Pl NW1 .**92** B2

St Andrew's Rd
W14 ....**154** B4

London NW9 ....**9** A2

London W3 ....**29** A3

St Andrew's Sq
W11 ....**31** A3

St Andrew St EC4 ..**107** C3

St Andrew & St Francis
CE Prim Sch NW2 ....**8** C2

St Andrews Way E3 ..**27** A1

St Andrew's Wharf
SE1 ....**139** A4

St Anne RC Prim Sch
E1 ....**99** B1

St Anne's CE Prim Sch
SW18 ....**59** A2

St Anne's Cl N6 ....**3** C1

St Anne's Ct W1 .....**105** B1

St Anne's Flats NW1 .**93** B4

St Anne's Pas E14 ...**33** B3

SE11 ....**162** C4

St Anne's Row E14 ..**33** B3

St Anne St E14 ....**33** B3

St Anne's Trad Est
E14 ....**33** B3

St Ann's Cres SW18 .**59** B1

St Ann's Gdns NW5 .**12** C2

St Ann's Hill SW18 ..**59** B1

St Ann's Ho WC1 .....**95** B3

St Ann's La SW1 ....**133** C1

St Ann's Park Rd
SW18 ....**59** B1

St Anns Rd SW13 ....**46** B2

St Ann's Rd W11 .....**30** C2

St Ann's St SW1 ....**133** C2

St Ann's Terr NW8 ...**79** C2

St Ann's Villas
W11 ....**112** A4

St Anselm's Rd 图
SW17 ....**72** A2

St Anselm's RC Prim Sch
SW17 ....**72** A2

St Anthony's Cl
EC2 ....**108** C1

图 London SW17 ......**72** A2

St Anthony's Ct
图 London SW17 ......**72** A2

Upper Tooting SW17 ...**72** C2

St Anthony's Flats
NW1 ....**83** B1

St Anthony's RC Prim
Sch SE22 . . . . .64 C1
St Asaph Ct SE4 . . . . . .65 C4
St Asaph Rd SE4 . . . . . .65 C4
St Aubins Ct N1 . . . . . .87 C4
St Augustine's CE High
Sch NW6 . . . . .23 C3
St Augustine's RC Prim
Sch NW6 . . . . .78 A1
St Augustine's RC Prim
Sch W6 . . . . .154 B3
St Augustine's Rd
NW1 . . . . .13 C1
St Austell Rd SE13 . . . .52 C1
St Barnabas CE Prim
Sch SW1 . . . . .145 C2
St Barnabas Cl 11
SE22 . . . . .64 A2
St Barnabas St
SW1 . . . . .145 C2
St Barnabas Terr
E9 . . . . .17 C3
St Barnabas Villas
SW8 . . . . .172 B4
St Bartholomew's Hospl
EC1 . . . . .108 B3
St Bede's RC Inf Sch
SW12 . . . . .73 C3
St Benets Cl SW17 . . . .72 C2
St Benet's Pl EC3 . .123 C4
St Bernadette RC Jun
Sch SW12 . . . . .73 B4
St Bernard Ho 8
E14 . . . . .42 B3
St Botolph St E1,
EC3 . . . . .110 C2
St Brelades Ct N1 . . . . .87 C4
St Bride's Ave EC4 . .108 A1
St Bride's Pas EC4 . .108 A1
St Bride St EC4 . . . .108 A2
St Catherines Cl
SW17 . . . . .72 A2
St Catherine's Ct 8
W4 . . . . .38 A3
St Catherine's Dr
SE14 . . . . .50 C1
St Catherines Mews
SW3 . . . . .144 C4
St Chad's St WC1 . . . . .94 C4
St Chad's St WC1 . . . . .94 B4
St Charles' Hospl
W10 . . . . .30 C4
St Charles Pl W10 . . . .31 A4
St Charles RC Prim Sch
W10 . . . . .30 C4
St Charles RC Sixth
Form Coll W10 . . . . .30 C4
St Charles Sq W10 . . . .30 C4
St Christina's Sch
NW8 . . . . .80 A2
St Christopher's Ho
NW1 . . . . .83 B1
St Christopher's Pl
W1 . . . . .103 C2
St Christopher's Sch
NW3 . . . . .11 C2
St Clair Ho 10 E3 . . . . .26 B2
St Clare St EC3 . . . .110 C1
St Clement Danes CE
Prim Sch WC2 . . . .106 C1
St Clements Ct 7
SE14 . . . . .50 C4
St Clement's Ct
EC3 . . . . .123 C4

St Clements Ct
London N7 . . . . .14 B2
8 London W11 . . . . . .30 C2
St Clement's La
WC2 . . . . .107 A1
St Clements Mans 5
SW6 . . . . .47 C4
St Clements St N7 . . . .14 C1
St Clement & St James
CE Prim Sch
W11 . . . . .31 A1 112 A1
St Columb's Ho 11
W10 . . . . .31 A4
St Crispins Cl NW3 . . .12 A4
St Cross St EC1 . . . .107 C4
St Cuthbert's Rd
NW2 . . . . .10 B2
St Cuthbert with St
Matthias Prim Sch
SW5 . . . . .142 A2
St Davids Ct 27
SE16 . . . . .40 A1
St David's Sq E14 . . . . .42 A1
St Dionis Rd SW6 . .165 A2
St Dominic RC Prim Sch
NW5 . . . . .12 B3
St Dominics Prim Sch
Sch E9 . . . . .18 A2
St Donatt's Rd SE14 .51 B2
St Dunstan's Alley
EC3 . . . . .124 A3
St Dunstan's Ave
W3 . . . . .28 C2
St Dunstan's Ct
EC4 . . . . .107 C1
St Dunstan's Gdns
W3 . . . . .28 C2
St Dunstan's Hill
EC3 . . . . .124 A3
St Dunstan's La
EC3 . . . . .124 A3
St Dunstan's Rd W6 .39 C1
St Edmund RC Sch
E14 . . . . .41 C2
St Edmund's Cl
NW8 . . . . .80 C3
St Edmund's Ct
NW8 . . . . .80 C3
St Edmund's Sq
SW13 . . . . .47 B4
St Edmund's Terr
NW8 . . . . .80 C3
St Edward's RC Prim
Sch NW1 . . . . .90 B1
St Elizabeth's RC Prim
Sch TW10 . . . . .54 B1
St Elmo Rd W12 . . . . .38 B4
St Elmos Rd SE16 . . .41 A4
St Ermin's Hill
SW1 . . . . .133 B2
St Ervan's Rd W10 . .31 B4
St Eugene de Mazenod
RC Prim Sch NW6 .23 C4
St Faith's CE Prim Sch
SW18 . . . . .59 B2
St Faith's Rd SE24 . . .75 A3
St Francesca Cabrini
Prim Sch SE23 . . . . .65 B1
St Francis Ho NW1 . .83 B1
St Francis of Assisi RC
Prim Sch W11 . . . . .30 C2
St Francis RC Prim Sch
SE15 . . . . .49 C3
St Francis Rd SE22 . .64 A3

St Francis Xavier Sixth
Form Coll SW12 . . . .61 A1
St Gabriel's CE Prim Sch
SW1 . . . . .146 C1
St Gabriel's Rd NW2 .9 C3
St George Ho
SW11 . . . . .169 C3
St George's Ave N7 .13 C4
St George's Battersea
CE Prim Sch SW8 .161 A1
St George's Cath
NW1 . . . . .92 B4
St George's Cath RC Jun
& Inf Sch SE1 . . . . .136 A2
St George's CE Prim Sch
SE5 . . . . .48 C3
St George's Circ
SE1 . . . . .136 A2
St George's Ct SE1 .136 A2
SW3 . . . . .144 A4
SW7 . . . . .128 C1
St Georges Dr SW15 .58 B3
St George's Dr
SW1 . . . . .146 B2
St George's Field
W2 . . . . .102 B1
St George's Gr
SW17 . . . . .71 C1
St Georges Hanover Sq
Sch W1 . . . . .117 C3
St George's Ho
NW1 . . . . .83 A1
St George's La
EC3 . . . . .124 A4
St Georges Mews 7
NW1 . . . . .12 B1
St George's Mews
SE1 . . . . .135 C2
St George's RC Cath
SE1 . . . . .135 C2
St George's RC Sec Sch
W9 . . . . .78 B1
St George's Rd
SE1 . . . . .136 A1
St Georges Rd W4 .37 C4
St George's Rd TW9 .54 B4
St George's Residences
4 SW2 . . . . .62 C2
St George's Ct
EC4 . . . . .108 A2
St Georges Sq 1
E14 . . . . .33 A2
St George's Sq SE8 .41 B2
SW1 . . . . .147 B1
St George's Square
Mews SW1 . . . . .147 B1
St George St W1 . .118 B4
St Georges Terr
NW1 . . . . .12 B1
St George's Way
SE15 . . . . .49 A4
St George the Martyr CE
Prim Sch WC1 . . . . .95 A1
St Gerards Cl SW4 . .61 B2
St German's Pl SE3 .53 C2
St Giles Cir WC2 . . .105 C2
St Giles Coll WC1 .106 A4
St Giles High St
WC2 . . . . .105 C2
St Giles Hospl SE5 . .49 A2
St Giles Pas WC2 . . .105 C1
St Giles Rd SE5 . . . . .49 A2
St Giles Twr 3 SE5 . .49 A2
St Gilles Ho 15 E2 . . .25 C3
St Helena Ho WC1 . . .95 B3
St Helena Rd SE16 . .40 C2

St Helena St WC1 . . . .95 B3
St Helen's Gdns
W10 . . . . .30 C3
St Helen's Pl EC3 . .110 A2
St Helen's RC Prim Sch
SW9 . . . . .62 C4
St Helier Ct 4 N1 . . . .24 A4
St Hilda Cl SW17 . . . . .72 A2
St Hilda's Cl NW6 . . . . .9 C1
St Hilda's Rd SW13 .47 A4
St Hilda Wharf 1 E1 .32 B1
St Hubert's Ho 1
E14 . . . . .41 C3
St Hughes Cl SW17 . .72 A2
St James Ct 2 . . . . . .99 C3
St James' Ct SW1 .133 A2
St James Ct 10 W4 .36 C1
St James' Ct W4 . . . . .37 C3
St James Hatcham CE
Prim Sch SE14 . . . . .51 A2
St James Independent
Schs W14 . . . . .140 B4
St James Ind Mews
SE1 . . . . .153 C1
St James' Mans
NW6 . . . . .10 C1
St James Mews E14 .42 B3
St James's App EC2 .98 A2
St James's Ave E2 . . .25 B3
St James's CE Prim Sch
SE16 . . . . .49 B2
St James School Flats
5 N7 . . . . .14 B4
St James's Cl NW8 . .80 C3
Upper Tooting SW17 .72 B2
St James's Cloisters 2
SE22 . . . . .64 B3
St James's Cres
SW9 . . . . .62 C4
St James's Dr
Balham SW12,SW17 .72 B4
Upper Tooting SW17 .72 B3
St James's Gdns
W11 . . . . .31 A1 112 A2
St James's Gr
SW11 . . . . .169 A2
St James's Market
SW1 . . . . .119 B3
St James's Palace
SW1 . . . . .119 A1
St James's Park
SW1 . . . . .133 B3
St James's Park Sta
SW1 . . . . .133 B2
St James's Pas
EC3 . . . . .110 B1
St James's Pl SW1 .118 C1
SE16 . . . . .153 C4
St James's Sq
SW1 . . . . .119 A2
St James's St SW1 .118 C2
St James's & St
Michael's CE Prim Sch
W2 . . . . .114 C4
St James St W6 . . . . .39 B1
St James's Terr
NW8 . . . . .80 C3
4 Upper Tooting
SW12 . . . . .72 C3
St James's Terrace
Mews NW8 . . . . .80 C3
St James's Wlk EC1 .96 A2
St James The Great RC
Prim Sch SE15 . . . . .49 B2

St Joan of Arc RC Prim
Sch N5 . . . . .15 B3
St John CE Prim Sch
SE17 . . . . .151 A3
St John Cl SW6 . . . .155 B2
St John Evangelist RC
Prim Sch N1 . . . . . . .86 A2
St John of Jerusalem CE
Prim Sch E9 . . . . . . .17 B1
St John's Angell Town
CE Prim Sch SW9 .173 B1
St John's Ave
London NW10 . . . . . .21 B4
Putney SW15 . . . . . . .57 C2
St John's CE Prim Sch
E2 . . . . .25 B3
Fulham SW6 . . . . . .164 B3
St John's Church Rd
E9 . . . . .17 B3
St Johns Concert Hall
SW1 . . . . .134 A1
St John's Cres SW9 .62 C4
St Johns Ct 33 E1 . . . .32 A1
St John's Ct
London N4 . . . . .6 A2
London N5 . . . . .15 A4
5 London NW3 . . . . .11 B2
London SE13 . . . . . . .52 B1
London W6 . . . . .39 A2
St John's Dr SW18 . . .71 A3
St John's Est SE1 . . .138 C3
St John's Gdns
W11 . . . . .31 B2 112 C3
St John's Gr
3 Barnes SW13 . . . . .46 B1
London N19 . . . . .4 B2
1 Richmond TW9 . . . .54 A3
St John's (Highbury
Vale) CE Prim Sch
N5 . . . . .6 A1
St John's Hill SW11 .59 C3
St John's Hill Gr
SW11 . . . . .59 C3
St Johns Ho 5
SE17 . . . . .48 C4
St John's La EC1 . . .108 B4
St John's Mans E5 .17 B3
St John's Park Mans
N19 . . . . .4 B1
St John's Path EC1 .96 A1
St John's Pk SE3 . . . .53 C3
St John's Pl EC1 . . . .96 A1
St John's Rd E16 . . . .35 C3
London SW11 . . . . . . .60 A3
Richmond TW9 . . . . . .54 A3
St John's Sq EC1 . . . .96 A2
St Johns Sta SE8 . . . .51 C1
St John's & St Clements
CE Prim Sch SE15 .64 C4
St John St EC1 . . . . . .96 A2
St John Terr W10 . . . .22 C1
St John & St James CE
Prim Sch E9 . . . . . . .17 B3
St John's (Upper
Holloway) Prim Sch
N19 . . . . .4 C2
St John's Vale SE8 . . .51 C1
St John's Villas
W8 . . . . .128 B3
London N19 . . . . .4 C2
St John's Way N19 . . .4 C3
St John's Wood Ct
NW8 . . . . .89 C3

St John's Wood High St
NW8 ....80 A1
St John's Wood Pk
NW8 ....79 B4
St John's Wood Prep
Sch NW8 ....90 B3
St John's Wood Rd
NW8 ....89 C3
St John's Wood Sta
NW8 ....79 B2
St John's Wood Terr
NW8 ....80 A2
St John the Baptist CE
Prim Sch N1 ...24 A3
St John the Divine CE
Jun & Inf Sch SE5 .48 A3
St Joseph's Cl W10 .31 A4
St Josephs 🔢
NW8 ....21 B3
St Joseph's Flats
NW1 ....93 B4
St Joseph's Ho W6 .39 C2
St Joseph's Hospice
E9,E8 ....25 A4
St Joseph's RC Jun & Inf
Sch
SE16 ....139 B3
SE16 ....40 B3
St Joseph's RC Jun Sch
SE5 ....48 B3
St Joseph's RC Prim Sch
SE10 ....43 A1
SE8 ....51 C3
SW3 ....144 C3
W9 ....88 C3
WC2 ....106 B2
London N19 ......4 A3
London NW10 .....8 A1
London SW18 ....58 C2
St Joseph's St
SW8 ....170 B4
St Joseph's Vale
SE3 ....67 C4
St Jude CE Prim Sch
SE24 ....63 A2
St Judes Ho 🔢 W10 .23 B2
St Jude's Prim Sch
SE1 ....136 A1
St Jude's Rd E2 ....25 A3
St Jude's & St Paul's
Prim Sch N1 ...16 A3
St Jude St N16 ...16 A3
St Julian's Rd NW6 .23 C4
St Katharine's Ho
N1 ....85 B2
St Katharine's Way
E1 ....125 B3
St Katherine's Prec
NW1 ....82 A2
St Katherine's Row
EC3 ....110 B1
St Katherine's Wlk 🔢
W11 ....30 C1
St Kilda's Rd N16 ....7 A3
St Laurence's Cl
NW6 ....22 C4
St Lawrence Ct N1 .87 C4
St Lawrence Ho
SE1 ....138 B2
St Lawrence St E14 .34 B1
St Lawrence Terr
W10 ....31 A4
St Lawrence Way
SW9 ....173 C2
St Leonard's Ct N1 .97 C4

St Leonards Ct
SW14 ....55 B4
St Leonard's Hospl
N1 ....24 A3
St Leonard's Rd E14 34 B4
St Leonards Rd
SW14 ....55 B4
St Leonard's Rd
NW10 ....20 C1
St Leonard's Sq
NW5 ....12 C2
St Leonard's St E3 .27 A2
St Leonard's Terr
SW3 ....145 A1
St Loo Ave SW3 ...158 B4
St Loo Ct SW3 ....158 C4
St Luke's Ave SW4 .61 C3
St Luke's CE Prim Sch
E14 ....42 C2
St Luke's CE Prim Sch
EC1 ....96 C3
W9 ....23 B2
Redhill TW9 .....44 C2
St Luke's Cl EC1 ...97 A2
St Luke's Ct W11 ...31 B3
St Luke's Hospl W1 .92 C1
St Luke's Mews
W11 ....31 B3
St Luke's Prim Sch
E16 ....35 B1
St Luke's Rd W11 ..31 B4
St Luke's Sq E16 ...35 B1
St Luke's St SW3 .144 B2
St Margaret's Cres
SW15 ....57 A2
St Margaret's Ct
SW15 ....57 A3
St Margaret's La
W8 ....128 A1
St Margarets Lo
W3 ....37 A4
St Margaret's Rd
London NW10 ...22 B2
London SE4 .....66 B3
St Margaret's Sch
NW3 ....11 A4
St Margaret St
SW1 ....134 A3
St Mark's CE Prim Sch
SE11 ....163 A4
St Marks Cl 🔢 SE10 .52 B3
St Mark's Cres NW1 .81 C4
St Marks Gate E9 ..18 B1
St Mark's Gr SW10 156 B2
St Marks Ho 🔢
SE17 ....48 C4
St Mark's Hospl EC1 .96 B4
St Mark's Pl W11 ...31 A3
St Mark's Prim Sch
N19 ....5 A2
St Mark's Rd W11 ..31 A3
London W10 .....30 C4
St Mark's Rise E8 ..16 B3
St Mark's Sq NW1 ..81 B3
St Mark St E1 .....111 A1
St Martin-in-the-Fields
High Sch for Girls
SW2 ....74 C3
St Martin's Almshouses
NW1 ....82 C4
St Martin's Cl NW1 ..82 C4
St Martins Ct N1 ...24 A4
St Martin's Ct WC2 120 A4
West Norwood SE27 ..75 A2
St Martin's La
WC2 ....120 A3

St Martin's Le Grand
EC1 ....108 C2
St Martin's Pl WC2 120 A3
St Martin's Rd
SW9 ....172 C2
St Martin's St WC2 119 C3
St Martin's Way
SW17 ....71 B1
St Mary Abbots CE Prim
Sch W8 ......128 A3
St Mary Abbot's Pl
W14 ....126 C1
St Mary Abbot's Pl
W14 ....127 A1
St Mary Abbots Terr
W14 ....127 A1
St Mary at Hill
EC3 ....124 A3
St Mary Axe EC3 ..110 B2
St Marychurch St
SE16 ....40 B4
St Mary Graces Ct
E1 ....125 A3
St Marylebone CE Sch
The W1 .....103 B3
St Mary le Bow
Church* EC2 ..109 A1
St Mary- le-Park Ct
SW11 ....158 B1
St Mary Magdalene CE
Prim Sch
W2 ....100 B4
London N7 ....14 C2
London SE15 .....50 A1
St Mary Magdalens CE
Prim Sch SE4 ...66 A3
St Mary Magdalens RC
Prim Sch SW14 ..55 C4
St Mary Magdalen's RC
Jun Sch NW2 ....9 A2
St Mary Newington Cl
SE17 ....152 B2
St Mary of the Angels
Sch
W2 ....31 C3 113 A4
St Mary RC Prim Sch
W10 ....23 A1
St Mary's Bryanston
Square CE Sch
NW1 ....102 C4
St Mary's CE Prim Sch
N1 ....86 B4
London NW10 .....8 A2
Putney SW15 ....57 C4
St Mary's Est 🔢
SE16 ....40 B4
St Mary's Flats NW1 .93 B4
St Mary's Gate W8 128 A1
St Mary's Gdns
SE11 ....149 C4
St Mary's Gr
Barnes SW13 ....47 A4
Chiswick W4 .....45 A4
London N1 ....15 A2
Richmond TW10,TW9 .54 B3
St Mary's Ho N1 ...86 B4
St Mary's Hospl
W2 ....101 C2
St Mary's Kilburn CE
Prim Sch NW6 ..23 C4
St Mary's Lewisham CE
Prim Sch SE13 ..67 A2
St Mary's Mans
W2 ....101 B4
London NW10 ....21 A4

St Mary's Medical Sch
W2 ....101 C2
St Mary's Mews
NW6 ....11 A1
St Mary's Path N1 ..86 B4
St Mary's Pl W8 ..128 A1
St Mary's RC Prim Sch
Chiswick W4 .....46 A4
London SW4 .....61 B2
London W8 .....170 B4
London W14 .....39 C3
St Mary's Rd
London NW10 ....21 A4
London NW11 .....1 A4
London SE15 .....50 B1
St Mary's Stoke
Newington CE Prim
Sch N16 ....7 A2
St Mary's Terr W2 101 B4
St Mary St & St Michael
Prim Sch E1 ....32 B3
St Mary St & St Pancras CE
Prim Sch NW1 ..83 B1
St Mary's Twr EC1 ..97 A1
St Mary's Wlk
SE11 ....149 C4
St Matthews CE
Prim Sch
SE1 ....136 C1
St Matthew's 🔢
SE17 ....48 C4
St Matthew's Lo
NW1 ....83 A2
St Matthew's Rd
SW2 ....62 B2
St Matthew's Row
E2 ....24 C1 99 B2
St Matthews
Westminster
SW1 ....133 C2
St Matthew St
SW1 ....133 B1
St Matthias CE Prim Sch
E2 ....98 C2
St Matthias's CE Prim
Sch N16 ....16 A4
St Maur Rd SW6 ..165 A3
St Michael's Alley
EC3 ....109 C1
St Michael's CE Prim
Sch
NW1 ....82 C3
London N6 ....3 C4
Wandsworth SW18 ..70 B4
St Michaels Ct E14 .34 B4
St Michael's Ct NW11 .1 B4
St Michael's Flats
NW1 ....83 B1
St Michael's Gdns
W10 ....31 A4
St Michael's RC Sch
SE16 ....139 B3
St Michael's Rd NW2 .9 B4
London SW9 ....172 C2
St Michael's St
W2 ....102 A2
St Mildred's Ct
EC2 ....109 B1
St Monica's RC Prim Sch
N1 ....98 B4
St Nicholas' Flats
NW1 ....83 B1
St Nicholas Ho SE8 .51 C4
St Nicholas St SE8 ..51 C2

St Norbert Gn SE4 ..66 A3
St Norbert Rd SE4 ..66 A3
St Olaf's Rd SW6 ..154 B1
St Olaves Ct W2 ...114 A3
St Olave's Ct EC2 ..109 B1
St Olave's Est SE1 .138 B4
St Olave's Gdns
SE11 ....149 B4
St Olave's Mans
SE11 ....149 A4
St Olav's Sq 🔢 SE16 .40 B4
St Osmund's RC Prim
Sch SW13 ......46 B2
St Oswald's Pl
SE11 ....148 C1
St Oswulf St SW1 ..147 C3
St Owen Ho SE1 ...138 B2
St Pancras Almshouses
🔢 NW5 ....12 B3
St Pancras Commercial
Ctr NW1 ....83 A4
St Pancras Hospl
NW1 ....83 A3
St Pancras Sta WC1 .94 A4
St Pancras Way
NW1 ....83 B4
St Patrick's RC Inf Sch
E1 ....32 A1
St Patrick's RC Prim Sch
NW5 ....13 A3
St Paul's Ave SE16 ..32 C1
London NW2 ......9 B2
St Paul's Cath*
EC4 ....108 C1
St Paul's Cath Sch
EC4 ....108 C1
St Paul's CE Prim Sch
SE17 ....150 C2
London NW3 .....12 B1
London W6 ......39 B1
St Paul's Church Yd
EC4 ....108 C1
St Pauls Ct W5 .....36 B4
St Pauls Cres NW1 .13 C1
St Paul's Ct
🔢 London N19 ....5 A2
London SW4 .....61 C4
St Paul's Dr E15 ...19 C3
St Paul's Girls' Sch
W6 ....39 C2
St Pauls Mews NW1 .13 C1
St Pauls Pl N1 .....15 C2
St Pauls Rd N1 ....15 B2
St Paul's Sch SW13 .38 C1
St Paul's Sta EC2 .108 C2
St Paul St N1 ....87 A3
St Paul's Terr SE17 .48 A4
St Pauls View NW1 .95 B3
St Paul's Way E3 ...33 C4
St Paul's Way Com Sch
E3 ....33 C4
St Paul's Whitechapel
CE Prim Sch E1 .125 C3
St Paul's with St
Michael's Prim Sch
E8 ....24 C4
St Paul with St Luke CE
Prim Sch E3 ....33 B4
St Peter's Alley
EC3 ....109 C1
St Petersburgh Mews
W2 ....114 A3
St Petersburgh Pl
W2 ....114 A3
St Peter's CE Prim Sch
SE17 ....151 C1

St Peter's CE Prim Sch
continued
W9 .... 23 C1
St Peter's Church Ct
N1 .... 86 B4
St Peter's CI E2 ...... 24 C3
St Peters CI SW17 .. 72 A2
St Peters Ct SE4 ..... 51 B1
St Peter's Eaton Square
CE Sch SW1 .... 132 B1
St Peter's Gdns
SE27 .... 74 C1
St Peter's Gr W6 .... 38 C2
St Peters Ho WC1 ... 94 B3
St Peter's Ho
4 SE17 .... 48 C4
London N16 .... 7 A4
St Peter's London Docks
CE Prim Sch E1 ..... 32 B1
St Peter's PI W9 ..... 88 A1
St Peter's Prim Sch
W6 .... 38 C1
St Peter's Rd W6 .... 38 C1
St Peter's Sq E2 ..... 24 C3
London W6 .... 38 B1
St Peter's St N1 ..... 86 B3
St Peters & St Pauls RC
Prim Sch EC1 .... 96 B2
St Peter's Street Mews
N1 .... 86 B2
St Peter's Terr
SW6 .... 154 B1
St Peter's Villas 5
W6 .... 38 C2
St Peter's Way N1 ... 16 A1
St Philip Ho WC1 .... 88 A1
St Philip Sq SW8 ... 170 A1
St Philip's Rd E8 .... 16 C2
St Philip's Sch
SW7 .... 142 C4
St Philip St SW8 .... 170 A1
St Philip's Way N1 .. 87 A3
St Quentin Ho
SW18 .... 59 C1
St Quintin Ave W10 . 30 C4
St Quintin Gdns
W10 .... 30 B4
St Regis Hts NW3 ... 2 A1
St Richard of Chichester
RC Sec Sch NW1 ... 13 B1
St Rule St SW8 ...... 170 C1
St Saviours SW4 .... 61 A3
St Saviour's CE Prim Sch
E14 .... 34 A4
W9 .... 88 B3
London SE24 .... 63 B4
St Saviours Ho
SE1 .... 139 B3
St Saviour's RC Prim
Sch SE13 .... 67 B3
St Saviour's Rd SW2 . 62 B2
St Saviour's & St Olaves
CE Sch SE1 .... 137 C1
St Saviour's Wharf
SE1 .... 139 B4
St Scholastica's RC Prim
Sch E5 .... 7 C1
St Simon's Ave
SW15 .... 57 B2
St Stephen's Ave
W12 .... 39 A4
St Stephen's CE Prim
Sch
SW8 .... 162 C2
W2 .... 31 C4
London SE8 .... 51 C1

St Stephen's CE Prim
Sch *continued*
London W12 .... 39 B4
St Stephen's CI
NW8 .... 80 B3
London NW5 .... 12 B3
St Stephen's Cres
W2 .... 31 C3
St Stephen's Gdns
W2 .... 31 C3
5 Putney SW15 ..... 58 B2
St Stephen's Gr
SE13 .... 67 B4
St Stephens Ho 7
SE17 .... 48 C4
St Stephen's Mews
W2 .... 31 C4
St Stephen's Rd E3 . 26 B3
St Stephen's Row
EC4 .... 109 B1
St Stephen's Terr
SW8 .... 162 C1
St Swithin's La
EC4 .... 123 B4
St Swithun's Rd
SE13 .... 67 C2
St Thomas' CE Prim Sch
W10 .... 23 A1
London N16 .... 7 C3
St Thomas' Gdns
NW5 .... 12 C2
St Thomas Ho 2
E1 .... 32 C3
St Thomas More RC Sch
SW3 .... 144 C3
St Thomas of
Canterbury RC Prim
Sch SW6 .... 155 C3
St Thomas' Rd E16 .. 35 C3
St Thomas's Rd W4 .. 45 B4
St Thomas's Hospl
SE1 .... 134 C2
St Thomas's Hospl
Medical Sch SE1 ... 134 C1
St Thomas's PI 20
E9 .... 17 B1
St Thomas's Rd
London N4,N5 .... 5 C1
London NW10 .... 21 A4
St Thomas's Sq E9 .. 17 B1
St Thomas's St SE1 . 123 C1
St Thomas's Way
SW6 .... 155 A2
St Thomas the Apostle
Coll The SE15 .... 50 B2
St Ursula's Convent Sch
SE10 .... 52 C3
St Vincent De Paul Ho
20 E1 .... 32 B4
St Vincent De Paul RC
Prim Sch SW1 ..... 132 C1
St Vincent's RC Prim Sch
W1 .... 103 C3
Acton W3 .... 28 A2
St Vincent St W1 ... 103 C3
St William of York RC
Sec Boys Sch (Upper)
N4 .... 14 A1
Salamanca PI SE1 .. 148 C3
Salamanca St SE1 .. 148 C3
Salcombe Gdns
SW4 .... 61 A3
Salcombe Lo NW5 ... 12 C4

Salcombe Rd 28
N16 .... 16 A3
Salcombe Villas 13
TW10 .... 54 A2
Salcot N4 .... 5 B2
Salcott Rd SW11 .... 60 B2
Salehurst Rd SE4 .... 66 B1
Salem Ho 19 E9 ..... 17 C2
Salem Rd W2 .... 114 B4
Sale PI W2 .... 102 A2
Salesian Coll
SW11 .... 168 A3
Sale St E2 .... 24 C1 99 B2
Salford Ho 4 E14 ... 42 B2
Salford Rd SW12,
SW2 .... 73 C3
Salisbury CI SE17 .. 151 B4
Salisbury Ct EC4 ... 108 A1
SE16 .... 139 C1
London E9 .... 18 A3
London W4 .... 38 A2
Salisbury Ho 3 E14 . 34 A3
London N1 .... 86 A4
E1 .... 109 C4
SW1 .... 147 C2
Wimbledon SW19 ... 69 C1
Salisbury Mews
SW6 .... 154 C1
Salisbury PI SW9 ... 48 A3
Salisbury Rd TW9 ... 54 A3
Salisbury Sq EC4 .. 107 C1
Salisbury St NW8 ... 90 A1
10 Acton W3 .... 37 B4
Salisbury Terr SE15 . 65 B4
Salisbury Wlk N19 .. 4 B2
Salmon La E14 ...... 33 A3
Salmon St 6 E14 .... 33 B3
Saltcoats Rd W4 .... 38 A4
Saltdene N4 .... 5 B3
Salterford Rd SW17 . 72 C2
Salter Ho 10 E14 ... 22 C1
Salters Hall Ct
EC4 .... 123 B4
Salter St 10 E14 .... 33 C2
London NW10 .... 21 C2
Salterton Rd N7 ..... 5 B1
Saltoun Rd SW2,
SW9 .... 62 C3
Saltram Cres W9 ... 23 C2
Saltwell St E14 ..... 33 C2
Saltwood Gr SE17 .. 151 B1
Salusbury Prim Sch
NW6 .... 23 B4
Salusbury Rd NW6 .. 23 A4
Salutation Rd SE10 . 43 A2
Salvin Rd SW15 ..... 57 C4
Salway Ho SW8 .... 172 B4
Salway Rd E15 ...... 19 C2
Salween Ho 2 N16 . 15 C4
Samantha Cl E17 ... 40 A3
Sambrook Ho 19 E1 . 32 B4
Samels Ct W6 .... 38 C1
Samford Ho N1 ..... 85 B3
Samford St NW8 .... 90 A1
Sam Manners Ho 7
SE10 .... 43 A1
Sam March Ho 5
E14 .... 34 C3
Sampson St E1 ..... 125 C1
Samuel Cl E8 .... 24 B4
SE14 .... 50 C4
Samuel Ho 18 E8 ... 24 B4
Samuel Jones Ind Est 18
SE15 .... 49 A3
Samuel Lewis Bldgs
N1 .... 14 C2

Samuel Lewis Trust
Dwellings
SW3 .... 144 A3
SW6 .... 155 C2
6 London SE5 ...... 48 B2
Samuel Rhodes Sch
N1 .... 85 B4
Samuel Richardson Ho
W14 .... 140 C3
Samuel's Cl 2 W6 .. 39 B2
Samuel St SE15 ..... 49 B3
Sancroft Ct SW11 .. 168 B4
Sancroft Ho SE11 .. 149 A2
Sancroft St SE11 ... 149 A2
Sanctuary St SE1 .. 137 A4
Sanctuary The
SW1 .... 133 C2
SE1 .... 32 A1
SW1 .... 133 C2
Sandale Cl N16 ...... 6 C1
Sandall Ho 8 E3 .... 26 A3
Sandall Rd NW5 .... 13 B2
Sandalwood Cl 1
E1 .... 26 A1
Sandalwood Ho 5
NW3 .... 11 A2
Sandbourne NW8 ... 78 B4
4 London W11 ...... 31 C3
Sandbourne Rd SE4 . 51 A1
Sandbrook Rd N16 .. 7 A1
Sandby Ho 6 NW6 .. 23 C4
6 London SE5 ...... 48 C3
Sandcroft Ho SE11 . 149 A2
Sandell St SE1 ..... 135 B4
Sanderling Ct 20
SE8 .... 51 B4
Sanders Ho WC1 ... 95 B4
Sanders Way 3 N19 . 4 C3
Sandfield WC1 ...... 94 B3
Sandford Ct N16 ..... 7 A3
Sandford Row
SE17 .... 151 C2
Sandford St SW6 .. 156 B1
Sandford Wlk SE14 . 51 A4
Sandgate Ho 15 E5 . 17 A4
Sandgate La SW17,
SW18 .... 72 A3
Sandgate St SE15 .. 50 A4
Sandgate Trad Est
SE15 .... 50 A4
Sandham Ct SW4 .. 172 B3
Sandhills The
SW10 .... 157 A4
Sandhurst Ct SW2 .. 62 A3
Sandhurst Ho 14 E1 . 32 B4
Sandilands Rd
SW6 .... 166 A3
Sandison St SE15 ... 64 C4
Sandland St WC1 .. 107 A3
Sandlings Cl SE15 .. 50 A1
Sandmere Rd SW4 .. 62 A3
Sandon Ho 5 SW2 .. 74 A4
Sandown Ho 2 W4 . 37 B1
Sandpiper Cl SE16 .. 41 B4
Sandpiper Ct
14 E14 .... 42 B3
6 SE8 .... 51 C3
Sandridge Ct N4 .... 6 B2
Sandridge St 2 N19 . 4 B2

Sandringham Cl 1
SW19 .... 69 C3
Sandringham Ct
18 SE16 .... 32 C1
W1 .... 105 A1
W9 .... 89 A3
Putney SW15 .... 57 C1
Sandringham Flats
WC2 .... 119 C4
Sandringham Ho
W14 .... 140 A4
Richmond TW10 ..... 54 C2
Sandringham Rd
London E8 .... 16 B3
London NW11 .... 1 A4
London NW2 .... 9 A2
Sandrock Rd SE13 .. 66 C4
Sands End La SW6 . 166 B4
Sandstone TW9 ..... 44 C3
Sandstone Pl N19 .... 4 A2
Sandways 6 TW9 ... 44 C2
Sandwell Cres 2
NW6 .... 10 C2
Sandwell Mans 3
NW6 .... 10 C2
Sandwich Ho
9 SE16 .... 40 B4
WC1 .... 94 A3
Sandwich St WC1 ... 94 A3
Sandycombe Rd
TW9 .... 44 C1
Sandy La N6 .... 4 B4
Sandy's Row E1 .... 110 B3
Sanford La 3 N16 ... 7 B2
Sanford St SE14,SE8 . 51 A4
Sanford Terr N16 ..... 7 B1
Sangora Rd 17
SW11 .... 59 C3
Sankey Ho 2 E2 .... 25 B3
Sansom St SE5 ...... 48 C3
London SE5 .... 48 C2
Sans Wlk EC1 ...... 96 A2
Santley Ho SE1 ..... 135 C3
Santley St SW4 ..... 62 B3
Santos Rd SW18 .... 58 C2
Sapcote Trad Ctr
NW10 .... 8 B2
Saperton Wlk
SE11 .... 149 A4
Sapperton Ct EC1 ... 96 C2
Sapphire Ct E1 ..... 125 B4
Sapphire Rd SE8 .... 41 A2
Saracen St E14 ..... 33 C3
Sarah Ho 11 E1 ..... 32 A3
Roehampton SW15 .. 56 B3
Sarah Swift Ho
SE1 .... 137 C4
Sara Lane Ct 31 N1 . 24 A3
Saratoga Rd E5 ..... 17 B4
Sardinia St WC2 ... 106 C2
Sarjant Path SW19 . 69 C2
Sark Ho 8 N1 .... 15 B2
Sarnesfield Ho
SE15 .... 50 A4
Sarratt Ho W10 ..... 30 B4
Sarre Rd NW2 .... 10 B3
Sarsden Bldgs W1 . 103 C1
Sarsfeld Rd SW12,
SW17 .... 72 B3
Sartor Rd SE15 ..... 65 C3
Sarum Hall Sch
NW3 .... 12 A1
Sarum Ho W11 .... 113 A3
Satchwell Rd E2 .... 99 B3

Saul Ct **4** SE15 .... 49 B4
Saunders Cl **14** E14 .33 B2
Saunders Ho **11**
SW2 .... 74 C3
Saunders Ness Rd
E14 .... 42 C2
Saunders St SE11 ..149 B4
Savage Gdns **2** 124 B4
Savana N16 .... 7 A2
Savannah Cl 9
SE15 .... 49 B3
Savernake Ho N4 .... 6 C4
Savernake Rd NW3 .12 B4
Saville Rd W4 .... 37 C3
Savill Ho **2** SW4 .... 62 A2
Savona St SW8 ......160 C1
Savoy Bldgs WC2 .. 29 B2
Savoy Circus W3 ...29 B2
Savoy Ct SW5 ....141 C4
WC2 ....120 B3
Savoy Hill WC2 ....120 C3
Savoy Pier WC2 .....120 C3
Savoy Pl WC2 ....120 C3
Savoy Row WC2 .....120 C3
Savoy St WC2 ....120 C3
Savoy Steps WC2 ..120 C3
Savoy Way WC2 .....120 C3
Sawkins Cl SW19 ....70 A2
Sawley Rd W12 ....29 C1
Sawmill Yd E3 ....26 A4
Sawyer St SE1 ....122 B1
Saxby Rd SW2 ....74 A4
Saxonbury Ct
2 London N7 ....14 A3
10 London N7 ....13 C3
Saxoncroft Ho
SW16 .... 73 C1
Saxon Dr W3 ....28 A4
Saxonfield Cl SW2 ..74 B4
Saxon Hall W2 ....114 A3
Saxon Ho **4** SW4 ..61 C3
Saxon Rd E3 .... 26 B3
Saxton Cl SE13 ....67 C4
Sayer Ho SE4 ....66 A3
Sayes Court St **5** ..51 B4
Sayes Ct SE8 ....51 B4
Scafell NW1 ....92 C4
Scala St W1 ....105 A4
Scampston Mews **5**
W10 .... 30 C3
Scandrett St **30** E1 ..32 A1
Scarba Wlk N1 ....15 C2
Scarborough Rd N4 ..5 C3
Scarborough St
E1 ....111 A1
Scarlette Manor Wlk 10
SE24 .... 75 A2
Scarsbrook Ho **2**
SW2 .... 62 C1
Scarsdale Pl W8 ...128 A2
Scarsdale Villas
W8 ....127 C1
Scarth Rd SW13 ......56 B4
Scawen Rd SE8 ....41 A1
Scawfell St E2 ....24 B3
Sceptre Ho 9 E1 .....25 B1
Sceptre Rd E2 ....25 B2
Schofield Wlk SE3 ..53 C3
Sch of Nursing
W1 ....104 C4
Sch of Pharmacy
WC1 .... 94 B2
Scholars Rd SW12 ..73 B3
Scholefield Rd N19 .. 4 C3

Scholey Ho SW11 ...60 A4
Schomberg Ho
SW1 ....147 C4
Schonfeld Sq N16 .... 6 C3
School App E2 ....98 B4
Schoolbank Rd
SE10 .... 43 B3
School Bell Cloisters **15**
E3 .... 26 C2
Schoolbell Mews **16**
E3 .... 26 A3
School Flats SW8 ...172 A3
School Ho SE1 ....152 A4
Schoolhouse La **1** ..32 C2
School of Finance &
Management N1 ...14 B2
School Rd NW10 .....20 C1
School Sq SE10 ....43 B3
Schooner Cl E14 .....42 C3
1 SE16 .... 40 C4
Schubert Rd SW15 ..58 B2
Science Mus★
SW7 ....129 B1
Sclater St E1 ....99 A2
Scoles Cres SW2 .....74 C3
Scoresby St SE1 ....122 A1
Scorton Ho **2** N1 ...24 A3
Scotch Ho★ SW1 ...130 C3
Scoter Ct **22** SE8 ....51 B4
Scotia Bldg **16** E1 ..32 C2
Scotia Ct **3** SE16 ....40 B3
Scotia Rd **2** SW2 ..74 C4
Scotland Pl SW1 ....120 A1
Scotney Ho E9 ....17 B2
Scotson Ho SE11 ...149 B3
Scotswood St EC1 ..95 C2

Scott Ct
17 London N16 .... 7 C2
London SW11 ......170 B1
London W4 ....37 C4
Scott Ellis Gdns
NW8 .... 89 B3
Scott Ho N1 ....87 B4
NW8 .... 90 A1
London N7 ....14 B2
Scott Lidgett Cres
SE16 ....139 C3
Scotts Ct **6** W12 ....39 A4
Scott's Rd W12 ....39 A4
Scott's Sufferance
Wharf SE1 ....139 A3
Scott St E1 ....25 A1
Scott's Yd EC4 ....123 B4
Scoulding Ho **8**
E14 .... 41 C3
Scoulding Rd E16 ...35 C3
Scouler St E14 ....34 C2
Scout App NW10 ..... 8 A4
Scovell Cres SE1 ...136 C3
Scovell Rd SE1 ....136 C3
Scriven Ct **2** E8 .....24 B4
Scriven St E8 ....24 B4
Scrooby St SE6 ....67 A1
Scrope Bldg EC1 ...107 C3
Scrubs La NW10,
W10,W12 ....22 A2
Scrutton Cl SW12 ..73 C4
Scrutton St
EC2 ....24 A1 98 A1
Scutari Rd SE22 ......65 B2
Scylla Rd SE15 ....65 A4
Seabright St **4**
E2 ....25 A2
Seacole Cl W3 ....28 C4
Seaford Ho **3** SE16 .40 B3
Seaford St WC1 ....94 B3
Seaforth Cres N5 .....15 B3

Seaforth Lo **2**
SW13 .... 46 B1
Seaforth Pl SW1 ....133 A2
Seager Pl **3** E3 ......33 B4
Seagrave Lo SW6 ..155 C4
Seagrave Rd SW6 ..155 C4
Seagrove Cl E1 ....32 C4
Seal Ho SE1 ....137 C2
Seal St E8 ....16 B4
Searle Pl N4 .... 5 B3
Searles Cl SW11 ....158 B1
Searles Rd SE1 ....151 C4
Searson Ho SE17 ...150 B3
Sears St SE5 ....48 C3
Seasalter Ho **4**
SW9 ....173 B4
Seaton Cl
SW15 ....69 A3 150 A2
Seaton Point E5 ......16 C4
Seavington Ho
SE5 ....64 A4
Sebastian Ho **25** N1 .24 A3
Sebastian St EC1 .....96 B3
Sebbon St N1 ....15 A1
Sebright Ho **21** E2 ..24 C3
Sebright Sch E2 ......24 C3
Secker Ho SW9 ....48 A1
Secker St SE1 ....121 B1
Second Ave W10 .....23 A2
London W3 ....29 B1
Mortlake SW14 .....56 A4
Sedan Way SE17 ...152 A2
Sedding St SW1 .....145 B4
Seddon Ho EC2 .....108 C4
Seddon St WC1 ....95 A3
Sedgeford Rd W12 ..29 B1
Sedgewick Ho
SW19 .... 69 C2
Sedgley Ho N4 .... 5 B2
Sedgmoor Pl SE5 ...49 A3
Sedgwick St E9 ......17 C3
Sedleigh Rd SW18 ..58 B1
Sedlescombe Rd
SW6 ....155 B4
Sedley Ho SE11 ....149 A2
Sedley Pl W1 ....104 A1
Seething La EC3 ....124 B4
Sefkon St SW15 .....57 B4
Sekforde St EC1 ......96 A2
Selborne **3** 60 C4
Selborne Ho SE1 ...137 B3
Selborne Rd **1** SE5 .48 C1
Selby Ho
10 London SW4 ....61 B1
6 London W10 .... 23 A2
Selby St E1 ....24 C1 99 C1
Selden Ho **2** SE15 ..50 B1
Selden Rd SE15 ......50 B1
Selden Wlk N7 .... 5 B2
Seldon Ho SW1 .....146 C1
SW8 ....160 C1
Selfridges★ 103 C1
Selhurst Cl SW19 ...69 C3
Selina Ho NW8 ....89 C2
Selkirk Ho N1 ....84 C4
4 London N16 .... 7 A1
Sellons Ave NW10 ..21 B4
Selma Ho **2** W12 ...30 A3
Selman Ho **3** E9 ....18 A2
Selsdon Way E14 ...42 A3
Selsea Pl N16 ....16 A3
Selsey St E14 ....33 C4
Selwood Ho **1** N4 ... 6 C4
Selwood Pl SW7 ....143 B2
Selwood Terr SW7 143 B2
Selworthy Ho
SW11 ....167 C4

Selwyn Ave TW9 .....54 B4
Selwyn Ct **8** TW10 .54 B2
Selwyn Ho **3** SW15 .57 C2
Selwyn Rd E3 ....26 B3
London NW10 .... 8 A1
Semley Gate E9 ....18 B2
Semley Ho SW1 .....146 A3
Semley Pl SW1 ......146 A3
Senate St SE15 ....50 B1
Senators Lo **23** E3 ..26 A3
Sendall Ct **18** SW11 .59 C4
Senior St W2 ....100 A4
Senrab St E1 ....32 C3
Seraph Ct EC1 ....96 C4
Serenaders Rd
SW9 ....173 B1
Sergeant Ind Est The
SW18 .... 59 A1
Serica Ct **14** SE10 ..52 B3
Serjeant's Inn EC4 107 C1
Serlby Ct W14 ....126 C2
Serle St WC2 ....107 A2
Sermon La EC4 .....108 C1
Serpentine Ct 10
SE16 .... 40 C4
Serpentine Gallery★
W2 ....129 C4
Serpentine Rd W2 116 C1
Serpentine The★
W2 ....116 B1
Service Route No 1
E15 ....19 C1
Service Route No 2
E15 ....19 C1
Service Route No 3
E15 ....19 C1
Servite Ho SE13 ......52 A2
Service RC Prim Sch
SW10 ....156 C4
Setchell Rd SE1 .....152 C4
Setchell Way SE1 ..152 C4
Seth St **18** SE16 .....40 B4
Settlers Ct **2** E14 ...34 C2
Settles St E1 ....111 C2
Settrington Rd
SW6 ....166 A1
Seven Dials WC2 ...106 A1
Seven Mills Prim Sch
E14 .... 41 C4
Sevenoaks Rd SE4 .66 B1
Seven Sisters Rd N4,
N7,N15 ....6 B4
Seven Stars Cnr
W12 .... 38 C3
Severnake Cl E14 ...41 C2
Severn Way NW10 .. 8 B3
Severus Rd SW11 ...60 A3
Seville Ho E1 ....125 C1
Seville Mews N1 .....16 A1
Seville St SW1 ....131 A3
Sevington St W9 .....88 A1
Seward St EC1 ....96 C3
Sewardstone Rd E2 .25 B3
Sewell Ho **7** N16 ....16 A3
Sextant Ave E14 .....42 C2
Sexton's Ho **5** SE13 52 B4
Seymour Ct
London N16 .... 7 C3
Putney SW15 ....57 A3
Seymour Gdns SE4 .66 A4
Seymour Ho NW1 ...93 C3
WC1 .... 94 A2
London SW8 ....171 A2
Seymour Mews
W1 ....103 B2
Seymour Pl W1 .....102 C2

Seymour Rd
Acton W4 ....37 B2
Wandsworth SW18 .58 B1
Wimbledon SW19 ..69 C1
Seymour St W1 ......103 A1
SW1 ....103 A1
Seymour Wlk
SW10 ....156 C4
Seyssel St E14 ....42 B2
Shaa Rd W3 ....28 C2
Shackleton Ct
2 Dulwich SE21 ...75 C2
4 London W12 ....39 A4
5 Millwall E14 ....41 C1
1 ....32 B1
Shacklewell Ho **8**
E8 .... 16 B4
Shacklewell La E8 ..16 B3
Shacklewell Prim Sch
E8 .... 16 B4
Shacklewell Rd N16 16 B4
Shacklewell Row
E8 .... 16 B4
Shacklewell St E2 ...99 A3
Shad Thames SE1 ..139 A4
Shadwell Gdns E1 ..32 B2
Shadwell Pierhead
E1 .... 32 B2
Shadwell Sta E1 .....32 A2
Shaftesbury Ave
W1 ....119 C4
Shaftesbury Ct N1 ..87 B1
SE1 ....137 B1
1 London SE5 ......63 C3
Shaftesbury Gdns
NW10 .... 21 A1
Shaftesbury Ho
W2 ....114 B4
2 London N16 .... 7 A1
E14 .... 34 A3
Shaftesbury Mews
W8 ....127 C1
Shaftesbury Park
Chambers **1**
SW11 .... 60 C4
Shaftesbury Rd
London N4,N19 ..... 5 A3
Richmond TW9 .....54 A4
Shaftesbury St N1 ..87 B1
Shafteswood Ct
SW17 .... 72 B1
Shafto Mews SW1 ..131 A1
Shafton Rd E9 ....25 C4
Shaftsbury Ct SW6 166 B3
Shaftsbury Mews **2**
SW4 .... 61 B2
Shaftsbury Park Prim
Sch SW11 ....60 C4
Shafts Cl EC3 ....110 A1
Shahjalal Ho **18** E2 24 C3
Shakespeare Ave
NW10 .... 20 C4
Shakespeare Cres
NW10 .... 20 C4
Shakespeare Ho **3**
E9 .... 17 B1
Shakespeare Rd
London SE24 ....63 A3
London W3 ....28 B1
Shakespeare's Globe
Theatre (site of)
SE1 ....123 A2
Shakespeare Twr
EC2 ....109 A4
Shakspeare Mews **7**
N16 ....16 A4

Shakspeare Wlk
 N16 . . . . .16 A4
Shalbourne Sq E9 . . .18 B2
Shalcomb St SW10 .157 A3
Shalden Ho **6**
 SW15 . . . . .56 B1
Shalfleet Dr W10 . . .30 C2
Shalford Ho SW10 . . .21 C4
Shalford St N1 . . . . . .86 A2
Shalford Rd Se1 . . .137 C2
Shalimar Gdns W3 . .28 B2
Shalimar Lo W3 . . . . .28 B2
Shalimar Rd W3 . . . .28 B2
Shalstone Rd SW14,
 TW9 . . . . .55 A4
Shamrock St SW4 . . .61 C4
Shandon Rd SW4 . . .61 B1
Shand St SE1 . . . . . .138 B4
Shandy St E1 . . . . . . .25 C1
Shannon Ct
 London N16 . . . . .7 A1
 London NW10 . . . . . . .8 C2
Shannon Gr SW9 . . . .62 B3
Shannon Pl NW8 . . . .80 B2
Shanti Cl SW18 . . . . .70 C3
Shapla Prim Sch
 E1 . . . . .125 C3
Shardcroft Ave
 SE24 . . . . .63 A2
Shardeloes Rd SE14 .51 B1
Shard's Sq SE15 . . . .49 C4
Sharebourne Ho
 SW2 . . . . .62 C2
Sharmbrook Ho
 W6 . . . . .155 B4
Sharon Gdns E9 . . . .25 B4
Sharon Rd W4 . . . . . .37 C1
Sharp Ho SW8 . . . . . .61 A4
Sharples Hall St **8**
 NW1 . . . . .12 B1
Sharpness Ct **2**
 SE15 . . . . .49 B3
Sharratt St SE15 . . . .50 B4
Sharstead St SE17 .150 A1
Sharwell Ho SW18 . .59 A1
Sharwood WC1 . . . . .85 A1
Shaver's Pl SW1 . . .119 B3
Shawbury Ct SE22 . .64 B2
Shawbury Rd SE22 . .64 B2
Shaw Ct London N19 . .5 A2
 12 London SW11 . . .59 C4
 8 London W3 . . . . . .37 B3
Shawfield St SW3 . .144 B1
Shawford Ct **6**
 SW15 . . . . .68 C4
Shaw Rd SE22 . . . . . .64 A3
Shearling Way N7 . . .14 A2
Shearsmith Ho E1 . .125 C4
Shearwater Ct **24**
 SE8 . . . . .51 B4
Sheen Common Dr
 SW14,TW10 . . . . .54 C2
Sheen Court Rd
 TW10 . . . . .54 C3
Sheen Ct TW10 . . . . .54 C3
Sheendale Rd TW9 . .54 B3
Sheen Gate Gdns
 SW14 . . . . .55 B3
Sheen Gr N1 . . . . .85 B4
Sheen La SW14 . . . . .55 B3
Sheen Mount JMI Sch
 SW14 . . . . .55 A2
Sheen Pk TW10,TW9 .54 A3
Sheen Rd TW10,TW9 .54 A3
Sheen Wood SW14 . .55 B2
Sheepcote La
 SW11 . . . . .169 A1

Sheep La E8 . . . . .25 A4
Sheffield Ho **14**
 SE15 . . . . .49 B2
Sheffield Sq **3** E3 . .26 B2
Sheffield St WC2 . . .106 C1
Sheffield Terr
 W8 . . . . .31 C1 113 C1
Shelburne Ho
 N19 . . . . .4 C4
Shelburne Ct SW15 .57 C2
Shelburne Rd N7 . . . . .5 B1
Shelbury Rd SE22 . . .65 A2
Sheldon Cl SW8 . . . .162 A1
Sheldon Ho **8** E9 . .17 C2
Sheldon Rd NW2 . . . . .9 C4
Sheldrake Ho **15**
 SE16 . . . . .40 C2
Sheldrake Pl W8 . . .127 B4
Shelduck Ct **20** SE8 .51 B4
Shelford Pl N16 . . . . .6 C1
Shelgate Rd SW11 . .60 B2
Shell Cls ∫ SE11 . . .121 A1
Shelley Cl SE15 . . . . .50 A1
Shelley Ct SW3 . . . .159 A4
 London N4 . . . . .5 B3
Shelley Ho **2** E2 . . .25 B2
 SW1 . . . . .160 C4
 9 London N16 . . . . .16 A4
Shelley Rd NW10 . . . .20 C4
Shelley Sch SE11 . . .149 C3
Shellness Rd E5 . . . . .17 A3
Shell Rd SE13 . . . . . .67 A4
Shellwood Rd
 SW11 . . . . .168 C1
Shelmerdine Cl E3 . .33 C4
Shelton St WC2 . . . .106 A1
 Shene Bldg EC1 . . . .107 C3
Shene Int Sch SW14 .56 A3
Shenfield St N1 . . . . .24 A3
Shenley Rd SE5 . . . . .49 A2
Shepherd Cl W1 . . . .117 B4
Shepherdess Pl N1 . .97 A4
Shepherdess Wlk
 N1 . . . . .87 A1
Shepherd Ho
 10 E14 . . . . .34 A3
 London N7 . . . . .14 A2
Shepherd Mkt W1 . .118 A1
Shepherd's Bush
 (Central Line) Sta
 W12 . . . . .39 C4
Shepherd's Bush Gn
 W12 . . . . .39 B4
Shepherd's Bush (Hamm
 & City) Sta W12 . . . .30 B1
Shepherd's Bush Market
 W12 . . . . .39 B4
Shepherd's Bush Pl
 W12 . . . . .39 C4
Shepherd's Bush Rd
 W6 . . . . .39 B3
Shepherds Ct **6**
 W12 . . . . .39 C4
Shepherd's La E9 . . .17 C2
Shepherds Pl W1 . . .117 B4
Shepherd St W1 . . . .118 A1
Shepherd's Wlk
 NW3 . . . . .11 C4
Sheppard Dr SE16 . .40 A1
Sheppard Ho **20** E2 .24 C3
 4 London SW11 . . .59 C4
 8 Stretham SW2 . .74 C3
Shepperton Rd N1 . .87 B4
Sheppey Ho **10** E5 . .17 A4
Sheppey Wlk N1 . . . .15 B1

Shepton Ct SW11 . .167 C4
Shepton Hos **11** E2 . .25 B2
Sherard Ct N19 . . . . . .5 A1
Sherard Ho **2** E9 . . .17 B1
Sheraton St W1 . . . .105 B1
Sherborne Ho
 SW1 . . . . .146 B2
 SW8 . . . . .162 C1
Sherborne La EC4 . .123 C4
Sherborne St N1 . . . .87 B4
Sherbrooke Ho **8**
 E2 . . . . .25 B3
Sherbrooke Rd
 SW6 . . . . .154 B1
Sherbrooke Terr
 SW6 . . . . .154 B1
Shere Ho SE1 . . . . . .137 B2
Sherfield Gdns
 SW15 . . . . .56 B1
Sheridan Bldgs
 WC2 . . . . .106 B1
Sheridan Ct SW9 . . .172 C1
 London NW6 . . . . . . .11 B1
Sheridan Ho **10** E1 . .32 B3
 SE11 . . . . .149 C3
 7 London N16 . . . . .7 A1
Sheridan Pl SW13 . . .56 B4
Sheridan St **22** E1 . .32 A3
Sheridon Ct SW5 . . .142 A3
Sheringdale Prim Sch
 SW18 . . . . .70 B3
Sheringham NW8 . . .79 C4
Sheringham Ho
 NW1 . . . . .102 B4
Sheringham Rd N7 .14 C2
Sherlock Ct NW8 . . . .79 B4
Sherlock Holmes Mus
 NW1 . . . . .91 A1
Sherlock Mews
 W1 . . . . .103 B4
Sherrick Green Rd
 NW10 . . . . .9 A3
Sherriff Ct NW6 . . . .10 C2
Sherriff Rd NW6 . . . .10 C2
Sherrin Rd E10 . . . . .19 A4
Sherston Ct SE1 . . . .150 B4
 WC1 . . . . .95 B3
Sherwin Ho SE11 . . .163 B4
Sherwin Rd SE14 . . .50 C2
Sherwood Ho N4 . . . .6 B4
Sherwood Cl SW13 .57 A4
Sherwood Ct W1 . . .102 C3
 London SE13 . . . . . . .52 A1
 4 London SW11 . . .59 B4
Sherwood Gdns
 E14 . . . . .41 C2
 SE16 . . . . .40 A1
Sherwood St W1 . . .119 A4
Shetland Rd E3 . . . . .26 B3
Shillaker Ct W3 . . . . .29 B1
Shillibeer Pl W1 . . . .102 B3
Shillingford Ho **26**
 E3 . . . . .27 A2
Shillingford St **21**
 N1 . . . . .15 A1
Shillingstone Ho
 W14 . . . . .126 B1
Shinfield St W12 . . . .30 B3
Shipka Rd SW12 . . . .73 A3
Ship La SW14 . . . . . .45 B1
Shiplake Ho **2** E2 . .98 C3
Shipley Ho SW8 . . . .171 B1
Ship & Mermaid Row
 SE1 . . . . .138 A4
Ship St SE8 . . . . .51 C2

Ship Tavern Pas
 EC3 . . . . .124 A4
Shipton Ho **10** E2 . . .24 B3
 7 NW5 . . . . .12 C2
Shipton St E2 24 C3 99 A4
Shipwright Rd SE16 .41 A4
Shipwright Yd SE1 .124 A1
Shirbutt St E14 . . . . .34 A2
Shire Pl SW18 . . . . . .71 B4
Shirland Mews W9 . .23 B2
Shirland Rd W9 . . . . .23 C1
Shirley Gr SW11 . . . .60 C4
 London W4 **8** SE5 . . .48 C3
Shirley Ho **5** SE5 . . .48 C3
Shirley Rd W4 . . . . . .37 C4
Shirley St E16 . . . . . .35 B1
Shirlock Rd NW3 . . . .12 B4
Shoe La EC4 . . . . . . .107 C2
Shooters Hill Rd
 SE3,SE10 . . . . .53 A2
Shoot-Up Hill NW2 .10 A2
Shore Bsns Ctr **31**
 E9 . . . . .17 B1
Shoreditch Ct **8** E8 .16 B1
Shoreditch High St
 E2 . . . . .24 A1 98 B2
Shoreditch Sta
 E1 . . . . .24 B1 99 A1
Shoreham Cl SW18 .59 A2
Shore Gr SW8 . . . . . .61 A4
Shore Mews **30** E9 . .17 B1
Shore Pl E9 . . . . .17 B1
Shore Rd E9 . . . . .17 B1
Shorncliffe Rd
 SE1 . . . . .152 C2
Shorrolds Rd SW6 .155 A2
Shortcroft Mead Ct
 NW10 . . . . .8 C3
Shorter St EC3 . . . . .125 A4
Shortlands W6 . . . . . .39 C2
Short Rd W4 . . . . .46 A4
Shorts Gdns WC2 . .106 A1
Short St SE1 . . . . . . .135 C4
Shottendane Rd
 SW6 . . . . .165 B4
Shottfield Ave
 SW14 . . . . .56 A3
Shottsford **11** W11 . .31 C3
Shoulder of Mutton
 Alley **10** E14 . . . . . . .33 A2
Shouldham St W1 . .102 B3
Shreveport Ho **23**
 N19 . . . . .4 C4
Shrewsbury Ave
 SW14 . . . . .55 C3
Shrewsbury Cres
 NW10 . . . . .20 C4
Shrewsbury Ho
 SE11 . . . . .163 A3
 SW3 . . . . .158 A3
Shrewsbury Mews **33**
 W2 . . . . .31 C3
Shrewsbury Rd W2 .31 C3
Shrewsbury St W10 .22 B1
Shropshire Pl WC1 . .93 A1
Shroton St NW1 . . . .102 B4
Shrubland Rd E8 . . . .24 C4
Shrubs Ho SW1 . . . .147 C3
Shubbery Cl N1 . . . . .87 A3
Shurland Gdns SE15 .49 B3
Shuters Sq W14 . . . .140 C1
Shuttle St E1 24 C1 99 B1
Shuttleworth Rd
 SW11 . . . . .168 A2
Sibella Rd SW4 . . . . .171 C1
Sicilian Ave WC1 . . .106 B3
Sidbury St SW6 . . . .164 A4
Sidding Ho

Sha – Sim 251
Siddons Ho W2 . . . .101 C3
 6 London NW3 . . . . .12 B3
Siddons La NW1 . . . .91 A1
Sidford Ho SE1 . . . . .135 A1
Sidford Pl SE1 . . . . . .135 A1
Sidgwick Ho SW9 . .172 B1
Sidings Mews N7 . . .14 C4
Sidlaw Ho N16 . . . . . . .7 B3
Sidmouth Ho
 18 SE15 . . . . .49 C3
 W1 . . . . .102 B2
 8 Stretham SW2 . .74 C4
Sidmouth Par NW2 . . .9 B1
Sidmouth Rd NW2 . . .9 B1
Sidmouth St WC1 . . .94 C3
Sidney Boyd Ct
 NW6 . . . . .10 C1
Sidney Godley (VC) Ho
 51 E2 . . . . .25 B2
Sidney Gr EC1 . . . . . .86 A1
Sidney Ho **4** E2 . . . .25 B3
Sidney Miller Ct **3**
 W3 . . . . .28 A1
Sidney Rd SW9 . . . .173 A1
Sidney Sq E1 . . . . . . .32 B4
Sidney St E1 . . . . .32 B4
Sidworth St **6** E8 . . .17 A1
Siebert Rd SE3 . . . . .53 C4
Siege Ho **20** E1 . . . . .32 A3
Sigdon Rd E8 . . . . . . .16 C3
Signmakers Yd
 NW1 . . . . .82 B3
Silbury Ho **9** SE26 . .76 C1
Silbury St N1 . . . . . . .97 B4
Silchester Rd W10 . .30 C3
Silesia Bldgs E8 . . . .17 A1
Silex St SE1 . . . . . . .136 B3
Silk Mills Path SE13 .67 B4
Silk Mills Sq E3 . . . . .18 B2
Silk St EC2 . . . . .109 A4
Sillitoe Ho N1 . . . . . . .87 C3
Silsoe Ho NW1 . . . . . .82 B1
Silverbirch Wlk **1**
 NW3 . . . . .12 C2
Silverburn Ho **4**
 SW9 . . . . .48 A2
Silver Cl SE14 . . . . . .51 A3
Silver Cres W4 . . . . .37 A2
Silver Ct N19 . . . . .4 B1
Silverdale NW1 . . . . .92 C4
Silverdale Ct EC1 . . .96 A2
Silvermere Rd SE6 . .67 A1
Silver Pl W1 . . . . . . .119 A4
Silver Rd W12 . . . . . .30 C2
Silverthorne NW6 . . .78 B3
Silverthorne Rd
 SW8 . . . . .170 B1
Silverton Rd W6 . . . .47 D4
Silvertown Way E16 .35 C1
Silver Wlk SE16 . . . . .33 B1
Silvester Ho **17** E1 . .32 A3
 22 E2 . . . . .25 B2
 2 W11 . . . . .31 B3
Silvester Rd SE22 . .64 B2
Silvester St SE1 . . . .137 B3
Silwood St SE16 . . . .40 B1
Simla Ho SE1 . . . . . .137 C3
Simmons Ho **2**
 London N7 . . . . .5 B2
Simms Ct SW6 . . . . .58 A4
Simms Rd SE1 . . . . .153 C3
Simon Cl
 W11 . . . . . .31 A2 113 A4
Simon Ct W9 . . . . . . .23 C2
Simon Lo **51** SW19 .69 C3

Simon Marks (Jewish)
Prim Sch N16 . . . . . . .7 B2
Simons Wlk E15 . . . . .19 C3
Simpson Dr W3 . . . . .28 C3
Simpson Ho NW8 . . . .89 A3
SE11 . . . . .148 C1
Simpson's Rd E14 . . .34 A2
Simpson St SW11 . . .168 A1
Sinclair Ct N5 . . . . . .15 A2
Sinclair Gdns W14 . .39 C4
Sinclair Ho 1
SW12 . . . . .73 C3
Sinclair Mans 6
W12 . . . . .39 C4
Sinclair Rd W14 . . . .126 A2
Sinclairs Ho 14 E3 . . .26 B3
Singer St EC2 . . . . . .97 C3
Sion-Manning RC Sch for Girls
W10 . . . . .31 A4
London W10 . . . . .30 C4
Sir Abraham Dawes Cotts SW15 . . . . . . .58 A3
Sir Alexander Cl
W3 . . . . .29 B1
Sir Alexander Rd
W3 . . . . .29 B1
Sirdar Rd
W11 . . . . .31 A2 112 A3
Sir Francis Drake Prim Sch SE8 . . . . .41 A1
Sirinham Point
SW8 . . . . .163 A3
Sirius Bldg 11 E1 . . . .125 C3
Sir James Barrie Prim Sch SW8 . . . . .171 A3
Sir John Cass Foundation & Redcoat CE Sec Sch E1 . . .32 C4
Sir John Cass's Prim Sch EC3 . . . . .110 B1
Sir John Kirk Cl 13
SE5 . . . . .48 B3
Sir John Lillie Prim Sch
SW6 . . . . .154 B3
Sir Oswald Stoll Foundation The
SW6 . . . . .156 A2
Sir Thomas Abney Sch
N16 . . . . .6 C3
Sir Thomas More Est
SW3 . . . . .157 C3
Sir William Burrough Prim Sch E14 . . . . . .33 A3
Sir William Powell's Almshos SW6 . . . .58 A4
Sise La EC4 . . . . . . .109 B1
Siskin Ho 14 SE16 . . .40 C2
Sispara Gdns SW18 . .58 B1
Sissinghurst Ho 17
SE15 . . . . .50 B4
Sister Mabel's Way 14
SE15 . . . . .49 C3
Sisters Ave SW11 . . . .60 B3
Sistova Rd SW12 . . . .73 A3
Sisulu Pl SW9 . . . . . .62 C4
Site of Changing of the Guard SW1 . . . .132 C3
Sivill Ho E2 . . . . .99 A4
Siward Rd SW17 . . . .71 B1
Six Bridges Ind Est
SE1 . . . . .153 C1
Sixth Ave W10 . . . . . .23 A2
Skardu Rd NW2 . . . . . .10 A3

Skeena Hill SW18,
SW19 . . . . .70 A4
Skeggs Ho 5 E14 . . . .42 B3
Skegness Ho 3 N7 . . .14 B1
Skelbrook St SW18 . . .71 A3
Skelgill Rd SW15 . . . .58 B3
Skelton Cl 7 E8 . . . . .16 B2
Skelton Ho N16 . . . . .16 A3
Skelwith Rd W6 . . . . .47 C4
Skenfrith Ho SE15 . . .50 A4
Sketchley Gdns
SE16 . . . . .40 C1
Skiffington Cl SW2 . . .74 C3
Skinner Pl SW1 . . . .145 B3
Skinners Company
(Upper) N16 . . . . .7 C4
Skinners La EC4 . . . .123 A4
Skinner St EC1 . . . . . .95 C2
Skipsea Ho SW18 . . . .59 C1
Skipton Ho SE4 . . . . . .66 A3
Skipwith Bldg EC1 . .107 C3
Skipworth Rd E9 . . . . .25 B4
Skua Ct 22 SE8 . . . . . .51 B4
Skyline Ct SE1 . . . . .138 C2
Skylines E14 . . . . . . .42 B4
Slade Ct NW2 . . . . . . .10 A3
Sladen Pl 13 E5 . . . . .17 A4
Slade Wlk SE17 . . . . .48 B4
Slagrove Pl SE13 . . . .67 A2
Slaidburn St SW10 . .157 A3
Slaithwaite Rd SE13 . .67 B3
Slaney Ct NW10 . . . . .9 B1
Slaney Pl 8 N7 . . . . . .14 C3
Sleaford Ho 10 E3 . . . .26 C1
Sleaford Ind Est
SW8 . . . . .161 A1
Sleaford St SW8 . . . .161 A1
Sleat Ho 9 E3 . . . . . . .26 B3
Slievemore Cl 8
SW4 . . . . .61 C4
Sligo Ho 3 E1 . . . . . . .25 C1
Slingsby Pl WC2 . . . .120 A4
Slippers Pl SE16 . . . . .40 A3
Sloane Ave SW3 . . . .144 B3
Sloane Avenue Mans
SW3 . . . . .144 C3
Sloane Ct E SW3 . . . .145 B2
Sloane Ct W SW3 . . .145 B2
Sloane Gate Mans
SW1 . . . . .145 B4
Sloane Gdns SW1 . . .145 B3
Sloane Ho 7 E9 . . . . .17 B1
Sloane Sq SW1 . . . . .145 A3
Sloane Square Sta
SW1 . . . . .145 B3
Sloane St SW1 . . . . .131 A1
Sloane Terr SW1 . . . .145 B4
Sloane Terr Mans
SW1 . . . . .145 B4
Slomon Ho 2 W10 . . .23 A2
Sly St 7 E1 . . . . .32 A3
Smallbrook Mews
W2 . . . . .101 B1
Smalley Cl N16 . . . . . . .7 B1
Smart's Pl WC1,
WC2 . . . . .106 B2
Smart St E2 . . . . .25 C2
Smeaton Ct SE1 . . . .136 C1
Smeaton Rd SW18 . . .70 C4
Smeaton St E1 . . . . . .32 A1
Smedley St SW4 . . . .171 C2
Smeed Rd E3 . . . . .18 C1
Smiles Pl SE13 . . . . . .52 B1
Smith Cl SE16 . . . . . . .32 C1
Smithfield Mkt
EC1 . . . . .108 A3
Smithfield St EC1 . . .108 A3

Smithies Ct E15 . . . . .76 B3
Smith's Ct W1 . . . . . .119 B4
Smith Sq SW1 . . . . . .134 A1
Smith St SW3 . . . . . .144 C1
Smith's Yd SW18 . . . .71 B2
Smith Terr SW1 . . . . .144 C1
Smithwood Cl
SW19 . . . . .70 A2
Smithy St E1 . . . . .32 B4
Smithy Street Sch
E1 . . . . .32 B4
Smugglers Way
SW18 . . . . .59 A3
Smyrna Mans 8
NW6 . . . . .10 C1
Smyrna Rd NW6 . . . . .10 C1
Smythe St E14 . . . . . .34 A2
Snarsgate St W10 . . . .30 B4
Sneath Ave NW11 . . . .1 B4
Sneyd Rd NW2 . . . . . . .9 B4
Snowberry Cl E11 . . . .19 C4
Snowbury Rd SW6 . .166 B1
Snowden St
EC2 . . . . .24 A1 98 A1
Snow Hill EC1 . . . . . .108 A3
Snow Ho SE27 . . . . . . .75 A1
Snowman Ho NW6 . . .78 B4
Snowsfield Prim Sch
SE1 . . . . .138 A4
Snowsfields SE1 . . . .137 C4
Soames St SE15 . . . . .64 B4
Soane Ct 11 NW1 . . . .13 B1
Soane Ho SE17 . . . . .151 C1
Soane Mus WC2 . . . .106 C2
Soaphouse La TW8 . . .44 A3
Soho ★ W1 . . . . .105 C2
**Soho Parish CE Prim
Sch** W1 . . . . .119 B4
Soho Sq W1 . . . . . . .105 B2
Soho St W1 . . . . .105 B2
Sojourner-Truth Cl 11
E8 . . . . .17 A2
Solander Gdns
12 E1 . . . . .32 B2
Stepney E1 . . . . .32 A2
Soldene Ct N7 . . . . . .14 B2
Solebay St E1 . . . . . . .26 A1
Solent Ho 6 E1 . . . . . .26 A1
Solent Rd NW6 . . . . . .10 C3
Soley Mews WC1 . . . .95 B4
Solna Ave SW15 . . . . .57 B2
Solomon's Pas SE15 . .65 A4
Solon New Rd SW4 . . .62 A3
Solon Rd SW2 . . . . . .62 A3
Solway Ho 10 E1 . . . . .25 C1
Solway Rd SE22 . . . . .64 C3
Somali Rd NW2 . . . . . .10 B3
Somborne Ho SW15 . .68 C4
Sombrook Ho
SE11 . . . . .149 B3
Somer Ct SW6 . . . . . .155 B3
Somerfield Ho SE16 . .40 C1
Somerfield Rd N4 . . . . .6 A2
Somerford Gr N16 . . . .16 B4
Somerford Grove Est
N16 . . . . .16 B4
Somerford St E1 . . . . .25 A1
Somerford Way
SE16 . . . . .41 A4
Somerleyton Rd
SW9 . . . . .62 C3
Somers Cl NW1 . . . . . .83 B2
Somers Cres W2 . . . .102 A1
Somerset Gdns
London N6 . . . . .3 C4
London SE13 . . . . .52 A1

Somerset Ho WC2 . . .121 A4
London SW19 . . . . .70 A1
Somerset Lo SW15 . . .57 A3
Somerset Rd
London W4 . . . . .37 C3
Wimbledon SW19 . . . . .70 A1
Somerset Sq W14 . . .126 C3
Somers Pl SW2 . . . . . .74 B4
Somers Rd SW2 . . . . .62 B1
Somers Town Est
NW1 . . . . .83 A1
Somerton Ave TW9 . . .55 A4
Somerton Rd
London NW2 . . . . .1 A1
London SE15 . . . . .65 A3
Somerville Ave
SW13 . . . . .47 B4
Somerville Ho 10
SW15 . . . . .57 C1
Somerville Point
SE16 . . . . .41 B4
Sonderburg Rd 12
N7 . . . . .5 B2
Sondes St SE17 . . . . .48 C4
Sonia Gdns NW10 . . . .8 B4
Sonning Ho 22 E2 . . . .98 C3
Sophia Cl N7 . . . . . . .14 B2
Sophia Ho 9 W6 . . . . .39 B1
Sophia Sq 14 SE16 . . .33 A2
Sopwith Way
SW11 . . . . .160 A2
Sorrel La 10 E14 . . . . .34 C3
Sorrell Ct SE14 . . . . .51 A3
London SW9 . . . . .173 C2
Sotheby Rd N5 . . . . . .15 B4
Sotheran Cl E8 . . . . . .24 C4
Sotheron Pl SW6 . . . .156 B1
Soudan Rd SW11 . . . .168 C3
Souldern Rd 10
W14 . . . . .39 C3
South Acton Sta
W3,W4 . . . . .37 A2
South Africa Rd
W12 . . . . .30 A2
Southall Pl SE1 . . . . .137 B3
Southam Ho 8
W10 . . . . .23 A1
Southampton Bldgs
WC2 . . . . .107 B3
Southampton Pl
WC1 . . . . .106 B3
Southampton Row
WC1 . . . . .106 B4
Southampton St
WC2 . . . . .120 B4
Southampton Way
SE5 . . . . .49 A3
Southam St W10 . . . . .23 A1
South Audley St
W1 . . . . .117 C2
South Ave TW9 . . . . . .44 C1
South Bank Bsns Ctr
SW8 . . . . .161 C3
South Bank Univ
SE1 . . . . .136 B2
London SW8 . . . . .171 C4
South Bermondsey Sta
SE16 . . . . .40 B1
South Black Lion La
W6 . . . . .38 C1
South Bldg SW1 . . . .133 A2
South Block 11 E1 . . .32 B2
South Bolton Gdns
SW10 . . . . .142 B2

Southborough Ho
SE17 . . . . .152 B2
Southborough Rd
E9 . . . . .25 C4
South Building
SE10 . . . . .52 C3
Southbury NW8 . . . . . .79 A4
South Camden Com Sch
NW1 . . . . .83 B1
South Carriage Dr
SW1,SW7 . . . . .130 C4
South Colonnade
E14 . . . . .33 C1
Southcombe St
W14 . . . . .140 A4
Southcote Rd N19 . . .13 B4
Southcott Ho 51 E3 . .27 A2
W9 . . . . .89 A1
South Cres E16 . . . . . .27 C1
WC1 . . . . .105 B3
South Ct 17 SW15 . . .57 C1
South Eaton Pl
SW1 . . . . .145 C4
South Edwardes Sq
W8 . . . . .127 B1
South End W8 . . . . . .128 B2
South End Cl NW3 . . .12 A4
South End Gn NW3 . . .12 A4
South End Rd NW3 . . .12 A4
South End Row
W8 . . . . .128 B2
Southerngate Way
SE14 . . . . .51 A3
Southern Gr E3 . . . . . .26 B1
Southern Row W10 . . .23 A1
Southern St N1 . . . . . .84 C2
Southern Way SE10 . .43 B3
Southerton Rd W6 . . . .39 B2
Southey Ho SE17 . . . .151 A2
Southey Rd SW9 . . . .173 B4
Southfield Prim Sch
W4 . . . . .38 A4
Southfield Rd W4 . . . .37 C4
Southfields Com Coll
SW18 . . . . .70 C3
Southfields Rd
SW18 . . . . .58 C1
Southfields Sta
SW18 . . . . .70 B3
Southgate Ct 15 N1 . .15 C1
Southgate Gr N1 . . . .15 C1
Southgate Rd N1 . . . . .87 C4
South Gr N6 . . . . .3 C3
South Grove Ho N6 . . .3 C3
**South Hampstead High
Sch** NW3 . . . . .11 C2
**South Hampstead Jun
Sch** NW3 . . . . .11 B2
South Hampstead Sta
NW8 . . . . .11 B1
South Hill Pk NW3 . . .12 A4
South Hill Pk Gdns
NW3 . . . . .12 A4
Southill St E14 . . . . . .34 A3
South Island Pl
SW9 . . . . .163 B1
South Kensington Sta
SW7 . . . . .143 C4
South Lambeth Pl
SW8 . . . . .162 B4
South Lambeth Rd
SW8 . . . . .162 B2
Southlands Coll
SW15 . . . . .56 C2

Southlands Dr
SW19 ..... 69 C2
South Lo NW8 ..... 89 B4
South London
Montessori Sch
SW11 ..... 168 A4
Southmead Prim Sch
SW19 ..... 70 A3
Southmead Rd
SW19 ..... 70 A3
South Molton La
W1 ..... 104 A1
South Molton Rd
E16 ..... 35 C3
South Molton St
W1 ..... 104 A1
Southmoor Way E9 ..18 B3
Southolm St SW11 ..170 B3
South Par W4 ..... 37 C2
South Parade SW3 143 C2
South Park Mews
SW6 ..... 59 A4
South Pl EC2 ..... 109 C3
South Pl Mews
EC2 ..... 109 C3
South Quay Plaza
E14 ..... 42 A4
South Quay Sta E14 42 A4
South Rise W2 ..116 B4
South Row SE3 ..... 53 B1
South Sea St SE16 41 B3
Southside N7 ..... 13 C4
South Side W6 ..... 38 B3
Southside Ind Est
SW8 ..... 170 C4
Southside Quarter
SW11 ..... 168 C2
South Sq WC1 ..... 107 B3
South St W1 ..... 117 C2
South Tenter St
E1 ..... 111 A1
South Terr SW7 ..144 A4
South Thames Coll
London SW18 ..... 59 A2
Putney SW15 ..... 57 C2
Southvale Rd SE3 ..53 A1
Southview Ave NW10 .8 B3
South Villas NW1 ..13 C2
Southville SW8 ..171 C3
Southwark Bridge
SE1,EC4 ..... 123 A3
Southwark Bridge Office
Village SE1 ..... 123 A1
Southwark Bridge Rd
SE1 ..... 123 A2
Southwark Cath ★
SE1 ..... 123 B2
Southwark Coll
SE1 ..... 136 A4
SE15 ..... 50 A1
Southwark Coll
(Blackfriars Ctr)
SE1 ..... 122 A1
Southwark Coll
(Camberwell Ctr)
SE5 ..... 49 A3
Southwark Coll (Grange
Ctr) SE1 ..... 138 B3
Southwark Coll (Surrey
Docks Ctr) SE16 ..40 A3
Southwark Park Est
SE16 ..... 40 A2
Southwark Park Prim
Sch SE16 ..... 40 A3
Southwark Park Rd
SE16 ..... 153 B4
Southwark St 122 C1

Southwater Cl 6
E14 ..... 33 B3
Southwell Gdns
SW7 ..... 142 C3
Southwell Ho
8 SE16 ..... 40 A2
13 London N16 ..... 16 A3
Southwell Rd SE5 ..63 B4
South Wharf Rd
W2 ..... 101 C2
Southwick Mews
W2 ..... 101 C2
Southwick Pl W2 ..102 A1
Southwick St W2 ..102 A2
Southwick Yd W2 ..102 A1
Southwold Mans
W9 ..... 23 C2
Southwood Ave N6 ..4 A4
Southwood Ct EC1 ..96 A3
Southwood Ho
W11 ..... 112 A4
Southwood Hospl
(Geriatric) N6 ..... 3 C4
Southwood Hts N6 ..4 A4
Southwood La N6 ..3 C4
Southwood Lawn Rd
N6 ..... 4 A4
Southwood Park N6 .3 C4
Southwood Smith Ho 4
E2 ..... 25 A2
South Worple Way
SW14 ..... 55 C4
Southwyck Ho SW9 .62 C3
South Yd EC1 ..... 109 B4
Sovereign Cl E1 ..... 32 A2
Sovereign Cres
SE16 ..... 33 A2
Sovereign Ct
3 Richmond TW9 ..54 B3
Stepney E1 ..... 32 A2
Sovereign Ho 6 E1 .25 A1
Sovereign Mews 6
E2 ..... 24 B3
Sovereign Pk NW10 .20 B1
Spa Ct SE1 ..... 139 B1
Spafield St EC1 ..... 95 B2
Spalding Ho SE4 ..66 A2
Spanby Rd E3 ..... 26 C1
Spaniards Cl NW11 ..2 C3
Spaniards End NW3 .2 C3
Spaniards Rd NW3 ..2 B2
Spanish Pl W1 ..... 103 C2
Spanish Rd SW18 ..59 B2
Spa Rd SE16 ..... 139 A1
Sparke Terr 2 E16 .35 B1
Sparkford Ho
SW11 ..... 167 C4
Sparks Cl W3 ..... 28 C3
Sparsholt Rd N19 ..5 B3
Sparta St SE10 ..... 52 B2
Spa Sch SE1 ..... 153 B4
Spa View 3 SW16 ..74 B1
Speakers' Corner ★
W1 ..... 117 A4
Speakman Ho SE4 ..66 A4
Spear Mews SW5 ..141 C3
Spears Rd N19 ..... 5 A3
Spectrum Ho NW5 ..12 C4
Spedan Cl NW3 ..... 2 B1
Speechly Mews E8 ..16 B3
Speedwell St 3
SE8 ..... 51 C3
Speedy Pl WC1 ..... 94 A3

Speldhurst Rd
London E9 ..... 17 C1
London W4 ..... 37 C3
Spellbrook Wlk N1 ..87 A4
Spelman Ho E1 ..... 111 B3
Spelman St E1 ..... 111 B4
Spence Cl SE16 ..... 41 B4
Spencer Gdns SW14 55 B2
Spencer Ho
London NW3 ..... 2 C1
3 London 171 B1
2 Putney SW19 ..... 69 C3
Wimbledon SW19 ..69 C1
Spencer Mews W6 154 A4
Spencer Park Ct
SW18 ..... 59 C2
Spencer Pk SW18 ..59 C2
Spencer Pl SW1 ..133 A1
16 London N1 ..... 15 A1
Spencer Rd
Chiswick W4 ..... 45 B3
London SW18 ..... 59 C2
London W3 ..... 28 B1
Spencer Rise NW5 ..4 A1
Spencer St EC1 ..... 96 A3
Spencer Wlk
18 London NW3 ..11 B4
Putney SW15 ..... 57 C3
Spenlow Ho SE16 ..139 C2
Spenser Gr N16 ..... 16 A4
Spenser Mews SE21 75 C3
Spenser Rd SE24 ..63 A2
Spenser St SW1 ..133 A2
Spens Ho 4 WC1 ..94 C1
Spensley Wlk N16 ..6 C1
Spert St E14 ..... 33 A2
Spey St E14 ..... 34 B4
Spezia Rd NW10 ..21 C3
Spice Ct E1 ..... 125 C2
10 London SW11 ..59 B4
Spicer Cl SE5,SW9 .48 A1
Spice Quay Heights
SE1 ..... 124 C1
Spindrift Ave E14 ..42 A2
Spinnaker Ho E14 ..41 C4
Spinney The
Barnes SW13 ..... 47 A4
Streatham SW16 ..73 C1
Spire Ct 16 TW10 ..54 A1
Spire Ho W2 ..... 115 A4
Spirit Quay E1 ..... 32 A1
Spital Sq E1 ..... 110 B4
Spital St E1 ..... 99 B1
Spital Yd E1 ..... 110 B4
Splendour Wlk
SE16 ..... 40 B1
Spode Ho SE11 ..... 135 B1
Spode Wlk NW3 ..... 11 A3
Sporle Ct 6 SW11 ..59 C4
Sprewell SW15 ..... 58 A1
Spriggs Ho 14 N1 ..15 A1
Sprimont Pl SW3 ..144 C2
Springall St 16 SE15 50 A3
Springalls Wharf
SE16 ..... 139 B4
Springbank Wlk
NW1 ..... 13 C1
Spring Cott 10 W12 38 C4
Springdale Rd N16 .15 C4
Springett Ho 8
SW2 ..... 62 B2
Springfield Ct
London W3 ..... 12 A1
7 London NW3 ..28 B3
Springfield Ho
1 London SE5 ..... 49 A1
London W3 ..... 28 B1

Springfield Hospl
SW17 ..... 72 A1
Springfield La NW6 .78 A3
Springfield Rd NW8 .79 A3
Springfield Wlk
NW6 ..... 78 A3
Spring Gdns SW1 ..120 A2
London N5 ..... 15 B3
Spring Gr W4 ..... 44 C4
Spring Grove Rd
TW10 ..... 54 B2
Springhill Cl SE5 ..... 63 C4
Spring Ho WC1 ..... 95 B3
Spring Mews W1 ..103 A4
Springpark Dr N4 ..6 B3
Spring Pl NW5 ..... 13 A3
Springrice Rd SE13 .67 C1
Spring St W2 ..... 101 B1
Spring Terr TW10 ..54 A2
Springvale Ave TW8 36 A1
Springvale Terr 6
W14 ..... 39 C3
Springwater WC1 ..106 C4
Springwell Ave
NW10 ..... 21 B4
Spring Wlk E1 ..... 111 C4
Spruce Ct W5 ..... 36 A3
Spruce Ho 15 SE16 .40 C4
Sprules Rd SE4 ..... 51 A1
Spurgeon St SE1 ..137 B2
Spurling Rd SE22 ..64 B3
Spur Rd SE1 ..... 135 B4
Spurstowe Rd E8 ..17 A2
Spurstowe Terr E8 ..17 A3
Square Rigger Row 7
SW11 ..... 59 B4
Squarea The SW6 ..165 B3
Squarey St SW17 ..71 B1
Square Gdns SW18 .89 B3
Squires Ct SW4 ..... 172 B3
Squire's Mount NW3 .2 C1
Squirries Ho 13 SE16 64 B3
Squirrels The SE13 .67 C4
Squirries St
E2 ..... 24 C2 99 C3
Stables Way SE11 ..149 B2
Stable Way W10 ..... 30 B3
Stable Yd Rd SW1 ..133 A4
Stacey St WC2 ..... 105 C1
London N7 ..... 5 C1
Stack Ho SW1 ..... 145 C3
Stackhouse St
SW1 ..... 130 C2
Stacy Path 21 SE5 ..49 A3
Stadium St SW10 ..157 A1
Stafford Cripps Ho
30 E2 ..... 25 B2
SW6 ..... 155 A3
Stafford Ct SW8 ..172 A4
W8 ..... 127 C2
Stafford Ho SE1 ..153 A2
Stafford Mans
1 London SW4 ..... 62 A3
London W14 ..... 39 C3
Stafford Pl SW1 ..132 C2
Stafford Rd E3 ..... 26 B3
London 23 C2
Staffordshire St
London SE15 ..... 49 C2
London SE15 ..... 50 A2
Stafford St W1 ..... 118 C2
Stafford Terr W8 ..127 B2
Stag La SW15 ..... 68 B2
Stag Pl SW1 ..... 132 C2

Stagshaw Ho 17
SE22 ..... 64 A4
Stainer St SE1 ..... 123 C1
Staining La EC2 ..... 109 A2
Stainsby Rd E14 ..25 E2 25 B3
Stainsby Rd E14 ..... 33 C3
Stalbridge Flats W1 103 C2
Stalbridge Ho NW1 .82 C1
Stalbridge St NW1 ..102 B4
Stalham St SE16 ..... 40 A3
Stambourne Ho
SW8 ..... 172 B4
Stamford Bridge
Stadium (Chelsea FC)
SW6 ..... 156 A2
Stamford Brook Ave
W6 ..... 38 B3
Stamford Brook Gdns 1
W6 ..... 38 B3
Stamford Brook Mans 2
W6 ..... 38 B3
Stamford Brook Rd
W6 ..... 38 B3
Stamford Brook Sta
W6 ..... 38 B3
Stamford Cl 2 NW3 ..2 B1
Stamford Cotts SW10 156 B4
Stamford Ct W6 ..... 38 C2
Stamford Grove E 1
N16 ..... 7 C3
Stamford Grove W 7
N16 ..... 7 C3
Stamford Hill N16 ..7 B3
Stamford Hill Mans 1
N16 ..... 7 B3
Stamford Hill Sta
N16 ..... 7 A4
Stamford Hospl W6 38 C2
Stamford Lo 2 N16 ..7 B4
Stamford Mans 2
N16 ..... 7 C3
Stamford Rd N1 ..... 16 A2
Stamford St SE1 ..... 121 C2
Stamp Pl E2 ..... 98 C3
Stanard Cl N16 ..... 7 A4
Stanborough Ho 4
E3 ..... 27 A1
Stanborough Pas
E8 ..... 16 B2
Stanbridge Mans
SW15 ..... 57 B4
Stanbridge Rd
SW15 ..... 57 B4
Stanbrook Ct W1 ..118 C2
Stanbury Ct 10 NW3 12 B2
Stanbury Rd
London SE15 ..... 50 A1
London SE15 ..... 50 B1
Standard Pl EC2 ..... 98 B3
Standard Rd NW10 ..20 C1
Standen Rd SW18 ..70 C4
Standish Ho 6 W6 ..38 C2
Standish Rd W6 ..... 38 C2
Stanesgate Ho 20
SE15 ..... 49 C3
Stanfield Ho NW8 ..89 C2
Stanfield Rd 3 E3 ..26 A3
Stanford Ct SW6 ..166 B3
W8 ..... 128 B1
Stanford Pl SE1 ..... 152 A3
Stanford Rd W8 ..128 B2
Stanford St SW1 ..147 B3
Stanhope Cl 2
SE16 ..... 40 C4
Stanhope Gate
W1 ..... 117 C2

Stanhope Gdns
SW7 ....143 A4
Stanhope Ho SE8 ....51 B3
◆ Putney SW15 ....57 B2
Stanhope Mews E
SW7 ....143 A4
Stanhope Mews S
SW7 ....143 A3
Stanhope Mews W
SW7 ....143 A4
Stanhope Pl W2 ....102 C1
Stanhope Rd N6 ....4 B4
Stanhope Row W1 ..118 A1
Stanhope St NW1 ....92 C3
Stanhope Terr W2 ..115 C4
Stanier Cl SW5 ....141 A1
Stanlake Rd W12 ....30 B1
Stanlake Villas W12 .30 B1
Stanlake Villas W12 .30 B1
Stanley Cl SW8 ....162 C3
Stanley Cres
W11 ....31 B2 112 C4
Stanley Gdns W11 ..112 C4
London NW2 ....9 B3
London W3 ....38 A4
Stanley Gr SW11 ..169 C1
Stanley Ho 🖩 E14 ..33 C3
London SW8 ....171 B1
Stanley Mans
SW10 ....157 A4
Upper Tooting SW17 .72 B1
Stanley Rd E15 ....27 C4
London W3 ....37 B3
Mortlake SW14 ......55 A3
Stanley St SE14,SE8 .51 A3
Stanley Studios
SW10 ....157 A4
Stanley Terr 🖫 N19 ..5 A2
Stanmer St SW11 ..168 B2
Stanmore Gdns
TW9 ....54 B4
Stanmore Ho SW8 ..171 C2
Stanmore Pl NW1 ..82 B4
Stanmore Rd TW9 ..54 B4
Stanmore St N1 ....84 C4
Stannard Cotts 🖾
E1 ....25 B1
Stannard Mews E8 ..16 C2
Stannard Rd E8 ....16 C2
Stannary Pl SE11 ..149 C1
Stannary St SE11 ..149 C1
Stansbury Ho 🖪
W10 ....23 A2
Stansfeld Ho SE1 ..153 A3
Stansfield Rd SW9 ..62 B4
Stanstead Ho 🖪 E3 ..27 B1
Stanswood Gdns
SE5 ....49 A3
Stanton Ct N16 ....15 C4
Stanton Ho 🖫 SE10 ..52 B4
Stanton Rd SW13 ....46 B1
Stanway Ct 🖾 N1 ....24 A3
Stanway St N1 ......24 A3
Stanwick Rd W14 ..140 C3
Stanworth St SE1 ..139 A3
Stapelhurst Ho 🖫
E5 ....17 A3
Staplefield Cl 🖪
SW2 ....74 A3
Stapleford Cl SW19 .70 A4
Staplehurst Ct
SW11 ....60 B1
Staple Inn WC2 ....107 B3
Staple Inn Bldgs
WC2 ....107 B3

Staples Cl SE16 ....33 A1
Staple St SE1 ......137 C3
Stapleton Hall N4 ..5 B4
Stapleton Hall Rd N4 .5 B4
Stapleton Ho 🖫 E2 ..25 A2
Stapleton Rd SW17 .72 C1
Star Alley EC3 ....124 B4
Starboard Way E14 .41 C3
Starcross St NW1 ..93 A3
Starfield Rd W12 ..38 C4
Star & Garter Mans
SW15 ....57 C4
Starliner Ct N7 ....14 C2
Starling Ho NW8 ....80 A2
Star Pl E1 ....125 C3
Star Rd W14 ......140 C1
Star St W2 ....102 A2
Star Works NW10 ..21 C2
Star Yd WC2 ......107 B2
Statham Gr N16 ....6 C1
Statham Ho SW8 ..170 C4
Stathard Ho 🔟 E1 ..25 B1
Station App
London NW10 ....21 B2
Richmond TW9 ......44 C2
Station App Rd
SE1 ....135 B2
Station Approach Rd
W4 ....45 B3
Station Ave
🖬 London SW9 ......63 A4
🔟 Richmond TW9 ....44 C2
Station Cres SE3 ..43 C1
Station Ct 🖫 SE5 ..50 B1
Stationers Hall Ct
EC4 ....108 B1
Station Gdns W4 ..45 B3
Station Par
London NW2 ....9 B2
Richmond TW9 ......44 C2
🔟 Upper Tooting
SW12 ....72 C3
Station Pas SE15 ..50 B2
Station Pl N4 ......5 C2
Station Rd N19 ....4 B1
Barnes SW13 ....46 B1
London NW10 ....21 B3
London SE13 ....67 B4
Station Rise SE27 ..75 A2
Station St E15 ....19 C1
Station Terr
London NW2 ....22 C3
London SE5 ....48 B2
Staunton Ho SE17 ..152 A3
Staunton St SE8 ....51 B4
Staveley NW1 ......92 C4
Staveley Cl
London N7 ....14 B4
London SE15 ....50 B2
🔟 London SE15 ......50 B2
Staveley Gdns W4 ..45 C2
Staveley Rd W4 ....45 C3
Staverdale Lo W14 .127 A2
Staverdale Rd N5 ..15 A4
Staverton Rd NW2 ..9 B1
Stave Yard Rd SE16 .33 A1
Stavordale Rd N5 ..15 A4
Stayners Rd E1 ....25 C1
Steadman Ct EC1 ..97 A2
Stead St SE17 ....151 B3
Stean St E8 ....24 B4
Stebbing Ho 🖪
W11 ....30 C1
Stebondale St E14 ..42 B2

Stebon Prim Sch
E14 ....33 C4
Stedham Pl WC1 ..106 A2
Stedman Cl SW17 ..150 C3
Steele Rd
London NW10 ....20 B3
London W4 ....37 B3
Steele's Mews N
NW3 ....12 B2
Steele's Mews S
NW3 ....12 B2
Steele's Rd NW3 ..12 B2
Steel's La 🔟 E1 ....32 B3
Steen Way 🖪 SE22 .64 A2
Steep Hill SW16 ....73 C1
Steeple Cl SW6 ....164 B1
Steeple Ct 🔟 E1 ..25 A1
Steeple Wlk N1 ....86 C2
Steerforth St SE18 .71 B2
Steers Way SE16 ..41 A4
Stelfax Ho WC1 ....95 A4
Stellman Cl E5 ....7 C1
Stephan Ct E8 ....24 C4
Stephen Ct 🔟 SW19 .69 C3
Stephendale Rd
SW6 ....166 C1
Stephen Fox Ho 🔟
W4 ....38 A1
Stephen Hawking Sch
E14 ....33 A3
Stephen Mews W1 ..105 B3
Stephen Pl SW4 ....61 B4
Stephen Saunders Ct
SW11 ....60 A2
Stephens Ct SE4 ..66 A4
Stephenson Ho
SE1 ....136 C2
🖪 London SW2 ......12 B3
🔟 London NW5 ......13 A4
Stephenson St SE16 .35 A4
London NW10 ....21 B2
Stephenson Way
NW1 ....93 A2
Stephen St W1 ....105 B3
Stepney Cswy E1 ..32 C3
Stepney Day Hospl
E1 ....32 B3
Stepney Green Ct 🖪
E1 ....32 C4
Stepney Greencoat CE
Prim Sch The E14 .33 B3
Stepney Green Ct 🖪
E1 ....32 C4
Stepney Green Sch
E1 ....25 C1
Stepney Green Sta
E1 ....25 C1
Stepney High St E1 .32 C4
Stepney Way E1 ....32 B4
Sterling Gdns SE14 .51 A4
Sterling Pl W5 ....36 A2
Sterling St SW7 ..130 B2
Sterndale Rd W14 ..39 C3
Sterne St W12 ....30 C1
Sternhall La SE15 ..64 C4
Sternhold Ave
SW12,SW2 ....73 C2
Sterry St SE1 ....137 B3
Steve Biko Ct W10 .22 C1
Steve Biko Rd N7 ..5 C1
Stevedore St 🖪 E1 .32 A1
Stevenage Rd SW6 .47 C2
Stevens Ave E9 ....17 B2
Stevenson Cres
SE16 ....40 A1
Stevenson Ho NW8 .78 C4
London SW11 ......168 C1

Stevens St SE1 ....138 B2
Steventon Rd W12 ..29 B2
Steward St E1 ....110 B4
Stewart Headlam Prim
Sch E1 ....25 A1
Stewart Rd E15 ....19 C4
Stewart St E14 ....42 B4
Stew La EC4 ......122 C4
Steyne Rd W3 ....28 A1
Stifford Ho E1 ....32 B4
Stile Hall Gdns W4 .36 C1
Stile Hall Par 🔟
W4 ....36 C1
Stileman Ho 🖪 E3 ..33 B4
Stillingfleet Rd
SW13 ....46 C4
Stillington St SW1 .147 A4
Stillness Jun & Inf Schs
SE23 ....66 A1
Stillness Rd SE23 ..66 B1
Stirling Ct EC1 ....96 A2
Stirling Rd
London SW9 ....172 B1
London W3 ....37 A3
Stoatley Ho 🔟
SW15 ....68 C3
Stockbeck NW1 ....83 A1
Stock Exchange
EC2 ....109 C1
Stockfield Rd SW16 .74 B1
Stockholm Ho E1 ..125 C4
Stockholm Rd SE16 .40 B1
Stockholm Way E1 .125 B2
Stockhurst Cl SW15 .47 C1
Stockleigh Hall
NW8 ....80 B2
Stock Orchard Cres
N7 ....14 B3
Stock Orchard St
N7 ....14 B3
Stocks Ct 🖪 E1 ....25 C1
Stocks Pl 🔟 E14 ..33 B2
Stockton Ho 🔟 E2 ..25 A2
Stockwell Ave SW9 .62 B4
Stockwell Gdns
SW9 ....172 C3
Stockwell Gn SW9 .172 C1
Stockwell La SW9 ..172 C1
Stockwell Park Cres
SW9 ....173 A2
Stockwell Park Rd
SW9 ....173 A3
Stockwell Park Sch
SW9 ....172 C3
Stockwell Park Wlk
SW9 ....62 C4
Stockwell Prim Sch
SW9 ....62 B4
Stockwell Rd SW9 ..172 C2
Stockwell St SE10 ..52 B4
Stockwell Terr SW9 .172 C3
Stoddart Ho SW8 ..163 A3
Stodmarsh Ho 🖪
SW9 ....173 C4
Stoford Cl SW19 ..70 A4
Stokenchurch St
SW6 ....166 A3
Stoke Newington
Church St N16 ....7 A2
Stoke Newington Comm
N16 ....7 B2

Stoke Newington High
St N16 ....7 B1
Stoke Newington Rd
N16 ....16 B4
Stoke Newington Sch
N16 ....6 C1
Stoke Newington Sta
N16 ....7 B2
Stoke Pl NW10 ....21 B2
Stokesley St W12 ..29 B3
Stondon Pk SE23 ..66 A1
Stone Bldgs WC2 ..107 A3
Stonebridge Sch The
NW10 ....20 C4
Stonebridge Sh Ctr 🖪
NW10 ....20 C4
Stone Cl SW4 .....171 A1
Stonecutter St
EC4 ....108 A2
Stonefield N4 ......5 B2
Stonefield Mans N1 .85 B3
Stonefield St N1 ..85 C4
Stone Gate 🖪 NW5 .12 C2
Stonehill Cl SW14 ..55 C2
Stonehill's Mans 🖪
SW16 ....74 A2
Stonehouse N1 ....83 A3
Stonehouse Ct
EC2 ....110 B2
Stonehouse Ho 🔾
W2 ....31 C4
Stoneleigh Lo 🖪
TW9 ....44 B2
Stoneleigh Pl W11 ..30 C2
Stoneleigh St W11 ..30 C2
Stoneleigh Terr N19 .4 A2
Stonell's Rd SW11 ..60 B2
Stonenest St N4 ....5 B3
Stones End St SE1 ..136 C3
Stoneyard La E14 ..34 A2
Stoney La E1 ......110 B2
Stoney St SE1 ....123 B2
Stonhouse St SW4 ..61 C3
Stonor Rd W14 ....140 C3
Stopes St SE15 ....49 B3
Stopford Rd SE17 ..150 B1
Stopher Ho SE1 ....136 B3
Storace Ho 🔟 SW4 .62 A3
Storers Quay E14 ..42 C2
Store St WC1 .....105 B4
London SE15 ....50 B4
Storey Ct NW8 ....89 B3
Storey Ho 🔟 E14 ..34 A2
Storey's Gate SW1 .133 C3
Stories Rd SE5 ....64 A4
Storks Rd SE16 ....139 C1
Stormont House Sch
E5 ....17 A4
Stormont Rd
London N6 ....3 B4
London SW11 ......60 C3
Storrington WC1 ..94 B3
Story St N1 ....14 B1
Stothard Pl E1 ....110 B4
Stothard St 🔟 E1 ..25 B1
Stott Cl SW18 ....59 C1
Stoughton Cl SE11 .149 A3
Roehampton SW15 ..68 C3
Stourcliffe Cl W1 ..102 C2
Stourcliffe St W1 ..102 C1
Stourhead Cl 🔾
SW19 ....69 C4
Stour Rd E3 ....18 C1

Stowage SE8 ....52 A4
Stowe Ho 11 N16 ......7 A1
Stowe Rd W12 ....39 A4
Stracey Rd NW10 ....20 C4
Stradbroke Rd N5 ..15 B4
Stradella Rd SE24 ..63 B1
Straffan Lo 3 NW3 ...62 B2
Strafford Rd 8 SE8 41 B1
Strafford Rd W3 ....37 B4
Strafford St E14 ....41 C4
Strahan Rd E3 ......26 A2
Straightsmouth
SE10 ....52 B3
Straker's Rd SE15 ..65 A3
Strale Ho 17 N1 ....24 A4
Strand WC2 ....120 C4
Strand La WC2 ....121 A4
Strand-on-the-Green
W4 ....44 C4
Strand-on-the-Green
Sch W4 ....44 C4
Strang Ho N1 ......86 C3
Strangways Terr
W14 ....126 C1
Stranraer Way N1 ..14 A1
Strasburg Rd
SW11 ....170 B4
Stratford Bus Sta
E15 ....19 C1
Stratford Cir E15 ..19 C2
Stratford Ctr E15 ..19 C1
Stratford Gr SW15 57 C3
Stratford Pl W1 ...104 A1
Stratford Rd W8 ..127 C1
Stratford Sta E15 ..19 C1
Stratford Studios
W8 ....128 A1
Stratford Villas
NW1 ....13 C1
Stratford Workshops
E15 ....27 C4
Strathan Cl SW18 ..58 A1
Strathblaine Rd
SW11 ....59 C3
Strathdon Dr SW17 71 C1
Strathearn Ho W2 116 A4
Strathearn Pl W2 ..116 A4
Stratheden Par SE3 53 C3
Stratheden Rd SE3 53 C3
Strathleven Rd SW2 62 A2
Strathmore Ct NW8 90 A4
Strathmore Gdns
W8 ....113 C2
Strathmore Rd
SW19 ....70 C1
Strathnairn St SE1 153 C3
Strathray Gdns
NW3 ....12 A2
Strath Terr SW11 ..60 A3
Strathville Rd SW18 71 A2
Stratton Cl 3 N1 ...16 A1
Strattondale St E14 42 B3
Stratton St W1 ....118 B2
Strauss Rd W4 ......37 C4
Streamline Mews
SE22 ....76 C3
Streatham Cl SW16 74 A2
Streatham & Clapham
High Sch SW16 ...73 C1
Streatham Ct SW16 74 A1
Streatham St WC1 106 A2
Streatham Hill SW2 74 A3
Streatham Hill &
Clapham High Sch
SW2 ....74 B3
Streatham Hill Sta
SW2 ....74 A4
Streatham Pl SW2 ..74 A4

Streatham St WC1 106 A2
Streatham & Tooting
Adult Inst SW16 ..74 B2
Streathbourne Rd
SW17 ....72 C1
Streatham Wells Prim
Sch SW2 ....74 B2
Streatleigh Par 4
SW16 ....74 A2
Streatley Pl
London NW3 ....11 C4
12 London NW3 ...11 B4
Streatley Rd NW6 ..10 B1
Streimer Rd E15 ...27 B3
Strelley Way W3 ...29 A2
Stretton Mans 16
SE8 ....51 C4
Strickland Ct SE15 64 C4
Strickland Ho E2 ..99 A3
Strickland Row
SW18 ....71 C4
Strickland St SE8 ..51 C2
Stringer Hos 19 N1 24 A4
Strode Ho 8 SW2 ..74 C3
Strode Rd SW6 ....154 A2
London NW10 ......8 C2
Strome Ho NW6 ....78 A1
Stronsa Rd W12 ....38 B4
Strood Ho SE1 ....137 C3
Stroud Cres SW15 ..68 C1
Stroud Green JMI Sch
N4 ....5 C2
Stroud Green Rd N4 ..5 C3
Stroudley Ho SW8 171 A4
Stroudley Wlk E3 ..27 A2
Stroud Rd SW19 ...70 C1
Strout's Pl E2 ......98 C4
Strudwick Ct SW4 172 B3
Strutton Ground
SW1 ....133 B1
Strype St E1 ....110 C3
Stuart Ave W5 ......36 B4
Stuart Ho W14 ....140 A4
1 London E9 ....17 C1
5 London SW4 .....62 A3
Stuart Mill Ho N1 ..84 C1
Stuart Rd
London NW6 ....23 C2
London SE15 ......65 B3
London W3 ....28 B1
Wimbledon SW19 ..70 C1
Stubbs Dr SE16 ....40 A1
Stubbs Ho 1 E2 ...25 C2
London N4 ....5 B3
Stucley Pl 18 NW1 13 A1
Studdridge St
SW6 ....165 C2
Studd St N1 ....86 A4
Studholme Ct NW3 ..10 C4
Studholme St SE15 50 A3
Studio Pl SW1 ....131 A3
Studios The NW8 ..171 C1
4 London SW4 ....61 B3
Studland SE17 ....151 B2
Studland Ho E14 ..33 A3
Studland St W6 .....39 A2
Studley Cl E5 ......18 A3
Studley Ct 9 E14 ..34 C2
Studley Rd SW4 ...172 B2
Stukeley St WC2 ..106 B2
Stunnell Ho 2 SE14 50 C4
Sturdee Ho 3 E2 ..24 C3
Sturdy Ho 4 E3 ....26 A3
Sturdy Rd SE15 ....50 A1
Sturgeon Rd SE17 150 C1
Sturge St SE1 .....136 C4
Sturmer Way N7 ...14 B3

Sturminster Ho
SW8 ....163 A1
Sturry St E14 ......34 A3
Sturt St N1 ....87 A1
Stutfield St E1 ....111 C1
Stuttle Ho E1 ....99 B1
Styles Gdns SW9 ..63 A4
Styles Ho SE1 ....122 A1
Sudbourne Prim Sch
SW2 ....62 B2
Sudbourne Rd SW2 62 B2
Sudbrooke Rd
SW12 ....60 C1
Sudbury Ct SW8 ..171 C4
London E5 ....17 C4
Sudbury Ho SW18 ..59 A2
Sudeley St N1 ......86 B1
Sudlow Rd SW18 ..58 C2
Sudrey St SE1 ....136 C3
Suffield Ho SE17 ..150 B2
Suffolk La EC4 ....123 B4
Suffolk Pl SW1 ....119 C2
Barnes SW13 .....46 C3
London NW10 .....8 A1
Suffolk Rd
London NW10 ......8 A1
Suffolk St SW1 ....119 C2
Sugar House La E15 27 B3
Sugar Loaf Wlk 6
E2 ....25 B2
Sugden Rd SW11 ..60 C3
Sulby Ho SE4 ......66 A3
Sulgrave Gdns 1
W6 ....39 B4
Sulgrave Rd W6 ...39 B3
Sulina Rd SW2 ....74 A4
Sulivan Ct SW6 ...165 B1
Sulivan Ent Ctr
SW6 ....58 C4
Sulivan Prim Sch
SW6 ....165 C1
Sulivan Rd SW6 ...58 C4
Sulkin Ho 3 E2 ....25 C2
Sullivan Cl SW11 ..60 A4
Sullivan Ct SW5 ..141 C4
London N16 ....7 B3
SW1 ....160 B4
Sullivan Rd SE11 ..149 A3
Sultan St SE5 ......48 B3
Sumatra Rd NW6 ..10 C2
Sumburgh Rd SW12 60 C1
Summercourt Rd
E1 ....32 B3
Summerfield Ave
NW6 ....23 A3
Summer Ho SE13 ..67 C3
Summerhouse Rd
N16 ....7 A2
Summerlands Ave
W3 ....28 B2
Summerley St
SW18 ....71 A2
Summers St EC1 ..95 B1
Summit Ct NW2 ....10 A3
Summit Est N16 ....7 C4
Sumner Ave SE15 ..49 B2
Sumner Bldgs SE1 122 C2
Sumner Ct SW8 ..172 A4
Sumner Ho 1 E3 ..34 A4
Sumner Pl SW7 ...143 C3
Sumner Place Mews
SW7 ....143 C3
Sumner Rd SE15 ..49 B3
Sumner St SE1 ....122 C2
Sumpter Cl NW3 ...11 B2
Sun Alley 6 TW9 ..54 A3
Sunbeam Cres W10 22 B1

Sunbeam Rd NW10 .20 C1
Sunbury Ave SW14 .55 C3
Sunbury Ct 3 SE14 50 C4
Sunbury Ho 2 E2 ..98 C3
Sunbury La SW11 .167 C4
Sunbury Workshops
E2 ....98 C3
Sun Ct EC3 ....109 C1
Sunderland Ct SE22 76 C4
Sunderland Ho 20
W2 ....100 A4
Sunderland Terr
W2 ....100 A2
Sundew Ave W12 ..29 C2
Sundra Wlk 20 E1 ..25 C1
Sundridge Ho 4 E9 17 C1
Sunlight Sq 22 E2 ..25 A2
Sunningdale Ave
W3 ....29 A2
Sunningdale Cl 22
SE16 ....40 A1
Sunningdale Gdns
W8 ....127 C1
Sunninghill Ct 9
W3 ....37 B4
Sunninghill Rd
SE13 ....52 A1
Sunnyhill Cl E5 ....18 A4
Sunnymead Rd
SW15 ....57 A2
Sunnyside 8 NW2 ..1 B1
Sunnyside Ho 2
NW2 ....1 B1
Sunnyside Rd N19 ..4 C4
Sun Pas SE16 .....139 B2
Sunray Ave SE5,
SE24 ....63 C3
Sun Rd W14 ....140 C1
Sunset Rd SE5 ....63 C3
Sun St EC2 ....109 C4
Sun St Pas EC2 ...110 A3
Sunwell Ct SE15 ...50 A2
Surat St E2 ....24 C2 99 C3
Surma Cl E1 ....24 C1 99 C1
Surrendale Pl W9 ..23 C1
Surrey Canal Rd
SE14,SE16,SE8 ...50 C4
Surrey Cres 1 W4 ..36 C1
Surrey La SW11 ...168 B3
Surrey Quays Rd
SE16 ....40 C4
Surrey Quays Sh Ctr
SE16 ....40 C3
Surrey Quays Sta
SE16 ....40 C2
Surrey Rd SE15 ...65 C2
Surrey Row SE1 ..136 B4
Surrey Sq SE17 ...152 B2
Surrey Square Inf Sch
SE17 ....152 A2
Surrey Square Jun Sch
SE17 ....152 A2
Surrey St WC2 ....121 A4
Surrey Terr SE17 ..152 B2
Surrey Water Rd
SE16 ....32 C1
Surridge Ct SW9 ..172 B2
Surr St N7 ....14 A3
Susan Constant Ct 3
E14 ....34 C2
Susan Lawrence Ho
5 E12 ....34 C2
Susannah St E14 ..34 B3
Sussex Cl N19 ......5 A2
Sussex Ct SE10 ....52 B4

Sussex Ct continued
W2 ....101 B1
3 Barnes SW13 ..46 B1
Sussex Gdns W2 ..101 C1
Sussex Ho
London NW3 ......12 A2
Richmond TW9 ....44 B1
Sussex House Sch
SW3 ....144 C3
Sussex Lo W2 .....101 C1
Sussex Mans SW7 143 B3
WC2 ....120 B4
Sussex Mews E
W2 ....101 C1
Sussex Mews W
W2 ....115 C4
Sussex Pl NW1 .....90 C2
W2 ....101 C1
23 London W6 ....39 B1
Sussex Sq W2 ....115 C4
Sussex St SW1 ...146 B2
Sussex Way N19 ....4 C3
London N7,N19 ....5 A2
Sutherland Ave W9 88 B2
Sutherland Ct
2 W9 ....23 C1
London N16 ....6 C1
Sutherland Gdns
SW14 ....56 A4
Sutherland Gr SW18,
SW19 ....70 B4
Sutherland Ho W8 128 A1
3 London NW6 ...11 B2
7 Putney SW15 ...69 B4
Sutherland Pl W2 ..31 C3
Sutherland Point 1
E5 ....17 A4
Sutherland Rd E3 ..26 B3
Chiswick W4 ......46 A4
Sutherland Row
SW1 ....146 B2
Sutherland Sq
SE17 ....150 C1
Sutherland St SW1 146 B2
Sutherland Wlk
SE17 ....151 A1
Sutterton St N7 ...14 B2
Sutton Court Rd
W4 ....45 B4
Sutton Ct
Chiswick W4 ......45 B4
8 London E5 .....17 A4
Sutton Est SW3 ..144 B2
Sutton Est The W10 30 B4
Sutton La N1 ......37 A1
Sutton La S W4 ...45 B4
Sutton Pl E9 ....17 B3
Sutton Row W1 ...105 C2
Sutton Sq E1 ......17 B3
Sutton St E1 ....32 B3
Suttons Way EC1 ..97 A1
Sutton Way W10 ..30 B4
Sutton Wlk SE1 ...120 C2
Swaby Rd SW17,
SW18 ....71 B2
Swaffield Prim Sch
SW18 ....71 B4
Swaffield Rd SW18 71 B4
Swain's La N6 ......4 A2
Swainson Rd W3 ..38 B4
Swallow Cl SE14 ..50 C2
Swallow Ct 4 W9 ..31 C4
Swallowfield NW1 ..92 B3
Swallow Ho NW8 ..80 A2

Swallow Pl W1 . . . .**104** B1
Swallow St W1 . . . . .**119** A3
Swanage Ct **5** N1 . . .**16** A1
Swanage Ho SW8 . .**162** C1
Swanage Rd SW18 . .**59** B1
Swanbourne SE17 . .**150** C3
Swanbourne Ho
NW8 . . . .**90** A2
Swan Ct E14 . . . .**33** B3
SW3 . . . .**144** B1
Swan Ho **5** N1 . . . . .**86** B4
Swan Ctr SW17 . . . . . .**71** B1
Swandon Way
SW18 . . . .**59** A3
Swanfield St E2 . . . . .**99** A3
Swan Ho N1 . . . .**86** C4
Swan La EC4 . . . . . .**123** C3
Swan Lane Pier
EC4 . . . .**123** C3
Swanlea Sec Sch
. . . .**28** B1
Swanley Ho SE17 . . .**152** B2
Swan Mead SE1 . . . . .**138** A1
Swan Mews SW9 . . . .**172** C2
Swanmore Ct SW18 .**59** B1
Swanne Ho **12** SE10 .**52** B3
Swan Pas E1 . . . .**125** B3
Swan Pl SW13 . . . . . .**46** B1
Swan Rd SE16 . . . .**40** B4
Swanscombe Ho **5**
W11 . . . .**30** C1
Swanscombe Point **2**
E16 . . . .**35** B2
Swanscombe Rd
London W11 . . . .**30** C1
5 London W4 . . . . . .**38** A1
Swan St SE1 . . . .**137** A3
Swanton Gdns
SW19 . . . .**69** C3
Swanwick Cl SW15 . . .**68** B4
Swan Wlk SW3 . . . . .**158** C4
Swan Yd N1 . . . .**15** A2
Swaton Rd E3 . . . . . .**26** C1
Swaythling Ho **2**
SW15 . . . .**56** B1
Swedenborg Gdns
E1 . . . .**32** A2
Sweden Gate SE16 . .**41** A2
Swedish Sch The
SW13 . . . .**46** B4
Sweeney Cres SE1 . .**139** A3
Sweyn Pl SE3 . . . .**53** C1
Swift Ho **2** E1 . . . . . .**32** B3
9 SW9 . . . .**163** C2
10 London N16 . . . . .**7** A1
Swift St SW6 . . . . . .**164** C4
Swinbrook Rd W10 . . .**31** A4
Swinburne Ct **4**
SE5 . . . .**63** C3
Swinburne Ho **16**
E2 . . . .**25** B2
Swinburne Rd
SW15 . . . .**56** C3
Swindon St W12 . . . . .**30** B1
Swinford Gdns SW9 .**63** A4
Swingfield Ho **5**
E9 . . . .**25** B4
Swinley Ho NW1 . . . . .**92** B4
Swinnerton St E9 . . . .**18** A3
Swinton Ho E2 . . . .**99** B3
Swinton Pl WC1 . . . . . .**94** C4
Swinton St WC1 . . . . . .**94** C4
Swiss Cottage SW3 . .**11** C1
Swiss Cottage Sch
NW8 . . . .**79** C4

Swiss Cottage Sta
NW3 . . . .**11** C1
Swiss Re Building★
EC2 . . . .**110** B1
Swiss Terr **1** NW3 . . .**11** C1
Sybil Phoenix Cl
SE8 . . . .**40** C1
Sybil Thorndike Casson
Ho SW5 . . . .**141** C1
Sybil Thorndike Ho **7**
N1 . . . .**15** B2
Sycamore Ave E3 . . . .**26** B4
Sycamore Cl W3 . . . . .**29** A1
Sycamore Ct NW6 . . . .**23** C4
London N19 . . . .**4** C1
4 London SE6 . . . . .**48** B2
Sycamore Gdns W6,
W12 . . . .**39** A3
Sycamore Gr SE6 . . . .**67** B1
Sycamore Ho
17 SE16 . . . .**40** C4
1 London N16 . . . . . .**6** C2
10 London NW3 . . . . .**12** B2
London W6 . . . .**39** A4
Sycamore Lo SW15 . . .**57** A4
Sycamore Mews **4**
SW4 . . . .**61** B4
Sycamore St EC1 . . . . .**96** C1
Sycamore Wlk **1**
W10 . . . .**23** A1
Sydenham Hill SE21,
SE22,SE23,SE26,SE19 .**76** C1
Sydenham Hill Sta
SE21 . . . .**76** B1
Sydner Mews N16 . . . .**16** B4
Sydner Rd N16 . . . . . .**16** B4
Sydney Cl SW3 . . . . .**143** C3
Sydney Ho **4** W4 . . . .**38** A2
Sydney Mews SW3 . .**143** C3
Sydney Pl SW7 . . . . .**143** C3
Sydney Rd TW10,
TW9 . . . .**54** A3
Sydney St SW3 . . . . .**144** A2
Sylva Ct **3** SW15 . . . .**69** C4
Sylvan Gr NW2 . . . .**9** C4
SE15 . . . .**50** A4
Sylvester Ho **7** E8 . . .**17** A2
Sylvester Path **5**
E8 . . . .**17** A2
Sylvester Rd E8 . . . . . .**17** A2
Sylvia Cotts **3** SE8 . . .**51** C2
Sylvia Pankhurst Ho **14**
E2 . . . .**25** C3
Sylvia Young Theatre
Sch NW1 . . . .**90** B1
Symes Mews NW1 . . . .**82** C2
Symington Ho **1** SE1 .**137** B1
Symington Mews
E9 . . . .**17** C3
Symister Mews N1 . . . .**98** A4
Symons St SW3 . . . . .**145** A3
Symphony Ho **18**
W10 . . . .**23** A2
Syringa Ho SE4 . . . . . .**66** B4

T

Tabard Ct **3** E14 . . . . .**34** B3
Tabard Ho **1** SE1 . . .**137** C2
Tabard St SE1 . . . . . .**137** B2
Tabernacle St EC2 . . . .**97** C2
Tableer Ave SW4 . . . . .**61** C2
Tabley Rd N7 . . . .**14** A4
Tabor Rd W6 . . . .**39** A3
Tachbrook Est
SW1 . . . .**147** C1

Tachbrook Mews
SW1 . . . .**146** C4
Tachbrook St SW1 . . .**147** A3
Tack Mews SE4 . . . . . .**66** C4
Tadema Ho NW8 . . . . .**89** C1
Tadema Rd SW10 . . . .**157** A1
Tadmor St W12 . . . . . .**30** C1
Tadworth Ho SE1 . . . .**136** A3
Taeping St E14 . . . .**42** A2
Taft Way **44** E3 . . . . . .**27** A2
Tailworth St E1 . . . . . .**111** B4
Tait Ct **8** E3 . . . .**26** B4
2 London N19 . . . . . .**13** B4
Tait Ho SE1 . . . .**121** C1
2 London N19 . . . . . .**4** C4
Takhar Mews
SW11 . . . .**168** B2
Talacre Rd NW5 . . . . . .**12** C2
Talbot Ct EC3 . . . . . .**123** C4
Talbot Grove Ho **9**
W11 . . . .**31** A3
Talbot Ho E14 . . . .**34** A3
London N7 . . . .**5** B1
Talbot Pl SE3 . . . .**53** A1
Talbot Rd W11 . . . .**31** B3
W2 . . . .**31** C3
London SE22 . . . .**64** A3
Talbot Sq W2 . . . .**101** B1
Talbot Wlk W11 . . . . . .**31** A3
London NW10 . . . .**8** A2
Talbot Yd SE1 . . . . . .**123** B1
Talcott Path **3**
SW2 . . . .**74** C3
Talfourd Pl SE15 . . . . .**49** B2
Talfourd Rd SE15 . . . . .**49** B2
Talgarth Rd W14 . . . .**140** B2
London W6 . . . .**39** C1
Talia Ho E14 . . . .**42** B3
Talina Ctr SW6 . . . . . .**166** C3
Talleyrand Ho SE5 . . . .**48** B1
Tallis St EC4 . . . .**121** C4
Talma Rd SW2 . . . .**62** C3
Talmudical Coll N16 . . .**6** C4
Talmud Torah Sch
N16 . . . .**7** B4
Talwin St E3 . . . .**27** A2
Tamar Cl E3 . . . .**26** B4
Tamar Ho **10** E14 . . . .**42** B3
SE11 . . . .**149** C2
Tamarind Ct **8** W3 . . .**28** B3
Tamarind Ho **4**
SE15 . . . .**49** C3
Tamarind Yd E1 . . . . .**125** C2
Tamarisk Sq W12 . . . .**29** B2
Tamworth N7 . . . .**14** A2
Tamworth St SW6 . . .**155** B3
Tangier Rd TW10 . . . . .**55** A4
Tangley Gr SW15 . . . . .**68** B4
Tangmere WC1 . . . .**94** C3
Tanhurst Ho **27**
SW2 . . . .**74** A4
Tankerton St WC1 . . . .**94** B3
Tanner Ho SE1 . . . . . .**138** B3
Tanner's Hill SE8 . . . . .**51** C2
Tanner St SE1 . . . . . .**138** B3
Tanners Yd **22** E2 . . . .**25** A3
Tannery Ho E1 . . . . . .**111** B4
Tannington Terr N5 . . . .**5** C1
Tansley Cl N7 . . . .**13** C3
Tanswell St SE1 . . . . .**135** B3
Tantallon Rd SW12 . . .**72** C3
Tant Ave E16 . . . .**35** B1
Tanza Rd NW3 . . . .**12** B4
Tapley Ho SE1 . . . . . .**139** B3
Taplow NW3 . . . .**11** C1
Taplow Ho **2** E2 . . . . .**98** C3
Taplow St N1 . . . .**87** A1

Tappesfield Rd
SE15 . . . .**65** B4
Tapp St **1** E1 . . . .**25** A1
Taranto Ho **11** E1 . . . .**32** C4
Tarbert Rd SE22 . . . . .**64** A2
Tarbert Wlk E1 . . . .**32** B2
Tarling Ho **7** E1 . . . . .**32** A3
Tarling Rd E16 . . . .**35** B1
Tarling St E1 . . . .**32** B3
Tarnbrook Ct SW1 . . .**145** B3
Tarn St SE1 . . . .**136** C1
Tarns The NW1 . . . .**92** C4
Tarplett Ho **22** SE14 .**50** C4
Tarragon Cl SE14 . . . . .**51** A3
Tarranbrae NW6 . . . . . .**10** A1
Tarrant Ho E2 . . . .**25** B2
Tarrant Pl W1 . . . .**102** C3
Tarrantt Ho W14 . . . . .**126** B2
Tarriff Cres SE8 . . . . . .**41** B2
Tarrington Cl SW16 . . .**73** C1
Tartan Ho **6** E14 . . . . .**34** B3
Tarver Rd SE17 . . . . . .**150** B2
Tarves Way SE10 . . . . .**52** A3
Tasker Ho **8** E14 . . . . .**33** B4
Tasker Rd NW3 . . . . . .**12** B3
Tasman Ct **3** E14 . . . .**42** A2
Tasman Ho **17** E1 . . . .**32** A1
Tasman Rd SW9 . . . . . .**62** A4
Tasso Rd W6 . . . .**154** A4
Tasso Yd W6 . . . .**154** A3
Tatchbury Ho **9**
SW15 . . . .**56** B1
Tate Britain★ SW1 . . .**148** B3
Tate Ho **6** E2 . . . .**25** C3
Tate Modern★
EC4 . . . .**122** B4
Tatham Pl NW8 . . . . . .**79** C2
Tatnell Rd SE23 . . . . . .**66** A1
Tatton Cres E5,N16 . . . .**7** B4
Tatum St SE17 . . . . . .**151** C3
Tauheed Cl N4 . . . .**6** B2
Taunton Ho W2 . . . . .**100** C1
Taunton Mews NW1 . . .**90** C2
Taunton Pl NW1 . . . . . .**90** C2
Taverner Ho N16 . . . . . .**6** C1
Taverners Cl W11 . . . .**112** A1
Taverner Sq **4** N5 . . . .**15** B4
Tavern La SW9 . . . . . .**173** C2
Tavistock Cl N16 . . . . . .**16** A3
Tavistock Cres W11 . . .**31** B4
Tavistock Ho WC1 . . . . .**93** C2
Tavistock Ho **1**
W11 . . . .**31** B3
Tavistock Mews **1**
W11 . . . .**31** B3
Tavistock Pl WC1 . . . . .**94** A2
Tavistock Rd W11 . . . . .**31** B4
London NW10 . . . .**21** B3
Tavistock Sq WC1 . . . . .**93** C2
Tavistock St WC2 . . . .**120** B4
Tavistock Terr N19 . . . .**4** C1
Tavistock Twr SE16 . . .**41** A3
Taviton St WC1 . . . .**93** B2
Tavy Cl SE11 . . . .**149** C2
Tawny Way SE16 . . . . .**40** C2
Taybridge Rd SW11 . . .**60** C3
Tayburn Cl E14 . . . .**34** B3
Tay Ho **3** E3 . . . .**26** B3
Tayler Ct NW8 . . . .**79** B4
Taylor Ct E15 . . . .**76** B3
Taylor Ho **10** SW2 . . .**74** C3
Taylor's Gn W3 . . . .**29** A3
Taylor's La NW10 . . . . . .**8** A1
Tayport Cl N1 . . . .**14** A1
Tayside Ct **8** SE5 . . . .**63** C3
Teak Cl SE16 . . . .**33** A1

Tealby Ct N7 . . . .**14** B2
Teal St **30** SE8 . . . . . .**51** B4
Teale St E2 . . . .**24** C3
Teather St **5** SE5 . . . .**49** A3
Tebbs Ho **14** SW2 . . . .**74** C4
Ted Roberts Ho **24**
E2 . . . .**25** A3
Tedworth Gdns
SW3 . . . .**144** C1
Tedworth Sq SW3 . . .**144** C1
Teesdale Cl E2 . . . .**25** A3
Teesdale St E2 . . . .**25** A3
Teesdale Yd **28** E2 . . .**25** A3
Tee The W3 . . . .**29** A3
Teignmouth Cl **6**
SW4 . . . .**61** C3
Teignmouth Rd NW2 . . .**9** C2
Telegraph Hill NW3 . . . .**2** A1
Telegraph Pl E14 . . . . .**42** A2
Telegraph Rd SW15 . . .**69** B4
Telegraph St EC2 . . . .**109** B2
Telfer Cl **3** W3 . . . . . .**37** B4
Telfer Ho EC1 . . . .**96** B3
Telferscot JMI Sch
SW12 . . . .**73** C3
Telferscot Prim Sch
SW12 . . . .**73** C3
Telferscot Rd SW12 . . .**73** C3
Telford Ho SE1 . . . . . .**137** A1
SW2 . . . .**74** A3
Telford Avenue Mans **7**
SW2 . . . .**74** A3
Telford Ho SE1 . . . . . .**136** C2
8 W10 . . . .**31** A4
Telford Parade Mans **7**
SW2 . . . .**74** A3
Telford Rd W10 . . . . . .**31** A4
Telford Terr SW1 . . . .**160** C4
Telford Way W3 . . . . . .**29** A4
Tell Gr SE22 . . . .**64** B3
Telscombe Ho
SW11 . . . .**169** B3
Temair Ho **1** SE10 . . .**52** B3
Temeraire St SE16 . . . .**40** B4
Temperley Rd SW12 . . .**72** C4
Templar Ho NW2 . . . . .**10** B2
Templars Ho E15 . . . . .**19** A3
Templar St SE5 . . . . . .**48** A1
Temple Ave EC4 . . . . .**121** C4
Temple Ct **1** SW8 . . .**162** A1
13 London N7 . . . .**4** B1
Temple La EC4 . . . . . .**107** C1
Temple Lo **1** London SW4 .**60** A4
Templemead St W3 . . .**29** A3
Templemead Ho E9 . . .**18** A4
Temple Pl WC2 . . . . . .**121** A4
Temple Rd London W4 . .**37** B3
Richmond TW9 . . . .**54** B4
Temple Sheen
SW14 . . . .**55** B2
Temple Sheen Rd
SW14 . . . .**55** B3
Temple St E2 . . . .**25** A3
Temple Sta WC2 . . . .**121** B4
Templeton Cl **2**
N16 . . . .**16** A3
Templeton Pl SW5 . . .**141** C3

Temple West Mews
SE1 . . . . 136 A1
Templewood Ave
NW3 . . . . 2 A1
Templewood Gdns
NW3 . . . . 2 A1
Templewood Point
NW2 . . . . 1 B2
Tenbury Ct SW12 . . . . 73 C3
Tenby Ho N7 . . . . 100 C1
London N7 . . . . 14 C4
Tench St E1 . . . . 32 A1
Tenda Rd SE16 . . . . . . 40 A2
Tendring Ho SW2 . . . . 62 C1
Tenham Ave SW2 . . . . 73 C2
Tenison Ct W1 . . . . . 118 C4
Tenison Way SE1 . . . . 121 B1
Tenniel Cl W2 . . . . . . 114 B4
Tennis St SE1 . . . . . . 137 B4
Tennyson Ct SW6 . . . 166 B3
Tennyson Ho SE17 . . 150 C2
Tennyson St SW8 . . . 170 A1
Tensing Ho N1 . . . . . . 15 A2
Tenterden Ho
SE17 . . . . 152 B1
Tenterden St W1 . . . . 104 B1
Tenter Ground E1 . . . 110 C3
Tent St E1 . . . . 25 A1
Terborch Way 6
SE22 . . . . 64 A2
Terling Ho W10 . . . . . . 30 B4
Terling Wlk N1 . . . . . . 86 C4
Terminus Pl SW1 . . . . 132 B1
Tern Ho 8 SE15 . . . . . 49 B2
Terrace Ave NW10 . . . 22 B2
Terrace Gdns SW13 . . 46 B1
Terrace La TW10 . . . . . 54 A1
Terrace Rd E9 . . . . 17 B1
Terrace The EC4 . . . . 107 C1
NW6 . . . . 23 C4
9 SE8 . . . . 41 B2
SW13,SW14 . . . . 46 A1
Terrapin Ct SW17 . . . . 73 A1
Terrapin Rd SW17 . . . 73 A1
Terrick Rd W12 . . . . . . 30 A3
Territorial Ho
SE11 . . . . 149 C3
Terry Ho SW2 . . . . 74 C3
Tersha St TW9 . . . . . . 54 B3
Tessa Sanderson Pl 6
SW8 . . . . 61 A4
Testerton Wlk 3
W11 . . . . 30 C2
Tetcott Rd SW10 . . . . 156 C1
Teversham La
SW8 . . . . 172 B4
Teviot St E14 . . . . 34 B4
Teyham Ct SW11 . . . . 60 B1
Thackeray Ct SW3 . . . 144 C2
W14 . . . . 126 C1
Thackeray Ho WC1 . . . 94 A2
Thackeray Mews 18 E8 16 C2
Thackeray Rd SW8 . . 170 B1
Thackeray St W8 . . . . 128 B2
Thalia Cl SE10 . . . . 52 C4
Thame Rd SE16 . . . . . . 40 C4
Thames Ave SW10 . . . 167 A4
Thames Bank SW14 . . 45 B1
Thames Circ E14 . . . . . 41 C2
Thames Cres W4 . . . . 46 A3
Thames Ct 19 SE15 . . . 49 B3
Thames Hts SE1 . . . . 138 C4
Thameside Ctr TW8 . . 44 B4
Thames Link Ho 3
TW9 . . . . 54 A3
Thames Pl SW15 . . . . 57 C4

Thames Quay E14 . . . . 42 A4
SW10 . . . . 167 A3
Thames Rd W4 . . . . . . 44 C4
Thames Reach W6 . . . 47 B4
Thames St SE10 . . . . . 52 A4
Thames Village W4 . . 45 B2
Thanet Ho WC1 . . . . . . 94 A3
⚀ West Norwood
SE27 . . . . 75 A1
Thanet Lo NW2 . . . . . 10 A2
Thanet St WC1 . . . . . . 94 A3
Thane Villas N7 . . . . . . 5 B1
Thane Works N7 . . . . . 5 B1
Thavie's Inn EC4 . . . . 107 C2
Thaxted Ct N1 . . . . 87 C1
Thaxted Ho SE16 . . . . 40 B2
Thaxton Rd W14 . . . . 155 A4
Thayer St W1 . . . . 103 C2
Theatre Mus W2 9 . . 120 B4
Theatre St SW11 . . . . 60 B4
Theberton St N1 . . . . . 86 A4
Theed St SE1 . . . . 121 C1
Thelbridge Ho 20
E3 . . . . 27 A2
Theobald's Rd
WC1 . . . . 106 C3
Theobald's Rd 5
SW15 . . . . 56 C2
Theodore Rd SE13 . . . 67 C1
Therapia Rd SE22 . . . . 65 B1
Theresa Rd W6 . . . . . . 38 C2
Therfield Ct N4 . . . . . . 6 B2
Thermopylae Gate
E14 . . . . 42 A2
Theseus Ho 2 E14 . . . 34 C3
Theseus Wlk N1 . . . . . 86 B1
Thessaly Ho SW8 . . . 160 C1
Thessaly Rd SW8 . . . 171 A4
Thesus Ho 2 E14 . . . . 34 C3
Thetford Ho SE1 . . . . 138 C2
Thetis Terr TW9 . . . . . 44 C4
Third Ave
London W10 . . . . 23 A2
London W3 . . . . 29 B1
Thirleby Rd SW1 . . . . 133 A1
Thirlmere NW1 . . . . . . 92 B4
Thirlmere Ho 20
N16 . . . . 15 C4
Thistle Gr SW7 . . . . . 143 A1
Thistle Ho 6 E14 . . . . 34 B3
Thistlewood Cl 3 N7 . 5 B2
Thistly Ct SE8 . . . . 52 A4
Thomas Baines Rd
SW11 . . . . 59 C4
Thomas Burt Ho 8
E2 . . . . 25 A2
Thomas Buxton Jun &
Inf Sch E1 . . . . 24 C1
Thomas Doyle St
SE1 . . . . 136 B2
Thomas Fairchild Comm
Sch N1 . . . . 86 C2
Thomas Ho
3 London E9 . . . . 17 B2
4 SW4 . . . . 62 A3
Thomas Hollywood Ho
4 E2 . . . . 25 B3
Thomas Jones Prim Sch
W11 . . . . 31 A3
Thomas More Ho
EC2 . . . . 108 C3

Thomas More Sq
E1 . . . . 125 B3
Thomas More St
E1 . . . . 125 B2
Thomas North Terr 3
E16 . . . . 35 B2
Thomas Pl W8 . . . . . . 128 A1
Thomas Rd E14 . . . . . . 33 C4
Thomas Road Ind Est
E14 . . . . 33 C3
Thomas's London Day
Schs SW11 . . . . 167 C3
Thomas's Prep Sch
Clapham SW11 . . . . . 60 B3
Thomson Ave E6 . . . . . 48 B3
Thomson Rd SE17 . . . 152 A3
Thorburn Ho SW1 . . . 131 B3
Thorburn Sq SE1 . . . . 153 B3
Thoresby Ho N16 . . . . 6 C1
Thoresby St N1 . . . . . . 97 A4
Thornaby Ho 15 E2 . . 25 A2
Thornbill Ho 7
SE15 . . . . 49 C3
Thornbury Cl N16 . . . 16 A3
Thornbury Ct W11 . . 113 B4
Thornbury Ho N6 . . . . 4 B3
Thornbury Rd SW2 . . 62 A1
Thornbury Sq N6 . . . . 4 B3
Thorncliffe Ct SW2 . . 62 A1
Thorncliffe Rd SW2 . . 62 A1
Thorncombe Rd
SE22 . . . . 64 A2
Thorncroft St SW8 . . 162 A1
Thorndale Ho N16 . . . 7 A3
Thorndean St SW18 . . 71 B2
Thorndike Cl
SW10 . . . . 156 C2
Thorndike Ho SW1 . . 147 B2
Thorndike St SW1 . . . 147 B3
Thorne Cl E16 . . . . 35 C3
34 E2 . . . . 25 B2
Thorne Pas 7
SW13 . . . . 46 B1
Thorne Rd SW8 . . . . . 162 B1
Thorness Ct SW18 . . . 59 B1
Thorne St SW13,
W4 . . . . 56 A4
Thornewill Ho 7
E1 . . . . 32 B2
Thorney Cres
SW11 . . . . 157 C1
Thorney Ct W8 . . . . . 128 C3
Thorney Hedge Rd
W4 . . . . 37 A2
Thorney St SW1 . . . . . 148 A4
Thornfield Ho 3
E14 . . . . 33 C2
Thornfield Rd W12 . . . 39 A4
Thornford Rd SE13 . . 67 B2
Thorngate Rd W9 . . . . 23 C1
Thornham Gr E15 . . . 19 C3
Thorn Ham Ho
SE1 . . . . 137 C2
Thornham St SE10 . . . 52 A4
Thornhaugh St
WC1 . . . . 93 C1
Thornhill Bridge Wharf
N1 . . . . 84 C3

Thornhill Cres N1 . . . 14 B1
Thornhill Gr N1 . . . . . 14 C1
Thornhill Ho
London N1 . . . . 14 C1
⓰ London W4 . . . . . . 38 A1
Thornhill Prim Sch
N1 . . . . 14 C1
Thornhill Rd N1 . . . . . 85 B4
Thornhill Sq N1 . . . . . 14 C1
Thornicroft Ho
9 SW9 . . . . 173 A1
Thornley Pl 2 SE10 . . 43 A1
Thornsett Rd SW18 . . 71 A3
Thornton Ave
London W4 . . . . 38 A2
Streatham SW2 . . . . . 73 C3
Thornton Ct N7 . . . . . . 13 C3
Thornton Gdns
SW12 . . . . 73 C3
Thornton Ho SE17 . . . 152 A3
Thornton Pl W1 . . . . . 103 A4
Thornton Rd
Mortlake SW14 . . . . . 55 C4
Streatham SW12,SW2 73 C3
Thornton St SW9 . . . 173 B2
Thornville St SE8 . . . . 51 C2
Thornwood Rd SE13 . 67 C2
Thornycroft Ct TW9 . . 44 B1
Thorold Ho 2 SE1 . . . 136 C4
6 Streatham SW2 . . . 74 A4
Thorparch Rd
SW8 . . . . 161 C1
Thorpebank Rd
W12 . . . . 29 C1
Thorpe Cl W10 . . . . . . 31 A3
Thorpedale Rd N4 . . . 5 B3
Thorpe Ho N1 . . . . 85 A3
Thorverton Rd NW2 . . 1 A1
Thoydon Rd E3 . . . . . . 26 A3
Thrale St SE1 . . . . 123 A1
Thrasher Cl 20 E8 . . . 24 B4
Thrawl St E1 . . . . 111 A3
Thrayle Ho 2 SW9 . . . 62 B4
Threadgold Ho 5
N1 . . . . 15 C2
Threadneedle St
EC2,EC3 . . . . 109 C1
Three Colts La E2 . . . . 25 A1
Three Colt St E14 . . . . 33 B2
Three Cups Yd
WC1 . . . . 107 A3
Three Kings Yd
W1 . . . . 118 A4
Three Mill La E3 . . . . . 27 B2
Three Nun Ct EC2 . . . 109 B2
Three Oak La SE1 . . . 138 C4
Threshers Pl W11 . . . . 112 A4
Thring Ho SW9 . . . . . 172 C2
Throgmorton Ave
EC2 . . . . 109 C2
Throgmorton St
EC2 . . . . 109 C2
Thrush St SE17 . . . . . 150 C2
Thurland Rd SE16 . . . 139 B2
Thurland Rd SE16 . . . 139 B2
Thurleigh Ave
SW12 . . . . 60 C1
Thurleigh Ct SW12 . . 60 C1
Thurleigh Rd SW12 . . 60 C1
Thurloe Cl SW7 . . . . . 144 A4
Thurloe Ct SW3 . . . . . 144 A3
Thurloe Pl SW7 . . . . . 143 C4
Thurloe Place Mews
SW7 . . . . 143 C4
Thurloe Sq SW7 . . . . . 144 A4
Thurloe St SW7 . . . . . 143 C4
Thurloe St SW7 . . . . . 143 C4

Thurlow Ho ⓱
SW16 . . . . 74 A1
Thurlow Park Rd
SE21,SE24 . . . . 75 B2
Thurlow Rd NW3 . . . . 11 C3
Thurlow St SE17 . . . . 152 A1
Thurlow Terr NW5 . . . 12 C3
Thurlow Twrs SE27 . . 74 C1
Thurnscoe NW1 . . . . . 82 C3
Thurry Gdns
SW19 . . . . 69 C2
Thursley Ho ⓰ SW2 . . 74 B4
Thurso Ho NW6 . . . . . 78 A1
Thurston Ind Est
SE13 . . . . 67 A4
Thurston Rd SE8,
SE13 . . . . 52 A1
Thurtle Rd E2 . . . . 24 B3
Tibbatts Rd E3 . . . . . . 27 A1
Tibbets Cl SW19 . . . . . 69 C3
Tibbet's Corner
SW19 . . . . 69 C4
Tibbet's Ride SW19 . . 69 C4
Tiber Gdns N1 . . . . . . 84 B3
Tickford Ho NW8 . . . . 90 A3
Tidal Basin Rd E16 . . . 35 B2
Tidbury Ct SW8 . . . . . 160 C1
Tidemill Prim Sch
SE8 . . . . 51 C3
Tideswell ⓰ NW5 . . . 12 C2
Tideswell Rd SW15 . . 57 B3
Tideway Ct 9 SE16 . . . 32 C1
Tideway Ho E14 . . . . . 41 C4
Tideway Ind Est
SW8 . . . . 161 A3
Tideway Wharf
SW13 . . . . 46 A1
Tideway Yd SW13 . . . 46 A1
Tidey St E3 . . . . 33 C4
Tidworth Ho ⓱
SE22 . . . . 64 A4
Tidworth Rd E3 . . . . . . 26 C1
Tierney Rd SW2 . . . . . 74 A3
Tierney Terr SW2 . . . . 74 A3
Tiger Ho WC1 . . . . 93 C4
Tiger Way E5 . . . . 17 A4
Tilbury Cl ⓲ SE15 . . . 49 B3
Tilbury Ho 4 SE14 . . . 50 C4
Tildesley Rd SW15 . . . 57 B1
Tilehurst NW1 . . . . 92 B3
Tilehurst Rd SW17,
SW18 . . . . 71 C3
Tile Kiln La N6 . . . . 4 B3
Tileyard Rd N7 . . . . . . 14 A1
Tilford Gdns SW19 . . 69 C3
Tilford Ho 8 SW2 . . . 74 B4
Tilia Rd E5 . . . . 17 A4
Tilia Wlk 21 SW9 . . . . 63 A3
Tilleard Ho 4 W10 . . . 23 A2
Tiller Ho 20 N1 . . . . . . 24 A4
Tiller Rd E14 . . . . 41 C3
Tillet Sq SE16 . . . . 41 A4
Tillet Way 6 E2 . . . . . 99 B4
Tilling Ho 8 SE15 . . . 65 A4
Tillman Ho 3 SW2 . . . 74 B3
Tillman St E1 . . . . 32 A3
Tillotson Ct SW8 . . . . 161 C1
Tilney Ct EC1 . . . . 97 A2
Tilney Gdns 12 N1 . . . 15 C2
Tilney St W1 . . . . 117 C2
Tilson Cl 2 SE5 . . . . . 49 A3
Tilson Gdns SW2,
SW4 . . . . 74 A4
Tilson Ho SW2 . . . . . . 74 A4
Tilton St SW6 . . . . 154 B3

Tiltwood The W3 . . . 28 B2
Timberland Cl 15
SE15 . . . . .49 C3
Timberland Rd E1 . . .32 A3
Timber Mill Way
SW4 . . . . .61 C4
Timber Pond Rd
SE16 . . . . .40 C4
Timber St EC1 . . . . . .96 C2
Time Sq E8 . . . . .16 C3
Timothy Cl 1 SW4 . .61 B2
Timothy Rd E3 . . . . . .33 B4
Timsbury Wlk 5
SW15 . . . . .68 C3
Tina Ct SW16 . . . . . . .74 C1
Tindal St SW9 . . . . . .48 A2
Tinniswood Cl N5 . . .14 C3
Tinsley Rd E1 . . . . . . .32 B4
Tintagel Cres SE22 . .64 B3
Tintagel Ct EC1 . . . . .96 A1
Tintern Cl SW15 . . . .58 A2
Tintern Ho NW1 . . . .82 B1
SW1 . . . . .146 A3
Tintern St SW4 . . . . .62 A3
Tinworth St SE11 . .148 B2
Tipthorpe Rd SW11 .60 C4
Tiptree 7 NW1 . . . . .13 A1
Tisbury Ct W1 . . . . .119 B4
Tisdall Pl SE17 . . . .151 C3
Tissington Ct 4
SE16 . . . . .40 C2
Titan Bsns Est 3
SE8 . . . . .51 C3
Titan Ct TW8 . . . . . . .36 B1
Titchborne Row
W2 . . . . .102 B1
Titchfield Rd NW8 . .80 C4
Titchwell Rd SW18 . .71 C3
Tite St SW3 . . . . . . .158 C4
Titmuss St W12 . . . .39 B4
Tiverton Rd NW6,
NW10 . . . . .22 A4
Tiverton St SE1 . . . .136 C2
Tivoli Ct SE16 . . . . . .33 B1
Tobago St E14 . . . . . .41 C4
Tobin Cl NW3 . . . . . . .12 A1
Toby La E1 . . . . .26 A1
Todber Ho W14 . . . .126 B2
Todds Wlk N7 . . . . .5 B2
Tokenhouse Yd
EC2 . . . . .109 B2
Toland Sq SW15 . . . .56 C2
Tolchurch 2 W11 . . .31 C3
Tollbridge Cl W10 . . .23 A1
Tollet St E1 . . . . .25 C1
Tollgate Dr SE21 . . . .76 A2
Tollgate Ho NW6 . . . .78 A2
Tollhouse Way N19 . . .4 B2
Tollington Ct N4 . . . . .5 B2
Tollington Pk N4 . . . . .5 B2
Tollington Pl N4 . . . . .5 B2
Tollington Rd N7 . . . .14 B4
Tollington Way N7 . . .5 A1
Tolmers NW1 . . . . . . .93 A2
Tolpaide Ho SE11 . .149 B3
Tolsford Rd E5 . . . . . .17 A3
Tom Groves Cl E15 . .19 C3
Tom Hood Cl E15 . . .19 C3
Tom Jenkinson Rd 5
E16 . . . . .35 C1
Tomline Ho SE1 . . . .122 C1
Tomlin's Gr E3 . . . . . .26 C2
Tomlinson Cl E2 . . . .99 A3
  5 London W4 . . . . .37 A1

Tomlin's Terr E14 . . .33 A3
Tomlins Wlk 4 N7 . . .5 B2
Tompion Ho EC1 . . . .96 B2
Tompion St EC1 . . . . .96 B3
Tom Smith Cl SE10 . .53 A4
Tomson Ho SE1 . . . .138 C2
Tom Williams Ho
SW6 . . . . .154 C3
Tonbridge Hos WC1 .94 A3
Tonbridge St WC1 . . .94 A3
Toneborough NW8 . .78 B3
Tonsley Hill SW18 . . .59 A2
Tonsley Pl SW18 . . . .59 A2
Tonsley Rd SW18 . . . .59 A2
Tonsley St SW18 . . . .59 A2
Took's Ct EC4 . . . . . .107 B2
Tooley St SE1 . . . . . .124 A1
Tooting Bec SW17 . . .72 C1
Tooting Bec Sta
SW17 . . . . .72 C1
Topham Ho 6 SE10 .52 B3
Topham St EC1 . . . . .95 B2
Topiary Sq TW9 . . . . .54 B4
Topmast Point E14 . .41 C4
Torbay Ct 1 NW1 . . .13 A1
Torbay Mans NW6 . . .23 B4
Torbay Rd NW6 . . . . .10 B1
Torbay St 15 NW1 . . .13 A1
Tor Ct W8 . . . . .127 C4
Tor Gdns W8 . . . . . .127 B4
Tornay Ho N1 . . . . . . .84 C2
  London E9 . . . . .17 B1
Torquay St W2 . . . .100 A3
Torrens Ct SE5 . . . . .63 C4
Torrens Rd SW2 . . . .62 B2
Torrens St EC1 . . . . . .86 A1
Torres Sq E14 . . . . . .41 C1
Torriano Ave NW5 . . .13 C3
Torriano Cotts NW5 .13 B3
Torriano Jun & Inf Schs
NW5 . . . . .13 C3
Torridge Gdns SE15 .65 B3
Torridon Ho NW6 . . .78 A1
Torrington Pl E1 . . .125 C2
WC1 . . . . .105 B4
Torrington Sq WC1 . .93 C1
Tortington Ho 1
SE15 . . . . .50 A3
Torwood Rd SW15 . . .56 C2
Tothill Ho SW1 . . . .147 C4
Tothill St SW1 . . . . .133 C3
Totland Ho SW18 . . . .59 A1
Tottan Terr E1 . . . . . .32 C3
Tottenhall 5 NW1 . . .12 C1
Tottenham Court Rd
W1 . . . . .105 A4
Tottenham Court Road
Sta W1 . . . . .105 C2
Tottenham Mews
W1 . . . . .105 A4
Tottenham Rd N1 . . .16 A2
Tottenham St W1 . .105 A4
Totteridge Ho
SW11 . . . . .167 C2
Touchard Ho N1 . . . .97 C3
Toulmin St SE1 . . . .136 C3
Toulon St SE5 . . . . . .48 B3
Toulouse Ct 2
SE16 . . . . .40 A1
Tournay Rd SW6 . . .155 A2
Toussaint Wlk
SE16 . . . . .139 C2
Tovy Ho SE1 . . . . . . .153 B1
Towcester Rd E3 . . . .27 B1
Tower 42 ★ EC2 . . .110 B1
Tower Bldgs 22 E1 . .32 A1

Tower Br App E1,
EC3 . . . . .124 C3
Tower Bridge ★
E1,EC3,SE1 . . . . .124 C2
Tower Bridge Bsns
Complex SE16 . . . . .40 A3
Tower Bridge Bsns Sq
SE16 . . . . .40 A2
Tower Bridge Piazza
SE1 . . . . .124 C1
Tower Bridge Prim Sch
SE1 . . . . .138 C4
Tower Bridge Rd
SE1 . . . . .124 C1
Tower Bridge Sq
SE1 . . . . .138 C4
Tower Cl NW3 . . . . . .11 C3
Tower Ct NW8 . . . . . .80 B2
WC2 . . . . .106 A1
London E5 . . . . .7 B4
Towergate SE1 . . . . .152 A4
Tower Gateway Sta
EC3 . . . . .124 C4
Tower Hamlets Coll
E1 . . . . .32 B4
E1 . . . . .32 C3
E14 . . . . .34 A2
E14 . . . . .34 A3
Tower Hill EC3 . . . .124 C3
Tower Hill Sta EC3 .124 C4
Tower Hill Terr
EC3 . . . . .124 C3
Tower Mans SE1 . . .138 C1
Tower Mews E5 . . . . .18 A3
Tower Millennium Pier
EC3 . . . . .124 B2
Tower Mill Rd 1
SE15 . . . . .49 A3
Tower Rd NW10 . . . . .8 C1
Tower Rise TW9 . . . . .54 A4
Tower Royal EC4 . . .123 B4
Tower Pl TW10 . . . . .54 A2
Tower St WC2 . . . . .106 A1
Towers The
London NW5 . . . . . . .13 A4
  1 Richmond TW9 . .54 B3
Tower Terr SE4 . . . . .66 A3
Tower The ★ EC3 . . .124 C3
Tower Wharf SE1 . . .138 C4
Tower Wlk SE1 . . . . .152 A4
Towncourt Path N4 . . .6 B3
Townhall Ave 3
W4 . . . . .37 C1
Town Hall Rd SW11 . .60 B4
Townley Rd SE22 . . .64 A2
Townley St SE17 . . .151 B2
Townmead Bsns Ctr
SW6 . . . . .59 B4
Townmead Rd
London SW6 . . . . . .166 C3
Richmond TW9 . . . .45 A1
Townsend Ho SE1 . .153 C3
Townsend Ind Est
NW10 . . . . .20 B3
Townsend Prim Sch
SE17 . . . . .152 A3
Townsend St SE1,
SE17 . . . . .152 A4
Townsend Yd N6 . . . . .4 A3
Townshend Ct NW8 . .80 B2
Townshend Est
NW8 . . . . .80 A2
Townshend Rd
NW8 . . . . .80 A3
Richmond TW9 . . . .54 B3
Townshend Terr
TW9 . . . . .54 B3

Towns Ho 4 SW4 . . .61 C4
Towton Rd SE27 . . . .75 B2
Toxteth Ho N4 . . . . . . .6 B4
Toynbee St E1 . . . . .110 C3
Tracey Ave NW2 . . . . .9 B3
Tracy Ho 12 E3 . . . . .26 B2
Tradescant Ho 18
E9 . . . . .17 B1
Tradescant Rd
SW8 . . . . .162 B1
Tade Twr E8 . . . . .59 B4
Trade Wharfs Cl E1 125 C2
Trading Estate Rd
NW10 . . . . .20 B1
Traemore Ct SW16 . .74 C1
Trafalgar Ave SE15 . .49 B4
Trafalgar Cl 1
SE16 . . . . .41 A2
Trafalgar Gdns E1 . . .32 C4
W8 . . . . .128 B2
Trafalgar Gr SE10 . . .52 C4
Trafalgar Ho SE17 . .151 A2
Trafalgar Mews E9 . .18 B2
Trafalgar Rd SE10 . . .43 A1
Trafalgar Sq ★
SW1 . . . . .119 C2
Trafalgar St SE17 . .151 C2
Trafalgar Way E14 . . .34 B1
Trafford Cl E15 . . . . . .19 A3
Trafford Ho N1 . . . . . .87 C2
Tragail SW15 . . . . . . .58 A2
Traitors Gate E1 . . .124 C2
Tralee Ct 5 SE16 . . .40 A1
Tramway Ave E15 . . .19 C1
Trance Way W3 . . . . .36 C3
Tranmere Ho 7 N7 . . .14 C3
Tranmere Rd SW17,
SW18 . . . . .71 B2
Tranquil Pass SE3 . . .53 B1
Tranquil Vale SE3 . . .53 A1
Transept St NW1 . . .102 B3
Transom Cl SE16 . . . .41 A2
Transom Sq E14 . . . .42 A1
Tranton Rd SE16 . . . .40 A3
Trappes Ho 2 SE16 .40 A2
Travel Clinic, Hospl for
Tropical Diseases
WC1 . . . . .93 A1
Travers Ho 6 SE10 .52 C4
Travers Rd N7 . . . . . . .5 C1
Travis Ho SE10 . . . . .52 B2
Treadgold Ho 7
W11 . . . . .30 C2
Treadgold St W11 . . .30 C2
Treadway St E2 . . . . .25 A3
Treasury Buildings
SW1 . . . . .134 A4
Treaty St N1 . . . . .84 C3
Trebeck St W1 . . . . .118 A1
Treborough Ho
W1 . . . . .103 B4
Trebovir Rd SW5 . . .141 C3
Treby St E3 . . . . .26 B1
Trecastle Way 3
N7 . . . . .13 C4
Tredegar Rd E3 . . . . .26 B3
Tredegar Sq E3 . . . . .26 B2
Tredegar Terr E3 . . . .26 B2
Trederwen Rd E8 . . . .24 C4
Treen Ave SW13 . . . .56 B4
Trees The N16 . . . . . . .6 C4
Trefil Wlk N7 . . . . . . .14 A4
Trefoil Rd SW18 . . . .59 B2
Tregarvon Rd SW11 .60 C3
Trego Rd E9 . . . . .18 C1
Tregothnan Rd SW9 62 A4

Tregunter Rd
SW10 . . . . .142 C1
Treherne Ct SW9 . . .48 A2
Trehern Rd 12
SW14 . . . . .55 C4
Trehurst St E5 . . . . . .18 A3
Trelawney Est E9 . . . .17 B2
Trelawney Ho SE1 . .136 C4
Trelawn Rd SW2 . . . .62 C2
Trellis Sq 1 E3 . . . . .26 B2
Tremadoc Rd SW4 . .61 C3
Tremaine Cl SE4 . . . .51 C1
Trematon Ho SE11 . .149 C2
Tremlett Gr N19 . . . . .4 B1
Tremlett Mews N19 . .4 B1
Trenchard St SE10 . .42 C1
Trenchold St SW8 . .162 A3
Trendell Ho 4 E14 . .33 C3
Trenmar Gdns
NW10 . . . . .22 A2
Trenmar Lo NW10 . . .22 A2
Trentham St SW18 . .70 C3
Trent Ho SE15 . . . . . .65 B3
Trent Rd SW2 . . . . . . .62 B2
Treport St SW18 . . . .71 A4
Tresco Ho SE11 . . . .149 B2
Tresco Rd SE15 . . . . .65 A3
Tresham Cres NW8 . .90 A2
Tresham Wlk E9 . . . . .17 B3
Tresidder Ho 10
SW4 . . . . .73 C4
Tressel Cl 20 N1 . . . .15 A1
Tressillian Cres SE4 .66 C4
Tressillian Rd SE4 . . .66 C4
Trevanion Rd W14 . .140 B2
Trevelyan Gdns
NW10 . . . . .22 B4
Trevelyan Ho 18 E2 .25 C2
SE5 . . . . .48 A3
Treveris St SE1 . . . . .122 B1
Treverton St W10 . . .22 C1
Treverton Twr W10 . .30 C4
Trevers Ho 11 24 C1 99 C1
Treville St SW15 . . . .69 A4
Trevithick Ho
3 SE16 . . . . .40 A2
SW8 . . . . .171 B4
3 London NW5 . . . . .13 A4
Trevithick St SE8 . . . .51 C4
Trevor Pl SW7 . . . . .130 B3
Trevor Roberts Tutorial
Coll NW8 . . . . .11 C1
Trevor Sq SW7 . . . . .130 B3
Trevor St SW7 . . . . .130 B3
Trevose Ho SE11 . . .149 A2
Trewint St SW18 . . . .71 B2
Triangle Est The
SE11 . . . . .149 C1
Triangle Ho SE1 . . . .138 C4
Triangle Pl SW4 . . . . .61 C3
Triangle 7 E8 . . . . . .25 A4
Triangle The E8 . . . . .25 A4
EC1 . . . . .96 B2
London N19 . . . . .4 C4
Trident Ho 9 E14 . . .34 B3
Trident St SE16 . . . . .40 C2
Trieste Ct SW12 . . . .72 B3
Trigon Rd SW8 . . . .163 A2
Trimdon NW1 . . . . . . .83 A3
Trimmer Wlk 8
TW8 . . . . .44 A4
Trim St SE8 . . . . .51 B4
Trinder Gdns N19 . . . .5 A3
Trinder Rd N4,N19 . . .5 A3
Trinidad Ho 17 E14 . .33 B2
Trinidad St E14 . . . . .33 B2

Trinity Church Rd
SW13 ....47 A4
Trinity Church Sq
SE1 ....137 A2
Trinity Cl
London SE13 ....67 C3
3 London SW4 ....61 B3
Trinity Cotts TW9 ..54 B4
Trinity Cres TW7 ...72 C2
Trinity Ct **2** N1 ....24 A4
WC1 ....94 C2
Trinity Gdns E16 ...35 B2
London SW2,SW9 ...62 B3
Trinity Gn E1 ....32 B4
Trinity Gr **8** SE10 ..52 B2
Trinity Ho SE1 .....137 A2
Trinity Homes **14**
SW2 ....62 B3
Trinity Mews SE18 .70 C3
Trinity Pl EC3 .....124 C3
Trinity Rd
Richmond TW9 .....54 B4
Wandsworth SW17,
SW18 ....72 A3
Trinity Rise SE24,
SW2 ....75 A4
Trinity Sq EC3 ....124 B4
Trinity St **18** E16 ...35 C4
SE1 ....137 B2
Trinity St Mary's CE
Prim Sch SW12 ....72 C3
Trinity Way W3 ....29 B2
Trio Pl SE1 ....137 A3
Tristan Ct **11** SE8 ..51 B4
Triton Ct EC2 ......97 C1
Triton Ho **2** E14 ...42 A2
Triton Sq NW1 .....92 C2
Triton Rd SE21,
SE27 ....75 C1
Trocette Mans SE1 .138 B2
Trojan Ct NW6 .....10 A1
Trojan Ind Est NW10 .8 B2
Troon Cl **3** SE16 ...40 A1
Troon Ho **11** E14 ...33 A3
Troon St E1 ....33 A3
Tropical Ct **2** W10 .22 C2
Trossachs Rd SE22 .64 A2
Trothy Rd SE1 .....153 C3
Trotman Ho SE14 ...50 B2
Trott St SW11 .....168 B3
Trotwood Ho **3**
SE16 ....40 A4
Troubridge Ct **12**
W4 ....37 B1
Troutbeck NW1 .....92 B3
Troutbeck Rd SE14 .51 A2
Trouville Rd SW4 ...61 B1
Trowbridge Rd E9 ..18 B2
Trower Ho **5** E9 ...18 A2
Troy Ct W8 ....127 B2
Troyes Ho NW3 ....12 B3
Troy Town SE15 ....64 C4
Troy Town Flats
SE15 ....64 C4
Truman's Rd **24** N16 .16 A3
Trump St EC2 .....109 A1
Trundle St SE1 ....136 C4
Trundleys Rd SE8 ..51 A4
Trundley's Rd SE8 ..40 C1
Trundley's Terr SE8 .40 C2
Truro Ho **28** W2 ...31 C4
Truro St NW5 ......12 C2
Trussley Rd W6 ....39 B3
Trust Wlk SE21 ....75 A3
Tryon Cres E9 .....25 B4
Tryon St SW3 .....144 C2

Tubbs Rd NW10 ....21 B3
Tudor Cl London N6 ..4 B4
London NW3 ....12 A2
London SW2 ....62 B1
Tudor Ct **5** SE16 ...32 C1
London N1 ....16 A2
London W5 ....36 C4
Tudor Est NW10 ....20 A3
Tudor Gdns SW14 ..56 A4
Tudor Gr E9 ....17 B1
Tudor Ho
14 London E9 ....17 B1
London W14 ....39 C2
Tudor Mews **2**
NW10 ....8 C2
Tudor Rd E9 ....25 A4
Tudor St EC4 .....121 C4
Tudor Way W3 .....36 C4
Tudwell St **2** E3 ...26 B4
Tufnell Park Mans **2**
N7 ....13 C4
Tufnell Park Prim Sch
N7 ....13 C4
Tufnell Park Rd
N19,N7 ....13 C4
Tufnell Park Sta
N19 ....13 C4
Tufton St SW1 ....134 A1
Tufton St SW1 ....134 A1
Tuke Sch SE15 .....50 A2
Tullis Ho **12** E9 ...17 B1
Tulse Hill
Streatham SW2 ....75 A3
Tulse Hill SW2,SE24 .74 C4
Tulse Hill Sta SE27 .75 A3
Tulse Ho SW2 .....62 C1
Tulsemere Rd SE21,
SE27 ....75 C4
Tunbridge Ct **1**
SE26 ....76 C1
Tunbridge Ho EC1 ..96 A4
Tunis Rd W12 .....30 A1
Tunley Gn **16** E14 ..33 B4
Tunley Rd
London NW10 .....21 A4
Upper Tooting SW12,
SW17 ....72 C2
Tunnel Avenue Trad Est
SE10 ....42 C4
Tunnel Rd SE16 ....40 B4
Tunstall Ct **14** TW9 .44 B2
Tunstall Rd SW9 ...62 B3
Tunstall Wlk **10**
TW8 ....44 A4
Tunworth Cres
SW15 ....56 B1
Tupman Ho SE16 ..139 B3
Turberville Ho **1**
SW9 ....62 B4
Turenne Cl SW18 ...59 B3
Turin St **2** E2 ......24 C2 99 B3
Turk's Head Yd
EC1 ....108 A4
Turks Row SW3 ...145 A2
Turle Rd N4 ....5 B2
Turlewray Cl N4 ....5 B3
Turnagain La EC4 ..108 A2
Turnberry Cl **2**
SE16 ....40 A1
Turnberry Quay **13**
E14 ....42 A3
Turnchapel Mews **1**
SW4 ....61 A4
Turner Cl **7** SW9 ..48 A2
Turner Ct **15** SE16 ..40 B4
5 London SE5 .....63 C3
Turner Ho NW8 .....80 A2
SW1 ....147 C3

Turner Ho continued
WC2 ....120 B3
London N4 ....5 B3
Turner Lo **10** SW19 .69 C3
Turner Pl SW11 ....60 A2
Turner St E1 ....32 A4
Turner St E1 ....32 A4
E16 ....35 B3
Turneville Rd W14 .154 C4
Turney Rd SE21 ....75 C4
Turney Sch SE21 ...75 B4
Turnham Green Sta
W4 ....38 A2
Turnham Green Terr
W4 ....38 A2
Turnham Ho SE4 ...66 A3
Turnham Prim Sch
SE4 ....66 A3
Turnmill Ho **8** SW2 .62 C2
Turnmill St EC1 ...108 A4
Turnour Ho **9** E1 ...32 A3
Turnpike Cl SE8 ...51 B3
Turnpike Ho EC1 ...96 B3
Turnpin La **2** SE10 .52 B4
Turpentine La
SW1 ....146 B1
Turpin Ho SW11 ..170 A4
Turpin Way N19 .....4 C3
Turquand St SE17 .151 A3
Turret Gr SW4 .....61 B4
Turville Ho NW8 ....90 A2
Turville St **2** E2 ...98 C2
Tuscan Ho **20** E2 ...25 B2
Tuskar St SE10 ....43 A1
Tuttle Ho SW1 ....147 C1
Tweeddale Ct E15 ..76 B3
Tweed Ho E14 .....27 B1
Tweezer's Alley
WC2 ....121 B4
Twelvetrees Cres
E3 ....27 B1
Twig Folly Cl E2 ...25 C3
Twilley St SW18 ...71 A4
Twine Ct E1 ....32 B2
Twisden Rd NW5 ...13 A4
Twyford CE High Sch
W3 ....28 A1
Twyford Ho N5 ......6 A1
Twyford PL WC2 ..106 C2
Twyford St N1 .....84 C4
Twynholm Mans
SW6 ....154 A2
Tyburn Tree (site of)
W2 ....116 C3
Tyburn Way W1 ...117 A4
Tyer's Est SE1 ....138 A4
Tyers Gate SE1 ...138 A3
Tyers St SE11 ....148 C2
Tyers Terr SE11 ...149 A1
Tyler Cl E2 ....24 B3
Tyler St SE10 ....43 A1
Tylney Ho **10** E1 ...32 A3
Tymperley Ct SW19 .70 A3
Tyndale La N1 .....15 A1
Tyndale Mans N1 ..15 A1
Tyndale Terr **13** N1 .15 A1
Tyndale Ct E14 ....42 A1
Tyneham Cl **10**
SW11 ....60 C4
Tynemouth St
SW6 ....166 C2
Tyne St E1 ....111 A2
Tynsdale Rd NW10 ...8 A2
Tynte Ct E9 ....18 A3
Tynwald Ho **14** SE26 .76 C1
Type St E2 ....25 C3

Tyrawley Rd SW6 ..166 A4
Tyrells Ct **4** SE22 ..64 C1
Tyrrell Ho SW1 ....161 A4
Tyrrell Rd SE22 ...64 C3
Tyrwhitt Rd SE4 ...66 C4
Tysoe St EC1 ......95 C3
Tyssen Rd N16 .....7 B1
Tyssen Sch N16 ....7 C2
Tyssen St N1 ......24 A3
London E8 ....16 B2
Tytherton **5** E2 ...25 B3
Tytherton Rd N19 ..4 C1

U

Uamvar St E14 ....34 A4
Udall St SW1 .....147 A3
Udimore Ho W10 ..30 B4
Uffington Rd NW10 .22 A4
Ufford St SE1 ....135 C4
Ufton Gr N1 ......15 C1
Ufton Rd N1 ......16 A1
Uhura Sq **10** N16 ...7 A1
Ujima Ct N19 ....5 A3
Ullin St E14 ....34 B4
Ullswater SW15 ....57 C1
Ullswater Ho SE15 .50 B4
Ullswater Rd
Barnes SW13 .....46 C3
West Norwood SE27,
SW16 ....75 A2
Ulster Pl NW1 .....92 A1
Ulundi Rd SE3 .....53 A4
Ulva Rd SW15 .....57 C3
Ulverscroft Rd SE22 .64 C2
Ulverstone Rd SE27 .75 A2
Ulysses Rd NW6 ...10 B3
Umberston St E1 ...32 A3
Umbria St SW15 ...56 C1
Una Ho **7** NW5 ...13 A2
Under Cliff SE10 ...52 B2
Undercliff Rd SE13 .67 A4
Underhill Ho **4** E14 .33 C4
Underhill Pas NW1 .82 B4
Underhill St NW1 ..82 B3
Undershaft EC3 ...110 A1
Underwood Ho W6 .39 A3
Underwood Rd
E1 ....24 C1 99 C1
Underwood Row
N1 ....97 A4
Underwood St N1 ..97 A4
Undine Rd E14 ....42 A2
Unicorn Bldg **14** E1 .32 C2
Unicorn Sch TW9 ..44 B2
Union Cl E11 ....19 C4
Union Ct
London SW4 .....172 A1
18 London N2 ...31 C4
2 Richmond TW10 .54 A2
Union Dr E1 ....26 A1
Union Gr SW8 ....171 C1
Union Mews SW9 .172 A1
Union Rd SW8 ....171 C1
Union Sq N1 ....87 A3
Union St E15 ....27 C4
SE1 ....122 C1
Union Wlk E2 .....98 A4
Union Yd W1 .....104 B1
Unity Cl NW10 .....9 A2
Unity Mews NW1 ...83 B2
Univ College Hospl
(Annexe) N1 .....103 C4
Univ Coll Jun Sch
NW3 ....11 B4
Univ Coll London
W1 ....105 A4
WC1 ....93 C1

Univ Coll London
continued
WC1 ....94 B2
University Coll Hospl
WC1 ....93 A1
University Coll Sch
NW3 ....11 B3
University Mans
SW15 ....57 C4
University of North
London (Tufnell Park
Hall) N7 ....4 B1
University St WC1 ..93 A1
Univ of East London
E15 ....27 C4
Univ of Greenwich
Rachel Mcmillan
Campus SE8 ......51 C4
Univ of Greenwich The
SW15 ....68 C4
Univ of London
WC1 ....94 A3
Univ of London (King's
Coll Hall) SE5 ....63 C4
Univ of London (Queen
Mary & Westfield Coll)
E1 ....26 A1
Univ of Westminster
NW1 ....92 C2
NW8 ....90 A1
W1 ....103 B4
W1 ....104 B2
Unwin Cl SE15 .....49 C4
Unwin Rd SW7 ...129 C2
Upbrook Mews
W2 ....101 A1
Upcerne Rd SW10 .157 A1
Upcott Ho **23** E3 ...27 A2
2 London E9 ....17 B1
Upgrove Manor Way **8**
SE24 ....74 C4
Upham Park Rd W4 .38 A2
Upland Rd SE22 ...64 C1
Uplands Cl SW14 ..55 A2
Upnall Ho **16** SE15 .50 B4
Upnor Way SE17 ..152 B2
Upper Addison Gdns
W14 ....126 A4
Upper Belgrave St
SW1 ....131 C2
Upper Berkeley St
W1 ....103 A1
Upper Brockley Rd
SE4 ....51 B1
Upper Brook St
W1 ....117 B4
Upper Caldy Wlk **14**
N1 ....15 B2
Upper Cheyne Row
SW3 ....158 A4
Upper Clarendon Wlk **12**
W11 ....31 A3
Upper Dengie Wlk
N1 ....86 C4
Upper Grosvenor St
W1 ....117 B3
Upper Ground SE1 .121 B2
Upper Gulland Wlk **10**
N1 ....15 B2
Upper Harley St
NW1 ....91 C1
Upper Hawkwell Wlk
N1 ....87 A4
Upper Holloway Sta
N19 ....4 C2

Upper James St
W1 .... **119** A4
Upper John St W1 **119** A4
Upper Mall W6 ...... **39** A1
Upper Marsh SE1 **135** A2
Upper Montague St
W1 .... **102** C3
Upper North St E3,
E14 .... **33** C4
Upper Park Rd NW3 **12** B3
Upper Phillimore Gdns
W8 .... **127** B3
Upper Rawreth Wlk
N1 .... **87** A4
Upper Richmond Rd
SW15 .... **57** B3
Upper Richmond Rd W
TW10,SW14,SW15 **55** B3
Upper St N1 .... **86** A3
Upper St Martin's La
WC2 .... **120** A4
Upper Tachbrook St
SW1 .... **147** A4
Upper Terr NW3 ..... **2** B1
Upper Thames St
EC4 .... **123** A4
Upper Tollington Pk
N4 .... **5** C3
Upper Tooting Park
Mans **17** SW17 ...**72** C2
Upper Tooting Rd
SW17 .... **72** B2
Upper Tooting Rd
SW17 .... **72** B1
Upper Tulse Hill
SW2 .... **74** B3
Upper Wimpole St
W1 .... **103** C4
Upper Woburn Pl
NW1,WC1 .... **93** C2
Upstall St SE5 ..... **48** A2
Upton Cl NW2 .... **1** A1
Urlwin St SE5 ...... **48** B4
Urlwin Wlk SW9 .... **48** A2
Urmston Dr SW19 ... **70** A3
Urmston Ho **9** E14 **42** B2
Ursula Mews N4 ..... **6** B3
Ursula St SW11 ... **168** A3
Urswick Rd E5,E9 .. **17** B3
Usborne Mews
SW8 .... **163** A2
Usher Rd E3 .... **26** B3
Usk Rd SW11 .... **59** B3
Usk St E2 .... **25** C2
Utopia Village NW1 **81** B4
Uverdale Rd SW10 **157** A1
Uxbridge Rd W12 .. **30** A1
Uxbridge St
W8 .... **31** C1 **113** B2

V

Vaine Ho **4** E9 .... **18** A2
Vale Cl W9 .... **88** C3
Vale Ct W9 .... **88** C3
  London W3 .... **29** B1
Vale End SE22 ..... **64** B3
Vale Est The W3 ... **29** A1
Vale Gr London N4 . **6** B4
  London W3 .... **28** C1
Valens Ho **1** SW2 **74** C3
Valentia Pl SW9 ... **62** C3
Valentine Ho **11**
SW4 .... **61** B1
Valentine Pl SE1 **136** A4

Valentine Rd E9 .... **17** C2
Valentine Row
SE1 .... **136** A3
Vale of Health NW3 . **2** C1
Vale Rd N4 .... **6** B4
Vale Rise NW11 ..... **1** B3
Vale Row N5 .... **6** A1
Vale Royal N7 ..... **14** A1
Vale The SW3 ..... **157** C4
  London NW11 ...... **1** A3
  London W3 .... **29** A1
Valetta Rd W3 ..... **38** B4
Valette Ho E9 ..... **17** B2
Valette St E8 ..... **17** A2
Valiant Ho **1** SW11 **167** C3
Vallance Rd
  E1 .... **24** C1 **99** C1
Valliere Rd NW10 .. **21** C2
Valmar Rd SE5 ..... **48** B2
Valmar Trad Est **7**
SE5 .... **48** B2
Valois Ho SE1 ..... **138** C2
Valonia Gdns SW18 **58** B1
Vanbern Ho NW5 ... **12** C2
Vanbrugh Ct SE11 **149** C3
Vanbrugh Fields
SE3 .... **53** B3
Vanbrugh Hill SE10,
SE3 .... **53** B3
Vanbrugh Ho **8** E9 **17** B1
Vanbrugh Park Rd
SE3 .... **53** B3
Vanbrugh Park Rd W
SE3 .... **53** B3
Vanbrugh Pk SE3 ... **53** B3
Vanbrugh Rd W4 ... **37** C3
Vanbrugh Terr SE3 **53** B2
Vanburgh Ho **1**
E1 .... **110** C4
Vancover Ho **13** E1 **32** A1
Vanderbilt Rd SW18 **71** B3
Vanderbilt Villas **3**
W12 .... **39** C4
Vandome Cl E16 ... **35** C3
Vandon Ct SW1 ... **133** A2
Vandon Pas SW1 .. **133** A2
Vandon St SW1 ... **133** A2
Vandyke Cl SW15 .. **57** C1
Vandy St EC2 ...... **98** A1
Vane Cl NW3 .... **11** C4
Vane St SW1 ...... **147** A4
Vange Ho **10** W10 . **30** B4
Van Gogh Ct E14 .. **42** C3
Vanguard Bldg **12**
E14 .... **41** C4
Vanguard St SE8 .. **51** C2
Vanguard Trad Cent
E15 .... **27** B4
Vanneck Sq SW15 .. **56** C2
Vansittart St **7**
SE14 .... **51** A3
Vanston Pl SW6 .. **155** C2
Vantage Mews E14 **34** B1
Vantrey Ho SE11 .. **149** B3
Varcoe Rd SE16 ... **40** B1
Vardens Rd SW11 .. **59** C3
Varden St E1 ...... **32** A3
Vardon Cl W3 ...... **28** C3
Vardon Ho SE10 ... **52** B2
Varey Ho E1 .... **26** C2
Varley Ho **5** NW6 . **23** C4
Varma Ct SE3 ...... **54** C1
Varndell St NW1 ... **92** C4
Varsity Row SW14 . **45** B1
Vassal Ho E3 ...... **26** A2
Vassall Rd SW9 .. **163** C1
Vat Ho SW8 .... **162** B2
Vauban Est SE16 . **139** A1
Vauban St SE16 .. **139** A1

Vaudeville Ct N4 ... **5** C2
Vaughan Ave W6 ... **38** B2
Vaughan Est E2 .... **98** C4
Vaughan Ho SE1 .. **136** A4
Vaughan Rd SE5 ... **63** B4
Vaughan St SE16 .. **41** B4
Vaughan Way E1 .. **125** C2
Vaughan Williams Cl
SE8 .... **51** C3
Vauxhall Bridge Rd
SW1 .... **147** A3
Vauxhall Cross
SW1,SE1 .... **148** B1
Vauxhall Gr SW8 . **148** B1
Vauxhall Prim Sch
SE11 .... **149** A2
Vauxhall St SE11 . **149** A2
Vauxhall Sta SE11 **148** B1
Vauxhall Wlk SE11 **148** C2
Vawdrey Cl E1 ..... **25** B1
Vaynor Ho N7 ...... **14** A4
Vectis Ct SW18 .... **59** A1
Veda Rd SE13 ...... **66** C3
Velde Way **1** SE22 **64** A2
Vellacott Ho W12 .. **30** A3
Velletri Ho **17** E2 . **25** C3
Venables St NW8 .. **101** C4
Vencourt Pl W6 .... **38** C2
Venetian Rd SE5 ... **48** B1
Venice Ct **5** SE5 .. **48** B3
Venn Ho N1 .... **85** A3
Venn St SW4 .... **61** B3
Ventnor Rd SE14 .. **50** C3
Venue St E14 ...... **34** B4
Vera Ct W2 .... **100** A2
Vera Rd SW6 ..... **164** B4
Verbena Gdns W6 .. **38** C1
Verdi Ho **2** NW6 .. **23** A3
Vere Bank SW19 ... **70** B3
Vereker Rd W14 .. **140** B1
Vere St W1 .... **104** A1
Verity Cl W11 ...... **31** A3
Verity Ho **15** E3 .. **26** B2
Vermeer Ct E14 .... **42** C3
Vermont Rd SW18 . **59** A1
Verne Ct **9** W3 ... **37** B3
Verney Ho NW8 ... **90** A2
Verney Rd SE16 ... **40** A1
Verney Way SE16 .. **40** A1
Vernon Ct NW2 ..... **1** B1
Vernon Ho SE11 .. **149** A1
Vernon Mews W14 **140** B3
Vernon Pl WC1 ... **106** B3
Vernon Rd E3 ...... **26** B3
  Mortlake SW14 ... **55** C4
Vernon Rise WC1 .. **95** A4
Vernon Sq WC1 .... **95** A4
Vernon St W14 ... **140** B3
Vernon Yd
W11 ..... **31** B2 **112** C4
Verona Ct **10** SE14 **50** C4
  London W4 .... **38** A1
Veronica Ho SE4 .. **66** B4
Veronica Rd SW17 . **73** A2
Verran Rd SW12 ... **73** A4
Verulam Ho **1** W6 . **39** B4
Verulam St EC1 ... **107** B4
Vervain Ho **2** SE15 **49** C3
Verwood Ho SW8 . **163** A1
Verwood Lo **4** E14 **42** C2
Vesage Ct EC1 ... **107** C3
Vesey Path **16** E14 **34** A3
Vespan Rd W12 .... **38** C4
Vesta Rd SE4,SE14 **51** A1
Vestry Mews **12** SE5 **49** A2
Vestry Rd SE5 ..... **49** A2

Vestry St N1 .... **97** B4
Viaduct Pl **28** E2 . **25** A2
Viaduct St E2 ..... **25** A2
Vian St SE13 ...... **67** A4
Vibart Gdns SW2 .. **74** B4
Vibart Wlk N1 ..... **84** B4
Vicarage Ave SE3 . **53** C3
Vicarage Cres
SW11 .... **167** B3
Vicarage Ct **8**
  7 Putney SW15 ... **68** C4
Vicarage Dr SW14 . **55** C3
Vicarage Gate W8 **114** A1
Vicarage Gdns SW14 **113** C1
  Mortlake SW14 ... **55** C3
Vicarage Gr SE5 ... **48** C2
Vicarage Gr SE5 ... **48** C2
Vicarage Wlk
SW11 .... **167** C4
Vicar's Cl E9 ...... **25** B4
Vicars Hill SE13 ... **67** A3
Vicar's Rd NW5 ... **12** C3
Viceroy Ct NW8 ... **80** B2
Viceroy Rd SW8 .. **172** A4
Vic Johnson Ho **14**
E3 .... **26** B4
Vickery Ct EC1 .... **97** A2
Vickery Ho **10** SW4 **62** A3
Victor Cazalet Ho
N1 .... **86** A4
Victoria & Albert Mus★
SW7 .... **129** C1
Victoria Arc SW1 . **132** B1
Victoria Ave EC2 . **110** B3
Victoria Bldgs **13**
E8 .... **25** A4
Victoria Coach Sta
SW1 .... **146** A3
Victoria Cotts E1 . **111** B4
  7 Richmond TW9 **44** C2
Victoria Ct E1 ... **125** B3
  5 London SW4 ... **61** C1
  London W3 .... **36** C4
Victoria Dr SW19 .. **69** C3
Victoria Emb SE1 **121** A1
Victoria Emb WC2 **120** B2
Victoria Gdns
W11 ...... **31** C1 **113** B2
Victoria Gr W8 ... **128** C2
Victoria Gr Mews
W2 .... **114** A3
Victoria Ho SW1 . **146** A2
  6 London SW4 ... **61** C1
  2 London SW8 . **162** C2
Victoria Ind Est W3 **29** A4
Victoria Mans
  8 London N7 .... **14** C3
  London NW10 ..... **9** A1
Victoria Mews NW6 **23** C4
  Wandsworth SW18 **71** B3
Victorian Gr N16 ... **7** A1
Victorian Rd N16 ... **7** B1
Victoria Park Ct **11**
E9 .... **17** B1
Victoria Park Ind Ctr
E3 .... **27** B3
Victoria Park Lofts
E9 .... **18** A1
Victoria Park Rd E9 **17** C1
Victoria Park Sq E2 **25** B2
Victoria Pas NW8 . **89** B2
Victoria Rd NW6 .. **23** B4
  NW8 .... **128** C2
  London N4 .... **5** B3
  London NW10 ...... **22** A2
  Mortlake SW14 ... **55** C4
Victoria Rise SW4 . **61** A4
Victoria Sq SW1 . **132** B2

Victoria St SW1 .. **133** A1
Victoria Sta SW1 **146** B4
Victoria Terr
  London N4 .... **5** C3
  London NW10 ..... **21** A1
Victoria Villas TW9 **54** B3
Victor Rd NW10 .. **22** A2
Victory Day Sch
SW1 .... **169** C4
Victory Pl **6** E14 . **33** A2
  SE17 .... **151** B4
Victory Prim Sch
SE17 .... **151** A4
Victory Way SE16 . **41** A4
Victory Wharf E14 **33** A2
Victory Wlk SE8 ... **51** C2
Video Ct N4 .... **5** A4
View Cl N6 .... **3** B4
Viewfield Rd SW18 **58** B1
Vigo St W1 .... **118** C3
Viking Cl **12** E3 .. **26** A3
Viking Ho **3** SE5 . **48** B1
Village Cl NW3 .... **11** C3
Village Mount **18**
NW3 .... **11** B4
Village Sch The
NW3 .... **12** B2
Village The SW11 . **60** B4
Village Way SE21 . **63** C1
Villa Rd SW9 ...... **62** C4
Villa St SE17 ..... **151** C1
Villiers Ct SW11 .. **168** B4
Villiers Rd NW2 .... **8** C2
Villiers St WC2 ... **120** B2
Vince Ct N1 .... **97** C3
Vincent Ct SW9 .. **173** A3
  W1 .... **102** C2
  London N4 .... **5** A3
Vincent Rd W3 ..... **37** B3
Vincents Cl SE16 .. **41** A4
Vincent Sq SW1 . **147** B4
Vincent St SE16 ... **35** B2
  SW1 .... **147** C4
Vincent Terr N1 ... **86** B2
Vince St EC1 ...... **97** C3
Vine Ct E1 .... **111** C3
Vinegar St E1 ..... **32** A1
Vinegar Yd SE1 .. **138** A4
Vine Hill EC1 ..... **95** B1
Vine La SE1 ...... **124** B1
Vine Rd SW13 ..... **56** B4
Vine Sq W14 ..... **141** A1
Vines Sch The
SW11 .... **60** C3
Vine St EC3 ...... **110** C1
  W1 .... **119** A3
Vine St Bridge EC1 **95** C1
Vineyard Path
SW14 .... **55** C4
Vineyard The
TW10 .... **54** A1
Vineyard Wlk EC1 . **95** B2
Viney Ct **9** SW4 .. **61** C1
Vine Yd SE1 ...... **137** A4
Viney Rd SE13 ..... **67** A4
Vining St SW2,SW9 **62** C3
Vinson Ho N1 ...... **87** C1
Vintners Ct EC4 . **123** A4
Viola Sq W12 ...... **29** B2
Violet Cl **14** SE8 .. **51** B4
Violet Hill NW8 .... **78** C1
Violet Hill Ho NW8 **78** C1
Violet Rd E3 .... **27** A1
Violet St E2 .... **25** A1
Virgil Pl W1 ...... **102** C3

Virgil St SE17 ......**135** A2
Virginia Ct **7** SE16 ...**40** C4
Virginia Ho **8** E14 ...**34** B2
Virginia Prim Sch
 E2 ....**98** C3
Virginia Rd E2 ......**98** C3
Virginia St E1 ......**125** C3
Virginia Wlk SW2 .....**62** B1
Viscount Ct **18** W11 ..**31** C3
Viscount St EC1 .....**108** C4
Vittoria Ho N1 ......**85** A3

Vittoria Prim Sch
 N1 ....**85** B2
Vivian Ho N4 ....**6** C4
Vivian Rd E3 ....**26** A3
Virginia Sq SE15 ....**65** A4
Vogans Mill S1 ......**139** A4
Vogler Ho **2** E1 .....**32** B2
Vollasky Ho E1 .....**111** B4
Voltaire
 2 London SE5 ....**49** B2
 15 Richmond TW9 ...**44** B2
Voltaire Ct SW11 ...**169** C2
Voltaire Rd SW4 ....**61** C4
Volt Ave NW10 ....**21** A2
Vorley Rd N19 ....**4** B2
Voss St E2 ....**24** C2 **99** C3
Voyager Bsns Est
 SE16 ....**139** B2
Vulcan Rd SE4 .....**51** B1
Vulcan Sq E14 ......**41** C2
Vulcan Terr SE4 .....**51** B1
Vulcan Way N7 .....**14** B2
Vyner Ct E5 ....**7** C2
Vyner Rd W3 ....**28** C2
Vyner St E2 ....**25** A4

W

Wadding St SE17 ....**151** B3
Waddington Rd E15 **19** C2
Waddington St E15 **19** C2
Wade Ho SE1 ....**139** B3
Wadeson St E2 .....**25** A3
Wade's Pl E14 ......**34** A2
Wadham Gdns NW3 **80** A4
Wadham Rd SW15 .**58** A3
Wadhurst Rd W4 ...**37** C3
Wager St E3 ....**26** B1
Waghorn St SE15 ...**64** C4
Wagner St SE15 ....**50** B3
Wainford Cl SW19 ..**69** C3
Wainwright Ho **3**
 E1 ....**32** B1
Waite St SE15 ......**49** B4
Waithman St EC4 ..**108** A1
Wakefield Ho **6**
 SE15 ....**49** C2
Wakefield Mews
 WC1 ....**94** B3
Wakefield St WC1 ..**94** B3
Wakeford Cl SW4 ..**61** B2
Wakeham St **9** N1 **15** C2
Wakehurst Rd SW11 **60** B2
Wakeling Ho **8**
 SE27 ....**75** A1
Wakeling St **13** E14 **33** A3
Wakelin Ho **10** N1 ..**15** A1
Wakeman Rd NW10 **22** C2
Wakley St EC1 .....**96** A4
Walberswick St
 SW8 ....**162** B1
Walbrook EC4 ......**123** B4
Walbrook Ct **22** N1 .**24** A3
Walburgh St E1 ....**32** A3
Walcorde Ave
 SE17 ....**151** A3

Walcot Gdns SE11 ..**149** B4
Walcot Ho **9** SE22 ..**64** A4
Walcot Sq SE11 ...**149** C4
Walcott St SW1 ....**147** A4
Waldeck Gr SE27 ....**75** A1
Waldeck Rd
 Brentford W4 ......**44** C4
 Mortlake SW14 ....**55** B4
Waldeck Terr SW14 **55** B4
Waldegrave Ho **5**
 SW15 ....**57** B2
Waldemar Ave
 SW6 ....**164** B2
Waldemar Avenue Mans
 SW6 ....**164** A3
Walden Ct SW8 ....**171** C4
Walden Ho SW1 ...**145** C3
 London SW11 .....**169** B2
Walden St E1 ......**32** A3
Waldo Cl SW4 ......**61** B2
Waldo Rd NW10 ....**22** A2
Waldron Ho **7** SW2 **62** B2
Waldron Mews
 SW3 ....**157** C4
Waldron Rd SW18 ..**71** B1
Walerand Rd SE13 ..**52** B1
Waleran Flats SE1 **152** A4
Wales Cl SE15 .....**50** A4
Wales Farm Rd W3 **28** C4
Waley St **1** E1 .....**33** A4
Walford Ho **1** E1 ..**32** A3
Walford Rd N16 ....**16** A4
Walham Ct **15** NW3 **12** B3
Walham Gr SW6 ...**155** B2
Walham Green Arc
 SW6 ....**155** C2
Walham Yd SW6 ...**155** B2
Walker Ho NW1 ....**83** B1
Walker Mews SW2 **62** C2
Walkerscroft Mead
 SE21 ....**75** B3
Walker's Ct W1 ...**119** B4
Walkers Lo **7** E14 ..**42** B4
Walker's Pl SW15 ..**58** A3
Walkinshaw Ct **14**
 N1 ....**15** B1
Walkynscroft **7**
 SE15 ....**50** A1
Wallace Collection*
 W1 ....**103** B2
Wallace Ho N7 .....**14** B2
Wallace Rd N1,N5 ..**15** B2
Wallbutton Rd SE4 **51** A1
Wall Ct N4 ....**5** B3
Waller Rd SE14 ....**50** C1
Wallett Ct **9** NW1 .**13** B1
Wallflower St W12 ..**29** B2
Wallgrave Rd SW5 **142** A3
Wallingford Ave
 W10 ....**30** C3
Wallis Alley SE1 ...**137** A4
Wallis Cl SW11 ....**59** C4
Wallis Rd E9 ....**18** C2
Wallorton Gdns
 SW14 ....**55** C3
Wallside EC2 .....**109** A3
Wall St N1 ....**15** C2
Wallwood St E14 ..**33** B4
Walmer Ho **8** W10 **30** C3
Walmer Pl W1 ....**102** C4
Walmer Rd
 W11 ......**31** A2 **112** A3
 London W10 ......**30** B3
Walmer St NW1 ...**102** C4
Walm La NW2 ....**9** B2
Walnut Cl SE8 ......**51** B4

Walnut Tree Cl
 SW13 ....**46** B2
Walnut Tree Ho
 SW10 ....**156** B4
Walnut Tree Rd
 SE10 ....**43** A1
 Brentford TW8 ....**44** B4
Walnut Tree Walk Prim
 Sch SE11 ....**149** B4
Walnut Tree Wlk
 SE11 ....**149** B4
Walpole Ct
 London NW6 ......**11** B1
 7 London W14 ....**39** C3
Walpole Gdns W4 ..**37** B1
Walpole Mews NW8 **79** B3
Walpole St SW3 ...**145** A2
Walsham Cl N16 ....**7** C3
Walsham Ho SE17 **151** B2
 SE14 ....**50** C1
Walsham Rd SE14 ..**50** C1
Walsingham NW8 ..**79** C4
Walsingham Lo
 SW13 ....**46** C2
Walsingham Mans
 SW6 ....**156** B2
Walsingham Pl
 SW4,SW11 ....**60** C1
Walt Besant Ho **2**
 E1 ....**25** C1
Walter Ct **3** W3 ...**28** B3
Walter Green Ho
 SE15 ....**50** B2
Walter Ho SW10 ..**157** B2
Walter Northcott Ho **2**
 London NW6 ......**10** C3
Walters Cl SE17 ...**151** A3
Walters Ho N1 .....**86** B4
 10 SE17 ....**48** A4
 8 London SE5 .....**49** A1
Walter St E2 ....**25** C2
Walters Way SE23 .**65** C1
Walter Terr E1 .....**32** C3
Walterton Rd W9 ..**23** C1
Waltham Green Ct
 SW6 ....**156** A1
Waltham Ho NW8 ..**78** C4
 London SW9 ......**173** A1
Walton Cl SW8 ....**162** B2
Walton Gdns W3 ..**28** A4
Walton Ho E2 ......**99** A2
 London N7 ....**5** B1
 London SW18 .....**58** C1
Walton Pl SW3 ...**130** C2
Walton St SW3 ...**130** B1
Walton Way W3 ...**28** A4
Walt Whitman Cl **6**
 SE24 ....**63** A3
Walworth Pl SE17 **151** A1
Walworth Rd SE17 **151** A2
Walworth Sch
 SE17 ....**152** B1
Wanborough Dr
 SW15 ....**69** A3
Wandle Ct **8** W12 ..**38** A4
Wandle Ho NW8 ..**102** A4
 Wandsworth SW18 **71** A4
 Wandle Prim Sch
 SW18 ....**71** A3
Wandle Way SW18 .**71** A3
Wandon Rd SW6 ..**156** B1
Wandsworth Bridge Rd
 SW6 ....**166** A2

Wandsworth Common
 Sta SW12 ....**72** B4
Wandsworth Common
 West Side SW18 ...**59** B2
Wandsworth Gyratory
 SW18 ....**59** A2
Wandsworth High St
 SW18 ....**59** A2
Wandsworth Plain
 SW8 ....**162** A1
Wandsworth Rd
 SW8 ....**171** A1
Wandsworth Town Sta
 SW18 ....**59** A3
Wangford Ho **13**
 SW9 ....**63** A3
Wanless Rd SE24 ..**63** B3
Wanley Rd SE5 ....**63** C3
Wansbeck Rd E3,E9 **18** B1
Wansdown Pl SW6 **156** A2
Wansey St SE17 ...**151** A3
Wapping Dock St **19**
 E1 ....**32** A1
Wapping High St
 E1 ....**32** A1
Wapping La E1 ....**32** A1
Wapping Wall E1 ..**32** B1
Warbeck Rd W12 ...**39** A4
Warburton Cl **6** N1 **16** A2
Warburton Ct SE15 **64** C4
Warburton Ho **5**
 E8 ....**25** A4
Warburton Rd **8**
 E8 ....**25** A4
Warburton St **6** E8 **25** A4
Wardalls Ho **12** SE8 **51** B4
Wardell Ho **3** SE10 **52** B4
Warden Rd NW5 ...**12** C2
Wardens Gr SE1 ..**122** C1
Wardle St E9 ......**17** C3
Wardley St SW18 ..**71** A4
Wardlow **3** NW5 ...**13** A4
Wardo Ave SW6 ...**164** A4
Wardour Mews
 W1 ....**105** A1
Wardour St W1 ....**105** B1
Ward Point SE11 ..**149** B3
Ward Rd E15 ......**27** C4
 N19 ....**4** B1
Wardrobe Pl EC4 .**108** B1
Wardrobe Terr
 EC4 ....**122** B4
Wareham Ct **2** N1 .**16** A1
Wareham Ho SW8 **162** C2
Warfield Rd NW10 .**22** C2
Warfield Yd **5**
 NW10 ....**22** C2
Wargrave Ho E2 ...**98** C3
Wargrave Rd SE23 **65** C4
Waring Ho E2 ......**99** C3
Warley Ho N1 .....**15** C2
Warley St E2 ......**25** C2
Warlock Rd W9 ....**23** C1
Warlters Cl N7 .....**14** A4
Warlters Rd N7 ....**14** A4
Warltersville Mans
 N19 ....**5** A4
Warltersville Rd N4,
 N8,N19 ....**5** A4
War Memorial Homes
 W4 ....**45** C2
Warmington Rd
 SE24 ....**63** B1
Warmsworth NW1 .**82** C4

Warncliffe Ho **3**
 SW15 ....**57** B2
Warndon St SE16 ..**40** B2
Warneford St E9 ...**25** A4
Warner Ho NW8 ...**88** C4
 4 London E9 ......**17** C2
 London SE13 .....**52** A1
Warner Pl E2 ..**24** C2 **99** B3
Warner Rd SE5 ....**48** B2
Warner St EC1 ....**95** B1
Warnford Ho SW15 **56** A1
Warnham WC1 ....**94** C3
Warnham Ho **6**
 SW2 ....**74** B4
Warple Mews W3 ..**38** A4
Warple Way W3,
 W12 ....**38** A4
Warren Ave SW14,
 TW10 ....**55** A3
Warren Cl SE21 ....**75** B4
Warren Ct N1 .....**85** B2
Warrender Rd N19 **13** B4
Warren Gdns E15 ..**19** C3
Warren Ho **2** E3 ..**27** A2
Warren Mews W1 ..**92** C1
Warren St W1 .....**92** C1
Warren Street Sta
 NW1 ....**93** A2
Warriner Gdns
 SW11 ....**169** B3
Warrington Cres
 W9 ....**88** C2
Warrington Gdns
 W9 ....**88** C2
Warrington Pl E14 **34** B1
Warspite Ho **3** E14 **41** A2
Warton Rd E15 ....**27** A4
Warwick W14 .....**141** A3
Warwick Ave W9 ..**88** C1
Warwick Avenue Sta
 W9 ....**88** C2
Warwick Chambers
 W8 ....**127** B2
Warwick Cres W2 ..**100** C4
Warwick Ct WC1 ..**107** A3
 London NW2 .....**10** A3
Warwick Dr SW15 ..**57** A4
Warwick Gdns
 W14 ....**141** A4
Warwick Ho
 London N4 ....**6** B3
 London SW9 .....**173** B1
 5 Putney SW15 ....**69** B4
Warwick House St
 SW1 ....**119** C2
Warwick La EC4 ..**108** B1
Warwick Mans
 SW5 ....**141** B3
Warwick Park Sch
 SE15 ....**49** B2
Warwick Pl W9 ...**100** C4
Warwick Pl N SW1 **146** C3
Warwick Rd W14,
 SW5 ....**141** A4
Warwick Row SW1 **132** C2
Warwickshire Path
 SE8 ....**51** B3
Warwick Sq EC4 ..**108** B2
 SW1 ....**146** C2
Warwick Sq Mews
 SW1 ....**146** C3

Warwick St W1 ....119 A4
Warwick Way SW1 .146 B3
Warwick Yd EC1 ....97 A1
Wasdale NW1 ....92 B3
Washbrook Ho SW2 62 C1
Washington Cl **68**
E3 ....27 A2
Washington Ho
SW1 ....130 C3
Washington Rd
SW13 ....46 C3
Watchfield Ct **7**
W4 ....37 B1
Watcombe Cotts
TW9 ....44 C4
Watercress Pl N1 ...16 A1
Waterden Cres **9** ...18 C3
Waterden Rd E15 ...18 C2
Waterford Rd SW6 156 A1
Watergate EC4 ....123 A4
Watergate Sch
SE13 ....67 A3
Watergate St SE8 ..51 C4
Watergate Wlk
WC2 ....120 B2
Water Gdns The
W2 ....102 B2
Waterhead NW1 ....92 C4
Waterhouse Cl
London NW3 ......11 C3
London W6 ....39 C1
Wateridge Cl E14 ..41 C3
Water La SE14 .....50 C3
Waterloo Bridge
SE1,WC2 ....121 A3
Waterloo Cl E9 .....17 B3
Waterloo East Sta
SE1 ....121 C1
Waterloo Gdns E2 ..25 B3
Waterloo Int Sta
SE1 ....121 C1
Waterloo Pier SE1 .134 C4
Waterloo Pl SW1 ...119 B2
Waterloo Rd SE1 ...135 C4
Waterloo Sta SE1 ..135 B4
Waterloo Terr N1 ...15 A1
Waterlow Ct NW11 ..2 A4
Waterlow Rd N19 ....4 B3
Waterman Bldg **4**
E14 ....41 C4
Waterman St SW15 .57 C4
Waterman Way E1 ..32 A1
Watermead Ho E9 ..18 B3
Watermeadow La
SW6 ....166 C1
Water Mews SE15 ..65 B3
Watermint Quay N16 .7 C4
Water's Edge SW6 ..47 B2
Waterside Cl E3 .....26 B4
SE16 ....139 C3
Waterside Cl SE13 ..67 C3
Waterside Pl NW1 ..81 C4
Waterside Point
SW11 ....158 B2
Waterson St E2 .....98 C4
Waters Pl SW15 ....47 B1
Water St WC2 ......121 B4
Water Tower Ho
W8 ....113 B1
Water Tower Pl N1 ..86 A3
Waterview Ho E14 ..33 A4
Waterworks Rd
SW2 ....62 B1
Watford Cl SW11 ..168 B4
Watford Rd E16 ....35 C4

Watkin Ho N16 ......7 B4
Watkinson Rd N7 ...14 B2
Watling Ct EC4 ....109 A1
Watling Gdns NW2 ..10 A2
Watling St EC4 ....109 A1
4 SE15 ....49 A4
Watney Cotts SW14 55 B4
Watney Mkt E1 .....32 A3
Watney Rd SW14 ...55 B4
Watney St E1 ....32 A3
Watson Cl N16 ......15 C3
Watson Ho **5** SW2 ..74 A4
Watson's Mews
W1 ....102 B3
Watson's St SE8 ...51 C3
Watts Gr E3 ....34 A4
Watts Ho **6** W10 ....31 A4
Watts St E1 ....32 A1
SE15 ....49 B2
Wat Tyler Rd SE10 .52 C2
Wavel Ct **7** E1 ......32 B1
7 Streatham SW16 .74 A1
Wavel Mews NW6 ..11 A1
Wavendon Ave W4 .37 C1
Waveney Ave SE15 .65 A3
Waveney Cl E1 ....125 C2
Waveney Ho SE15 ..65 A3
Waverley Ct **8** W1 ..103 C4
8 London NW6 .....10 A1
Waverley Pl N4 .....5 C2
Waverley Rd N8 .....5 A4
Waverley Sch (lower)
SE22 ....65 A1
Waverley Sch (Upper)
SE15 ....65 B2
Waverly Ct NW3 ....12 B3
Waverton Ho **8** E3 ..26 B4
Waverton Rd SW18 .71 B4
Waverton St W1 ...118 A2
Wavertree Ct **9**
SW2 ....74 A3
Wavertree Rd SW2 .74 B3
Waxham NW5 ......12 B3
Waxlow Rd NW10 ..20 C3
Wayford St SW11 .168 B1
Wayland Ave E8 ....16 C3
Wayland Ho SW9 .173 B2
Waylett Ho SE11 ..149 B1
Waylett Pl SE27 ....75 A1
Wayman Ct E8 .....17 A2
Waynflete Sq
12 London W10 ....30 C2
18 London W10 ....30 C3
Waynflete St SW18 .71 B2
Wayside London NW11 1 A3
Mortlake SW14 ....55 B2
Weald Ct **10** SE16 ..40 A1
Weardale Ho N4 ....6 B4
Weardale Rd SE13 ..67 C3
Wearmouth Ho **1**
E3 ....33 B4
Wear Pl **4** E2 ....25 A2
Wearside Rd SE13 ..67 A3
Weatherbury **6** W2 .31 C3
Weatherbury Ho **9**
N19 ....4 C1
Weatherley Cl E3 ..33 B4
Weaver Ct **4** E2 ....25 A1
Weaver St E1 .24 C1 99 B1
Weavers Way NW1 .83 B4
8 London NW1 ....13 C1
Webb Ct W3 ....37 A4
Webber Row SE1 ..136 A3
Webber St SE1 ....136 A3

Webb Est E5 ....7 C4
Webb Ho SW8 ....161 C1
Webb Pl NW10 .....21 B2
Webb Rd SE3 ......53 B4
Webb's Rd SW11 ..60 B2
Webb St SE1 ......138 A1
Webheath **6** NW6 ..10 A1
Webster Ho **10** N16 .16 A3
Webster Rd SE16 .139 C1
Wedderburn **46**
E2 ....25 C1
Wedderburn Rd
NW3 ....11 C3
Wedgewood Ho
SW1 ....146 C1
Wedgewood Mews
W1 ....105 C1
Wedgewood Wlk
NW3 ....11 A3
Wedgwood Ho
17 E2 ....25 C2
SE11 ....135 B1
Wedlake St W10 ...23 A1
Wedmore Gdns N19 .4 C2
Wedmore St N19 ....4 C1
Weech Rd NW6 ....10 C4
Weedington Rd
NW5 ....12 C3
Weedon Ho W12 ...29 C3
Weekley Sq SW11 ..59 C4
Weighhouse St
W1 ....103 C1
Weimar St SW15 ...57 C4
Weir Ho **8** SW12 ...73 B4
Weir Rd
Streatham SW12 ..73 B4
Wimbledon SW18,
SW19 ....71 A1
Weir's Pas NW1 ....93 C4
Weiss Rd SW15 ....57 C4
Welbeck Ct W14 ..140 C4
Welbeck Mans **10**
NW6 ....10 C3
Welbeck St W1 ....104 A2
Welbeck Way W1 ..104 A2
Welby Ho N19 ....4 C4
Welby St SE5 ......48 A2
Welford Ct
12 London NW1 ....13 A1
London SW8 .....170 C1
Welland Ho SE15 ..65 B3
Welland Mews E1 .125 C2
Welland St SE10 ...52 B4
Wellclose Sq E1 ...125 C4
Wellclose St E1 ...125 C3
Well Ct EC4 ....109 A1
Wellday Ho **7** E9 ...18 A2
Weller Ho SE16 ...139 B3
Weller St SE1 .....136 C4
Wellesley Ave W6 ..39 A3
Wellesley Ct W9 ...88 C4
Wellesley Ho NW1 .93 B3
Wellesley Pl NW1 ..93 B3
Wellesley Rd
London NW5 ......12 C3
London W4 ....37 A1
Wellesley St E1 ....32 C4
Wellesley Terr N1 ..97 A4
Wellfit St **5** SE24 ..63 A3
Wellgarth Rd NW11 ..1 C2
Wellington Arch
SW1 ....131 C4
Wellington Bldgs
46 E3 ....26 C2
SW1 ....145 C1
Wellington Cl
London SE14 ......50 C2
London W11 ....31 C3

Wellington Ct NW8 .79 C1
SW1 ....130 C3
SW6 ....166 B3
WC2 ....120 A4
Wellington Gr SE10 .52 C3
Wellington Ho **18**
NW3 ....12 B3
Wellington Hospl
(North) NW8 ......79 C1
Wellington Hospl
(South) NW8 ......79 C1
Wellington Mans
N16 ....16 B3
Wellington Mews
London SE22 .....64 C3
Streatham SW16 ..73 C1
Wellington Mus (Apsley
Ho) SW1 ....131 C4
Wellington Prim Sch
E3 ....26 C2
Wellington Rd NW8 .79 C1
London NW10 .....22 C2
Wimbledon SW19 ..70 C2
Wellington Row
E2 ....24 C2 99 B4
Wellington Sq
SW3 ....144 C2
Wellington St
WC2 ....120 C4
Wellington Terr **2**
E1 ....32 A1
Wellington Way E3 .26 C2
Well La SW14 ......55 B2
Well Rd NW3 ....2 C1
Wells Ct **5** N1 ......23 C3
London N1 ....16 A3
10 London NW3 ...11 B4
Wells Ho EC1 ......96 A4
8 SE16 ....40 B3
8 W10 ....23 A1
Wells Ho The NW3 .11 C4
Wells House Rd
NW10 ....29 A4
Wellside Gdns
SW14 ....55 B2
Wells Mews W1 ...105 A2
Wells Pl SW18 .....71 B4
Wells Rd W12 ......39 B4
Wells Rise NW8 ....80 C3
Wells Sq WC1 ......95 A3
Wells St W1 ....105 A2
Wells Terr N4 ....5 C2
Wells Way SE5 .....49 A4
SW7 ....129 B2
Wells Yd **2** N7 ......14 C3
Well Wlk NW3 ....2 C1
Wellwood Ct SW15 .57 B3
Welsford St **51** 153 B3
Welsh Ho **10** E1 ...32 A1
Welshpool Ho **8**
E8 ....24 C4
Welshpool St **1** E8 .25 A4
Welstead Ho **6** E1 .32 A3
Welstead Way W4 ..38 B2
Weltje Rd W6 ......38 C1
Welton Ho E1 ......32 C4
London SE5 ....49 A2
Welwyn St E2 ......25 B2
Wembury Rd N6 ....4 A4
Wemyss Rd SE3 ...53 B1
Wendell Park Prim Sch
W12 ....38 B4
Wendell Rd W12 ...38 B4
Wendle Ct SW8 ...162 A3

Wendling NW5 .....12 B3
Wendon St E3 .....26 B4
Wendover SE17 ...152 A1
Wendover Ct **4** NW2 .1 C1
W1 ....103 B3
London W3 ....20 B1
Wendover Ho W1 .103 B3
Wendover Rd NW10 21 B3
Wenham Ho SW8 .160 C1
Wenlake Ho EC1 ...96 C2
Wenlock Ct N1 .....87 C1
Wenlock Rd N1 .....87 A1
Wenlock St N1 .....87 B1
Wennington Rd E3 .25 C3
Wensdale Ho E5 .....7 C2
Wensleydale Ho **8**
N4 ....6 B4
Wentworth Cres
SE15 ....49 C3
Wentworth Ct W6 .154 A3
Wandsworth SW18 .59 A1
Wentworth Dwellings
E1 ....110 C2
Wentworth Mews
E3 ....26 B2
Wentworth St E1 ..111 A3
Werrington St NW1 .83 A1
Werter Rd SW15 ...58 A3
Wesleyan Pl NW5 ..13 A4
Wesley Ave NW10 ..20 C2
Wesley Cl SE17 ...150 B3
London N7 ....5 B2
Wesley Ho SE24 ...63 C1
Wesley Rd NW10 ..20 B4
Wesley Sq W11 ....31 A3
Wesley St W1 .....103 C3
Wessex Ct SW11 ..57 C2
Wessex Gardens Prim
Sch NW11 ....1 A3
Wessex Ho SW11 ..1 A3
4 London N19 ......4 C1
Wessex St E2 ......25 B2
Wessex Way NW11 ..1 A3
Westacott Cl N19 ...4 C3
West Acton Prim Sch
W3 ....28 A3
West Arbour St E1 .32 C3
West Bank N16 .....7 A4
West Barnes Rd NW2 10 A3
West Block **41** E1 ..32 B2
Westbourne Ave
W3 ....28 C3
Westbourne Cres
W2 ....115 B4
Westbourne Ct
W2 ....100 C2
Westbourne Gdns
W2 ....100 A2
Westbourne Gr
W11 ....100 A1
W2,W11 .31 C3 113 A4
Westbourne Gr Mews **7**
W11 ....31 C3
Westbourne Gr Terr
W2 ....100 A2
Westbourne Ho
SW1 ....146 A2
Westbourne Park Rd
W11 ....31 B3
W2 ....31 C3
Westbourne Park Sta
W11 ....31 B4
Westbourne Park Villas
W2 ....31 C4
Westbourne Rd N7 .14 B2

Westbourne St
W2 ....**115** B4
Westbourne Terr
W2 ....**101** A2
Westbourne Terr Mews
W2 ....**100** C3
Westbourne Terr Rd
W2 ....**100** C3
Westbridge Cl W12 ...**29** C1
Westbridge Prim Sch
SW11 ....**168** A4
Westbridge Rd
SW11 ....**168** A4
West Brompton Sta
SW5 ....**141** C1
Westbrook Ho
5 E2 ....**25** B2
5 London SW4 ....**61** B3
Westbury St SW4 ...**61** A1
Westbush Ct **1**
W12 ....**39** A4
West Carriage Dr
W2 ....**116** A2
West Central Ave
NW10 ....**22** A2
West Central St
WC1 ....**106** A2
Westchester Ho
W2 ....**102** C1
Westcliff Ho **8** N1 ..**15** C2
Westcombe Ct **1**
SE3 ....**53** B3
Westcombe Hill
SE3,SE10 ....**53** C4
Westcombe Park Rd
SE3 ....**53** C3
Westcombe Park Sta
SE3 ....**43** C1
Westcott Ho **1** E14 ..**34** A2
Westcott Rd SE17 ...**48** A4
West Cotts W6 .....**10** C3
Westcroft Cl NW2 ..**10** A4
Westcroft Ct **8** W6 ..**38** C2
Westcroft Sq W6 ....**38** C2
Westcroft Way NW2 ..**10** A4
West Cromwell Rd
W14 ....**141** A2
West Cross Route
W10,W11 ....**30** C2
Westdean Cl SW18 ..**59** A1
Westdown Rd E15 ...**76** B4
West Dulwich Sta
SE21 ....**75** C3
West Eaton Pl
SW1 ....**145** B4
West Eaton Pl Mews
SW1 ....**145** B4
West Ella Rd NW10 ...**8** A1
West End Ct NW6 ...**11** A1
West End La NW6 ...**11** A2
Westerdale Ct N5 ...**15** A4
Westerdale Rd **2**
SE10 ....**43** C1
Westerham NW1 ....**82** C3
Westerham Ho
SE1 ....**137** C2
Western Ave **3**
NW11 ....**1** A4
Western Avenue Bsns
Pk W3 ....**20** A1
Western Ct
4 London W3 ......**28** C3
London W9 ....**23** B3
Western Eye Hospl The
NW1 ....**102** B4
Western Ho **1** W9 ....**23** B1
Western La SW12 ...**72** C4
Western Mews W9 ...**23** B1

Western Pl **13** SE16 ..**40** B4
Western Rd
London NW10 ......**20** B1
London SW9 ....**62** C4
Western Terr W6 ...**38** C1
Western Wharf **1**
SE15 ....**49** C4
Westferry Cir E14 ...**33** C1
Westferry Rd E14 ...**41** C3
Westferry Sta E14 ...**33** C2
Westfield NW3 ......**10** C4
Westfield Ct SW10 ..**156** C1
Westfield Ct **1**
W10 ....**22** B2
Westfield Ho **6**
SE16 ....**40** C2
Westfields SW13 ....**56** B4
Westfields Ave
SW13 ....**56** A4
Westfields Sch
SW13 ....**56** B4
Westfield Way **1** E1 ..**26** A1
West Garden Pl
W2 ....**102** B1
Westgate Bsns Ctr
2 W10 ....**23** A1
London W10 ....**22** C1
Westgate Ct **13**
SW9 ....**62** C4
Westgate St E8 .....**25** A4
Westgate Terr
SW10 ....**156** B4
West Gdns E1 ......**32** A2
West Gr SE10 ......**52** C2
Westgrove La SE10 ..**52** B2
West Halkin St
SW1 ....**131** B2
West Hall Rd TW9 ...**45** A2
West Hampstead Mews
NW6 ....**11** A2
West Hampstead Sta
NW6 ....**10** C2
West Hampstead
Thameslink Sta
NW6 ....**10** C2
West Harding St
EC4 ....**107** C2
Westhay Gdns
SW14 ....**55** A2
West Heath Ave
NW11 ....**1** C3
West Heath Cl NW3 ..**1** C1
West Heath Ct NW11 ..**1** C3
West Heath Dr NW11 ..**1** C3
West Heath Gdns
NW3 ....**1** C1
West Heath Rd NW3 ..**2** A1
West Hill N6 ....**3** C4
Putney SW15 ......**58** A1
Westhill Ct W11 ....**113** A4
West Hill Ct N6 .....**3** C1
Westhill Pk London N6 **3** B2
London N6 ....**3** C2
West Hill Prim Sch
SW18 ....**58** C2
West Hill Rd SW18 ..**58** B1
West Ho **9** SW2 ....**73** B4
Westhope Ho **2** **99** C3
Westhorpe Rd
SW15 ....**57** B4
West House Cl
SW19 ....**70** A3
West India Ave E14 ..**33** C1
West India Dock Rd
E14 ....**33** C2

West India Ho **1**
E14 ....**33** C2
West India Quay Sta
E14 ....**33** C2
West Kensington Ct
W14 ....**140** C2
West Kensington Mans
W14 ....**140** C1
West Kensington Sta
W14 ....**140** C2
West La SE16 ....**40** A4
Westlake **16** SE16 ...**40** B2
Westland Pl N1 .....**97** B4
Westlands Terr **3**
SW12 ....**61** B1
Westleigh Ave
SW15 ....**57** B2
West London Stad The
W12 ....**30** A4
Westly Ct NW2 ......**9** C2
Westmacott Ho
NW8 ....**89** C1
West Mall W11 .....**113** C2
Westmark Point **13**
SW15 ....**69** A3
Westmead SW15 ....**57** A1
West Mews SW1 ...**146** C3
Westmill Ct N4 ......**6** B2
Westminster Abbey★
SW1 ....**134** A2
Westminster Abbey
Choir Sch SW1 ...**133** C2
Westminster Boating
Base SW1 ....**161** B4
Westminster Bridge
SE1,SW1 ....**134** B3
Westminster Bridge Rd
SE1 ....**135** C3
Westminster Cath★
SW1 ....**132** C1
Westminster Cath Choir
Sch SW1 ....**147** A4
Westminster Cath RC
Prim Sch SW1 ....**147** C2
Westminster City Hall
SW1 ....**133** A2
Westminster City Sch
SW1 ....**132** C1
Westminster Ct
22 SE16 ....**32** C1
London SE18 ......**58** C2
Westminster Gdns
SW1 ....**148** A4
Westminster Kingsway
Coll
WC1 ....**94** C3
London NW1 .....**169** C4
Westminster Pier
SW1 ....**134** B3
Westminster Sch
SW1 ....**134** A2
Westminster Sta
SW1 ....**134** B3
Westmore Ct SW15 ..**58** A2
Westmoreland Ho
NW10 ....**21** C2
Westmoreland Pl
SW1 ....**146** B1
Westmoreland Rd
SE17 ....**48** C4
Barnes SW13 ....**46** C2
Westmoreland St
W1 ....**103** C3
Westmoreland Terr
SW1 ....**146** B1
West Norwood Sta
SE27 ....**75** A1

Westonbirt Ct **6**
SE15 ....**49** B4
Weston Ct N4 ......**6** B1
Weston Ed Ctr The
SE5 ....**48** B1
West One Ho W1 ...**104** C4
Weston Ho **9** E9 ....**25** B4
4 London NW6 ....**10** A1
Weston Rd W4 .....**37** B3
Weston Rise N1,
WC1 ....**95** A4
Weston St SE1 .....**137** C4
West Rise W1,
W2 ....**102** C1
Westover Hill NW3 ...**1** C2
Westover Rd SW18 ..**59** B1
West Park Ave TW9 ..**45** A2
West Park Rd TW9 ..**44** C2
West Parkside SE10 ..**43** B3
West Point SE1 ....**153** B2
Westpoint SW15 ....**57** C1
Westpoint Trad Est
W3 ....**28** A4
Westport St E1 .....**32** C3
West Poultry Ave
EC1 ....**108** A3
West Quarters W12 ..**29** C3
West Rd SW3 ......**159** A4
London SW4 ....**61** C2
West Row W10 .....**23** A1
Westrow SW15 .....**57** B1
West Sheen Vale
TW9 ....**54** B3
Westside **1** W3 ....**28** A1
West Smithfield
EC1 ....**108** B3
West Sq SE11 .....**136** A1
West St E2 ....**25** A3
WC2 ....**105** C1
West Temple Sheen
SW14 ....**55** A2
West Tenter St E1 ..**111** A1
Westvale Mews W3 ..**38** A4
Westview
London NW10 ......**8** B3
London W10 ....**30** B4
Westville Rd W12 ...**38** C4
West Warwick Pl
SW1 ....**146** C3
Westway W10,W12 ..**29** C2
Westway (Elevated Rd)
W10 ....**31** B4
Westway Lo **9** SW2 ..**74** A4
Westwell **4** SW5 ...**31** C4
Westwick Gdns
W14 ....**39** C4
Westwood Gdns
SW13 ....**56** B4
Westwood Ho
5 London N4 ....**6** C4
London N4 ....**30** B1
Westwood Rd SW13 ..**56** B4
Wetherby Gdns
SW5 ....**142** C3
Wetherby Mans
SW5 ....**142** A2
Wetherby Mews
SW5 ....**142** B2
Wetherby Pl SW7 ..**143** A3
Wetherell Rd E9 ...**25** C4
Wetland Centre The
SW13 ....**47** A3
Wevco Wharf SE15 ..**50** A4
Wexford Ho **2** E1 ...**32** B4
Wexford Rd SW12 ..**72** B4
Weybourne St
SW18 ....**71** B2

Weybridge Ct **19**
SE16 ....**40** A1
Weybridge Ho N4 ....**6** B4
Weybridge Point
SW11 ....**169** A2
Weydown Cl SW19 ..**70** A3
Weyhill Ho **27** SE5 ..**48** B1
Weyhill Rd E1 .....**111** C2
Wey Ho NW8 ......**89** C1
Weymouth Ct **5** E2 ..**24** B3
3 Streatham SW2 ..**74** B4
Weymouth Ho
SW8 ....**162** C1
Weymouth Mews
W1 ....**104** A3
Weymouth St W1 ..**104** A4
Weymouth Terr E2 ..**24** B3
Whadcoat St N4 ....**5** C2
Whadden Ho **10**
SE5 ....**64** A4
Whaddon Ho SW1 ..**131** A3
Wharfdale Rd N1 ...**84** B2
Wharfedale Ct **5**
E5 ....**17** C4
Wharfedale St
SW10 ....**142** A1
Wharf Pl E2 ....**25** A4
Wharf Rd E15 ......**27** C4
N1 ....**86** C2
Wharfside Rd E16 ..**35** A4
Wharf St E16 ......**35** A4
Wharton Cl NW10 ...**8** A2
Wharton Ho SE1 ...**138** C2
Wharton St WC1 ...**95** A3
Whateley Rd SE22 ..**64** B2
Wheatland Ho **7**
SE22 ....**64** A4
Wheatlands Rd
SW17 ....**72** C1
Wheatley Ho
London NW5 ......**13** A4
3 Putney SW15 .....**68** C4
Wheatley St W1 ...**103** C3
Wheat Sheaf Cl E14 ..**42** A2
Wheatsheaf La
SW8 ....**162** B2
London SW6 ....**47** B3
Wheatsheaf Terr
SW6 ....**155** A1
Wheatstone Ho **7**
W10 ....**31** A4
Wheatstone Rd
W10 ....**31** A4
Wheeler Ct **6**
SW11 ....**59** C4
Wheeler Gdns N1 ..**84** B4
Wheelwright St N7 ..**14** B1
Wheldon Ct SE1 ...**138** C4
Wheler Ho E1 ......**98** C1
Wheler St E1 ..24 **B1**/**98** C1
Whellock Rd W4 ...**38** A3
Whetstone Park
WC2 ....**106** C2
Whewell Rd N19 ....**5** A2
Whichcote St SE1 ..**121** B1
Whidborne Bldgs
WC1 ....**94** A3
Whidborne Cl SE8 ..**51** C1
Whidborne St WC1 ..**94** B3
Whippingham Ho **17**
E3 ....**26** B2
Whiskin St EC1 .....**96** A3
Whistler Mews **2**
SE15 ....**49** B3

Whistlers Ave
SW11 . . . .**157** C1
Whistler St N5 . . . . . .**15** A3
Whistler Twr
SW10 . . . .**156** C1
Whistler Wlk
SW10 . . . .**157** A2
Whiston Ho **10** N1 . . .**15** A1
Whiston Rd E2 . . . . . .**24** C4
Whitbread Ctr EC1 . .**97** A1
Whitbread Rd SE4 . . .**66** B3
Whitburn Rd SE13 . . .**67** B3
Whitby Ave NW10 . . . .**20** A2
Whitby Ct N7 . . . .**14** A4
Whitby Ho NW8 . . . . . .**78** C3
Whitby St E1 . . . .**98** C2
Whitcher Cl SE14 . . . .**51** A4
Whitcher Pl NW1 . . . .**13** B2
Whitchurch Ho **16**
    W10 . . . .**30** C3
Whitchurch Rd W11 .**30** C2
Whitcomb Ct W1 . . .**119** C3
Whitcombe Mews
    TW9 . . . .**45** A2
Whitcomb St WC2 . .**119** C3
Whiteadder Way
    E14 . . . .**42** A2
Whitear Wlk E15 . . . .**19** C2
Whitebeam Cl
    SW9 . . . .**163** A1
Whitebeam Ho **3**
    NW3 . . . .**12** B2
White Bear Pl NW3 . .**11** C4
White Bear Yd EC1 . .**95** B1
Whitechapel High St
    E1 . . . .**111** A2
Whitechapel Rd
    E1 . . . .**32** A4 **111** B3
Whitechapel Sta E1 .**32** A4
Whitechurch La
    E1 . . . .**111** B2
White City W10 . . . . . .**30** B2
White City Cl W12 . . .**30** B2
White City Est **21**
    W12 . . . .**30** A2
White City Rd W12 . .**30** B2
White City Sta W12 . .**30** B2
Whitecliff Ho SW18 . .**59** A1
White Conduit St
    N1 . . . .**85** C2
Whitecross PI EC2 . .**109** C4
Whitecross St EC1 . . .**97** A1
Whitefield Cl SW15 . .**58** A1
Whitefriars St EC4 .**107** C1
Whitehall SW1 . . . . .**134** A4
Whitehall Ct SW1 . .**120** B1
Whitehall Gdns
    SW1 . . . .**120** A1
    Chiswick W4 . . . .**45** A4
Whitehall Mans **3**
    N19 . . . .**4** B3
Whitehall Park Rd
    W4 . . . .**45** A4
Whitehall Pk N19 . . . .**4** B3
Whitehall Pl WC2,
    SW1 . . . .**120** A1
White Hart Ct EC2 .**110** A3
White Hart La
    London NW10 . . . .**8** B2
    Mortlake SW13 . . . . .**56** A4
White Hart St EC4 .**108** B1
    SE11 . . . .**149** C2
White Hart Yd SE1 .**123** B1
Whitehaven St NW8 .**90** A1
Whitehead Cl SW18 .**71** B4

Whitehead Ho **8**
    SW15 . . . .**57** C2
Whitehead's Gr
    SW3 . . . .**144** B3
White Ho
    London SW11 . . . . . .**167** C2
    3 Streatham SW4 . .**73** C4
Whitehorn Ho **6** E1 .**32** B1
White Horse La E1 . .**32** C4
Whitehorse Mews
    SE1 . . . .**136** A2
Whitehorse Rd E1 . . .**33** A4
White Horse Rd E1 . .**33** A3
White Horse St
    W1 . . . .**118** B1
White Horse Yd
    EC2 . . . .**109** B2
White Ho The NW1 . .**92** B2
White Kennett St
    E1 . . . .**110** B2
Whitelands Coll,
    Roehampton, Univ of
    Surrey SW18 . . . .**70** A4
Whitelands Ho
    SW3 . . . .**145** A2
Whiteley Ho **9**
    SW4 . . . .**73** C4
Whiteleys Ctr W2 . .**100** A2
White Lion Ct EC3 .**110** A1
White Lion Hill
    EC4 . . . .**122** B4
White Lion St N1 . . . .**85** C1
White Lion Yd W1 . .**118** A4
Whitelock Ho **21** E9 .**17** C2
Whiteness Ho SW9 .**173** B4
White Post La
    E9 . . . .**18** C2
White Post St SE14,
    SE15 . . . .**50** B3
White's Grounds
    SE1 . . . .**138** B4
White's Grounds Est
    SE1 . . . .**138** B4
White's Row E1 . . . .**110** C3
White's Sq SW4 . . . . .**61** C3
Whitestone La NW3 . .**2** B1
Whitestone Wlk NW3 .**2** B1
Whitethorn St E3 . . . .**33** C4
Whitfield Gdns
    W1 . . . .**105** A4
Whitfield Ho NW8 . . .**90** A1
Whitfield Pl W1 . . . . .**93** A1
Whitfield Rd SE10,
    SE3 . . . .**52** C2
Whitfield St W1 . . . .**105** A4
Whitgift Ho SE11 . . .**148** C4
    SW11 . . . .**168** A4
Whitgift St SE11 . . .**148** C4
Whitington Ave
    EC3 . . . .**110** A1
Whitley Ho SW1 . . . .**161** A4
Whitlock Dr SW19 . . .**70** A3
Whitman Ho **20** E2 . .**25** B2
Whitman Rd E3 . . . . . .**26** A1
Whitmore Comm Sch
    N1 . . . .**87** B3
Whitmore Gdns
    NW10 . . . .**22** B3
Whitmore Ho **20** E1 .**24** A4
Whitmore Rd N1 . . . . .**24** A4
Whitnell Ct **7**
    SW15 . . . .**57** C2
Whitnell Way SW15 . .**57** C2
Whitney Ho **6** SE22 .**64** A4
Whitstable Ho **11**
    W10 . . . .**30** C3
Whitsters Ho SE1 . .**138** C4

Whittaker Ct SW4 . .**172** B3
Whittaker St SW1 . .**145** B3
Whittaker Way
    SE1 . . . .**153** C4
Whittingham Ct W4 .**46** A3
Whittingstall Mans
    SW6 . . . .**165** A3
Whittingstall Rd
    SW6 . . . .**165** A3
Whittington Hospl The
    N19 . . . .**4** B2
Whittlebury Ho N4 . . .**6** B4
Whittlesey St SE1 . .**121** C1
Whitton NW3 . . . .**12** B1
Whitton Wlk E3 . . . . .**26** C2
Whitworth Ho SE1 . .**137** A1
Whitworth St SE10 . .**43** A1
Whorlton Rd SE15 . . .**65** A4
Whytlaw Ho **11** E3 . .**33** B4
Wicker St **2** E1 . . . . .**32** A3
Wickfield Ho **6** SE16 . .**139** C3
Wickford Ho **5** E1 . .**25** B1
Wickford St E1 . . . . . .**25** B1
Wickham Cl E1 . . . . . .**32** B4
Wickham Gdns SE4 . .**66** B4
Wickham Ho SW15 . .**57** C1
Wickham Mews SE4 .**51** B1
Wickham Rd SE4 . . . .**66** B4
Wickham St SE11 . .**148** C2
Wick La E3 . . . .**26** C4
    London E3 . . . .**18** B1
Wicklow Ho N16 . . . . .**7** B3
Wicklow St WC1 . . . . .**94** C4
Wick Mews **1** E9 . . . .**18** A2
Wick Rd Hackney E9 . .**17** C2
    London E9 . . . .**18** B2
Wick Sq E9 . . . .**18** B2
Wickstead Ho TW8 . .**36** B1
Wicksteed Ho SE1 . .**137** A1
Wickway Ct **7** SE15 .**49** B4
Wickwood St SE5 . . . .**48** A1
Widdenham Rd N7 . . .**14** B4
Widecombe Ho **39**
    SE5 . . . .**48** B1
Widegate St E1 . . . .**110** B3
Widford **8** NW1 . . . . .**13** A2
Widford Ho N1 . . . . . .**86** A1
Widley Rd W9 . . . .**23** C1
Widnes Ho **6** N7 . . . .**14** C3
Wigmore Hall W1 . .**104** A2
Wigmore Pl W1 . . . .**104** A2
Wigmore St W1 . . . .**103** C2
Wigram Ct SW11 . . .**168** A4
Wigram Ho **8** E14 . . .**34** A2
Wigton Pl SE11 . . . .**149** C1
Wilberforce Ho **4**
    SW11 . . . .**59** C4
Wilberforce Prim Sch
    W10 . . . .**23** A2
Wilberforce Rd
    London N4 . . . .**6** A2
    London N4,N5 . . . .**6** A3
Wilbraham Ho **3**
    SW8 . . . .**162** A1
Wilbraham Pl SW1 .**145** B4
Wilby Mews
    W11 . . . .**31** B1 **113** A2
Wilcox Cl SW8 . . . . .**162** B2
Wilcox Ho **6** E3 . . . . .**33** B4
Wilcox Pl SW1 . . . . .**133** A1
Wilcox Rd SW8 . . . .**162** A2
Wildcroft Manor
    SW15 . . . .**69** B4
Wildcroft Rd SW15 . .**69** B4
Wild Ct WC2 . . . .**106** C2
Wilde Cl E8 . . . .**24** C4
Wilde Pl SW18 . . . . . .**71** C4

Wilderness Mews
    SW4 . . . .**61** A3
Wilderton Rd N16 . . . .**7** A4
Wild Goose Dr SE14 .**50** B2
Wilding Ho **17** E9 . . .**17** C2
Wild's Rents SE1 . . .**138** A2
Wild St WC2 . . . .**106** C1
Wildwood Gr NW3 . . .**2** C3
Wildwood Rd NW11 . .**2** B4
Wildwood Rise NW11 .**2** B3
Wildwood Terr NW3 . .**2** C3
Wilfred Fienburgh Ho
    N7 . . . .**13** C4
Wilfred St SW1 . . . .**132** C2
Wilfrid Gdns W3 . . . . .**28** B4
Wilkes Rd **3** TW8 . . .**44** A4
Wilkes St E1 . . . .**111** A4
Wilkie Ho SW1 . . . .**147** C2
Wilkins Ho SW1 . . . .**160** C4
Wilkinson Ho N1 . . . . .**87** C1
Wilkinson St SW8 . .**162** C1
Wilkinson Way W4 . .**37** C4
Wilkin St NW5 . . . . . .**13** A2
Wilks Pl N1 . . . .**24** A3
Willan Wall E16 . . . . .**35** B2
Willard St SW8 . . . . . .**61** A4
Willbury Ho **4** N7 . . .**13** C3
Willcott Rd W3 . . . . . .**28** A1
Willenfield Rd
    NW10 . . . .**20** B3
Willesden Community
    Hospl The NW10 . . . . .**8** C1
Willesden Green Sta
    NW2 . . . .**9** B2
Willesden High Sch
    NW10 . . . .**22** A4
Willesden Junction Sta
    NW10 . . . .**21** B2
Willesden La NW2,
    NW6 . . . .**9** C2
Willes Rd NW5 . . . . . .**13** A2
Willesden Terr NW2 . . .**9** B2
William Banfield Ho **2**
    SW6 . . . .**164** C2
William Booth Meml
    Training Coll SE5 . . .**48** C1
William Brown Ct
    SE27 . . . .**75** A2
William Caslon Ho **28**
    E2 . . . .**25** A3
William Channing Ho **6**
    E2 . . . .**25** A2
William Davis Prim Sch
    E2 . . . .**24** C1 **99** B2
William Dromey Ct
    NW6 . . . .**10** B1
William Dunbar Ho
    NW6 . . . .**23** B3
William Ellis Sch
    NW5 . . . .**3** C1
William Ellis Way
    SE16 . . . .**139** C1
William Evans Ho **8**
    SE8 . . . .**40** C2
William Gdns SW15 . .**57** A2
William Guy Gdns **47**
    E3 . . . .**27** A2
William Harvey Ho **1**
    SW19 . . . .**70** A3
William Hunt Mans
    SW13 . . . .**47** B4
William IV St WC2 . .**120** A3
William Margrie Cl **1**
    SE15 . . . .**49** C1
William Mews
    SW1 . . . .**131** A3

William Morris Acad
    W6 . . . .**39** C1
William Morris Ho
    W6 . . . .**47** C4
William Morris Way
    SW6 . . . .**166** C1
William Patten Prim Sch
    N16 . . . .**7** B2
William Pl **31** E3 . . . .**26** B3
William Rathbone Ho **5**
    E2 . . . .**25** A2
William Rd NW1 . . . . .**92** C3
William Rushbrooke Ho
    SE16 . . . .**153** B4
William Saville Ho **2**
    NW6 . . . .**23** B3
Williams Cl SW6 . . .**154** B2
Williams Ho **8** E3 . . .**26** C2
    6 E9 . . . .**25** B4
    8 Streatham SW2 . . .**74** C3
Williams La SW14 . . .**45** B1
Williamson Cl SE10 . .**43** B1
Williamson Ct
    SE17 . . . .**150** C1
Williamson St N7 . . . .**14** A4
William Sq **18** SE16 . .**33** A2
William St SW1 . . . .**131** A3
William Tyndale Prim
    Sch N1 . . . .**15** A1
William Winter Ct **20**
    SW2 . . . .**74** C4
Willingham Cl **4**
    NW5 . . . .**13** B3
Willingham Terr
    NW5 . . . .**13** B3
Willington Rd SW9 . .**62** A4
Willis Ho **7** E14 . . . . .**34** A2
Willis St E14 . . . .**34** A3
Willoughby Hall
    Dyslexia Ctr NW3 . . .**11** C4
Willoughby Ho
    E1 . . . .**32** A1
    EC2 . . . .**109** B3
Willoughby Rd NW3 .**11** C4
Willoughby St
    WC1 . . . .**106** A3
Willoughbys The
    SW14 . . . .**56** A3
Willow Ave SW13 . . . .**46** B1
Willowbank SW6 . . . .**58** A4
Willow Bridge Rd
    N1 . . . .**15** B2
Willow Cotts TW9 . . .**44** C4
Willow Ct EC2 . . . .**98** A2
    Chiswick W4 . . . .**46** A3
    London N7 . . . .**14** B3
    London SW9 . . . .**173** B3
    10 London W2 . . . . . .**31** C4
    8 Streatham SW16 . . .**74** B1
Willowdene SE15 . . . .**50** A3
    London N6 . . . .**3** B4
    London SE15 . . . .**50** A2
Willow Farm La
    SW15 . . . .**57** A4
Willow Hall NW3 . . . .**11** C4
Willow Ho
    9 London NW3 . . . . . .**12** B2
    London W10 . . . .**22** C1
Willow Lo
    Fulham SW6 . . . .**47** C2
    Putney SW15 . . . .**57** A4
Willow Lodge **10**
    SW8 . . . .**61** A4

Willow Pl SW1 ....147 A4
Willow Rd
London NW3 ......11 C4
London W5 ......36 A4
Willow St
EC2 ....24 A1 98 A2
Willows Terr NW1 ..21 B3
Willow Tree Cl E3 ..26 B4
Wandsworth SW18 ...71 A3
Willow Vale W12 ...29 C1
Willow Way SW11 ..30 C2
Willow Wlk SE1 ...152 C4
Willsbridge Ct 1
SE15
Willshaw St SE14 ...51 C2
Wilman Gr E8 ....16 C1
Wilmcote Ho W2 ..100 A4
Wilmer Gdns N1 ...24 A4
Wilmer Ho 3 E3 ..26 A3
Wilmer Lea Cl E15 ..19 C1
Wilmer Pl N16 .....7 B2
Wilmers Ct 5
NW10 ......20 C4
Wilmington Ave W4 43 C3
Wilmington Sq WC1 95 B3
Wilmington St WC1 95 B3
Wilmot Cl SE15 ...49 C3
Wilmot Pl NW1 ....13 B1
Wilmot St E2 .....25 A1
Wilna Rd SW18 ....71 B4
Wilsham St
W11 ....31 A1 112 A2
Wilshaw Ho 10 SE8 .51 C3
Wilson Gr SE16 ....40 A4
Wilson Ho
London NW6 ....11 B1
London SW8 ....171 B1
Wilson Rd SE5 ....49 A2
Wilson's Pl E14 ...33 B3
Wilson's Rd W6 ...39 C1
Wilson St EC2 ....109 C4
Wilton Ct 2 E14 ...33 B3
Wilton Est E8 .....16 C2
Wilton Ho 8 SE22 .64 A4
Wilton Mews SW1 .131 C2
Wilton Pl SW1 ....131 B3
Wilton Rd SW1 ...146 C4
Wilton Row SW1 ..131 B3
Wilton Sq N1 .....87 B4
Wilton St SW1 ....132 A2
Wilton Terr SW1 ..131 B2
Wilton Villas N1 ...87 B3
Wilton Way E8 ....16 C2
Wiltshire Cl 2 SW3 144 C3
Wiltshire Ct 2 N4 ...5 B3
Wiltshire Rd SW9 ..62 C4
Wiltshire Row N1 ..87 C3
Wimbart Rd SW2 ..74 B4
Wimbledon Lawn Tennis
Mus SW19 ......70 A1
Wimbledon Park Ct
SW19 ......70 B3
Wimbledon Park First
Sch SW19 ......71 A2
Wimbledon Park Rd
SW18,SW19 .....70 B3
Wimbledon Park Side
SW19 ......69 C3
Wimbledon Park Sta
SW19 ......70 C1
Wimbledon Stadium
Bsns Ctr SW17 ...71 A1

Wimbledon Windmill
Mus SW19 ......69 B1
Wimbolt St
E2 ....24 C2 99 B4
Wimborne Ho E16 .35 B2
NW1 ......90 B1
SW8 ......163 A1
Upper Tooting SW12 .73 B1
Wimbourne Ct N1 ..87 B2
Wimbourne St N1 ..87 B2
Wimpole Mews
W1 ......104 A3
Wimpole St W1 ...104 A2
Winans Wlk SW9 ..173 B1
Winant Ho 17 E14 .34 A2
Wincanton Rd
SW18 ......70 B4
Winchelsea Cl
SW15 ......57 C2
Winchelsea Ho 11
SE16 ......40 B4
Winchelsea Rd
NW10 ......20 C4
Winchendon Rd
SW6 ......165 A4
Winchester Ave
NW6 ......10 A1
Winchester Cl
SE17 ......150 B3
Winchester Ct W8 .128 A4
Winchester Ho
E3 ......26 B2
SW3 ......157 C3
W2 ......100 C1
6 London E8 ....16 B3
London Rd N6 ....4 B3
London NW3 ....11 C1
Winchester Sq
SE1 ......123 B2
Winchester St
SW1 ......146 B2
Acton W3 ......37 B4
Winchester Wlk
SE1 ......123 B2
Winchfield Ho
SW15 ......56 B1
Winch Ho SW10 ..157 A2
Winchilsea Ho NW8 .89 C3
Wincott St SE11 ..149 C3
Windermere NW1 ..92 B4
2 Putney SW15 ...57 C1
Windermere Ave
NW6 ......23 A4
Windermere Ct
SW13 ......46 B4
Windermere Ho 3 E3 26 B1
Windermere Point 3
SE15 ......50 B3
Windermere Rd N19 4 B2
Windham Rd TW9 ..54 B4
Windlass Pl SE8 ...41 A2
Windlesham Gr
SW19 ......69 C3
Windmill WC1 ....106 C4
Windmill Alley 7
W4 ......38 A2
Windmill Cl SE1 ..153 C4
London NW2 .....1 A1
3 London SE13 ..52 B1
Windmill Ct NW2 ..10 A2
Windmill Dr SW4 ..61 A2
Windmill Hill NW3 ..2 B1
1 London NW3 ...11 B4
Windmill Ho SE1 ..121 C1
Windmill La E15 ...19 C2

Windmill Pas 10
W4 ......38 A2
Windmill Rd
London SW18 ....59 C1
London W4 ......38 A2
Roehampton SW19 ..69 A1
Windmill Row
SE11 ......149 B1
Windmill St W1 ...105 B3
Windmill Wlk SE1 .121 C1
Windrose Cl SE16 ..40 C4
Windrush Cl
Chiswick W4 .....45 B3
London SW11 ....59 C3
Windrush Ho NW8 .101 C4
Windrush Rd NW10 20 C4
Windsock Cl 11
SE16 ......41 B2
Windsor Ct 20 SE16 .32 C1
SW3 ......144 B2
W2 ......114 A4
Fulham SW6 .....58 A4
London NW3 .....10 C4
London SW11 ...167 C2
2 London SE16 ..58 C2
4 London SW4 ...61 B3
Windsor Gdns W9 ..23 C1
Windsor Ho E2 ....25 C2
N1 ......87 A2
NW1 ......92 B4
London NW2 .....10 A2
4 London W11 ...37 B1
Windsor Pl SW1 ..147 A4
Windsor Rd
London N7 ......5 A1
London N7 ......9 A2
Richmond TW9 ...44 B1
Windsor St N1 ....86 B4
Windsor Terr N1 ...97 A4
Windsor Way W14 .140 A4
Windsor Wharf E9 ..18 B3
Windsor Wlk SE5 ..48 C1
Windspoint Dr SE15 50 A4
Windus Rd N16 ....7 B3
Windus Wlk N16 ...7 B3
Wine Cl E1 ......32 B2
Wine Office Ct
EC4 ......107 C2
Winfield Ho SW11 .167 C3
Winford Ct 13 SE15 49 C2
Winford Ho E3 ....18 B1
Winforton St SE10 .52 B2
Winfrith Rd SW18 .71 B3
Wingate Ho 20 E3 .27 A2
8 London N16 ...15 C4
Wingate Rd W6 ...39 A3
Wingfield Ct 10 E14 34 C2
Wingfield Ho 2 ...98 C3
NW6 ......78 A2
Wingfield Mews
SE15 ......64 C4
Wingfield St SE15 ..64 C4
Wingford Rd SW2 ..62 A1
Wingham 6 NW5 ..12 C2
Wingmore Rd SE24 63 B4
Wingrad Ho 16 E1 .32 B4
Wingrave SE17 ....151 B3
Wingrave Rd W6 ..47 B4
Wingreen NW8 ....78 B4
Winicotte Ho W2 ..101 B4
Winifrede Paul Ho 7
E9 ......17 B3
Winkley St 8 E2 ...25 A3
Winnett St W1 ...119 B4

Winnington Ho
8 SE5 ......48 B3
19 W10 ......23 A1
Winscombe St N19 ..4 A2
Winsham Gr SW11 .60 C2
Winsham Ho NW1 ..93 C4
Winslade Rd SW2 ..62 A2
Winsland Mews
W2 ......101 B2
Winsland St W2 ...101 B2
Winsley St W1 ....105 A2
Winslow SE17 ....152 A1
Winslow Rd W6 ...47 B4
Winstanley Rd
SW11 ......59 C4
Winston Ho WC1 ..93 C1
Winston Rd N16 ...15 C4
Winston Wlk 4 ....37 C2
Winterbourne Ho
W11 ......112 A3
Winter Box Wlk
TW10 ......54 B2
Winterbrook Rd
SE24 ......63 B1
Winterfold Cl SW19 70 A2
Winterleys 7 NW6 .23 B3
Winterslow Ho 20
SE5 ......48 B1
Winterton Ho 19 E1 32 B3
Winterton Pl
SW10 ......157 A4
Winterwell Rd SW2 62 A2
Winthorpe Rd SW15 58 A3
Winthrop Ho 10
W12 ......30 A2
Winthrop St E1 ...32 A4
Winton Prim Sch
N1 ......84 C1
Wirral Ho 15 SE26 .76 C1
Wisden Ho SW8 ..163 A3
Wise Rd E15 .....27 C4
Wiseton Rd SW17 .72 B3
Wisley Ho SW1 ...147 B2
Wisley Rd SW11 ..60 C2
Wisteria Rd SE13 ..67 C3
Wistow Ho 12 E2 ..24 C4
Witanhurst La N6 ...3 C3
Witan St E2 .....25 A2
Witchwood Ho 11
SW9 ......62 C4
Witcombe Point 18
SE15 ......49 C2
Witham Ct SW17 ..72 B1
Witham Ho 19 SE5 .48 B1
Witherington Rd
N5 ......14 C3
Withers Pl EC1 ...97 A2
Withycombe Rd
SW19 ......69 C4
Withy Ho 4 E1 ...25 C1
Witley Ho 2 SW2 ..74 B4
Witley Point 8
SW15 ......69 A3
Witley Rd N19 ....4 B2
Wittering Ho
SW11 ......169 A2
Wivenhoe Cl SE15 .65 A4
Wix Prim Sch SW4 .61 A3
Wix's La SW4 ....61 A3
Woburn Ct 22 SE16 40 A1
Richmond TW9 ...54 B4
Woburn Pl WC1 ...94 A1
Woburn Sq WC1 ...93 C1
Woburn Wlk WC1 ..93 C3
Wodehouse Ave
SE15 ......49 B2

Wodehouse Ct 10
W10 ......37 B3
Woking Cl SW15 ..56 B3
Wolcot Ho NW1 ...83 A1
Wolfe Cres 32 SE16 40 C4
Wolfe Ho 13 W12 ..30 A2
Wolfson Ct SE1 ...139 A4
London NW11 .....1 A4
Wolftencroft Cl
SW11 ......59 C4
Wollaston Cl SE1 ..150 C4
Wolseley Ave SW18,
SW19 ......70 C2
Wolseley Gdns W4 .45 A4
Wolseley Rd W4 ...37 B2
Wolseley St SE1 ..139 A3
Wolsey Ct NW6 ...11 B1
Wolsey Mews NW5 13 B2
Wolsey Rd N1 ....15 C3
Wolsey St E1 ....32 B4
Wolverley St E2 ...25 A2
Wolverton SE17 ..152 A2
Wolverton Gdns
W6 ......39 C2
Wontner Cl 3 N1 ..15 B1
Wontner Rd SW12,
SW17 ......72 B2
Woodall Cl 23 E14 .34 A2
Woodberry Down 4 ..6 B4
Woodberry Down Com
Prim Sch N4 .....6 B4
Woodberry Gr N4 ..6 B4
Woodbine Terr E9 ..17 B2
Woodborough Rd
SW15 ......57 A3
Woodbourne Ave
SW16 ......73 C1
Woodbourne Cl
SW16 ......74 A1
Woodbridge Cl 10 N7 5 B2
Woodbridge Ct N16 .6 C1
Woodbridge St EC1 96 A2
Woodchester Sq
W2 ......100 A4
Woodchurch Ho
SW9 ......173 B4
Woodchurch Rd
NW6 ......11 A1
Wood Cl E2 ....24 C1 99 B2
Woodcock Ho 4
E14 ......33 C4
Woodcote Ho 4
SE8 ......51 B4
Woodcott Ho 1
SW15 ......68 C4
Woodcroft Mews
SE8 ......41 A2
Wood Dene 3 SE15 50 A2
Woodfall Rd N4 ...5 C2
Woodfall St SW3 ..144 C1
Woodfarrs SE5 ....63 C3
Wood Field NW3 ..12 B3
Woodfield Ave
SW16 ......73 C1
Woodfield Ct SW16 73 C1
Woodfield Ctr The
SW16 ......73 C1
Woodfield Gr SW16 73 C1
Woodfield Pl W9 ..23 B1
Woodfield Rd W9 ..31 B4
Woodger Rd W12 ..39 B4
Woodhall NW1 ....92 C3
Woodhall Ave SE21 76 B1
Woodhall Dr SE21 .76 B1
Woodhall Ho SW18 59 C1

Woodheyes Rd NW10 ...8 A3
Wood Ho 6 NW6 ...23 B3
London SW4 ...171 C2
Woodhurst Rd W3 ...28 B2
Woodison St E3 ...26 B1
Wood La W12 ...30 B2
Woodland Cres
SE16 ...53 A4
18 SE16 ...40 C4
Woodland Gr SE10 ...43 A1
Woodlands SW4 ...61 A3
Woodlands Ave W3 ...28 A1
Woodlands Ct
NW10 ...22 C4
Woodlands Gt SE18 58 B2
Woodlands Park Rd
SE10 ...53 A4
Woodlands Rd
SW13 ...56 B4
Woodland Rd 2 E8 ...16 B2
Woodlands The N6 ...15 B4
Woodlands Way
SW15 ...58 B2
Woodland Wlk
9 SE10 ...43 A1
London NW3 ...12 A3
Woodlane High Sch
W12 ...30 A3
Woodlawn Cl SW15 58 B2
Woodlawn Rd SW6 .47 C2
Woodlea Rd N16 ...7 A1
Woodleigh Gdns
SW16 ...74 A1
Woodmans Gr NW10 .8 B3
Woodmans Mews
W12 ...30 A4
Woodmere Cl 10
SW11 ...60 C4
Woodpecker Mews
SE13 ...67 C3
Woodpecker Rd 8
SE14 ...51 A4
Wood Point 8 E16 .35 C4
Woodquest Ave
SE24 ...63 B2
Woodruff Ho SW2 ...62 C1
Woodrush Cl 4
SE14 ...51 A3
Woodseer St E1 ...111 A4
Woodsford SE17 ...151 B1
Woodsford Sq
W14 ...126 B4
Woodstar Ho 8
SE15 ...49 C3
Woodstock Ave
NW11 ...1 A4
Woods Ho SW8 ...170 C4
Wood's Mews W1 ...117 B4
Woodsome Rd NW5 .4 A1
Wood's Pl SE1 ...138 B1
Woodspring Rd
SW19 ...70 A2
Wood St EC2 ...109 A2
Wood St SE15 ...50 A2
London W4 ...38 A1
Woodstock Ct
SE11 ...149 A2
Woodstock Gr W12 .39 C4
Woodstock Ho 2
N5 ...15 B4
Woodstock Mews
W1 ...103 C3
Woodstock Rd
London N4 ...5 C3
London NW11 ...1 B3

Woodstock Rd continued
London W4 ...38 A3
Woodstock St W1 ...104 A1
Woodstock Terr
E14 ...34 A2
Woodthorpe Rd
SW15 ...57 A3
Woodview Cl N4 ...6 A4
Woodville Ct 3
SE10 ...52 B2
Woodville Ho SE1 ...138 C2
Woodville Rd NW6 ...23 B3
London N16 ...16 A3
London NW11 ...1 A4
Woodwarde Rd
SE22 ...64 A1
Woodwell St SW18 .59 B2
Wood Wharf SE10 ...52 B4
Woodyard Cl NW5 ...12 C3
Woodyard La SE21 ...76 A4
Woolcombes Ct 3
SE16 ...32 C1
Wooler St SE17 ...151 C2
Woolf Ct 7 W3 ...37 B3
Woolf Mews WC1 ...94 A3
Woolley Ho SW9 ...63 A4
Woollon Ho 1 E1 ...32 B3
Woolmore Prim Sch
E14 ...34 B2
Woolmore St E14 ...34 B2
Woolneigh St SW6 166 A1
Woolpack Ho 1 E9 .17 B2
Woolridge Way E9 .17 B1
Woolstaplers Way
SE16 ...153 B4
Woolstone Ho 7
E2 ...24 C4
Woolven Ho SE3 ...53 B4
Wooster Gdns E14 .34 C3
Wootton St SE1 ...121 C1
Worcester Ct 44
W2 ...31 C4
Worcester Dr W4 ...38 A4
Worcester Gdns
SW11 ...60 B2
Worcester Ho
SE11 ...135 B1
W2 ...100 C1
3 Putney SW15 ...69 B4
Worcester Mews 2
NW6 ...11 A2
Wordsworth Ho
NW6 ...23 C2
Wordsworth Pl 11
NW5 ...12 B3
Wordsworth Rd
SE1 ...153 A3
London N16 ...16 A4
Worfield St SW11 ...158 B1
Worgan St SE11 ...148 C2
SE16 ...40 C2
Working Men's Coll The
NW1 ...82 C2
World's End Pas
SW10 ...157 B2
World's End Pl
SW10 ...157 B2
Worlidge St W6 ...39 B1
Worlingham Rd
SE22 ...64 B3
Wormholt Park Prim
Sch W12 ...29 C2
Wormholt Rd W12 ...29 C2
Wormwood St EC2 110 A2
Wornington Rd
W10 ...31 A4

Wornum Ho 3
NW6 ...23 A3
Woronzow Rd NW8 .80 A3
Worple St SW14 ...55 C4
Worple Way TW10 ...54 A3
Worship St
EC2 ...24 A1 98 A1
Worsley Gr E5 ...16 C4
Worsopp Dr SW4 ...61 B2
Worth Gr SE17 ...151 B1
Worthington Ho
EC1 ...95 C4
10 Streatham SW2 ...74 C4
Wotton Ct 18 E14 ...34 C2
Wotton Rd 8 SE8 ...51 B4
Wouldham Rd E16 .35 B3
Wrayburn Ho SE16 139 C3
Wray Cres N4 ...5 B2
Wray Ct N4 ...5 B2
Wray Ho 11 SW2 ...74 A3
Wren Ave NW2 ...9 B4
Wren Ho E3 ...26 B3
SW1 ...147 B1
Wren Landing E14 ...33 C1
Wrenn Ho SW13 ...47 B4
Wren Rd SE5 ...48 C2
Wren St WC1 ...95 A2
Wrentham Ave
NW10 ...22 C3
Wren View N6 ...4 B3
Wrestlers Ct EC3 ...110 A2
Wrexham Rd E3 ...26 C3
Wrigglesworth St
SE14 ...50 C3
Wright Cl SE13 ...67 C3
Wright Ho SW15 ...57 A2
Wright's Gn SW4 ...61 C3
Wright's La W8 ...128 A2
Wright's Rd E3 ...26 B3
Wrights Wlk SW14 .55 C4
Wrotham Ho SE1 ...137 C2
Wrotham Rd 11
NW1 ...13 B1
Wrottesley Rd
NW10 ...21 C3
Wroughton Rd
SW11 ...60 B1
Wroxton Rd SE15 ...50 B1
Wulfstan St W12 ...29 B3
Wyatt Cl SE16 ...41 B4
Wyatt Dr SW13 ...47 A3
Wyatt Ho NW8 ...89 C1
London SE3 ...53 B1
Wyatt Park Mans 1
SW2 ...74 A2
Wyatt Park Rd SW2 .74 A2
Wyatt Rd N5 ...6 B1
Wybert St NW1 ...92 C2
Wycherley Cl SE3 ...53 B3
Wychwood End N6 ...4 B4
Wychwood Ho N4 ...6 B4
Wye St SW11 ...167 C1
Wyfold Rd SW6 ...154 A1
Wyke Rd E3 ...18 C1
Wyldes Cl NW11 ...2 B3
Wyllen Cl E1 ...25 B1

Wymering Mans 6
W9 ...23 C2
Wymering Rd W9 ...23 C2
Wymondham Ct
NW8 ...79 C4
Wymond St SW15 ...57 B4
Wynan Rd E14 ...42 A1
Wynard Terr SE11 ...149 A2
Wyndham Cres N19 .4 B1
Wyndham Deedes Ho 27
E2 ...24 C3
Wyndham Ho SW1 145 B3
Wyndham Mews
W1 ...102 C3
Wyndham Pl W1 ...102 C3
Wyndham Rd SE5 ...48 B3
Wyndham St W1 ...102 C4
Wyndham Yd W1 ...102 C3
Wyneham Rd SE24 .63 C2
Wynford Rd N1 ...85 A2
Wynne Ho SE14 ...50 C2
Wynne Rd SW9 ...173 B1
Wynnstay Gdns
W8 ...127 C2
Wynter St SW9 ...173 A1
Wynter St SW11 ...59 B3
Wynton Pl W3 ...28 A3
Wynyard Ho SE11 ...149 A2
Wynyatt St EC1 ...96 A4
Wytham Ho NW8 ...89 C1
Wythburn Ct W1 ...102 C2
Wythburn Pl W1 ...102 C2
Wyvil Prim Sch
SW8 ...162 B2
Wyvil Rd SW8 ...162 A2
Wyvis St E14 ...34 A4

Y

Yabsley St E14 ...34 B1
Yaldam Ho SE1 ...152 A3
Yalding Ho 20 E5 ...17 A3
Yalding Rd SE16 ...153 B4
Yale Ct NW6 ...11 A3
Yardley St WC1 ...95 B3
Yarmouth Pl W1 ...118 A1
Yarnfield Sq 14
SE15 ...49 C2
Yarrow Ho 10 E14 ...42 B3
London W10 ...30 B4
Yatesbury Ct E5 ...18 A3
Yates Ct NW2 ...9 C2
Yates Ho 2 E2 ...99 C4
Yatton Ho W10 ...30 B4
Yeadon Ho W10 ...30 B4
Yearby Ho W10 ...22 B1
Yeate St N1 ...15 C1
Yeats Cl NW10 ...8 A2
Yeldham Ho W6 ...39 C1
Yeldham Rd W6 ...39 C1
Yelverton Rd
SW11 ...167 C1
Yeoman Ho SE27 ...75 A1
Yeoman Ho 1 SE1 ...153 A2
Yeoman's Row
SW3 ...130 B1
Yeoman St SE8 ...41 A2
Yeoman's Yd E1 ...125 A4
Yeo St E3 ...34 A4
Yeovil Ho London N7 .5 B2
London W10 ...22 B1
Yerbury Prim Sch
N19 ...4 C1
Yerbury Rd N19 ...4 C1
Yesodey Hatorah Sch
N16 ...7 B4
Yewfield Rd NW10 ...8 B2

Yew Gr NW2 ...9 C4
Yew Ho SE14 ...51 B1
Yew Tree Rd W12 ...29 B2
Yoakley Rd N16 ...7 A2
Yoke Cl N7 ...14 A2
Yonge Pk N4,N7 ...5 C1
York Ave SE17 ...151 A2
Mortlake SW14 ...55 B2
York Bldgs WC2 ...120 B3
York Bridge NW1 ...91 B2
York Cl 6 SE5 ...48 B1
York Gate NW1 ...91 C1
York Gr SE15 ...50 B2
York Hill SE27,SW16 .75 A1
York Ho N1 ...84 C1
SE1 ...135 A1
SW3 ...145 A2
W1 ...102 C4
W8 ...128 A4
London N5 ...14 C3
3 London N7 ...13 C2
London W3 ...28 B2
Richmond TW10 ...54 C2
Richmond TW9 ...44 C2
York House Pl W8 128 A4
York Mans NW1 ...90 C1
SW5 ...146 B2
W1 ...103 B4
York Mews SW11 ...169 C4
York Mews NW5 ...13 A3
York Pl WC2 ...120 B3
London SW11 ...59 C4
York Place Mans
NW1 ...103 A4
York Rd SE1 ...135 A4
SW11,SW18 ...59 C4
London W3 ...28 C3
4 Richmond TW10 ...54 B2
York Rise NW5 ...4 A1
York Road Bsns Ctr
SW11 ...167 A1
Yorkshire Cl N16 ...7 A1
Yorkshire Grey Yd
WC1 ...106 C3
Yorkshire Rd E14 ...33 A3
York Sq 6 E14 ...33 A3
York St W1 ...103 A4
York St Chambers
W1 ...102 C4
York Terr E NW1 ...91 C1
York Terr W NW1 ...91 B1
Yorkton St E2 ...24 C3
York Way N1 ...84 B3
London N1,N7,NW1 ...14 A1
York Way Ct N1 ...84 B3
Young's Bldgs EC1 ...97 A2
Youngs Ct SW11 ...169 C3
Young St W8 ...128 A3
Yoxall Ho W10 ...22 B1
Yukon Rd SW12 ...73 A4
Yuletide Cl NW10 ...8 A2

Z

Zampa Rd SE16 ...40 B1
Zander Ct E2 ...24 C2 99 C4
Zangwill Ho NW6 ...23 B3
Zealand Ho 11 SE5 .48 B1
Zealand Rd E3 ...26 A3
Zennor Rd SW12 ...73 B3
Zenoria St SE22 ...64 B3
Zetland Ho W8 ...128 A2
Zetland St E14 ...34 B4
Zion Ho 6 E1 ...32 B3
Zoar St SE1 ...122 C2
Zodiac Ho 3 E3 ...26 C1
Zoffany St N19 ...4 C2

List of numbered locations

This atlas shows thousands more place names than any other London street atlas. In some busy areas it is impossible to fit the name of every place.

Where not all names will fit, some smaller places are shown by a number. If you wish to find out the name associated with a number, use this listing.

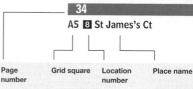

34

A5 **8** St James's Ct

Page number | Grid square | Location number | Place name

1

B1 **1** Mortimer Cl
2 Sunnyside Ho
3 Sunnyside
4 Prospect Pl
B4 **1** Berkeley Ct
2 Exchange Mans
3 Beechcroft Ct
4 Nedahall Ct
C1 **1** Portman Hts
2 Hermitage Ct
3 Moreland Ct
4 Wendover Ct

2

B1 **2** Stamford Cl

4

1 Hunter Ho
2 Fisher Ho
3 Lang Ho
4 Temple Ho
5 Palmer Ho
B2 **1** Flowers Mews
2 Sandridge St
3 Bovingdon Cl
4 Laurel Cl
5 Forest Way
6 Larch Cl
7 Pine Cl
8 Alder Mews
10 Aspen Cl
B3 **1** Calvert Ct
2 Academy The
3 Whitehall Mans
4 Pauntley St
5 Archway Hts
6 Pauntley Ho
C1 **1** Melchester Ho
2 Norcombe Ho
3 Weatherbury Ho
4 Wessex Ho
5 Archway Bsns Ctr
C2 **1** Bowerman Ct
2 Hargrave Mans
3 Church Garth
4 John King Ct
C3 **1** Louise White Ho
2 Levison Way
3 Sanders Way

5

C4 **1** Eleanor Rathbone Ho
2 Christopher Lo
3 Monkridge
4 Marbleford Ct
5 High London
6 Garton Ho
7 Hilltop Ho
8 Caroline Martyn Ho
9 Arthur Henderson Ho
10 Margaret Mcmillan Ho
11 Enid Stacy Ho
12 Mary McArthur Ho
13 Bruce Glasier Ho
14 John Wheatley Ho
15 Keir Hardie Ho
16 Monroe Ho
17 Iberia Ho
18 Lygoe Ho
19 Shelbourne Ho
20 Arkansas Ho
21 Lafitte Ho
22 Shreveport Ho
23 Packenham Ho
24 Orpheus Ho
25 Fayetville Ho
26 Bayon Ho

5

A1 **1** Northview
2 Tufnell Park Mans
A2 **1** Christie Ct
2 Ringmer Gdns
3 Kingsdown Rd
4 Cottenham Ho
5 St Paul's Ct
6 Rickthorne Rd
7 Stanley Terr
A3 **1** Beeches The
2 Lambton Ct
A4 **1** Marie Lloyd Gdns
2 Jessie Blythe La
3 Leyden Mans
4 Brambledown
5 Lochbie
6 Edith Cavell Ct
B2 **1** Berkeley Wlk
2 Lazar Wlk

3 Thistlewood Cl
4 Tomlins Wlk
5 Andover Ho
6 Barmouth Ho
7 Chard Ho
8 Methley Ho
9 Rainford Ho
10 Woodbridge Cl
11 Allerton Ho
12 Falconer Wlk
13 Sonderburg Rd
B3 **1** Lawson Ct
2 Wiltshire Ct
3 Hutton Ct
C2 **1** Brookfield
2 Churnfield

6

B4 **1** Finmere Ho
2 Keynsham Ho
3 Kilpeck Ho
4 Knaresborough Ho
5 Leighfield Ho
6 Lonsdale Ho
7 Groveley Ho
8 Wensleydale Ho
9 Badminton Ho
C2 **1** Chestnut Cl
2 Sycamore Ho
3 Lordship Ho
4 Clissold Ho
5 Beech Ho
6 Laburnum Ho
7 Ormond Ho
C4 **1** Selwood Ho
2 Menilp Ho
3 Ennerdale Ho
4 Delamere Ho
5 Westwood Ho
6 Bernwood Ho
7 Allerdale Ho
8 Chattenden Ho
9 Farningham Ho
10 Oakend Ho

7

A1 **1** Gujarat Ho
2 Marton Rd
3 Painsthorpe Rd
4 Selkirk Ho
5 Defoe Ho

6 Edward Friend Ho
7 Sheridan Ho
8 Barrie Ho
9 Arnold Ho
10 Macaulay Ho
11 Stowe Ho
12 Carlyle Ho
13 Shaftesbury Ho
14 Lillian Cl
15 Swift Ho
16 Dryden Ho
17 Scott Ct
18 Kingsfield Ho
19 Uhura Sq
A3 **1** Godstone Ct
2 Farnham Ct
3 Milford Ct
4 Cranleigh Ct
5 Haslemere Ct
6 Belmont Ct
7 Hockworth Ho
8 Garratt Ho
9 Fairburn Ho
B1 **1** Lawrence's Bldgs
2 Cottage Wlk
3 Batley Pl
B2 **1** Garnham St
2 Garnham Ho
3 Sanford La
4 Sandford Wlk
5 Abney Gdns
6 Fleet Wood
B3 **1** Stamford Hill Mans
2 Montefiore Ct
3 Berwyn Ho
4 Clent Ho
5 Chiltern Ho
6 Laindon Ho
7 Pentland Ho
B4 **1** Regent Ct
2 Stamford Lo
3 Holmwood Ct
C1 **1** Ravenscourt
2 Mellington Ct
3 Rendlesham Ho
4 Florence Ct
5 Burnaston Ho
C2 **1** Cazenove Mans
2 Chedworth Ho
3 Aldergrove Ho
4 Abbotstone Ho

5 Briggeford Cl
6 Inglethorpe Ho
7 Ashdown Ho
C3 **1** Stamford Grove E
2 Stamford Mans
3 Grove Mans
4 Stamford Grove W

8

A1 **1** Beveridge Rd
C2 **1** Regency Mews
2 Tudor Mews

10

A1 **1** Fountain Ho
2 Kingston Ho
3 Waverley Ct
4 Weston Ho
5 Mapes Ho
6 Athelstan Gdns
7 Leff Ho
B1 **1** Alma Birk Ho
2 Brooklands Ct
3 Brooklands Court Apartments
4 Cleveland Mans
5 Buckley Ct
6 Webheath
C1 **1** Linstead St
2 Embassy Ho
3 Acol Ct
4 Kings Wood Ct
5 Douglas Ct
6 King's Gdns
7 Carlton Mans
8 Smyrna Mans
9 New Priory Ct
10 Queensgate Pl
11 Brondesbury Mews
C2 **1** Dene Mans
2 Sandwell Cres
3 Sandwell Mans
4 Hampstead West
5 Redcroft
C3 **1** Orestes Mews
2 Walter Northcott Ho
3 Polperro Mans
4 Lyncroft Mans
5 Marlborough Mans
6 Alexandra Mans

13 Jethou Ho
14 Upper Caldy Wlk
15 Caldy Wlk
16 Alderney Ho
17 Marquess Rd S
18 Oronsay Rd
19 Upper Gulland Wlk
20 Gulland Wlk
21 Church Rd
B3 1 Pearfield Ho
2 Larchfield Ho
3 Beresford Terr
4 Pondfield Ho
5 Ashfield Ho
6 Elmfield Ho
B4 1 Fountain Mews
2 Woodstock Ho
3 Henson Ct
4 Taverner Sq
C2 1 John Kennedy Ct
2 John Kennedy Lo
3 Ball's Pond Pl
4 Haliday Wlk
5 Rona Wlk
6 Threadgold Ho
7 Wakeham St
8 Saffron Ct
9 Callaby Terr
10 Tilney Gdns
11 Westcliff Ho
12 Ilford Ho
13 Ongar Ho
14 Greenhills Terr
15 Romford Ho
C4 1 Ledo Ho
2 Salween Ho
3 Prome Ho
4 Arakan Ho
5 Rangoon Ho
6 Mandalay Ho
7 Karen Ho
8 Wingate Ho
9 Jubet Ho
10 Orde Ho
11 Chindit Ho
12 Mabel Thornton Ho
13 Crawshay Ho
14 Avon Ho
15 Connaught Mans
16 Jonson Ho
17 Herrick Ho
18 Donne Ho
19 Grasmere Ho
20 Thirlmere Ho

16

A1 1 Dorchester Ct
2 Wareham Ho
3 Dorset Ct
4 Stratton Ct
5 Swanage Ct
6 Blandford Ct
7 Portland Ct
8 Oscar Faber Pl
9 Lancaster Ct
A2 1 Kingsland Gn
2 Kingsland Pas
3 Metropolitan Benefit Societies Almshouses
4 Nimrod Pas
5 De Beauvoir Ct
6 Warburton Ct
7 Buckingham Mews
A3 1 Hewling Ho
2 Matthias Ho

3 Port Royal Pl
4 Cressington Cl
5 King Henry's Ct
6 Bronte Ho
7 Sewell Ho
8 Lydgate Ho
9 Patmore Ho
10 Congreve Ho
11 Elton St
12 Conrad Ho
13 Southwell Ho
14 Neptune Ho
15 Campion Ho
16 Webster Ho
17 Meredith Ho
18 Beckford Ho
19 Ashley Ct
20 Hayling Ct
21 Millard Cl
22 Lydford Cl
23 Salcombe Rd
24 Truman's Rd
25 Templeton Cl
26 John Campbell Rd
27 Gillett St
28 Bradbury St
A4 1 Londesborough Ho
2 Knebworth Ho
3 Knebworth Rd
4 Bransby Ct
5 Imperial Ave
6 Leonard Pl
7 Shakspeare Mews
8 Binyon Ho
9 Shelley Ho
10 Browning Ho
11 Burns Ho
12 Andrew Marvell Ho
13 Wycliffe Ho
14 Blake Ho
15 Marlowe Ho
16 Fletcher Ho
17 Chaucer Ct
B1 1 Hilborough Rd
2 Shoreditch Ct
3 Evergreen Sq
B2 1 Prospect Ho
2 Woodland St
3 Crosby Wlk
4 Kirkland Wlk
5 Bowness Cl
6 Carlisle Wlk
7 Skelton Cl
8 Camerton Cl
9 Buttermere Wlk
10 Houghton Cl
11 Hayton Cl
B3 1 Miller's Terr
2 Chow Sq
3 Drysdale Flats
4 Gateway Mews
5 Birkbeck Mews
6 Winchester Pl
B4 1 Coronation Ave
2 Morris Blitz Ct
3 Shacklewell Ho
4 Alexandra Ct
C1 1 Aldington Ct
2 Bayton Ct
3 Rochford Wlk
C3 1 Kingsdown Ho
2 Glendown Ho
3 Moredown Ho
4 Blakeney Cl
5 Beeston Cl
6 Benabo Ct

7 David Devine Ho
8 Kreedman Wlk
9 Hermitage Row
10 Grafton Ct
11 Lushington Terr

17

A1 1 Fortescue Ave
2 Pemberton Pl
3 Weston Wlk
4 Bayford St Ind Ctr
5 Bayford St
6 Sidworth St
7 Helmsley St
A2 1 Bohemia Pl
2 Graham Mans
3 Marvin St
4 Boscobel Ho
5 Royal Oak Rd
6 Colonnades The
7 Sylvester Ho
8 Sylvester Path
9 Doctor Spurstowe Almshos
10 Great Eastern Bldgs
11 Sojourner-Truth Cl
A3 1 Birchington Ho
2 Bicknor Ho
3 Boxley Ho
4 Adisham Ho
5 Cranbrook Ho
6 Marden Ho
7 Broome Ho
8 Crandale Ho
9 Cheriton Ho
10 Ditton Ho
11 Langley Ho
12 Dymchurch Ho
13 Elham Ho
14 Bodney Mans
15 Pembury Ct
16 Downs Ct
17 Perrywood Ho
18 Stapelhurst Ho
19 Pegwell Ho
20 Yalding Ho
21 Northbourne Ho
22 Monkton Ho
23 Milsted Ho
24 Athlone Ct
25 Clarence Pl
26 Gould Terr
27 Quested Ct
28 Brett Pas
29 Marcon Ct
A4 1 Sutherland Point
2 Embley Point
3 Downs La
4 Gaviller Pl
5 Robert Owen Lo
6 Apprentice Way
7 Arrowe Ct
8 Gilwell Ct
9 Sutton Ct
10 Kinnoull Mans
11 Rowhill Mans
12 Sladen Pl
13 Mothers Sq The
14 Richborough Ho
15 Sandgate Ho
16 Sheppey Ho
B1 1 Pitcairn Ho
2 Lyme Grove Ho
3 Shakespeare Ho
4 Upcott Ho

5 Loddiges Ho
6 Parkinson Ho
7 Sloane Ho
8 Vanbrugh Ho
9 Cambridge Pas
10 Lyttleton Ho
11 Victoria Park Ct
12 Tullis Ho
13 Fairchild Ho
14 Forsyth Ho
15 Tradescant Ho
16 Mason Ho
17 Capel Ho
18 Cordwainers Ct
19 Bridgeman Ho
20 St Thomas's Pl
21 Barclay Ho
22 Clayton Ho
23 Danby Ho
24 Sherard Ho
25 Catesby Ho
26 Petiver Cl
27 Leander Ct
28 Philip Turner Est
29 Grendon Ho
30 Shore Mews
31 Shore Bsns Ctr
32 Kendal Ho
33 Classic Mans
34 Tudor Ho
35 Park Ho
36 Alpine Gr
37 Clarendon Ct
B2 1 Woolpack Ho
2 Elvin Ho
3 Thomas Ho
4 Hockley Ho
5 Retreat Ho
6 Butfield Ho
7 Brooksbank Ho
8 Cresset Ho
9 Brooksbank St
10 Lennox Ho
11 Milborne Ho
12 Collent Ho
13 Middlesex Pl
14 Devonshire Hall
15 Brent Ho
C1 1 Stuart Ho
2 Gascoyne Ho
3 Chelsfield Point
4 Sundridge Ho
5 Banbury Ho
C2 1 Musgrove Ho
2 Cheyney Ho
3 Haynes Ho
4 Warner Ho
5 Gilby Ho
6 Gadsden Ho
7 Risley Ho
8 Baycliffe Ho
9 Sheldon Ho
10 Offley Ho
11 Latimer Ho
12 Ribstone Ho
13 Salem Ho
14 Fieldwick Ho
15 Lever Ct
16 Matson Ho
17 Wilding Ho
18 Rennell Ho
19 Dycer Ho
20 Granard Ho
21 Whitelock Ho
22 Harrowgate Ho
23 Cass Ho

24 Lofts on the Park
C4 1 Cromford Path
2 Longford Ct
3 Overbury Ho
4 Heanor Ct
5 Wharfedale Ct
6 Ladybower Ct
7 Ilkeston Ct
8 Derby Ct
9 Rushmore Cres
10 Blackwell Cl

18

A2 1 Wick Mews
2 Wellday Ho
3 Selman Ho
4 Vaine Ho
5 Trower Ho
B2 1 Merriam Ave

19

C4 1 Mulberry Ct
2 Rosewood Ct
3 Gean Ct
4 Blackthorn Ct
5 Cypress Ct

20

1 Fitzsimmons Ct
2 Bernard Shaw Ho
3 Longlents Ho
4 Mordaunt Ho
5 Wilmers Ct
6 Stonebridge Sh Ctr

21

B3 1 New Crescent Yd
2 Harlesden Plaza
3 St Josephs Ct

22

C2 1 Westfield Ct
2 Tropical Ct
3 Chamberlayne Mans
4 Quadrant The
5 Queens Park Ct
6 Warfield Yd
7 Cherrytree Ho

23

A1 1 Sycamore Wlk
2 Westgate Bsns Ctr
3 Buspace Studios
4 Bosworth Ho
5 Golborne Gdns
6 Appleford Ho
7 Adair Twr
8 Gadsden Ho
9 Southam Ho
10 Norman Butler Ho
11 Thompson Ho
12 Wells Ho
13 Paul Ho
14 Olive Blythe Ho
15 Katherine Ho
16 Breakwell Ct
17 Pepler Ho
18 Edward Kennedy Ho
19 Winnington Ho
A2 1 Slomon Ho
2 Stansbury Ho

4 Tilleard Ho
5 Selby Ho
8 Mundy Ho
9 Macfarren Ho
10 Mounsey Ho
11 Courtville Ho
12 Croft Ho
13 Batten Ho
14 Bantock Ho
15 Banister Ho
16 Symphony Mews
17 Bliss Mews
A3 1 Lancefield Ct
2 Verdi Ho
3 Wornum Ho
B1 1 Western Ho
2 Russell's Wharf
B2 1 Boyce Ho
2 Farnaby Ho
3 Danby Ho
4 Purday Ho
5 Naylor Ho
6 St Judes Ho
7 Leeve Ho
8 Longhurst Ho
9 Harrington Ct
10 Mulberry Ct
11 Quilter Ho
12 Romer Ho
13 Kilburn Ho
B3 1 Claremont Ct
2 William Saville Ho
3 Western Ct
4 Bond Ho
5 Crone Ct
6 Wood Ho
7 Winterleys
8 Carlton Ho
9 Fiona Ct
C1 1 Westside Ct
2 Sutherland Ct
3 Fleming Ct
4 Hermes Cl
C2 1 Masefield Ho
2 Austen Ho
3 Fielding Ho
4 Park Bsns Ctr
5 John Ratcliffe Ho
6 Wymering Mans
7 Pavilion Ct
8 Nelson Ct
C3 1 Wells Ct
2 Cambridge Ct
3 Durham Ct
C4 1 Ryde Ho
2 Glengall Pass
3 Leith Yd
4 Daynor Ho
5 Varley Ho
6 Sandby Ho
7 Colas Mews
8 Bishopsdale Ho
9 Lorton Ho
10 Marshwood Ho
11 Ribblesdale Ho
12 Holmesdale Ho
13 Kilburn Vale Est
14 Kilburn Bridge

24
A3 1 Bracer Ho
2 Scorton Ho
3 Fern Cl

4 Macbeth Ho
5 Oberon Ho
6 Buckland Ct
7 Crondall Ct
8 Osric Path
9 Caliban Twr
10 Celia Ho
11 Juliet Ho
12 Bacchus Wlk
13 Malcolm Ho
14 Homefield St
15 Crondall Pl
16 Blanca Ho
17 Miranda Ho
18 Falstaff Ho
19 Charmian Ho
20 Myrtle Wlk
21 Arden Ho
22 Sebastian Ho
23 Stanway Ct
24 Jerrold St
25 Rosalind Ho
26 Cordelia Ho
27 Monteagle Ct
28 John Parry Ct
29 James Anderson Ct
30 Ben Jonson Ct
31 Sara Lane Ct
32 Walbrook Ct
A4 1 Portelet Ct
2 Trinity Ct
3 Rozel Ct
4 St Helier Ct
5 Corbiere Ho
6 Kenning Ho
7 Higgins Ho
8 Cavell Ho
9 Girling Ho
10 Fulcher Ho
11 Francis Ho
12 Norris Ho
13 Kempton Ho
14 Nesham Ho
15 Crossbow Ho
16 Catherine Ho
17 Strale Ho
18 Horner Hos
19 Stringer Hos
20 Whitmore Ho
21 Nightingale Ho
22 Fletcher Ho
23 Arrow Ho
24 Archer Ho
25 Meriden Ho
26 Rover Ho
27 Bowyer Ho
28 Longbow Ho
29 Tiller Ho
30 Canalside Studios
31 Bishopgate
32 Holburn
B3 1 Queensbridge Ct
2 Godwin Ho
3 Kent Ct
4 Brunswick Ho
5 Weymouth Ct
6 Sovereign Mews
7 Dunloe Ct
8 Cremer Bsns Ctr
9 James Hammett Ho
10 Allgood St
11 Horatio St
12 Cadell Ho
13 Horatio Ho
14 Shipton Ho

B4 1 Hilborough Ct
2 Scriven Ct
3 Livermere Ct
4 Angrave Ct
5 Angrave Pas
6 Benfleet Ct
7 Belford Ho
8 Orme Ho
9 Clemson Ho
10 Longman Ho
11 Lowther Ho
12 Lovelace Ho
13 Harlowe Ho
14 Pamela Ho
15 Samuel Ho
16 Acton Ho
17 Loanda Cl
18 Phoenix Cl
19 Richardson Cl
20 Thrasher Cl
21 Mary Secole Cl
22 Canal Path
23 Pear Tree Cl
24 Hebden Ct
25 Charlton Ct
26 Laburnum Ct
27 Mansfield Ct
28 Garden Pl
C2 1 Lorden Wlk
C3 1 London Terr
2 Sturdee Ho
3 Maude Ho
4 Haig Ho
5 Jellicoe Ho
6 Ropley St
7 Guinness Trust Bldgs
8 Ion Ct
9 Moye Cl
10 Morrel Ct
11 Courtauld Ho
12 Drummond Ho
13 Atkinson Ho
14 Gurney Ho
15 Halley Ho
16 Goldsmith's Sq
17 Ken Wilson Ho
18 Shahjalal Ho
19 Crofts Ho
20 April Ct
21 Sebright Ho
22 Beechwood Ho
23 Gillman Ho
24 Cheverell Ho
25 Besford Ho
26 Dinmont Ho
27 Wyndham Deedes Ho
28 Sheppard Ho
29 Mary James Ho
30 Hadrian St
31 Blythendale Ho
32 George Vale Ho
33 Lion Mills
34 Pritchard Ho
C4 1 Broke Wlk
2 Rochemont Wlk
3 Marlborough Ave
4 Rivington Wlk
5 Magnin Cl
6 Gloucester Sq
7 Woolstone Ho
8 Marsworth Ho
9 Cheddington Ho
10 Linslade Ho

11 Cosgrove Ho
12 Blisworth Ho
13 Eleanor Ct
14 Wistow Ho
15 Muscott Ho
16 Boxmoor Ho
17 Linford Ho
18 Pendley Ho
19 North Church Ho
20 Debdale Ho
21 Broadway Market Mews
22 Welshpool Ho
23 Ada Ho

25
A1 1 Rochester Ct
2 Weaver Ct
3 Greenheath Bsns Ctr
4 Glass St
5 Herald St
6 Northesk Ho
7 Codrington Ho
8 Heathpool Ct
9 Mocatta Ho
10 Harvey Ho
11 Blackwood Ho
12 Rutherford Ho
13 Bullen Ho
14 Fremantle Ho
15 Pellew Ho
16 Ashington Ho
17 Dinnington Ho
18 Bartholomew Sq
19 Steeple Ct
20 Orion Ho
21 Fellbrigg St
22 Eagle Ho
23 Sovereign Ho
24 Redmill Ho
25 Grindal Ho
26 Collingwood Ho
A2 1 Charles Dickens Ho
2 Adrian Bolt Ho
3 William Rathbone Ho
4 Southwood Smith Ho
5 Rushmead
6 William Channing Ho
7 John Cartwright Ho
8 Charles Darwin Ho
9 Thomas Burt Ho
10 John Fielden Ho
11 Gwilym Maries Ho
12 Joseph Priestley Ho
13 Wear Pl
14 John Nettleford Ho
15 Thornaby Ho
16 Stockton Ho
17 Barnard Ho
18 Gainford Ho
19 Stapleton Ho
20 James Middleton Ho
21 Kedleston Wlk
22 Queen Margaret Flats
23 Hollybush Ho
24 Horwood Ho
25 Norden Ho
26 Newcourt Ho

27 Seabright St
28 Viaduct Pl
29 Sunlight Sq
A3 1 Dinmont St
2 Marian St
3 Claredale Ho
4 Bradley Ho
5 Connett Ho
6 Winkley St
7 Temple Dwellings
8 Argos Ho
9 Helen Ho
10 Lysander Ho
11 Antenor Ho
12 Paris Ho
13 Nestor Ho
14 Hector Ho
15 Ajax Ho
16 Achilles Ho
17 Priam Ho
18 Peabody Est
19 Cambridge Cres
20 Peterley Bsns Ctr
21 Beckwith Ho
22 Parminter Ind Est
23 Ted Roberts Ho
24 Cambridge Ct
25 West St
26 Millennium Pl
27 William Caslon Ho
28 Hugh Platt Ho
29 Mayfield Ho
30 Apollo Ho
31 Tanners Yd
32 Teesdale Yd
A4 1 Welshpool St
2 Broadway Ho
3 Regents Wharf
4 London Wharf
5 Warburton Ho
6 Warburton St
7 Triangle Rd
8 Warburton Rd
9 Williams Ho
10 Booth Cl
11 Albert Cl
12 King Edward Mans
13 Victoria Bldgs
B1 1 William's Bldgs
2 Donegal Ho
3 Frederick Charrington Ho
4 Wickford Ho
5 Braintree Ho
6 Doveton Ho
7 Doveton St
8 Cephas Ho
9 Sceptre Ho
10 Bancroft Ho
11 Stothard St
12 Redclyf Ho
13 Winkworth Cotts
14 Ryder Ho
15 Hadleigh Ho
16 Hadleigh Cl
17 Amiel St
18 Stathard Ho
19 Barbanel Ho
20 Colebert Ho
21 Kenton Ho
22 Ibbott St
23 Stannard Cotts
24 Rennie Cotts
25 Rickman St
26 Rickman Ho

27
27 Pemell Cl
28 Pemell Ho
29 Leatherdale St
30 Gouldman Ho
31 Lamplighter Cl
32 Hamilton Lo
33 Cleveland Gr
34 Montgomery Lo
35 Bardsey Pl
36 Cromwell Lo
37 Colin Winter Ho
38 Allport Mews
B2 1 Mulberry Ho
2 Gretton Ho
3 Merceron Ho
4 Montfort Ho
5 Westbrook Ho
6 Sugar Loaf Wlk
7 Museum Ho
8 Globe Terr
9 Moravian St
10 Shepton Hos
11 Mendip Hos
12 Academy Ct
13 Pepys Ho
14 Swinburne Ho
15 Moore Ho
16 Morris Ho
17 Burns Ho
18 Milton Ho
19 Whitman Ho
20 Shelley Ho
21 Keats Ho
22 Dawson Ho
23 Bradbeer Ho
24 Forber Ho
25 Hughes Ho
26 Silvester Ho
27 Rogers Est
28 Pavan Ct
29 Stafford Cripps Ho
30 Sidney Godley (VC) Ho
31 Butler Ho
32 Butler St
33 Thorne Ho
34 Bevin Ho
35 Tuscan Ho
B3 1 Evesham Ho
2 James Campbell Ho
3 Thomas Hollywood Ho
4 James Docherty Ho
5 Ebenezer Mussel Ho
6 Jameson Ct
7 Edinburgh Cl
8 Roger Dowley Ct
9 Sherbrooke Ho
10 Calcraft Ho
11 Burrard Ho
12 Dundas Ho
13 Ponsonby Ho
14 Barnes Ho
15 Paget Ho
16 Maitland Ho
17 Chesil Ct
18 Reynolds Ho
19 Cleland Ho
20 Goodrich Ho
21 Rosebery Ho
22 Sankey Ho
23 Cyprus Pl
24 Royston St

26 Stainsbury St
27 Hunslett St
28 Baildon
29 Brockweir
30 Tytherton
31 Malmesbury
32 Kingswood
33 Colville Ho
B4 1 Halkett Ho
4 Christ Church Sq
5 Swingfield Ho
6 Greenham Ho
7 Dinmore Ho
8 Anstey Ho
9 Weston Ho
10 Carbroke Ho
15 Bluebell Cl
16 Cherry Tree Cl
17 Georgian Ct
20 Regency Ct
21 Norris Ho
C1 1 Raynham Ho
2 Pat Shaw Ho
3 Colmar Cl
4 Withy Ho
5 Stocks Ct
6 Downey Ho
7 Bay Ct
8 Sligo Ho
9 Pegasus Ho
10 Barents Ho
11 Biscay Ho
12 Solway Ho
13 Bantry Ho
14 Aral Ho
15 Pacific Ho
16 Magellan Ho
17 Levant Ho
18 Adriatic Ho
19 Genoa Ho
20 Hawke Ho
21 Palliser Ho
22 Ionian Ho
23 Weddell Ho
C2 1 Stubbs Ho
2 Holman Ho
3 Clynes Ho
4 Windsor Ho
5 Gilbert Ho
6 Chater Ho
7 Ellen Wilkinson Ho
8 George Belt Ho
9 Ayrton Gould Ho
10 O'Brian Ho
11 Sulkin Ho
12 Jenkinson Ho
13 Bullards Ho
14 Sylvia Pankhurst Ho
15 Mary Macarthur Ho
16 Trevelyan Ho
17 Wedgwood Ho
18 Pemberton Ho
19 Walter Besant Ho
20 Barber Beaumont Ho
21 Brancaster Ho
22 Litcham Ho
C3 1 Kemp Ho
2 Piggott Ho
3 Mark Ho
4 Sidney Ho
5 Pomeroy Ho
6 Puteaux Ho
7 Doric Ho
8 Modling Ho
9 Longman Ho
10 Ames Ho
11 Alzette Ho
12 Offenbach Ho
13 Tate Ho
14 Norton Ho
15 St Gilles Ho
16 Harold Ho
17 Velletri Ho
18 Bridge Wharf
19 Gathorne St
20 Bow Brook The
21 Palmerston St
22 Peach Walk Mews
23 Lakeview
24 Caesar Ct

26
A1 1 Formosa Ho
2 Galveston Ho
3 Arabian Ho
4 Greenland Ho
5 Coral Ho
6 Anson Ho
7 Lindop Ho
8 Moray Ho
9 Azov Ho
10 Sandalwood Cl
11 Broadford Ho
A3 1 Bunsen Ho
2 Bunsen St
3 Beatrice Webb Ho
4 Margaret Bondfield Ho
5 Wilmer Ho
6 Sandall Ho
7 Butley Ct
8 Josseline Ct
9 Dalton Ho
10 Brine Ho
11 Ford Cl
12 Viking Cl
13 Stanfield Rd
14 Ruth Ct
15 School Bell Cloisters
16 Schoolbell Mews
17 Medhurst Cl
18 Olga St
19 Conyer St
20 Diamond Ho
21 Daring Ho
22 Crane Ho
23 Exmoor Ho
24 Grenville Ho
25 Hyperion Ho
26 Sturdy Ho
27 Wren Ho
28 Ardent Ho
29 Senators Lo
30 Hooke Ho
31 Mohawk Ho
32 Ivanhoe Ho
33 Medway Mews
B2 1 Trellis Sq
2 Sheffield Sq
3 Howcroft Ho
4 Astra Ho
5 Byas Ho
6 George Lansbury Ho
7 Regal Pl
8 Coborn Mews
9 Cavendish Terr
10 Buttermere Ho
11 Buttermere Ho
12 Tracy Ho
13 Hanover Pl
14 Coniston Ho
15 St Clair Ho
16 Verity Ho
17 Icarus Ho
18 Whippingham Ho
19 Winchester Ho
20 Hamilton Ho
21 Longthorne Ho
B3 1 Roman Square Mkt
2 John Bond Ho
3 McKenna Ho
4 Dennis Ho
5 McBride Ho
6 Libra Rd
7 Dave Adams Ho
8 Tay Ho
9 Sleat Ho
10 Ewart Pl
11 Brodick Ho
12 Lunan Ho
13 Mull Ho
14 Sinclairs Ho
15 Driftway Ho
16 Clayhall Ct
17 Berebinder Ho
18 Stavers Ho
19 Barford Ho
20 Partridge Ho
21 Gosford Ho
22 Gullane Ho
23 Cruden Ho
24 Anglo Rd
25 Dornoch Ho
26 Dunnet Ho
27 Enard Ho
28 Fraserburgh Ho
29 Forth Ho
30 Ordell Ct
31 William Pl
B4 1 Hampstead Wlk
2 Waverton Ho
3 Elton Ho
4 Locton Gn
5 Birtwhistle Ho
6 Clare Ho
7 Magpie Ho
8 Atkins Ct
9 Tait Ct
10 Ranwell Ho
11 Ranwell Cl
12 Tufnell Ct
13 Pulteney Cl
14 Vic Johnson Ho
C1 1 Fairmont Ho
2 Healy Ho
3 Zodiac Ho
4 Buick Ho
5 Consul Ho
6 Bentley Ho
7 Cresta Ho
8 Daimler Ho
9 Riley Ho
10 Jensen Ho
11 Lagonda Ho
12 Ireton St
13 Navenby Wlk
14 Burwell Wlk
15 Leadenham Ct
16 Sleaford Ho
C2 1 Jarret Ho
2 Marsalis Ho
3 Lovette Ho
4 Drapers Almshouses
5 Mallard Point
6 Creswick Wlk
7 Bevin Ho
8 Huggins Ho
9 Williams Ho
10 Harris Ho
11 Marina Ct
12 Electric Ho
13 Matching Ct
14 Wellington Bldgs
15 Grafton Ho
16 Columbia Ho
17 Berkeley Ho

27
A1 1 Broxbourne Ho
2 Roxford Ho
3 Biscott Ho
4 Stanborough Ho
5 Hillstone Ct
A2 1 Bradley Ho
2 Prioress Ho
3 Alton Ho
4 Foxley Ho
5 Munden Ho
6 Canterbury Ho
7 Corbin Ho
8 Barton Ho
9 Jolles Ho
10 Rudstone Ho
11 Baxter Ho
12 Baker Ho
13 Insley Ho
14 Hardwicke Ho
15 Glebe Terr
16 Priory St
17 Sadler Ho
18 Ballinger Point
19 Henshall Point
20 Dorrington Point
21 Warren Ho
22 Fairlie Ct
23 Regent Sq
24 Hackworth Point
25 Priestman Point
26 Wingate Ho
27 Nethercott Ho
28 Thelbridge Ho
29 Bowden Ho
30 Kerscott Ho
31 Southcott Ho
32 Birchdown Ho
33 Upcott Ho
34 Langmead Ho
35 Limscott Ho
36 Northleigh Ho
37 Huntshaw Ho
38 Chagford Ho
39 Ashcombe Ho
40 Shillingford Ho
41 Patrick Connolly Gdns
42 Lester Ct
43 Franklin St
44 Taft Way
45 Washington Cl
46 Elizabeth Ho
47 William Guy Gdns
48 Denbury Ho
49 Holsworthy Ho

28
A1 1 Lantry Ct
2 Rosemount Ct

21 Jean Pardies Ho
22 Clichy Ho
23 Le Moal Ho
24 Odette Duval Ho
25 Dagobert Ho
26 Charles Auffray Ho
27 Boisseau Ho
28 Paymal Ho
C1 1 Clarence Mews
2 Raleigh Ct
3 Katherine Cl
4 Woolcombes Ct
5 Tudor Ct
6 Quayside Ct
7 Princes Riverside Rd
8 Surrey Ho
9 Tideway Ct
10 Edinburgh Ct
11 Falkirk Ct
12 Byelands Cl
13 Gwent Ct
14 Lavender Ho
15 Abbotshade Rd
16 Bellamy's Ct
17 Blenheim Ct
18 Sandringham Ct
19 Hampton Ct
20 Windsor Ct
21 Balmoral Ct
22 Westminster Ct
C2 1 Barnardo Gdns
2 Roslin Ho
3 Glamis Est
4 Peabody Est
5 East Block
6 Highway Trad Ctr The
7 Highway Bsns Pk The
8 Cranford Cotts
9 Ratcliffe Orch
10 Scotia Bldg
11 Mauretania Bldg
12 Compania Bldg
13 Sirius Bldg
14 Unicorn Bldg
15 Keepier Wharf
C3 1 Pattison Ho
2 St Thomas Ho
3 Arbour Ho
4 Bladen Ho
5 Antill Terr
6 Billing Ho
7 Dowson Ho
8 Lipton Rd
9 Chalkwell Ho
10 Corringham Ho
11 Ogilvie Ho
12 Edward Mann Cl
13 Lightermans Mews
C4 1 Roland Mews
2 Morecambe Cl
3 Stepney Green Ct
4 Milrood Ho
5 Panama Ho
6 Galway Ho
7 Caspian Ho
8 Darien Ho
9 Rigo Ho
10 Flores Ho
11 Taranto Ho
12 Aden Ho
13 Frances Grey Ho
14 Master's St
15 Diggon St

33
A2 1 St Georges Sq
2 Drake Ho
3 Osprey Ho
4 Fleet Ho
5 Gainsborough Ho
6 Victory Pl
7 Challenger Ho
8 Conrad Ho
9 Lock View Ct
10 Shoulder of Mutton Alley
11 Frederick Sq
12 Helena Sq
13 Elizabeth Sq
14 Sophia Sq
15 William Sq
16 Lamb Ct
17 Lockside
18 Ionian Bldg
20 Regents Gate Ho
A3 1 Coltman Ho
2 Repton Ho
3 Causton Cotts
4 Darnley Ho
5 Mercer's Cotts
6 Troon Ho
7 Ratcliffe Ho
8 Wakeling St
9 York Sq
10 Anglia Ho
11 Cambria Ho
12 Caledonia Ho
13 Ratcliffe La
14 Bekesbourne St
15 John Scurr Ho
16 Regents Canal Ho
17 Basin App
18 Powlesland Ct
A4 1 Waley St
2 Edith Ramsay Ho
3 Andaman St
4 Atlantic Ho
5 Pevensey Ho
6 Solent Ho
7 Lorne Ho
8 Cromarty Ho
9 Greaves Cotts
10 Donaghue Cotts
11 Ames Cotts
B2 1 Hamilton Ho
2 Imperial Ho
3 Oriana Ho
4 Queens Ct
5 Brightlingsea Pl
6 Faraday Ho
7 Ropemaker's Fields
8 Oast Ct
9 Mitre The
10 Bate St
11 Joseph Irwin Ho
12 Padstow Ho
13 Bethlehem Ho
14 Saunders Cl
15 Roche Ho
16 Stocks Pl
17 Trinidad Ho
18 Grenada Ho
19 Kings Ho
20 Dunbar Wharf
21 Limekiln Wharf
B3 1 Dora Ho
2 Flansham Ho
3 Gatwick Ho
4 Ashpark Ho

5 Newdigate Ho
6 Salmon St
7 Midhurst Ho
8 Redbourne Ho
9 Southwater Cl
10 Aithan Ho
11 Britley Ho
12 Cheadle Ho
13 Elland Ho
14 Butler Ho
15 Fitzroy Ho
16 Leybourne Ho
B4 1 Wearmouth Ho
2 Elmslie Point
3 Grindley Ho
4 Stileman Ho
5 Baythorne St
6 Wilcox Ho
7 Robeson St
8 Couzens Ho
9 Perley Ho
10 Whytlaw Ho
11 Printon Ho
12 Perkins Ho
13 Bowry Ho
14 Booker Cl
15 Tunley Gn
16 Callingham Cl
17 Tasker Ho
C2 1 West India Ho
2 Birchfield Ho
3 Elderfield Ho
4 Thornfield Ho
5 Gorsefield Ho
6 Arborfield Ho
7 Colborne Ho
8 East India Bldgs
9 Compass Point
10 Salter St
11 Kelly Ct
12 Flynn Ct
13 Mary Jones Ho
14 Horizon Bldg
15 Berber Pl
C3 1 Landin Ho
2 Charlesworth Ho
3 Gurdon Ho
4 Trendell Ho
5 Menteath Ho
6 Minchin Ho
7 Donne Ho
8 Denison Ho
9 Anglesey Ho
10 Gough Wlk
11 Baring Ho
12 Hopkins Ho
13 Granville Ho
14 Gladstone Ho
15 Russell Ho
16 Pusey Ho
17 Overstone Ho
18 Stanley Ho
19 Old School Sq
C4 1 Bredel Ho
2 Linton Ho
3 Matthews Ho
4 Woodcock Ho
5 Limborough Ho
6 Maydwell Ho
7 Underhill Ho
8 Meyrick Ho
9 Ambrose Ho
10 Carpenter Ho
11 Robinson Ho
12 Bramble Ho
13 Bilberry Ho

14 Bracken Ho
15 Berberis Ho
16 Busbridge Ho
17 Metropolitan Cl
18 Invicta Cl
19 Bellmaker Ct

34
A2 1 Westcott Ho
2 Corry Ho
3 Malam Gdns
4 Devitt Ho
5 Leyland Ho
6 Wigram Ho
7 Willis Ho
8 Balsam Ho
9 Finch's Ct
10 Poplar Bath St
11 Lawless St
12 Storey Ho
13 Abbot Ho
14 Landon Wlk
15 Goodhope Ho
16 Goodfaith Ho
17 Winant Ho
18 Lubbock St
19 Goodwill Ho
20 Martindale Ho
21 Holmsdale Ho
22 Norwood Ho
23 Constant Ho
24 Woodall Cl
A3 1 Colebrook Ho
2 Essex Ho
3 Salisbury Ho
4 Maidstone Ho
5 Osterley Ho
6 Norwich Ho
7 Clarissa Ho
8 Elgin Ho
9 Shaftesbury Lo
10 Shepherd Ho
11 Jeremiah St
12 Elizabeth Cl
13 Chilcot Cl
14 Fitzgerald Ho
15 Vesey Path
16 Ennis Ho
17 Kilmore Ho
A4 1 Sumner Ho
2 Irvine Ho
3 David Ho
4 Brushwood Ho
5 Limehouse Cut
6 Colmans Wharf
7 Foundary Ho
8 Radford Ho
B2 1 Discovery Ho
2 Mountague Pl
3 Virginia Ho
4 Collins Ho
5 Lawless Ho
6 Carmichael Ho
7 Commodore Ho
8 Mermaid Ho
9 Bullivant St
10 Anderson Ho
11 Mackrow Wlk
12 Robin Hood Gdns
B3 1 Langdon Ho
2 Balfron Twr
3 Tabard Ct
4 Delta Bldg
5 Kilbrennan Ho
6 Thistle Ho
7 Heather Ho

8 Tartan Ho
9 Trident Ho
B4 1 Mills Gr
3 Duncan Ct
C2 2 Settlers Ct
3 Susan Constant Ct
4 Adventurers Ct
5 Bartholomew Ct
6 Atlantic Ct
7 Cape Henry Ct
8 Wotton Ct
9 Studley Ct
10 Wingfield Ct
C3 1 Lansbury Gdns
2 Thesus Ho
3 Theseus Ho
4 Adams Ho
5 Sam March Ho
6 Arapiles Ho
7 Athenia Ho
8 Jervis Bay Ho
9 Helen Mackay Ho
10 Gaze Ho
11 Ritchie Ho
12 Circle Ho
13 Dunkeld Ho
14 Braithwaite Ho
15 Rosemary Dr
16 Sorrel La
17 East India Dock Road Tunnel

35
B1 1 Newton Point
2 Sparke Terr
3 Montesquieu Terr
4 Crawford Point
5 Rathbone Ho
6 George St
7 Emily St
8 Fendt Cl
9 Sabbarton St
B2 1 Radley Terr
2 Rathbone Mkt
3 Thomas North Terr
4 Bernard Cassidy St
5 Mary St
6 Hughes Terr
7 Swanscombe Point
8 Rawlinson Point
9 Kennedy Cox Ho
10 Cooper St
C1 1 Capulet Mews
2 Pepys Cres
3 De Quincey Mews
4 Hardy Ave
5 Tom Jenkinson Rd
6 Kanamel St
7 Kennacraig Cl
8 Gatcombe Rd
9 Badminton Mews
10 Holyrood Mews
11 Britannia Gate
12 Dalemain Mews
C2 1 Clements Ave
2 Martindale Ave
C4 1 Odeon Ct
2 Edward Ct
3 Newhaven La
4 Ravenscroft Cl
5 Douglas Rd
6 Ferrier Point

7 Harvey Point
8 Wood Point
9 Trinity St
10 Pattinson Point
11 Clinch Ct
12 Mint Bsns Pk

36
A1 **1** Burford Ho
2 Hope Cl
3 Centaur Ct
4 Phoenix Ct
C1 **1** Surrey Cres
2 Forbes Ho
3 Haining Cl
4 Melville Ct
5 London Stile
6 Stile Hall Par
7 Priory Lo
8 Kew Bridge Ct
9 Meadowcroft
10 St James Ct
11 Rivers Ho

37
A1 **1** Churchdale Ct
2 Cromwell Cl
3 Cambridge Rd S
4 Oxbridge Ct
5 Tomlinson Cl
6 Gunnersbury Mews
7 Grange The
8 Gunnersbury Ct
A4 **1** Cheltenham Pl
2 Beaumaris Twr
3 Arundel Ho
4 Pevensey Ct
5 Jerome Twr
6 Anstey Ct
7 Bennett Ct
8 Gunnersbury Ct
B1 **1** Arlington Park Mans
2 Sandown Ho
3 Goodwood Ho
4 Windsor Ho
5 Lingfield Ho
6 Ascot Ho
7 Watchfield Ct
8 Belgrave Ct
9 Beverley Ct
10 Beaumont Ct
11 Harvard Rd
12 Troubridge Ct
B2 **1** Chiswick Green Studios
2 Bell Ind Est
3 Fairlawn Ct
4 Dukes Gate
5 Dewsbury Ct
6 Chiswick Terr
B3 **1** Blackmore Twr
2 Bollo Ct
3 Kipling Twr
4 Lawrence Ct
5 Maugham Ct
6 Reade Ct
7 Woolf Ct
8 Shaw Ct
9 Verne Ct
10 Wodehouse Ct
11 Greenock Rd
12 Garden Ct

13 Barons Gate
14 Cleveland Rd
15 Chapter Ct
16 Carver Cl
17 Beauchamp Cl
18 Holmes Ct
B4 **1** Belgrave Cl
2 Buckland Wlk
3 Frampton Ct
4 Telfer Ct
5 Harlech Twr
6 Corfe Twr
7 Barwick Ho
8 Charles Hocking Ho
9 Sunninghill Ct
10 Salisbury St
11 Jameson Ho
C1 **1** Chatsworth Lo
2 Prospect Pl
3 Townhall Ave
4 Devonhurst Pl
5 Heathfield Ct
6 Horticultural Pl
7 Merlin Ho
8 Garth Rd

38
A1 **1** Glebe Cl
2 Devonshire Mews
3 Binns Terr
4 Ingress St
5 Swanscombe Rd
6 Brackley Terr
7 Stephen Fox Ho
8 Manor Gdns
9 Coram Ho
10 Flaxman Ho
11 Thorneycroft Ho
12 Thornhill Ho
13 Kent Ho
14 Oldfield Ho
A2 **1** Chestnut Ho
2 Bedford Ho
3 Bedford Cnr
4 Sydney Ho
5 Bedford Park Cnr
6 Priory Gdns
7 Windmill Alley
8 Castle Pl
9 Jonathan Ct
10 Windmill Pas
11 Chardin Rd
12 Gable Ho
A3 **1** Fleet Ct
2 Ember Ct
3 Emlyn Gdns
4 Clone Ct
5 Brent Ct
6 Abbey Ct
7 Ormsby Lo
8 St Catherine's Ct
A4 **1** Longford Ct
2 Mole Ct
3 Lea Ct
4 Wandle Ct
5 Beverley Ct
6 Roding Ct
7 Crane Ct
B1 **1** Miller's Ct
2 British Grove Pas
3 British Grove S
4 Berestede Rd
5 North Eyot Gdns
B2 **1** Flanders Mans

2 Stamford Brook Mans
3 Linkenholt Mans
4 Prebend Mans
5 Middlesex Ct
B3 **1** Stamford Brook Gdns
2 Hauteville Court Gdns
3 Ranelagh Gdns
C2 **1** Hamlet Ct
2 Derwent St
3 Westcroft St
4 Black Lion Mews
5 St Peter's Villas
6 Standish Ho
7 Chambon Pl
8 Court Mans
C4 **1** Victoria Ho
2 Lycett Pl
3 Kylemore Ct
4 Alexandra Ct
5 Lytten Ct
6 Becklow Mews
7 Northcroft Ct
8 Bailey Ct
9 Spring Cott
10 Landor Wlk
11 Laurence Mews
12 Hadyn Park Ct
13 Askew Mans

39
A2 **1** Albion Gdns
2 Flora Gdns
3 Lamington St
4 Felgate Mews
5 Galena Ho
6 Albion Mews
7 Albion Ct
8 King Street Cloisters
9 Dimes Pl
10 Clarence St
11 Hampshire Hog La
12 Marryat Ct
A4 **1** Westbush Ct
2 Goldhawk Mews
3 Sycamore Ho
4 Shackleton Ct
5 Drake Ct
6 Scotts Ct
B1 **1** Bridge Avenue Mans
2 Bridgeview
3 College Ct
4 Beatrice Ho
5 Amelia Ho
6 Edith Ho
7 Joanna Ho
8 Mary Ho
9 Adela Ho
10 Sophia Ho
11 Henrietta Ho
12 Charlotte Ho
13 Alexandra Ho
14 Bath Pl
15 Elizabeth Ho
16 Margaret Ho
17 Peabody Est
18 Eleanor Ho
19 Isabella Ho
20 Caroline Ho
21 Chancellors Wharf
22 Sussex Pl

B2 **1** Phoenix Lodge Mans
2 Samuel's Cl
3 Broadway Arc
4 Brook Ho
5 Hammersmith Broadway
B4 **1** Verulam Ho
2 Grove Mans
3 Frobisher Ct
4 Library Mans
5 Pennard Mans
6 Lanark Mans
7 Kerrington Ct
8 Granville Mans
9 Romney Ct
10 Rayner Ct
11 Sulgrave Gdns
12 Bamborough Gdns
C3 **1** Grosvenor Residences
2 Blythe Mews
3 Burnand Ho
4 Bradford Ho
5 Springvale Terr
6 Ceylon Rd
7 Walpole Ct
8 Bronte Ct
9 Boswell Ct
10 Souldern Rd
11 Brook Green Flats
12 Haarlem Rd
13 Stafford Mans
14 Lionel Mans
C4 **1** Vanderbilt Villas
2 Bodington Ct
3 Kingham Cl
4 Clearwater Terr
5 Lorne Gdns
6 Cameret Ct
7 Bush Ct
8 Shepherds Ct
9 Rockley Ct
10 Grampians The
11 Charcroft Ct
12 Addison Park Mans
13 Sinclair Mans

40
A1 **1** Hockney Ct
2 Toulouse Ct
3 Lowry Ct
4 Barry Ho
5 Lewis Ct
6 Gainsborough Ct
7 Renoir Ct
8 Blake Ct
9 Raphael Ct
10 Rembrandt Ct
11 Constable Ct
12 Da Vinci Ct
13 Gaugin Ct
14 Michelangelo Ct
15 Monet Ct
16 Weald Cl
17 Jasmin Lo
18 Birchmere Lo
19 Weybridge Ct
20 Florence Ho
21 Gleneagles Ct
22 Sunningdale Ct
23 Muirfield Ct
24 Turnberry Ct
25 St Andrews Ct
26 Kingsdown Cl
27 St Davids Cl

28 Galway Cl
29 Edenbridge Cl
30 Birkdale Cl
31 Tralee Ct
32 Woburn Ct
33 Belfry Cl
34 Troon Cl
35 Holywell Cl
A2 **1** Market Pl
2 Trappes Ho
3 Thurland Ho
4 Ramsfort Ho
5 Hambley Ho
6 Holford Ho
7 Pope Ho
8 Southwell Ho
9 Mortain Ho
10 Radcliffe Ho
11 Southwark Park Est
12 Galleywall Road Trad Est
13 Trevithick Ho
14 Barlow Ho
15 Donkin Ho
16 Landmann Ho
17 Fitzmaurice Ho
18 Dodd Ho
A3 **1** Perryn Rd
2 Chalfont Ho
3 Prestwood Ho
4 Farmer Ho
5 Gataker St
6 Gataker Ho
7 Cornick Ho
8 Glebe Ho
9 Matson Ho
10 Hickling Ho
11 St Andrews Ho
A4 **1** Butterfield Ho
2 Janeway Pl
3 Trotwood Ho
4 Cranbourn Ho
5 Cherry Garden Ho
6 Burton Ho
7 Morriss Ho
8 King Edward The Third Mews
9 Cathay St
10 Rotherhithe St
B2 **1** Damory Ho
2 Antony Ho
3 Roderick Ho
4 Pedworth Gdns
5 Beamish Ho
6 Gillam Ho
7 George Walter Ho
8 Richard Ho
9 Adron Ho
10 Westlake
11 McIntosh Ho
B3 **1** Blick Ho
2 Neptune Ho
3 Scotia Ct
4 Murdoch Ho
5 Edmonton Ct
6 Niagara Ct
7 Columbia Point
8 Ritchie Ho
9 Wells Ho
10 Helen Peele Cotts
11 Orchard Ho
12 Dock Offices
13 Landale Ho
14 Courthope Ho
B4 **1** Mayflower St
2 St Mary's Est

3 Rupack St
4 Frank Whymark Ho
5 Adams Gardens Est
6 Hatteraick St
7 Hythe Ho
8 Seaford Ho
9 Sandwich Ho
11 Winchelsea Ho
12 Kenning St
14 Western Pl
15 Ainsty St
16 Pine Ho
17 Beech Ho
18 Larch Ho
19 Seth St
20 Turner Ct
20 Risdon Ho
21 Risdon St
22 Aylton Est
23 Manitoba Ct
24 Calgary Ct
25 Irwell Est
26 City Bsns Ctr
27 St Olav's Sq
C2 **1** John Kennedy Ho
2 Brydale Ho
3 Balman Ho
4 Tissington Ct
5 Harbord Ho
6 Westfield Ho
7 Albert Starr Ho
8 John Brent Ho
9 William Evans Ho
10 Raven Ho
11 Egret Ho
12 Fulmar Ho
13 Dunlin Ho
14 Siskin Ho
15 Sheldrake Ho
16 Buchanan Ct
17 Burrage Ct
18 Biddenham Ho
19 Ayston Ho
20 Empingham Ho
21 Deanshanger Ho
22 Codicote Ho
C4 **1** Schooner Cl
2 Dolphin Cl
3 Clipper Cl
4 Deauville Ct
5 Colette Ct
6 Coniston Ct
7 Virginia Ct
8 Derwent Ct
9 Grantham Ct
10 Serpentine Ct
11 Career Ct
12 Lacine Ct
13 Fairway Ct
14 Harold Ct
15 Spruce Ho
16 Cedar Ho
17 Sycamore Ho
18 Woodland Cres
19 Poplar Ho
20 Adelphi Ct
21 Basque Ct
22 Aberdale Ct
23 Quilting Ct
24 Chargrove Cl
25 Radley Ct
26 Greenacre Sq
27 Leaf Sq
28 Stanhope Cl
29 Hawke Pl
30 Drake Cl

31 Brass Talley Alley
32 Monkton Ho
33 James Ho
34 Wolfe Cres

41
A2 **1** Trafalgar Ct
2 Hornblower Cl
3 Cunard Wlk
4 Caronia Ct
5 Carinthia Ct
6 Freswick Ho
7 Graveley Ho
8 Husbourne Ho
9 Crofters Ct
10 Pomona Ho
11 Hazelwood Ho
12 Cannon Wharf Bsns Ctr
13 Bence Ho
14 Clement Ho
15 Pendennis Ho
16 Lighter Cl
17 Mast Ct
18 Rushcutters Ct
19 Boat Lifter Way
B1 **1** Gransden Ho
2 Daubeney Twr
3 North Ho
4 Rochfort Ho
5 Keppel Ho
6 Camden Ho
7 Sanderson Ho
8 Berkeley Ho
9 Strafford Ho
10 Richman Ho
11 Hurleston Ho
12 Grafton Ho
13 Fulcher Ho
14 Citrus Ho
B2 **1** Windsock Ct
2 Linberry Wlk
3 Lanyard Ho
4 Golden Hind Pl
5 James Lind Ho
6 Harmon Ho
7 Pelican Ho
8 Bembridge Ho
9 Terrace The
10 George Beard Rd
11 Colonnade The
12 Pepys Ent Ctr
C1 **1** Hudson Ct
2 Shackleton Ct
3 Perry Ct
4 Maritime Quay
C2 **1** Olympian Ct
2 Aphrodite Ct
3 Mercury Ct
4 Poseidon Ct
5 Neptune Ct
6 Artemis Ct
7 Hera Ct
8 Ares Ct
9 Cyclops Mews
10 Magellan Pl
11 Britannia Rd
12 Deptford Ferry Rd
13 Ironmonger's Pl
14 Radnor Wlk
15 Ashdown Wlk
16 Rothsay Wlk
17 Dartmoor Wlk
18 Ringwood Gdns
19 Dockers Tanner Rd
20 Apollo Bldg

21 Nova Bldg
C3 **1** St Hubert's Ho
2 John Tucker Ho
3 Clare Grant Ho
4 Gilbertson Ho
5 Bowsprit Point
6 Scoulding Ho
7 Cord Way
8 Cressall Ho
9 Alexander Ho
10 Kedge Ho
C4 **1** Jefferson Bldg
2 Waterman Bldg
3 Pierpoint Bldg
4 Franklin Bldg
5 Bellamy Ct
6 Bosun Cl
7 Edison Bldg
8 Vanguard Bldg

42
A2 **1** Brassey Ho
2 Triton Ho
3 Warspite Ho
4 Rodney Ho
5 Conway Ho
6 Exmouth Ho
7 Akbar Ho
8 Arethusa Ho
9 Tasman Ct
B2 **1** Betty May Gray Ho
2 Castleton Ho
3 Urmston Ho
4 Salford Ho
5 Capstan Ho
6 Frigate Ho
7 Galleon Ho
8 Barons Lo
B3 **1** Cardale St
2 Hickin St
3 John McDonald Ho
4 Thorne Ho
5 Skeggs Ho
6 St Bernard Ho
7 Kimberley Ho
8 Kingdon Ho
9 Lingard Ho
10 Yarrow Ho
11 Sandpiper Ct
12 Nightingale Ct
13 Robin Ct
14 Heron Ct
B4 **1** Llandovery Ho
2 Rugless Ho
3 Ash Ho
4 Elm Ho
5 Cedar Ho
6 Castalia Sq
7 Walkers Lo
8 Antilles Bay
9 Alice Shepherd Ho
10 Oak Ho
11 Ballin Ct
12 Martin Ct
13 Grebe Ct
14 Kingfisher Ct
C2 **1** Verwood Lo
2 Fawley Lo
3 Lyndhurst Lo
4 Blyth Cl
5 Farnworth Ho
6 Francis Cl

43
A1 **1** Bellot Gdns
2 Thornley Pl
3 King William La
4 Bolton Ho
5 Miles Ho
6 Mell St
7 Sam Manners Ho
8 Hatcliffe Almshouses
9 Woodland Wlk
10 Earlswood Cl
B1 **1** Baldrey Ho
2 Christie Ho
3 Dyson Ho
4 Cliffe Ho
5 Moore Ho
6 Collins Ho
7 Lockyer Ho
8 Halley Ho
9 Kepler Ho
C1 **1** Layfield Ho
2 Westerdale Rd
3 Mayston Mews

44
A4 **1** Ferry Sq
2 Wilkes Rd
3 Albany Par
4 Charlton Ho
5 Albany Ho
6 Alma Ho
7 Griffin Ct
8 Cressage Ho
9 Tunstall Wlk
10 Trimmer Wlk
11 Running Horse Yd
12 Mission Sq
13 Distillery Wlk
B2 **1** Primrose Ho
2 Lawman Ct
3 Royston Ct
4 Garden Ct
5 Capel Lo
6 Devonshire Ct
7 Celia Ct
8 Rosslyn Ho
9 Branstone Ct
10 Lamerton Lo
11 Kew Lo
12 Dunraven Ho
13 Stoneleigh Lo
14 Tunstall Ct
15 Voltaire
C2 **1** Clarendon Ct
2 Quintock Ho
3 Broome Ct
4 Lonsdale Mews
5 Elizabeth Cotts
6 Sandways
7 Victoria Cotts
8 North Ave
9 Grovewood
10 Hamilton Ho
11 Melvin Ct
12 Power Ho
13 Station Ave
14 Blake Mews

46
B1 **1** Melrose Rd
2 Seaforth Lo
3 St John's Gr
4 Sussex Ct
5 Carmichael Ct
6 Hampshire Ct
7 Thorne Pas
8 Beverley Path

47
C4 **1** Cobb's Hall
2 Dorset Mans
3 St Clements Mans
4 Bothwell St
5 Hawksmoor St

48
A1 **1** Langport Ho
2 Iveagh Ho
3 Newark Ho
4 Edgehill Ho
5 Hopton Ho
6 Ashby Ho
7 Nevil Ho
A2 **1** Fairbairn Gn
2 Hammelton Gn
3 Foxley Sq
4 Silverburn Ho
5 Butler Ho
6 Dalkeith Ho
7 Turner Cl
8 Bathgate Ho
9 Black Roof Ho
A4 **1** Faunce Ho
2 Garbett Ho
3 Harvard Ho
4 Doddington Pl
5 Kean Ho
6 Jephson Ho
7 Cornish Ho
8 Bateman Ho
9 Molesworth Ho
10 Walters Ho
11 Cruden Ho
12 Brawne Ho
13 Prescott Ho
14 Chalmer's Wlk
15 Copley Cl
B1 **1** Bergen Ho
2 Oslo Ho
3 Viking Ho
4 Jutland Ho
5 Norvic Ho
6 Odin Ho
7 Baltic Ho
8 Nobel Ho
9 Mercia Ho
10 Kenbury Gdns
11 Zealand Ho
12 Elsinore Ho
13 Norse Ho
14 Denmark Mans
15 Dane Ho
16 Canterbury Cl
17 York Cl
18 Kenbury Mans
19 Parade Mans
20 Winterslow Ho
21 Lilford Ho
22 Cutcombe Mans
23 Bartholomew Ho
24 Guildford Ho
25 Boston Ho
26 Hereford Ho
27 Weyhill Ho
28 Lichfield Ho
29 Lansdown Ho
30 Honiton Ho
31 Pinner Ho
32 Baldock Ho
33 Widecombe Ho

48 B1

34 Nottingham Ho
35 Witham Ho
36 Barnet Ho

B2 1 Bertha Neubergh Ho
2 Mornington Mews
3 Badsworth Rd
4 Sycamore Ct
5 Elm Tree Ct
6 Samuel Lewis Trust Dwellings
7 Valmar Trad Est
8 Keswick Ho
9 Mitcham Ho

B3 1 Boundary Ho
2 Day Ho
3 Burgess Ho
4 Carlyle Ho
5 Myers Ho
6 Thompson's Ave
7 Palgrave Ho
8 Winnington Ho
9 Brantwood Ho
10 Lowell Ho
11 Jessie Duffett Ho
12 Otterburn Ho
13 Crossmount Ho
14 Venice Ct
15 Bowyer St
16 Livingstone Ho
17 Gothic Ct
18 Coniston Ho
19 Harlynwood
20 Carey Ct
21 Finley Ct
22 Grainger Ct
23 Hayes Ct
24 Moffat Ho
25 Marinel Ho
26 Hodister Cl
27 Arnot Ho
28 Lamb Ho
29 Kipling Ho
30 Keats Ho
31 Kenyon Ho
32 New Church Rd
33 Sir John Kirk Cl

C1 1 Selborne Rd

C2 1 Joiners Arms Yd
2 Butterfly Wlk
3 Cuthill Wlk
4 Colonades The
5 Artichoke Mews
6 Peabody Bldgs
7 Brighton Ho
8 Park Ho
9 Peabody Ct
10 Lomond Ho
11 Lamb Ho
12 Kimpton Ct
13 Belham Wlk
14 Datchelor Pl
15 Harvey Rd

C3 1 Masterman Ho
2 Milton Ho
3 Pope Ho
4 Chester Ct
5 Marvel Ho
6 Flecker Ho
7 Landor Ho
8 Evelina Mans

34 Habington Ho
35 Langland Ho
36 Drinkwater Ho
37 Procter Ho
38 Shirley Ho
39 Drayton Ho
40 Bridges Ho
41 Cunningham Ho
42 Hood Ho
43 Herrick Ho
44 Dekker Ho
45 Sansom St

C4 1 Houseman Way
2 Coleby Path
3 Jago Wlk
4 Queens Ho
5 Arnside Ho
6 Horsley St
7 St Peter's Ho
8 St Johns Ho
9 St Marks Ho
10 St Stephens Ho
11 St Matthew's Ho
12 Red Lion Cl
13 Boyson Rd
14 Bradenham

49

A1 1 Springfield Ho
2 Craston Ho
3 Walters Ho
4 Edgecombe Ho
5 Fowler Ho
6 Rignold Ho
7 Chatham Ho

A2 1 Barnwell Ho
2 Brunswick Villas
3 St Giles Twr
4 Bentley Ho
5 Dawson Ho
6 Dryden Ho
7 Mayward Ho
8 Longleigh Ho
9 Fairwall Ho
10 Bodeney Ho
11 Sandby Ho
12 Vestry Mews
13 Netley
14 Lakanal
15 Racine

A3 1 Tower Mill Rd
2 Tilson Ho
3 Dorton Cl
4 Granville Sq
5 Farnborough Way
6 Hordle Prom W
7 Samuel Jones Ind Est
8 Dibden Ho
9 Marchwood Cl
10 Pilgrims Cloisters
11 Beacon Ho
12 Teather St
13 Stacy Path
14 Rumball Ho
15 Ballow Cl
16 Rill Ho

A4 1 Pearse St
2 Watling St
3 Gandolfi St
4 Andoversford Ct
5 Downend Ct

B2 1 Colbert
2 Voltaire
3 Finch Mews
4 Charles Coveney Rd

5 Crane St
6 Curlew Ho
7 Mallard Ho
8 Tern Ho
9 Crane Ho
10 Falcon Ho
11 Bryanston Ho
12 Basing Ct
13 Marcus Ho
14 Sheffield Ho

B3 2 Whistler Mews
3 Painswick Ct
4 Sharpness Ct
5 Hordle Prom N
6 Mattingly Way
7 Calypso Cres
8 Samuel St
9 Hordle Prom S
10 Cinnamon Cl
11 Savannah Ct
12 Thames Ct
13 Amstel Ct
14 Danube St
15 Tilbury Cl
16 Hordle Prom E
17 Indus Ct
18 Oakcourt
19 Palm Ct
20 Rowan Ct
21 Blackthorn Ct
22 Pear Ct
23 Lidgate Rd

B4 1 Willsbridge Ct
2 Cam Ct
3 Quedgeley Ct
4 Saul Ct
5 Quenington Ct
6 Westonbirt Ct
7 Wickway Ct

C1 1 William Margrie Cl
2 Choumert Sq
3 Parkstone Rd
4 Atwell Rd

C2 2 Angelina Ho
3 Jarvis Ho
4 Richland Ho
5 Honeywood Ho
6 Wakefield Ho
7 Primrose Ho
8 Hardcastle Ho
9 Dunstall Ho
10 Purdon Ho
11 Flamborough Ho
12 Lambrook Ho
13 Witcombe Point
14 Yarnfield Sq
15 Winford Ct
16 Portbury Cl
17 Robert Keen Cl

C3 1 Thornbill Ho
2 Vervain Ho
3 Woodstar Ho
4 Tamarind Ho
5 Hereford Retreat
6 Haymerle Ho
7 Furley Ho
8 Applegarth Ho
9 Freda Corbett Cl
10 Rudbeck Ho
11 Henslow Ho
12 Lindley Ho
13 Collinson Ho
14 Sister Mabel's Way
15 Timberland Cl
16 Hastings Cl
17 Neville Cl

18 Sidmouth Ho
19 Budleigh Ho
20 Stanesgate Ho
21 Braemore Ho
22 Ely Ho

C4 1 Bowles Rd
2 Western Wharf
3 Northfield Ho
4 Millbrook Ho
5 Denstone Ho
6 Deerhurst Ho
7 Caversham Ho
8 Battle Ho
9 Cardiff Ho
10 Bridgnorth Ho
11 Exeter Ho
12 Grantham Ho
13 Aylesbury Ho
14 Royston Ho

50

A1 1 Walkynscroft
2 Ryegates
3 Hathorne Cl
4 Pilkington Rd
5 Russell Ct
6 Heaton Ho
7 Magdalene Cl

A2 1 Willowdene
2 Pinedene
3 Oakdene
4 Beechdene
5 Hollydene
6 Wood Dene
7 Staveley Cl
8 Carnicot Ho
9 Martock Ct
10 Kendrick Ct

A3 1 Tortington Ho
2 Credenhill Ho
3 Bromyard Ho
4 Hoyland Cl
5 Willowdene
6 Ashdene
7 Acorn Par
8 Carlton Gr
9 Springall St
10 Harry Lambourn Ho

B1 1 Honiton Gdns
2 Selden Ho
3 Hathway Ho
4 Hathway St
5 Station Ct

B3 1 Ambleside Point
2 Grasmere Point
3 Windermere Point
4 Roman Way
5 Laburnham Cl
6 Romney Cl
7 Hammersley Ho
8 Hutchinson Ho
9 Hammond Ho
10 Fir Tree Ho
11 Glastonbury Ct
12 Highbridge Ct
13 Filton Ct
14 Chiltern Ct
15 Cheviot Ct

B4 1 Penshurst Ho
2 Reculver Ho
3 Mereworth Ho
4 Camber Ho
5 Chilam Ho
6 Otford Ho
7 Olive Tree Ho
8 Aspen Ho

9 Lewis Silkin Ho
10 Richborough Ho
11 Dover Ho
12 Eynsford Ho
13 Horton Ho
14 Lamberhurst Ho
15 Canterbury Ind Pk
16 Upnall Ho
17 Sissinghurst Ho
18 Rochester Ho
19 Leybourne Ho
20 Lullingstone Ho

C3 1 Richard Anderson Ct
2 Palm Tree Ho
3 Edward Robinson Ho
4 Antony Ho
5 Gerrard Ho
6 Palmer Ho
7 Pankhurst Cl

C4 1 Harrisons Ct
2 Grantley Ho
3 Sunbury Ct
4 Tilbury Ho
5 Graham Ct
6 Connell Ct
7 St Clements Ct
8 Henderson Ct
9 Jemotts Ct
10 Verona Ct
11 Heywood Ho
12 Francis Ct
13 Hind Ho
14 Donne Ho
15 Carew Ct
16 Burbage Ho
17 Newland Ho
18 Dobson Ho
19 Dalton Ho
20 Greene Ct
21 Redrup Ho
22 Tarplett Ho
23 Stunnell Ho
24 Gasson Ho
25 Bryce Ho
26 Barnes Ho
27 Barkwith Ho
28 Bannister Ho
29 Apollo Ind Bsns Ctr

51

A3 1 Batavia Ho
2 Marlowe Bsns Ctr
3 Batavia Mews
4 Woodrush Cl
5 Alexandra St
6 Primrose Wlk
7 Vansittart St
8 Granville Ct
9 Cottesbrook St

A4 1 Portland Ct
2 Phoenix Ct
3 Rainbow Ct
4 Hawke Twr
5 Woodpecker Rd

B3 1 Austin Ho
2 Exeter Way
3 Crossleigh Ct
4 Mornington Pl
5 Maple Ho

B4 1 Chester Ho
2 Lynch Wlk
3 Arlington Ho
4 Woodcote Ho
5 Cornbury Ho

6 Prospect Pl
7 Akintaro Ho
8 Mulberry Ho
9 Laurel Ho
10 Linden Ho
11 Ashford Ho
12 Wardalls Ho
13 Magnolia Ho
14 Howard Ho
15 Larch Cl
16 Ibis Ct
17 Merganser Ct
18 Wotton Rd
19 Kingfisher Sq
20 Sanderling Ct
21 Dolphin Twr
22 Mermaid Twr
23 Scoter Ct
24 Shearwater Ct
25 Brambling Ct
26 Kittiwake Ct
27 Guillemot Ct
28 Marine Twr
29 Teal Ct
30 Lapwing Twr
31 Cormorant Ct
32 Shelduck Ct
33 Eider Ct
34 Pintail Ct
35 Tristan Ct
36 Skua Ct
37 Rosemary Ct
38 Violet Ct
39 Diana Ct
C2 1 Admiralty Cl
2 Harton Lo
3 Sylvia Cotts
4 Pitman Ho
5 Heston Ho
C3 1 Sandpiper Ct
2 Flamingo Ct
3 Titan Bsns Est
4 Rochdale Way
5 Speedwell Ct
6 Reginald Pl
7 Fletcher Path
8 Frankham Ho
9 Cremer Ho
10 Wilshaw Ho
11 Castell Ho
12 Holden Ho
13 Browne Ho
14 Lady Florence Ctyd
15 Covell Ct
C4 1 Dryfield Wlk
2 Blake Ho
3 Hawkins Ho
4 Grenville Ho
5 Langford Ho
6 Mandarin Ct
7 Bittern Ct
8 Lamerton St
9 Armada St
10 Armada Ct
11 Benbow Ho
12 Oxenham Ho
13 Caravel Mews
14 Hughes Ho
15 Stretton Mans

52
A3 1 Finch Ho
2 Jubilee The
3 Gordon Ho
4 Haddington Ct
5 Maitland Cl

6 Ashburnham Retreat
B1 1 Ellison Ho
2 Pitmaston Ho
3 Windmill Ct
4 Hertmitage The
5 Burnett Ho
6 Lacey Ho
B2 1 Penn Almshouse
2 Jarvis Ct
3 Woodville Ct
4 Darnell Ho
5 Renbold Ho
6 Lindsell St
7 Plumbridge St
8 Trinity Gr
9 Hollymount Cl
10 Cade Tyler Ho
11 Robertson Ho
B3 1 Temair Ho
2 Glaisher St
3 Prince of Orange La
4 Lombard Ho
5 St Marks Cl
6 Ada Kennedy Ct
7 Arlington Pl
8 Topham Ho
9 Darnell Ho
10 Hawks Mews
11 Royal Pl
12 Swanne Ho
13 Maribor
14 Serica Ct
15 Queen Elizabeth College
B4 1 Greenwich Mkt
2 Turnpin La
3 Durnford St
4 Sexton's Ho
5 Bardsley Ho
6 Wardell Ho
7 Clavell St
8 Stanton Ho
9 Macey Ho
10 Boreman Ho
C4 1 Frobisher Ct
2 Hardy Cotts
3 Palliser Ho
4 Bernard Angell Ho
5 Corvette Sq
6 Travers Ho
7 Reade Ho
8 Maze Hill Lo

53
B3 1 Westcombe Ct
2 Kleffens Ct
3 Ferndale Ct
4 Combe Mews
5 Mandeville Cl
6 Heathway
7 Pinelands Cl
C3 1 Mary Lawrenson Pl
2 Bradbury Ct
3 Dunstable Ct
C4 1 Nethercombe Ho
2 Holywell Cl

54
A1 1 Lancaster Cotts
2 Lancaster Mews
3 Bromwich Ho
4 Priors Lo
5 Richmond Hill Ct
6 Glenmore Ho

7 Hillbrow
8 Heathshot
9 Friars Stile Pl
10 Spire Ct
11 Ridgeway
12 Matthias Ct
A2 1 Lichfield Terr
2 Union Ct
3 Carrington Lo
4 Wilton Ct
5 Egerton Ct
6 Beverley Lo
7 Bishop Duppa's Almshouses
8 Regency Wlk
9 Clearwater Ho
10 Onslow Avenue Mans
11 Michels Almshouses
12 Albany Pas
13 Salcombe Villas
A3 1 St John's Gr
2 Michel's Row
3 Michelsdale Dr
4 Blue Anchor Alley
5 Clarence St
6 Sun Alley
7 Thames Link Ho
8 Benns Wlk
B1 1 Chester Cl
2 Evesham Ct
3 Queen's Ct
4 Russell Wlk
5 Charlotte Sq
6 Jones Wlk
7 Hilditch Ho
8 Isabella Ct
9 Damer Ho
10 Eliot Ho
11 Fitzherbert Ho
12 Reynolds Pl
13 Chisholm Rd
B2 1 Alberta Ct
2 Beatrice Rd
3 Lorne Rd
4 York Rd
5 Connaught Rd
6 Albany Terr
7 Kingswood Ct
8 Selwyn Ct
9 Broadhurst Cl
B3 1 Towers The
2 Longs Ct
3 Sovereign Ct
4 Robinson Ct
5 Calvert Ct
6 Bedford Ct
7 Hickey's Almshouses
8 Church Estate Almshouses
9 Richmond International Bsns Ctr
10 Abercorn Mews

55
A3 1 Hershell Ct
2 Deanhill Ct
3 Park Sheen
4 Furness Lo
5 Merricks Ct
C4 1 Rann Ho
2 Craven Ho
3 John Dee Ho
4 Kindell Ho

5 Montgomery Ho
6 Avondale Ho
7 Addington Ct
8 Dovecote Gdns
9 Firmston Ho
10 Glendower Gdns
11 Chestnut Ave
12 Trehern Rd
13 Rock Ave

56
B1 1 Allenford Ho
2 Swaythling Ho
3 Tatchbury Ho
4 Penwood Ho
5 Bramley Ho
6 Shalden Ho
7 Dunbridge Ho
8 Denmead Ho
9 Charcot Ho
10 Portswood Pl
11 Brockbridge Ho
12 Hurstbourne Ho
C2 1 Theodore Ho
2 Nicholas Ho
3 Bonner Ho
4 Downing Ho
5 Johsen Ho
6 Fairfax Ho
7 Devereux Ho
8 David Ho
9 Leigh Ho
10 Clipstone Ho
11 Mallet Ho
12 Arton Wilson Ho

57
B2 1 Inglis Ho
2 Ducie Ho
3 Warncliffe Ho
4 Stanhope Ho
5 Waldegrave Ho
6 Mildmay Ho
7 Mullens Ho
C1 1 Balmoral Ct
2 Glenalmond Ho
3 Selwyn Ho
4 Keble Ho
5 Bede Ho
6 Gonville Ho
7 Magdalene Ho
8 Armstrong Ho
9 Newnham Ho
10 Somerville Ho
11 Balliol Ho
12 Windermere Ho
13 Little Combe Cl
14 Classinghall Ho
15 Chalford Ct
16 Garden Royal
17 South Ct
18 Anne Kerr Ct
19 Ewhurst
C2 1 Geneva Ct
2 Laurel Ct
3 Cambalt Ho
4 Langham Ct
5 Lower Pk
6 King's Keep
7 Whitnell Ct
8 Whitehead Ho
9 Halford Ho
10 Humphry Ho
11 Jellicoe Ho
C3 1 Olivette St
2 Mascotte Rd

59 C3 **277**

3 Glegg Pl
4 Crown Ct
5 Charlwood Terr

58
A2 1 Claremont
2 Downside
3 Cavendish Ct
4 Ashcombe Ct
5 Carltons The
6 Draldo Ho
7 Millbrooke Ct
8 Coysh Ct
9 Keswick Hts
10 Lincoln Ho
11 Avon Ct
B2 1 Burlington Mews
2 Cumbria Ho
3 St Stephen's Gdns
4 Atlantic Ho
5 Burton Lo
6 Manfred Ct
7 Meadow Bank
8 Hooper Ho
C2 1 Pembridge Pl
2 Adelaide Rd
3 London Ct
4 Windsor Ct
5 Westminster Ct
6 Fullers Ho
7 Bridge Pk
8 Lambeth Ct
9 Milton Ct
10 Norfolk Mans
11 Francis Snary Lo
12 Bush Cotts
13 Downbury Mews
14 Newton's Yd

59
A2 1 Fairfield Ct
2 Blackmore Ho
3 Lancaster Mews
4 Cricketers Mews
B4 1 Molasses Ho
2 Molasses Row
3 Cinnamon Row
4 Calico Ho
5 Calico Row
6 Port Ho
7 Square Rigger Row
8 Trade Twr
9 Ivory Ho
10 Spice Ct
11 Sherwood Ct
12 Mendip Ct
13 Chalmers Ho
14 Coral Row
C3 1 Burke Ho
2 Fox Ho
3 Buxton Ho
4 Pitt Ho
5 Romsey Ho
6 Beverley Ho
7 Florence Ho
8 Linden Ct
9 Dorcas Ct
10 Johnson Ct
11 Agnes Ct
12 Hilltop Ct
13 Courtyard The
14 Old Laundry The
15 Oberstein Rd

16 Fineran Ct
17 Sangora Rd
18 Harvard Mans
C4 **1** Benham Cl
2 Milner Ho
3 McManus Ho
4 Wilberforce Ho
5 Wheeler Ct
6 Sporle Ct
7 Holliday Sq
8 John Parker Sq
9 Carmichael Cl
10 Fenner Sq
11 Clark Lawrence Ct
12 Shaw Ct
13 Sendall Ct
14 Livingstone Rd
15 Farrant Ho
16 Jackson Ho
17 Darien Ho
18 Sheppard Ho
19 Ganley Ct
20 Arthur Newton Ho
21 Chesterton Ho
22 John Kirk Ho
23 Mantua St
24 Heaver Rd

60

A4 **1** Kiloh Ct
2 Lanner Ho
3 Grifton Ho
4 Kestrel Ho
5 Kite Ho
6 Peregrine Ho
7 Hawk Ho
8 Inkster Ho
9 Harrier Ho
10 Eagle Hts
11 Kingfisher Ct
12 Lavender Terr
13 Temple Ho
14 Ridley Ho
15 Eden Ho
16 Hertford Ct
17 Nepaul Rd
C1 **1** Rayne Ho
2 St Anthony's Ct
3 Earlsthorpe Mews
C4 **1** Shaftesbury Park
Chambers
2 Selborne
3 Rush Hill Mews
4 Marmion Mews
5 Crosland Ct
6 Craven Mews
7 Basnett Rd
8 Woodmere Cl
9 Tyneham Cl

61

A4 **1** Turnchapel Mews
2 Redwood Mews
3 Phil Brown Pl
4 Bev Callender Cl
5 Keith Connor Cl
6 Tessa Sanderson Pl
7 Daley Thompson
Way
8 Rashleigh Ct
9 Abberley Mews
10 Willow Lodge
11 Beaufoy Rd

B1 **1** Joseph Powell Cl
2 Cavendish Mans
3 Westlands Terr
4 Cubitt Ho
5 Hawkesworth Ho
6 Normanton Ho
7 Eastman Ho
8 Couchman Ho
9 Poynders Ct
10 Selby Ho
11 Valentine Ho
12 Gorham Ho
13 Deauville Mans
14 Deauville Ct
B2 **1** Timothy Ct
2 Shaftesbury Mews
3 Brook Ho
4 Grover Ho
5 Westbrook Ho
6 Hewer Ho
7 Batten Ho
8 Mandeville Ho
9 George Beare Lo
B3 **1** Polygon The
2 Windsor Ct
3 Trinity Ct
4 Hanscomb Mews
5 Studios The
6 Bourne Ho
B4 **1** Clapham Manor Ct
2 Clarke Ho
3 Gables The
4 Sycamore Mews
5 Maritime Ho
6 Floris Pl
C1 **1** Parrington Ho
2 Savill Ho
3 Blackwell Ho
4 Bruce Ho
5 Victoria Ct
6 Victoria Ho
7 Belvedere Ct
8 Ingram Lo
9 Viney Ct
10 Bloomsbury Ho
11 Belgravia Ho
12 Barnsbury Ho
C3 **1** Kendoa Rd
2 Felmersham Cl
3 Abbeville Mews
4 Saxon Ho
5 Gifford Ho
6 Teignmouth Cl
7 Holwood Pl
8 Oaklands Pl
C4 **1** Chelsham Ho
2 Lynde Ho
3 Greener Ho
4 Towns Ho
5 Hugh Morgan Ho
6 Roy Ridley Ho
7 Lendal Terr
8 Slievemore Cl
9 Cadmus Cl

62

A2 **1** King's Mews
2 Clapham Court Terr
3 Clapham Ct
4 Clapham Park Terr
5 Queenswood Ct
6 Oak Tree Ct
7 Park Lofts
A3 **1** Morris Ho
2 Gye Ho
3 Clowes Ho

4 Thomas Ho
5 Stuart Ho
6 Storace Ho
7 Bedford Ho
8 Ascot Ct
9 Ascot Par
10 Ashmere Ho
11 Ashmere Gr
12 Vickery Ho
13 Stafford Mans
14 Beresford Ho
A4 **1** Callingham Ho
2 Russell Pickering
Ho
3 Lopez Ho
4 Coachmaker Mews
B2 **1** Beatrice Ho
2 Florence Ho
3 Evelyn Ho
4 Diana Ho
5 Brixton Hill Ct
6 Austin Ho
7 Manor Ct
8 Camsey Ho
9 Romer Ho
10 Gale Ho
11 Byrne Ho
12 Farnfield Ho
13 Marchant Ho
14 Rainsford Ho
15 Springett Ho
16 Mannering Ho
17 Waldron Ho
B3 **1** Freemens Hos
2 Roger's
Almshouses
3 Gresham
Almshouses
4 Exbury Ho
5 Glasbury Ho
6 Dalbury Ho
7 Fosbury Ho
8 Chalbury Ho
9 Neilson-Terry Ho
10 Pavilion Mans
11 Daisy Dormer Ct
12 George Lashwood
Ct
13 Marie Lloyd Ct
14 Trinity Homes
15 Lethaby Ho
16 Edmundsbury Ct
Est
17 Regis Pl
18 Belvedere Ct
19 Alpha Ho
20 Beta Pl
21 Cedars Ho
B4 **1** Turberville Ho
2 Thrayle Ho
3 Percheron Ct
4 Draymans Ct
C1 **1** Eccleston Ho
2 Scarsbrook Ho
3 Purser Ho
4 Rudhall Ho
5 Hardham Ho
6 Heywood Ho
7 Haworth Ho
8 Birch Ho
9 Lonsdell Ho
10 Lomley Ho
11 Laughton Ho
12 Bascome St
13 Dudley Mews
14 Herbert Mews

16 Blades Lo
17 Dick Shepherd Ct
18 Charman Ho
19 Morden Ho
20 Bishop Ct
21 Blackburn Ct
22 Leigh Ct
23 John Conwey Ho
C2 **1** Crownstone Ct
2 Brockwell Ct
3 Nevena Ct
4 St George's Resi-
dences
5 Hanover Mans
6 Fleet Ho
7 Langbourne Ho
8 Turnmill Ho
9 Cossar Mews
10 Carter Ho
C3 **1** Electric Mans
2 Electric La
3 Connaught Mans
4 Clifton Mans
5 Hereford Ho
6 Chaplin Ho
7 Brixton Oval
8 Lord David Pitt Ho
9 Marcus Garvey Way
10 Montgo Cl
11 Bob Marley Way
12 Leeson Rd
C4 **1** Buckmaster Cl
2 Albemarle Ho
3 Goodwood Mans
4 Angell Park Gdns
5 Fyfield Rd
6 Howard Ho
7 Harris Ho
8 Broadoak Ct
9 Burgate Ct
10 Witchwood Ho
11 Blacktree Mews
12 Chartham Ct
13 Chilham Ct
14 Northgate Ct
15 Westgate Ct
16 Dover Mans

63

A3 **1** Mahatma Ganhi Ind
Est
2 Dylan Rd
3 Bessemer Park Ind
Est
4 Pablo Neruda Ind
Est
5 Langston Hughes
Cl
6 Walt Whitman Cl
7 James Joyes Wlk
8 Alice Walker Cl
9 Louise Bennett Cl
10 Chadacre Ho
11 Burwood Ho
12 Pyrford Ho
13 Wangford Ho
14 Ashford Ho
15 Kenwood Ho
16 Moyne Ho
17 Elveden Ho
18 Carrara Wlk
19 Broughton Dr
20 Tilia Wlk
21 Angela Davis Ind
Est
A4 **1** Mallams Mews
2 Amberley Ct

3 Harper Ho
4 Leicester Ho
5 Station Ave
6 Wellfit St
7 Loughborough Ct
8 Belinda Rd
9 Higgs Ind Est
C3 **1** Shaftesbury Ct
2 Mayhew Ct
3 Morris Ct
4 Swinburne Ct
5 Perth Ct
6 Tayside Ct
7 Matlock Ct
8 Hunter Ct
9 Turner Ct

64

A2 **1** Velde Way
2 Delft Way
3 Arnhem Way
4 Isel Way
5 Kempis Way
6 Terborah Way
7 Steen Way
8 Deventer Cres
9 Nimegen Way
10 Hilversum Cres
11 St Barnabas Cl
A4 **1** Harfield Gdns
2 Karen Ct
3 Seavington Ho
4 Appleshaw Ho
5 Birdsall Ho
6 Whitney Ho
7 Wheatland Ho
8 Wilton Ho
9 Walcot Ho
10 Whadden Ho
11 Melbrook Ho
12 Ledbury Ho
13 Tidworth Ho
14 Riseholme Ho
15 Ringmer Ho
16 Petworth Ho
17 Stagshaw Ho
18 Ivybridge Ho
19 Inwood Ho
20 Gatcombe Ho
21 Gatebeck Ho
22 Felbridge Ho
23 Cowdray Ho
B3 **1** Dulwich Mews
2 St James's Clois-
ters
C2 **1** Dorothy Charrington Ho
2 Keswick Ct
3 Kendall Ct
4 Halliwell Ct

65

A4 **1** Tilling Ho
2 Goodwin Ho
3 Citron Terr
4 Cheam St
C3 **1** Laxton Path
2 Barlings Ho
3 Bayfield Ho
4 Coston Wlk
5 Coverham Ho
6 Gateley Ho
7 Dereham Ho
8 Greenwood Ho
9 Hilton Ho
10 Goodall Ho

11 Horsley Ho
2 Jordan Ho

68
1 Farnborough Ho
2 Rushmere Ho
3 Horndean Cl
4 Highcross Way
5 Timsbury Wlk
6 Foxcombe Rd
7 Ryefield Path
8 Greatham Wlk
9 Gosport Ho
10 Stoatley Ho
11 Milland Ho
12 Clanfield Ho
13 Fareham Ho
14 Grayswood Point
C4 1 Woodcott Ho
2 Lyndhurst Ho
3 Wheatley Ho
4 Allbrook Ho
5 Bordon Wlk
6 Chilcombe Ho
7 Vicarage Ct
8 Shawford Ct
9 Eastleigh Wlk
10 Kings Cl

69
A3 1 Ramsdean Ho
2 Purbrook Ho
3 Portsea Ho
4 Blendworth Point
5 Eashing Point
6 Hindhead Point
7 Hilsea Point
8 Witley Point
9 Buriton Ho
10 Grately Ho
11 Hascombe Ho
12 Dunhill Point
13 Westmark Point
14 Longmoor Point
15 Cadnam Point
B4 1 Cumberland Ho
2 Devonshire Ho
3 Cornwall Ho
4 Norfolk Ho
5 Leicester Ho
6 Warwick Ho
7 Sutherland Ho
8 Worcester Ho
9 Rutland Ho
C3 1 Sandringham Cl
2 Eastwick Ct
3 Oatlands Ct
4 Banning Ho
5 Grantley Ho
6 Caryl Ho
7 Duncombe Ho
8 Chilworth Ct
9 Kent Lo
10 Turner Lo
11 Marlborough
12 Parkland Gdns
13 Lewesdon Cl
14 Pines Ct
15 Ashtead Ct
16 Mynterne Ct
17 Arden
18 Stephen Ct
19 Marsham Ct
20 Doradus Ct
21 Acorns The

22 Heritage Ho
23 Conifer Ct
24 Spencer Ho
25 Chartwell
26 Blenheim
27 Chivelston
28 Greenfield Ho
29 Oakman Ho
30 Radley Lo
31 Simon Lo
C4 1 Brett Ho
2 Brett House Cl
3 Sylva Ct
4 Ross Ct
5 Potterne Ct
6 Stourhead Cl
7 Fleur Gates
8 Greenwood

70
A3 1 William Harvey Ho
2 Highview Ct
3 Cameron Ct
4 Galgate Ct
5 Green Ho The
6 King Charles Wlk
7 Florys Ct
8 Augustus Ct
9 Albert Ct
10 Hertford Lo
11 Mortimer Lo
12 Allenswood
13 Ambleside

72
C2 1 Upper Tooting Park Mans
2 Cecil Mans
3 Marius Mans
4 Boulevard The
5 Freshfield Mans
6 Holdernesse Rd
C3 1 Heslop Ct
2 St James's Terr
3 Boundaries Mans
4 Station Par
5 Old Dairy Mews
C4 1 Hollies Way
2 Endlesham Ct

73
A3 1 Holbeach Mews
2 Hildreth Street Mews
3 Coalbrook Mans
4 Hub Buildings The
A4 1 Meyer Ho
2 Faraday Ho
3 Hales Ho
4 Frankland Ho
5 Graham Ho
6 Gibbs Ho
7 Anslie Wlk
8 Rokeby Ho
9 Caister Ho
10 Ivanhoe Ho
11 Catherine Baird Ct
12 Marmion Ho
14 Devonshire Ho
B4 1 Limerick Ct
2 Homewoods
3 Jewell Ho
4 Glanville Ho
5 Dan Bryant Ho
6 Olding Ho

7 Quennel Ho
8 Weir Ho
9 West Ho
10 Neville Ct
C3 1 Sinclair Ho
2 MacGregor Ho
3 Ingle Ho
4 St Andrews Mews
C4 1 Riley Ho
2 Bennett Ho
3 White Ho
4 Rodgers Ho
5 Dumphreys Ho
6 Homan Ho
7 Prendergast Ho
8 Hutchins Ho
9 Whiteley Ho
10 Tresidder Ho
11 Primrose Ct
12 Angus Ho
13 Currie Ho

74
A1 1 De Montfort Par
2 Leigham Hall Par
3 Leigham Hall
4 Endsleigh Mans
5 John Kirk Ho
6 Raebarn Ct
7 Wavel Ct
8 Homeleigh Ct
9 Howland Ho
10 Beauclerk Ho
11 Bertrand Ho
12 Drew Ho
13 Dowes Ho
14 Dunton Ho
15 Raynald Ho
16 Sackville Ho
17 Thurlow Ho
18 Astoria Mans
A2 1 Wyatt Park Mans
2 Broadlands Mans
3 Stonehill's Mans
4 Streatleigh Par
5 Dorchester Ct
A3 1 Beaumont Ho
2 Christchurch Ho
3 Staplefield Cl
4 Chipstead Ho
5 Coulsdon Ho
6 Conway Ho
7 Telford Avenue Mans
8 Telford Parade Mans
9 Wavertree Ct
10 Hartswood Ho
11 Wray Ho
A4 1 Picton Ho
2 Rigg Ho
3 Watson Ho
4 MacArthur Ho
5 Sandon Ho
6 Thorold Ho
7 Pearce Ho
8 Mudie Ho
9 Miller Ho
10 Lycett Ho
11 Lafone Ho
12 Lucraft Ho
13 Freeman Ho
14 New Park Par
15 Argyll Ct
16 Dumbarton Ct
17 Kintyre Ct

8 Cotton Ho
10 Crossman Hos
20 Cameford Ct
21 Parsons Ho
22 Brindley Ho
23 Arkwright Ho
24 Perry Ho
25 Brunel Ho
26 New Park Ct
27 Tanhurst Ho
B1 1 Carisbrook Ct
2 Pembroke Lo
3 Willow Ct
4 Poplar Ct
5 Mountview
6 Spa View
B3 1 Charlwood Ho
2 Earlswood Ho
3 Balcombe Ho
4 Claremont Cl
5 Holbrook Ho
6 Gwynne Ho
7 Kynaston Ho
8 Tillman Ho
9 Regent Lo
10 Hazelmere Ct
11 Dykes Ct
B4 1 Archbishop's Pl
2 Witley Ho
3 Outwood Ho
4 Dunsfold Ho
5 Deepdene Lo
6 Warnham Ho
7 Albury Lo
8 Tilford Ho
9 Elstead Ho
10 Thursley Ho
11 Brockham Ho
12 Capel Lo
13 Leith Ho
14 Fairview Ho
15 Weymouth Ct
16 Ascalon Ct
17 China Mews
18 Rush Common Mews
C3 1 Valens Ho
2 Loveday Ho
3 Strode Ho
4 Ethelworth Ct
5 Harbin Ho
6 Brooks Ho
7 Godolphin Ho
8 Sheppard Ho
9 McCormick Ho
10 Taylor Ho
11 Saunders Ho
12 Talcott Path
13 Derrick Ho
14 Williams Ho
15 Baldwin Ho
16 Berkeley Ct
17 Churston Cl
18 Neil Wates Cres
19 Burnell Ho
20 Portland Ho
C4 1 Ellacombe Ho
2 Booth Ho
3 Hathersley Ho
4 Brereton Ho
5 Holdsworth Ho
6 Dearmer Ho
7 Cherry Cl
8 Greenleaf Cl
9 Longford Wlk

76 C1 **279**

10 Scarlette Manor Wlk
11 Chandlers Way
12 Upgrove Manor Way
13 Ropers Wlk
14 Tebbs Ho
15 Bell Ho
16 Worthington Ho
17 Courier Ho
18 Mackie Rd
19 Hamers Ho
20 Kelyway Ho
21 Harriet Tubman Cl
22 Estoria Cl
23 Leckhampton Pl
24 Scotia Rd
25 Charles Haller St
26 Sidmouth Ho
27 Hunter Ct
28 Onslow Lo
29 William Winter Ct
30 Langthorne Lo

75
A1 1 Thanet Ho
2 Chapman Ho
3 Beaufoy Ho
4 Easton Ho
5 Roberts Ho
6 Lloyd Ct
7 Kershaw Ho
8 Wakeling Ho
9 Edridge Ho
10 Jeston Ho
11 Lansdowne Wood Cl
C2 1 Coppedhall
2 Shackleton Ct
3 Bullfinch Ct
4 Gannet Ct
5 Fulmar Ct
6 Heron Ct
7 Petrel Ct
8 Falcon Ct
9 Eagle Ct
10 Dunnock Ct
11 Dunlin Ct
12 Cormorant Ct

76
C1 1 Tunbridge Ct
2 Harrogate Ct
3 Bath Ct
4 Leamington Ct
5 Porlock Ho
6 Cissbury Ho
7 Eddisbury Ho
8 Dundry Ho
9 Silbury Ho
10 Homildon Ho
11 Highgate Ho
12 Richmond Ho
13 Pendle Ho
14 Tynwald Ho
15 Wirrall Ho
16 Greyfriars

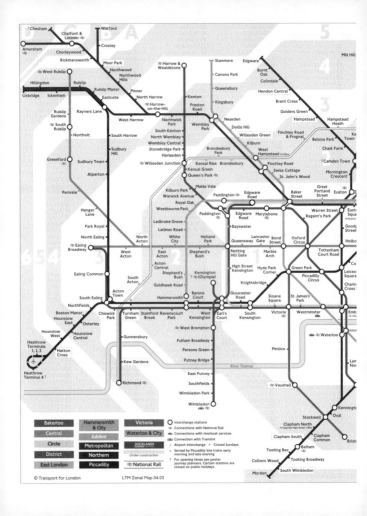

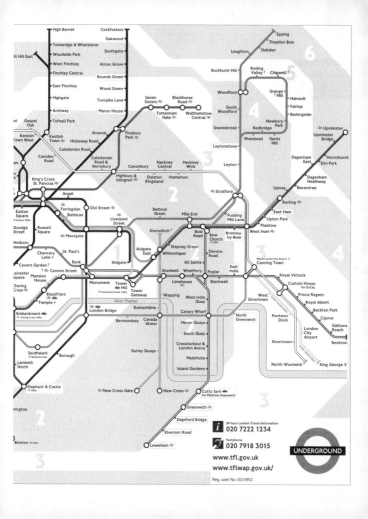

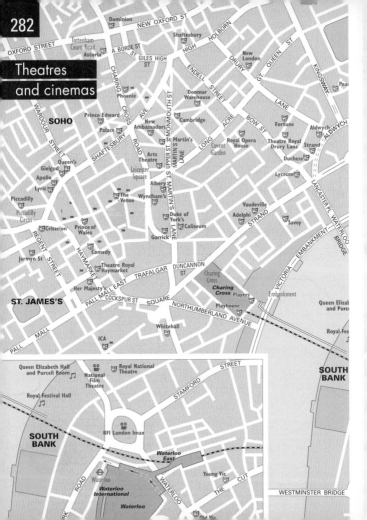

Theatres
and cinemas